# Teaching and
# Schooling in America

## Pre- and Post-September 11

### Allan C. Ornstein
*St. John's University*

Boston | New York | San Francisco
Mexico City | Montreal | Toronto | London | Madrid | Munich | Paris
Hong Kong | Singapore | Tokyo | Cape Town | Sydney

Vice President: Paul A. Smith
Executive Editor and Publisher: Stephen D. Dragin
Editorial Assistant: Barbara Strickland
Marketing Manager: Tara Whorf
Manufacturing Buyer: JoAnne Sweeney
Cover Administrator: Linda Knowles
Electronic Composition: Omegatype Typography, Inc.

For related titles and support materials, visit our online catalog at
www.ablongman.com.

Between the time Website information is gathered and published, some sites may have closed.
Also, the transcription of URLs can result in typographical errors. The publisher would
appreciate notification where these occur so that they may be corrected in subsequent editions.

**CIP data not available at the time of publication.**

**ISBN: 0-205-36711-9**

Printed in the United States of America

10 9 8 7 6 5 4 3 2 1     07 06 05 04 03 02

# Dedication

The attacks on the World Trade Center and the Pentagon were an act of war and a threat to the democracies of the world. Some 2,900 people from more than 80 countries died, the vast majority being Americans. It was an event that has become the turning point in our understanding of the shrinking global village and the fluidity of international boundaries. The event influenced the content of this book. In fact, this may be the first, or one of the first education books that deals with the political, social, and cultural aspects of September 11, 2001, and how it relates to teaching and schooling.

Americans expressed solidarity and support to all the victims and the relatives of the victims. Every victim was the most important person in the world to someone. Stunned leaders around the world expressed outrage and presented a united front. Around the world, millions of people mourned and offered sympathy to a grieving nation and the families who lost loved ones. School children across the nation expressed all kinds of care and support for the victims and their families.

There are no adequate words to describe the aftermath—at the site of the World Trade Center rubble—and the profound grief for all those who died. Unquestionably, this is a land of diversity, and we celebrate, worship, and mourn in different ways. All of our different religions have customs for dealing with death and for grieving, and to help us cope with personal loss. So we have our funerals, burials, and methods for cremating and dispersing ash. We eat, drink, smile, cry, and come together to comfort one another. Some of us suffer in silence, and some suffer for years, remembering our loved ones. I ask you to turn to pages 37–43 and read about death and remembering the dead.

Given my own sentiments, I dedicate this book to Mary Wieman and to all those who suffered and died in the airplanes and at the Pentagon and the World Trade Center. Mary was incinerated in the WTC, somewhere below the 75th floor, and her body was never found.

Goodbye, Mary. I will miss your smile, your wit, your laughter, your energy—and all your lovely, feisty remarks.

# Contents

*Chapter* **3**

# Theories of Learning  107

# Preface

Most education textbooks are ho-hum, middle of the road, antiseptic, and designed not to unravel the reader. The idea is to play it safe and walk the white line, right down the middle of the political continuum, and to write flat and dry prose. The trick is to twist the truth and to be politically correct, especially when it comes to gender, race, ethnicity, and religion. Well, folks, I started to think about the status quo and whether the field of education needed another boring, middle-of-the-road book. I decided to betray convention and make some waves. So, prepare yourself for an unusual voyage—one that will rock and roll and probably upset many readers in some places of the text. Why? The nature of the subject matter is controversial and the prose is written free from a technocratic style—one that is critical, honest, and passionate.

To my knowledge, there hasn't been a philosophical or social foundations (or curriculum issues or social policy) textbook in this country that has challenged traditional, popular, and politically correct opinion as the one you are about to read. I am going to uncork some complicated ideas with "unfakeable" opinion and a genuine seriousness. As an author, I'm sometimes in your face—asking you to examine and reexamine the issues of teaching and schooling. When you finish reading this book, most of you will be exhausted, but if I have it my way, you will have a different opinion about teaching and schooling.

Reading this book is not a quick read. For those who were brought up with classic comics as substitutes for classic literature, relied on cliff notes or summary versions, or now prefer some novel that entertains and says nothing (what I call mass-market trash), this book will drive you up the wall. And, for those who prefer to listen to "hair metal" or "hip hop" music instead of reading one of Ibsen's short plays or Kafka's short stories (or worse do not know Ibsen or Kafka), this book will nip and bite you. At best, the passages and pages will be a minor ordeal—at worst, a real ordeal.

Let me set the record straight. This is not going to be an easy book to read. I am not going to entertain you, nor am I going to waste your time and bore you and talk about mundane subjects. This is a book that expects you to think, to criticize, to question, to evaluate, and to reevaluate—to grapple with ideas and issues and to ask "Why?" and "What if?" Asking *why* and *what if* questions forces people to reflect and modify their *ideas* and *values*. It leads to self-realization, self-improvement, and self-invention. Hopefully, this book will rattle your brains, turn your thinking upside down and inside out, and transform your views about education and society—and life in general. And, that's what every author should aim to do, and that's what every good book should do for the reader.

Getting down to specifics, *Teaching and Schooling in America: Pre- and Post-September 11* is concerned with life and death, peace and war, good and evil, miseducation and education, achievement and aptitude, and equality and inequality. The book is about ideas, and it will force you to think and rethink about the issues of schooling and society. *Teaching and Schooling* examines 2,500 years of historical, philosophical, social, and educational thought. It starts with the ancient Greeks and Romans and ends with post-September 11 society, including American, Chinese, Indian, and Arabic cultures.

At the level of society, specific topics deal with religion, morality, justice, colonialism, global poverty, rape and plunder, and other horrors of the twentieth century—war, death camps, and racial/ethnic hatred—and now the new century with terrorism and cloning. At the educational level, the focus is on race, gender, class, social stratification, school finance, black-white achievement gaps, affirmative action, quotas, reparations, computers, satellite communications, and global education and understanding.

I doubt if this book will ever win an award, make the *New York Times* best-seller list, or Book-of-the-Month Club, not because I'm a lowbrow writer or myth maker, but because education books are not designed for a mass audience. This book is a tribute to America because it is so different from all other countries. Here, people from all over the world have been accepted and have the opportunity to rise from rags to riches, at least to live a decent life, free from tyranny, famine, and despair. This book is also a wake-up call about global issues that American educators fail to address and that I perceive as threatening the American way of life. I write as an ideological warrior, recounting struggles of life and ideas and ideology that have impacted the global village, as well as in the promised land—which I call America.

# Introduction

Let me make a few comments. You are about to read a highly opinionated book, and you are invited to write to me. I guarantee to read all comments. Don't worry: You gotta say what you gotta say. Just don't get too fiesty. You can send your comments to me at St. John's University, 8000 Utopia Parkway, Jamaica, NY 11439.

In the chapters you are about to read, you will encounter some theories and ideas, as well as some generalizations and comments that are bound to raise some eyebrows. This is a serious book, dealing with the "grand generalizations" about life and death, peace and war, good and evil, inequality and equality, race, culture, and gender over several centuries. In effect, this is a serious statement about education—about teaching and schooling. It is a book that requires from the author a certain amount of experience and wisdom that comes with age, as well as knowledge of the humanities and social sciences.

As people gain knowledge and deal with "grand ideas"—what is known about the nature of life, the human condition, and the behavior of human species—it becomes problematical and makes many of us, including myself, sometimes critical and cynical. Indeed, we live in an age of complaint, both liberal and conservative reaction, and the need to advocate "causes" and "reform." The dictum of Ecclesiastes prevails: "For in much wisdom is much grief and he that increaseth knowledge increaseth sorrow."

A century has passed since John Dewey published his little book, *The School and Society* (1899), whereby he outlined the need to educate the whole child and the need for schools to emphasize character building, community membership, and democracy. More than 200 years have passed since Jefferson introduced the ideals of universal education: to serve as the *the great equalizer* of the human condition, as the *balance wheel* for social mobility, and the *means of Enlightenment;* to defend against the rise of despots, monarchs, and the aristocracy, which was pervasive in Europe at that time; and to ensure some form of *equality, freedom,* and *democracy,* since the common man had to have the knowledge to make intelligent decisions.

Fifty years later, Horace Mann began his quest and hammered his boundless faith in the public school movement. Here was a total faith in the power of education to shape the nation, and to permit children of humble origin to attend school for free and to achieve places of distinction in society. Mann's theory of universal education represented a mix of American progressivism, Jeffersonian democracy, Christian moralism, and business and industrialist sentimentalism. He was able to convince large segments of American society that the public school was an institution worthy of support, and that all children should attend regardless of rank. Like Jefferson before and Dewey later, Mann understood the relationship between education and democracy, education and equality, and education and morality.

More than 300 years have passed since the British conquest of New Netherlands in which was later to be called New York, and America has been compared to ancient Athens in terms of culture, freedom, and faith in the common man, and to ancient Rome in terms of political and military power. Little wonder that the United States has fired such enthusiasm and optimism from visitors abroad, like Alexis de Tocqueville and James Bryce, and even today from Tony Blair and British historian Niall Ferguson, as well as from immigrants for centuries of every color, mixture of blood, folk heritage, and language.

And with all this American optimism and power, the barbarians have always been at the gates of civilized society. War is inevitable. Rape and plunder are instruments of war. Most people die in vain and are forever forgotten. The human condition is such that throughout history and around the world evil has prevailed over good, inequality has prevailed over equality, social injustice has often prevailed over justice. Very little has changed in terms of the distribution of goods and services. Around the globe, the working class and peasant class are still pushing stones up the hill, as in the days of the Pharaoh some 5,000-plus years ago. Approximately one-fourth of 1 percent still control 50 percent of all the resources of their particular society, as it was 5,000 years ago, except in the United States and Canada, where the figure is about 5 percent. Still, the United States comprises 4 percent of the world's population and consumes 25 percent of the world's resources. Since 1966, when the first international tests were administered, U.S. junior high and senior high school students have ranked at the bottom or near bottom in math and science, compared to their counterparts in advanced and industrialized countries.

This book makes one harsh statement after another and forces you to reflect and think about life, about schools, and about society. Many of my words and phrases are vivid and sharp, nonlinear, and politically controversial. Other words and phrases exhibit sorrow, grief, and contempt regarding man's inhumanity toward man, toward all the vile behavior exhibited by nations and people.

I suspect some of you will oppose some of my thoughts, and rightfully so, since the ideas deal with political and economic ideology, philosophical and social conditions, and the nature of teaching and schooling. If I have erred, I hope I have erred toward the moral and humanistic side. If you feel my point of view is slanted or biased, try to see the merits or value of it without accepting it as "truth." A few of you might even feel that the voyage is too difficult, that the comparisons and analysis are not so simple, but require thinking and assume an understanding of philosophy, history, sociology, psychology, economics, and an overall literacy background. Indeed, some of you have been hoodwinked by mindless and antiseptic books. You may now feel life is too difficult and there is no need to read a book in education that requires a literate mind. If you cannot be entertained by glossy pictures and smiling faces, or with sidebars of cartoons or case studies, then you might rationalize that you should not be bothered or expected to read or think about serious issues. For this reason, a few of you might not appreciate the epic story and linguistic juggernaught you are about to experience.

Now I'm not trying to be smug or small-minded. I'm just telling it like it is. Rather than impressing you with wine and roses, or false optimism, the fact is, this is not intended to be light reading, or a "Dick and Jane" reader. For those with an urge to be politically correct on all topics, you will find plenty to be upset with—not willing to admit to your own form of racial, ethnic, religious, or gender prejudice. Finally, there will be some who find fault that the content lacks restraint, sobriety, and optimism, and that my expressions are somewhat disruptive and upsetting—extreme topics that deal with war zones, extermination camps, racial lynching, rape and plunder, famine, human stupidity and human misery, political and economic oppression, religious fanaticism, and death.

Let me briefly respond to all my potential critics. For decades, maybe even centuries, we have managed well enough without any of those controversial topics or gems. Life has become pretty flat and dull when reading typical education texts. That the context has become so oblique and middle-of-the-road is a tribute to mainstream society that publishers wish to convey a neutral or positive picture of the human condition; to some extent, the situation also reflects the thoughts of many educators who are too unwilling or uncomfortable to deal with complicated topics, uncomfortable truths, and tough-minded positions. What I have tried to do is to say no to convention and popularity—and I have tried to move the issues from the private to public sector, from what is politically acceptable or neutral to what is philosophically honest and poignant.

Of course, I do expect that some of you will enjoy the twists and turns in the metaphors and phrases—the word inventions, passionate talk, purposeful topics, and serious judgments about schools and society, and life in general. But some of you may come out of the closet and even risk and say in class how refreshing it is to find someone who is so pro-American, who extends the debate beyond racial and gender issues, beyond issues of "relevancy," and deals with 2,500 years of life—the past, present, and future. Indeed, this book represents a fateful shift—content that deals with many critical and complicated issues, and issues that are moved from the political arena to the moral realm.

For those who find this book rewarding, I would also like to hear from you. Recall, my address is noted in the earlier pages of the introduction. It will be nice to know that some of you believe in my good intentions. And, for my students, I realize life can be difficult, but you are going to have to read the book and earn your grade—no matter how much you tell me you enjoyed reading the book.

Finally, a note of appreciation is extended to Dean Jerry Ross and Chair Gene Geisert who provided the leadership and intellectual atmosphere and time for writing this book. I am also indebted to Leeanne G-Bowley who had to deal with my handwriting and who typed the manuscript. In addition, I thank the following reviewers: Stacey L. Edmonson, Sam Houston State University; Gerald L. Gutek, Loyola University, Chicago; and William R. Martin, George Mason University. And finally, there is the woman, Esther, who understands my thoughts.

Allan Ornstein

# Improving
# Teaching

## Chapter 1

## *Focusing Questions*

1. In what ways is theory related to practice? In what ways are they different?

2. Do you prefer a scientific or artistic approach to teaching? Why?

3. What aspects of teaching are not evaluated in a teacher-product model? What aspects of teaching are not evaluated in a teacher-content model?

4. How would you define an expert teacher and a novice teacher? How do experts and novices differ in the role they assume in classrooms?

5. What purpose do stories, biographies, and reflective practices serve for improving teaching?

6. How does humanism (or humanistic teaching) contribute to the improvement of the learning condition?

7. How would you describe a moral teacher?

8. To what extent should teachers discuss and honor the dead in their classrooms?

## EPISODE *A*

To help you appreciate the discussion in this chapter, try this exercise: Make a list of teachers you have had about whom you have pleasant memories. List those teachers in whose classes you were not happy. As you read this chapter, think about how the attitudes and behaviors of the teachers on the two lists correspond to research findings and information that follows about effective and ineffective teachers.

In the early stages of research, up to the mid-1970s, theorists and researchers were concerned with *teacher processes*—that is, what the teacher was doing while teaching. They attempted to define and explain good teaching by focusing on teacher styles, teacher interactions, teacher personality, teacher characteristics, and/or teacher methods. A supervisor might observe or evaluate a teacher's blackboard work and movement around the classroom, while another supervisor might focus on the teacher's attire or whether the shades of the window were even. From about 1975 to 1990, researchers shifted their concerns to *teacher products*—that is, student outcomes—and the assessment focused on teacher effects and teacher productivity. It no longer mattered whether teachers' blackboard penmanship was straight, slanted, or colored, or whether teachers wore jackets and ties or dresses below or above the knees, or for that matter whether teachers stood on their heads or drew cartoons to motivate students. What counted was student achievement. As we move into the twenty-first century, theorists are attempting to analyze the culture, language, and thoughts of teachers, combine (rather than separate) teaching and learning processes, and use qualitative methods to assess what they call *teacher contexts*.

Discussion will move to still another level, one that deals with the topics of morality, remembrance of the dead, and related issues of violence, rape, war, and genocide—and why and how teachers need to deal with these issues. A good part of my thinking, to be candid, is related to September 11, 2001 (9-11). The world has changed, especially for Americans, and teachers need to understand and deal with the post-September 11 world. Given our population, and the fact that our schools are expected to bring together diverse children and therefore Americans of every race, ethnicity, and religion, our children need to learn the concepts of democracy, patriotism, human rights, and justice. Our teachers need to adopt the professional role as educator, social commentator (or possibly critic), and intellectual leader in the exchange of the aforementioned ideas and values. There is no turning back the clock, and there is no other feasible choice. America has changed, and to paraphrase President John Kennedy, "We are all New Yorkers."[1]

## Review of the Research on Teaching

Over the years, thousands of studies have been conducted to identify the behaviors of successful teachers and of unsuccessful teachers. However, teaching is a complex act; what works in some situations with some students may not work in different

---

1. On June 26, 1963, President Kennedy spoke to hundreds of thousands of Berliners in front of the Berlin Wall. As he paid tribute to Berliners, he stated "I am a Berliner."
Sandra Feldman, president of the American Federation of Teachers, sums up this point about New York in her weekly commentary in the *New York Times* and *Education Week*. Rudy Giuliani made the same point on several occasions when he was mayor of New York, leading the city and nation during the WTC crisis. We are a nation of many nations and New York City best typifies it by its diversity. The city is a world-class city, comprising some 8 million people who speak more than 50 different languages and dialects and come from more than 150 different countries and whose roots and culture span the entire globe.

school settings with different subjects, students, and goals. There will always be teachers who break many of the rules, procedures, and methods and yet are profoundly successful. There will always be teachers who enroll in a host of education courses, follow all the rules, and still be unsuccessful.

Biddle and Ellena maintain that we cannot distinguish between "good" and "poor" or "effective" and "ineffective" teachers, that no one knows for sure or agrees what the competent teacher is, and that few authorities can "define, prepare for, or measure teacher competence."[1] They point out that disagreement over terms, problems in measurement, and the complexity of the teaching act are major reasons for the negligible findings in judging teacher behavior. The result is that much of the data have been confusing, contradictory, or confirmations of common sense (a democratic teacher is a good teacher), and that so-called acceptable findings have often not been repudiated.[2]

The more complex or unpredictable one views teaching as being, the more one is compelled to conclude that it is difficult to agree on generalizations about successful teaching. Because we are unable to agree on or precisely define what a good teacher is, we can use almost any definition (or a list of characteristics, behaviors, or methods) so long as it makes sense, seems logical, and can be tested and validated. ("Good teaching is like a stroll in the park" or "Good teaching is as easy as learning how to ride a bicycle" cannot easily be tested or validated, but it can serve as a metaphor.) Other researchers assert that appropriate teaching behaviors can be defined (and learned by teachers), that good or effective teachers can be distinguished from poor or ineffective teachers, and that the magnitude of the effect of these differences on students can be determined.[3] They conclude that the kinds of questions teachers ask, the way they respond to students, their expectations of and attitudes toward students, their classroom-management techniques, their teaching methods, and their general teaching behaviors (sometimes referred to as *classroom climate*) all make a difference.

However, in some cases the positive effects teachers have on student performance may be masked or washed out by the relative negative effects of other teachers in the same schools. Thus, it is difficult to separate or control the effects of other teachers in the same schools and it is more difficult to separate or control the effects of secondary school teachers on students than elementary school teachers who work with one class for almost the entire day and school year. The teacher may not be the only variable, or even the major one, in the teaching-learning equation (home environment is more important), but he or she can make a difference, and it can be positive or negative.

1. Bruce J. Biddle and William J. Ellena, *Contemporary Research on Teacher Effectiveness* (New York: Holt, Rinehart and Winston, 1964), p. 3.

2. Allan C. Ornstein, "Successful Teachers: Who They Are," *American School Board Journal* (January 1993), pp. 24–27; Ralph T. Putnam and Hilder Borko, "What Do New Views of Knowledge . . . Say About Research on Teaching," *Educational Researcher* (January–February 2000), pp. 4–16; and Grant Wiggins, *Educative Assessment* (San Francisco: Jossey-Bass, 1998).

3. David A. Jacobsen, Paul Eggen, and Donald P. Kauchak, *Methods for Teaching,* 6th ed. (Columbus, OH: Merrill, 2002); Thomas L. Good and Jere E. Brophy, *Looking in Classrooms,* 7th ed. (Boston: Addison-Wesley, 1997).

Here it should be noted that negative teacher influences have greater impact than do positive ones, in that students can be turned into nonlearners and experience loss of self-concept, composure, and academic focusing ability in a matter of weeks as a result of a hostile or intimidating teacher. Other symptoms might be exhibited by sudden nail biting, increased sibling rivalry, and sudden outbursts at home or excuses for not doing homework or completing school assignments. In general, negative stimuli (loss of sleep, food, or water) can have major effects on humans in short periods of times compared to the positive stimuli (proper sleep, food, and water) that have positive influence on humans over long periods of time. In other words, the effects of a nurturing, supportive, and positive school environment influence the learner over a long period of time but the outcome(s) can be easily modified, curtailed, or neutralized by negative stimuli that last for only a short time, or by one teacher.

If teachers do not make a difference, then the profession has problems. For example, if teachers do not make a difference, the notions of teacher evaluation, teacher accountability, and teacher performance are nonworkable. Sound educational policy cannot be formulated, and there is little hope for many education students and little value in trying to learn how to teach. However, even if we are convinced that teachers have an effect, it is still true that we are unable to assess with confidence the influence a particular teacher has on student performance because the learning variables are numerous and the teaching interactions are complex.

## Theory versus the Practice of Teaching

The test of a good theory is whether it can guide practice. In reverse, good practice is based on theory. *Practice* refers to the methods, strategies, and skills that apply to the working world, when a person is on the job and actively involved in his or her profession. These procedures are teachable and can be applied in different situations. When applied, they should result in the practitioner (teacher) being considered successful or effective. *Theory* refers to the knowledge gained by research and experience that is generalizable and whereby potential users (teachers) can make informed estimates of the probable effects of various practices.[1] Without theory, we cannot assess whether a particular method or strategy will suit the purpose or effect we are trying to achieve. In the absence of theory, we operate haphazardly, intuitively, and instinctively. This is not always bad, but it is often difficult to put confidence in our judgments while teaching because of its swift, complex, and multidimensional nature; in fact, Philip Jackson claims there are at least 1,000 daily student-teacher interac-

---

1. Paul Cobb and Janet Bowers, "Cognitive and Situated Perspectives in Theory and Practice," *Educational Researcher* (March 1999), pp. 4–14; Allan C. Ornstein, "Theory and Practice of Curriculum," *Kappan Delta Pi Record* (Fall 1987), pp. 15–16; and Ornstein, "Teacher Effectiveness Research: Theoretical Considerations," in H. C. Waxman and H. J. Walberg, eds., *Effective Teaching: Current Research* (Berkeley, CA: McCutchan, 1991), pp. 63–80.

tions shaping elementary classrooms.[1] The nature of teaching, therefore, makes it difficult to repeat and interpret what we are doing when we teach.

Regardless of theories, those who work with or prepare teachers in one way or another have to deal with practice—that is, with what works. Good theories are workable for practitioners, make sense, can be applied to the real world of classrooms and schools, and are generalizable to a varied number of settings or situations. Theories that are not workable and generalizable are not good theories and cannot be translated into practice. (Similarly, unless a practice becomes part of a larger theory, it remains unique to a given time, situation, or person.) Theories about teaching may not provide specific answers or quick solutions to vexing problems; theories must be adjusted to the situation, given the fact that people (teachers and students) and situations (classrooms and schools) differ—they are not nuts and bolts on an assembly line or tiny transistors in a computer that can be shaped precisely to specifications. Thus, we commonly hear teachers saying, "That's all good theory, but it doesn't working practice."

In defense of teachers, most teaching experts have difficulty fusing theory and practice. Perhaps we have trouble connecting theory and practice because the methods of inquiry lend themselves more to the theoretical discussion and less to practical matters. Also, promoting good theory is recognized as a worthwhile endeavor, but a repertoire of good practice is often misconstrued by theoreticians as a cookbook approach or as "dos and don'ts" that are second rate or unimportant. Despite the claims of some theoreticians, we seem unable to make the leap from theory to practice, from the textbook and college course to the classroom and school. Good theory in teaching often gets lost as practitioners try to apply what they have learned in college to the classroom setting—in a search for practical solutions to common everyday problems. On the other hand, good practice—what is sometimes called *craft knowledge* (or practical wisdom)—often gets ignored by researchers who feel such knowledge is unimportant, fragmentary, or relevant only to specific situations.

Good theory sometimes gets ignored by teachers because it deals with generalizations that don't always work in specific situations. Faced by the mountains of research, the minutiae of facts, the growing information awed by watchful academics, the researcher often takes refuge in a few learned journals and narrowly specialized details and dissertations. Only the professor who is on the cutting edge or unusually nimble minded can attempt to synthesize or theorize in one sweeping sequence the great events and ideas that have influenced the field of study, the destinies of people, or trends that shape social systems. Anyone who can think and dwell on this abstract level will not give much concern to a particular situation or event at the classroom level.

The conflict between theory and practice is keenly noted by Joseph Schwab, who maintains that the differences cannot be reconciled. The strength of theory lies in "it's generality, system, and economy." The practical, however, is "concrete, variable, and particular." A theory can be likened to a map, but "the road we drive has bends and

---

1. Philip W. Jackson, *Life in Classrooms,* 2nd ed. (New York: Teachers College Press, 1990).

potholes not included on the map."[1] We may understand the child's achievement scores, social class, and personality type—all based on good theories—yet we need to take into account specific classroom conditions—that is, practice. Not everyone can make the leap, particularly because of professional knowledge and partially because of lack of insight skills.

No college course can really teach what Matthew Lipman calls "self-correcting skills." This is the ability to discern when there are special limitations to a theory given certain circumstances, and when a "configuration" (i.e., a theory) needs to be modified due to circumstances, or that the circumstances are atypical so only portions of the theory are applicable.[2] A related problem is that under the guise of good theory, certain principles or methods can become prescriptive: We develop specific policies and pedagogy for teachers to follow at the expense of allowing teachers (who know their students) to make adaptive, flexible, and intuitive decisions.

Indeed, there is no one way of teaching, and there is no one way of learning. There are different teaching styles and teaching methods, and there are different learning styles and ways of thinking about and solving problems. In other words, there are many roads to Rome, and many acceptable ways for organizing classrooms and teaching students. Under the misguided notion of agreed-upon theory (or generic teaching methods), we sometimes disenfranchise, deprofessionalize, and make teachers impotent: unable to innovate, unable to meet the needs of their students, and unable to deviate from an evaluation instrument, checklist, or a predetermined set of behaviors or methods.

The danger occurs when a teaching theory or principle turns into a prescription, or when a particular philosophy, thought, or behavior becomes a mandate. It occurs when a school principal or supervisor expects all teachers to be evaluated by a specific model or method with little room for deviation or differences. This is exactly what happened in the first third of the twentieth century when the behavioral psychology of E. L. Thorndike and John Watson won the teaching-learning war of ideas, and the progressive ideas of John Dewey and William Kilpatrick lost. This is what is happening today under various sequenced-teaching, merit reward, performance-based, and standard-based education systems.

The problem of translating theory into practice is further aggravated by researchers and professors, many of whom are more concerned with the teacher "knowing how" than with the teacher "knowing why." Nate Gage, for example, "refers to the difference between being able to state factual propositions [or theory] and being able to perform skills or operations" in the classroom. The one kind of knowledge does not necessarily follow from the other; this is the reason why teaching texts and courses can stress either theory or practice (without the other component).

    1. Joseph J. Schwab, "The Practical: Arts of Eclectic," *School Review* (May 1971), pp. 494, 496.
    2. Matthew Lipman, "Critical Thinking—What Can It Be," in A. C. Ornstein and Linda S. Behar-Horenstein, *Contemporary Issues in Curriculum,* 2nd ed. (Boston: Allyn and Bacon, 1999), pp. 145–152.

According to Gage, "much of the teacher education program is given over to providing teachers with a great deal of knowledge that certain things are true, in the subject [grade levels] to be taught."[1] It is keenly illustrated when beginning teachers ask for a list of "dos and don'ts" or "tips" on how to teach. This kind of knowledge is often sought after and acquired by beginning teachers at the expense of theory that could help them understand the basic principles and phenomena underlying their work. To some extent, then, many teachers focus on the trees (or small items) rather than the forest (or big picture); they focus on what is workable or practical (for a particular situation) at the expense of what is abstract or generalizable (to many situations).

The problem is further compounded by teachers, supervisors, and administrators who feel that practical considerations (e.g., getting Johnny in his seat) are more worthwhile than theory; most teachers and supervisors view theory as impractical and how-to approaches as helpful. Thus, while many theoreticians ignore the practitioners, at the same time many practitioners ignore the theoreticians. The fact is, many theoretical discussions of teaching are divorced from practical application in the classroom, and many practical discussions of teaching rarely consider theoretical relationships. Professors tend to talk among themselves and their students about theory, and practitioners tend to talk to themselves about practice.

*Practice* involves selecting strategies and methods that apply to specific situations. *Theory* involves principles and propositions that can be generalized to many situations. The problem is that every situation is unique. This becomes especially evident when practitioners try to apply the theory they learn from reading the professional literature. Adopting the right method for the appropriate situation is not an easy task and involves a good deal of common sense and experience, which no one can learn from a theoretical discussion. No matter how good our theories may be, they are not always predictable or generalizable from one situation to another. All we need to do is to change one variable in the situation and the interaction of subsequent variables differ from another situation, hence, we enter into a new arena with a host of possibilities that cannot always be predicted or controlled.

Two prominent educators offer a perspective relevant to this discussion. Different teachers in the same school may be assigned to similar classes with students of similar abilities and interests, but they exhibit different perceptions of their students, different behaviors, different academic tasks, and different instructional resources.[2] Some teachers may have better knowledge of their students, and others may have better knowledge of their subject matter. Moreover, different teachers and different students have different personalities, creating different classroom climates. All these variations and interactions occur in various nonlinear ways and result in a hall of mirrors where there is no end. To be sure, teaching is dynamic, always evolving,

1. N. L. Gage, *The Scientific Basis of At of Teaching* (New York: Teachers College Press, 1978), p. 44; Gage, "Confronting Counsels of Despair for Behavioral Sciences," *Educational Researcher* (April 1996), pp. 5–15, 22.

2. David K. Cohen and Deborah L. Ball, "Making Change: Instruction and Improvement," *Phi Delta Kappan* (September 2001), pp. 73–77.

influenced by how teachers use their knowledge of students and subject matter, and what educational theories and practices they rely on.

Another problem is that the field of education, and the vast array of social sciences, have a growing number of revisionist and radical theorists who have imposed novel interpretations on research and theory. As this new group sees it, there are no acceptable or universal "truths," and successful theory requires but a clear eye unclouded by preconceptions. Progress occurs when the fetters of traditional research methods and theoretical principles are shaken off, and observable facts impress themselves on an open mind. This perspective allows postmodern and postcolonialist theorists to portray lack of traditional research and traditional theory as an advantage: One is free from biases, less trammeled, and more open to fresh perspectives than someone who has been seduced by a technocratic or scientific mode of thinking that dates back to the laws of Newton and rationalism of Descartes.

The trouble is, however, without some prior theoretical framework, observations, life experiences, practical applications, and so on are by themselves worthless (at least limited), for they cannot be tied to a coherent whole or a method that others can learn and use. There is nothing to look for, nothing to give observations or outcomes a framework or significance; therefore, one can invent any explanation and one can claim any method as plausible. Far from hindering the search for truth, good theory (and the scientific method) provides the soil in which practice can grow and benefit practitioners.

One last note: If there are no acceptable or universal truths to guide our thinking, as many postmodernists claim, all rational thought is suspect and all rival interpretations have merit. We are left with "chaos theory" or what I would call irrationality—a stage of bizarre thoughts resembling *The Planet of the Apes*: where the apes are smarter than humans. If there are no agreed-upon theories, if there are no accepted virtues and ideas, then we might as well return to the Dark Ages. False universals become acceptable or at least credible, so, for example, Machiavelli's, *The Prince* is considered a jokester, Milton's Satan is morally neutral, and Stalin is a military genius. In schools and society, similarly, it becomes acceptable to beat kids into submission and so they learn to respect their teachers and parents—and the rhetoric for acceptance can be found in Puritan doctrine and early American education.

Teachers need to examine various principles based on sound, agreed-upon theory. They should try different approaches for different subjects and grade levels, and ultimately develop their own variations of what works for their students, based on craft knowledge or professional judgments and insights.[1] Teachers need to understand they exhibit many theories in the classroom, sometimes without even realizing it. They need to be encouraged to assess the effectiveness of various theories, and then to modify them for their own classroom setting, students, and subjects. They need to view

1. Marilyn Cochran-Smith and Susan L. Lytle, "Research on Teaching and Teacher Research," *Educational Researcher* (March 1990), pp. 2–11; Deanne Kuhn, "A Developmental Model of Critical Thinking," *Educational Researcher* (March 1999), pp. 16–25.

teaching beyond a linear or prescribed activity wherein teacher behaviors are considered "causes" and student learning as "effects" or "outcomes."[1] Theory, by itself, often views teaching as a discrete set of behaviors or processes that can be counted, categorized, or observed at the expense of human relationships between the teacher and students. Practice, by itself, often views teaching as a set of "dos and don'ts," based on a limited situation, and cannot easily be translated to a larger situation with different teachers and students.

Both theoreticians and practitioners must understand that the principles and ideas of a theory are situational and vary according to the school setting and classroom situation. It is one thing to learn about a theory, but it is different when we attempt to apply what we have learned—whereby the teacher must attend simultaneously to diverse students' needs and abilities, the demands of the curriculum and subject matter standards, and the ideas or requirements of the pedagogy. Well-designed theories must be tempered by practice or the reality of the classroom, which is a rapid, multifunctioned, and hard-to-measure series of human interactions.

## Improving Theory and Practice

The idea of blending theory with practice is an ideal rooted in the "science of education" based on the methods of finding facts, testing ideas, and reasoning out solutions to problems. The idea was introduced at the turn of the twentieth century by Charles Judd, the first Department Head of Education at the University of Chicago, and his colleague John Dewey.[2] In turn, their ideas can be traced back to Greek philosophers of ancient Athens, and these philosophers in turn may have been influenced by Egyptian and Persian thinkers. Many of the solutions to our education problems today—to beef up the curriculum, to focus on ideas more than facts, to hold teachers accountable, and to impose state-mandated tests—have been discussed through the ages by Socrates, Plato, and Aristotle in ancient Greece, by Quintilian and Cicero in Rome, by Arab scholars in Baghdad, Cairo, and Toledo, and by Christian scholars at the universities in Bologna, Cambridge, and Paris. In short, our theories of education are rooted in 3,000 or more years of history.

The resultant logic is that teachers today can be better trained to blend theory with practice. As experts point out, teachers are assigned to classrooms and isolated for the bulk of the day and the bulk of their careers with brief excursions for an in-service course taught at a university by some college professor who may know his or her theory but who hasn't seen a classroom for the last 10 years or more and is divorced from

1. Allan C. Ornstein, "Analyzing and Improving Teaching," in H. C. Waxman and H. J. Walberg, eds., *New Directions for Teaching Practice and Research* (Berkeley, CA: McCutchan, 1999), pp. 17–62.
2. John Dewey, *How We Think* (Boston: D. C. Heath, 1910); Dewey, *The Source of Science* (New York: Liveright, 1929); and Charles H. Judd, *Introduction to the Scientific Study of Education* (Boston: Ginn, 1918).

reality.[1] They might also be taught on a school site by some school supervisor who reads one or two journal articles and then makes a leap about some "new" theory or practice, as if he or she was an "expert."

Isolation among teachers is a real problem, especially for beginning teachers who need the assistance of colleagues, mentors, and supervisors. New employees outside education usually are trained on the job, are mentored, and carry reduced loads for an extended period of time. If teachers are to blend theory with practice, to make the leap from the college classroom to the school classroom, they are going to have to be treated as professionals and given sufficient time to work together and grow as professionals.

We know that being observed by a supervisor once or twice a year is insufficient, and we know that teachers who are mentored during the first year or two are more likely to remain in the profession longer and be considered more effective than those not mentored.[2] We also know that reading a book about teaching is not the same as getting feedback from colleagues who have observed you, or reviewing and analyzing your own teaching on video. What it boils down to is the need to examine theory and practice in a safe setting among colleagues who understand the problems of the particular students, subject, and school; to refine teaching skills and methods with the assistance of partners or mentors; and to be treated as a professional by fellow teachers and supervisors. It is not about pay; it is about professional pride. It is not about getting an A in some education course; it is about recognition and appreciation for a job well done by those who work with you and supervise you.

## The Science versus the Art of Teaching

We cannot agree on whether teaching is a science or an art. Some readers may say that this is a hopeless dichotomy, similar to that of theory versus practice, because the real world rarely consists of neat packages and either-or situations. Those who view teaching as a science put the emphasis on methods of research or analysis, breaking it down into empirical units and smaller behaviors or components to understand causes and effects. Those who prefer to view teaching as an art use such words as *creativity, feelings, emotions, attitudes,* and *human connections and relationships* to describe what it represents.

Nate Gage uses this distinction between *teaching as a science* and *teaching as an art* to describe the elements of predictability in teaching and what constitutes "good" teaching. A science of teaching, he contends, "implies that good teaching will some

---

1. Elliot W. Eisner, "The Art and Craft of Teachers," *Educational Research* (April 1983), pp. 4–14; Susan Moore Johnson, "Can Professional Certification for Teachers Reshape Teaching as a Career," *Phi Delta Kappan* (January 2001), pp. 393–399.

2. Mary Hatwood Futrell, "The Ability to Persuade People to Change," *Phi Delta Kappan* (February 2001), pp. 465–467; Gerald K. LeTendre et al., "Teachers' Work," *Educational Researcher* (August–September 2001), pp. 3–16.

day be attainable by closely following vigorous laws that yield high predictability and control." Teaching is more than a science, he observes, because it also involves "artistic judgment about the best ways to teach." When teaching leaves the laboratory or textbook and goes face to face with students, "the opportunity for artistry expands enormously."[1] No science can prescribe successfully at all the twists and turns as teaching unfolds, or as teachers respond with judgment, insight, or sensitivity to promote learning. These are expressions of art that depart from the rules and principles of science.

Is such a limited scientific basis of teaching even worthwhile to consider? Yes, but the practitioner must learn as a teacher to draw not only from his or her professional knowledge (which is grounded in scientific principles) but also from a set of personal experiences and resources (craft knowledge) that are uniquely defined and exhibited by the teacher's own personality and "gut" reaction to classroom events that unfold (which form the basis for the art of teaching). For Philip Jackson, the hunches, judgments, and insights of the teacher, as he or she responds spontaneously to events in the classroom, are as important as—and perhaps even more important than—the science of teaching.[2] The routine activities of the classroom, the social patterns and dynamics among students, and the accommodations and compromises between students and teachers are much more important than any science about teaching, because it is the everyday routines and relationships that determine the process and outcomes of teaching.

To some extent, the act of teaching must be considered intuitive and interactive, not prescriptive or predictable. According to Elliot Eisner, teaching is based primarily on feelings and artistry, not scientific rules. In an age of science and technology, there is a special need to consider teaching as an art and craft. Eisner condemns the scientific movement in psychology, especially behaviorism, and the scientific movement in education, especially school management, as reducing the teaching act to trivial specifications. He regards teaching as a "poetic metaphor," more suited to satisfying the soul than informing the head, more concerned with the whole than with a set of discrete skills or stimuli. The role of a teacher, he claims, should not be that of a puppeteer, an engineer, or a manager; rather, it is "to orchestrate the dialogue [as the conductor of a symphony] moving from one side of the room to the other."[3] The idea is to perceive patterns in motion, to improvise within the classroom, and to avoid mechanical or prescribed rules. The need is to act human, to display feelings, and to affirm and value our students. The idea is to be able to smile, clap, and laugh with your students while you teach them. Sadly, many teachers lack the self-confidence to openly express their emotions, feelings, or real personality.

Louis Rubin has a similar view of teaching—that effectiveness and artistry go hand in hand. The interplay of students and teacher is crucial and cannot be predetermined with carefully devised strategies. Confronted with everyday problems that

1. Gage, *The Scientific Basis of the Art of Teaching*, pp. 15, 17.
2. Jackson, *Life in Classrooms*.
3. Eisner, "The Art and Craft of Teachers," p. 8. Also see Elliot W. Eisner, *The Kind of Schools We Need* (Portsmouth, NH: Heinemann, 1998).

cannot be easily predicted, the teacher must rely on intuition and on "insight acquired through long experience."[1] Rubin refers to such terms as "with-it-ness," "instructional judgments," "quick cognitive leaps," and "informal guesses" to explain the difference between the effective teacher and the ineffective teacher. Recognizing the limits to rationality, he claims that for the artistic teacher a "feel for what is right often is more productive than prolonged analysis." In the final analysis, Rubin compares the teacher's pedagogy with the "artist's colors, poet's words, sculptor's clay, and musician's notes"[2] in all of which certain amount of artistic judgment is needed to get the right mix, medium, or blend.

Other researchers are more extreme in their analysis of teaching solely as an art, providing romantic accounts and tales of successful teaching and teaching strategies, described in language that could hardly be taken for social science research. They consider the act of teaching akin to drama, an aesthetic and kinesthetic endeavor, and feel that those who wish to teach should audition in a teaching studio and be trained as performing artists. Good teaching is likened to good theater, and a good teacher is likened to a good actor.[3]

Seymour Sarason describes the teacher as a performing artist. Like an actor, conductor, or artist, the teacher attempts to *instruct* and *move* the audience.[4] More significantly, this author maintains that the actor, artist, or teacher attempts to *transform* the audience in terms of thinking and instilling new ideas. This transformation alters the audience's outlook toward objects or ideas, encouraging them to think—and to ask "why?" and "what if?" Revolutionary thought, I believe, is built on poetry, music, art, movies, and speeches. And ultimately, it is the aesthetics, ideas, and values (the art, music, food, customs, laws, and thoughts) that define who we are. Hence, it is teachers in the broadest sense, including actors, artists, poets, writers, and of course parents, that make us think and that make the difference for society because they instill us with ideas and values.

Given the metaphor of the *performing artist*, a certain amount of talent or innate ability is needed to be effective, along with sufficient rehearsal and caring behavior. But knowledge or understanding of the audience is also needed. *Mr. Holland's Opus* makes the point. The teacher was unsuccessful in the beginning of the movie, despite his knowledge of music, compassion, and desire to give the students his "all." In the second half of the movie, however, through some "magic" awakening, he redefined his methods (science of teaching) and acting (art of teaching), with the result that the audience (students) became interested and learned to appreciate good music. Mr. Holland originally thought the problem was in the minds of the audience. Not until he

1. Louis J. Rubin, *Artistry of Teaching* (New York: Random House, 1985), p. 61.

2. Ibid., pp. 60, 69.

3. Jonathan Cohen, *Educating Minds and Hearts* (New York: Teachers College Press, 1999); Robert Fried, *The Passionate Teacher* (Boston: Beacon Press, 1995); and Fried, *The Passionate Learner* (Boston: Beacon Press, 2001).

4. Seymour B. Sarason, *Teaching as a Performing Art* (New York: Teachers College Press, 1999).

realized that it was the other way around, that it was his attitude that needed to be improved, was he successful.[1]

In *The King and I*, the British teacher was successful from the outset of the movie, despite cultural differences and gender inequalities of the society (Siam). Not only was she caring and compassionate, but she also understood her students. She was able to adapt to their needs, interests, and abilities—and affirm their individuality. The song *Getting to Know You* illustrates the point. She reminded some of us of the old school teachers we had when we were kids, perhaps as the loving and joyful teacher expressed in Sylvia Ashton-Warner's *Teacher,*[2] written some 40 years ago, or perhaps as a combination of my two favorite elementary school teachers, whom I remember fondly and to whom I dedicated one of my books: Mrs. Katz, "a warm, friendly, and understanding teacher," and Mrs. Schwartz, "a tough, nurturing school marm who drilled the facts and enforced the rules."[3]

Both movies underscore the need for teachers to understand students, and that good teaching is about making connections with the audience: Either through previous learning (pedagogical knowledge) or practical experience (craft knowledge), the teacher must know how students think and feel. A certain amount of training helps to understand students, but it is only a starting point. A successful teacher first understands and accepts himself or herself, then understands and accepts others. Arthur Jersild summed it up some 50 years ago: "Self understanding requires something quite different from the methods . . . and skills of know-how . . . emphasized in education [courses]." Planning pedagogical methods and techniques are helpful, but what is also needed "is a more personal kind of searching, which will enable the teacher to identify his own concerns and to share the concerns of his students."[4] Thus, teaching is not just an academic or cognitive enterprise; it involves people and an affective (feelings, attitudes, and emotions) or artistic component that has little to do with pedagogical or scientific knowledge.

The more we consider teaching as an art, packed with emotions, feelings, and excitement, the more difficult it is to derive rules or generalizations. If teaching is more an art than a science, then principles and practices cannot be easily codified or developed in the classroom or easily learned by others. Hence, there is little reason to offer instructional method courses in education. If, however, teaching is more a science, or at least partly a science, then pedagogy is predictable to that extent. It can be observed and measured with some accuracy, and the theory and research can be applied to the practice of teaching (as a physician applies scientific knowledge to the practice of medicine) and also learned in a college classroom or on the job. See Teaching Tips 1.1.

1. Ibid.
2. Sylvia Ashton-Warner, *Teacher* (New York: Simon and Schuster, 1964).
3. Allan C. Ornstein, *Strategies for Effective Teaching*, 2nd ed. (Dubuque, IA: Brown and Benchmark, 1995), dedication page.
4. Arthur Jersild, *When Teachers Face Themselves* (New York: Teachers College Press, 1955), p. 3.

# *Teaching Tips* 1.1

## The Good and Brophy Teacher Effectiveness Model

Over the last 25 years, Thomas Good and Jere Brophy have identified several factors related to effective teaching and student learning. They focus on basic principles, or the science of teaching. Many of these principles border on classroom-management techniques and structured learning settings, suggesting that good discipline and "businesslike," "organized," and "direct" teacher behaviors lead to success in the classroom.

1. *Clarity* about instructional goals (objectives)
2. Knowledge about *content* and ways for teaching it
3. *Variety* in use of teaching methods and media
4. *"With-it-ness,"* awareness of what is going on, alertness in monitoring classroom activities
5. *Overlapping,* sustaining an activity while doing something else at the same time
6. *Smoothness,* sustaining proper lesson pacing and group momentum, not dwelling on minor points or wasting time dealing with individuals, and focusing on all the students
7. *Seatwork* instructions and management that initiate and focus on productive task engagement
8. Holding students *accountable* for learning; accepting responsibility for student learning
9. *Realistic expectations* in line with student abilities and behaviors
10. *Realistic praise,* not praise for its own sake
11. *Flexibility* in planning and adapting classroom activities
12. *Task orientation* and businesslike behavior in the teacher
13. *Monitoring* of students' understanding; providing appropriate feedback, giving praise, asking questions
14. Providing student *opportunity* to learn what is to be tested
15. Making comments that help *structure learning* of knowledge and concepts for students; helping students learn how to learn

But a word of caution is needed. The more we rely on artistic interpretations or on old stories and accounts about teachers, the more we fall victim to fantasy, wit, and romantic rhetoric, and the more we depend on hearsay and conjecture rather than on social science or objective data in evaluating teacher competency. On the other hand, the more we rely on the scientific interpretations of teaching, the more we overlook those commonsense and spontaneous processes of teaching, and the sounds, smells, and visual flavor of the classroom. The more scientific we are in our approach to teaching, the more we ignore what we cannot accommodate to our empirical assumptions or principles. What sometimes occurs, according to Eisner, is that the educationally significant but difficult to measure or observe is replaced by what is insignificant but comparatively easy to measure or observe.[1]

1. Elliot W. Eisner, "The Promise and Perils of Alternative Forms of Data Representation," *Educational Researcher* (August–September 1997), pp. 4–11.

It is necessary to blend artistic impressions and relevant stories about teaching, because good teaching involves emotions and feeling, with the objectivity of observations and measurements and the precision of language. There is nothing wrong with considering good teaching to be art, but we must also consider it to lend itself to a prescriptive science or practice. If it does not, then there is little assurance that prospective teachers can be trained to be teachers—told what to do, how to instruct students, how to manage students, and so forth—and educators will be extremely vulnerable to public criticism and to people outside the profession telling them how and what to teach.

True knowledge of teaching is achieved by practice and experience in the classroom. According to some observers, the beliefs, values, and norms—that is, the knowledge teachers come to have the most faith in and use most frequently to guide their teaching—are those consistent with traditions that have "worked" in the classroom. Although it seems to be more commonsensical than highly specialized and theoretical, the process still includes the receiving and using of data that can be partially planned and scientifically analyzed. We also assume there are generic professional and technical skills that can be taught to teachers and that can be designed and developed in advance with underlying scientific principles and research-based data. Some would refer to this as "pedagogical knowledge" or "craft knowledge" as opposed to subject-matter or content-based knowledge.

Indeed, the real value of scientific procedures may not be realized in terms of research or theoretical generalizations that can be translated into practice. Research and pedagogical knowledge may have limited potential for teachers, but it can help them become aware of the problems and needs of students. Scientific generalizations and theories may not always be applicable to specific teaching situations, but such propositions can help in the formulation of a reliable and valid base for teaching in classrooms. Scientific ideas can serve as a starting point for discussion and analysis of the art of teaching.

## Teacher Contexts: New Research, New Paradigms

For the last 50 years or more, research on teacher behavior has been category based, focused on specific teacher behaviors, characteristics, or effects. It focused on either the *processes* of teaching (how the teacher was behaving in the classroom) or the *products* of teaching (student outcomes). As the 1990s unfolded, the research on teaching examined the multifaceted nature and *context* of teaching: the relationship of teaching and learning, the subject-matter knowledge of the teacher, how knowledge was taught, and how it related to pedagogy.

The new emphasis on teaching goes beyond what the teacher is doing; it explores teacher thinking from the perspective of teachers themselves. The teacher is depicted as one who copes with a complex environment and simplifies it, mainly through experience, by attending to a small number of tasks and synthesizing various kinds of information that continually evolve. The impact of professional knowledge (that is, both pedagogical knowledge and subject matter—knowing what you know and how well you know it) is now considered important for defining how teachers and students construct meaning for their respective academic roles and perform tasks related to those roles.[1]

An alternative for understanding the nature of teaching has evolved—one that combines teaching and learning processes, incorporates holistic practices, and goes beyond what teachers and students appear to be doing to inquire about what they are thinking. This model relies on language and dialogue—not mathematical or statistical symbols and not observational instruments or rating scales (now criticized as "technocratic" and "male-dominated" research techniques)—to provide conceptual categories and organize the data. It uses the approaches that critical pedagogists, feminists, reconceptualists, neomarxists, and postliberal theoreticians have advocated: metaphors, stories, biographies and autobiographies, conversations (with experts), voices (or narratives), and reflective practices.[2]

The new research, which has blossomed in the last 10 years, looks at teaching from the "inside." It focuses on the personal and practical knowledge of teachers, the culture of teaching, and the language and thoughts of teachers. It also elevates their status and role as a practitioner-researcher, and thus enhances their professional role and professional development.

## Metaphors

Teachers' knowledge, including the ways they speak about teaching, not only exists in propositional form but also includes figurative language or metaphors. The thinking of teachers consists of personal experiences, images, and jargon, and therefore figurative language is central to the expression and understanding of the teachers' knowledge of pedagogy.[3]

*Metaphors* of space and time figure in the teachers' descriptions of their work ("pacing a lesson," "covering the content," "moving on to the next part of the lesson"). The studies on teacher style represent concepts and beliefs about teachers that can be considered as metaphors: the teacher as a "boss," "coach," "comedian," or "maverick." The notions of a "master" teacher, "lead" teacher, "star" teacher, "talented" teacher or "expert" teacher are also metaphors or descriptors used by researchers to describe outstanding or effective teachers.

1. Allan C. Ornstein, "Beyond Effective Teaching," *Peabody Journal of Education* (Winter 1995), pp. 2–23; Ornstein, "The New Paradigm in Research on Teaching," *Education Forum* (Winter 1995), pp. 124–129.

2. Marilyn Cochran-Smith and Susan L. Lytle, "The Teacher Research Movement: A Decade Later," *Educational Researcher* (October 1999), pp. 15–25; Ornstein, "Beyond Effective Teaching."

3. Kathy Carter, "The Place of Story in the Study of Teaching," *Educational Researcher* (January 1993), pp. 5–12; Christopher Clark, "Real Lessons from Imaginary Teacher," *Journal of Curriculum Studies* (September–October 1991), pp. 429–434; and Cindy Dooley, "Teaching as a Two-Way Street: Discontinues Among Metaphors, Images, and Classroom Realities," *Journal of Teacher Education* (November–December 1998), pp. 97–107.

Metaphors are used to explain or interpret reality. In traditional literature, this process of understanding evolves through experience and study—without the influence of the researchers' personal or cultural biases. But the use of metaphors can also be conceptualized in the literature of sociology to include ideas, values, and behaviors that derive in part from a person's knowledge and life experiences—all which can be conceptualized or described in terms of political, cultural, and ideological terms.[1]

Using metaphors, however, is somewhat problematic, since traditional researchers and professors consider it "loosey-goosey" or vague; others consider it biased or tainted, especially when it comes to describing schools in a political or social context. Many have adapted the language of metaphors to be current but continue to profess what they know, the old conventional wisdom, and still use traditional research models. Hence, there is a gap between academics' "espoused" theories and theories in use. There is a gap in terms of what is intellectually interesting and provocative for readers and what is realistic and relevant for teachers—what leads to academic discourse in college and what is acceptable in schools.

The extreme use of metaphors that have a political, cultural, or ideological meaning is represented by intelligent and accomplished educators who have a natural aptitude to push the envelope and stretch reality. Henry Giroux advocates a "theory of radical pedagogy" based on a ideological construct that promotes resistance and opposition of subordinate groups against dominate groups. He seeks to shift the explanation of school failure among minority groups and at-risk students from a psychological and educational analysis to a political and cultural analysis.[2] Although his ideas are stimulating, his writing in places comes perilously close to incoherent.

Ivan Illich's metaphor is about the "deschooling of society." He completely rejects school as a viable agency: If schools were eliminated, education could be open to all (through peer matching, skill centers, and community networks) and could become a genuine instrument of "human liberation."[3] Learners would no longer have an obligatory curriculum imposed on them; they would be liberated form institutional and "capitalistic indoctrination."

Peter McLaren is perhaps more extreme, stating that U.S. schooling promotes a perverse social order, in that "it strives through its curriculum to create a culture of desire"—not to nurture a communal consensus but rather to hide from students and the general public the gaps in our society. "Unfortunately, we still mistake the disease (capitalism), for the cure (democracy)."[4] Given the global reaches of capitalism and its agents, what he calls "global carpet baggers" who profit from human suffering and

---

1. Michael W. Apple, *Cultural Politics and Education* (New York: Teachers College Press, 1996); James A. Banks, *Teaching Strategies for Ethnic Studies* (Boston: Allyn and Bacon, 1997); and Margaret Smith Crocco et al., *Pedagogues of Resistance: Women Educator Activities* (New York: Teachers College Press, 1999).

2. Henry A. Giroux, *Theory and Resistance in Education* (Westport, CT: Bergin & Garvey, 1983).

3. Ivan Illich, *Deschooling Society* (New York: Harper and Row, 1971).

4. Peter McLaren, "Critical Pedagogy and the Pragmatics of Justice," in M. Peters, ed. *Education and the Postmodern Condition* (Westport, CT: Bergin & Garvey, 1995), pp. 91–92.

short-term profits at the expense of the planet's resources and ecological health, he urges a Marxian end to capitalism—the latter which he calls a "Frankensteinian" monster.[1]

All of these metaphors are academically interesting and provoke discussion in class, but to what extent they are relevant to school teachers is another question. It is hard to imagine that well-intentional and dedicated teachers, intent on reading and teaching the children in their classrooms, are perverse, act as prison guards, and/or are political lackeys, as these critics would have us believe. In the end, the metaphors and accompanying analysis these critical pedagogists and neomarxists delineate were argued in 1932 when George Counts asked progressive educators to consider social and economic problems—and to change the social order.[2]

## Stories

Increasingly, researchers are telling stories about teachers—their work and how they teach—and teachers are telling stories about their own teaching experiences. Most *stories* are narrative and descriptive in nature; they are rich and voluminous in language, and those by and about teachers make a point about teaching that would otherwise be difficult to convey with traditional research methods. The stories told are rich in meaning and reflect the belief that there is much to learn from "authentic" teachers who tell their stories about experiences they might otherwise keep to themselves or fail to convey to others.[3]

Stories have an important social or psychological meaning. Stories of teachers allow us to see connections between the practice of teaching and the human side of teaching. The stories of individual teachers allow us to see their knowledge and skills enacted in the real world of classrooms, and lead us to appreciate their emotional and moral encounters with the lives of the people they teach.

There are three types of stories. Stories by novelists, playwriters, and filmmakers entertain us; they may be based on some true account about a teacher (e.g., Jaime Escalante in *Stand and Deliver*) or they may be completely fictional, such as with the teachers in *Blackboard Jungle, Mr. Novak, Room 222,* or more recently *Dangerous Minds* and *Dead Poets' Society*. Although such stories capture the lives of a teacher, in a given time and place, they are fictionalized and idealized; in the words of two commentators, they are "romantic versions of teachers and classrooms [in which problems] are resolved artifically." They help us "capture some truths" about teach-

1. Peter McLaren and Ramin Farahmandpur, "Reconsidering Marx in Post-Marxist Times: A Review for Postmodernism?" *Educational Researcher* (April 2000), p. 25.

2. George S. Courts, *Dare the Schools Build a New Social Order?* (New York: Day, 1932).

3. Freema Elbaz, "Research on Teacher's Knowledge: The Evolution of Discourse," *Journal of Curriculum Studies* (January–February, 1991), pp. 1–19; Ornstein, "Beyond Effective Teaching"; and John K. Smith, "The Stories Educational Researchers Tell About Themselves," *Educational Researcher* (June–July 1997), pp. 4–11.

ing in a "poignant way";[1] the stories are emotionally engaging, and they serve as excellent advertising and recruiting material for the teaching profession. Such stories help illustrate the *art* of teaching.

Stories by teachers such as Bel Kaufman, Herbert Kohl, Johnathan Kozol, and Sylvia Ashton-Warner have become bestsellers because of their rich descriptions, personal narratives, and vivid accounts of the very essence of teaching. These stories are aesthetic and visual landscapes of teaching and learning, and are often missed or ignored by clinically based and traditional researchers. Still others criticize such personal teacher stories for lacking scholarly reliability and validity—flaws critics see as grounded in personal egoism or exaggeration. In short, the story is told from one viewpoint; there is one world, one context, one interpretation. Truth and accuracy are dependent on the history and social lens of one person—the storyteller, who sometimes exhibits a selective and cloudy memory.

Stories of teachers by researchers are less descriptive, less emotional, and less well known. Nevertheless, they are still personal and rich encounters of teachers, and they provide us with teachers' knowledge and experiences not quite on their own terms, but in a deep way that helps us understand what teaching is all about. These stories provide unusual opportunities to get to know and respect teachers as persons on an emotional as well as an intellectual level. Most important, these stories represent an important shift in the way researchers are willing to convey teachers' pedagogy and understanding of teaching. However, some researchers point out that field-based observers and authors construct different realities, so that different storytellers can write different versions of the same teacher.[2] But the author is only one variable. Subject matter, students, and school settings can also lead to a striking contrast in portrayal and interpretation of the same teacher or school among different storytellers.

One needs to ask whether interviewees (i.e., teachers) can recall their experiences, in some cases many months or years ago. Are the stories being filtered through a biased lens? What is being omitted? Embellished? Did the researcher change the stories in transcribing, selecting, and editing the interviews? Did the researcher lead the interviewee in a way as to slant the story to fit the interviewer's message?[3] Can

---

1. Allan C. Ornstein and Thomas L. Lasley, *Strategies for Effective Teaching,* 3rd ed. (Boston: McGraw-Hill, 2000), p. 6. Note there are other stories, not directly related to teaching, that can also help us understand children and youth, and the need for teacher-student connections: classics such as *Grease, West Side Story, Back to the Future,* and more recently *A Walk to Remember.*

2. Antoinette Errante, "But Sometimes Your Not Part of the Story," *Educational Researcher* (March 2000), pp. 16–27; Margaret C. Neddels and N. L. Gage, "Essence and Accident in Process-Product Research on Teaching," in H. C. Waxman and H. J. Walberg, eds., *Effective Teaching: Current Research* (Berkeley, CA: McCutchan, 19991), pp. 3–32.

3. David Coulter, "The Epic and the Novel: Dialogism and Teacher Research," *Educational Researcher* (April 1999), pp. 4–13; Errante, "But Sometimes Your Not Part of the Story."

researchers faithfully and objectively tell someone else's story? How does the researcher's politics, social lens, or lack of experience play on the outcomes? When transcribing the story, from tape to print, what part of the story is omitted, modified, or actually altered? What is the difference between telling a story and writing (and editing) it? How much of the actual context or history is absent? Is one story or a series of stories, from 5 or 10 subjects, as valuable as the results of research involving 1,000 subjects in 10 or 25 schools? These are serious questions that traditional or "technocratic" researchers would raise when confronted with field-based or qualitative research.

## Biographies and Autobiographies

Stories written by researchers about teachers tend to be *biographical* and stories written by teachers about themselves tend to be *autobiographical*. Both biography and autobiography encompass a "whole story" and represent the full depth and breadth of a person's experiences as opposed to commentary or fragments. Unity and wholeness emerge as a person brings past experiences to make present action meaningful—understandable in terms of what a person has undergone.[1]

The essence of an autobiography is that it provides an opportunity for people to convey what they know and have been doing for years, and what is inside their heads, unshaped by others. Whereas the biography is ultimately filtered and interpreted by a second party, the autobiography permits the author (in this case, the teacher) to present the information in a personal way on his or her own terms. As human beings, we all have stories to tell. Each person has a distinctive biography or autobiography shaped by a host of experiences, practices, and a particular viewpoint or way of looking at the world (in this case, classrooms and schools). For teachers, this suggests a particular set of teaching experiences and practices, as well as a particular style of teaching and pedagogy.

A biography or an autobiography of a teacher may be described as the life story of one teacher who is the central character based in a classroom or school, and of the classroom dynamics and school drama that unfolds around the individual. These types of stories are concerned with limited longitudinal aspects of personal and professional experiences that can bring much detailed and insightful information to the reader. They help us to reconstruct teachers' and students' experiences that would not be available by reading typical professional literature on teaching; they describe the human dimension of teaching.

The accounts in biographies and autobiographies suggest that the author is in a position of "authority" with respect to the particular segment of the life being described. Thus, the thoughts and experiences of the author take on a sense of reality

---

1. Georgy Hilocks, *Ways of Thinking, Ways of Teaching* (New York: Teachers College Press, 1999); Donna Kagan, "Research on Teacher Cognition," in A. C. Ornstein, ed., *Teaching: Theory and Practice* (Boston: Allyn and Bacon, 1995), pp. 226–238; and Thomas S. Popkewitz, *Struggling for the Soul* (New York: Teachers College Press, 1998).

and objectivity not always assumed in other stories.[1] However, when teachers write an autobiography (as opposed to someone else writing the story in biography form), they run the risk of being considered partial or writing self-serving descriptions of their teaching process. This point is illustrated in the stories by Kohl and Kozol, who also write off their colleagues as indifferent, incompetent, and/or racist (while the authors are the "knights in silver armor").

Thus, Madeline Grumet suggests that researchers publish multiple accounts of a teacher's knowledge and pedagogy, instead of a single narrative. The problem is that this approach suggests taking stories out of the hand of teachers.[2] Joint publications between teachers and researchers may be appropriate in some situations and a method for resolving this problem.[3]

## The Expert Teacher

The *expert teacher* concept involves new research procedures—such as simulations, videotapes, and case studies—and new language to describe the work, prestige, and authority of teachers. The research usually consists of small samples and in-depth studies (an analysis of what transpired), in which expert (sometimes experienced) teachers are distinguished from novice (sometimes beginning) teachers. Experts usually are identified through administrator nominations, student achievement scores, or teacher awards (e.g., Teacher of the Year). *Novice teachers* commonly are selected from groups of student teachers or first-year teachers.

Dreyfus and Dreyfus delineate five stages from novice to expert across fields of study. In stage 1, the novice is inflexible and follows principles and procedures the way they were learned. The advanced beginner, stage 2, begins to combine theory with on-the-job experiences. By the third stage, the competent performer becomes more flexible and modifies principles and procedures to fit reality. At stage 4, the proficient performer recognizes patterns and relationships and has a holistic understanding of the

1. David Coulter, "Teaching as Communicative Action," in V. Richardson, ed., *The Handbook of Research Teaching*, 4th ed. (Washington, DC: American Educational Research Association, 2000); Myles Horton, Judith Kohl, and Herbert Kohl, *The Long Overhaul: An Autobiography* (New York: Teachers College, 1998); and Anna Neumann and Penelope L. Peterson, *Learning From Our Lives: Women Research and Autobiography in Education* (New York: Teachers College Press, 1997).

2. Madeline R. Grumet, "The Politics of Personal Knowledge," *Curriculum Inquiry* (Fall 1987), pp. 319–329.

3. Kathy L. Carter, "The Place of Story in the Study of Teaching," *Educational Researcher* (January 1993), pp. 5–12; Donna Kagan and Deborah J. Timmins, "The Genesis of a School-University Partnership," *Educational Forum* (Winter 1995), pp. 48–62; and Ornstein, "Beyond Effective Teaching."

processes involved. Experts, stage 5, have the same big picture in mind but respond effortlessly and fluidly in various situations.[1]

Data derived from recent studies suggest that expert and novice teachers teach, perceive, and analyze information about teaching in different ways. Whereas experts are able to explain and interpret classroom events quickly, novices provide detailed descriptions of what they did or saw and refrain from making interpretations. Experts recall or see multiple interactions and explain interactions in terms of prior information and events, whereas novices recall specific facts about students or what happened in the classroom; they sometimes get bogged down on detail on insignificant events. Researchers point out that "expert teachers make classroom management and instruction look easy," although we know that teaching is a complex act, requiring the teacher "to do many many things at the same time."[2]

The information from experts is rich in conversational and qualitative information, but limited in statistical analysis and quantifiable information. What experts (or experienced teachers) say or do about teaching is now considered important for building a science of teaching. Studies of expert and novice teachers show that they differ in many specific areas of teaching and instruction.

1. *Experts are likely to refrain from making quick judgments about their students and tend to rely on their own experiences and gut feelings.* Novices, on the other hand, tend to lack confidence in their own judgments and are not sure where to start when they begin teaching. For example, experts are rarely concerned about what colleagues have to say and make their own decisions about teaching and instruction. Novices rely on the advice of others and are unsure about where to start and what practices work under what conditions. Whereas experts respond in a fluid way as events unfold, novices think more about the circumstances and are sometimes paralyzed by inaction or inappropriate action.

2. *Experts tend to analyze student cues in terms of instruction.* Novices tend to analyze student cues in terms of classroom management. Expert teachers assess student responses in terms of monitoring student learning, providing feedback or assistance, and identifying ways instruction can be improved. Novices fear loss of control in the classroom. When given the opportunity to reassess their teaching on videotape, the latter focus on cues they missed that deal with students' inattentiveness or misbehavior. Although negative student cues appear to be of equal importance to experts and novices, positive cues figure prominently in the discussion on expert teachers.

3. *Experts make the classroom their own, often changing the instructional focus and methods of the previous teacher.* Novices tend to follow the previous teacher's footsteps. Experts talk about starting over and breaking old routines; they tell us about how to get students going and how to determine where the students are in terms

1. Hubert L. Dreyfus and Stuart E. Dreyfus, *Mind Over Machine* (New York: Free Press, 1986).
2. Katherine S. Cushing, Donna S. Sabers, and David C. Berliner, "Investigation of Expertise in Teaching," *Educational Horizons* (Spring 1992), p. 109.

of understanding content. Novices, on the other hand, have trouble assessing where the students are, what their capabilities are, and how and where they are going. They rely more on test data and student profiles to determine what instructional practices to adopt, whereas experts look at the data in context with their own experience and knowledge of how to organize instruction.

**4.** *Experts engage in a good deal of intuitive and improvisational teaching.* They begin with a simple plan or outline and fill in the details as the teaching-learning process unfolds, and as they respond to students. Novices spend much more time planning, stay glued to the content, and are less inclined to deviate or respond to students' needs or interests while the lesson is in progress.

**5.** *Experts seem to have a clear understanding of the types of students they are teaching and how to teach them.* In a sense, they seem to "know" their students before they meet them. Novices do not have a well-developed idea of the students they are teaching. Whereas novices have trouble beginning the new term, experts routinely find out just what it is the students already know and proceed accordingly.

**6.** *Expert teachers are less egocentric and more confident about their teaching.* Novices pay more attention to themselves and the parents of students, worrying about their effectiveness as teachers and about potential discipline problems. Experts are willing to reflect on what they were doing, admit what they did wrong, and comment about changes they would make. Although novices recognize mistakes and contradictions in their teaching, they are defensive about their mistakes and seem to have many self-concerns and doubts about where and how to improve.[1]

Finally, experts tend to be aware of and integrate the scientific and artistic elements of teaching, as well as the theoretical and practical elements; they are not expert solely on a technical or rational basis. Novices have some knowledge of theory but are often unable to apply it to practice, and they need more professional experience to modify it to their personalities (and students' personalities) or to use pieces of it based on their own teaching style. Novices have a better understanding of the science of teaching, because of their courses in methods and student teaching, but they need experience and maturity to appreciate the art of teaching—along with the imaginative, innovative, and creative aspects of teaching.

## Voice

The notion of *voice* sums up the new linguistic tools for describing what teachers do, how they do it, and what they think when they are teaching. *Voice* corresponds with

1. D. Jean Clandinin and F. Michael Connelly, "Teachers' Professional Knowledge Landscapes," *Educational Researcher* (April 1996), pp. 24–30; Kathy Carter, Walter Doyle, and Mark Riney, "Expert-Novice Differences in Teaching," in A. C. Ornstein, ed., *Teaching: Theory and Practice,* pp. 257–271; and Donna S. Sabers, Katherine S. Cushing, and David C. Berliner, "Differences Among Teachers in a Task Characterized by Simultaneity, Multidemensionality, and Immediacy," *American Educational Research Journal* (Spring 1991), pp. 63–88.

such terms as the *teacher's perspective, teacher's frame of reference,* and *getting into the teacher's head.* The concern with voice permeates teacher empowerment and the work of researchers who collaborate with teachers in teacher research projects. The idea of voice should be considered against the backdrop of previous teacher silence and impotence in deciding on issues and practices that affect their lives as professionals. The fact that researchers are now willing to give credibility to teachers' knowledge, teachers' practices, and teachers' experiences helps redress an imbalance that in the past gave little recognition to teachers. Now, teachers have a right and a role in speaking for themselves and about teaching.[1]

Although there are some serious attempts to include teachers' voices, the key issue is to what extent these new methods permit the "authentic" expression of teachers to influence the field of teacher effectiveness research and teacher preparation programs. In the past, it has been difficult for teachers to establish a voice, especially one that commanded respect and authority, in the professional literature. The reason is simple: The researchers and theoreticians have dominated the field of inquiry and decided on what should be published.

With the exception of autobiographies and stories written by teachers, the voices of teachers generally are filtered through and categorized by researchers' writing and publications. For decades, firsthand expressions of teacher experiences and wisdom (sometimes conveyed in the form of advice or recommendations) were considered nothing more than "recipes" or lists of "dos and don'ts"—irrelevant to the world of research on teaching. Recently, however, under umbrella terms such as *teacher thinking, teacher processes, teacher cognition,* and *teacher practices,* it has become acceptable and even fashionable to take what teachers have to say, adapt it, and turn it into *professional knowledge, pedagogical knowledge, teacher knowledge,* and *craft knowledge.* Although researchers are now collaborating with practitioners, taking teacher views seriously, and accepting teachers on equal terms as part of teacher-training programs, teachers still do not always receive credit where it is due. Whereas in scholarly publications researchers and professors are named as coauthors, practitioners may be acknowledged only by pseudonyms such as "Nancy" or "Thomas." The culture of schools and universities, and of teachers and professors, should be compatible enough to bridge this gap in the near future.

Many of the new voices embody a critique and criticism of prevailing institutions (such as schools and schools of education) and relationships of power and inequality (including relationships between students and teachers, teachers and administrators, men and women, etc.). There is a tendency to analyze relationships in dominate and subordinate forms that serve particular interest groups.[2] The words *critical, radical, feminist, postliberal, neomarxist, transcendentalist,* and *spiritual* can be added to the narratives and voices to signify this new ethnographic trend.

1. Elbaz, "Research on Teacher's Knowledge"; Andy Hargreaves, "Revisiting Voice," *Educational Researcher* (January–February 1996), pp. 12–19. Also see Vito Perrone, *Lessons for New Teachers* (Boston: McGraw-Hill, 2000).

2. Patricia Burdell and Beth Blue Swadener, "Critical Narrative and Autoethnography in Education," *Educational Researcher* (August–September 1999), pp. 21–26.

Some of the new voices mainly deal with personal testimony and conversations of the political left—their biographies, ideological tracts, and ethnographic practices. Still others want to "decolonize" traditional research-practitioner relationships, as well as dethrone scientific and empirical authority while elevating the notions of subjectivity and qualitative methods.[1] These new voices focus on racial prejudice and bigotry, multiculturalism and gender discourse, political domination and oppression, and corporate, capitalistic, and military excess.[2] They tend to frown on 400 years of science, rooted in the ideas of Newtonian physics, the quantum measurements of Einstein and Fermi, as well as the logic and rational thinking of Bacon, Locke, and Descartes in Europe and Thomas Jefferson, Ben Franklin, and John Marshall in the United States (who exemplified the Age of Reason).

These new voices prefer the existentialist thinking of the twentieth century (Camus, Kierkegaard, and Sartre), radicalized linguistics (the oppressed gain a political voice), and discourse concerning social and cultural issues (class, race, gender, and gender preference). They frown on disciplinary boundaries and reject traditional and contemporary educators (both their practices and pedagogy) for their inability to deal with oppressive ideology (or what I would call "ugly-isms") such as militarism, colonialism, imperialism, racism, and so on. These radical critics blame teachers for remaining on the sidelines while most people bleed socially and economically and live a miserable existence.[3] (Remember, outside the United States and the West, the vast majority of people live in poverty or near poverty.) They would prefer that teachers, in their role as change agents, storm the barricades, which makes little sense given the conservative nature of teachers and the fact that as they get older they curb their philosophical and political idealism and make compromises for the practical reality of feeding their families.

These radical voices would say their ideas are rooted in the Frankfurt School (1920s and 1930s), which included Eric Fromm, Jurgen Habermas, Kurt Lewin, Herbert Marcuse, and Karl Popper (mostly western Marxists) living in Germany, most of whom immigrated to the United States during the rise of Nazism. They are also influenced by Latin America critics such as Paulo Friere, Che Guevara, and Ivan Illich (also neomarxists).[4] In terms of education, their ideas are rooted in old-fashioned

1. Gary L. Anderson and Kathy Herr, "The New Paradigm Wars," *Educational Researcher* (June–July 1999), pp. 12–21; Burdell and Swadener, "Critical Personal Narrative . . . in Education."

2. For a brief review of these issues, as purported by these educators, see Carl A. Grant, ed., *Multicultural Research: A Reflective Engagement with Race, Class, Gender, and Sexual Orientation* (Philadelphia: Falmer, 1999); Donaldo Macedo and Lilia Bartolome, *Dancing with Bigotry* (New York: St. Martin's Press, 2000); and William F. Pinar, ed. *Contemporary Curriculum Discourses* (New York: Peter Lang, 1999).

3. Personally, I would settle for teachers to encourage dialogue, protect dissent, and teach about democracy, morality, and the virtues of heroism and patriotism exemplified by the police and firefighters involved in the WTC tragedy.

4. See Henry Giroux, *Theory and Resistance in Education: A Pedagogy for the Opposition* (Westport, CT: Bergin & Garvey, 1983); Giroux, *Impure Acts: The Practical Politics of Cultural Studies* (New York: Routledge, 2000); and Peter McLaren, *Che Guevara, Paulo Freire, and the Pedagogy of Revolution* (Lanham, MD: Rowman & Littlefield, 2000).

Reconstructionist philosophy—namely, the ideas of George Counts and Harold Rugg, who spoke against the prevailing social and political order, spoke against existing economic and racial discrimination, and sought to reform schools and society.[1] What is often considered fresh, thought provoking, and radical is really based on the old ideas of Counts and Rugg, updated with a little more vim and vinegar—and with slightly more hostility against the Establishment.

Some of these new researchers see themselves as "border-crossers"; that is, they teach in several departments within the educational field, draw on several social sciences as their source of knowledge, and sometimes bounce around (often isolated in their respective institutions) from university to university until they feel accepted. Their voices are based on poststructural, postcolonial, postcritical, and postmodern theories—a collection of heightened consciousness, theoretical and political discourse, phenomenological and qualitative methods, and race and gender politics as the basis of their knowledge, constructs, and paradigms.

Right now, these "border-crossers" seek to reframe, redefine, and reconceptualize their respective fields in education (and other social sciences). In doing so, they threaten some colleagues on a professional and personal level—partially because of political ideology (and the way they perceive the world) and partially because of personality differences. Thus, these critics often remain isolated in their departments and universities. Often, they mix politics with their professional relations and have trouble getting along with their colleagues who perceive the world from another perspective—more traditional, conservative, and/or empirical. Some of these people can be considered crusaders who have made impressive contributions to their fields—and we are richer for it.

## Reflection

The terms *reflection* and *reflective practice* are partly based on the works of Carl Rogers and David Schon, studying the actions and thoughts of workers in a variety of fields who learn to analyze and interpret events in ways that guide their own development and day-to-day practice. According to these authors, each person is capable of examining questions and answers needed to improve his or her own professional performance. Through open-mindedness and maturity, and with the help of colleagues, individuals can discover new ideas and illuminate what they already understand and know how to do.[2] Such reflection, in effect, combines the essentials of self-evaluation and peer evaluation: It can provide clearer perceptions of oneself and others and provide explanations and reasons behind teacher and student behavior.

It is through reflection that teachers focus on their concerns, come to better understand their own teacher behavior, and help themselves or colleagues improve as

---

1. Counts, *Dare the Schools Build a New Social Order?;* Harold Rugg, *Culture and Education in America* (New York: Harcourt, 1931).
2. Vicki K. Laboskey, *Development of Reflective Practice* (New York: Teachers College Press, 1994); Rachel C. Livsey and Parker J. Plamer, *The Courage to Teach: A Guide to Reflection and Renewal* (San Francisco: Jossey-Bass, 1999).

teachers. Through reflective practices in group settings, or forums, teachers learn to listen carefully to each other, which also helps provide insight into one's own work. In turn, as researchers hear teachers reflect on their practices, what they do in the classroom, and the basis for those actions, they are in the position to translate the teachers' practical knowledge and particular point of view into theoretical knowledge and integrate it with other teacher viewpoints.

Thus, as teachers probe and further examine specific teaching situations, a language of practice can emerge that allows us to better understand how teachers cope with the complexity of their work. Here, the key is to make sense of what teachers have to say, to clarify and elaborate on particular scripts or situations, and to delineate what meaning these reflections have for the teachers themselves and other professionals.

Now, the problem is that aspiring teachers are not encouraged to be reflective. Teacher preparation programs, according to John Goodlad, do not develop the skills of discourse, debate, self-analysis, introspection, elaboration, and the like for teachers to engage in personal reflection and professional renewal.[1] There is no set procedure, no case studies, no course in which teachers can come together and reflect on teaching concerns. As beginning teachers enter their chosen occupation, they are socialized into a culture of staff meetings that feature little dialogue about teacher or school improvement. Rather, most of the discussion is about school bureaucracy, school regulations, state requirements, and so on—and getting paperwork and records in on time. Such trivial staff activities, year after year, takes its toll on teachers. Listening to teachers talk about records, reports, and regulations—and all the other features of bureaucracy—is common shop talk, lounge talk, and cafeteria talk.

In describing what takes place in the classroom, teachers do not seem to have a precise vocabulary to assess what is happening when they teach, and therefore they have difficulty in reflecting on their practice. According to Phil Jackson, teachers use fleeting cues, such as "You could tell from their faces that the students were interested in the lesson" or "The students seem motivated and asked questions"—to describe what takes place in class.[2] Even worse, most teachers are unable to provide detailed descriptions or analysis of their own behavior or students' behavior. Their reflections are superficial; rarely, if ever, do they consider multiple factors or that their actions have multiple influences on their students. All these facts of classroom life reduce the ability of teachers to reflect and explore ways to improve. It is even more difficult for beginning teachers who tend to deal in absolute, and not relative, viewpoints.

The data suggest that because of lack of experience, beginning teachers operate at a low level of reflection and are more close-minded than experienced teachers. The latter are more open to change and have the confidence to admit when they don't know the answer, and they are more able to appreciate multiple factors and understand multiple perspectives.[3] There is also a need for teachers to analyze and discriminate

1. John I. Goodlad, *Teachers for Our Nation's Schools* (San Francisco: Jossey-Bass, 1994).

2. Jackson, *Life in Classrooms.*

3. Dorene D. Ross, "First Steps in Development of a Reflective Approach," *Journal of Teacher Education* (March–April 1998), pp. 22–30.

between average, above-average, and exceptional teaching, to help themselves and others improve their performance, and to cope with personal issues related to professional self-concept and identity (and other adjustment problems related to the job). The best way to deal with these matters is for teachers to reflect—to take stock of their strengths and weaknesses as teachers, to honestly engage in self-examination, to be observed and mentored and to observe and mentor others, and finally to make adjustments that deal with the lifestyle of teachers. See Teaching Tips 1.2.

## EPISODE *B*

## Reconceptulizing Teaching

To argue that good teaching boils down to a set of prescriptive behaviors, methods, or proficiency levels, that teachers must follow a "new" research-based teaching plan or evaluation system, or that decisions about teacher accountability can be assessed in terms of students passing some standardized or a multiple-choice test is to miss the human aspect of teaching—the "real stuff" of what teaching is all about.

Stress on assessment and evaluation systems illustrate that behaviorism has won at the expense of humanistic psychology. It also suggests that school administrators, policymakers, and researchers would rather focus on the *science* of teaching—where behaviors and outcomes can be observed, counted, or measured—than on the *art* of teaching with its humanistic and hard to measure variables.

Robert Linn contends that assessment of teachers and students can be easily mandated, implemented, and reported, and thus have wide appeal under the guise of "reform." Although these assessment systems are supposed to improve education, they don't necessarily do so.[1] Real reform is complex and costly (for example, reducing class size, raising teacher salaries, introducing special reading and tutoring programs, extending the school day and year), and it takes time before the results are evident. People, such as politicians and business leaders, who seem to be leading this latest wave of reform want a quick, easy, and cheap fix. Thus, they will always opt for assessment, since it is simple and inexpensive to implement. It creates heightened media visibility, the feeling that something is being done, and the "Hawthorne effect" or novelty tends to elevate short-term gains. This assessment focus (which is a form of behaviorism) also provides a rationale for teacher education programs, because it suggests we can separate the effects of teachers from other variables and identify good teaching. Yet it is questionable, given our current knowledge of teaching and teacher education, and the human factor that goes with teaching and learning, whether new teachers can be properly prepared both in terms of academic rigor and practical reality.

---

1. Robert L. Linn, "Assessment and Accountability," *Educational Researcher* (March 2000), pp. 4–15.

# *Teaching Tips* 1.2

## Observing Other Teachers to Improve Teaching Practices

Beginning teachers (even student teachers) can supplement their pedagogical knowledge and practice by observing experienced teachers organize their classrooms and instruct students. Below is a list of questions beginning teachers (as well as student teachers) can consider when observing other teachers.

### Student-Teacher Interaction

- What evidence was there that the teacher understood the needs of the students?
- What techniques were used to encourage students' respect for each others' turn to talk?
- What student behaviors in class were acceptable and what were unacceptable?
- How did the teacher motivate students?
- In what way did the teacher see things from students' points of view?

### Teacher-Learning Process

- Which instructional methods interested the students?

- How did the teacher provide for transitions between instructional activities?
- What practical life experiences (or activities) were used by the teacher to integrate concepts being learned?
- How did the teacher minimize student frustration or confusion concerning the skills of concepts being taught?
- In what ways did the teacher encourage creative, imaginative work from students?
- What instructional methods were used to make students think about skills, ideas, or answers?
- How did the teacher arrange the groups? What social factors were evident within groups?
- How did the teacher integrate subject matter with other subjects?

### Classroom Environment

- How did the teacher use classroom space/equipment effectively?
- What did you like and dislike about the physical environment of the classroom?

---

For those in the business of preparing teachers, there is a need to provide a research base and rationale showing that teachers who enroll and complete a teacher education program are more likely to be effective teachers than those who lack such training. There are several alternative certification programs for teachers in more than 40 states, in which nearly 5 percent (as high as 16 percent in Texas and 22 percent in New Jersey) of the nationwide teaching force entered teaching.[1] This fact makes teachers of teachers (professors of education) take notice and try to demonstrate that their teacher preparation programs work and that they can prepare effective teachers. Indeed, there is need to identify teacher behaviors and methods that work under certain conditions—leading many educators to favor behaviorism (or prescriptive

---

1. Abbey Goodnough, "Regents Create a New Path to Teaching," *New York Times*, July 15, 2000, pp. B4, 7.

ideas and specific tasks) and assessment systems (close-ended, tiny, measurable variables) that correlate teaching behaviors (or methods) and learning outcomes.

A growing body of literature informs us that traditional certification programs and education courses make little difference in teacher effectiveness; therefore, they should be curtailed to allow alternative certification programs to expand. For the time being, Linda Darling-Hammond assures us that the bulk of the research suggests that teachers who are versed both in pedagogical knowledge as well as subject knowledge are more successful in the classroom than teachers who are versed only in subject matter. It is also true that teachers who hold standard certificates are more successful than teachers who hold emergency licenses or who attend "crash" programs in the summer and are then temporarily licensed.[1] Some of us become disheartened and troubled by the amount of state interference in teacher certification permitted by schools of education that other professional schools would not permit.

Being able to describe detailed methods of teaching and how and why teachers do what they do should improve the performance of teachers. Much of the new research, however, hardly tells the whole story of teaching—what leads to teacher effectiveness and student learning. Being able to describe teachers' thinking or decision making and to analyze their stories and reflective practices suggest that we understand and can improve teaching. The new research on teaching—with its stories, biographies, reflective practices, and qualitative methods—provides a platform and publication outlet for researchers. It promotes their expertise (which in turn continues to separate them from practitioners) and permits them to continue to subordinate teaching to research. It also provides a new paradigm for analyzing teaching, since the older models (teacher styles, teacher personality, teacher characteristics, teacher effectiveness, etc.) have become exhausted and repetitive. The issues and questions related to the new paradigm create new educational wars and controversy between traditional and nontraditional researchers, between behaviorists and phenomenologists, and between quantitative and qualitative advocates. It is questionable, however, whether this new knowledge base about teaching really improves teaching and learning or leads to substantial and sustained improvement.

## The Need for Humanistic Teaching

The focus of teacher research should be on the learner, not the teacher; on the feelings and attitudes of the student, not on knowledge and information (since feelings and attitudes will eventually determine what knowledge and information are sought after and acquired); and on long-term development and growth of the students, not on short-term objectives or specific teacher tasks. But if teachers spend more time focusing on the learners' feelings and attitudes, as well as on social and personal growth,

---

1. Linda Darling-Hammond, "The Challenge of Staffing Our Schools," *Educational Leadership* (May 2001), pp. 12–17; Linda Darling-Hammond, Barnett Berry, and Amy Thoreson, "Does Teacher Certification Matter?" *Education Evaluation and Policy Analysis* (Spring 2001), pp. 57–77.

teachers may be penalized when cognitive student outcomes (little pieces of information) are correlated with their behaviors and methods in class.

Especially when they are young, students need to be encouraged and nurtured by their teachers. Most are too dependent on approval from significant adults (i.e., parents and teachers). Parents and teachers need to help young children and adolescents establish a source for self-esteem by focusing on their strengths, supporting them, discouraging negative self-talk, and helping them take control of their lives in context with their own cultures and values.

People (including children) with high self-esteem achieve at high levels, and the more one achieves, the better one feels about oneself. The opposite is also true: Students with low self-esteem and who fail to master the subject matter get down on themselves and eventually give up. In short, student self-esteem and achievement are directly related. If teachers can nurture students' self-esteem, almost everything else will fall into place, including achievement scores and academic outcomes. Regardless of how smart or talented a child is, if he or she has personal problems, then cognition will be detrimentally effected.

This builds a strong argument for creating successful experiences for students to help them feel good about themselves. The long-term benefits are obvious: The more students learn to like themselves, the more they will achieve; and the more they achieve, the more they will like themselves. But that takes time and a lot of nurturing; and it doesn't show up on a standardized test within a semester or school year. Moreover, it doesn't help the teacher who is being evaluated by a content- or test-driven school administrator who is looking for results now. And it certainly doesn't benefit the teacher who is being evaluated by a behaviorist instrument, such as how many times he or she attended departmental meetings, whether the shades in the classroom were even, if his or her instructional objectives were clearly stated, or whether homework was assigned or the computer was used on a regular basis.

It is obvious that certain behaviors contribute to good teaching. The trouble is that there is little agreement on exactly what behaviors or methods are most important. Some teachers gain theoretical knowledge of "what works," but are unable to put the ideas into practice. Some teachers with similar preparation act effortlessly in the classroom and others consider teaching a chore. All this suggests that teaching cannot be described in terms of a checklist of a precise model. It also suggests that teaching is a humanistic activity that deals with people (not tiny behaviors or competencies) and how people (teachers and students) behave in a variety of classroom and school settings.

Research on teacher effectiveness provides a vocabulary and system for improving our insight into good teaching, but there is a danger that some of us might become too rigid in our view of teaching. Following only one teacher model or evaluation system can lead to too much emphasis on specific behaviors that can be easily measured or prescribed in advance. This comes at the expense of ignoring humanistic behaviors that cannot be easily measured or prescribed in advance, such as aesthetic appreciation, emotions, values, and moral responsibility.

Although some educators recognize that humanistic factors influence teaching, we continue to define most teacher behaviors in terms of behaviorist and cognitive factors.

Most teacher evaluation instruments tend to deemphasize the human side of teaching because it is difficult to observe or measure. In an attempt to be scientific, to predict and control behavior, we sometimes lose sight of the attitudes and feelings of teachers and their relations with students. As Maxine Greene asserts, good teaching and learning involve feelings, insights, imagination, creative inquiries—an existential and philosophical encounter—that cannot be readily quantified. By overlooking hard-to-measure aspects of teaching, we miss a substantial part of teaching—what Greene calls the "stuff" of teaching, what Eisner calls the "artful elements" of teaching, and what others refer to as drama, tones, and flavor.[1]

Teacher behaviors that correlate with measurable outcomes often lead to rote learning, "learning bits" rather than the whole picture, and to memorization and automatic responses instead of high-order learning. These evaluation models seem to miss moral and ethical outcomes, as well as social, personal, and self-actualizing factors related to learning and life—in effect, the affective domain of learning and the psychology of being human. In their attempt to observe and measure what teachers do, and to detail whether students improve their performance on reading or math tests, these models ignore the learners' imaginations, fantasies, and intuitive thinking; their dreams, hopes, and aspirations; and how teachers have an impact on these hard-to-define and measure but very important aspects of students' lives.

In providing feedback and evaluation for teachers, many factors need to be considered so the advice or information does not fall on deaf ears. Teachers appreciate feedback processes whereby they can improve their teaching, so long as the processes are honest and professionally planned and administered, so long as teachers are permitted to make mistakes, and so long as more than one model of effectiveness is considered so that they can adopt recommended behaviors and methods to fit their own personalities and philosophies of teaching.

Teachers must also be permitted to choose from a wide range of research and theory, and to discard other teacher behaviors that conflict with their own personality and philosophy without the fear of being considered ineffective. Many school districts, even state departments of education, have developed evaluation instruments and salary plans based exclusively on prescriptive and product-oriented behaviors. Even worse, teachers who do not exhibit these behaviors are often penalized or labeled as "marginal" or "incompetent."[2] There is an increased danger that many more school districts and states will continue to jump on this bandwagon and make decisions based on prescriptive behaviors research without recognizing or giving credibility to other teacher behaviors or methods that might deal with feelings, emotions, and personal connections with people—what some educators label as "fuzzy" or "vague" criteria.

1.  Maxine Greene, *The Dialectic of Teaching* (New York: Teachers College Press, 1998); and Elliot W. Eisner, *The Educational Imagination,* 4th ed. (New York: Macmillan, 1999).

2.  Ornstein, "Beyond Effective Teaching." Also see Allan C. Ornstein, ed., *Teaching: Theory into Practice* (Boston: Allyn and Bacon, 1995).

## Examples of Humanistic Teaching

In traditional terms, humanism is rooted in the fourteenth- and fifteenth-century Renaissance period of Europe, where there was a revival of classical humanism expressed by the ancient Greek and Latin culture. The philosophies and educators of the Renaissance, like the medieval scholastics before them (who were governed and protected by the church) found wisdom in the past and stressed classical manuscripts. Unlike the scholastics, they were often independent of the church and were concerned with the experiences of *humans* rather than God-like or religious issues.[1]

In the early twentieth century, humanistic principles of teaching and learning were envisioned in the theories of progressive education: in the *child-centered* lab school directed by John Dewey at the University of Chicago from 1896 to 1904; in the *play-centered* methods and materials introduced by Maria Montessuri, which were designed to develop the practical, sensory, and formal skills of prekindergarten and kindergarten slum children of Italy starting in 1908; and the *activity-centered* practices of William Kilpatrick, who, in the 1920s and 1930s, urged that elementary teachers organize classrooms around social activities, group enterprises, and group projects, and allow children to say what they think.

All of these progressive theories were highly humanistic and stressed the child's interests, individuality, and creativity—in short, the child's freedom to develop naturally, freedom to develop without teacher domination, and freedom from the weight of rote learning. But progressivism failed because, in the view of Lawrence Cremin, there weren't enough good teachers to implement progressive thought in classrooms and schools.[2] To be sure, it is much easier to stress knowledge, rote learning, and right answers than it is to teach about ideas, to consider the interests and needs of students, and to give them freedom to explore and interact with each other without teacher constraints.

By the end of the twentieth century, the humanistic teacher was depicted by William Glasser's "positive" and "supportive" teacher who could manage students without coercion and teach without failure.[3] It was also illustrated by Robert Fried's "passionate" teachers and Vito Perrone's "teacher with a heart"—teachers who live to teach young children and refuse to submit to apathy or criticism that may infect the school in which they work.[4] These teachers are dedicated and caring; they actively

---

1. The religious scholar of the medieval period, versed in scriptures and theological logic, was no longer the preferred model; rather it was the courtier—a liberally educated man of style, wit, and elegance; a diplomat, politician, or successful merchant. See Baldesar Catiglione, *The Book of the Courtier*, rev. ed. (Garden City, NY: Doubleday, 1959). Machavelli's *The Prince* is a perfect example of the preferred philosophy, advise, and behavior for this Renaissance period.

2. Lawrence A. Cremin, *The Transformation of the School* (New York: Random House, 1961).

3. William Glasser, *Schools Without Failure* (New York: Harper & Row, 1969); Glasser, *The Quality School* (New York: Harper Collins, 1990).

4. Fried, *The Passionate Teacher*; Vito Perrone, *Teacher with a Heart* (New York: Teachers College Press, 1998).

engage students in their classrooms and they affirm their identities. The students do not have to ask whether their teacher is interested in them, thinks of them, or knows their interests or concerns. The answer is definitely *yes*.

The humanistic teacher is also portrayed by Ted Sizer's mythical teacher called "Horace," who is dedicated and enjoys teaching, treats learning as a humane enterprise, inspires his students to learn, and encourages them to develop their powers of thought, taste, and character.[1] Yet, the system forces Horace to make a number of compromises in planning, teaching, and grading, which he knows he would not make if we lived in an ideal world (with more than 24 hours in a day). Horace is a trouper; he hides his frustration. Critics of teachers don't really want to hear him or face facts; they don't even know what it is like to teach. Sizer simply states, "Most jobs in the real world have a gap between what would be nice and what is possible. One adjusts."[2] Hence, most caring, dedicated teachers are forced to make some compromises, take some shortcuts, and make some accommodations. So long as no one gets upset, and no one complains, the system permits a chasm between rhetoric (the rosy picture) and reality (slow burnout).

There is also the humanistic element in Nel Noddings's ideal teacher who focuses on the nurturing of "competent, caring, loving, and lovable persons." To that end, she describes teaching as a caring profession in which teachers should convey to students the caring way of thinking about oneself, siblings, and strangers; animals, plants, and physical environment. She stresses the affective aspect of teaching: the need to focus on the child's strengths and interests, and the need for an individualized curriculum built around the child's abilities and needs.[3] Caring, according to Noddings, cannot be achieved by a formula or checklist. It calls for different behaviors in different situations—from tenderness to tough love. Good teaching, like good parenting, requires continuous effort, trusting relationships, and continuity of purpose—the purpose of caring, appreciating human connections, and respecting people and ideas from a historical, multicultural, and diverse perspective.[4]

Actually, the humanistic teacher is someone who highlights the personal and social dimension in teaching and learning, as opposed to the behavioral, scientific, or technological aspects. One might argue that everything the teacher does is "human" and that the expression *humanistic teaching* is a cliché. However, I would also use the term in a "loose" sense to describe the teacher who emphasizes the arts as opposed to the sciences, and people instead of numbers. Although the teacher understands the value of many subjects, including the sciences and social sciences, he or she feels there is the need for students to understand certain *ideas* and *values*, some rooted in 3,000 years of philosophy, literature, art, music, and theater. Without cer-

---

1. Theodore R. Sizer, *Horace's Compromise* (Boston: Houghton Mifflin, 1985).
2. Ibid., p. 20.
3. Nel Noddings, *The Challenge to Care in Schools* (New York: Teachers College Press, 1992).
4. Nel Noddings, *Educating Moral People* (New York: Teachers College Press, 2001); Noddings, *The Challenge to Care in Schools*.

tain agreed-upon content—what Arthur Bestor and Allan Bloom would call the "liberal arts," what E. D. Hirsh and Diane Ravitch would call "essential knowledge," and what Robert Hutchins and Mortimer Adler would call "the Great Books"—our heritage would crumble and we would be at the mercy of chance and ignorance. Moreover, our education enterprise would be subject to the whim and fancy of local fringe groups.

Humanistic education, according to Jacques Barzun, the elegant and eloquent writer of history and humanism, leads to a form of knowledge that helps deal with the nature of life, but it does not guarantee a more gracious or noble life. "The humanities will not sort out the world's evils and were never meant to cure [our] troubles. . . . They will not heal diseased minds or broken hearts any more than they will foster political democracy or settle international disputes." The so-called humanities (and I add, the humanistic teacher) "have meaning," according to Barzun, "because of the inhumanity of life; what they depict is strife and disaster"[1] (and I add, by example, help us deal with the human condition and provide guidelines for moral behavior, good taste, and the improvement of civilization).

On a schoolwide level, I would argue that humanism means that we eliminate the notion that everyone should go to college, since it creates frustration, anger, and unrealistic expectations among large numbers of children and youth. According to Paul Goodman, it requires that society find viable occupational options for noncollege graduates, and jobs that have decent salaries, respect, and social status.[2] It suggests, according to John Gardner, that we recognize various forms of excellence—the excellent teacher, the excellent artist, the excellent plumber, the excellent bus driver—otherwise, we create a myopic view of talent and subsequent tension that will threaten a democratic society.[3] It also means that we appreciate and nurture different student abilities, aptitudes, and skills—what Howard Gardner calls "multiple intelligences."[4]

We need to provide more options and opportunities for children and youth, not only preparation for jobs related to verbal and math skills or aptitudes (the ones usually emphasized in schools and tested on tests) but also skills and aptitudes that produce poets, painters, musicians, actors, athletes, mechanics, and public speakers or politicians. Both authors believe in performance and merit, although John Gardner calls it "talent" (what Howard Gardner calls "intelligence," and what I call "skills and aptitude"). John Gardner is more concerned about the social consequences if we emphasize only academic performance as a criterion for success and status. Similarly, Howard Gardner feels that emphasis on verbal-logical-mathematical learning is rooted in classic Piagetian theory, which ignores a pluralistic approach to cognition and a wider range of domains conducive to different cultures.

1. Jacques Barzun, *Teachers in America,* rev ed. (Lanham, MD: University Press of America, 1972).

2. Paul Goodman, *Compulsory Mis-Education* (New York: Horizon Press, 1964).

3. John Gardner, *Excellence: Can We Be Equal Too?* (New York: Harper & Row, 1962).

4. Howard Gardner, *Frames of Mind: The Theory of Multiple Intelligences* (New York: Basic Books, 1983).

## Moving from Humanistic to Moral Thought

If we fail to adapt a more caring and compassionate view of teaching and schooling, then we fall victim to excessive competitiveness and materialism—and eventually to class differences that divide society into dominant and subordinate groups. Pursuant to neomarxist and radical postmodern thinking, we create a permanent underclass living in "squalid" (Kozol's words), "dehumanizing" (Friere's words) and "colonialized" (Giroux's and McLaren's words) conditions. The outcome: a society in which a disproportionate number of low-achieving students, poor, minority, and special needs children are locked into future low-end jobs, unemployment, or what Oscar Lewis, some 40 years ago, referred to as the "culture of poverty," whereby poverty is transferred from generation to generation.[1] In short, we have a new subordinate group—the "have nots"—construed as dumb and lazy, and deskilled by a school system and society that encourage competitiveness and judge people on different characteristics and different outcomes.

This human situation is tolerated by the majority of the populace because egalitarianism, social justice, and human dignity are wrongly conceived or ignored. Our prejudices become ingrained in our thinking because they become institutionalized by society. Moreover, we come to rely on "scientific objectivity" to excuse or defend educational and social practices that generate and then perpetuate these dominant-subordinate conditions. There should be no room in this country, or in any society that claims to be civilized, for second-class citizenship, or even for people who think of themselves as such. There have been enough second-class citizens in the world.

Through the ages, the vast majority of humans have been barbarians, slaves, serfs, peasants, extremely poor, and uneducated. Almost one-half to one percent of the population—the monarchs and nobility, popes and cardinals, military leaders and generals, czars, and capitalists—have possessed more than 50 percent of the wealth and resources existing within their particular period of history, and in many countries and civilizations the percent of wealth among the ruling class has topped 90 percent. Even today, 1.2 billion people (or 20 percent) of the world's population live on less than one dollar a day, and 50 percent of the developing countries (4.5 billion people) live on less than two dollars a day—the greatest percentages in South Asia, sub-Saharan Africa, and Latin America.[2] These poor people live under wretched conditions that very few of us, except for a few scholars and human rights workers, fully comprehend. But it is this poverty and hopelessness in developing countries, the resulting difference in quality of life and culture, that leads to deep and lasting hatred toward the more prosperous western world and a form of madness where people don't care if they die or are blown to pieces.

Too many people in this country, and in other countries, have been forced to give up their identities, to move from their world to another world, to assimilate: to pass for white, Christian, or "straight." No one should have to pretend for a lifetime, to live

1. Oscar Lewis, "The Culture of Poverty," *Scientific American* (October 1996), pp. 19–25.

2. "Poverty and Globalization," Center for Global Studies Conference, St. John's University, April 26, 2001. Based on 1998 World Bank Data.

in a closet, to disown one's family, ethnic group, or religion—never to return to one's people. Of course, one can argue that ethnocentrism and religious zeal are also sources of the worst atrocities. True believers come in all shades, stripes, and ideologies—and there has been a steady oversupply of lawless opportunists and willing executioners, no matter how low their position in the chain of command may be, who take pleasure in the destruction and annihilation of other people.

Some of you might consider this interpretation as an attempt to instill neomarxist, postmodern, or illusory rhetoric in the discussion, but I contend that lack of humanism and moral teaching has resulted in lack of conscience and caring throughout the ages and throughout the globe. The outcomes are similar for all time: human suffering, oppression, fanaticism, and wholesale slaughter of human life, under a political or religious ideology that mocks the individual and preaches hatred, brute force, and terrorism. It represents the exploitive and "dark side" of the human psyche, inflicted on humans by humans for centuries, from Roman gladiator arenas to African slave ships, from European serfdom and mass peasantry to the burning of witches and the hanging of blacks and gays in the United States.

Of course, the Japanese atrocities in Nanking, the battle in the Ukraine, the Holocaust in Europe, the purges of Stalin and Mao, the Killing Fields of Pol Pot and the tribal wars and civil wars of Africa are the darkest pages of history, totally irrational and extreme forms of evil that cannot be fully understood with only words. Narratives from victims, photographs, and films must become part of the discourse to fully comprehend the extent of this rampant barbarism and blasphemy. Blaming today's generation for another generation's sins is not the answer, but learning from old injustices and immorality is valuable so that we don't repeat history, so that we become more a civil and compassionate society.

## Remembering the Dead

All of us have lived most of our lives in the twentieth century, and all the lost souls who no longer exist because of human cruelty and hatred must be remembered. Most of the voices and faces we never knew; therefore, it is easy to become detached from their demise and to treat them as an abstract statistic. In fact, the larger the number of dead—thousands or millions—the easier it is to become "clinical" or "objective" (by adding zeros) because the mind is unable to fathom the reality and enormity of the deed, unless, of course, a loved one was part of the cruel nature of history. Among the dead are some who were famous for something and are in our encyclopedias, but the vast majority have been forgotten and funneled into anonymity. All that can be hoped for is the poet, painter, or musician to make use of the forgotten through their pen, canvas, or lyrics in order for the living to gain understanding. In this connection, it is for the teacher to educate the next generation—to make use of these forgotten and transitory people, to help them return among the living just for a brief moment, to help explain the order of magnitude of lost lives and a counting system of the dead that involves five, six, or seven zeros.

Educators who grew up in the twentieth century must now teach students of the twenty-first century that the most cruel and vile acts were committed in the twentieth century—much worse than the vestiges of the World Trade Center. The worst deeds were committed in the twentieth century, despite that it comprised the most educated populace, because countries produced the most efficient machines to kill the most people. And, after surrounded by mass murder, rape, and pillage, we become detached from these violent and deathward-leaning acts; we deal with these encounters by abstracting and anatomizing them through a variety of academic subjects and topics. We keep them under lock and key so our young children and students have almost no real knowledge of Nanking, the Ukraine,[1] the Holocaust, Stalin's and Mao's purges, the Killing Fields, or more recently Kosovo, Angola, and Rwanda. Even at home— Antietam (4,000+ dead), Gettysburg (50,000+), Pearl Harbor (2,300), and now the World Trade Center (2,900)—the dead are generally forgotten, as if they never existed, except by individuals who knew someone or buried someone.

It is questionable whether we have a complete language to capture all the torture, pillage, and plunder, all the vile deeds humans have imposed on other humans—in the name of God, the empire or monarch, the nation-state, or some new order. Czeslaw Milosz, the leading Polish poet and the most electrifying international poet of the twentieth century (not mentioned in U.S. classrooms, and unknown by 99.9 percent of the U.S. English and history teachers) comes closest to describing the terror of the twentieth century as to make other poetry (about life and death, peace and war) written in the West seen trite. In his last book, a collection of 70 years of writing poetry, the 91-year-old poet confronts the truth. "If I could at last [say] what [I feel]/ if I could [yell:] people! I have lied by pretending it was not there./ It was there, day and night." This time he speaks to God. "You are closing down my five senses, slowing,/ and I am an old man lying in darkness." Experiencing one activity after another, never really being free, he writes: "I always ran forward, composing poems,"[2] and thus escaping from the bleak and bitter reality of his homeland and continent.

1. I assume most readers need help with Nanking and the Ukraine. Japan invaded Nanking, the capital of China, in 1939. Approximately two million Chinese people died. Women were beaten, raped, and murdered. Children and men were bayoneted, used as target practice, and set on fire, and then the city was torched. There was no sense of guilt by the Japanese, since they were fighting for the Emperor (like fighting for the king, the Fuhrer, God, or country). The Japanese regarded the Chinese as animals, subhuman, and similar to rats or bugs (no different from the way Serbs, gypsies, homosexuals, Armenians, Jews, and people of black and yellow color have been depicted by the enemy).

In the Ukraine, over a three-year period, seven million people were starved, tortured, and slaughtered, mostly civilians, by the German army, Russian partisans, and Ukrainian partisans. The Ukrainian people were depicted by the conquering Germans as subhuman—one German soldier worth hundreds of Ukrainian civilians. The Ukrainian people depicted the Russian partisans as barbarians and thieves, roaming the countryside and stealing, raping, plundering, and shooting their own people.

There is no adequate way of describing these events (and other events mentioned) in a few sentences. The best I can do is to mourn these people in passing, to indulge in the uneasy business of dwelling on the ugly deeds of people who would rather we forget, not dwell on their deeds, or not remember the people they murdered.

2. Czeslaw Milosz, *New and Collected Poems: 1931–2001* (New York: HarperCollins, 2001).

As teachers, we must make sense of our past through our philosophy, history, literature, art, poetry, and music. We are required to ask our students to think about the true believers and zealots, and the willing oppressors and opportunists who have ravaged the earth. We must pay homage to the millions who perished in the wars and witch hunts, the purges and extermination camps of the twentieth century. We must hear their voices, see their faces, and understand their final thoughts of life in the midst of background screams, muzzled groans, sad goodbyes, and then the stench of death to fully comprehend the barbaric deeds of humans, and how many more times throughout all time evil has prevailed over good.

Indeed, I am reminded of an old soldier, a World War II veteran, discussing the Battle of the Bulge (275,000 dead). He couldn't remember how he celebrated his last birthday or why he just opened the refrigerator, but he could vividly recount the conditions of the battlefield as if it had happened yesterday: gray foreboding clouds, the snow-covered grass, the cold nipping at his toes and fingers, the rubble of the dead around him, the eyes of the enemy, the tatter of machine guns on the front, and the smell of fuel oil and ashes of annihilation mixed in the countryside air.

In detail, the veteran could still recall the names and faces of the fallen dead around him, the color of their eyes, their smiles and sorrows, what they had on their minds the night before they died, and the outstretched arms and last words of his doomed comrades, 18, 19, and 20 years old. In a flash, all their hopes were destroyed. They never had a chance to live their lives, to have children and grandchildren; they were all taken away and now forgotten—except by him. For that moment of recollection, there was nothing impersonal or abstract about the slaughter—the excruciating combat, the lost voices and souls, and the sense of madness around him. Tears were flowing from the old man's eyes, and his voice was breaking down; it was only the human spirit and his memory that kept him going.

I am reminded of another veteran, a survivor of the Battle of Normandy, walking along the gravesites, remembering his fallen comrades and lamenting: No one wins in war. There are only losers—on all sides. "Here lies John; here lies Fred; they gave away all their tomorrows. They died so we could live." I can't recall the old soldier's name. It was either Wally Parr or Charlie Klein. It could have also been Gunther Kraus or Helmut Schmidt. It could have also been an Englishman, a Canadian, or a French soldier. There is little difference. The ancient Greeks summed it up, "War is a human plague," as the historian Herodotus said. War is "a curse from Zeus," so the poet Hesiod concluded. "War is senseless butchery" was the theme of Thucydides's history. Let me vault through time, to the present. War is the antithesis of life, peace, and hope; it breeds death, destruction, and despair. War is the evil in all of us; it is innate to the human condition; it allows fathers and mothers to bury and remember their sons as heroes.[1]

Wartime letters and diaries, written by ordinary people—many with little or average education—have become part of our history, a way of understanding the folly and tragedy of war. Trapped in foxholes and trenches, charging open battlefields and

---

1. I am aware of the need for political correctness and gender equality, but as I told the editor, about 99 percent of the soldiers throughout history have been males. I rejected the word *daughters*.

beachheads, crawling on their bellies, fatigued and ill-fed, in jungles and frozen waste-lands, these soldiers often wrote home, sharing their fears and hopes, describing the horrors and heat of war, often in simple, sad, and surreal ways. Every "civilized" country has its share of letters, written by soldiers still alive, hoping to come home alive, often having a feelings they would die on the battlefield. American soldiers are heroes, and every country has its soldier heroes, even our enemies who we dehumanize, who fight for sacred rights or a holy cause. Yet, I cannot remember a teacher in my 12 years of schooling ever mentioning one wartime letter or diary, one excerpt where the groans and agonies of a soldier were mentioned—never even when we were talking about Yorktown, Bull Run, or the Battle of the Bulge. I am still unable to discern whether the chief reason was due to teacher ignorance, laziness, or lack of creativity.

Across centuries, across cultures, we dispose of the dead in different ways. We bury them, burn them, mummify them, and place them on logs and send them out to sea. Some dead have been left in the fields for animals to eat. Some have been thrown into pits, sewers, and rice fields—some hundreds at a time, some one at a time. Many of us weep at funerals; others drink, dance, or converse with the dead while they are still in our midst; and still others converse with them long after their death. Funerals help define our culture and who we are, that a person belongs somewhere and some place in time. Coming together and remembering the dead—summing up the person's life, and contemplating or worshipping, believing that the soul merges with the universe (Hinduism), is part of a stream without an end (Buddhism), or rises to heaven (Christianity)—is an important ritual. Regardless of culture or religion, the dead matter to the living.

As teachers, we must try to provide some reassurance to our students that the dead did not die in vain, good can prevail over evil, and morality can topple immorality. Although we should not be weighted down by the past, we must remember all the nameless and voiceless people who suffered and died a senseless or terrible death before their time, and keep the specter and memory of the nations, tribes, and political and religious zealots that committed the acts of violence against these victims. We must fight off fading memories and amnesia so that we have a chance to prevent, or at least reduce, the animalistic nature in us, the resulting blasphemy and evil that has characterized so many of the inhabitants of the last century.

We should inspire our students and help them deal with the nature of life and death; this is one of our most important professional roles. Yet, it ought to come as no surprise that we rarely connect with our students in this way. Is it because we have no passion, lack a sense of history or loyalty to an ideal, have a desire to omit death from our classroom discussions, or merely shy from moral messages? I personally think it is all of these reasons, and thus we fail the memory of the people of the last century and previous centuries who unjustly died before they were supposed to die.

Part of why we fail to remember the dead (and related numbers, stories, and comparisons) is that the deeds have taken place beyond our borders. It is much easier to deal "objectively" with the carnage of humanity from a global perspective rather than from an American perspective. Americans have managed to live through 225 years of turbulent history without experiencing foreign invasions, mass bombings, social anarchy, or widespread disease. We have been blessed by oceans that until very recently protected us from the wreckage and slaughter of humans experienced by the rest of the world. We are the "moderns" that Aristotle and Plato idealized. We have a political system that allows for peaceful changes, an economic system that fosters mobility and merit so that the working and middle class can rise to the top and be counted, and an educational system that educates everyone, not only the social elite or men, and promotes a productive and entrepreneur workforce—all which add to the quality of our life and reduce the possibility of inhumane behavior. What happened at the World Trade Center is heart-breaking and barbaric, but is incomparable to the loss of lives on a worldwide perspective. (Remember that Hiroshima exterminated 70,000 Japanese citizens in a nuclear moment. In our own country, 50,000 soldiers died at Gettysburg in three days.)

Writer James Atlas, editor of the Viking/Penguin Books, states, "The loss of life in the financial heart of New York was . . . nearly beyond our capacity to tolerate, but—if you take the long view—nothing out of the ordinary."[1] But many people would argue that the WTC tragedy has global implications and is one of the worst terrorist attacks on a civilian population.[2] Others might equate civilians killed in the WTC with civilians killed by U.S. bombings in Afghanistan, since their views could be colored by their own life experiences and view of history. Still others would argue, including one military historian, grieved relatives and friends may not care whether the victims were killed by terrorists or by armies pursuing a "just" cause (What is just?) by "unjust" means.[3]

Atlas speaks again: "The history of mankind is a history of anonymous and random slaughter—civilizations we think of as 'civilized' were no exception. When Caesar marched on Rome, in a small part of a single day he killed 50,000 of the enemy."[4] These distinctions may matter for philosophers, social critics, and military historians, but try discussing these differences to the dead and their descendants. For some, Americans are pursuing a "just" cause; for others, Americans (and the West) are perceived as "big bullies." Historical accident and life experiences have a lot to do with perceptions. The ancient world was a killing field; so was the medieval world with its social anarchy, plagues, and wars; and so is the modern world—only more terrible—because

1. James Atlas, "Among the Lost: Illusions of Immortality," *New York Times,* October 7, 2001, Sect. 4, p. 5.
2. One might peruse an intellectual discussion between indiscriminate terror (like the WTC) and brutal acts of war on civilian populations (Sherman's march through Georgia, the Allied bombing of Dresden and Berlin, the American bombing of Hiroshima and Tokyo, and the Serbian cleansing of Bosnia and Kosovo). Distinctions can become blurred by historical interpretation, political fragmentation, and/or philosophical speculation. For a brief discussion about the distinctions of terrorism and civilian warfare, see Michel Ignatieff, "Barbarians at the Gates," *New York Times Book Review,* February 7, 2002, p. 8. He argues that one event deals with civilians massacred deliberately and without warning during a time of peace; the other events deal with acts of war, uniformed soldiers, and a response to a declared war.
3. Caleb Carr, *The Lessons of Terror: A History of Warfare Against Civilians* (New York: Random House, 2001).
4. Atlas, "Among the Lost: Illusions of Immorality."

of technological efficiency. It is a lesson that U.S. teachers have generally avoided. From the destruction of ancient Greece by the Persians to the destruction of the third Reich by the Allied Powers, the so-called civilized world has been plundered—and has experienced more darkness than light, more destruction than peace, and more evil than good. Americans fail to understand the barbaric and inhumane side of civilization because of their nation's fortunate accidents of history, geography, and world politics.

Who is to blame for all of this death and destruction? How do we make sense of all this folly and tragedy? How do we deal with inhumanity? How do we mediate between past and present, between people lost and people now alive? Can the answers be found in Ecclesiastes or the Bhagavad-Gita?[1] On a secular basis, can the answers be found by reading Plato, Shakespeare, Darwin, Freud, Tolstoy, or Buber? Is it mainly a matter of religious, racial, and ethnic hatred? Does it boil down to 2,000 or more years of shifting borders and bad history? Should we put the blame on nationalism, imperialism, colonialism—or any other "ism"? Or is it just simple greed or fanaticism perpetuated by madmen, monarchs, and church-going men? Can it be a simple fact the *id* (people's aggression) is more powerful than the *super ego* (people's consciences)? Perhaps it's the might of *realpolitik*—armies, embassies, and families—that men and women of power must inevitably collide?

American students wind up living in a fantasy land, unaware that the rest of the world in the majority of the moments in history has experienced needless deaths and the illusion of justice. It is a feature of the texture of the world's daily lives, caused by humankind's ill-treatment of the slave, the serf, the peasant, the worker. Since the time of cave dwellers, the underclass has always been prevalent and subordinate and has been first to die in European and nonwestern conflicts, because of either political or religious rage, and in one battle after another, in one century after another. Cemeteries and burial grounds dot the global landscape; town squares and main streets are ripe with memories of the dead.

The underclass (or mass) are left to believe and have faith, to read the Bible, to listen to their clergy, to walk in the valley of death without fear, to hope at the "endpoint" there is bliss and contentment and that the soul is eternal. And for those of us, today, who don't believe and still need to grieve or be reassured, there is the world of healers and soothsayers—pop gurus, yogis, herbalists, and nutritionists, as well as traditional counselors, psychologists, and pharmacists. And if anyone still has trouble sleeping at nights, or needs psychic relief, there is always a new book by Deepak Chopra, the Dali Lama, or Guriemayi—even talk shows hosted by Oprah, Donahue, and other celebrities.

All religions provide hope and soothe the mind. In many societies, religion is a method of preventing uprisings against the ruling class. In most cases, such thinking helps sedate and control the masses to accept their station in life, to forget the anonymous slaughter of people, and to rationalize the willingness for other people to die for some ideological cause or crusade. All one has to do is believe in the hereafter and

---

1. Written between the fourth and third centuries B.C., it is one of the best-known religious Indian writings, still chanted in Hindu temples. The title means "Song of the Lord" and deals with personal responsibility and mastery of the self in the midst of life's challenges.

a better, eternal life to help accept one's misery and exploitation on earth. As Marx and Lenin would argue, religion reduces the potential for revolution by the proletariat class and the eventual overthrow of the ruling class; however, Marx and Lenin would still eliminate religion, since they view it as a competing ideology of communism.[1]

No wonder Edward Gibbon, Oswald Spengler, and Arnold Toynbee can easily talk and write for hundreds of pages about the cycles of history, the transience of civilizations, and the rise and fall of empires and monarchs. It is reflected in the immorality of those in power (power corrupts) and the disquieting behavior of people and nation states. History everywhere is full of needless death, the face of evil, the procession of one ideology after another conquering the minds, thoughts, and behavior of individuals except perhaps in America, where it might be argued that common sense, free thought, and individualism are encouraged and flourish as part of the nation's intellectual thought and social fiber.[2]

As teachers, we often fail in our role to elaborate on the agony of our history, that the need to reduce the ruthlessness and atrocities of humans rests with the present generation. All the people who are alive today are connected to the past like a cloud that sweeps through the constellations—and eventually disappears. Among the thinkers of society, and especially among our writers, poets, and artists, as well as our teachers, there should be a thirst for knowledge that remembers the dead and then goes beyond the borders of the dead to elaborate on life and improve the human condition. Indeed, we now have a cemetery in our midst to remind us that we are no longer untouchable, and to dispel the illusion that we can stand alone and continue to prosper while ignoring the rest of the world.

## Students' Learning Opportunities

Ed Patak contends that introducing students to this kind of "content" before they are emotionally mature and intellectually sophisticated has exactly the opposite effect of what is intended.[3] There is a tendency to identify with the aggressor and those in power, and to laugh at or ridicule the victim. Premature and excessive emphasis on

---

1. There is an enormous injustice of "have" and "have nots"—perpetuated, condoned, and justified by the pharaohs and caesars, kings and queens, nobility and landed gentry, the Church, the Brahmins of India, the military generals and corrupt government officials of the nonwestern world, the American robber barons and capitalists of the nineteenth and twentieth centuries—exemplified by the Rockefellers, Vanderbilts, Goulds, and Millikens of big business and Wall Street. The only way teachers historically fit into the world of "haves" is as underpaid caretakers of the system. (John Holt uses the term *prison guard;* Paul Goodman uses the term *arm of the law* to describe the teacher's role; and Willard Waller likens the teacher image to *the army officer*—neat, clean, and a little stiff.)

2. Of course, this is an idealistic view of America, and depends to some extent on what side of the fence you sit, whether you eat "three squares" and whether you come from Winnetka, Illinois; the Watts section of Los Angeles; Manhasset, New York; or the middle of "Motown" in Michigan.

3. Comments made by Ed Patak to Author, September 6, 2001.

the "dark" side of history and society informs unsophisticated students about which groups represent "legitimate" targets for hate.

But we cannot protect the new generation from the chambers of horrors that have characterized most of our history. We cannot continue to allow only a little darkness to spill out in our classrooms, to keep the horrors hemmed in by limiting the dark side of human behavior to a few sentences or paragraphs in a textbook or a few comments in class. Patak may represent the majority view among educators; it is certainly the safe view. However, I would rely on Piaget's principles of cognition—that the child's formal mental operations (or advanced stage of cognition) develops between ages 11 to 15, whereby the adolescent is capable of analyzing ideas, engaging in abstract operations, and clarifying values. Even before the age of 11, the concepts of right and wrong, fairness, and basic democratic laws and principles are understood. Similarly, Piaget's theory of moral development, along with Kohlberg's notion of moral reasoning and moral ideology, suggest that teens can understand the principles of ethics, contractual obligations, conscience, and justice. There is some variation, of course, which has to do with the student's family, religion, and cultural background— that is, biases and prejudices which develop outside the school. But this is exactly what the teacher has to overcome; it is part of the teacher's role.

Let me put it in a different way: Blind hatred, erroneous claims of superiority, and ideological fanaticism—where the individual is drowned out by the mass, made impotent, then dehumanized and/or slaughtered—represents the "ugly" side of humanity. It can be depicted as the opposite to the music of Bach; the art of Michelangelo; the stories of Cervantes and Shakespeare; the philosophy of Kant, Lock, and Rousseau; the poems of Frost, Dickinson, and Lao-Tzu; and the spiritual messages of Mohammed, Buddha, and Gandhi. Teachers, in the past, have emphasized the good side of humanity. I'm urging that both sides need to be explored. By ignoring the ugly side of civilization, teachers unwittingly create a void among future generations—a lack of humanity, compassion, and moral constraint.

The ideals of right and wrong, justice and goodness are rooted in western morality, in Greek and Judeo-Christian ideas, as well as in Eastern philosophy and religious thought, and should be incorporated into the curriculum. Education without concern for certain universal and humanistic truths, values, and ways of behaving hinders the moral fiber of society. Taken to the next step, it leads to natural aggression, based on biological and animal instincts, to more ruthless behavior among people and more needless deaths. Freud would say this means the *id* has gained the upper hand over the *super ego* (personal and social conscious). In the worst-case scenario, rational and ethical constraints are lifted; then comes the rise of Nietsche's "superman" complex and the subsequent rationale for racism, imperialism, colonialism, fanaticism, and militarism. The artifacts of these "isms" is the death of hundreds of millions of people (50 million people alone in World War II, including 292,000 Americans) and the destruction of hundreds of nation-states and racial, ethnic, and religious groups. In fact, the slaughter has been going on before ancient Greece and Rome were built; before Agamemnon, Ulysses, and Achilles rode into battle; even before the great empires of China and Egypt, since we came out of the caves.

So we come to one of the great thinkers of modern times—Charles Darwin and his studies on the behaviors of animals and humans. Darwin's evolutionalism needs to be adjusted in terms of humankind's limitless acts of rage, anonymous slaughter, and wholesale violence. Humans may have the potential for more rational, imaginative, and spiritual thinking than our cousins—the chimpanzee, monkey, and ape—but there is something that creeps over our minds and spirit whereby we kill our own human species. This unnamed something in our genes or DNA creates the potential for the most vile acts of aggression and violence against our own species—and puts us below the evolutionary scale of our cousins.[1]

People in power—political, military, and religious leaders—have historically and indiscriminately created one killing field after another—treating people and nations as flies or dots on the world landscape. No person or nation can rationalize or defend such violence committed by humans on humans, committed in the name of some nation-state, religion, or ideology. As one *New York Times* critic observes, only a well-developed moral framework will allow people to determine what is good and evil, what is worth defending, and what bad should be eliminated.[2] Terms such as *reconceptualism, neomarxism, postmodernism, postcolonialism, Green Peace,* and so on are fashionable descriptors but do not provide the intellectual tools needed to deal with vile acts of aggression that need moral rebuttal.

After teaching some 5,000 teachers over my professional career, I am convinced that teachers generally lack independent thought and are influenced more by bureaucratic bigness, popular ideas, and the media. Most are intellectually unprepared to deal with the human gene that fosters the potential for aggression and violence and that shapes human behavior. Our traditional education theories and philosophies tend to paint a rosy picture about schools and society, and often equivocate over ideas that need moral rebuttal. We are more concerned, as teachers, over debates about subject-versus student-centered curricula, basic skills, essential knowledge, high-stake testing, and accountability. In an era of outcome-based education and standard-based education, we have no time to deal with the larger issues of morality or justice. The sentiment expressed by the headmaster at Roxbury Latin School in Boston puts it in perspective for teachers. Humans are "mean, nasty, brutish, selfish, and capable of great cruelty and meanness. We have to hold a mirror to students and say, 'This is what you are. Stop it.' "[3]

1. As part of his theory on "the survival of the fittest," Darwin tried to disguise this aspect of human behavior. The fact is, he was English and his country was consumed with territorial, monarch, and church-related power struggles, which in the seventeenth century alone led to the death of tens of millions of subjects and soldiers—an extraordinary number considering the total world population was less than two billion. Rising from a nation poorer than Venice and weaker than Spain and France, Great Britain became the most imperialist nation, trying to fill the appetite of Queen Victoria, who reigned for some 50 years, so that before World War I its empire would encircle the globe. See Simon Schama, *A History of Britain* vol. II (New York: Miramax Books, 2001); and *Victoria and Albert,* Public Television, October 24, 2001.

2. Judith Shulevitz, "A War with the World," *New York Times Book Review,* October 21, 2001, p. 39.

3. Washington Javis quoted in Alfie Kohn, "A Critical Examination of Character Education," in A. C. Ornstein and L. Behar-Horenstein, eds., *Contemporary Issues in Curriculum,* 2nd ed. (Boston: Allyn and Bacon, 2000), p. 179.

With moral constraints, people's aggressive instincts are played out in board rooms and on Wall Street; on high school, college, and professional football fields and wrestling arenas; at suburban pee-wee soccer fields and on big-city asphalt basketball fields; and on the nation's highways and byways. Most of us would refer to these behaviors as socially acceptable, or wink at them as part of American culture; only a few of us might have trouble accepting these behaviors.

But the teaching of knowledge without morality leads to extreme competitiveness, human stratification, and survival of the fittest. In other words, unchecked emphasis on performance where the same students always "win" and another group always "loses," or the labeling, categorizing, and tracking of students and noting differences among people (smart, dumb; superior, inferior) suggest a school system and a society that encourages, even fosters, all the wrong "isms." In fact, almost all militant and imperialist societies stress their own efficiency and superiority over other societies—nothing more than excuses and theories for explaining or justifying humans' inhumanity to humans. Even worse, this type of thinking and behavior is often derived from and supported by "scientific explanations," laws, religious theology, or political ideology—doctrines created by people to suppress other people.

Teaching and schooling should be committed to a higher purpose—a humanistic/moral purpose, designed not only to enhance academic grades but also personal and social responsibility. It should be built around people and community—around respecting, caring, and having compassion toward others. It means that teachers in the classroom deal with social and moral issues, with the human condition, and good and evil. It means that students be encouraged to ask "Why?" as opposed to being expected to give the "right" answer. The question should start with family conversation but must be nurtured in school during the formative years of learning so a sense of social and moral consciousness is developed. But precisely on this score our teachers and schools register a disturbing deficit, originally because it was thought to tread on the spiritual domain and now because there is little time to inquire about and discuss important ideas and issues since the curriculum is test driven by trivia items of knowledge and short-answer questions.

## Teaching in Historical Context

Asking "Why?" according to one historian, is the existential question that every individual must be permitted to ask and to receive an appropriate and meaningful answer from those in power or who mete out justice. If the question is denied, then the individual has few or no basic rights.[1] It is the purest form of totalitarianism, where the individual is trivialized—as in the Roman empire, where the ruling classes' main amusement was watching human beings get eaten by animals or fight each other to the death; as in the cattle cars to the concentration camps of Auschwitz and Dachau, where the individual was reduced to a serial number and whose remains were often retrofitted into soap products, lamp shades, and gold rings; and as in the ethnic cleansing and rape of Bosnia, Kosovo, and Rwanda.

1. Fritz Stern, "The Importance of 'Why,' " *World Policy Journal* (Spring 2000), pp. 1–8.

And how many of us can locate Rwanda on a map? Does anyone among us know where Auschwitz and Dachau were located? How many—except a few elderly statesmen, scholars, and descendents of the victims—care? Given the luxury of late birth and geographical distance, who among us are expected to do more than cite a few numbers or statements to put the horrors of humanity into some context or understanding? Who cares about the sufferings of all the folk groups, tribes, and nations? How many of us know the names of one or two people who died in Nanking, Pearl Harbor, the Holocaust, at Juno or Utah Beach, in the Killing Fields, or in Croatia or Kosovo? Who can cite one name that appears on the Arc de Triumph or on the Vietnam Memorial "wall"? Why is it that Jewish refugees from Europe often refer to their original homeland as a graveyard? Who can recall or ever knew the name of the pilot (Paul Tibbots) who dropped the A-bomb on Hiroshima—what his thoughts were as he approached the target, or after the carnage and cloud of dust?

Of the more than 100 million soldiers and civilians who died in war (or related civilian activities) in the last century, who among us care to know or can explain what happened or why it happened to these people—in what I would call the most gruesome and ruthless century with the most vile deeds and crimes against humanity? How do we weigh the smug claims of western technology and industry with the millions who died beside railroad tracks and in battle trenches? Americans don't seem to care, don't seem to know, don't seem to understand. We need to revamp our mindset. We need to grapple with these questions, especially since our geographical fortress has been breached.

Now, we all die—but many of us die when we are not ready to die, nor are we given any maps or charts of the journey. Modern philosophy, history, and literature have sanitized these deaths. We have more details (dates, names, and places) than we can process, so that those who were murdered, raped, gassed, and executed have been generalized into nonindividuals. The lucky ones were cared for by people, but the caregivers rarely knew anything about the history of the dying individuals, anything about who they were, and sometimes did not even know their names. It's an old story, repeated several times in different places and periods of history, yet it must be examined by teachers and students so there is a better chance of preventing, or at least reducing, this common madness in society.

Americans, of course, are not innocent, given our inhumane and criminal treatment of Native Americans—namely, the near extermination and remaining dismemberment of an entire Indian civilization under the banner of westward expansion. There is also the subhuman treatment of blacks during 100 years of slavery, followed by the exclusion of blacks from American society during the post-Reconstruction and Jim Crow era—keenly illustrated by separate drinking fountains and toilets and segregated schools and housing and other public facilities.

We all know when injustices are being perpetuated, but we often don't act or want to deal with it. Throughout the ages, people have deceived themselves by remaining indifferent or looking the other way in the midst of the worst atrocities and crimes—connoting a human or moral character flaw. Periodically, a nation or ethnic group has to pay a heavy price and be held accountable for their actions or inactions. Although the past has taught us how not to act, we periodically fall from civilized to uncivilized practices, our "dark side" checkmates our "good side" (the music of Bach, the stories of Shakespeare, etc.), because of our aggressive and competitive nature to beat the next person. So long as people have bread on their tables and sufficient clothes on their backs, they often remain silent, look the other way, or become true believers—in effect, blindsided by inaction and the vile deeds of others.

Moral practices start with the family and continue with the church and community, but teachers must play an active role if we are to be more a compassionate, caring, and just society. They need to encourage open debate concerning the thorniest issues of the present and past, to hold discussions without attacks or stereotypes, and to build a sense of community (what the French call *civisme*) and character. We must flee from our comfortable classroom niches, go beyond facts, raise thoughtful questions that stem from meaningful readings, and transcend beyond the cognitive domain into the moral universe. We must promote this type of teaching at all grade levels.

Our readings in school should have a moral flavor—to encourage discussion, thinking, and ultimately the transformation of the learner. Even at the primary grade level, it must not be wasted by assigning *See Spot Run* or *A Sunday Trip to Granny's;* rather, the emphasis should be on folktales and stories, such as *Jack and the Beanstalk, Rumpelstiltskin, Seasons,* and *The Mouse and the Wizard*—from all parts of the world.

The relationship between history, literary criticism, and philosophy raises many questions about human conditions and civilizations. These ideas express the nature of humanity and society, considered by some to be part of the Great Books, Junior Great Books, or Great Ideas program. Call it what you want—these readings deal with moral conscience and historical consciousness, and this is what students should be reading.

The idea is for the teacher to capture the students' imaginations, to have them explore ideas and issues, support arguments and draw conclusions—what could be called *critical thinking.* At the same time, students need to examine, analyze, and interpret morally laden books to help understand the evil or dark side of humans—what happens when morality is dethroned for greed, hatred, some god, or ideology; when excellence or efficiency is pushed to an extreme in which all trains are expected to run on time and all soldiers are expected to follow orders and even die for the glory of some god, the nation, or principles of old politicians.

Much of history has been rewritten for religious or nationalistic reasons; or for apologies and excuses that what happened was historically inevitable or historically justifiable; or because "those people" were different from us, backward and uneducated; or "they" had too much power and money—whatever hocus-pocus rationale is used to distort the truth and alter beliefs. Teachers must decide what is important in the curriculum—what has been omitted and what needs to be included for discussion. Often, big-city teachers are rendered impotent in this professional role, and the curriculum is imposed on them from the central office—by a few bureaucrats (former teachers and principals) who eventually lose touch with the community, classroom reality, and the needs of students.

Regardless of our politics and idiosyncratic judgments, as professionals we need to become more involved in curriculum development and decide how the content in class achieves a balanced portrait of the past and present, of other people and nations. Unlocking these thoughts and dealing with these issues will depend in part on the frame of mind, the politics, and the subject expertise of teachers. Nonetheless, we need to take a position, hopefully a moral position appropriate for a changing and diverse society, a society that is willing to face and deal with its problems. Students must be encouraged by their teachers to raise questions, take positions, and act morally responsible. To some extent, it is a position originally set forth by old Reconstructionists such as John Dewey, George Counts, and Ted Brameld.

The writer, poet, musician, and teacher need to summon the shades of the past to fight off anonymity and amnesia. Through selected readings, or even through film (for students who are unable to read fluently), we need to restore our fading and faltering memories, to show that the dead who were taken before their time did not die in vain. A war memorial or plaque is not the answer. It may serve political or nationalistic interests and raise the spectre (genre) of jingoism, but it cannot convey the moral lessons of the past. It can evoke tears and stimulate pride, but it cannot lead to critical and analytical thought, to clarify arguments, to explain and defend concepts and ideas, to maintain purposeful and critical discussion.

The writer, poet, musician, and teacher must remember the people who lived and died. As teachers, we must capture the agony and lessons of history, the myths of as well as the goodness of humanity through our philosophy, history, literature, music, and art. We must retain the vestiges of the lost world, where people died terrible deaths as victims of war, famine, poverty, nationalism, racism, or religious fanaticism, and try to make sense of all the senseless crimes people have committed and are still capable of committing.

The people who shaped my world and your world, for the greater part, no longer exist. We have 25 or 30 years as teachers to make an imprint on the next generation, to remember the millions who are not in the encyclopedias and who no longer exist, to pass on their thoughts and deeds to the next generations. As teachers, the necessity of our work requires that we understand what is at stake—improving and enriching society by making the next generation care about what is morally right—and to motivate them to accomplish great things that exhibit the "good side" of what is human. In simple terms, today's youth will determine our future and the type of society we become.

Moving from literature and philosophy to active teaching and learning means that students must be encouraged and rewarded for moral and community action—for helping others and volunteering their time and service. It means that students involved in character development and civic service receive the same attention and recognition that we give to top academic students and star quarterbacks. It calls for special assemblies, special scholarships, and special staff development programs that promote civil behavior and self-restraint, the desire to help others, and the expectation for social/civic involvement. It means that we give character development and civic service—helping and caring for others, contributing and giving back to the school and community—as much attention as we give academics and sports in school. Collectively, critics might argue that some of these ideas or values reflect religious doctrine, and, unless you believe in the preaching of Moses, Muhammad, or St. Augustine, they are behaviors that extend beyond the schoolhouse. Nonsense. I would argue that they reflect the attributes of a good person and a responsible person, and of what "citizenship" is about.

I am not talking about a special course or program to meet some "service-learning" requirement; rather, I am referring to a school ethos or a common philosophy that teachers and administrators support. The idea must permeate throughout the entire school—expected and required for all students. It means coming to agreement on basic moral virtues, character education, and community or civic education, and this content becomes part of the formal curriculum.[1] One or two teachers attempting to teach moral responsibility or civic participation cannot effect long-term change; it takes a team effort and a schoolwide policy. It demands nothing less than a reconceptualization of the roles, expectations, and activities of students and teachers involved in the life of schools and communities. The idea flows back to the "seven cardinal principles" of secondary education, the progressive philosophy of the 1910s and 1920s, and the old core curriculum of the 1930s and 1940s, which promoted the study of moral and social issues, social responsibility at the school and community levels, and civic education and youth service for the community and nation.

It also means that we consider the basic elementary school, which focuses on the child and community and where schools are kept small so people work together and feel connected and empowered; it means the school provides emotional and social support for children (beyond academics), where the focus is on the whole child and where teachers teach the importance of values, ethics, and moral responsibility.[2] It suggests that a moral and civil society is a requirement for democracy to work, so keenly described 150 years ago by Alex de Tocqueville's classic treatise on *Democracy in America* and reemphasized (85 years ago) by John Dewey in *Democracy and Education*. It means we teach the importance of connecting with nature and the ecology of our planet—to preserve our resources and ensure our future. It requires that we bring competitiveness and social cohesion, excellence and equality, as well as material wealth and poverty into harmony—not an easy task. Finally, we need to look into the future: The bomb is an eclipse, but the products of technology and biological sciences—from medicines and foods, to better babies (altering the DNA of generations to come), to extending life (by eliminating/adding genes or inserting stem cells or computer chips)—offer new ways to play God and leave us with many moral issues about which to ponder.

1. See Spencer Kagan, "Teaching for Character and Community," *Educational Leadership* (October 2001), pp. 50–55. Kagan urges three sets of virtues: *personal*, such as good judgment, hard work, integrity, and courage; *relationships*, such as caring, kindness, helpfulness, honesty, and tolerance; and *community*, including citizenship, responsibility, loyalty, and trustworthiness. My own belief is that every school and community should agree on its own list of virtues or moral concepts and then incorporate them into the curriculum.

2. Ernest L. Boyer, "The Basic School: Focusing on the Child," *Elementary Principal* (January 1994), pp. 29–32.

## Final Words

All of us are filled with memories of people who lived and died, and all of us can personally identify with our own racial, ethnic, religious, or other group that has suffered from the ruthless behavior of others. All of us who perceive ourselves as members of a minority group understand the notions of subordination and suffering. We experience our own transitoriness and mortality every day as we read in the news or see on television the acts of violence committed by people toward other people.

The wisdom of the Bible and the virtues of religious leaders provide me with little comfort or hope, because the people who should know better and who preach hope are often burdened by their own biases, prejudices, and ill feelings toward other people who summon up different interpretations of the past and present. Although the clergy can be construed as teachers, their mission and agenda center on faith and ideology, and their methods historically have been used to promote this way of thinking—a sort of mind control of the individual—the same methods adopted by modern-day totalitarian nations. Indeed, one idea merely replaces another idea.

As I describe a cruel and sad world—flawed by its own stupidity, hatred, crimes, slaughter, and a host of "isms"—I provide the notion for teachers to speculate about their own roles and what education is all about or should be about. Hopefully, a deep sense of human guilt and teacher triumph of consciousness of humanity will help future citizens of the world be more responsible in terms of character and compassion. Indeed, it is the teacher's role to keep revisiting history, to fight off amnesia, and to become a spokesperson for the dead, and thus improve the human condition. It is a professional role rarely, if ever, described in the education literature; it is an idea worth considering—in a world where the United States is at the zenith of its power but would rather hide from the evils of the world and no longer can.

Finally, I am reminded of an old saying that was popular when I was a young man: "We don't know what World War III will be fought with, but World War IV will be fought with rocks."[1] I am reminded of last goodbyes—"I love you," "I will wait for you in heaven," "Tell ____ I will forever miss her," and so on. I am reminded of Carl Sandburg's *Grass*—all the wars, all the dead, and all the grass that keeps growing; and I think of James Joyce's *The Dead*—describing the demise of the ordinary people, "falling faintly through the universe." I wonder how many teachers have read Sandburg or Joyce. I suspect the majority have not.

On a more personal level, I feel the presence of Yevgeni Yevuschenko, who saw himself and his ancestors "persecuted, spat on, and slandered" for centuries in Europe. It culminated in his homeland, Mother Russia, with the death of tens of thousands in Belostock (the most violent pogrom) and hundreds of thousands at Babi Yar (a mass murder and mass grave). "Like one long soundless scream . . . I'm every old man executed here, As I am every child murdered." So few people seem to care, so few remember, so few even know about Yevuschenko or Belostock and Babi Yar.

1. Francis X. Clines, "A New Form of Grieving," *New York Times,* September 16, 2001, Sect. 4 p. 3.

Yet, because of the long roads and caravans traveled by my ancestors, I recall that so many people in so many lands, since ancient Egypt, Persia, and Rome, have been thrown back by the boot, the sword, and the law—by a soldier, crusader, king, or despot. I have no patience for hearing false excuses or false proclamations in the name of hatred, stupidity, or herd behavior. I have no pity for fools, zealots, and tyrants who strip people of their dignity and then put them to death. Even worse, I fear some in power who are given to genocidal impulses and are bent on reducing whole villages to rubble and destroying whole cultures and civilizations to nothing more than a line or two in some high-toned poem like *The Waste Land* or *Babi Yar*. I have no faith in arms control agreements and international peace organizations to keep the peace.

I am reminded of all the English teachers trying to teach classic poems and *The Iliad, King Lear, Gulliver's Travels,* and *The Death of Ivan Illych*—the best that has been thought and said in our culture. Then, I think of all the bored students, squirming and sweating in their seats, dozing and doodling, watching the clock tick by tick and missing the bittersweet phrases and lost opportunity to reflect on ways ordinary and tragic. The leaves turn brown; the years come and go. I'm sure there will be more heaps of needless deaths and graveyards way before these kids start growing downward and outward.

I long for a simpler day: *Little House on the Prairie, Leave It to Beaver, Gilligan's Island,* and *Ozzie and Harriet*. But the clock cannot be turned back. In another instant, I recall Mickey and Minnie and Uncle Miltie; Huey, Louie, and Dewey; Captain Video, Captain Kangaroo, and Howdy Doody. They were all perky, cute, and innocent. And what about *Here's to You, Mrs. Robinson,* Marilyn and Jolt'n Joe, *Where Have All the Flowers Gone?* What happened to *Yellow Submarine, Strawberry Fields,* and *Blackbird Singing in the Dead of the Night*. Has anyone seen my childhood heroes—Jackie, Pee Wee, Duke, and the other "Boys of Summer"? Can you tell me where? What these images represent is a knowledge of a more innocent time, a brief period in American history most notably forgotten in a post–9-11 world, a period in my youth when American optimism and good fortune resonated around the world.

I can also recall playing catch with Dad and stickball in the school yard with Jack and Larry. Then there was Mrs. Katz, Mrs. Schwartz, and Miss Hess from P.S. 42 Queens, and Mr. Faulkner, Mr. Tietz, and Miss Gussow from Far Rockaway High School. All my favorite teachers are gone, too, but I thought it would be the right thing to do, in the dearness of remembering a simpler period and vanishing era, to recall the names of teachers, largely forgotten, who taught for 25 to 30 years and made a difference to thousands of kids from my generation. All of you can cherish the names of other teachers who made a difference in your lives—and all of you can ponder the larger role of teaching in the changing world we live in.

## $\mathcal{S}$ummary

1. Research on teaching has shifted from the *process* of teaching to the *products* of teaching and, now, to the *context* of teaching.

2. Differences between theory and practice of teaching need to be clarified. Researchers and professors of education tend to focus

on the theory of teaching, whereas teachers prefer the practical aspects.

3. A problem with determining teacher effectiveness is that we cannot agree whether teaching is a science or an art. Whereas the science of teaching is predictable and prescriptive, the art of teaching in intuitive and based on personal experience.

4. Since the 1990s, there has been a shift in the research on teaching—based on language and dialogue: metaphors, stories, biographies, autobiographies, expert opinions, voice, and reflection. All these methods dismiss traditional and quantitative methods of examining teacher behavior, and promote qualitative and ethnographical method of research.

5. We need to promote caring, supporting, and empathetic teachers who are willing to allow students to develop their natural curiosity and talents. We should avoid plans, methods, and evaluation systems that lock us into prescriptive or predetermined behaviors. We might think of teaching as a human endeavor involving human relationships between students and teachers.

6. The idea of teaching should no longer be divorced from moral roles. The teacher's obligation is to help students learn, to help them think about ideas and values that improve society, and to develop moral character and civic responsibility.

7. Part of moral teaching deals with remembering the dead—how and why they died.

## Discussion Questions

1. How would you reconcile or integrate theory and practice in your own teaching?

2. What can be done to improve the science-art relationship? What scientific components are important for teaching? What artistic components are important?

3. What makes for an interesting teacher metaphor? What trust, if any, do you have in the autobiography of a teacher?

4. How would you compare expert teachers with novice teachers?

5. What behaviors do you think best describe a humanistic teacher? Moral teacher?

## Things to Do

1. Discuss in class: To what extent is teaching a science or art? Defend the possession you have taken.

2. Recall three or four of your favorite teachers. Compare their characteristics. Why do you think these people were your favorite teachers? What are the most successful characteristics of good teachers?

3. Observe two or three teachers (or professors) while they teach. Categorize them as novice, advanced beginning, competent, proficient, or expert. Defend your reasoning.

4. Interview several experienced teachers concerning recommended teaching methods. To what extent do these methods coincide with humanistic teaching? To what extent do they contradict humanistic teaching?

5. What can be done to make teachers more aware of the moral issues involved in teaching? Discuss this question with members of your class.

## Recommended Readings

1. Eisner, Elliot W. *The Kind of Schools We Need* (Portmouth, NH: Heinemann, 1998). The relationship of qualitative methods, humanistic teaching, and school reform.

2. Molnar, Alex, ed. *The Construction of Children's Character* (Chicago: University of Chicago Press, 1997). Strategies for implementing and assessing character education.

3. Noddings, Nel. *Educating Moral People* (New York: Teachers College Press, 2001). Establishing a school environment that supports moral education and moral behavior.

4. Sarason, Seymour. *Teaching as a Performing Art* (New York: Teachers College Press, 1999). An examination of teaching as an art.

5. Schlechty, Philip C. *Inventing Better Schools* (San Francisco: Jossey-Bass, 2001). How to improve schools, including mission statements, goals, strategic planning, and the need for administrative leadership.

6. Soder, Roger, John I. Goodlad, and Timothy J. McMannon, eds. *Developing Democratic Character in the Young* (San Francisco: Jossey-Bass, 2001). How schools can create the climate necessary for democracy, and the connection between democracy, character development, and education.

7. Waxman, Hersholt C., and Herbert J. Walberg, eds. *New Directions for Teaching Practice and Research* (Berkeley, CA: McCutchan, 1999). Current research on effective teaching, with focus of teaching as a science.

# Teaching and Teacher Accountability

## Chapter 2

## *Focusing Questions*

1. Why is it important to establish the relationship between teacher behavior and student learning?

2. What problems are involved in defining good teaching? What measurement problems are related to defining good teaching?

3. How would you compare the advantages and disadvantages of using observation instruments, rating scales, and student achievement tests for determining teacher effectiveness?

4. Which group of raters do you prefer for your own teacher evaluation: students, colleagues, supervisors, or researchers? Why?

5. Why do national and state tests often reflect problems involving curriculum validity?

6. Why do most standardized tests measure knowledge rather than not high-order thinking processes?

7. What are the reasons for the failure of compensatory education? What measures or policies would you suggest for improving of compensatory education programs?

8. Why did reformers move from advocating compensatory education to advocating accountability?

9. Who should be held accountable? For what?

## EPISODE *A*

Probably no aspect of education has been discussed with greater frequency, with as much concern, or by more educators and parents than how to define, identify, and measure good teaching. Facets of the problem have been studied by school districts and teams of researchers for the last 75 years. But findings about the competence and performance of teachers are inconclusive.

There is general agreement that the goal should be a highly competent teacher in every classroom, but there is considerably less agreement on the meaning and the evaluation of competence. Here, it is important to remember that from the 1920s to the 1970s, identifying and observing the *characteristics* of effective teachers was in widespread use as a prime method for evaluating teachers. The characteristics, sometimes called *behaviors,* were often developed as lists and based on conventional wisdom. Donald Medley summed up this period for evaluating teachers. "In no instance was any evidence advanced to show that teachers possessing these characteristics were actually more effective in helping pupils achieve any of the goals of education than teachers who lacked them."[1]

Given today's heated discussion about research on teacher effectiveness and rewarding or holding them accountable, it is difficult to imagine that characteristics and behaviors were listed as a means for defining teacher competency. When I started my teaching career some 40 years ago, the lists were still being used. It was what a teacher *did* in the classroom that mattered—that he or she appeared friendly and personal, came to class on time, stated clear objectives, incorporated visuals, and used the blackboard in a neat and organized manner. Hence, the focus was on behavior, or the *process* of teaching (see Chapter 1).

Since most of this research found its way into teacher preparation programs, a good deal of education method courses were based on "dos" and "don'ts," sentimental advice, and custom. Undoubtedly, most of the knowledge base about teaching was questionable, based more on the personality of the teacher providing advice or the opinions of the professor in charge of the educational courses.

## Do Teachers Make a Difference?

Not until the mid-1970s did it become apparent that productive research on teacher effectiveness had to focus on both teacher behavior or what the teacher did (process), and student learning or the outcomes of teaching (products)—what is now called *process-product* research on teaching. The fundamental question became whether teachers actually influence student outcomes and, if so, to what extent. Although the question seems silly on the surface, it is not. Indeed, there is need to establish the relative contribution of teacher behavior to student learning for several reasons.

**1.** *It provides teacher educators a rationale for their job.*    Teacher educators must screen and prepare future teachers, as well as provide in-service education for experienced teachers. If teachers have little or no impact on student outcomes, then there

1. Donald M. Medley, "The Effectiveness of Tenders," in P. L. Peterson and H. J. Walberg, eds., *Research on Teaching* (Berkeley, CA: McCutchan, 1979), p. 13.

is no reason to guard professional "gates" with credentials or to make such a fuss about teacher education. If teachers have minimal or no clear impact on students, then there is little or no reason to provide pedagogical knowledge in order to enhance professional competence. Also, there is little reason for being upset or raise questions about alternative certification programs.

**2.** *It provides a rationale for recent reforms regarding teacher evaluation, teacher performance, and teacher competence.*   If teachers have little effect on student outcomes, or if replicable findings of teacher effectiveness cannot be found, then all the new reform policies at best are theoretical exercises and at worst politicize the evaluation of teachers. If such data are lacking, then various methods for effective teaching have been sold as unproven, and sound teacher evaluation policies cannot be formulated. Moreover, assessing teachers or making judgments about their performance cannot be supported; making inferences about "low-performing/high-performing," "incompetent/competent" or "master" teachers, are premature. The absence of teacher influence on student learning suggests that remediation, probation, and other personnel decisions cannot be statistically or legally supported, and it is difficult for supervisors and administrators to give constructive evaluation and feedback to teachers.

**3.** *It provides support for the ideas that teacher differences exist and that teachers make a difference.*   For the last 25 years the prominent view is that teachers influence student outcomes. This new research assumes that the *process* (teacher behaviors and/or methods) can be controlled, modified, or taught, and that teacher-student interactions can be analyzed and predicted. It also assumes that what teachers do in the classroom does affect students and that narrowly defined teacher behaviors and/or methods affect student *outcomes,* which can also be measured.[1]

**4.** *It provides a rationale for holding teachers accountable, developing standard-based education, and assessing each year the teachers' (and schools') contribution to what students know, can do, and will do.*   If we are to hold teachers accountable, compare schools (or school districts,) and provide rewards (or penalties) for teacher or school performance, then we need to asses student learning and growth and in relationship to teacher performance (behaviors and/or methods) and school performance (the composite of teacher performance). Although the use of process-product research can unwittingly result in mechanical behaviors and "sets of rules" that are inappropriate to many teaching and learning styles, researchers believe that standardized tests are informative and can show the relationship between teacher performance and student achievement for different teachers and students.[2]

1.  Allan C. Ornstein, "Teacher Effectiveness Research," in H. C. Waxman and H. J. Walberg, eds., *Effective Teaching: Current Research* (Berkeley, CA: McCutchan, 1991), pp. 63–80.
2.  Barbara Gleason, "Pay for Performance," *Educational Leadership* (February 2000), pp. 82–85; Elizabeth Spalding, "Performance Assessment and the New Standards Project," *Phi Delta Kappan* (June 2000), pp. 758–765.

## Contextual Problems in Evaluating Teachers

It is no easy task to determine effective teachers because we are dealing with numerous contextual variables, such as subjects, students, classrooms, and schools. Failure to control accurately for these variables and their interaction effects leads to inconsistent research findings and difficulty in recommending methods for good teaching. Let us briefly consider these four variables.

### Subject Matter

The nature of *subject matter* influences teacher behaviors and methods; the math and foreign language teacher often relies on practice and drill and on strict monitoring of student performance, whereas the art and music teacher relies on freedom of expression, and the social studies and English teacher relies on discussion of ideas and issues. In math and foreign language, *part-to-whole* learning is essential, but in social studies and English literature, *whole-to-part* learning is more appropriate. Of course, student ability is a factor—namely, low-achieving students rely on and need more monitoring and feedback, as well as concrete experiences and part to whole learning experiences.

From data derived from standardized tests in reading, math, and other subjects, we are told by test advocates that, over time, generalizations can be made about the performance of teachers and schools. Some observers call this *value-added* teaching and testing, a way of profiling academic growth for each student and the impact of each teacher and school on student learning. By separating important factors and through sophisticated statistical procedures, such as previous learning and related student factors, it is maintained that estimates can be made about the effectiveness of teachers and schools. It is further claimed that we can separate the effects of the second-grade teacher on students who are now in the fourth or fifth grade.[1] The problem is, test content, scales, and item difficulty, over time or from one test to the next or even written within the same subject, are not constant.[2] Moreover, the effects of family life, peer group, community life, and socioeconomic status are rarely considered in these value-added profiles, and these factors are more important than what the teacher or school does.

### Students

Different students imply different social classes, personalities, behaviors, abilities, and needs—and it would seem that teacher behavior would be relative to different *stu-*

---

1. John H. Holloway, "A Value Added View of Pupil Performance," *Educational Leadership* (February 2000), pp. 84–85; Chris Pipho, "The Value Added Side of Standards," *Phi Delta Kappan* (January 1998), pp. 341–342.

2. A. S. Bryk et al., *Academic Productivity of Chicago Public Elementary Schools* (Chicago: Consarium on Chicago School Research, 1998).

*dent* characteristics. For example, the warm or businesslike teacher has a different effect on different learners with different abilities and needs. One of the most ambitious studies on teacher-student interaction was conducted by Ned Flanders. Every three seconds, observers sorted teacher talk into *indirect* or *direct* behavior. Flanders found that indirect teachers tended to overlap with the warm teacher, and direct teachers tended to overlap with the businesslike teacher. Students in the indirect classrooms learned more and exhibited more independent attitudes toward learning than students in direct classrooms.[1]

Ned Flanders's direct teacher would be more suitable among low-achieving students who need direction, monitoring, and continuous and positive feedback to satisfy their esteem and encouragement to work on academic tasks. Flanders's indirect teacher would be more suitable among high-achieving students who are not necessarily concerned with the right answers, but would prefer discussing ideas, inquiring, and experimenting on their own. In most cases, practice and drill, and strict monitoring of these students would be a waste of time and, in fact, would probably lead to classroom-management problems.

As an important side note, Flanders found that as much as 80 percent of the classroom time is consumed by teacher talk. I would venture to guess that most prospective and beginning teachers tend to exhibit direct behaviors, since they talk too much. In fact, education students and student teachers often associate good teaching with some form of lecturing, since most of their recent teaching models are professors who often do a lot of talking—too much talk for younger students who lack maturity, attentiveness, and focus ability to cope with a passive learning situation for any length of time.

## Classroom Complexity

A source of difficulty in assessing teacher behavior is that the act of teaching is extremely complex, involving an interaction process between teacher and student(s), where the cause-effect relationships and sequence of responses occur multidimensionally and so rapidly that it is nearly impossible to accurately categorize or even focus on prescribed behaviors. The teacher's behavior is more or less spontaneous, reacting to the students with hunches and on an intuitive basis. Trying to break down and analyze the teaching act as some logical or rational behavior, with precise and predictive categories or processes, is perhaps too difficult and suggests educational folly. One educator writes, "In the small but crowded classroom, events come and go with astonishing rapidity," with the teacher engaging in about "200 to 300 interpersonal interchanges every hour of her working day." Although some of these interchanges are somewhat repetitive, "the content and sequence of these interchanges cannot be predicted or preplanned with any exactitude."[2]

1. Ned A. Flanders, *Teacher Influence, Pupil Attitudes, and Achievement* (Washington, DC: U.S. Governemnt Printing Office, 1965).
2. Philip W. Jackson, *Life in Classrooms,* 2nd ed. (New York: Teachers College Press, 1990), p. 149.

Gage and Unruh state the problem in a similar manner: "The uncontrived character, speed and uncontrollability of teaching moves in the 'interactive' phase [between teacher and students] make the formulation of teaching . . . seem merely metaphysical, not to be taken literally."[1] In addition, the rhythm of the classroom may not correspond with an orderly set of behaviors that can precisely be identified and measured. Covert behaviors, transitions, gestures, and body language may be too subtle or convey different meanings to different teachers and students, especially among researchers who are unfamiliar with the specific features and tone of the classroom, or even among supervisors who infrequently observe teachers.

In short, classrooms are not neat and orderly places, and teaching cannot be reduced to a set of predetermined behaviors, although many educational theorists claim they can or should be. This does not mean that there is no logic in teaching; rather, the underlying events seem too ambiguous, unpredictable, and/or complex to reduce to a precise set of behaviors that can be accurately described by present behavioral science methods or used by supervisors to make decisions about teacher merit, promotion, or retention. For the moment, let us call teaching, at least in part, a craft that relies on behaviors and methods (processes) that researchers have not yet learned to translate into terms that teachers always find helpful or that supervisors can primarily use to make important career decisions about teaching.

## School Settings

When it comes to setting, the issue is historical and social in nature. Certain teaching theories and teacher behaviors become dated as the years progress. The assertive teacher in the past was able to make a point with his or her hands, a ruler, or commands. All of us can remember being taught by teachers who laid down the law the first day, explaining the rules and routine, and firmly held the line with stern disciplinarian measures that today would be grounds for a lawsuit with the student(s) supported by a child advocate, civil rights, and/or tort lawyer.

In the 1932 classic book *The Sociology of Teaching*, Willard Waller discusses how to maintain control over students. He views students as *subordinate*, and teachers as the *dominant* figures in the classroom. He warns that "pupils who habitually forget to obey rules should have their memory stimulated by something more effective than an admonition." Later on, he warns, "Get order. Drop everything else, if necessary, until order is secured. Stretch your authority to the breaking point. . . . Pile penalty upon penalty for misdemeanors, and let the 'sting' of each penalty be double that of its predecessor."[2] Do you think this sounds a little excessive or overzealous? Back then, and up to the 1950s, Waller's insights were considered a benchmark study in the social life of the school. Today, the same suggestions would get the teacher into legal difficulty, possibly even on probation.

1. N. L. Gage and W. R. Unruh, "Theoretical Formulation for Research," *Review of Educational Research* (June 1967), p. 361.

2. Willard Waller, *The Sociology of Teaching*, rev. ed. (New York: John Wiley, 1965), p. 307.

The ban on movement extends to the entire school in the vast majority of inner-city schools. Charles Silberman, in his 1970 best-selling book, *Crisis in the Classroom,* describes a typical big-city high school where "no student may walk down the corridor without a form, signed by a teacher, telling where he is coming from, and the time to the minute, during which the pass is valid." In most schools, he continues, "the toilets are kept locked except during class breaks, so that a student not only must obtain a pass but must find a custodian and persuade him to unlock the needed facility."[1]

The contrast in suburban and middle-class schools is clear; a parent or visitor to the schools in Scarsdale, New York, or Winnetka, Illinois, might be struck by the relaxed social atmosphere in the hallways and classrooms, in part because these students generally possess inner controls and do not require strict rules and routines as with most inner-city students who often lack inner controls. Simply put, children and youth who grow up under different living conditions—in terms of social, cultural, and economic circumstances—will exhibit different indices of social and educational deprivation, as well as learning styles, abilities, and needs. Both on an individual and group basis, children and youth who come from impoverished and marginal settings, compared to their counterparts who grow up in advantaged homes and communities, will exhibit different cognitive abilities and social behavior. What starts as slight differences in behavior in the early grades add up and accumulate as large differences by junior high school and high school in terms of discipline and students' control of their own impulses. To put it in different terms, the most effective teacher in Scarsdale, New York, or Winnetka, Illinois, when thrust into Harlem, New York, or Southside, Chicago, might very well quit in the middle of the term because of frustration or battle fatigue. And, teacher behaviors considered effective among inner-city teachers—such as highly organized and structured approaches (practice and drill, seatwork, and monitoring of students' work)—will rarely work in middle-class, suburban school settings.[2]

In light of the four contextual variables, research on teaching is summed: "A realistic theory of teacher behavior has not yet evolved. . . . This has left the field with a rather confusing series of scattered and unfinished attempts at developing the necessary theoretical basis for teacher education,"[3] teacher evaluation, and teacher accountability.

## Criterion Problems in Evaluating Teachers

The terms used to judge teacher effectiveness are often misleading and vague. Investigators use different terms in trying to judge teacher effectiveness, and the definitions

---

1. Charles E. Silberman, *Crisis in the Classroom* (New York: Random House, 1970), p. 131.
2. See Allan C. Ornstein and Thomas L. Lasley, *Strategies for Effective Teaching,* 3rd ed. (Boston: McGraw-Hill, 2000).
3. Fred A. J. Korthagen and Jos P. A. M. Kessels, "Linking Theory and Practice," *Education Researcher* (May 1999), p. 8.

and usage of terms vary among different researchers. In other words, not only are there different behaviors and methods but there is also lack of agreement of what terms to use. Even when there is agreement, the terms do not necessarily have the same meaning. As previously discussed, Ned Flanders uses the term *direct* to describe an *ineffective* a teacher who lectures, criticizes, and gives orders. Several other researchers (Brophy and Good, Doyle, Rosenshine, etc.) consider *direct* teachers as *effective*—providing structured tasks, prompts, cues, clear transitions, and teacher-led practices.[1] Although the concepts or behaviors may be reliable for a particular study, the definitions of teacher behavior and related categories of one study usually cannot be compared with another study, because we are dealing with different contextual variables (subjects, students, classrooms, and school settings).

The problem is that confusion over terms and categories, interchangeability of definitions, and similarities and dissimilarities overlap among and between teacher behaviors and methods. These discrepancies, this inability to agree on operational terms, produce a lack of generalization in the findings and cause teacher behavior instruments to be confusing and misleading. As Bruce Biddle asserts, "The proliferation of similar but unidentical lists for categorizing teacher performance suggests that the investigators themselves do not know what to make of [their own] findings."[2] And, if the researchers have trouble interpreting and making sense of their own data, there should be little wonder why the teachers are unaffected by the research. In fact, school people often (with good reason) ignore the research on teacher behavior; they rely on their own experiences, common sense, inner strength, and self-understanding in dealing with problems and improving their performance. See Teaching Tips 2.1.

In addition, according to Needels and Gage, when researchers build on data—from study to study—the complexity of the data increase. The idea is to try to find fairly stable patterns to make generalizations, but this process is complex and confusing because "many factors in the students' lives in addition to teaching affect learners." Researchers try their best to control for such factors, either statistically or though random assignment of teachers and students, but rarely are they successful.[3]

## Common Research Problems

If we take the position that teaching can be analyzed and evaluated, or that teachers can be held accountable for their performance, then we must deal with a host of research problems. The fact is, however, many teachers complain that the research on

1. Walter Doyle, "Classroom Organization and Management," in M. Wittrock, ed., *Handbook of Research on Teaching*, 3rd ed. (New York: Macmillan, 1986), pp. 392–431; Thomas L. Good and Jere E. Brophy, *Looking in Classrooms*, 7th ed. (New York, Longman, 1997); and Barak Rosenhine and Carol Meister, "Reciprocal Teaching: A Review of the Research," *Review of Educational Research* (Winter 1994), pp. 479–530.

2. Bruce J. Biddle, "Methods and Concepts in Classroom Research," *Review of Educational Research* (June 1969), p. 348.

3. Margaret C. Needels and N. L. Gage, "Essence and Accident in Process-Product Research on Teaching," in Waxman and Walberg, *Effective Teaching*, pp. 3–31.

# Teaching Tips 2.1

## Helping Teachers Resolve Problems

Effective teachers are able to cope with frustrations and problems that arise on the job. Regardless of the amount of satisfaction they obtain from teaching, there are dissatisfying aspects of the job. What follows is a list of mental health strategies in the form of questions that are a mix of psychology 101 and common sense 101 for self-understanding. They are presented to help teachers deal with problems or dissatisfactions that may arise on the job—to become more satisfied and self-actualized as teachers.

1. *Are you aware of your strengths and weaknesses?* The ability to make realistic self-estimates is crucial, given the fact that your students and colleagues will observe and make judgments about your behavior, attitude, and abilities. Learn to see yourself as others see you and to compensate for or modify areas that need to be improved.
2. *Do you make use of resources?* As a teacher, you will come across many different textbooks, workbooks, tests, and materials. You will need to make judgments about their value and how best to utilize these resources for your own professional growth.
3. *Are you aware of your social and personal skills?* You will need to understand the attitudes and feelings of your students and parents, as well as your colleagues and supervisors, and how to adopt and work cooperatively with them.
4. *Can you function in a bureaucratic setting?* Schools are bureaucracies, and you must learn the rules and regulations as well as the norms and behaviors of the school. As a teacher, you are an employee of an organization that has certain expectations of you.
5. *Do you take out your frustrations in class?* Don't vent your problems or dissatisfac-

tions on your students. It solves nothing and adds to your own teaching problems.
6. *Do you make wise choices?* You will need to understand and apply the decision-making process purposefully and logically. Learn to be consistent and rational when making choices. Think about the impact your decisions have on others in the school.
7. *Do you understand your roles as a teacher?* Your role as a teacher goes far beyond teaching a group of students in class. Teaching occurs in a particular social context, and much of what you do and are expected to do is influenced by this context. Different students, supervisors, administrators, parents, and community members expect you to perform varied roles, depending on the realities, demands, and expectations of the school's culture.
8. *Do you expose yourself to new professional experiences?* Broaden your professional experiences. Volunteer for workshops and exchange teaching ideas. Devote time to study and travel.
9. *Can you cope with school forms and records?* Schools expect you to complete a host of forms, reports, and records accurately and on time. The quicker you become familiar with this work, the smoother it will be for you.
10. *Can you study and learn from someone else with similar problems?* It helps to talk to or observe colleagues with similar problems to see what they are doing wrong so as to avoid making the same mistakes, or what they are doing right so as to learn what to do.
11. *Do you look for help on specific questions?* Often, teacher dissatisfaction pertains to a specific problem—for example, the inability to maintain discipline. Consulting with an experienced colleague or supervisor sometimes helps.

continued

*Teaching Tips 2.1* **Continued**

12. *Do you participate in group discussions?* Since many problems of teachers are similar, pool ideas and experience. Even the gripe session in the teachers' lounge has benefits for venting or expressing one's dissatisfaction and learning that others have similar problems.

13. *Are you able to organize your time?* There are only so many hours in a day, and many demands and expectations are imposed on you as a person and a professional. You will need to make good use of time, to set priorities, to plan, and to get your work done.

14. *Can you separate your job from your personal life?* Never let the teaching job (or any job) over-

whelm you to the point that it interferes with your personal life. There are times when you will have to stay late after school working with students, parents, or colleagues or spend extra hours at home grading papers and tests, preparing lessons, and performing clerical tasks, but for your own mental health, be sure you have time left for you private, family, and social life.

15. *Have you developed a professional identity?* Professional identity involves an understanding of the relation between your professional roles, knowledge of yourself and how others perceive you, and understanding of your teaching style and relationship with colleagues.

teaching is not relevant to the reality of the classroom, because the following problems are not easy to resolve:

1. The variables we use to assess successful teaching not only vary, but even when they reappear in similar form in different studies, the *meanings differ*. For example, student variables, such as low/high socioeconomic status, connote different meanings for different investigators, as do more global terms dealing with student personalities and attitudes, critical thinking, classroom climate, and so on. These are constructs that entail a diversity of specifics as to defy precise definition and exact quantification. And, if we were to break them down into precise, agreed-upon, quantifiable constructs, the number of variables would vastly increase to the point of trivia, and the importance of each would be reduced to the specific study.

2. Once we start to analyze various or *multiple relationships* among teacher-student variables, we come to numerous interactions and still other new and untested interactions. The process is endless; we enter into a hall of mirrors that extends to infinity. How far we carry our analysis depends on our knowledge and purposes; nonetheless, the relationships are not linear or clear, but rather aggregate and complex.

3. Teaching behaviors that have sometimes been found to be effective bear a *curvilinear relation* to achievement (or any other outcome). A behavior that is effective when used in moderation or when used under certain circumstances can produce negative results when used too much or under different circumstances. For example, praise usually has positive effect, but too much praise or false praise can have detrimental effects on student performance.

4. Nearly all researchers who assess teacher effectiveness have relied on student gains in achievement as a correlate for success. The researchers have used the *mean residual gain of classrooms or schools,* paying little attention to the gains among individual students. How do the gains break down? Does the mean gain for a class as a whole represent the gain for boys and girls equally well; for low ability, average-ability, and high-ability students; for black, brown and white students? Questions concerning the relationship between teacher effectiveness and student variation have not really been investigated. It is possible, for example, that the high gain of one group of students is being cancelled by the low gain of another group at the classroom or school level.

5. Many teacher *behaviors that increase achievement on standardized tests* (behaviors such as convergent questions, drill, and teacher-initiated discourse) are dissimilar—indeed, almost opposite from those behaviors (such as open-ended questions, problem-solving activities, and student-initiated discourse) that tend to increase high-order cognitive learning and creativity. In teaching toward the test to raise student outcomes, the latter behaviors are often considered wasteful and time consuming; the idea is to review knowledge and factual information that correspond with low-level thinking and the test questions on most standardized tests.

6. Standardized achievement tests are extensively used as a criterion by which to measure student outcomes. These tests, as a group, tend to be highly reliable and valid for measuring student achievement on a national, state, or city basis. They usually have adequate *curriculum content* validity and are predictive of academic success for a large student population. The trouble is, they usually do not reflect what is taught in a teacher's classroom. These tests are designed to measure cumulative achievement or knowledge of content at the national, state, or city level; they are not appropriate for *instructional content* at the classroom or school level, or for measuring what students have learned over a short period of time, such as a semester or school year.

7. There is *disagreement about what effects a teacher is called on to produce.* Should a teacher's effectiveness be defined in terms of long-range, broad educational goals or short-term, specific outcomes on the student? Should a teacher be called on for equal behaviors or outcomes with all types of students, subjects, or grade levels, or should differences be allowed in working with the inner-city, the disabled, the exceptional student; in reading, math, science, art, or physical education (certain subjects are more difficult to effect changes in achievement over similar periods of time); with sixth-graders or tenth-graders (for the older child, it is more difficult it is to effect changes in achievement)? Until effects desired of the teacher are decided on, no adequate definition of teacher effectiveness or performance is possible.

8. *Teacher effects are indistinguishable from the effects of other teachers or agents, as well as parents and peer groups.* Certainly the home life of the child, especially the parents' education, counts more than the teacher's behavior. The teacher does not operate in isolation from other teachers or people. The long-term effects of a teacher are confounded by the fact of time, and the short-term effects of a teacher often are unobservable because instruments are unable to measure accurately the changes in learning in short-time intervals.

# The Measurement Problem

In addition to the limitations of finding acceptable teacher behaviors, there is lack of agreement on how to measure teacher behavior or what methods to use relative to determining success in the classroom. Methods of measuring and correlating teacher behavior generally fall into three broad areas: (1) observations, (2) rating scales, and (3) student tests of achievement.

## Observations

The observation of teacher behavior is costly and time consuming, because it takes a significant amount of time (depending on the observer's purpose and expertise) to obtain a sense of reality of what is happening in the classroom. The high number of interpersonal interchanges between the teacher and students limits the person who is attempting to describe the context of the teacher's behavior. Moreover, the observations of the person often do not coincide with the rhythm, pace, or verbal messages of the teacher-student exchanges. The observer is limited by human overload, without guarantee that the perceptions of these swift and complex interchanges are accurate. Does a 5-minute, 10-minute, or even 30-minute observation of a teacher, on one, two, or three occasions, translate into reality? Does the observation instrument—checking or circling some indicators, behaviors, or coded sentences or interactions—coincide with what is really occurring in the classroom? Often the observer, or the observation instrument being used to code the behaviors, does not capture the full flavor of the teacher's and students' behaviors, the interaction effects, or whether the behaviors represent a cognitive or social effect.[1]

There are four other basic limitations concerning observations: (1) the reliability of the observer; (2) the tendency of the teacher to put on an act while being observed; (3) the presence of the observer creating a "Hawthorne effect"—namely, the teacher and students are aware of a study or another person in the room and their behaviors change; and (4) the influence of the observer's own values and interpretations of what constitutes a good teacher. Even the position of the observer is a fact to consider. When sitting in the back of the room, the observer sees a number of heads and shoulders and his or her vision of the students is partially blocked. When sitting at the side or front of the room, the observer's presence is accentuated, and behavioral changes among the subjects are more likely to occur.

Most researchers do consider the reliability of the observer; that is, they ensure the observer is consistent in describing what occurs in the classroom, although what they are trained to see may be limited to the observation instrument and describe only a fraction of classroom reality. But supervisors who observe teachers for purpose of

---

1. Allan C. Ornstein, "Theoretical Issues Related to Teaching," *Education and Urban Society* (November 1989), pp. 96–105; Ornstein, "How Good Are Teachers in Affecting Student Outcomes," *NASSP Bulletin* (December 1992), pp. 61–70; and Jane Stallings and H. Jerome Freiberg, "Observation for the Improvement of Teaching," in Waxman and Walberg, *Effective Teaching*, pp. 107–134.

evaluation are not tested for observer reliability. Most of us merely make the assumption they are reliable and knowledgeable in what they do. This, of course, is a simple and naïve view of the social world. Actually, observers tend to see what they expect to see in the classroom. In other words, their observations are colored by a "halo effect"—where they see what they expect to see and evaluate the teacher in the direction of their general impression of the teacher. The supervisor has a bias about the teacher before entering the classroom, and "observes" (not always accurately) specific items that coincide with the original bias. A person has to be pretty fair-minded and experienced to put his or her biases aside and objectively observe and evaluate someone else; some people are, others are not.

A related problem with observing is that conclusions about the teacher are based on only a few observations. The content, activities, and resulting teacher-student interactions that take place in a classroom change on a regular basis, so that teacher behaviors vary on a regular basis. Just how stable, consistent, or valid one's descriptions of teacher behaviors are when based on a few observations is a legitimate concern. The changes in teacher behavior from day to day may be subtle and most likely a function of changing content and which students are absent or present, but there may be marked differences over the term or school year. Observers vary in reliability but research suggests that across time (three to six months) the target is 70 percent reliable with the same observer; however, with different observers, the reliability decreases.[1] Indices of .90 have been reported, however.[2]

Observation Techniques    There are three common observational techniques: categorical checklists, specimen record techniques, and open-ended forms. With the *categorical checklist,* the observer emphasizes a number of specified teacher or student behaviors. Scoring is sometimes made at intervals or within time units (e.g., every two or three seconds) and sometimes on a five- or seven-point continuum suggesting a bipolar list of behaviors such as "authoritarian" to "democratic" or "boring" to "stimulating." This process tends to ignore the richness and variations of the interaction process. Even worse, the observer is confined to a particular list of behaviors or categories that may or may not even correspond with the reality and rhythm of the classroom or student achievement.

In using the *specimen record technique,* the observer focuses on a specific person (teacher or student) and records all things that the person says or does. The limitations here are that the observer ignores the rest of the classroom, which has an impact on the observed individual(s). Also, the descriptions tend to avoid interpretive

1. Ibid. See also Hersholt C. Waxman and Shwu-Yong L. Huang, "Classroom Observation Research and the Improvement of Teaching Practices," in H. C. Waxman and H. J. Walberg, eds., *New Directions for Teaching Practice and Research* (Berkeley, CA: McCutchan, 1999), pp. 107–130.

2. Michael J. Dunkin and Bruce J. Biddle, *The Study of Teaching* (New York: Holt, Rinehart, 1974); Thomas R. Guskey, *Evaluating Professional Development* (Bloomington, IN: Phi Delta Kappan, 1999); and Stallings and Freiberg, "Observation for the Improvement of Teaching."

or explanatory remarks, which are often essential in fully understanding the intent and effects of behavior.

With the *open-ended form,* the observer may concentrate on whatever he or she wants to write about or describe, ranging from the evenness (or unevenness) of the window shades to the teacher's attire. At the end of the session or day, the observer summarizes his or her data in journalistic style and frequently has a postevaluation conference with the teacher. This method is frequently used in schools, yet it is perhaps the most unreliable and invalid observational technique. The observer goes into the room with a host of biases and preconceived attitudes about the teacher. Since there are no controls, and no checklists, categories, or behaviors to focus on or use as a guide during the observation, there is more latitude for the observer to see what he or she wants or expects to see.[1]

Actually, each of us has a preferred set of biases, and regardless of the observational technique (whether we do or do not have a specific list or coded set of behaviors to interpret), we tend to concentrate on our favored items and bypass the others. We can concentrate on the color of the chalk, blackboard penmanship, the teacher's voice, or the classroom bulletin board. Although it might be pointed out that some of these problems can be reduced with the introduction of visual and auditory tapes to play back, the mechanical problems and cost of recording do not make the video approach as attractive as it might first seem. Moreover, the recordings are produced and replayed by the observer and filtered through his or her eyes and ears; therefore, they still incorporate and reflect contaminating factors.[2]

## Rating Scales

Rating scales are probably the most common technique used for measuring teacher behavior. A large number of rating instruments have been used, ranging from high to low reliability and validity. The instruments used in most schools usually have no evidence of reliability or validity, and are usually based on policy or custom. On a typical form, the students, other teachers, supervisors or administrators, and sometimes parents or consultants are asked to rate a teacher's abilities or performance. However, different groups markedly disagree in their judgments in identifying good teachers. This is not surprising in view of the fact that such judges are human and handicapped by their own personal biases and beliefs of what is or should be a good teacher. Often, they lack firsthand information concerning the classroom situation (except the students) and sufficient knowledge or understanding of teaching or of the subject field to make sound judgments.

The rater is also human and his or her rating is affected by a host of contaminating factors. On a more technical level, ratings are distorted by the (1) "halo effect,"

---

1. Allan C. Ornstein, "Research on Teaching: Measurements and Methods," *Education and Urban Society* (February 1986), pp. 176–181; Ornstein, "Historical and Philosophical Considerations in Determining Teacher Effectiveness," in A. C. Ornstein, ed., *Teaching: Theory into Practice* (Boston: Allyn and Bacon, 1995), pp. 1–24.

2. Ibid.

where the rater evaluates or reacts to each item in the direction of the general impression of the teacher; (2) "error of leniency," a tendency of the rater to rate low or high, no matter what the reason, just like some teachers or professors grade the same students high, and others grade them low; (3) "error of central tendency," whereby the rater is reluctant to make extreme judgments about others (teachers) and either rates in the middle, average, or "three" on a five-point scale; and (4) "constant error," whereby the rater tends to rate others in the opposite direction of his or her attitudes and behaviors (e.g., the rater who is businesslike tends to rate the teacher as less businesslike or the rater who is not businesslike tends to rate the teacher as more businesslike). Other factors that tend to affect raters are (1) gender, (2) race (ethnicity), (3) age, (4) intelligence, (5) understanding of directions, (6) understanding of purpose, (7) sufficient time to complete the ratings, (8) possession of traits being measured, and (9) different criteria raters employ for assessing the same trait or behavior.[1]

The teacher-raters' reference group is also a factor, whether the reference group is perceived as different or the same. Sometimes raters have two different attitudes—one for friends and relatives, and one for formal questionnaires. Raters are not always motivated or honest. Because raters are human, their judgments are imperfect; they are susceptible to selective perceptions, memory, and lack of sensitivity to what may be important. Many raters are impressed more by personality than actual performance. People not only become duped and misjudge physicians or lawyers by their bedside manner or what they promise but they also rate friendly and socially adept teachers higher on performance than their skills and abilities would otherwise suggest.

Despite the hazards associated with rating scales, the majority of supervisors and administrators rely on them in providing feedback to their teachers (after a classroom visit or at the end of a school year) and in identifying the "best" and "worst" teachers. The reasons for using rating instruments in the schools seem in part a function of tradition, the ease in which the inventories can be distributed and tallied, and the fact that many ratings can be used to arrive at a composite score about the teacher.

Students as Raters   When students are raters, there is concern that they lack the maturity and ability to distinguish between teacher personality and teacher performance. If a teacher is likeable or exhibits good interpersonal skills, students tend to be more positive in rating teachers. If a teacher has a personality that is less than favorable or is a tough grader, then teacher performance tends to be depressed. Although it is nearly impossible to control for teacher personality because personality is widely varied and multifaceted, it is feasible to control for grades when scoring student ratings of teachers. (For example, lenient graders often have higher student evaluations.)

Nonetheless, students are the best raters of teachers (and professors) because they see them over an extended period of time and under varied circumstances. (The Hawthorne effect is reduced to zero.) Their sample size is large ($n = 25$ or 30 in one class), compared to a supervisor or researcher ($n = 1$); therefore, the data are more reliable and valid. Furthermore, extreme scores (based on politics, gender, race, religion,

1. Ornstein, "Research on Teaching: Measurements and Methods."

or personality differences) should be eliminated or reduced by the large number of student ratings.

Students are the consumers of education, and their feelings and attitudes (even if misguided) directly influence learning and are therefore more important than the ratings by teachers, supervisors, or researchers. Regardless of how knowledgeable the other raters are, they can be misled or fooled by the infrequent observations of the teacher, and by virtue of the teacher (and students) putting on an act. Moreover, there is no sure way to offset the personal biases of one rater—the "halo" effect, "error of leniency," politics, and or differences in personality or philosophy.

Frequently, student raters are dismissed on the bases of immaturity. The fact is that they tend to be most difficult raters to please, since they have high expectations of their teachers to teach and are required to sit in their seats daily for an extended period of time. Whereas the researcher or supervisor can leave the room at will, and only observes the teacher once or twice to make an assessment, the students are "trapped" for the term or year. They cannot be fooled by the teacher putting on an act to impress the one- or two-time observer.[1]

Although the students' view of good teaching may not always coincide with the view of professionals, students tend to be more honest than adults, who often have their own agenda and set of biases. To be sure, teacher ratings can be used as a potential device to get the "goods" on selected teachers (if ratings are "poor") because of politics or philosophy within a department or school, whereas if ratings are positive, the results will not benefit the same teachers if they are at odds with the administration. Rarely do students have hidden agendas or politics to guide their teacher ratings as do adults who work with and evaluate other adults.

## Student Tests

Policymakers and business executives seem united about establishing the relationship between teacher performance and student achievement. Two related high-stake testing trends have evolved—one aimed at students and the other at teachers and administrators. By 2000, every state except Iowa had established standards in at least some subjects, and 44 had standards in the four academic areas of English, history, math, and science. By 2003, students in 26 states will not graduate from high school without passing a statewide test. There are 13 states that have already linked standardized testing in elementary school with grade promotion and options for getting extra instruction in after-school classes, summer school, and retaking tests.[2]

Obviously, to promote someone who cannot read or do math is no favor to the child in the long run, especially as learning gaps widen over years. Some critics would agree it means blaming the victim, or that there is a cultural or racial bias since a dispropor-

---

1. James H. MacMillan, *Essential Assessment Concepts for Teachers and Administrators* (Thousand Oaks, CA: Corwin Press, 2001); Ornstein and Lasley, *Strategies for Effective Teaching.*

2. Abigail Thernstom, "Testing and its Enemies," *National Review* (September 11, 2000), pp. 38–41.

tionate number of poor and minority students fail these statewide, "gate-keeping" tests. Others would merely argue that promoting students who cannot academically function in class is like allowing them to fall into a bottomless pit with no escape or pushing them into a pool, deeper and deeper, even though they cannot swim.

Without question, state and national tests are being used as "school report cards," with the results sent to parents, published in local newspapers, used as a source for school district funding and sometimes for teachers' and administrators' jobs. Because the public often concludes that high-scoring districts are better than low-scoring districts, it is not surprising that educators seriously consider these results. Some have been caught excluding low-performing students from taking the tests (labeling them as "learning disabled" or "special education" status), teaching the test, extending test time beyond the limits, and altering scores to improve their school standing and their own job status. Parents who wish to buy or sell a home in a particular school district consider these results.

Similarly, numerous states have implemented pay-for-performance incentives tied to improvement in student achievement. The plans vary—bonuses for master teachers, improvement of low-performing teachers who improve, and rewards for teachers whose schools meet improvement targets, as well as for teachers in inner-city schools whose students improve academic outcomes. In 2000, the school district allocating the most money for academic improvement was New York ($29 million) and the state investing the most money for student progress was California ($577 million). Nationally, about half the rewards for increased student achievement are earmarked for schools—mainly to spend on curriculum materials and computers. The remaining bonuses go directly to teachers and administrators (as much as $25,000).[1]

Some states are not above watering down the exam or changing the standards so more students can pass and the state and schools can look better for public consumption, or so there are no charges of racial discrimination because more whites pass than minorities. The federal courts have put pressure on some states to place a moratorium on using tests to hold students back until they can prove the tests are reliable and valid.[2] One way to deal with the matter is the New York state solution. In 1999, 97 percent of students statewide and 95 percent in New York City (90 percent minority enrollment) passed the New York English Regents exam for graduation. In the past, the average passing rate was 70 percent statewide and less than 50 percent citywide. Why the improvement now? The state decided to lower the passing grade to 55 from the traditional 65 in previous years.[3] Not only does the percent passing

1. Anne Blackman et al., "School Testing," *Time* (September 11, 2000), pp. 49–54; Gleason, "Pay for Performance"; and Ben Keller, "Most California Schools to Bet Cash for Meeting Test Targets," *Education Week* (October 11, 2000), p. 24.

2. Linda Jacobson, "State Leaders Push to Sell Public on Shift in Standards for Schools," *Education Week* (November 8, 2000), pp. 1, 28, 29; Erik W. Robelen, "Parents Seek Civil Rights Pride of High-Stake Test in LA," *Education Week* (October 11, 2000), p. 14.

3. "Regents Exam Scores Offer Mixed Picture," *New York Times* (November 10, 2000), pp. A-1.

falsely imply excellence in New York schools but it also takes the federal heat off probing or challenging the state test.

A major concern is that high school mandatory testing does not raise student achievement. In a review of high-stakes testing, one researcher concludes that the states that participated in high-stakes testing evidenced similar reading and math test scores compared to states without tests, based on the National Education Longitudial Study from 1988 to 1992. Actually, the tests had negative effects on students in the bottom 20 percent of the achievement curve. For example, students in the bottom 10 percent of the achievement curve were 33 percent more likely to drop out of school in states that were tested compared to nontest states. For the 11 to 20 percent bottom, they were 25 percent more likely to drop out.[1] In some big cities, such as Chicago, Detroit, and New York, children who fail standardized tests are now forced to attend summer school or are threatened with retention. Critics point out that this "big stick" policy doesn't work. Not only should the use of a single test score not be used to determine important policy decisions for students but also retention only increases dropout rates and narrows the scope of the curriculum.[2]

## Technical Problems of Testing

The high-stakes testing movement raises concerns about fairness, reliability, and validity. The typical standardized test in reading, math, or other subject area comprises a small amount of test items: 40 to 50 items, or sometimes fewer. The tests do an excellent job in providing comparisons among students as to what they have learned at a given point in time, but they are not designed to show changes or gains in scores over short periods of time.[3]

The magnitude of differences between pre- and posttests tend to be small, and it is difficult to obtain reliable scores when the magnitude of differences is small. It is also possible that the ability to get good scores on posttests merely reflects guessing or coaching, since getting correct 3 or 4 extra items out of 40 or 50 results in marked improvement. When changing raw scores into grade equivalent scores, the difference (3 or 4 items) can be as much as one-half to one grade equivalent, depending on the particular test.[4] This means that Johnny can be reading at the fifth-grade level on the

1. Brian A. Jacob, "Getting Tough? The Impact of High School Graduation Exams," *Educational Evaluation and Policy Analysis* (Summer 2001), pp. 99–121.

2. Gerald W. Bracey, "Raising Achievment of At-Risk Students—Or Not," *Phi Delta Kappan* (February 2002), pp. 431–432; Jacob, "Getting Tough."

3. George F. Madaus, "The Distortion of Teaching and Testing," *Peabody Journal of Education* (Spring 1988), pp. 24–46; W. James Popham, "Why Standardized Tests Don't Measure Educational Quality," *Educational Leadership* (March 1999), pp. 8–15.

4. Allan C. Ornstein, "The Evolving Accountability Movement," *Peabody Journal of Education* (Spring 1989), pp. 12–20; Henry S. Dyer, "Toward Objective Criteria of Professional Accountability in the Schools in the Schools," *Phi Delta Kappan* (December 1970), pp. 206–211; and Robert E. Stake, "Testing Hazards in Performance Contracting," *Phi Delta Kappan* (June 1971), pp. 583–589.

pretest with 23 correct items and at the sixth-grade level on the posttest with 27 correct items. Most teachers do not like to have their year's work summarized by little change in performance—based on 3 or 4 items on a test. Even more disturbing, when the test items cover only a small sample of the universe of what is supposed to be taught, those teachers who coach or teach to the test have a skewed impact on students showing performance gains, and the outcomes have little to do with teacher effectiveness. Indeed, it is unfair to raise the question of ethics; it boils down to the purpose of teaching and what is expected from teachers.

The *learning calendar* is also important. It is common knowledge that fall and winter are the most rapid periods of learning, and that summer is the slowest period; in fact, most students regress in the summer. The first month of school is the time for getting things organized and reviewing subject matter lost during the summer. Testing students in September or October would yield a low artificial test result. Testing students in March or April would yield the highest artificial score; after April, there tends to be a drop because instruction tends to compete with other distractions.[1] Not only is learning uneven or lopsided during the school year but it is also a basis for miscalculating real gains in performance.

Programs using an annual testing cycle (fall to fall or spring to spring) to measure student progress in achievement tend to exhibit significantly smaller gains than programs that use a fall to spring test cycle. The second method leads to inflated gains,[2] and characterizes today the vast majority of accountability plans. To be sure, it is inappropriate to compare pretest scores in September with posttest scores in April or May, clear and simple, unless the goal is to corrupt the results—along with student exclusion, grade equivalent conversion errors, mean regression effects, cuts in scores or lower passing criteria, modification of testing conditions or the time, change of tests, coaching or teaching to the test (or the "narrowing" of the curriculum), and outright altering of scores. Depending on your philosophy and sense of ethics, some or all of these factors are acceptable and others are not. Recording progress every few months during the year would be technically preferred, but most educators would be opposed to "all that testing," and the school district or state would raise questions about the extra costs and time lost for teaching.

Obviously, children learn year-round, but it is an unreasonable expectation that most children learn one school year of content in the course of one school year. Such an expectation leads to a simplistic view of human growth and learning. Not only do children and youth develop and learn in spurts, some more rapidly than others at a particular age, but also slow learners generally need more time and assistance than average or high-achieving learners to grasp the same material; in fact, this is the philosophy

1. Robert L. Linn et al., "The Validity of the Title I Evaluation and Reporting System," in E. R. House, ed. *Evaluation Studies Review*, Vol. 7 (Beverly Hills: Sage, 1982), pp. 427–442; John Merrow, "Undermining Standards," *Phi Delta Kappan* (May 2001), pp. 652–659; and Stake, "Testing Hazards in Performance Contracting."

2. Robert L. Linn, "Assessments and Accountability," *Educational Researcher* (March 2000), pp. 4–15; Lorrie A. Shepard, "The Role of Assessment in a Learning Culture," *Educational Researcher* (October 2000), pp. 4–14.

and pedagogy behind mastery learning. In addition, all learning is based on prior learning, and children with learning deficits should not be expected to learn at the same rate as others with no learning deficits. A seventh-grade class with a one-year average deficit in reading and a range of reading scores from grades 5 to 9 provides a different and most likely less difficult change deficit problem than another seventh-grade class with the same one-year deficit in reading but with a range of reading ability from grades 3 to 9. The reading deficit of the second class is much more difficult to deal with because of the lower scores and greater range of abilities, and maturation and instruction are not going to have the same effect on learning how to read. In short, we cannot equate differences in difficulty in reasoning deficits of different magnitudes or the extreme levels of poor student performance.[1]

*Regression effects* toward the mean on the posttest are also unrelated to teaching. For example, if Mary's reading score is at the 40 percentile, statistically she has a 10 percent chance of reaching the 50th percentile on the next test without being taught by the teacher. If a student answered only 20 items correctly out of 50 on the initial test, being able to answer an extra 5 questions on the posttest is easier for her (because of chance variation) than students who had almost all the items correct on the first test. Being able to answer an extra 5 questions would place lower-performing students (i.e., 20 items correct) much higher on relative improvement than would a gain score of 5 questions when the initial score was 40 correct answers. However, when pre- and posttesting low-achieving students, changes in standardized tests scores for these students may be the result of chance variation or guessing, because both scores are based on a small sample of test items. Practice, coaching, or teaching to the posttest would have much greater effect for the slower-achieving students, since they have greater room or potential for improvement, and make the teacher appear to be more effective.

In short, regression effects make the low-achieving students and their teachers look better the next time tested. A similar situation can be observed with children who are very poor tennis players or swimmers. A little extra time in a small group, or preferably on an individual basis, coupled with an understanding instructor, can lead to marked improvement in a short period of time. However, the rate of improvement cannot be sustained. As players became more proficient, it takes more effort and more practice to exhibit slight improvement—or gains in performance.

Another pre- and posttest problem is created by *cellar* and *ceiling effects*. The first of these effects refers to a test that is so difficult that it does not measure accurately at the bottom, and the second of these effects refers to a test that fails to measure at the top because it is too easy. Similarly, students who initially make extremely low scores gain little on posttests, as do students who initially score extremely high. Students who really don't know, who are really incompetent, will not learn under normal conditions and with normal instruction. They need small classes, special tutoring, and psychological counseling to deal with self-esteem and learning problems. For stu-

1. Judy Carr and Douglas E. Harris, *Succeeding With Standards* (Alexandria, VA: Association for Supervision and Curriculum Development, 2001); Grant P. Wiggins, *Assessing Student Performance* (San Francisco: Jossey-Bass, 1999).

dents who initially score high, instruction has minimal impact because there is little room for gains on posttests; these students actually learn a great deal on their own with or without instruction or effective teaching.

Students who are slightly below or slightly above average are often hardworking and have potential for the most improvement, and they will most likely take advantage of instruction, showing more relative improvement on posttests than the lowest- and highest-achieving students. Given the same quality of instruction, if students are ability grouped, teachers assigned to one ability group rather than another will be found to be more "effective" on posttest results. Those classes with average or near-average students will show greater gains, all things being equaled.

The fact that so few test items are used in standardized tests results in a problem with *curriculum validity*. Statewide and nationwide tests do not necessarily reflect the knowledge and skills that teachers emphasize at the local or district level. One can argue that schools need to align their instruction to standardized achievement tests, but in view of the nation's student diversity, especially in urban areas, and with the wide range of abilities among students within and among different school districts, attempting to fit all sizes into one size (one-size-fits-all assessments) is wishful thinking.

Similarly, we all know that textbooks drive the curriculum at all grade levels, and in most cases dominate the nature and sequence of instruction. Comparing five well-known nationally standardized achievement tests in mathematics for grades 4 to 6, researchers conclude that between 50 and 80 percent of what is measured on standardized tests are not suitably addressed in the texts.[1]

One reason for the mismatch between test items and text information is that textbook authors are driven by the nationwide marketplace. They try to incorporate a wide breadth of materials to satisfy the potential users or the largest market, and at the expense of depth of treatment. For example, U.S. math textbooks address 175 percent more topics than do German textbooks and 350 percent more than Japanese textbooks. Similarly, U.S. science textbooks cover 930 percent more topics than German textbooks and 433 percent more topics than Japanese textbooks.[2] The fact that both German and Japanese students significantly outperform American students on international tests in math and science at all grade levels is one issue; the other issue is that American textbooks (which American teachers use) have an unmanageable number of topics so that items that appear on U.S. standardized tests (and international tests) have been, at best, mildly discussed, and in many cases glanced over. German and Japanese textbooks, on the other hand, have the blessing of the ministry of education and are aimed at a national audience—one reason for focused or agreed-upon topics.

**Thinking and Testing**    In general, standardized tests measure knowledge items, because it is difficult to construct short-answer questions that measure higher levels of

---

1. D. J. Freeman et al., "Do Textbooks and Tests Define a Natural Curriculum in Elementary School Mathematics," *Elementary School Journal* (May 1983), pp. 501–513.
2. Mike Schmoker and Robert J. Marzano, "Realizing the Promise of Standards-Based Education," *Educational Leadership* (March 1999), pp. 17–21.

thinking. In a review of 6,942 test items on standardized tests, Marzano and Costa found that less than 15 percent of the items represented thinking beyond simple retrieval or memory of information. Only 7 out of 22 high-order cognitive processes could be identified on standardized tests.[1]

Since teacher performance and the school's reputation is based on student test scores, what gets emphasized on the tests—basic knowledge and low-level cognitive operations—are items that can be easily measured. Since the tests ignore moral and ethical content, socialization, aesthetics (art and music), and values (respect for others, charity, compassion, etc.), the decision for teaching is easy: Ignore this content in class; focus instead on the test items, basic knowledge and information, at the expense of imaginative or creative thought, critical thinking, and the development of the whole child.

With the need for test preparation (some teachers devote several months of class time to test preparation, the amount varying with the stakes involved), there is little time left for making rocket ships in science, talking about the moral issues in *Of Mice and Men* in English, or discussing Picasso's portrayal of women in art. Even with today's emphasis on multicultural education and diversity, there is no time to examine the implications of Crevecoeur's 1782 *Letters of an American Farmer.* "I could point out to you a man whose grandfather was an Englishman, whose wife was Dutch, whose son married a French woman, and whose present four sons have wives of different nations." In America, he continued, "individuals of all nations are melted into a new race of men."

As the states set up standards and rush to hold students or teachers accountable, will teachers have the time and confidence to ask an Irishman, Croatian, or Vietnamese refugee, or a third-generation Holocaust survivor, What does the Statue of Liberty mean to you? Is there sufficient time to ask, Why are so few women in the United States remembered by statues and monuments? With emphasis on completing workbooks and worksheets, practicing and taking tests, will teachers have time to ask moral questions or to deal with and make sense of the tragedy of September 11 and America's response? Advocates, however, claim that the alignment of curriculum to standards and what students are supposed to learn results in a more "rigorous" curriculum. Try to refute the CEO or politician who claims this is how it is: The bottom line counts; thinking is secondary.

Some states (Illinois, New York, Michigan, and others) are beginning to develop standardized tests in reading that attempt to determine how well readers think—to make inferences and to analyze, synthesize, and predict. To assess the readers' cognitive processes is important for determining how students read and for helping them become better readers. The same is true in math, science, history, and other subject areas. The problem, however, is that instead of reading and discussing novels, students are taught how to skim reading passages for key words. Instead of learning how to problem solve in math, conduct experiments in science, or analyze trends and ideas in history, students now practice how to interpret charts and graphs in an attempt to

---

1. Robert J. Marzano and Arthur L. Costa, "Question: Do Standardized Tests Measure General Cognitive Skills? Answer: No," *Educational Leadership* (May 1998), pp. 66–71.

prepare them for neutral or "culturally fair" content in standardized tests. But when students are required to explain their answers, or make inferences and predictions, many students who usually test in the highest percentiles on standard multiple-choice tests perform poorly compared to low-achieving students. This is because the answers contain some gray; the answers are not clearly right or wrong. When there is need to carefully consider multiple options or possible answers, low-achieving students have almost the same chance as high-achieving students of guessing the correct answer.

Theoretically, test items that are answered correctly by a very large number or a very small number of students are not appropriate for inclusion in a standardized test. In both cases, insufficient distinctions are made among students. The majority of items on standardized tests should be in midrange of difficulty.[1] Now, if we follow this reasoning to the end, the better teachers do in teaching important content, the less likely these items will be on standardized tests measuring such knowledge and skills. Put in different terms, what most teachers stress in class and teach should not be tested, because distinctions among students cannot be made. The test items are too easy. That means that if teachers are doing a good job, and teaching the content everyone else is teaching, it is less likely to show up on a standardized test.

## Environmental Factors

Even worse, a case can be made that test items that make students think or figure out complicated answers do not reflect the curriculum but rather the innate abilities of students to respond correctly. Therefore, these items should be omitted from tests because they measure, according to James Popham, "what students come to school with, not what they learn there." Through circular or atypical reasoning, test items that deal with analysis and problem solving do not contribute to valid measures of how well children have been taught; rather, Popham would argue, they reflect "innate intellectual skills that are not readily measurable in school."[2] Similarly, Diane Ravitch would argue that students should have fully learned in school what is being tested; "otherwise, their test scores merely reflect whether they come from an educated family."[3]

We are left with a troubling conclusion: Standardized test items that measure knowledge and low-level information are valid indicators of what children learn in school and indicators of teacher performance; test items that measure high-order thinking are not appropriately aligned with the curriculum, because this is not what or how most teachers teach. We may give lip service in teacher education courses about critical thinking and creativity, but this often does not coincide with classroom reality; facts and knowledge are stressed in classrooms and schools more often than high-order thinking or abstract thinking.

1. Norman Gronlund, *Assessment of Student Achievement,* 6th ed. (Boston: Allyn and Bacon, 1998); W. James Popham, *Modern Educational Measurement,* 3rd ed. (Boston: Allyn and Bacon, 2000).
2. Popham, "Why Standardized Tests Don't Measure Educational Quality," p. 13.
3. Diane Ravitch, "In Defense of Testing," *Time* (September 11, 2000), p. 54.

Terms and concepts that are taken for granted in middle-class society—such as a fourth-grade test item that depends on understanding that cherries and lemons have pits, and celery and radishes are seed-free plants—will affect student scores but will have nothing to do with instruction or content learned in school or in class. The difference between *who* and *which* should be taught by the eighth grade, but knowing actually when to use these words depends more on language usage at the dinner table and previous readings at home than the present performance of the eighth-grade teacher. Teaching high school students to locate where $x$ and $y$ coordinates intersect on a graph is nearly impossible if they lack basic skills in math, unless there are resources available for one-to-one tutoring or highly enriched, small study groups that meet on a regular basis.

The fact is, many items on standardized tests assess various degrees of knowledge and skills learned outside of school, which are more likely to be learned in community settings and within the family. Moreover, Ben Bloom contends that home environment and a student's school achievement show correlations of .7 to .8, and E. D. Hirsh maintains that among students learning current knowledge, the correlation with prior knowledge is .8.[1] If Bloom and Hirsh are correct, then the teacher effect on student achievement is minimal, since we know that subsequent learning in school is in a large part determined by previous learning. As the student progresses through the grades, the effect of the teacher diminishes and basically becomes irrelevant.

Again, the work of Bloom is paramount in understanding that there are limits within which cognition, as it is stabilized and reinforced, may be influenced by classroom or school conditions. From birth to age 4, the individual develops 50 percent of his or her potential for learning; from ages 4 to 8, another 30 percent is developed, and between ages 8 and 17, the remaining 20 percent appears. Put in other terms, student achievement can be affected by the environment six times more at age 4 than at age 17—that is, by 2.5 IQ points per year at age 4 and only .4 IQ point per year from age 8 to 17.[2]

Thus, deprivation at the preschool level has greater consequences on future learning than deprivation in the 10 years from age 8 to 17, because learning (or failure to learn) is based on previous learning and cumulative; the academic gaps widens with age (so that the need for early intervention is crucial.) Taken to its logical end, junior high and high school teachers are off the hook and should not held accountable. It is silly, therefore—actually politically outrageous—to hold teachers accountable for learning deprivation that has accumulated over several previous years. To effect real changes, we need to extend schooling downward to age 3 and extend it over the summer months for primary students (grades 1 to 3) who lack basic skills so that they can be caught up and not fall further behind over the summer months as most students do.

---

1. Benjamin S. Bloom, "The Two Signing Problem," *Educational Researcher* (June–July 1984), pp. 4–16; E. D. Hirsh, "Seeking Breadth and Depth in the Curriculum," *Educational Leadership* (October 2001), pp. 22–25. (Note that .7 and .8 are considered high correlations; a perfect correlation is 1.)

2. Benjamin S. Bloom, *Stability and Change in Human Characacteristics* (New York: Wiley, 1964).

## Problems, Prospects, and Professionalism

When teachers try to tell the public that standardized tests will provide a misleading indicator of teacher performance, they are accused of running from their professional responsibilities and encouraging teacher incompetence by default. What's more, recent public opinion polls reveal that the vast majority of parents (more than 75 percent) are aware of local school standards, believe schools have been "careful and reasonable" in setting academic standards, and support student testing and accountability (for students and teachers alike) that goes with it. Only 18 percent believe teachers spend too much time preparing students for tests, at the expense of real learning.[1]

Only a few educators raise concerns about the appeal of state and national standards, and relating teacher performance to student test scores; these popular trends may (1) discredit many teachers and schools without raising questions about joint responsibility of students, parents, and communities; (2) deprofessionalize teachers and turn them into technocrats who must follow the drum beat of externally imposed "expert" judgments; (3) reduce monetary resources and services spent on education; and (4) divert educators' and the public's attention from real steps needed to improve education for all students.[2]

Some educators would refer to all these test-driven suggestions as part of "outcome-based education," others as "results-driven education," and still others as "competency-based education." The commonality is school improvement—or improving teaching and learning—through collaborative and collegial efforts. By teachers working together, responding to problems, creating or revising standards, aligning curriculum and instruction with standards, being recognized and rewarded for their efforts, teachers can play an important role in improving education. For their own professional status and welfare, teachers must insist on a stronger voice in determining standards at the district and school levels. We must leave important decisions about teaching in their hands, not with external groups nor bureaucrats from state capitals or Washington, DC.

To gloss over the teachers' voice, to minimize their professional knowledge and experience, is to make teachers impotent and demoralize them on an individual and group (or professional) basis. According to Harry Broudy, the image of the teacher as the surrogate, loving, tender, and understanding substitute parent, an interpretation of the *in loco parentis,* or of the person hired by the school to discharge and follow administrative-approved behavior breeds "a mischievous sentimentalism" that deflates the idea of teacher professionalism.[3] Teachers should not be expected to vibrate sympathetically with every fad or dictum imposed upon them by "experts" or the political and business community. Most of these voices of reform (past and present) have

1. David J. Hoff, "Polls Dispute a 'Backlash' to Standards," *Education Week* (October 11, 2000), pp. 1, 16; John Leo, "A Tempest in an Ink Spot," *U.S. News and World Report* (October 16, 2000), p. 18.

2. Sandra Feldman, "Stark Differences," *New York Times* (October 29, 2000), p. 7; Deborah Meier, *Will Standards Save Public Education?* (Boston: Beacon Press, 2000); and Robelen, "Parents Seek Civil Rights Probe of High-Stakes Tests."

3. Harry S. Broudy, *The Real World of the Public Schools* (New York: Harcourt, Brace, 1972).

not taught, and don't really know what it is like to teach; they have no right to impose educational standards, to chastise or admonish teachers for their performance in class or with their students. All of these new standards and testing doctrines dribble down to a legalism and policy that undercuts teachers and forces them to emphasize tiny pieces of information at the expense of real teaching and learning.

**EPISODE** $\beta$

## Educational Accountability

Although there are many definitions of *accountability*, the term is rooted in the educational trends of the 1970s and 1980s; in the ideas of Leon Lessinger and U.S. Commissioner of Education, Sidney Marland, both of whom translated business concepts of accountability into the educational arena; and in the competency-based education movement that attempted to determine minimum standards for student and teacher performance. At its height in the mid-1980s, 35 states administered tests for grade promotion as a "gate-keeping role" and/or for high school graduation. In those days, the legislation made students the focal point for rewards and penalties, although in a few cases the test results were used to make decisions about school funding. Similarly, 21 states required competency tests in general academic knowledge or in basic skills as an exit requirement from a teacher education program, and 37 required it for professional certification.[1] The idea of competency testing came under attack because of alleged discriminatory test results (minority students and teachers failed in greater percentages) and the testing program had no impact on improving student achievement.

Although there are several definitions, for most educators *accountability* means that students, teachers, and/or schools must exhibit some standard, competency level, or performance level, and educators must devise methods of relating teacher performance or student expenditures to student outcomes. For many years, the quality of education was measured by the total number of dollars spent per student or the achievement scores of the students. Now, achievement standards are being introduced, students are being tested, the curriculum is being aligned to these tests, schools are being compared, and students and educators are being made to answer for results.

Demands for accountability have increased over the recent years for the following reasons:

1. An increasing number of parents realize that schooling is important for success and that their children are not learning well enough.
2. The public has the impression that school people are accountable to no one but themselves.

1. *The Condition of Education 1989*, vol. 1 (Washington, DC: U.S. Government Printing Office, 1989); Chris Pipho, "The Sting of High Stake Testing and Accountability," *Phi Delta Kappan* (May 2000), pp. 645–646.

3. School costs continue to rise. People feel overtaxed and want to know where their dollars are being spent.
4. Some educators and policymakers claim that we need to develop an information system to identify effectiveness indicators and to evaluate teachers and schools based on those indicators. Here, the important criterion for success is not teacher or school input characteristics but student output or results.
5. The push for accountability is heightened by the demand for excellence. The clamor for higher academic standards and increased academic productivity reflects our growing concern about student achievement scores on international tests and our economic inability to compete internationally on a long-term basis. Hence, there is recognition that human capital and economic capital are interlinked.
6. Some educators assert that modes of proof can be established for assessing standards. Instead of vague promises to increase student learning, precise standards can be stated that specify what students are expected to gain from their educational experiences.
7. Several states, and now the federal government, have mandated test-driven curriculum standards and cause-effect relationships to assess performance. Although there are usually multiple causes for student achievement, the demand is for local educators to measure performance of teachers and schools, then to penalize or reward performance.

## Accountability in Historical Context

Although accountability is a relatively new concept in the educational literature, the original idea dates back to the ancient Greek philosophers. As the cup of hemlock touched Socrates' lips back in 339 B.C., history recorded for the first time the act of holding a teacher accountable for what he was teaching. Fewer than 400 years later, another great teacher, Jesus Christ, was held accountable for His teachings. In 1925, John Scopes was held accountable by the community for teaching about the theory of evolution, which resulted in his trial and conviction. Each of us is able to recall cases, even closer to home, concerning the dismissal of a teacher on the grounds that his or her reading list, learning activities, or political, moral, or religious interpretations ran contrary to the values of the community. This concept of accountability (holding a teacher responsible for the personal views he or she expresses) is certainly not new.

Accountability also has a history of going back into time—accountability for what should be taught and how it should be taught. In the medieval universities, professors and tutors were paid directly by the students. The law students of Bologna during the mid-thirteenth century extracted this form of accountability. Writes one observer, "The students who had the whip hand kept their professors to a punctual observance of the lecture timetable, under threat of financial penalties, and revenged themselves on unpopular teachers by boycotts."[1] In the United States, we can go as

1. Frederich Herr, *The Medieval World* (New York: American Library, 1961), p. 244. (Note that this student control was not characteristic of all medival universites—at least not at the universities of Paris and Salerno.)

far back as the Old Deluder Satan Act of 1647. Enacted by the Massachusetts Bay Colony, it held each town accountable for teaching the children to read the Bible. A fine of five pounds was levied for noncompliance. On still another level, there has always been an implied form of accountability (and educational standards) in terms of educational goals, compulsory attendance, student assessment, teacher certification requirements, teacher ratings, professional duties of teachers and school administrators, evaluation of programs, and budget costs. Accountability has always been with us, although the names and definitions have varied over time.

A 1922 Wisconsin contract, calling for a salary of $75 a month, outlined conditions that held teachers accountable for a host of behaviors that need to be analyzed in context with the times: the Model T Ford, the protest marches of Susan B. Anthony, the growing pains of organized labor, and Sinclair Lewis's *Main Street* and *Babbit*. As part of the contract provisions, it expressly warned teachers (1) not to get married; (2) not to keep company with men; (3) not to loiter downtown in ice-cream parlors; (4) not to smoke or drink beer, wine, or whiskey; (5) not to dress in bright colors; (6) not to dye their hair; (7) not to wear dresses shorter than two inches above the ankle; (8) not to wear face powder or paint the lips; and (9) not to leave town at any time without the permission of the chairman of trustees.[1]

In the past (as illustrated by the preceding examples), the teacher was held responsible for exhibiting certain behaviors and what should or should not be taught. The responsibility for learning what was taught resided with the learner. But a concept of accountability based on the ability of the educational delivery system to assure successful student learning is a product of our times. It grows out of our recognition of the societal problems arising in part from the failure of our schools to come to grips with the learning problems of students who are not succeeding. It is evident to many that our educational institutions are failing to produce the egalitarian society heralded as perhaps the prime educational goal.

## Compensatory Education and Egalitarianism

To reach the goal of egalitarian society, school reformers (segments of liberal and minority groups) since the beginning of the War on Poverty and civil rights movement in the 1960s have raised the cry of equal educational opportunity and institutional (school) responsibility for assuring successful learning. Both equal educational opportunity and institutional responsibility found support in the prevailing psychological theories of environmentalism and behaviorism. Americans have long put great faith in the role of environment to shape our lives and the extent to which people and society can be improved through changes in the environment; behaviorism provided the tool for modifying behavior to suite the altered environment. The early compensatory programs of the 1960s, followed by the Elementary and Secondary Education Acts (ESEA) of 1965, served as outlets for the environmentalists' idea of cognitive development and the behaviorists' theory of changing human characteristics. In 1970, the program budget for Title I of the ESEA was over $1 billion per year, actually $1.3 billion, or 10.5 percent of the $12.5 billion federal budget in education. By 1998,

1. *Chicago Tribune* (September 28, 1975), Sect. 1, p. 3.

spending on programs for Title I (also briefly called Chapter I and renamed Title I) was $7.8 billion, or 10 percent of the $76 billion dollar budget.[1] For 2002, amid increased military and home security spending and consolidation of many federal programs, ESEA funding reached $10.2 billion, reflecting the elements of President's Bush's prized "Reading First Program" and "Leave No Child Behind" plan.[2]

During this 37-year period (1965–2002), the Consumer Price Index increased about four times, but compensatory funding soared 11.5 times. Funding for Title I, or disadvantaged students, has become big business—with a host of bureaucratic layers and jobs and subsequent advocates for compensatory funding. In the name of a variety of environmental and behavioral theories, as well as President Johnson's dream of the "Great Society," compensatory programs proliferated as educators and social designers rushed to make claims to federal monies, spending billions of dollars based on hunches and sometimes sloppy program designs. Although compensatory programs from the Johnson era to the Bush administration had a great deal in common, the latter was the first president to raise the difficult issue on how to define *failing schools*, although resolving it during these four decades has always remained unclear.

In the early years, one educator summarized compensatory funding as an "ineffective free for all . . . with few federal strings attached to the expenditures."[3] Program after program seemed to make little difference, perhaps the only consistent thread running through the programs was the demand that more money be spent. Only gradually, after some 15 or 20 years, did we come to the first stage of wisdom: confession of how little we know about improving the education of inner-city students—namely, poor and minority students. And, almost 40 years later, after spending nearly half a trillion dollars on compensatory education, one educator concluded there was "no answer to the question of whether increases in school funding would change measured [student] achievement." Educators are still unable to determine "how economic circumstances affect educational outcomes." Obviously, there are a number of "other variables that ought to be considered," such as the characteristics of families, peer groups, and student population.[4]

## The Evaluation (and Failure) of Compensatory Education

The evaluation of compensatory education began with its most prominent program. When the Westinghouse–Ohio University report was published in 1969, the Office of Education, along with some members of the reform community, tried to obscure

1. *Digest of Education Statistics 1998* (Washington, DC: U.S. Government Printing Office, 1998), Table 361, pp. 400–401; *Digest of Education Statistics 2000* (Washington, DC: U.S. Government Printing Office, 2001), Table 361, p. 407.

2. Erik W. Robelen, "Amid Crisis, Outlook for ESEA Overhaul Unclear," *Education Week* (September 26, 2001), pp. 25–26; Robelen, "Congress Refocuses on ESEA," *Education Week* (October 3, 2001), pp. 27, 31. Also see *Digest of Education Statistics 2000*, Table 363, p. 414; Edwork/force.housegov/issues/107th/education/nclb.

3. Howard A. Glickstein, "Federal Educational Programs and Minority Groups," *Journal of Negro Education* (Summer 1969), p. 305.

4. Sarah E. Turner, "A Comment of Poor School Funding, Child Poverty, and Mathematics Achievement," *Educational Researcher* (June–July 2000), pp. 15, 17.

the findings. The report evaluated Head Start programs, still considered a success at that time by reformers. The report concluded that from a sample of children from 104 Head Start centers, there was no significant difference in learning between Head Start children and a matched control group, and that the program failed to help disadvantaged learners catch up to their middle-class counterpart or to alleviate any of their cognitive deficiencies.[1] Then came the summary analysis of compensatory results by Richard Fairley, the Director of the Office of Education's Division of Compensatory Education: Of more than 1,200 educational projects evaluated between 1970 and 1972, only 10 were found successful on the basis of measurable data.[2]

Although several reasons were suggested for the disappointing results of compensatory programs, they could be summed: As programs were extended to larger numbers of children, the impact was watered down, efforts were not intensive, teachers were ill trained, classes were too large, and early gains tended to "fade out" after a few years of schooling.[3]

When Arthur Jensen brought up the role of heredity as a contributing factor in learning, and the major reason why compensatory education failed, shock waves were felt through the education community.[4] He was quickly branded as a "racist" and encountered a great deal of harassment and abuse at the hands of many reformers. Jensen maintained that compensatory education, which was costing taxpayers billions of dollars a year, had failed and would continue to do so because it was trying to compensate disadvantaged children by using learning processes and pedagogical methods for students who had facility in abstract thought. Curriculum and instruction had to be revamped, he argued, to fit the needs and abilities of the disadvantaged more closely—namely, to use concrete materials and methods.[5] Some 20 years later, without referring to the generic component or comparisons of mental abilities between or among racial groups, many of these concrete methods would be considered appropriate under the guise of "direct instruction" and "mastery learning"—which included such strategies as structured tasks, practice opportunities, monitoring performance, and providing prompt feedback—all which became part of the "effective teacher" literature.

During this period, Richard Herrnstein was severely condemned as one of "Hitler's propagandists" for touching lightly on the racial implication of IQ, suggesting that there was evidence of a genetic factor in education and social-class dif-

1. Westinghouse Learning Corporation and Ohio University, *The Impact of Head Start* (Washington, DC: U.S. Government Printing Office, 1969).

2. Richard L. Fairley, "Accountability's New Test." *American Education* (June 1972), pp. 33–35. Also see *Compensatory Education and other Alternatives in Urban Schools* (Washington, DC: U.S. Government Printing Office 1972).

3. Allan C. Ornstein, Daniel U. Levine, and Doxy A. Wilkenson, *Reforming Metropolitan Schools* (Pacific Palisades, CA: Goodyear, 1975).

4. Arthur R. Jensen, "How Much Can We Boost IQ and Scholastic Achievement," *Harvard Educational Review* (Spring 1969), pp. 1–123.

5. Arthur R. Jensen, "IQ Tests Are Not Culturally Based for Blacks and Whites," *Phi Delta Kappan* (June 1976), pp. 675–676. Also see Jensen, "How Much Can We Boost IQ and Scholastic Achievement?"

ferences.[1] Fifteen years later, Herrnstein experienced worse ridicule. He coauthored with Charles Murray *The Bell Curve,* and argued that hereditary affected intellectual development, social behavior, and personality; it was also the key factor for determining inequality in education and income. The fact that there were differences in a person's characteristics, abilities, and motivation meant there had to be differences in education outcomes. The closer a society comes to the ideal of equal opportunity, the more those with high IQs will rise to the top and those with low IQs will remain at the bottom. Equality would never eliminate education or economic differences. Compensatory education could not neutralize the effects of low IQ and education deprivation. Given the social and political period, the authors feared the decline of merit and competency as the push for egalitarianism called for equal results.[2]

In the meantime, the Brookings Institute had become a haven for the deposed liberals of the New Frontier and the Great Society. The 1972 Brookings study, by Charles Schultz, was a confession, topic by topic, of liberal regret. According to the authors, no person alive could say what education and social programs in schools and communities had been successful. Chapter by chapter, we learned about the failure of one governmental program after another, including compensatory education, job training, urban renewal, and welfare, each of which cost the taxpayers millions of dollars a year.[3]

The same year, the Rand Corporation, another organization staffed mainly by many liberal social scientists, published a report by Harvey Averch and associates about schools and other related programs in the educational poverty industry. The analysis suggested that, with respect to school financing, we were already spending too much in terms of what we were getting in return. In the early stages of school and related compensatory programs, input increments had a high marginal return, but they gradually diminished until the exchange of input for output was no longer equal, and finally to the point where input was wasted because there was virtually no increase in output. It was concluded that, in many areas of education, we had reached a "flat area," less output in relations to input, or worse, no return.[4]

Then, Daniel Moynihan, former advisor on domestic policies to former Presidents Johnson and Nixon, raised the issue that educational and social spending was suffused with waste and confusion, that the money spent on compensatory education and antipoverty programs went to the people running the programs and not to the poor. He also criticized extra spending on education, pointing out that close to 70 percent of the operating expenses of the public schools went toward salaries, and any increase in educational spending would go mainly to teachers and school administrators.

1. Richard J. Herrnstein, "IQ," *Atlantic* (September 1971), pp. 43–64; Herrnstein, *IQ in the Meritocracy* (Boston: Little, Brown, 1971).

2. Richard J. Herrnstein and Charles Murray, *The Bell Curve* (New York: Free Press, 1994).

3. Charles L. Schultz et al., *Setting National Priorities: The 1973 Budget* (Washington, DC: Brookings Institute, 1972).

4. Harvey A. Averch et al., *How Effective in Schooling?* (Santa Monica, CA: Rand Corporation, 1972).

Moynihan argued that there was no need to increase social spending because it was a failure and the only people who really benefited were a new class of middle-class bureaucrats who were paid to dispense the services and who claimed they were the only ones qualified because of race to dispense these services. He argued that if one-third of the $31 billion spent by the federal government alone in 1971 on social programs for the poor had gone directly to the poor, there would no longer be any poverty in the United States (as the poverty level was defined). Without mentioning accountability, there was the implied assumption of the need for accountability in terms of curbing spending and obtaining intended results.[1]

Some 40 years later, after continuous massive funding of compensatory education (Title I) programs, particularly early childhood and Head Start programs, the debate continues to draw a good deal of controversy and attention: whether these programs are successful—or not. (Head Start is the most visible program, serving 21 million students at risk from 1965 [its inception] to 2002; it has been a Clinton and Bush priority, now serving 915,000 children annually.)[2] Despite increased funding, high program visibility, and constant attempts to improve the delivery system, there is a critical mass of educators who argue that all these programs have no significant effect. Moreover, the research that shows positive results is scientifically invalid, pure and simple, and designed to mask failure.[3]

If you need to venture or guess why, then consider reputations and careers of the advocates, the jobs and dollars at stake, and the general need to be positive and believe something will work to improve the education of students at risk, which is the heart of social reform and social justice. The harshest critic, Stanley Pogrow, states the issue in bleak terms: "Despite the widespread rhetoric of 'we know what works,' it turns out that learning gaps between minority students and white students on the National Assessment of Educational Progress (NAEP)," considered the premier standardized test that reveals the best information on achievement at the national level, "actually increased in the 1990s, and the reading of the lowest quartile actually declined."[4] In other words, we are pouring more money into compensatory and early childhood education, and going backwards.

1. Daniel P. Moynihan, "Equalizing Education: In Whose Benefit?" *Public Interest* (Fall 1972), pp. 69–89; Moynihan, "The Schism in Black America," *Public Interest* (Spring 1972), pp. 3–24.

2. Linda Jacobson and Darcia Harris Bowman, "Early Childhood Education Advocates Say President's Budget Fails to Meet His Rhetoric," *Education Week* (February 13, 2002), p. 32; Sharon L. Kagon and Lynda G. Hallmark, "Early Care and Education Policies in Sweden: Implications for the United States," *Phi Delta Kappan* (November 2001), pp. 237–245, 254.

3. Paul Barton, "Raising Achievement and Reducing Gaps," *A Report to the National Education Goals Panel,* March 2002; Mark Berends, *Implementation and Perfomance in New American Schools* (Santa Monica, CA: Rand Corporaion, 2001); and Jonathan Jacobson, *Educational Achievement and Black-White Inequality* (Washington, DC: U.S. Government Printing Office, 2001).

4. Stanley Pogrow, "Success for All Is a Failure," *Phi Delta Kappan* (February 2002), p. 463.

Educators involved in directing compensatory and early childhood programs, and who have spent the last 15 to 20 years doing so, make it clear that there is substantial evidence that such programs work, and that many evaluators have made the same conclusion. Robert Slavin, associated with "Success for All," is one of the best-known advocates. His data in Baltimore, Miami, and Houston show that his reading skills programs works with tens of thousands of students, especially with black and Hispanic students.[1] Similarly, James Comer has developed an early childhood program called the "School Development Program," which emphasizes parental and community participation, enhances social and psychological services, organizes teachers to improve their expectations and instructional practices, and improves school climate. Originally established in New Haven (CT), his model has been adapted in many large cities, such as Chicago, Detroit, and Los Angeles.[2]

We would like to believe that early compensatory programs work, simply because of our 37-year investment; it also coincides with conventional wisdom—the theories of cognitive psychology and the environmental influence on education outcomes, as opposed to a hereditarian theory that infers little hope and creates social tension. If we can send people to the moon, and if we want to promote our values to the "have-nots" of the world, or if we want to improve our rankings on international tests and the output of our own labor force, these early childhood programs *have* to work. If education cannot reverse the effects of poverty, or if achievement levels cannot be raised, then we will need to rethink our school policies and the concept of equality. Personally, I find Karl Alexander and his colleagues' research the kindest explanation for the failure of compensatory education and how education outcomes for students at risk can be improved.[3]

Test results for grades 1 through 5 in high poverty schools almost always test poorly against nonpoverty schools. "Their students lag behind in the early grades and fall further back over time."[4] But the greatest disparities seems to be associated with summer gains made by middle-class and upper-middle-class children, because of family support structures and language skills that are continuously rehearsed in these homes, compared to lower-class children whose gains, on average, are flat or slightly dip in the summer. Hence, the effects of early childhood programs become blurred when

1. Eric A. Hurley et al., "Effects of Success for All on TAAS Reading Scores: A Texas Statewide Evaluation," *Phi Delta Kappan* (June 2001), pp. 750–756; Robert E. Slavin, "Mounting Evidence Supports the Achievment Effects of Success for All," *Phi Delta Kappan* (February 2002), pp. 469–471, 480.

2. James P. Comer, "Educating Poor Minority Children," *Scientific American* (November 1988), pp. 42–48; Thomas D. Cook et al., "Comer's School Development Program in Chicago," *American Educational Research Journal* (Summer 2000), pp. 535–597.

3. Karl L. Alexander, Doris R. Entwisle, and Linda S. Olson, "Schools, Achievment, and Inequality: A Seasonal Perspective," *Educational Evaluation and Policy Analysis* (Summer 2001), pp. 171–191; Doris R. Enwisle, Karl L. Alexander, and Linda S. Olson, *Children, Schools, and Inequality* (Boulder, CO: Westview Press, 1997).

4. Alexander et al., "Schools, Achievement, and Inequality," p. 171.

achievement is compared on an annual basis. The gains in achievement of children at risk depend less on home resources during the school year than do lack of gains in the summer months when they are not attending school. The need is to reform the school calender and require summer school for primary-grade children who lack basic cognitive skills and thus support at-risk children's learning year-round.

## The Economists Enter the Arena

Several economists eventually introduced their ideas—in terms of "inputs" and "outputs" of education. In the early 1970s, Kenneth Boulding presented an input-output thesis in a report to the American Educational Research Association, noting that extra input in school programs was not yielding more output. The point of maximum return had long been passed, and the possibility of increasing school productivity seemed improbable. Private industry operating in the same manner as the school industry would have long since closed down because of the losses.[1]

Peter Drucker made a similar point about governmental spending for educational and social programs. There was little in the record to substantiate the bright beliefs of the 1960s, and the argument that the reason for the failure of these programs was that not enough money was spent. There was no evidence that extra money was the answer, as some reform groups had proclaimed, but there was sufficient data to support the claim that money already spent had no appreciable results. Implied in his analysis was the need to measure the costs versus effectiveness of these programs. He claimed the need to test our ideas before expanding them, to define our goals and priorities, to coordinate effectively the activities, and to postpone making promises until the programs were evaluated and the results were in. Without ever mentioning the word *accountability*, Drucker employed the jargon of accountability and in effect advocated it.[2]

Enter Milton Friedman. In the 1960s and 1970s, he began to preach a doctrine that included school choice and privatization of schooling. He argued that public schools were failing to educate a large segment of children and that competition among schools would raise the overall level of education quality and school outcomes. The idea was to allow the laws of marketplace: Effective schools would stay in business, and ineffective schools would be forced to close their doors and go out of business. Friedman's ideas would take hold in the 1990s with the rise of educational vouchers, tuition tax credits, school choices, and charter schools.

A large number of production models—that is, analysis based on inputs and outputs—have continued to have an impact on the field. The conclusions are contradictory. Most noted, on the conservative scale, is Eric Hanushek, who concludes in several studies, over a 15-year period (1985–2000) that the effects of additional funding in education result in nonsignificant differences. Money alone makes little differ-

1. Kenneth Boulding, "The School Industry as a Possible Pathological Economy," paper presented at the Annual AERA Conference, New York, February 1971.

2. Peter F. Drucker, "Can the Businessmen Meet Our Social Needs," *Saturday Review* (March 13, 1973), pp. 41–44.

ence in student outcomes; the need is to address family, peer groups, and student responsibilities.[1]

On the other hand, positive findings have been reported during the same 15-year period: School funding does increase school output, and compensatory funding can have long-lasting results if programs are planned and implemented properly and if additional services are sustained throughout elementary grades.[2] The actual gains in achievement vary considerably, however: how far behind participants start out, cooperation and education of the parents, how much students read at home, motivation of the students, and exactly what variables (things that money can buy) are considered in the analysis.

## From Compensatory Education to Accountability

Although the political left and right started their ideological movements from opposite ends of the continuum, it was inevitable that they should discover each other in the middle or at least somewhere on the continuum. Although their ends were opposed, they found they had much in common with their quest for accountability. Whereas the reform community advocated more money and various programs, the conservative voice believed the programs were generally unworkable because of the difficulties of changing human nature and thus sought better utilization of resources and money. For both the advocates and critics of compensatory education, it was a simple step to accountability.

Indeed, the controversy over compensatory education led into accountability with the 1970 amendments to Title I of the ESEA, which included a form of responsibility at all levels. Although directed at compensatory spending, it moved the funded schools toward accountability by requiring expenditure and staff data on a school basis. It also required administrators of Title I money to set performance criteria, then to evaluate the programs in line with such criteria. In defending the rationale for this amendment, one government evaluator wrote, "Teachers will have a number of sets of data to work with in evaluating their own teaching—and the success or failure of the program they are involved in."[3] Here, it is easy to see how transfer was made in the compensatory movement and evaluating the programs to accountability and evaluating teachers and administrators (and the law Bush enacted in 2001).

In the same vein, both those on the left and those on the right of the political continuum generally accepted Leon Lessinger's statement of holding "an agent [school

1. Eric A. Hanushek, "Moving Beyond Spending Fetishes," *Educational Leadership* (November 1995), pp. 60–64; Hanushek, "A More Complete Picture of School Resource Policies," *Review of Educational Research* (Fall 1996), pp. 397–409; and Hanushek, "Assessing the Empirical Evidence on Class Size Reductions from Tennessee and Non-Experimental Research," *Educational Evaluation and Policy Analysis* (Summer 1999), pp. 143–164.

2. Lorin W. Anderson and Leonard O. Pellices, "Synthesis of Research on Compensatory and Remedial Education," *Educational Leadership* (September 1990), pp. 10–16; Larry V. Hedges and Robert Greenwald, "Have Times Changed? The Relationship between School Resources and Student Performance," in G. Burtless, ed., *Does Money Matter?* (Washington, DC: Brookings Institute, 1966), pp. 74–92; and Robert E. Slavin, "Putting the School Back in School Reform," *Educational Leadership* (December–January 2001), pp. 22–27.

3. Fairley, "Accountability's New Test," p. 34.

person, board of education, private company, etc.] answerable for performing according to agreed-upon terms, within an established time period, and with stipulated use of resources and performance standards."[1] According to Lessinger, the school was a malfunctioning machine, and there was need for school systems to adopt private enterprise accountability procedures. It is only a small transition to go from Lessinger's definition of and reasons for accountability to the related demands made by the political left and right in the new millenium.

Thus, one advocate group writes, today: "Successful standards-based reform depends on clear standards, well-crafted tests and fair accountability." Students, teachers, and parents alike need to fully understand what students are expected to learn. "We need a consistent way of measuring progress, . . . and the system should connect incentives and supports with results."[2] Still another advocate intends that "the biggest indicators that standards are here to stay are the public's demand for accountability and dramatic increase in the public's access to information about students."[3] National and state testing results are available on the Internet, so we can now find out how schools compare. Eventually, we will start a monitoring system that compares teachers within schools: Whether we focus on standards or not, the information age permits us to focus on a detailed accountability program that tracks student and teacher performance in multiple ways throughout the year. Robert Marzano agrees: "We're entering an era of accountability that has been created by technology and the idea of information explosion."[4] Inputting data, then tracking and holding the teacher (not the student) accountable is becoming feasible and popular.

With both ends of the political continuum urging some form of accountability, it is safe for almost anyone to advocate accountability, knowing full well he or she will encounter much support and little criticism with politically active groups. Now, with government and business groups also pushing accountability, the concept takes on a new and heightened image, and almost everyone else falls into line and joins the marching bandwagon.

Although the accountability movement means different things to different people, both 20 years ago and today, it has become a unifying theme related to management by objectives, cost-effectiveness audits, competency-based education, outcome-based education, pay for performance, curriculum alignment, high-stakes testing, national or state testing, school improvement, and standards-based education. The fact that accountability means so many different things makes it acceptable to many education reformers and people in many political circles. The issue, today, is not whether to have standards or accountability, but what kind of standards and accountability will prevail. See Teaching Tips 2.2.

1. Leon M. Lessinger, "Engineering Accountability for Results in Public Education." *Phi Delta Kappan* (January 1970), p. 217.

2. Matthew Gandal and Jennifer Vranek, "Standards Here Today, Here Tomorrow," *Educational Leadership* (September 2001), p. 7.

3. Marge Scherer, "How and Why Standards Can Improve Achievement: A Conversation with Robert J. Marzano," *Educational Leadership* (September 2001), p. 18.

4. Ibid.

# *Teaching Tips 2.2*

## Improving Standards-Based Education and Assessing Teacher Performance

Given the popularity of standards-based education, we are forced to come up with some criteria for judging teacher performance. Twelve recommendations are made here. We need the following:

1. A method to align national and state education standards with the local curriculum.
2. An improved method to correlate student scores with teacher performance.
3. A method to analyze data that will generate a "values added" correlation between individual teachers and student learning gains over time.
4. An appropriate appraisal of the data that indicates patterns of performance of students and teachers, and discerns teacher influence from other in-school factors as well as out-of-school factors, such as socioeconomic status, parental factors, and so on.
5. A corrective approach to help new teachers and experienced teachers whose students consistently exhibit poor learning (including but not limited to coaching and mentoring, staff development programs, and reassignment).
6. Methods for improving teachers' communication and cooperation so that teachers can share results openly, discuss issues, and encourage peer recognition.
7. Supplementary assessment of teacher performance to recognize and encourage

teacher excellence, based on student, parental, and supervisory evaluations.
8. Steps by the school to provide math and reading tutoring, summer school, homework centers, additional after-school and Saturday morning classes, and smaller classes for students who need help; money should never be taken away from low-performing schools, which is self-defeating and tantamount to punishing the victims.
9. Methods to avoid pitting teachers against each other in the same school for merit or bonuses; instead, we must reward schools (not individual teachers) or entire teaching staffs to foster teamwork and collegiality.
10. Professional opportunities and school time to design, implement, and/or revise standards and assessment procedures that coincide with the students' needs and abilities of the local schools.
11. Agreement of teachers and parents in establishing their own standards (more local control) in context with state and national goals and benchmarks, as well as methods for achieving them.
12. Districtwide processes that favor decisions about teaching by teachers, including the alignment of curriculum and instruction with standards and the improvement and evaluation of teacher performance.

## Old Wine, New Labels

The present accountability movement places responsibility on teachers and schools for delivery of an instructional program that assures student performance and holds school people responsible for performing according to agreed-upon terms.

Compensatory education implied something was wrong with the child; with accountability, if the program fails, the teachers or schools are at fault. For the compensatory advocates, accountability, now coupled with standards and pay-for-performance agreements, serve as a means of transferring the burden of blame to educators and as a second chance to prove the value of compensatory education to the many detractors who feel and oppose the cost of government spending in taxes and rising inflation. For the critics of compensatory spending, accountability was and still is a way of enhancing educational dollars, to establish modes of proof, and to hold down taxes.

The education establishment today points to an educational crisis: Many inner-city students are not learning, despite our compensatory efforts, and American students continuously fall behind on international tests. As in the post-*Sputnik* era, when we had to beef up the curriculum to beat the Soviets, there is a sense of urgency and concern about a rising tide of mediocrity, keenly expressed in *A Nation at Risk* in 1983; *Time for Results,* the governors' reports in 1986 and 1991 to the nation; *Goals 2000,* outlined in 1990, 1994, and 1997 by former Presidents Bush and Clinton; and the $26.4 billion package for the No Child Left Behind Act, enacted in 2001 by President George W. Bush.

Our concern has reached near hysteria, illustrated by alarming figures that characterize the decline of American education in the last 20 years—for example, declining SAT scores, increased remedial courses at the college level, and the international tests and "report cards" that illustrate that American students have trouble competing with their counterparts in Europe and Asia (see Figure 2.1). The deficiencies have came to light at a time when the demand for highly skilled military personnel and workers in labor and industry is accelerating rapidly, there is a growing concern that the United States may be overtaken by other industrialized nations in terms of economic output, and our war with terrorism may drain our economy at the expense of human and educational services.

When the Soviets launched *Sputnik* (1957), it was a turning point in U.S. history and foreign policy. American schools responded by beefing up the curriculum and stressing academics, testing students, and motivating and pushing above-average and gifted and talented students into college tracks and special programs, particularly math and science courses.[1] September 11, 2001, represented another turning point, not only in our history and foreign relations but also in terms of teaching our children the need to understand each other and other cultures, and to appreciate patriotism and the democratic principles and values of our nation. September 11 also bolstered the conservative trend, starting with *A Nation at Risk* (1983), to push for higher standards (now national standards), high-stakes testing (now national and statewide testing), and improved performance among teachers (including cash

---

1. Valerie E. Lee, *Restructuring High Schools for Equity and Excellence* (New York: Teachers College Press, 2001); Tom Loveless, *The Tracking Wars* (Washington, DC: Brookings Institution, 1999).

─────────────── FIGURE *2. 1* ───────────────
## Academic Achievement of American Students

1. Schools and colleges have shifted away from requiring students to take what had been the standard academic core curriculum for graduation 30 years ago: foreign language, mathematics, science, English, and history. Elective courses and remedial courses have replaced many standard academic courses.

2. Grade inflation is on the rise, and students are required to complete less homework. (In 1998, 75 percent of high school students completed less than one hour of homework a night.) At the college level, 40 percent of the students study fewer than 30 minutes a day and 17 percent confess to studying less than one hour a week.

3. As reported by the National Assessment of Education Progress (NAEP), only 29 percent of all fourth-graders read proficiently at their grade level in 1999, but the figure is 13 percent among minority students. The achievement gap widens as students progress through the grade levels. By the end of high school, black and Hispanic students perform at the level white students do in the eighth grade. This achievement gap parallels the Coleman data, published in 1966. Despite all our additional efforts in the last 35 or more years, achievement gaps by race continue to represent the crux of inequality in our society.

4. Again, as reported by NAEP tests, math and science proficiency improved for 9- and 13-year-olds between 1970 and 1999; it decreased with 17-year-olds. Among twelfth-grade students, only 14 percent were capable of performing at grade level in math and only 7.5 percent were capable of advanced work such as calculus or statistics.

5. Average achievement scores on the Scholastic Aptitude Test (SAT) demonstrated a virtually unbroken decline from 1963 to 1994. Average verbal scores fell over 40 points (466 to 423) and mathematics scores dropped 13 points (492 to 479). In the last five years, however, there has been an increase of 58 points total (verbal and math combined), largely because of changes in content and lengthening test time of the reading and math sections 15 minutes each. Scores were also realigned so that the middle of both the verbal and math scales was about 500—in other words a lowering of the mean or benchmark.

6. International comparisons of student achievement, since in the 1970s, reveal that on 19 academic tests, U.S. students were never first or second and, in comparison with other industrialized nations, were last seven times. In 1988, twelfth-graders scored last in math (averaging 94 points below first-ranked Korea) and next to last in science (averaging 71 points below first-ranked Korea). In 1998 (Third International Mathematics and Science Study), U.S. twelfth-graders scored below their peers in 19 of 21 countries in math and below their peers in 16 of 21 countries in science.

continued

FIGURE *2.1*

**Continued**

7. Although high school completion in 1998 had increased among adults from 78 percent to 85 percent in the last 20 years, some 23 to 25 million U.S. adults were functionally illiterate by the simplest test of everyday reading and writing.* International adult literacy surveys show that about 21 percent of all 17-year-olds in the United States are considered functionally illiterate, and this illiteracy rate jumps to 40 percent among minority youth. About one-third of 17-year-olds cannot place France on a map of the world, and only 22 percent of high school graduates can write a reasonably coherent paragraph.

8. Business and military leaders complain that they are required to spend millions of dollars annually on costly remedial education and training programs in the basic skills, or the three Rs. Between 1975 and 1995, remedial mathematics courses in four-year colleges increased by 75 percent, and, by 1995, constituted one-fourth of all mathematics courses taught in these institutions. By 1999, more than 1.6 million, or 20 percent of, college students in two- and four-year colleges were enrolled in "learning strategies" courses—a euphemism for "remedial courses"—another 900,000, or 11 percent, were being tutored individually or in groups. As many as 25 percent of the recruits in the armed forces cannot read at the ninth-grade level. Teaching "learning strategies" and "study skills" has become a cottage industry at the high school, college, and armed service levels—what was once called "remedial education" before political correction entered the education arena.

9. All these sordid figures pile up and stare at us, despite the fact that our student-teacher ratios were 17:1 in 1998, which put us seventh lowest in the world (whereas such countries as Japan and Korea have higher student-teacher ratios—19:1 and 28:1, respectively) and that our pupil expenditures for education were the second highest in the world (second only to first-ranked Switzerland).

*However, most of these illiterate adults are immigrants, dropouts, or suffer from significant mental or physical impairments. See Dennis Baron, "Will Anyone Accept the Good News in Literacy?" *Chronicle of Higher Education* (February 1, 2002), p. B10.

*Sources: Digest of Education Statistics 2000* (Washington, DC: U.S. Government Printing Office, 2001); *The Condition of Education, 2001* (Washington, DC: U.S. Government Printing Office, 2001); "Learning How to Learn," *New York Times Education Life* (November 1, 2000), Section 4A, pp. 12, 16. Also see Fred Lunenburg and Allan C. Ornstein, *Educational Administration: Concepts and Practices,* 3rd ed. (Belmont, CA: Wadsworth, 2000), pp. 253–254; *Predictions of Freshmen Grade-Point Average from the Revised and Recented SAT I,* Research Report No. 2000-1 (New York: The College Board, 2000); and William C. Symonds, "How to Fix America's Schools," *Business Week* (March 19, 2001), pp. 66–76, 80.

bonuses to teachers and schools in some 15 states as of 2001). A drop in scores in some states means that the teachers or schools are in trouble; outside agencies and consultants are brought in with authority over the principal along with power to transfer or dismiss teachers. In still other cases, for-profit education firms are awarded contracts to administer the schools.[1]

In the words of "business talk," we are told today what is missing in education is "efficiency," "cost effectiveness," "competency," "performance-based standards," and "accountability." What is good for General Motors and IBM is good for teachers and schools! (I wonder if the same people would include Enron's or Global Crossings financial strategies used to falsify earnings or Arthur Andersen's financial/fraudulent accounting tricks.) It is the same kind of jargon expressed by *machine theory* during the early twentieth century. Efficient operation of schools became a major goal, and administrators gained reputations for eliminating small classes, increasing student-teacher ratios, keeping down teacher salaries, and cutting costs in other ways.

Machine theory was originally a business concept promoted by Frederick Taylor to increase the efficiency of workers and to reduce costs. Workers were followed by supervisors with stopwatches, and efficiency "experts" introduced time-and-motion studies.[2] Workers were pit against workers, and treated like "nuts and bolts" rather than humans. There is little difference today in how some school reformers, especially from business and government, treat teachers—with little regard for human relations and professionalism, instead imposing strict supervision of teachers, performance goals, and task requirements for generating efficiency and getting the job done.

According to Taylor, employers were to be paid according to a standard unit of production, based on a norm established by the industry. Inefficient workers either had to improve or expect to be reassigned or fired,[3] not much different than today with accountability and standards movement. Machine theory 2000 seeks to reward or penalize teachers (and school administrators) for performance based on some "objective" criteria or standard unit of production, called *student achievement,* established by the education testing experts—and again supported by business interests.

From the works of Franklin Bobbitt, who translated machine theory into education terms in the 1920s, to the writings of Raymond Callahan's "Cult of Efficiency," in the 1960s, this type of administrative efficiency prevailed as the most prominent school of thought among administrators.[4] It was highlighted by organizational theories that emphasized administrative control, efficiency, specialization, authority, division of labor, objectives and performance goals, and balanced budgets. It was evidenced in the practice by hundreds of thousands of self-contained classrooms of 30 to 40 students sitting in chairs with tables arranged in precise rows and bolted to the floor—a rigid and efficient way of organizing students and placing the teacher in front of the room as the authority figure for controlling students.

1. Allan C. Ornstein, *Pushing the Envelope: Critical Issues in Education* (Columbus, OH: Merrill, 2003).

2. Fredrick W. Taylor, *The Principles of Scientific Management* (New York: Harper and Row, 1911).

3. Ibid.

4. Franklin Bobbitt, *The Curriculum* (Boston: Houghton Mifflin, 1918); Bobbitt, *How to Make a Curriculum* (Boston: Houghton Mifflin, 1924); and Raymond E. Callahan, *The Cult of Efficiency* (Chicago: University of Chicago Press, 1962).

Machine theory is also illustrated by the historical roots of accountability reflected by Lessinger's business management model for holding down costs, implementing audits, demonstrating modes of proof, and increasing results (that is, student achievement). His model was based on reducing school failure and developing accountability through or variety of student output measures. Objectives were to be written for the purpose of measuring the consequences of any given program and the performance of personnel at any given time. The "training" components of education were the basic skills that lended themselves to precise definition and assessment.

Today, machine theory is best illustrated by Florida's obsession with input-output data that assigns grades, from A to F, to each school based on test results. Writes Paul George, the "principals have become data-driven organizational leaders. . . . District offices provide race, gender, . . . subject, and grade level" computerized information. Principals and teachers attempt to meet output goals on a weekly and monthly basis "rather than in years." Principals and teachers know "they have to make identifiable progress almost immediately; a series of low school grades can, and does, result in the principal's removal."[1]

Across the country, the emphasis on work specifications, scheduling, production, and work time is illustrated by statewide and school district attempts to *standardize* curriculum and instruction, even the amount of time teachers should spend on teaching a topic or unit to ensure that agreed-upon content is taught. Along with standardization comes *alignment* to tests, even the amount of days or scheduled periods teachers need to spend reviewing and/or teaching toward them. The argument is that high standards (or "efficiency machinery") may hold the promise of giving all students opportunity to attain essential knowledge, skills, and concepts, as well as monitor and promote student output on a large scale ("mass production"). But it fails to consider that students differ in terms of abilities, readiness levels, interests, learning styles, and learning rates; therefore, content and instruction should differ—what some educators would call "adaptive instruction" or "differentiated instruction."

Some critics are concerned that in the quest to bolster test scores, average and gifted students will be pushed to the background or even ignored, since it is assumed they will achieve acceptable outcomes on statewide tests—which leads to an erroneous assumption that they must be learning.[2] Parents in the middle- and upper-class school districts have also raised concerns. They believe in standards—the essence of their culture of high achievement and meritocracy and what led to their own economic success—but they object to the content of tests, how the curriculum has been distorted and crowds out higher-order learning, the number of tests, and the way the tests are scored and used to judge students, teachers, schools, and real-estate values.[3]

---

1. Paul S. George, "A+ Accountability in Florida," *Educational Leadership* (September 2001), p. 29.

2. Richard J. Stiggins, "Assessment Crisis: The Absence of Assessment for Learning," *Phi Delta Kappan* (June 2002), pp. 758–765; Susan Winebrenner, "Gifted Students Need Education, Too," *Educational Leadership* (September 2000), pp. 52–56.

3. James Traub, "The Test Mess," *New York Times Magazine* (April 7, 2002), pp. 46–51, 60.

Ironically, these parents cannot phantom how statewide standards can benefit their children, since they are lower than the ones they accept for themselves or their schools; their focus is not on competency but excellence (exceeding production rates). Nonetheless, standards-based education has become the central theme for reform in the majority of states for the last five or more years, and the thrust of federal education policy since the Bush administration.

The testing industry constitutes another pressure group behind the accountability and standards-based testing movement, and it must also be considered as part of the equation of demanding tests for measuring academic achievement. According to one group of observers, the testing industry has doubled its amount of sales between 1975 and 1990, comprising nearly $750 million per year, because of increased testing of schools and colleges and related consultants and contractors.[1] Of course, testing students and holding teachers, administrators, and schools accountable to state and national standards will continue to increase the flow of dollars to the testing industry. (I estimate the testing industry will have tripled its earnings by 2003, as state and national testing increase as per federal legislation under the Bush administration.)

Real reform means breaking from many past theories that are considered "teacher proof"—that is, reforms that are implemented with little concern for or input from teachers, the idea that change can work whether teachers like the idea or not, and/or the belief that teachers are educational dispensaries charged with distributing facts or information deemed important by some administrative hierarchy or group of outside "experts." It's the kind of intellectual snobbery and bias that characterized school reform since *Sputnik*—since liberal arts professors have insisted they know more about pedagogy than professors of education, and professors of education have insisted they know more about teaching than classroom teachers.

Real reform means investing a great amount of money; reorganizing classrooms and schools; introducing additional reading, math, and tutoring programs; making kindergarten and prekindergarten part of the nation's universal education system; increasing the school day and school year; scheduling a Saturday morning school day for junior and senior high school students who need tutoring or help in reading and/or mathematics, requiring summer school for all students in grades 1 to 3 who lack basic reading and literacy skills to quickly reduce increasing academic deficits,[2] hiring more teachers and reducing class size; and changing teaching and learning habits

---

1. Walter Haney, George Madau, and Robert Lyons, *The Fractured Marketplace for Standardized Testing* (Boston: Kluwer Academic Publishing, 1993).
2. Grades 1 through 3 are crucial. If cognitive (and social) deficits cannot be remedied during this period, the academic gap will increase, because new learning is influenced by prior learning. What someone is capable of learning depends on being able to perform or master preequisite learning. According to cognitive and developmental learning theories, there are teachable moments, when a task, skill, or concept should be learned, based on age, and if not learned, it will impact negatively on future learning. Robert Havighurst, *Developmental Tasks and Education* (Chicago: University of Chicago, 1948) wrote a classic education text on this theory, and Erik Erikson, *Childhood and Society* (New York: W. W. Norton, 1950) presented the same theory of psychosocial development.

dominated by textbooks and teacher talk. As we learned 40 years ago, it is easier to put a man on the moon than to reform American schools. Reforming U.S. schools is like trying to put a square peg in a round hole. Everyone has an idea, but the ideas don't seem to work. A lot of people have a lot of good ideas, but no one wants to tread on someone's domain or upset the applecart. And you don't need to be a rocket scientist (or even a geometry teacher) to figure out why so many of our reform theories fall flat in practice—given the attitude the public has toward teachers.

It is much easier and cheaper for business and government, as well as parent and community groups, to spend a few million dollars on tests in each state and another few million dollars in rewards or bonuses for teachers than to invest in real reform. Assessment of teachers and students can be easily mandated as part of a bandwagon or reform movement without considering the diverse needs and nature of teaching or learning, and thus have wide appeal under the guise of "reform." Not only is reform costly and complex but it also takes time before the results are evident. The people leading the new wave of reform want results, and as cheaply as possible. Thus, according to Robert Linn, they will most often opt for assessment, since it is simple and inexpensive to implement. It can be rapidly planned and put into practice to correspond with the office of a governor, superintendent of instruction, or other elected officials. It creates heightened media visibility, a feeling that something is being done, to improve education, and it creates changes in the curriculum that are easy to legislate.[1]

As the trend marches forward, the *Hawthorne effect,* or novelty, tends to elevate short-term gains in the first few years with or without real improvement. This, of course, satisfies reformers until they find a new fad or reform slogan, as well as politicians who seek reelection. But in many cases, the gains are not real and cannot be sustained. So, we introduce the explanation called the *fade-out syndrome.* When gains are not evident, state standards are changed, the bar for success is reduced and "cut scores for passing" is lowered, and appeals are made for postponement of the tests. Claims are also made that the tests are unfair for numerous students, and we should not make them attend catch-up programs, repeat grades, or postpone their graduation, because they will more likely drop out of school.[2]

The fact is, our educational ideals have clashed with the real world of poverty, class, and caste. Indeed, there are many illiterate students who are unable to learn adequately under past and present family and school conditions; it is easier to publically discuss school problems than family problems. When we set unrealistic standards, or when we tie important decisions to one or two tests, we are bound to make faulty policy decisions. The solution goes back to joint responsibility of educating students (putting some of the responsibility on students and parents), improving education as a whole, and investing in real reform. Whether we can discuss all the issues in public and will spend the necessary funds reflects the kind of society we are and expect to become. Indeed, what has deteriorated most in the last 40 years (when the War on Poverty was introduced) is not our teaching or schooling, but the lives of our students,

1. Linn, "Assessment and Accountability."
2. Dan Seligman, "Accountability: The Backlash," *Forbes* (November 13, 2000), pp. 238–240.

and the quality of family relationships due to the increase in illegitimacy, and single-headed households related to poverty and divorce.[1]

And surely it is time to bring the huge problem of American poverty and minority status out of the closet and into the public arena. Between 20 and 25 percent of this nation's student population are classified as poor, and about 40 percent are classified as minority. In some cities, 25 percent of babies are born to teenage parents, and "there are no cities in Western Europe or in any industrialized nation that approaches these figures."[2] To think that teachers or schools can neutralize the enormous problems of housing, nutrition, health care, drugs, crime, and family instability is naïve. As one group of observers note, "We are imposing an enormous burden on America's public schools when we ask schools [and I add, teachers] some how to 'make up' for their poverty of their clients."[3] Similarly, it is doubtful if the power structure, especially wealthy white communities, will redistribute money or eagerly open their communities and schools to a large number of black inner-city students. "A great difference exists between tolerating black children and welcoming them."[4] Until these issues are faced directly, we will skim around the issue of reform and devise "adaptive" strategies, such as testing students and either blaming them or their teachers for problems beyond their control.

What does all this mean? One message is the possible "corporatization" of the education industry. Another message is that testing and standards are here to stay. Still another message is that teachers are going to be held accountable for their performance with or without their input. Educators must also guard against what currently some observers warn—the virtual *carte blanche* of the testing industry and outside "experts" dictating accountability policies and standards with little concern for or protection of teachers, and with little regulation from the teaching profession.[5] It is the same concern voiced 30 years ago by David Selden, in his role as president of the American Federation of Teachers. He equated the cry for accountability to "know-nothingness," with accountability advocates approaching education "with all the insight of an irate viewer 'fixing' a television set: Give it a kick and see what happens." No consideration is given to "the possibility that teaching and learning may be complex . . . and [require] the cooperative effort of everyone involved [including parents and students] if success is to be achieved."[6]

1. Robert Evans, "Family Matters," *Education Week* (May 22, 2002), pp. 37, 48; see Joe Queenan, "Nuclear Dad: Last of My Kind," *New York Times* (June 17, 2001), Sect. 9, pp. 1–2.

2. Anita Manning, "Health and Behavior," *USA Today* (September 25, 2001), p. 4.

3. Kevin J. Payne and Bruce J. Biddle, "Poor School Funding, Child Poverty, and Mathematics Achievement," *Educational Researcher* (August–September, 1999), p. 12.

4. Jerome E. Morris, "What is the Future of Predominantly Black Urban Schools?" *Phi Delta Kappan* (December 1999), p. 317.

5. Chris Gallagher, "A Seat at the Table: Teachers Reclaiming Assessment through Rethinking Accountability," *Phi Delta Kappan* (March 2000), pp. 502–507; Susan Ohanian, "News from the Test Resistance Trail," *Phi Delta Kappan* (January 2001), pp. 363–366.

6. David Selden, "Productivity, Yes, Accountablity, No," *Nation's Schools* (May 1971), p. 13.

## Teachers Taking Charge

If teachers are left standing by the side of the road, and remain indifferent and/or become impotent, then we can expect that teaching and learning will be reduced to the transmission of low-level knowledge and practice in discrete skills—all aimed at passing standardized tests at the state and national levels. Classroom performance will be aligned with rewards and punishments, rather than learning for the sake of learning and intrinsic motivation. We will have succumbed to Rensis Likert's classic principles of shaping employers, called the "lollipop–big stick" theory of motivation, and maximizing efficiency in "machine" terms of productivity and workers' (teachers' and administrators') pay.[1] We will be organized according to the theories of March and Simon: organizational controls, departmentalization, specific supervision, production rates and productivity standards, task identification, low-level tasks, with perceived consequences.[2]

We are faced with a dilemma: potential loss of professional dignity, control, and status—in an extreme view, reduced to a worker on the assembly line, dating back to the era of Taylor and Bobbitt. In more current terms, the teacher is expected to act as an autotran who shuffles papers and workbooks, drills students on tiny pieces of information, and reviews tests according to prescribed objectives. This preoccupation with testing, efficiency, and performance turns teachers into timekeepers, traffic managers, and technocrats who will rarely, if ever, be called on to provide professional input into matters that concern them. It is firmly rooted in school tradition and the way the public historically treats teachers—with a certain amount of distrust and disdain, as nonprofessionals and union workers,[3] and with presumed lack of knowledge to contribute about pedagogy or the science of teaching and other professional matters pertaining to curriculum, instruction, and learning.[4]

With almost everyone in favor of accountability and testing for students and teachers alike, the central business is no longer *learning,* whatever this vague term means; it is knowing the answer to pass a test. It has little to do with proof of understanding, application, or actual performance. (Knowing that an adjective modifies a noun, and identifying the adjective on a test, for example, does not mean or indicate that a student can write a sentence, develop a paragraph, or use formal English.) Why the student is made to learn this or that, or this before that is no concern or mystery for the student. The idea is to get the right answer—namely, the answer that the teacher is tuned in to or expects. The student senses that he is going to be taught what-

1. Renis Likert, "Developing Patterns of Management." *General Management Series* (New York: American Management Association, No. 182, 1956), pp. 3–29; Likert, *New Patterns of Management* (New York: McGraw-Hill, 1958).

2. James G. March and Herbert A. Simon, *Organizations* (New York: Wiley, 1966).

3. Broudy, *The Real World of Public Schools;* Susan M. Johnson, *Teachers at Work* (New York: Basic Books, 1990); and Myron Lieberman, *The Future of Public Education* (Chicago: University of Chicago Press, 1962).

4. John I. Goodlad, *A Place Called School* (New York: McGraw-Hill, 1984); Silberman, *Crisis in the Classroom;* and Gerald Grant and Christine E. Murray, *Teaching in America* (Cambridge, MA: Harvard University Press, 1999).

ever the teacher has decided she is going to teach (to pass an exam in order to be promoted or graduate), so there is a little reason or time to ask *why* or raise other questions. Similarly, the teacher is going to teach whatever the school district or state requires to keep her job or to be rewarded, so the questions of why or what is important to learn are also useless.

Right now, the state or school district says, "Here are the standards. You figure them out. You implement them." About the only professional decision or function left for teachers is to decide what part of the textbook or workbook can be skipped, and which resources to use in the instructional process. To assert their professional status, teachers must initiate conversations in schools and conferences at the state and regional levels about what students should know in different grade levels and subject areas. Teachers must be the ones, along with supervisors and principals, to coordinate standards with the curriculum, and not allow some business group or state department committee to seize complete control of standards or accountability systems (such as what has happened in Florida, Texas, and California.) No teacher should feel that mandated standards are driving the entire curriculum or all instructional time in class. It's a top-down model, rooted in Taylor's "machine theory" and in Lessinger's business notion of accountability.

Some educators (Robert Reys) argue that standards highlight the essential content of a subject, lead to the development of in-depth materials, and result in a pedagogy that engages students.[1] Other educators (E. D. Hirsh) maintain that standards provide teachers with the basic content that's worth knowing, lead to breadth and depth in the curriculum, and help narrow the test-score gap among different student populations.[2] Still other educators (Mary Anne Raywild) feel the accountability and testing movement is so strong that teachers cannot defend against it, so we had "better join it and try to shape it."[3]

Though the aim is to standardize the curriculum so that the public has an idea if and how schools are performing, this new reform movement has little to do with the deeper purpose of schooling, which is to enable students to improve their own lives and society, to obtain a broad education, to learn to get along with all types of people, to learn to think about and grapple with ideas, to develop a sense of morality, to become a whole person, not just a machine or a cog or a brain in industry.

Teachers' voices must be heard in matters that concern them and in finding ways to improve service to their clientele—which some might argue are students and others would maintain is society. Nevertheless, the field of teaching does not have clear norms and behaviors as to which of these clients is to be served, and the administrators are of little help, since they are employed by the organization (school district) and guided by self-interests and detached objective service to the organization.

1. Robert E. Reys, "Curricular Controversy with Math Wars," *Phi Delta Kappan* (November 2001), pp. 255–264.
2. E. D. Hirsh, "Seeking Breadth and Depth in the Curriculum," *Educational Leadership* (October 2001), pp. 22–25.
3. Mary Anne Raywild, "Accountability: What's Worth Measuring?" *Phi Delta Kappan* (February 2000), pp. 433–436.

It behooves teachers, then, to assert their professional knowledge and skills learned over a period of time, to insist on professional practices that are in the interest of their first client (students), and not to jump willy nilly and try to satisfy political and business groups that pronounce popular statements and policies and that imply low achievement is the fault of teachers or schools and therefore teachers and administrators must be held accountable. According to Edgar Schein, the need is for teachers to institute a process of self-diagnosis and evaluation to plan performance goals and how to adapt schools to achieve these goals. Logic dictates that if teachers are to maintain their role as professionals, they must insist on diagnosis and evaluation done by members of the school, with some help from outside, but it is not to be farmed out and they are not to lose control.[1]

Since teachers are on the front line and deal with the problems of teaching and learning on a daily basis, they need to develop their own planning and evaluative systems. This would make it clearer for determining what kinds of goals are feasible and what kind of student outcomes and teacher performance is realistic. The theories of planned change, cooperation, and communication are numerous, and what remains to be done is for teachers to take charge of their own profession, to live up to their roles as educators, for the good of their clients—students and society. Instead of keeping their noses clean, and going with the tide, it means they assert their collective and professional identity. Since the spirit of education necessities a sense of purpose and commitment, teachers must participate in the search for reform if the reform is to succeed.

Teachers carry the torch and divisity of freedom and democracy; it is the content and values they teach their students, the ideas and character they instill in their students, that determine what the country is all about, and whether its institutions and ideals will survive. Teachers have an important role in society, and they should not allow the public to forget it or beat them down with oversimplified accountability procedures that are designed to "scapegoat" or deprofessionalize them. Educators need to wake up—advance and protect their own interests and values as professionals, as well as the interests and values of the nation, especially since *Sputnik* and September 11. The latter incident, especially, was an assault on Americans' way of life, and just like people need to react as a nation to frontal attacks on their culture, pluralism, and democracy, teachers need to be imbued with professional indignation against those who would try to make them impotent as individual teachers and as a profession.

As a nation, we are always in a dilemma about whether we want to further stability (and support semi-facists or military leaders who support us) or further democracy (and risk revolution and possibly an anti-American policy). So often, if we want to further democracy on a global basis, the price is instability. Well, if we want to promote school and social reform, there is a certain price we have to pay, a certain amount of time and effort we have to invest, and a certain amount of instability and change we have to absorb and accept. As a nation, we must involve ourselves in places around the world to advance our interests and values; and when we don't take an ac-

1. Edgar H. Schein, *Organizational Culture and Leadership*, 3rd ed. (San Francisco: Jossy-Bass, 1996); Schein, *Professional Education*.

tive role, it is perceived as weakness. Similarly, teachers need to involve themselves if they are to retain their professional influence and status. If teachers remain silent, others will take over and dictate policy to them. Obviously, strong leadership is needed at the national level, both in politics and education. We have had strong presidents over the years, but we have had minor players in education; the last strong leader was Albert Shanker, former president of the American Federation of Teachers, who died several years ago (although some people might say that Lynne Cheney, William Bennett, Chester Finn, and Rod Paige are no slouches).

The idea of teachers participating in reform and taking change of their own destiny is not new—it dates back to the 1930s and the rise of Reconstructionist philosophy. George Counts stunned his contemporaries at the Progressive Education Association in 1932 when he got up to the podium and lamented that progressive education had not reformed schools and that it needed to "face squarely and courageously every social issue, come to grips with life in all its stark reality . . . , fashion a compelling and challenging vision of human destiny, and become less frightened than it is today at the bogies of imposition and indoctrination."[1] He called on teachers to reform schools and society, to become change agents, and to deal with issues of race, ethnicity, sexual inequality, unemployment, poverty, and political oppression—not a bad list, given the times. In effect, Counts asked teachers to become change agents and to help *reconstruct* society—a radical idea for any period and the basis for today's critical pedagogy, reconceptualist thinking, and neomarxism.

Theodore Brameld, 20 years later, signaled a similar challenge for teachers to take positions and become agents of education and social reform. Neutrality in classrooms and schools, that in which we often engage under the guise of objective and scientific inquiry, is not appropriate for the democratic process. Wrote Brameld, "Teachers and students have a right to take sides, to stand up for the best reasoned and informed partialities they can reach as a result of free, meticulous examination and communication of all relevant evidence." In particular, teachers "must measure up to their social responsibilities . . . and the profession [must] draw up on its strength and [take] control of schools" and lead the spirit for reform.[2]

In a satire on education entitled *The Saber-Tooth Curriculum,* Harold Benjamin (under the pseudoname J. Abner Peddiwell), described a society in which the major tasks for survival were catching fish, clubbing horses, and frightening saber-tooth tigers. The school in this society set up a curriculum to meet its needs—namely, teaching courses in these three areas of survival. Eventually conditions changed: The streams dried up, the horses and tigers disappeared, and social change necessitated learning new tasks for survival. But the curriculum continued to feature catching fish, clubbing horses, and frightening saber-tooth tigers.

The teachers knew better, but they remained silent as they "hung their heads and kicked their toes in the sand embarrassedly." They kept silent even though they knew

1. George S. Counts, *Dare to School Build a New Social Order?* (New York: Day, 1932), pp. 7–8.
2. Theodore Brameld, *Ends and Means in Education* (New York: Harper & Row, 1950), p. 70.

better that the goal of education was to teach "students to think." They kept silent because as one wise teacher claimed: "You'll get your neck out too far—you'll get your ears slapped down—you'll get fired, that's what you'll get." The wise teacher continued, "School teachers are not supposed to change people's ways so much that the people will change the rules . . . and don't forget that."[1]

Today, we live in a highly technical, bureaucratic, and information-based society. In an era of space technology, computers, and instant electronic communication, we cannot continue to advocate catching fish. Similarly, teachers cannot continue to stay on the sidelines and allow the times to engulf them. Reformers such as Counts, Brameld, and Benjamin have asked educators to act, to spearhead reform. Teachers failed in the past, thinking of their jobs and ways to keep their noses clean, to impress low-level bureaucrats and administrators. The challenge stares at educators again: Whether they permit a single test to measure teacher or school performance, or to ascertain the quality of teachers and schools, depends to a large measure on the collective influence and wisdom of teachers and their willingness to stand tall together. Of course, it is much easier to remain silent, watch the tide come in, and catch fish. Educators have an option: to rationalize and label this chapter as poppy-cock theory, hocus-pocus chatter, or quaint rhetoric. Or, at the next faculty meeting, or the next time they are sitting adjacent to their colleagues with coffee and bagels, they can raise questions. Reform starts with an idea, and it builds when committed people join together and advocate because of inspiration, idealism, or ideology.

1. Harold Benjamin, *The Saber-Tooth Curriculum* (New York: McGraw-Hill, 1939), pp. 109–110.

## Summary

1. Trying to identify good teaching, or the behaviors and methods of successful teachers, is contaminated by a host of research problems, including definition of terms, the subject matter, grade level, type of student, and context of schooling.

2. Three common methods of evaluating teachers are rating scales, observations, and student achievement tests. Students tend to be the most reliable raters of teachers, although there is a tendency to dismiss their opinions as immature and nonprofessional.

3. The nation's investment in education has produced little return with the majority of inner-city students, as evidenced by the predominant findings of the evaluation of compensatory education. For the greater part, these programs do not improve academic outcomes of target students. Educators are also concerned, on a national level, that a critical mass of students are unable to read, write, or perform math problems at basic literacy levels. This has resulted in a concern to beef up the curriculum and hold teachers and principals accountable, as evidenced by a host of government reports since *A Nation at Risk* was published in 1983 and now epitomized by President Bush's education plan to rely on test scores as a component of an accountability system.

4. The result of an accountability system is greater academic focus, national and state standards, and high-stakes testing. Indeed,

many reform (conservative) groups wish to curtail compensatory funding because they have lost confidence that these programs improve academic performance of poor and minority students. Other reform (liberal) groups wish to change the focus of responsibility from students and parents to teachers and administrators, thus also buying into the popularity of the national standards and accountability movements in education.

5. These twin movements rely on high-stakes tests, regardless of the fact that there are several problems inherent in these models, not least of which are several testing problems dealing with changes in learning; teaching toward the test; common problems of fairness, reliability, and validity; and talk about punishment of low-performing teachers and schools.

6. The concept of standards, testing, and holding workers (teachers/administrators) accountable is rooted in business efficiency models.

7. Philosophical and political questions plague standards-based education, testing, and accountability models. What standards? What test items? Knowledge or problem solving? Who should be held accountable? For what? To whom? To what extent should there be joint responsibility among various individuals and groups?

8. Given the public's distrust about the competency of teachers, and the lack of teacher power, there is concern that teachers will be held accountable without their input, pitting teachers against teachers and losing out on pay raises and possibly their jobs when their students fail some high-stakes test.

9. Teachers need to assert their professional identity and take greater responsibility in establishing accountability models and in diagnosing, implementing, and evaluating matters involved in teaching and learning and improving schools in general.

## *Q*uestions to *C*onsider

1. How would you describe the problems related to identifying and measuring good teachers?

2. To what extent would you prefer supervisory evaluations or student evaluations of your own teaching? Why?

3. What testing issues concern you the most as a student? a teacher? a parent?

4. What is your opinion about the reasons for the general failure of compensatory education?

5. Why are the questions "What standards?" "Who should be held accountable?" and "For what?" so complex?

## *T*hings to *D*o

1. Volunteer to teach a lesson in class for 10 minutes in front of your college classmates. Note whether there is agreement among class members about your teacher behavior and methods.

2. What assessment instruments do schools in your community (or your place of employment) use to measure teacher performance? What are the criteria used to determine teacher competency?

3. Use the Internet to find out what compensatory programs school districts in your state have adopted. Do improvements seem to be occurring? Why or why not?

4. Visit a local school and talk to teachers about standards and testing. Try to summarize their views in three or four major points.

5. Discuss in class the pros and cons of accountability in education.

## Recommended Readings

Berliner, David C., and Bruce J. Biddle. *The Manufactured Crisis* (Boston: Addison-Wesley-Longman, 1995). The failure of American schools is a myth or manufactured crisis.

Callahan, Raymond E. *Education and the Cult of Efficiency* (Chicago: University of Chicago Press, 1962). Efficiency in education has its roots in the early twentieth century and is best known by Callahan's book.

Kendall, John S., and Robert J. Marzano. *Content Knowledge: Standards and Benchmarks for K–12 Education,* 3rd ed. (Baltimore: Association for Supervision and Curriculum Development, 2000). Summaries of standards for each subject and grade level; a tool or guide for teachers and administrators interested in curriculum change.

Meier, Deborah. *Will Standards Save Public Education?* (Boston: Beacon Press, 2000). A heated debate about standards in education among eight well-known educators—point/counterpoint and advantages/disadvantages of the concept.

Orfield, Gary, and Mindy Kornhaber. *Raising Standards or Raising Barriers?* (Washington, DC: Brookings Institution, 2001). The book focuses on standards and high-stakes testing, and related issues of inequality.

Popham, W. James. *Modern Educational Measurement,* 3rd ed. (Boston: Allyn and Bacon, 2000). The uses and abuses of testing, and various assessment instruments, are discussed.

Wiggins, Grant. *Educative Assessment* (San Francisco: Jossey-Bass, 1998). Methods for designing standards for performance-based and accountability plans.

# Theories
# of Learning

## Chapter 3

## *Focusing Questions*

1. Why is the study of learning theories important for teachers?

2. How would you compare classical conditioning with operant conditioning?

3. In what way does modeling influence performance?

4. How would you compare behaviorism with cognitive psychology?

5. What are the differences and similarities between Piaget's thinking and Bruner's thinking?

6. What are the differences between moral knowledge, moral character, and moral development? How does value clarification foster moral thinking?

7. How can students learn how to learn? What cognitive processes contribute to learning?

8. What is critical thinking? How can teachers teach critical thinking?

## EPISODE A

Historically, two major theories of learning have been classified: (1) *behaviorism* or association theories, the oldest one of which deals with various aspects of stimulus-response and reinforcers, and (2) *cognitive psychology*, which views learners in relationship to the total environment and considers the way learners apply information. When behaviorist theories are discussed separately, learning tends to focus on conditioning, modifying, or shaping behavior through reinforcement and rewards. Much ideas about goals, objectives and standards, practice and drill, classroom management, and teacher education programs involve behaviorist theory. Behaviorists tend to be rational, scientific, and technocratic; therefore, they are more inclined to support the *science* of teaching and to focus on the *products* of teaching, rather than the *process*.

When cognitive psychology (or cognitive information processing) theories are stressed, the learning process focuses on the student's developmental stages, environmental experiences, and problem-solving strategies. Cognitive learning theorists tend to accept both the *science* and the *art* of teaching, and both the *processes* and the *products* of teaching; however, cognitive theories have been criticized by behaviorists as subjective, vague, and unscientific. Both schools of thought consider *phenomenological* aspects of learning that deal with the needs, attitudes, and feelings of the learner—what some educators might call the affective domain of learning.[1] Both theories are concerned with the relationship of the teaching-learning process, and teachers need to understand how the theories of each can contribute to this process. Questions of mutual interest to psychologists and teachers are the following: What are the most effective teaching methods for a specific group of students? How do teachers respond as they do to the efforts of students? What is the impact of prior experience on student learning? How do cultural experiences (or differences) influence student learning? How does age (or maturation) affect learning? How should curriculum and instruction be organized to enhance learning?

For the last 50 years, B. F. Skinner has been the most quoted learning psychologist.[2] His basic principle for learning is that the teacher can modify and shape student behavior by consistently and systematically rewarding appropriate behavior and eliminating rewards (sometimes punishing) for inappropriate behavior. The use of proper rewards and punishment forms the basis of learning, as well as manipulating the surface behavior (what is called *classroom management* in schools) of learners. Parents, teachers, and the clergy are always modifying and shaping the behavior of the young, just like CEOs, spouses, and drill sergeants modify and shape the behavior of adults.

Within the same 50-year period, Piaget has been the second most quoted learning psychologist. He has influenced the world of environmental and cognitive psychology, espousing the idea that learning can be inhibited or enhanced by experience.[3] During their waking hours, children and youth are always engaged in some form of learning; the need for the teacher is to shape their environment, to help them learn particular knowledge, concepts, and skills. The central problem is for the teacher to provide proper stimuli (methods, materials, media, etc.) on which to focus students' attention and efforts to enhance learning.

1. David Krathwohl et al., *Taxonomy of Educational Objectives, Handbook II: Affective Domain* (New York: McKay, 1964).

2. Whereas early behaviorists put emphasis on *reflexive* behavior, such as learning how to ride a bicycle or to swim, Skinner argued that such behavior accounted for only a portion of learning. He proposed another type of behavior called *operant* behavior because it operates in context with the environment.

3. See Ernest R. Hilgard, *Theories of Learning* (New York: Appleton, 1956); Johannes Kingma and Welko Tomic, *Advances in Cognition and Educational Practice*, Vol. 4 (Greenwich, CT: JAI Press, 1997).

# Behaviorism

The behaviorists, who represent traditional psychology, are rooted in philosophical speculation about the nature of learning—the ideas of Descartes, Locke, and Rousseau. They emphasize conditioning behavior and altering the environment to elicit selected responses from the learner. This theory dominated much of twentieth-century psychology.

## Classical Conditioning

The *classical conditioning* theory of learning emphasizes that learning consists of eliciting a response by means of previously neutral or inadequate stimuli; some neutral stimulus associated with an unconditioned stimulus at the time of response gradually acquires the ability to elicit the response. The classical conditioning experiment by Ivan Pavlov in 1903 and 1904 is widely known. In this experiment, a dog learned to salivate at the sound of a bell. The bell, a biologically neutral or inadequate stimulus, was presented simultaneously with food, a biologically nonneutral or specific stimulus. So closely were the two stimuli associated by the dog that the bell came to be substituted for the food, and the dog reacted to the bell as he originally had to the food.[1]

The implications for human learning were important. Some neutral stimulus (bell) associated with an unconditioned stimulus (food) at the same time of the response gradually acquired the association to elicit the response (salivation). The theory has led to a wealth of laboratory investigations about learning and has become a focal point in social and political discussions—for example, Aldous Huxley's futuristic novel *Brave New World* and the movies *The Deer Hunter, Jacob's Ladder, The Silence of the Lambs,* and *Robo Cop.*

On the American scene, James Watson used Pavlov's research as a foundation for building a new science of psychology based on behaviorism. The new science emphasized that learning was based on the science of behavior, what was observable or measurable, and not on cognitive processes. The laws of behavior were derived from animal and then human studies and were expected to have all the objectivity of the laws of science.[2]

For Watson and others, the key to learning was to condition the child in the early years of life, based on the method Pavlov had demonstrated for animals. Thus, Watson once boasted, "Give me a dozen healthy infants . . . and my own specified world to bring them up and I'll guarantee to take any one at random and train him to be any type of specialist I might select—a doctor, lawyer, artist . . . and yes into beggar man and thief, regardless of his talents . . . abilities, vocations and race."[3]

1. Ivan P. Pavlov, *Conditioned Reflexes,* tran. G. V. Anrep (London: Oxford University Press, 1927).

2. John B. Watson, *Behaviorism* (New York: Norton, 1939).

3. John B. Watson, "What the Nursery Has to Say about Instincts," in C. A. Murchison, ed., *Psychologies of 1925* (Worcester, MA: Clark University Press, 1926), p. 10.

## Connectionism

One of the first Americans to conduct experimental testing of the learning process was Edward Thorndike, who is considered the founder of behavioral psychology. At Harvard, Thorndike began his work with animals, a course of experimentation other behaviorists adopted as well.[1] Thorndike's work focused on testing the relationship between a stimulus and a response (classical conditioning). He defined *learning* as habit formation—as connecting more and more habits into a complex structure. *Teaching,* then, was defined by Thorndike as arranging the classroom so as to enhance desirable connections as bonds.

Three major laws of learning were developed by Thorndike: (1) the *law of readiness*—when a "conduction" unit is ready to conduct, to do so is satisfying and not to do so is annoying; (2) the *law of exercise*—a connection is strengthened in proportion to the number of times it occurs, and in proportion to average intensity and duration; and (3) the *law of effect*—responses accompanied by discomfort weaken the connection.[2]

The *law of readiness* suggests that when the nervous system is ready to conduct, it leads to a satisfying state of affairs; this has been misinterpreted by some educators as referring to educational readiness, such as readiness to read.[3] The *law of exercise* provides justification for drill, repetition, and review and is best illustrated today by instruction in basic math and foreign language classes and basic skill instructional approaches. Although reward and punishments were used in schools for centuries prior to Thorndike's formulation of the *law of effect* (people repeat responses that on previous occasions produced satisfying effects), his theory did make it more explicit and furnished justification for what was already being done. B. F. Skinner's operant model of behavior, programmed instruction, military training, and many current ideas based on providing satisfying (and unsatisfying) experiences to the learner, as well as reinforcement in the form of prompt feedback, are rooted in this law.

Thorndike maintained that (1) behavior was influenced more likely by conditions of learning; (2) attitudes and abilities of learners could change (and improve) over time through proper stimuli; (3) instructional experiences could be designed and controlled; and (4) it was important to select appropriate stimuli or learning experiences that were integrated and consistent, and that reinforced each other. For Thorndike, no one subject was more likely than another to improve the mind; rather learning was a matter of relating new learning to previous learning (an idea that John Dewey and Ralph Tyler later adopted). According to Thorndike, the view that one particular subject is better than another subject for "improvement of the mind . . . seems doomed to disappoint-

---

1. Edward L. Thorndike, *Animal Intelligence* (New York: Macmillan, 1911).

2. Edward L. Thorndike, *Psychology of Learning* (New York: Teachers College Press, 1913).

3. This law is the heart of connectionism—that learning is a process of developing and strengthening neural connections between stimuli and responses. Educational readiness, however, is based on the child's development, which is a cognitive theory. The need is to match appropriate learning tasks with the child's cognitive and social capabilities to achieve maximum learning.

ment." The fact is, "good thinkers" take certain subjects, not that certain subjects result in good thinking. "If the abler pupils should all study physical education and dramatic art, these subjects would seem to make good thinkers."[1]

Thus, Thorndike was critical of the "psychology of mental discipline," the dominate theory of learning during the turn of the twentieth century—advocated by traditional educators of the era. His attack meant that there was no hierarchy of subject matter and that learning involved constructs between stored knowledge, memories of experience, and new information or stimuli—a schema theory very similar to Piaget's notions of knowledge acquisition and comprehension.

But entrenched beliefs die hard. Traditional educators argued that certain subjects—such as Latin, classical studies, rhetoric, and mathematics—were most valuable for training the mind; that such training was transferable to various mental tasks of the learner; and that such subjects (or lack of these subjects) led to "superior" and "inferior" tracks. This view was criticized not only by Thorndike but also subsequently by John Dewey and other Progressive educators who felt such a mindset was rooted in traditionalism and elitism, and that the underlying philosophy taught students "docility, receptivity, and obedience."[2]

The two most prominent educators of the era (Thorndike and Dewey) objected to the mental discipline approach (a learning theory that maintained that the mind could be developed by certain tough subjects, similar to the way the body could be developed through exercise). However, for the next 50 years these ideas served as a basis for formulating the standard elementary and secondary curriculum with the concurrent belief that the right of students to an education should persist as far as their intellectual capabilities. Little recognition or provision was made for the less able student—well illustrated by the fact that as late as 1950, the high school dropout rate was as high as 40 percent and only 27 percent of 18- to 21-year-olds were enrolled in college.[3]

The 1895 Committee of Fifteen, the prestigious and conservative task force headed by Charles Eliot, then president of Harvard University, solidified this position. It was reported that "grammar, literature, arithmetic, geography and history [were] the subjects in the elementary school with the greatest value for training the mind."[4] This view set the tone for most of the entire twentieth century, especially during the post-*Sputnik* and Cold War era, when the subjects with the greatest value were considered to be math and science. Music, art, and physical education were considered secondary or unimportant, an idea that persists today in many schools where essentialist philosophy and back-to-basics have been revived under the banner of standards-based education and school reform.

1. Edward L. Thorndike, "Mental Discipline High School Studies," *Journal of Educational Psychology* (February 1924), p. 98.

2. John Dewey, *Experience and Education* (New York: Macmillan, 1938), p. 18.

3. Allan C. Ornstein and Francis P. Hunkins, *Curriculum: Foundations, Principles, and Issues,* 3rd ed. (Boston: Allyn and Bacon, 1998), p. 75.

4. Committee of Fifteen, "Report of the Subcommittee on the Correlation of Studies in Elementary Education," *Educational Review* (March 1895), p. 284.

## Operant Conditioning

Perhaps more than any other recent behaviorist, B. Frederick Skinner attempted to apply his theories to the classroom situation. Basing a major part of his theories on experiments with mice and pigeons, Skinner distinguished two kinds of responses: *elicited,* a response identifies with a definite stimulus, and *emitted,* a response that is apparently unrelated to an identifiable stimulus. When a response is elicited, the behavior is termed *respondent.* When it is emitted, the behavior is *operant*—that is, no observable or measurable stimuli explain the appearance of the response.[1] In operant conditioning, the role of the stimuli is less definite; often, the emitted behavior cannot be connected to a specific stimulus.

Reinforcers can be classified, also, as primary, secondary, or generalized. A *primary reinforcer* applies to any stimulus that helps satisfy a basic drive, such as for food, water, or sex. (This reinforcer is also paramount in classical conditioning.) A *secondary reinforcer* is important for students, such as getting approval from friends or teachers, receiving good grades, or winning school awards. Although secondary reinforcers do not satisfy primary drives, they can be converted into primary reinforcers, because of their choice and range, and thus Skinner refers to them as *generalized reinforcers.* Classroom teachers have a wide variety of secondary reinforcers at their disposal, ranging from words of praise or smiles to words of admonishment or punishment.

Operant behavior will discontinue when it is not followed by reinforcement. Skinner classifies reinforcers as positive or negative. A *positive reinforcer* is simply the presentation of reinforcing stimulus. A student receives positive reinforcement when a test paper is returned with a grade of A or a note that says, "Keep up the good work." A *negative reinforcer* is the removal or withdrawal of a stimulus. When a teacher shouts to the class "Keep quiet," and the students quiet down, the students' silence reinforces the teacher's shouting. Punishment, on the other hand, calls for the presentation of unpleasant or harmful stimuli or the withdrawal of a (positive) reinforcer, but it is not always a negative reinforcer.[2] Although Skinner believes in both positive and negative reinforcement, he tends to reject punishment because he feels it inhibits learning.

## Acquiring New Operants

Skinner's approach of selective reinforcement, whereby only desired responses are reinforced, has wide appeal to educators because he has demonstrated its application to the instructional and learning process. An essential principle in the reinforcement interpretation of learning is the variability of human behavior, which makes change possible. Individuals can acquire *new operants*—that is, behavior can be shaped or modified and complex concepts can be taught to students. The individual's capability for the desired response is what makes the shaping of behavior or the learning possible. Behavior and learning can be shaped through a series of successive approxima-

1. B. F. Skinner, *Science and Human Behavior* (New York: Macmillan, 1953).
2. B. F. Skinner, *Reflections on Behaviorism and Society* (Englewood Cliffs, NJ: Prentice-Hall, 1970); Skinner, *Science and Human Behavior.*

tions, or a sequence of responses that increasingly approximate the desired one. Thus, through a combination of reinforcing and sequencing desired responses, new behavior is shaped; this is what some people today refer to as *behavior modification.*

Although behavior modification approaches vary according to the student and the behavior being sought, they are widely used in conjunction with behavioral objectives, individualized instructional techniques, computerized learning, and classroom-management techniques. Student activities are specified, structured, paced, reinforced, rewarded, and frequently assessed in terms of learning outcomes or behaviors desired. With this approach, curriculum, as defined by Popham and Baker, is "all planned outcomes for which the school is responsible and the desired consequences of instruction."[1]

## Observational Learning and Modeling

Albert Bandura has contributed extensively to what we know today about how aggressive behavior can be learned from viewing human adults acting aggressively in real situations as well as in movies and television. The same children also learn nonaggressive behavior by observing humans of subdued temperaments.[2]

The repeated demonstration that people can learn and have their behavior shaped by observing another person or even a film (obviously, the influence of TV is immense) has tremendous implications for modifying tastes and attitudes (i.e., whether we deserve to take a break at McDonalds or Burger King), how we learn and perform, or whether as a society we want to develop soldiers or artists. For behaviorists, the idea suggests that cognitive factors are unnecessary in explaining learning; through *modeling,* students can learn how to perform at sophisticated levels of performance. They can learn how to ski, participate in democratic citizenry, engage in moral or caring behavior, or become the culprit in a shootout in the school cafeteria. While recognizing the value of reinforcement and reward, the learner needs mainly to attend to and acquire the necessary responses through observation and then to model the behavior later. See Teaching Tips 3.1.

Bandura is also associated with the theories of *vicarious learning.* Although most modeling is reinforced first by observation and then by imitating behavior, others learn by seeing other people rewarded or punished for engaging in certain behaviors.[3] We all know that our chances for winning the lottery is perhaps one out of 10 million, but seeing or reading about others rewarded makes many of us participate. Teachers use the same principle in rewarding certain behaviors in front of the class, providing verbal praise, or displaying a student's work on the bulletin board.

1. W. James Popham and Eva I. Baker, *Systematic Instruction* (Englewood Cliffs, NJ: Prentice-Hall, 1970), p. 48. Also see W. James Popham, *Classroom Assessment,* 2nd ed. (Boston: Allyn and Bacon, 1999).

2. Albert Bandura, *Social Learning Theory* (Englewood Cliffs, NJ: Prentice-Hall, 1977); Bandura, *Social Foundations of Thought and Action* (Englewood Cliffs, NJ: Prentice-Hall, 1986).

3. Ibid.

# *Teaching Tips* 3.1

## Behaviorism in Classroom Learning Situations

A wide range of behaviors can be used when applying behavioral theories in the classroom. The following suggestions have meaning for behaviorist teaching and learning situations:

1. Consider that behavior is the result of particular conditions; alter conditions to achieve desired behaviors.
2. Use reinforcement and rewards to strengthen the behavior you wish to encourage.
3. Consider extinction or forgetting by reducing the frequency of undesirable behaviors.
4. Reduce undesirable behaviors as follows:
   a. Withhold reinforcement or ignore the behavior.
   b. Call attention to rewards that will follow the desired behavior.
   c. Take away a privilege or resort to punishment.
5. When students are learning factual material, provide frequent feedback; for abstract or complex material, provide delayed feedback.
6. Provide practice, drill, and review exercises; monitor learners' progress.
7. Consider workbooks, programmed materials, and computer programs that rely on sequenced approaches.
8. When students struggle with uninteresting material, use special reinforcers and rewards to motivate them.
   a. Select a variety of reinforcers students enjoy (candy bars, bubble gum, baseball cards).
   b. Establish a contract for work to be performed to earn a particular award or grade.
   c. Provide frequent, immediate rewards.
9. Make use of observational learning.
   a. Select the most appropriate model.
   b. Model the behavior clearly and accurately.
   c. Insist that learners attend to what is being modeled.
   d. Provide praise when the desired behavior is exhibited.
   e. Have the learner practice the observed behavior.
   f. Provide corrective feedback during practice.
   g. Repeat demonstrations when necessary.
   h. Reinforce desired behaviors.
   i. Model behavior in similar settings in which learners will use the new skills.
10. Assess changes in learning and behavior.
    a. Diagnose learning problems.
    b. Establish levels of competency or mastery.
    c. Provide feedback.
    d. Integrate old tasks or skills with new ones.
    e. Reteach, when necessary.
    f. Take other actions.

## Hierarchical Learning

Robert Gagné has presented a hierarchical arrangement of eight types of learning sets or behaviors that has become a classic model. In fact, the model for learning has been adapted by the education, business, and military industries. The behaviors are based on prerequisite conditions, resulting in a cumulative process of learning. The eight types of learning and examples of each follow:

1. *Signal learning.* Classical conditioning, a response to a given stimulus. Example: Fear response to a rat.
2. *Stimulus response.* Operant conditioning (S-R), a response to a given stimulus. Example: Student's response to the command "Please sit."
3. *Motor chains.* Linking together two or more S-R connections to form a more complex skill. Example: Dotting the *i* and crossing the *t* to write a word with an *i* and a *t*.
4. *Verbal associations.* Linking together two or more words or ideas. Example: Translating a foreign word.
5. *Multiple discriminations.* Responding in different ways to different items of a particular set. Example: Discriminating between grass and trees.
6. *Concepts.* Reacting to stimuli in an abstract way. Examples: Forming and understanding words that categorize or classify other words, such as animals, grammar, and so on.
7. *Rules.* Chaining two or more stimulus situations or concepts. Examples: Animals have offspring. An adjective is a noun.
8. *Problem solving.* Combining known rules or principles into new elements to solve a problem. Example: Finding the area of a triangle given the dimensions of two sides.[1]

Gagné's hierarchy of learning represents a transition between behaviorism and cognitive psychology; the first four behaviors are behaviorist and the last four are mainly cognitive. Learning, according to Gagné, comprises a hierarchical sequence that orders instructional materials and methods from simple to complex. The idea is that general theories, principles, and/or concepts (what Jerome Bruner would describe as the "structure" of a subject) encompass specific ideas and knowledge—which need to be learned before advanced learning. Other learning theorists (including David Ausubel and Robert Marzano) maintain that by understanding general principles and concepts (Ausubel calls them "advance organizers"), a learner is able to learn more efficiently because it is easier to assimilate new information into prior information. Whereas Gagné and Bruner represent a *bottom-up* theory of learning, Ausubel and Marzano represent a *top-down* theory. A *middle* position delineated by Dewey is that information is best learned and remembered when it is related to students' experiences and has direct application to their immediate environment. All three approaches to learning are acceptable and used by teachers, depending on the students' abilities (and age) and content of subject matter.

Gagné also describes five *learning outcomes* that can be observed and measured and encompass all the domains of learning: (1) *intellectual skill*, "knowing how" to categorize and using verbal and mathematical symbols, forming concepts through

---

1. Robert M. Gagné, *The Conditions of Education*, 4th ed. (New York: Holt, Rinehart, 1987). The examples are provided by me.

rules and problem solving; (2) *information*, which can be described as "know what"—knowledge about facts, names, and dates; (3) *cognitive strategies,* skills needed to process and organize information, what today is called "learning strategies" or "learning skills"; (4) *motor skills,* the ability to coordinate movements and complex movements, which come with practice and coaching; and (5) *attitudes,* feelings and emotions learned through positive and negative experiences.[1]

The five outcomes overlap with the three domains (cognitive, psychomotor, and affective) of the *taxonomy of education objectives.* The first three of Gagné's capabilities mainly fall within the cognitive domain, motor skills correspond with psychomotor domain, and attitudes correspond with the affective domain. The mental operations and conditions involved in each of the five outcomes are different. Writes Gagné, "Learning intellectual skills requires a different design of instructional events from those required for learning verbal information or from those required for learning motor skills and so on."[2]

## The "Shock Machine"

Much of Stanley Milgram's professional life is surrounded by controversy because of his experiments on obedience conducted while at Yale University in 1962. As many as 65 percent of his subjects, who were ordinary residents of New Haven, Connecticut (including college graduates), were willing to follow orders and give what they thought were harmful electric shocks (up to 450 volts) to loudly protesting "victims" simply because some scientific-looking authority commanded them when the victim wrongly answered a question.[3] The victims were actors who did not actually receive the shocks, but the subjects were convinced during the experiment that they were instilling the electric shocks. At the end of the experiment, the subjects were debriefed about the real facts. Nonetheless, the experience was painfully real for most participants, and they felt enthusiastically involved.

Milgram's work does not receive attention in most psychology or learning texts because his experiment was considered highly provocative, involving questions about the ethics of the research and practices involving human subjects. He never took a single psychology course as an undergraduate and took only six graduate psychology courses at three different New York area universities in one summer in 1954. His experiment led to criticism in many newspapers, for the stress created among willing subjects, and the American Psychological Association (APA) temporarily suspended his application for membership. More than 10 years later, after a televised CBS special, Milgram received honors and awards, and his shock machine was placed on exhibit supported by the APA. His experiment has been replicated in dozens of countries over a 25-year period with similar devastating results and with no differences between

1. Robert M Gagné, Leslie J. Briggs, and Walter W. Wager, *Principles of Instructional Design,* 3rd ed. (New York: Holt, Rinehart, 1988).
2. Gagné, *The Conditions of Education,* p. 245.
3. Stanley Milgram, *Obedience to Authority* (New York: Harper, 1983); Milgram, *The Individual in a Social World* (New York: McGraw-Hill, 1991).

men and women,[1] subsequently raising issues about human behavior, brain washing, and mass conformity. From Hitler's, Stalin's, and Hirohito's willing believers, to the Serbian and Jihad soldiers, obedience to authority helps explain how ordinary people can blindly follow orders and commit some of the most brutal and horrific crimes (murder, torture, plunder, rape of innocent civilians), even to die doing it thinking they will be rewarded in the next life.

Implications of Obedience    Milgram's experiment is a gripping read and helps explain how people can follow orders, commit some of the worst crimes against humanity, then rationalize or defend their behavior ("We were merely following orders") and show little or no remorse. Going beyond the effects of behaviorism and stimulus-response experiments, we live in a culture where individual personal memories and publicly collected memories are given increasing importance in the media, in the courts, and among policymakers. We are asked by black Americans 150 years later not to forget about slavery, as a rationale for affirmative action, and we expect the Germans not to forget 55 years after the fact, and thus pay reparations for their crimes. Indeed, obedient people must sometimes pay for their mistakes.

In a letter from Mortimer von Falkenhausen in 1948 to a Jewish friend who escaped to America four weeks before *Kristallnacht,* the German pogrom of November 1938, he wrote: "What I will never be able to fathom is this fact that countless Germans, without a word of protest, let themselves descend to the level of sadistic criminals who murdered and raged like wild animals—and found such behavior perfectly normal."[2]

Of course, there is a difference between turning a blind eye or remaining silent and participating, or even worse, getting enjoyment or an adrenaline rush by giving electric shocks to people in a New Haven laboratory, Devil's Island, or Dachau. But the distinction becomes blurred when we focus on mass behavior, immorality, and the destructive consequences of blindly following orders of some leader. Why are so many people able to shed their consciences and rationalize amoral behavior? Is it peer pressure, custom, or the accidents of history? Or, is it just a matter of human frailty, an obscure genome that is embedded in 65 percent of human species (the New Haven percentage) willing to conform and show obedience?

Can human beings be programmed to operate any which way by a puppet producer or authority figure? Classical behaviorists say yes, and behaviorists might even say that with today's computerized and electronic world, we can program people and shrink-wrap them into a Microsoft-like disk with precise coded instructions on how to behave. Surely robots have no individuality, no souls, no spirit; but sometimes, individuals are programmed to behave as robots. Indeed, history makes it very clear that zealous soldiers, crusaders, cult followers, kamikaze pilots, and religious terrorists come in all sizes, shapes, and shades—and from all time periods and civilizations. The more someone is conditioned to be a follower or puppet, the more capable the person is to commit brutal acts and atrocities. The barbarians have always been

1. Thomas Blass, "The Milgram Paradigm after 35 Years," *Journal of Applied Social Psychology* (May 1999), pp. 955–978.
2. Fritz Stern, "The Importance of 'Why,' " *World Policy Journal* (Spring 2000), p. 3.

perched at the gates; failure to respond, inadequate, or irregular responses, breeds further barbarianism.[1]

Rather than saying no, most of us permit and some participate in abuses, hypocrisy, and evil behavior. Social and moral responsibility requires a certain minimum of inner strength and self-confidence; an ability of the individual to question authority, custom, and the dominant ideology within his or her society; and to be skeptical of the workings of big business, religion, and government. During the French Revolution, in which so much blood was spilled, Robespierre was asked, "Is there a voice inside you that every so often whispers in secret—you're lying, you're lying." Fifty years later, Victor Hugo raised a similar question in *Les Miserables,* by describing the fanaticism of Inspector Javier, who hunted down Jean Val Jean for 30 years because he stole a loaf of bread. The inspector's defense was the law, or, more accurately, the perversion of law. The law was used in France to cripple the minds and spirits of the enemies of the state. During the twentieth century, prisoners were shipped to Devil's Island, some because of criminal behavior and some because they questioned political authority or challenged the law. Over time, many of these people were reduced to the status of walking, mindless zombies.

And if it happened in France where the Age of Enlightenment once flourished, in a place where Franklin and Jefferson felt more at home than in Philadelphia or Monticello, then it can happen here, there, anywhere. Yes, the law can be perverted and used as an instrument to build and justify any ugly ideology or "ism," whereby the individual succumbs to the rule of authority and remains obedient to a cult figure, philosopher-king, guru, or outright "nut." Given this diagnosis of the human condition, especially the generic appeal to authority, and that many nations throughout history have needed warlike missions to stir the populace, one can better understand the likes of Bin Laden, Idi Amin, Hussain, Quadaffi, Castro, and Mao—and their control over the herd.

Ortega y Gasset's dictum, in *The Revolt of the Masses,* rings loud in describing how easily men and women can be conditioned to behave, how "the mass man will rule as well as be ruled." The truth is, most people on planet Earth, including most Americans, can adopt more easily to Sparta than Athens, more easily to the empire than the republic. The latter requires education and critical thought. As Alan Bloom asserts, we refuse to take positions on right or wrong, based on standards of truth; rather, we welcome no-fault choices. Our media and educational institutions are marked by easy-going, flippant indifference to critical thought and standards of excellence. We avoid an engagement with the great works and great minds of the past.[2] Our students lack educational depth and thus are prone to become docile, obedient, and conforming students in class and, later, docile, conforming, and obedient citizens. In most classrooms, right answers count, not critical thought. Pleasing the teacher (i.e., the authority figure) takes precedence over questioning the teacher—and regur-

---

1. Terrorism (such as surprise attacks on civilians during a time of peace) is a form of barbarianism. The only option left is to declare war. Of course, warfare can also be barbaric.

2. Alan Bloom, *The Closing of the American Mind* (New York: Simon and Schuster, 1987).

gitating from the textbook, regardless of the author's biases and social/political lens, is often expected from students and encouraged by the teacher.

## Brain Circuits, Choice, and Conditioning

Do people make conscious choices? The latest theory is that humans became conditioned by habit and routine—and lose their individual consciousness. As children develop, their brains develop internal methods of identifying objects and responding to people, and thus predicting how they move and respond to their environment. As stimuli flow from the external world to the brain, humans compare it to what they already know. If things are familiar or match up, there is little conscious awareness of the surrounding environment. If there is a surprise or a detour in our daily life experiences, the brain shifts to a new state and we become more conscious of what we are doing.

According to one recent estimate, 90 percent of what people do everyday coincides with habit or predictable events, so that we usually operate on "automatic" response. To use the vernacular, we become zombies much of the time. Animals use their brain circuits to determine what to attend to, what to react to, and what to ignore. Humans have bigger, more complex brains and make decisions about what to learn, what to eat, and other decisions in life, including assessing rewards or lack of rewards. Our behavior is conditioned by a set of expectations and reward systems. The best learning, according to this theory, takes place when the person is confronted with an unexpected event or unexpected reward, thus producing a dopamine rush. Fluctuating levels of rewards make people do things outside their conscious awareness.[1]

Money, for most people, is similar to drugs, food, or sex—or anything a person expects as a reward. Cookies and candy have a similar effect on small children. People crave it! Anything that people crave can be used as a vehicle for modifying behavior. Some people crave winning in sports because of recognition or money and will engage in unethical behavior; others crave power and will steal or kill to maintain it; still others crave martyrdom and will commit suicide for the Emperor, the Fuhrer, or Allah. Once the mind is hijacked (conditioned), where the person loses a sense of conscious awareness, he or she becomes capable of engaging in group behavior, even fanatic behavior. It can become emotionally depressing to realize what human beings are capable of doing to innocent fellow human beings. Once they lose sight of their individual thoughts or consciences and become part of group or mob behavior, then all forms of atrocities and vile deeds are possible. If it's a matter of conditioning people to commit murder, it is easier if it is fixed to some political or religious utopia. The Puritans killed witches who they believed had demonic power and were casting Satan's evil spells, and Moslem extremists want to murder Americans who they believe are the infidel. As one true believer puts it, "Nonmuslims are our enemy according to the Koran, so Americans are our enemy. We hate America. I believe in jihad"[2] (a holy war).

1. Sandra Blakeslee, "Hijacking the Brain Circuits," *New York Times* (February 19, 2002), Sect. F, p. 1.
2. Lynsey Addario, "Jihad's Women," *New York Times Magazine* (October 21, 2001), p. 40.

Once the brain becomes conditioned to crave a stimulus, the person becomes either self-destructive or highly dangerous. Because of craving, some people may regularly gamble, knowing the chances are they will lose money. Others will smoke, knowing there is a good chance they will die from it. Still others totally abdicate their individual identities and critical faculties and are willing to die for politics or religion based on faith, hope, or hatred. Nazism appealed to millions of Germans because it promised not only prosperity but also greatness, even salvation. Muslim extremism also eliminates individual thought and makes similar promises to its followers, with the end being paradise.

Hitler and the Germans believed the Jews posed a mortal threat and had to be eliminated. Bin Laden, his al-Qaeda network, and the extreme Muslim world believe America and the West's cultural messages pose a major threat and have to be destroyed. In both cases, the brain systems of political and religious followers have been short-circuited, to the extent they have lost their individual identities and consciences. What happened in Nazi Germany can be expected to happen to Moslem extremists—a downward spiral of hate, rage and self-pity, a notion of victimhood and imposed oppression, and the eventual shattering of their world. It doesn't take a genius to compare the rise of Hitler with Bin Laden, and/or the sneak attack at Pearl Harbor with events of 9-11.

**Human Conditioning and Biotechnology**   The old world of behaviorism and human conditioning intersect with the world of biotechnology, or what one scientist calls "our post-human future."[1] We are on the verge of discovering and implementing an alternative to thinking and behaving, based on prescribing Prozac, Ritalin, and other drugs to modify mental processes and behaviors. Even more controversial, we are about to alter normal evolution by intervening in the genetic process, designing babies, strengthening bodies, cloning, producing interspecies hybrids in food and animals, expanding stem cell research and anti-aging research. Here, science, psychology, philosophy, and politics collide as we try to establish policies in this milieu of biotechnology and medical research.[2]

On a simple level, our national past time has been affected by this brave new world, not only in terms of the way baseball derives its statistics but also in how many dads and sons bond as they talk about baseball box scores, discuss Topps baseball cards, and compete and strategize in fantasy leagues based on real players. Reliable estimates are that possibly one-third of major leagues players, most of them "heavy hitters," have been using steroids for the last 10 or more years.[3] Thus, baseball's records are collapsing at an astonishing rate from "beefed-up" bodies and numbers. Most fans know that Babe Ruth wasn't exactly sober every time he got up at the bat, even during Prohibition but did Hank Aaron use steroids? Mark McGuire, Sammy

---

1. Francis Fukuyama, *Our Posthuman Future: Consequences of the Biotechnology Revolution* (New York: Farrar, Straus, & Giroux, 2002).

2. Colin McGinn, "Machine Dreams," *New York Times Book Review* (May 5, 2002), p. 11.

3. Alan Schwarz, "Scoring Hits, Runs and Asterisks," *New York Times* (June 9, 2002), Sect. 4, p. 5.

Sosa, and Barry Bonds, our super-baseball heroes, seem to have beefed-up bodies. Most of our athletes are faster, stronger, smarter, and happier. Is all this improvement related only to food and exercise?

In our schools, about 26 percent of the student population is on Ritalin and other drugs to control hyperactivity and other so-called disruptive behavior.[1] The controversy over using medication, instead of psychological conditioning or behavioral modification, is debated in the professional literature and has ethical implications. And, there are other drugs that can enhance memory and that would make present learning theory outdated and mundane. Drugs, psychological therapy, and physical changes in the school environment, which shapes one's senses and performance, have the potential to make George Leonard's vision, *Education and Ecstasy,* a reality.[2]

On the level of society, we have reached a point that approaches Orwell's *1984* and Huxley's *Brave New World.* All our notions of human equality, human rights, and moral choices are being challenged as we develop new techniques for altering personality, behavior, the quality and growth of intellectual and physical attributes, and even the rate and vision of living. There is such a thing as the nature of man and the concept of balance (or the golden rule). I think Aristotle, and later Ruth Benedict and Kinsley Davis who wrote about *Patterns of Culture* (1934) and *Human Society* (1948), got the balance right. In this biotech work of ours, there are many philosophical and social questions that have global reach. If I was forced to bet on the optimism of Locke or the pessimism of Hobbes in terms of human nature and the future of the human species, sadly, I would opt for Hobbes's interpretation of the human condition, since I believe there is more potential for evil than good in the character of people, nation-states, empires, and spiritual institutions.

## Behaviorism and Teaching

Behaviorism still exerts an impact on education, although the influence has declined in the last 20 or 30 years. Teachers who are behaviorists use many principles of behaviorism in the classroom and in the creation of new programs. Although what influences learning differs for different students, teachers can adopt procedures to increase the likelihood that each student will find learning relevant and enjoyable. When new topics or activities are introduced, connections should be built on positive experiences each student has had. Things about which each student is likely to have negative feelings about should be identified and modified, if possible, to produce positive results.

Behaviorists believe that the curriculum should be organized so students experience success in mastering the subject matter. Of course, all teachers, regardless of their psychological camps, have this view. The difference is that behaviorists are highly prescriptive and diagnostic in their approach and they rely on step-by-step, structured methods of teaching; learning is monitored and broken down into small tasks with appropriate sequencing of tasks and reinforcement of desired behaviors.

1. N. L. Gage and David C. Berliner, *Educational Psychology,* 7th ed. (Boston: Houghton Mifflin, 2001).
2. George B. Leonard, *Education and Ecstasy* (New York: Delacorte Press, 1968).

It should be noted that behaviorist theories have been criticized as describing learning too simply and mechanically—and as perhaps reflecting overreliance on classical animal experimentation. Human learning involves complex thinking processes beyond respondent conditioning (or recall and habit) and operant conditioning (or emitted and reinforced behavior). A further concern, according to Robert Travers, is that there is little justification to define learning in terms of a "collection of small bits of behavior each of which has to be learned separately." Although behavior consists of organized sequences, it is not a collection of tiny bits of behavior. The stress on prescribed, lock-step procedures and tasks—and a "belief that a behavioral science should be definable in terms of observable events—[are] hardly justifiable today."[1]

The latter criticism may be an overstatement, because many behaviorists today recognize cognitive processes much more than classical or S-R theorists, and they are flexible enough to hold that learning can occur without the individual's having to act on the environment or exhibit overt behavior. To the extent that traditional behavioral theory can be faulted for having to rely on identifying all behavior, many contemporary behaviorists are willing to consider that cognitive processes partially explain aspects of learning.

But behaviorism is alive and well; it is linked to many current educational practices affecting classrooms and schools. Wrote Robert Glaser some 20-plus years ago:

> Much of the application of psychological theory currently going on in schools represents the earlier behavioristic approach. The concepts of behavioral objectives and behavior modification, for example, now pervade all levels of education, including special education, elementary school instruction in basic literary skills and personalized systems of instruction.[2]

The same statement could be made today; and it would be appropriate to add such behavioral approaches as mastery learning, outcome-based education, and standards-based education. In general, combining behaviorism with learning includes careful analyzing and sequencing of the learners' needs and behaviors. Principles of testing, monitoring, drilling, and feedback are characteristic. The learning conditions needed for successful outcomes are carefully planned through small instructional steps and sequences of responses that increasingly approximate the desired behavior or learning. The teacher emphasizes a carefully planned lesson, clearly stated objectives, coinciding with logically organized materials with emphasis on getting the "correct" answer or achieving clearly defined outcomes. The teacher monitors the progress of students on a regular basis, using individualized materials, tutoring, and small-group projects. These basic principles tend to coincide with today's basic skill training programs in reading and literacy, as well as methods of individualized instruction, direct instruction, continuous progress, instructional design, and competency-based education. These steps and sequences are shown in Table 3.1. Although these procedures

1. Robert M. Travers, *Essentials of Learning,* 5th ed. (New York: Macmillan, 1982), p. 505.

2. Robert Glaser, "Trends and Research Quotations in Psychological Research on Learning and Schooling," *Educational Researcher* (November 1979), p. 12.

===== TABLE *3.1* =====

## A Cognitive-Behaviorist Approach to Teaching and Learning

| Direct Instruction: Rosenshine Model | Mastery Learning: Block and Anderson Model | Guided Instruction: Hunter Model | Systematic Instruction: Good and Brophy Model |
|---|---|---|---|
| 1. *State learning objectives.* Begin lesson with a short statement of objectives. | 1. *Clarify.* Explain to students what they are expected to learn. | 1. *Review.* Focus on previous lesson; ask students to summarize main points. | 1. *Review.* Review concepts and skills related to homework; provide review exercises. |
| 2. *Review.* Introduce short review of previous or prerequisite learning. | 2. *Inform.* Teach the lesson, relying on whole-group instruction. | 2. *Anticipatory set.* Focus students' attention on new lesson; stimulate interest in new materials. | 2. *Development.* Promote student understanding; provide examples, explanations, demonstrations. |
| 3. *Present new materials.* Present new materials in small, sequenced steps. | 3. *Pretest.* Give a *formative* quiz on a no-fault basis; students can check their own papers. | 3. *Objective.* State explicitly what is to be learned; state rationale or how it will be useful. | 3. *Assess comprehension.* Ask questions; provide controlled practice. |
| 4. *Explain.* Give clear and detailed instructions and explanations. | 4. *Group.* Based on results, divide the class into mastery and nonmastery groups (80 percent is considered mastery). | 4. *Input.* Identify needed knowledge and skills for learning new lesson; present material in sequenced steps. | 4. *Seatwork.* Provide uninterrupted seatwork; get everyone involved; sustain momentum. |
| 5. *Practice.* Provide active practice for all students. | 5. *Enrich and correct.* Give enrichment instruction to mastery group; give corrective (practice/drill) to nonmastery group. | 5. *Modeling.* Provide several examples or demonstrations throughout the lesson. | 5. *Accountability.* Check the students' work. |
| 6. *Guide.* Guide students during initial practice; provide seatwork activities. | 6. *Monitor.* Monitor student progress; vary amount of teacher time and support for each group based on group size and performance. | 6. *Check for understanding.* Monitor students' work and check to see they understand directions or tasks. | 6. *Homework.* Assign homework regularly; provide review problems. |
| 7. *Check for understanding.* Ask several questions; assess student comprehension. | 7. *Posttest.* Give a *summative* quiz to nonmastery group. | 7. *Guided practice.* Periodically ask students questions or problems and check their answers. Again, monitor for understanding. | 7. *Special reviews.* Provide weekly reviews to check and enhance learning; provide monthly reviews to further maintain and enhance learning. |
| 8. *Provide feedback.* Provide systematic feedback and corrections. | 8. *Assess performance.* At least 75 percent of students should achieve mastery by the summative test. | 8. *Independent practice.* Assign independent work or practice when it is reasonably certain that students can work on their own with minimal frustration and understanding. | |
| 9. *Assess performance.* Obtain student success rate of 80 percent or more during practice session. | 9. *Reteach.* If needed, repeat procedures starting with corrective instruction (small study groups, individual tutoring, alternative instructional materials, extra homework, reading materials, practice and drill). | | |
| 10. *Review and test.* Provide for spaced review and testing. | | | |

are predetermined, linear, and planned in advance, some observers claim they have a cognitive flavor, too.

The contributions of behaviorists to both psychology and education, as well as teaching and learning, were great during the past century, and it is likely that behaviorism will continue to influence the teaching field. However, most behaviorists are aware that, as we learn more about learners and learning, we cannot adhere to rigid doctrines. Human beings are not pigeons or mice, the subjects of early behaviorists. We are a little more complicated in terms of thinking and behavior. Perspectives that allow for investigations of the mind and psyche have been incorporated into behaviorism. Cognitive developmental theories are being integrated into some behaviorists' approaches to human learning—often called cognitive psychology or cognitive science.

## Cognitive Psychology

Anytime we categorize any phenomena, we run the risk of misinterpretation. Today, most psychologists classify human growth and development as cognitive, social, psychological, and physical. And although an individual grows and develops along all these fronts, most psychologists agree that learning in school is mainly cognitive in nature. Despite this acknowledgment, some psychologists, known as *developmentalists,* are more concerned with the developmental aspect of human learning; others, known as *cognitive structuralists,* focus more on the way in which content is structured for learning; and a third major group, the *cognitive scientists,* investigates the various cognitive structures that individuals create in order to generate meaning and ultimately knowledge. *Constructivism,* a fashionable and overused term today, is nothing more than old-fashioned John Dewey, Jean Piaget, and Jerome Bruner mixed together with some new vocabulary in which students acquire learning strategies and integrate (or construct) new information with social experiences to form new knowledge. It represents the learners' awareness of and control over cognitive processes—usually high-order mental processes.

Constructivism is rooted in the pedagogy of progressivism and humanistic education. Curriculum and teaching are *student centered,* focusing on child-centered activities and projects (Pestallozi, Froebel, Kilpatrick, and Rugg), problem-solving methods (Dewey, Piaget, Sternberg, and Tyler), and discovery learning (Ausubel, Broudy, Bruner, and Vygotsky). These teaching and learning methods have been the basis of school reform since the turn of the twentieth century, coinciding with the rise of progressivism and the decline of perennialism (which dominated U.S. education for the first 150 years). In theory, the idea is to reduce or eliminate the teacher-centered, text-centered, and rote-centered method of instruction, and to change to a student-centered approach. In practice, however, many of the progressive and student-centered ideas have remained as reform slogans, printed in education textbooks, purported as recommendations among most professors of elementary education and educational psychology, but seldom adopted by teachers on a large scale.[1]

Most, if not all, psychologists and educators would agree that cognitive psychology (and constructivism) represents the dominant school of thought, and learning is the sum total of the results of human interactions with their world. However, there is no agreed-upon way to determine exactly to what extent the characteristics (cognitive, social, psychological, and physical) of an individual are the result of inherited limitations or potential (harmful or favorable circumstances), or his or her environment. Considerable controversy continues about the extent or role of heredity versus environment in determining cognitive outcomes (that is, IQ scores and achievement scores) in school. As an increasing number of educators view the results of schooling as more than just achievement scores, these debates are likely to intensify. It is essential that teachers be aware of these debates because the issue affects teaching and learning theories.

## Piaget's Cognitive Theory

Most *cognitive theory* is developmental; that is, it supposes that growth and development occur in progressive stages. Jean Piaget resents the most comprehensive view of this theory. The Swiss psychologist's work came to the attention of American educators during the 1950s and 1960s—coinciding with the rising influence of cognitive developmental psychology, environmentalist theories, and the subsequent compensatory education movement.

Like many other investigators today, Piaget describes cognitive development in terms of stages from birth to maturity. The overall stages can be summarized as follows:[2]

**1.** *Sensorimotor stage* (birth to age 2). The child progresses from reflex operations and undifferentiated surroundings to complex sensorimotor actions in relation to environmental patterns. The child comes to realize that objects have permanence; they can be found again. He or she begins to establish simple relations between similar objects.

**2.** *Preoperational stage* (ages 2 to 7). In this stage, objects and events begin to take on symbolic meaning. For example, a chair is for sitting; a sweater is for wearing, and so on. The child shows an increased ability to learn more complex concepts from experience so long as familiar examples are provided from which to extract criteria that define the concept. (For example, oranges, apples, and bananas are fruit; the child should have the chance to touch and eat them.)

**3.** *Concrete operations stage* (ages 7 to 11). The child begins to organize data into logical relationships and gains facility in manipulating data in problem-solving

1. For some of the reasons, see Lawrence A. Cremin, *The Transformation of American Schools* (New York: Random House, 1963); Larry Cuban, *How Teachers Taught* (New York: Longman, 1984); and John I. Goodlad, *Educational Renewal* (San Francisco: Jossey-Bass, 1998).

2. Jean Piaget, *The Psychology of Intelligence*, rev. ed. (London: Broadway, 1950).

situations. This learning situation occurs, however, only if concrete objects are available or if actual past experiences can be drawn upon. The child is able to make judgments in terms of *reversibility* and reciprocal relations (e.g., that the left and right are relative to spatial relations) and *conservation* (e.g., a long narrow glass may hold the same amount of water as short wide one).

**4.** *Formal operations stage* (age 11 and onward). This stage is characterized by the development of formal and abstract operations. The adolescent is able to analyze ideas and comprehend spatial and temporal relationships. The young person can think logically about abstract data, evaluate data according to acceptable criteria, formulate hypotheses, and deduce possible consequences from them. He or she can construct theories and reach conclusions without having had direct experience in the subject. At this stage (by age 15 to 16), there are few or no limitations on what the adolescent can learn; learning depends on his or her intellectual potential and environmental experiences. Theoretically, by age 16, a student should be able to learn any subject, including advanced courses in calculus, physics, statistics, or philosophy. The only possible barrier, besides the teacher's low expectations of the student, is in the lack of learner's prerequisite content. In short, there is no longer need to postpone "tough" or highly abstract subject matter.

Piaget's cognitive stages presuppose a *maturation process* in the sense that development is a continuation and is based on previous growth. The mental operations are sequential and successive. The stages are hierarchical, and they form an order of increasingly sophisticated and integrated mental operations. Although the succession of stages is constant, stages of attainment vary within certain limits that are a function of heredity and environment. Although hereditary or environmental factors may speed up or slow down cognitive development, they do not change the stages or the sequence.

Environmental experience is the key to Piaget's cognitive theories, as it was also the crux of Dewey's learning principles. The educator's role involves "the shaping of actual experience by environing conditions" and knowing "what surroundings are conducive to having experiences that lead to growth."[1] Three basic cognitive processes form the basis of the environmental and experiential theories of both Piaget and Dewey.

For Piaget, *assimilation* is the incorporation of new experiences into existing experiences; it represents a coordination of the child's experiences into his or her environment. But assimilation alone does not have the capacity to handle new situations and new problems in context with present cognitive structures. The child must organize and develop new cognitive structures in context with existing structures—that is, how he or she thinks. This is *accommodation,* whereby the child's existing structures are modified and adapted in response to his or her environment. *Equilibration* is the process of achieving balance between those things that were previously understood and those yet to be understood; it refers to the dual process of assimilation and accommodation of one's environment.[2]

1. Dewey, *Experience and Education,* p. 40.
2. Jean Piaget, *The Child's Conception of Physical Causality* (New York: Harcourt, 1932).

This coincides with Dewey's "conceptions of situation and interaction [which] are inseparable from each other" and which form the basis of continuity.[1] For Dewey, a *situation* represents the experiences of the environment affecting the child, similar to Piaget's assimilation. *Interaction* is concerned with current or latitudinal transactions taking place between the child and his or her environment, including his or her capacities to establish meaning, similar to Piaget's accommodation. *Continuity* refers to longitudinal learning or to situations and interactions that follow, similar to Piaget's equilibration.

## Bruner: Structure of Subject Matter

The notion of *structure of subject matter* advocated by Jerome Bruner and Phil Phenix during the post–World War II era encourages the teacher to teach "deep understanding" of the content, the basic logic or structure of each major discipline—the key relationships, concepts, principles, and research methods.[2] This is what Harry Broudy called "applicable knowledge," what Lee J. Schulman called "procedural knowledge," what E. D. Hirsh called "process," and what some old-fashioned educators, including John Dewey, might call "problem solving" and some more recent educators, such as Lauren Resnick and Robert Sternberg, might call "critical thinking."

The idea is to go beyond the realm of knowledge to a higher-order process—such as understanding, analysis, and problem solving by teaching the underlying concepts and principles of a subject. It is important to teach learners how to learn on their own, to inquire and hypothesize, by using the investigative methods of the subject to acquire and assimilate new information. The student who cultivates fluency with this mode of inquiry attains mastery of the content area and is able to continue, independently, self-paced learning in the subject area. As Jacques Barzum said more than half century ago, the results of a good education produce learners who are capable of, and very much inclined toward, lifelong growth and education.[3]

Age is not a hindrance. The process can start at the primary-grade levels. The need for the teacher is to teach the concepts and principles of the subject that are relevant and meaningful to the age (and abilities) of the student. For instance, first-graders may be asked by the teacher to rub their hands together and feel the heat produced—a concept that deals with high school physics but taught in a manner suitable for the child. For supporters of this approach, when learning science or mathematics, students would employ the methods of scientists or mathematicians. When studying history or geography, the students would employ the methods of historians and geographers. The goal is for students to become "little scholars" in their respective fields—and for high-achieving students to take more demanding coursework.

Subjects such as language arts, social studies, general science, and global studies are not considered "real" subjects, or what Bruner refers to as "disciplines," because

1. Dewey, *Experience and Education*, p. 43.
2. Jerome Bruner, *The Process of Education* (Cambridge, MA: Harvard University Press, 1959); Philip H. Phenix, *Realms of Meaning* (New York: McGraw-Hill, 1964).
3. Jacques Barzum, *Teacher in America* (Boston: Little, Brown, 1944).

they lack structure and a clear domain of knowledge. These are *broad field subjects,* an idea originally popularized in the 1940s and 1950s, and based on an interdisciplinary design in an effort to correct what many educators (including John Dewey and later Ralph Tyler) considered the fragmentation and compartmentalization of subject matter. Whereas the broad fields approach is an attempt to integrate content that appears to fit logically (language arts, social studies, etc.), the notion of "structure" and "disciplined knowledge" represents the content of a separate field of study (English, mathematics, history, science or foreign languages).

Piaget's equilibration forms the basis of Bruner's notion of a *spiral curriculum,* in which previous learning is the basis of subsequent learning, learning is continuous, and content in a subject field is related to and built and expands on a foundation (from grade to grade). Bruner is also influenced by Dewey, who uses the term *continuity* in learning to explain that what a person has already learned "becomes and instrument of understanding and dealing effectively with the situations that follow." Bruner uses the term *continuity,* in the same way as Piaget and Dewey, to describe the spiral curriculum: how subject matter and mental operations can be "continually deepened by using them in a progressively more complex form."[1]

Bruner considers that the act of learning consists of three related mental processes, similar to Piaget's cognitive processes:

1. *Acquisition* is the grasping of new information; it mainly corresponds to Piaget's assimilation. Such information may be new to one's store of data, may replace previously acquired information, or may merely refine or further qualify previous information.
2. *Transformation* is the individual's capacity to process new information so as to transcend or go beyond it. Means for processing such information are extrapolation, interpolation, or translation into another form; it overlaps somewhat with Piaget's accommodation.
3. *Evaluation* is the determination of whether information has been processed in a way that renders it appropriate for dealing with a particular task or problem. It closely corresponds with equilibration.

## Moral Education

How a person develops morally is partially, if not predominantly, based on cognition and mental operations and the way he or she interacts with family, schools, and society—more precisely, on the roles and responsibilities he or she learns and deems important based on contact with people and social institutions. Schools have traditionally been concerned with the moral education of children. In the nineteenth century, moral education became linked to obedience and conformity to rules and regulations. Standards of moral behavior were enforced by rewards and punishments

1. Bruner, *The Process of Education,* p. 13.

and were translated into grades in what at different times was called *morals and manners,* and later *citizenship, conduct,* or *social behavior.*

Until the late nineteenth century, public schools typically exhibited a strong, nonsectarian Protestant moral tone. This standard was reflected in activities such as Bible readings, prayers, and the content of the *New England Primer* (students memorized sermons and learned their ABCs through rote and drill) and McGuffey readers (that reflected old-fashioned industrial morality such as private property, hard work, diligence, and savings, as well as patriotism and love of country).

By the turn of the twentieth century, the schools shifted the notion of moral education to purely secular activities, such as student responsibility, student cooperation in class and student councils, flag salutes, assembly rituals, and community and school service. "Dick and Jane" eventually replaced the McGuffey readers and depicted middle-class values of the era—small-town life, a nuclear family with two children, a father as the breadwinner and mother as the housewife. Life was depicted in these books in terms of happy, neat, and white, with intact families living in a clean and pleasant home. People exhibited a Protestant, inner-directed (respect toward adult authority, community centered, work-success ethic, achievement orientation, future-time orientation), and moral life. Racial and ethnic diversity was excluded, or confined to a unit such as "Children from Other Lands." The civil rights movement of the 1960s and the subsequent rise of racial and ethnic studies ended the Dick and Jane series.

The point is, schools have never ignored moral education, but the values have reflected the majority culture. Teachers have avoided the teaching of morality because of its subjective nature and its potential trappings or overlap with religious indoctrination. Most moral teachings have been indirect, limited to modeling middle-class behavior and attitudes in the classroom and community, and the teaching of patriotism and heroism through history and English subject matter.

## Moral Knowledge

It is possible to give instruction in *moral knowledge* and ethics. Teachers can discuss philosophers such as Socrates, Plato, and Aristotle who examined the good society and the good person; the more controversial works of Immanuel Kant, Franz Kafka, and Jean-Paul Sartre; religious leaders such as Moses, Jesus, and Confucius; and political leaders such as Abraham Lincoln, Mohandas Gandhi, and Martin Luther King. Through the study of the writings and principles of these moral people, students can learn about moral knowledge. For young readers there are *Aesop's Fables* and *Jack and the Beanstalk.* For older children there are *Sadako, Up from Slavery,* and *The Diary of Anne Frank.* And for adolescents, there are *Of Mice and Men, A Man for All Seasons, Lord of the Flies, Death of a Salesman,* and *The Adventures of Huckleberry Finn.* All these books deal with moral and value-laden issues. Whose morality? Whose values? There are agreed-upon virtues—such as honesty, hard work, integrity, civility, caring, and so forth—that represent an American consensus. It is there—if we have sufficient moral conviction to find it.

Of course, when it comes to the likes of Huck Finn, we have created a red herring, where the likes of Bill O'Reilly meet Jesse Jackson. Is it a *racist* book that should be banned or a *masterpiece* (perhaps the number-one fiction book written by an American author) that should be read, discussed, and analyzed? Huck is a backwoods kid, not too bright, the precursor of the modern juvenile delinquent, a rebel who finds a moral cause without giving up his pranks or surrendering his identity.

Jim is a runaway slave, a clown and companion, living in a white man's world in a servant-type role, but, by reason of his place in society and his clever nature, he neither says all that he means nor means all he says. Acting as the clown, and with poetic imagination and humor, he is able to get along in his troubled world, and the reader learns to respect his wit, his jiving and joking and use of other compensatory devices. In some respects, Jim is the future "Amos" or "Andy," a rascally creature southern whites were prone to make him, who performed from behind an ethnic mask in the same way Will Smith was forced to play in *Men in Black,* Bruce Lee in *Green Hornet,* and Tonto in *The Lone Ranger.*

Think of Mark Twain as a minstrel—performing and mocking convention, dissecting the minds and matters of the day through jokes, tales, and gestures that circulated above the southern white folks along the Mississippi River and now the black folks in African American studies and nearly everyone in postcolonial and neo-marxist studies who condemn "whiteness."

We have become a sanitized society, where literacy passages considered sensitive or potentially offensive to minorities are bleeped out of school literature. What used to be called history, literature, art, or photography is often scrubbed according to whim or worry. With a click of a mouse, textbooks, tests, films, and even literary classics can be edited to fit what one critic now calls an "offenseless society," tailored to every school group and community. The cultural wars of old have shifted: The political and moral overtones "have given way to quieter, more modest strokes of revision or deletion. The parties on either side might be liberal, conservative or anything in between."[1] It becomes a little silly, however, when the New York State Board of Regents changes *thin* for *skinny* and *heavy* for *fat* on their standardized tests, when U.S. history guidelines develop a dialogue between George Washington and an Indian leader to demonstrate American pluralism, or when the religious right see witches, pagans, and devils in textbooks.[2]

The question arises: Can a school or society trying to depict all racial, ethnic, religious, and minority groups (including women, homosexuals, and those with disabilities) with dignity also nourish its literary and artistic culture? Schools can select a science text without reference to evolution, a history book that excludes the Holocaust, and now, with the computer, edit and omit passages that the community may find offensive in classics (Homer's *Odyssey,* Shakespeare's *Merchant of Venice,* Chekhov's *Rothchild's Fiddle,* William Faulkner's *Brer Tiger and the Big Wind*). The language cut is often part of the conversation of society. Rather than expecting students to question and analyze such statements, we have revisionary and doctored ver-

1. John Leland, "The Myth of the Offenseless Society," *New York Times* (June 9, 2002), Sect. 4, p. 4. Also see N. A. Kleinfield, "N.Y. Exam Strips Renounced Texts of Naked Literary Truths," *Chicago Tribune* (June 3, 2002), p. 17.
2. Daniel Henninger, "Ten Years After, Writers Get Word of the PC Wars," *Wall Street Journal* (June 14, 2002), p. 12.

sions of text, failing to recognize that outside classrooms and schools, the literature and lyrics flow without comment or question. Do we really create a purer school environment or purer society by omission? Since the Puritan era, American society has failed to filter out passages that deal with reality, what is sometimes considered politically or morally offensive.

Instead of asking moral questions and requiring students to grapple with issues of life, much of the routine of school is to teach prescribed content and skills—things students are expected to know. As John Goodlad has commented for a 10-year period, across the curriculum at all grade levels, students are expected to recall and memorize information, answer mundane questions in workbooks and textbooks, and pass multiple-choice and true-false tests.[1] The point is, Huck and Jim need to be heard, then analyzed and discussed, along with Homer, Shakespeare, Chekhov, and Faulkner.

According to Philip Phenix, the most important sources of moral knowledge are the laws and customs of society, and they can be taught in courses dealing with law, ethics, and sociology. However, *moral conduct* cannot be taught; rather, it is learned by "participating in everyday life of society according to recognized standards of society."[2] Although laws and customs and obedience are not always morally right, accepted standards do provide guidance for conduct and behavior.

The content of moral knowledge, according to Phenix, covers five areas: (1) *human rights,* involving conditions of life that ought to prevail; (2) *ethics* concerning family relations and sex; (3) *social relationships,* dealing with class, racial, ethnic, and religious groups; (4) *economic life,* involving wealth and poverty; and (5) *political life,* involving justice, equity, and power.[3] The way we translate moral content into moral conduct defines the kind of people we are. It is not our moral knowledge that counts; rather, it is our moral behavior in everyday affairs with people that is more important.

## Moral Character

A person can have moral knowledge and obey secular and religious laws but still lack moral character. *Moral character* is difficult to teach because it involves patterns of attitudes and behavior that result from stages of growth, distinctive qualities of personality, and experiences. It involves a coherent philosophy and the will to act in a way consistent with that philosophy. Moral character also means to help people and to accept their weaknesses without exploiting them; to see the best in people and to build on their strengths; to act with civility and courteousness in relations with classmates, friends, or colleagues; to express humility; and to act as an individual even if it means being different from the crowd (e.g., to say "no" when almost everyone says "yes").

Perhaps the real test of moral character is to cope with crisis or setback, to deal with adversity, and to be willing to take risks (that is, possible loss of jobs, even life itself) because of one's convictions. Courage, conviction, and compassion are the ingredients

1. John I. Goodlad, *A Place Called School* (New York: McGraw-Hill, 1984); Goodlad, *Educational Renewal* (San Francisco: Jossey-Bass, 1994).

2. Phenix, *Realms of Meaning,* pp. 220–221.

3. Ibid.

of character. What kind of person do you want to emerge as a result of your effort as a teacher? Teachers can engage in moral education and teach moral knowledge, but can they teach moral character? (See Teaching Tips 3.2.) In general, the morally mature person understands moral principles and accepts responsibility for applying these principles in real-life situations.

The world is full of people who understand the notion of morality but take the expedient way out or follow the crowd. Who among us (including our colleagues)

# *Teaching Tips* 3.2

## The Morally Mature Person

The Association for Supervision and Curriculum Development has written its description of the morally mature person. The characteristics it lists offer teachers a framework for classroom discussions and classroom interaction.

I. *Respects human dignity,* which includes
1. Showing regard for the worth and rights of all persons
2. Avoiding deception and dishonesty
3. Promoting human equality
4. Respecting freedom of conscience
5. Working with people of different views
6. Refraining from prejudice actions
II. *Cares about the welfare of others,* which includes
1. Recognizing interdependence among people
2. Caring for one's country
3. Seeking social justice
4. Taking pleasure in helping others
5. Working to help others reach moral maturity
III. *Integrates individual interests and social responsibilities,* which include
1. Becoming involved in community life
2. Doing a fair share of community work
3. Displaying self-regard and other moral virtues—self-control, diligence, fairness, kindness, honesty civility—in everyday life
4. Fulfilling commitments

5. Developing self-esteem through relationships with others
IV. *Demonstrates integrity,* which includes
1. Practicing diligence
2. Taking stands for moral principles
3. Displaying moral courage
4. Knowing when to compromise and when to confront
5. Accepting responsibility for one's choices
V. *Reflects on moral choices,* which includes
1. Recognizing the moral issues involved in a situation
2. Applying moral principles (such as the Golden Rule) when making moral judgments
3. Thinking about the consequences of decisions
4. Seeking to be informed about important moral issues in society and the world
VI. *Seeks peaceful resolution of conflict,* which includes
1. Striving for the fair resolution of personal and social conflicts
2. Avoiding physical and verbal aggression
3. Listening carefully to others
4. Encouraging others to communicate
5. Working for peace

*Source:* ASCD Panel on Moral Education, "Moral Education and the Life of the School," *Educational Leadership* (May 1998), p. 5.

possesses moral character? Who among our students will develop into morally mature individuals? To be sure, moral character cannot be taught by one teacher; rather, it takes a concerted effort by the entire school, cooperation among a critical mass of teachers within the school, and involves the nurturing of children and youth over many years. Ted and Nancy Sizer ask teachers to confront students with moral questions and moral issues about their own actions or inactions in ways that may be unsettling or difficult. As teachers, we need to address things that threaten the self-concept and self-esteem of students.[1] We need to deal with issues of inequity and social injustice, while promoting cooperative behaviors, intergroup relations, and respect for diversity among children and youth.

The Sizers want teachers to "grapple" with ideas, to "dig deep," to ask why things are so, to examine what evidence there is, and to explore what thoughts and actions mean. They hope that teachers will stop taking shortcuts in their preparation or testing/evaluation practices, and they hope that schools will reduce the "sorting" practice in ways that sometimes correspond with social (class or caste) groupings. Although some sorting of students is necessary, it should be flexible enough to respect students' and parents' wishes and to avoid stereotyping. In the end, the Sizers argue that students should not experience hypocrisy in classrooms and schools that claim all students are equal or all students can be what they can be, while at the same time discriminating against students of class, color, or low ability.

Schools must establish moral character as policy in which all teachers are expected to adopt. One or two teachers by themselves will have little impact. It takes a school community to implement a program of moral character, whereby students are taught that they are responsible for their actions and that values such as honesty, respect, tolerance, compassion, and a sense of justice are worthwhile and important concepts to learn and become benchmarks in life or calls for action.

Educators should not establish the attitude or take the easy way out and claim that the student population is too diverse and moral consensus cannot be reached, or that the best they can do is to hope to promote democratic principles, mutual respect, and critical thinking. That's all well and good, but it begs the issue that education is designed to socialize children and youth, and shape thinking for the good of society. To avoid tough moral issues, or to pooh-pooh character development, is to fall into Amy Gutman's trap, who believes that moral issues are inappropriate in public schools because of the diverse backgrounds and biases of students. It also means to adopt Nel Noddings's misguided notion that caring for strangers is more important than shaping minds and attitudes of students.[2]

There are some 7.5 million Muslims living in the United States who are diligent, law-abiding, and hard-working. It may be acceptable for Moslem students to assert their identity and wear their traditional facial scarf or headdress in their homes, mosques, or communities, but if they had never worn it in American public schools

1. Theodore R. Sizer and Nancy Faust Sizer, *The Students Are Watching: Schools and the Moral Context* (Boston: Beacon Press, 1999).

2. Amy Gutman, *Democratic Education*, rev. ed. (Princeton, NJ: Princeton University Press, 1999); Nel Noddings, *Educating Moral People: A Caring Alternative to Character Education* (New York: Teachers College Press, 2002.)

prior to 9-11, it is not now acceptable because it is potentially inflammatory and likely to invite disruption or violence.[1] Moslem students do not have to wear Air Jordan sneakers or Calvin Klein jeans to prove they are homogenized Americans. But freedom of speech does not allow someone to yell "fire" in a crowded and enclosed place, nor does it allow at a time of war for a group of students who may be profiled or wrongly associated with the enemy to put it in their classmates' face. To urge or protect this type of behavior is liberal jibberish and an afront to common sense.

Similarly, if people are to live in an environment of peace and mutual respect, then to disseminate the pictures of the barbaric murder of Danny Pearl (whose throat was cut on video because he was an American) on the Internet should be judged as morally repugnant and should not be excused by the protection of the First Amendment—not when the country is at war with terrorists who wish to topple our way of life. The corporate world had the technology to censor this inflammatory media, failed to, and must be judged morally contemptuous.

If all this seems to smell like some form of the Alien Sedation Acts, McCarthyism, or antidiversity, then you are missing the point. Students walking around and displaying Nazi tattoos in school, or with para-military garb in the postperiod of Columbine High School, should be stopped at the school doors and told to go home and cover up their tattoos and/or dress in a way that is nonthreatening.[2]

1. Had the scarf or headdress been worn regularly prior to 9-11, then it boils down to a religious or cultural issue (not political) that should be accepted by school authorities.

2. Hate dates back to primitive society when one group of cave-dwellers had more of something than another group or looked slightly different. Hatred based on religion, race, gender, sexual preference, and other characteristics is as old as recorded history. What is new, today, is that hate mongers have access to the worldwide Internet, which enables them (along with terrorists) to communicate around the globe and to use technology to bolster their messages.

There are more than 500 hate groups in the United States, with an estimated total membership of one to three million people who target people of color, Jews, women, homosexuals, and sometimes Catholics and immigrants, who are not considered Aryan and Protestant. Their central belief that the U.S. government and liberals are conspiring and imposing a new order designed to "mongrelize" America.

Several members of these hate groups were involved in the Oklahoma City tragedy that killed approximately 175 people. The crucifixion-type murder of gay student Matthew Shepard in Wyoming, the racially motivated truck-dragging of James Byrd in Texas, the shooting spree of Benjamin Smith in Illinois and Indiana, and the Columbine High School massacre in Colorado are examples of recent hate crimes.

Most hate crimes go unreported by the media. In 1995, the year the Oklahoma bombing took place, the FBI reported 100 hate crimes. By 2000, the number has soared to 1,000, either reflecting new reporting procedures or the increase and organization of hate groups. Approximately 350 radio stations, mainly in nonurban areas, carry one or more hate-related programs.

To dismiss all these groups as "kooks," "rednecks," "skinheads," or "neoNazis," or to make them appear to be odd or stupid, is to miss the point. Many are educated and excellent speakers, writers, and organizers. Schools currently do very little in dealing with these groups, to neutralize their hate rhetoric, to teach students to deal with hate related issues. The need is for community and civic groups to oppose these groups, and to work with schools and other social institutions, and to be vigilant against the far right gaining power of local school boards and town libraries. See Robert Hilliard, "Unmarking the New Face of Hate," *Expression* (Winter 2001), pp. 11–15.

Regardless of the position of the American Civil Liberties Union, school officials must take moral positions. There are certain events that are horrifying and represent the most evil aspects of human behavior. Students who laugh at pictures of the rape of Nanking, the Holocaust, the Killing Fields—or the incineration of the World Trade Center—should not be excused because of their ignorance, or religious, racial, or ethnic backgrounds; nor should they be provided with a school platform at the K–12 level to voice their "justification" or to get into a historical debate about racial superiority of certain groups. They are wrong on all moral accounts, pure and simple, given the tenets of a civilized society. Their minds are rot, and they are potential followers and instruments of others who preach hatred. It is the role of the teacher to shape their minds and attitudes, if at all possible, to the laws of living with and respecting others. Some of you may infer this is propaganda, or even fascism, and not what schools are about—claiming all American students should have the freedom to voice their opinion in class. And I answer, not when it reflects hate and mocks the death of thousands or millions of people.

There is enough evidence to believe that Aristotle and Plato would accept my view, given their idea of a good society—and what is ethical and rational behavior—and so would the U.S. Supreme Court as it is presently constituted. For all the victims who had to grasp their final moments, decent people understand that there needs to be some bit of good prevailing over evil. When a religious, racial, or ethnic group, or a nation, is aghast—and people can recall the background screams of the dying—children and youth do not need to be insulted or hear some banal rhetoric. The last vanishing moments of the dead should not be compromised by a political or religious message that espouses hate. Hate should not be allowed into the K–12 curriculum, even under the guise of freedom of expression.

Good moral character requires a clear set of values, but someone who has a clear set of values (i.e., Adolf Hitler, Bin Laden, or Enron CEO Kenneth Lay) may not be moral.[1] The values a person holds depend on many factors, including historical and social environment, education, and personality. Teachers and schools are always transmitting values to students, both consciously and unconsciously. Sometimes the transmission occurs through what educators call the "hidden curriculum," the unstated meanings conveyed by teacher attitudes and behavior, class routines, school policies, and the curriculum in general.[2]

1. The word *ethics* is concerned with the evaluation of human behavior. Enron executives had a habit of cooking the books, hiding debt, and making side deals to enrich their own pockets as the expense of their employees and the public. The company had a 64-page booklet, their own Code of Ethics, covering everything from honesty, workplace harmony and collegiality, commitment to environmental protection, conducting business affairs in accordance with "all applicable laws and in a moral and honest manner," and more. It is hard to discern who spoke with a greater "forked tongue" or who was more amoral—the executives at Philip Morris, Firestone, Worldcom, or Enron.

2. Clark Power and Lawrence Kohlberg, "Moral Development: Transforming the Hidden Curriculum," *Curriculum Review* (September–October 1986), pp. 26–32; Allan C. Ornstein, "The Irrelevant Curriculum: A Review from Four Perspectives," *NASSP Bulletin* (September 1988), pp. 14–17; and Frank Trocco, "Encouraging Students to Study Weird Things," *Phi Delta Kappan* (April 2000), pp. 628–631.

## Moral Development: Piaget and Kohlberg

Although some self-control of behavior may be seen in the preschool years, researchers agree that not until a child is about 4 years old do moral standards begin to develop at a rapid rate. During the period when a child begins to abandon behavior governed by what he or she wants to do at a particular moment, the child's conscience tends to be erratic, largely confined to prohibitions against specific behaviors and based on external sanctions. Before age 5, morality does not exist for children because they have little or no conception of rules. From about 5 to 6 years, a child's conscience becomes less confined to specific behaviors and begins to incorporate more generalized standards; it becomes determined less by external rewards or punishments and more by internal sanctions.[1]

**Piaget's Theory of Moral Development**   Piaget's theory was based on techniques of investigation that included conversing with children and asking them questions about moral dilemmas and events in stories. For example, he might ask a child, "Why shouldn't you cheat in a game?" Piaget's observations suggest that from ages 5 to 12, children's concepts of justice pass from rigid and inflexible notions of right and wrong, learned from parents, to a sense of equity in moral judgments. Eventually, it takes into account specific situations or circumstances.

As children grow older, they become more flexible and realize that there are exceptions to rules. As they become members of a larger, more varied peer group, rules and moral judgments become less absolute and rigid and more dependent on the needs and desires of the people involved. Wrote Piaget, "For very young children, a rule is a sacred reality because it is traditional; for the older ones it depends upon a mutual agreement."[2]

On the basis of numerous studies, Piaget concluded:

> There are three great periods of development of the sense of justice in the child. One period, starting at the age of 5 and lasting to the age 7–8, during which justice is subordinated to adult authority; a period contained approximately between 8–11, and which is that of progressive equalitarianism; and finally a [third] period that sets in toward 11–12, and during which purely equalitarian justice is tempered by consideration of equity.[3]

**Kohlberg's Theory of Moral Reasoning**   More recently, Lawrence Kohlberg studied the development of children's moral standards and concluded that the way people think about moral issues reflects their culture and their stage of growth. He outlined six de-

1. Bernadette Baker, "The Dangerous and the Good? Developmentalism, Progress, and Public Schooling," *American Educational Research Journal* (Winter 1999), pp. 797–834.
2. Jean Piaget, *The Moral Development of the Child* (New York: Free Press, 1965), p. 182.
3. Ibid., p. 314.

velopmental stages of moral judgment and grouped three moral levels that correspond roughly to Piaget's three stages of cognitive development:

1. *Preconventional level.* Children have not yet developed a sense of right or wrong. The level is comprised of two stages: (a) children do as they are told because they fear punishment and (b) children realize that certain actions bring rewards.
2. *Conventional level.* Children are concerned about what other people think of them, and their behavior is largely other-directed. The two stages in this level are (a) children seek their parents' approval by being "nice" and (b) children begin thinking in terms of laws and rules.
3. *Postconventional level.* Morality is based not only on other people's values but also on internalized precepts of ethical principles and authority. This level also includes two stages: (a) children view morality in terms of contractual obligations and democratically accepted laws and (b) children view morality in terms of individual principles of conscience[1] [as well as a higher being].

Unless a reasonable degree of moral development takes place during childhood and adolescence (i.e., unless standards of right and wrong are established), the child, and later the adult, is likely to engage in asocial and/or antisocial behavior. On the other hand, if the acceptance of others' standards or the internalization of standards and prohibitions is unduly strong, guilt may develop in association with a wide variety of actions and thoughts. Ideally, individuals work out an adequate sense of morality and at the same time avoid self-condemnation, in the context of the culture in which they live.

Kohlberg's theory has been widely criticized on the grounds that moral reasoning does not necessarily conform to development and involves many complex social and psychological factors, that particular moral behaviors are not always associated with the same reasoning (and vice versa), and that his prescriptions are culture bound and sexist. However, he has made researchers and practitioners aware of moral reasoning and has provided a moral theory, along with Piaget's, to guide teaching and learning.

Beyond Piaget and Kohlberg    Although Kohlberg found that his theories of moral reasoning have been replicated in various countries, and that it occurs in the same order and about the same ages cross cultures, he has been criticized that his early work was limited mainly to boys. For example, Carol Gilligan has maintained that boys and girls use different moral criteria. Male morality centers more on individual rights

1. Lawrence A. Kohlberg, "The Development of Children's Orientation Toward a Moral Order, I: Sequence in the Development of Moral Thought," *Vita Humana,* vol. 6 (1963), pp. 11–33; Kohlberg, "Development of Moral Character and Moral Ideology," in M. L. Hoffman and L. W. Hoffman, eds., *Review of Child Development,* vol. 1 (New York: Russell Sage Foundation, 1964), pp. 383–431.

and social justice, whereas female morality focuses on individual responsibilities, self-sacrifice, and caring.[1]

Kohlberg revised his research on the basis of the preceding criticism, but he (and others) failed to find any male-female significant differences in moral reasoning or moral maturity. Although there is no convincing evidence that women are more caring, cooperative, or altruistic,[2] as Gilligan has argued, these ideas have been embellished by Nel Noddings in her book *The Challenge to Care in Schools*[3] and by several feminists who advocate the virtue of caring within the family and in educational, social, and medical settings and the need to reduce competitive behavior in schools and society. Gilligan's ideas have become increasingly feminist and also seem to coincide with the everyday folk belief that "men are from Mars" and "women are from Venus," as well as in popular Broadway plays such as *I Love You. You're Perfect. Now Change* and *The Caveman*. If you ask her why love often falls apart, it is the fault of men, who feel they are the center of the universe and are guided by the male-centered tale of Oedipus.[4] My own male response: Ho-Hum.

The most important limitations to Piaget's and Kohlberg's theories is that they fail to distinguish between moral reasoning and actual behavior. Moral behavior does not necessarily conform to simple rules, guidelines, or developmental stages. The social context, an individual's overall personality and perception of reality, and the individual's motivation to behave morally are factors for consideration. (For example, there are always opportunities to cheat or steal, but there is also the possibility of getting caught.) But what is at stake? A 50-cent candy bar, a $10 CD, or the SAT test questions that may admit you into Harvard or Yale? Although certain aspects of moral reasoning account for moral behavior, the correlation can be weak—given social and personal variables. According to research, moral reasoning can be predicted much more precisely than moral behavior. The latter is more complex; furthermore, the link between moral reasoning and moral behavior is minimal.[5]

**Cheating: Just about Everyone Does It**    Besides mutual respect and understanding, what else do students owe each other? Given the competitive nature of grading and school ranking at the high school level, there is a tendency among students to cheat. According

---

1. Carol Gilligan, *In a Different Voice: Sex Differences in the Expression of Moral Judgment* (Cambridge, MA: Harvard University Press, 1982).

2. Alice H. Eagley and Maureen Crowley, "Gender and Helping Behavior," *Psychological Bulletin* (November 1986), pp. 283–308; J. G. Smetana, M. Killen, and E. Turiel, "Children's Reasoning About Interpersonal and Moral Conflicts," *Child Development*, vol. 68 (1998), pp. 629–644.

3. Nel Noddings, *The Challenge to Care in Schools* (New York: Teachers College Press, 1992).

4. Carol Gilligan, *The Birth of Pleasure* (New York: Alfred A. Knopf, 2002).

5. G. G. Bear and G. S. Rys, "Moral Reasoning, Classroom Behavior, and Sociometric Status Among Elementary School Children," *Developmental Psychology*, vol. 30 (1995), pp. 633–638; Muriel J. Bebeau, Jame R. Rest, and Darcia Narvaez, "Beyond the Promise: A Perspective on Research in Moral Education," *Educational Researcher* (May 1999), pp. 18–26.

to Noddings, "many students deny that cheating is wrong," and teachers fail to "protect students who are committed to fair competition."[1] We can blame the system, and argue that it fosters a competitive culture, which leads to winning at all costs. We can also blame parents for creating pressure to succeed, starting before their children enter school, when they begin lap reading and introducing them to foods and animals, and even American heroes with a page and picture for each letter of the alphabet.

A recent study at Duke University indicates that about 75 percent of college students acknowledge some academic dishonesty. Why? Typical responses are: "I guess the first time you do it, you feel bad. After a while, you get used to it." Another student states: "There are times when you need a little help."[2] We can discuss all the policies colleges have implemented to reduce cheating, ranging from signing pledges not to cheat to judiciary boards that have the right to suspend students. But now, with the Internet, there are a slew of students (literally hundreds of thousands) surfing sites for papers available to them for a few bucks a page—among them are Cheater.com and Schoolsucks.com (which boasts 10,000 hits per day).[3] In this world of Oz, professors are forced to fight back and enlist Internet services that can identify papers that have been lifted from one source or cut and paste from several sources.

The bottom line is that cheating reflects moral laxity that will not go away in a world where our heroes and star citizens cheat—or wink and nod. Athletes take drugs to enhance their performance because the result is higher salaries and more endorsements. Politicians lie and are often caught with their fingers in the cookie jar or hiding stuffed shoeboxes in their closets. Judges are bought and decisions are often based on politics and not the law. CEOs invent new accounting techniques to disguise losses, then proceed to cheat their employees and the general public out of hundreds of billions of dollars while they become millions of dollars richer. The clergy steals children's innocence one moment (creating havoc, fear, and guilt for the rest of those children's lives) and preach the gospel the next moment. Bishops—who knowingly covered up such actions, protected these priests, and allowed them to remain in the ministry, where they continue to abuse children—now worry about scandal.

Given the so-called pillars of society who are supposed to model moral behavior, who publicly adhere to a rigorous moral code, and who demand accountability from others but have not been held accountable for their own behavior, ask why children cheat. Once upon a time, when "Dick and Jane" taught most of us how to read and Dr. Seuss and "mad comics" reached out to "those other kids," when boys were naughty and girls were nice, and when children showed respect for their parents and teachers and other adults in positions of authority, and before the death of the traditional American family, cheating was a "no-no."

Given the modern world of technology, fast foods, and fast cars, along with sex, drugs, and MTV, students have little connection with the old values of society—what some kids today might label the "Stone Age" and what some educators might call the

1. Noddings, *The Challenge to Care in Schools*, p. 101.
2. Glenn C. Altschinler, "Battling the Cheats," *New York Times Education Life* (January 7, 2001), Sect. 4A, p. 15.
3. Ibid.

"pre-postmodern age." It is apparent that schools have mirrored the social transformation of society, including contemporary society, and so have students. William Bennett and Lynne Cheney, with their emphasis on American virtues and values, and even Jerry Falwell, who claims to have 16 million followers, cannot turn back the clock.

## Moral Freedom

Intellectuals love to generalize about U.S. culture: Do Americans live in a democratic and free society or are we materialistic and morally corrupt? Are we in a culture of victims, disbelief, and consumerism or are we a hard-working, god-fearing, and thrifty society? Do we still breed rugged individuals or have we become anxious conformists? Are we shamelessly permissive or tenaciously hanging on to our puritanical values? Many intellectuals would argue there is a cultural and moral war going on in our nation, illustrated by hot debates on welfare, immigration, labor, religion, homosexuality, and family life. Just about every educator, psychologist, sociologist, and journalist has something to say about these issues in context with "traditional," "emerging," and "postmodern" values.

Moral freedom, according to Alan Wolfe, defines the way we live and the type of society we are. Based on in-depth interviews in eight niche communities, all very different—from a small town in Iowa, a black community in Hartford (CT), a middle-class suburb in Ohio, to a gay district in San Francisco and a wealthy area in Silicon Valley—he focuses on changing morality in America. His conclusions are that Americans on all sides of the political continuum are engaged in reconciling individual freedom with a common morality.[1] Those on the political left welcome individual self-fulfillment and reduced powers of the police, and those on the right put devotion to God first and insist on law and order and strict penalties for criminal behavior. Moral relativists on the left support smoking bans, organic food, strict environment laws, and hate-crime legislation. Those on the right acknowledge the profit motive that drives industry, the need to search for oil in Alaska, and the importance of patriotism, forgiveness, and redemption—pretty close to what the McGuffey readers advanced some 150 years ago and to what William Bennett preaches today on television and in his books.[2]

In general, Americans are moral moderates. We seek high standards of virtuous behavior but not mandates or prescriptive laws. We strive to live the good, virtuous life, but we worry about the divorce rate and its effect on children. Respect for honesty is neutralized by the need to function in a perceived dishonest world. Morality is a form of common sense and law; it is eclectic, like religion in America.[3] It boils

1. Alan Wolfe, *Moral Freedom: The Impossible Idea That Defines the Way We Live Now* (New York: Norton, 2001).

2. See William J. Bennett, ed. *The Children's Book of Hearth and Home* (Chicago: Children's Press, 2002); Bennett, *Virtues of Courage in Adversity* (Nashville, TN: W Publishing Group, 2002).

3. Wendy Kaminer, "Have a Nice Life," *New York Times Book Review* (April 8, 2001), p. 14.

down to each of us as the individuals and how we relate to others. Americans tend to "personalize" religion, borrowing from traditional scriptures and new age spiritual movements. American teachers tend to "individualize" teaching and learning theories that suit their own personality and knowledge base. Likewise, Americans tend to "personalize" moral behavior, drawing from both conservative and liberal thinking, from ideals of godliness, self-discipline, and modern notions of self-fulfillment, sexual freedom, and counterculture ideals. A lot of this moderation stems from the fact that we are not a homogeneous population, driven by one religious or political ideal. We are a mixed breed of people with mixed traditional and liberal ideas about morality. In this mixed environment, teachers and schools must find their way—and not run away from teaching morality.

Since the 1960s and to the present, radical youth, cultural activists, black-power advocates, feminists, and homosexuals have rejected the concepts of puritan moral behavior, the political and social measures of the Establishment and traditional order. They have fashioned their own moral ideas and interpretations to counter the ones bequeathed to them. In many cases, conservative reaction in schools and society has been just as opinionated and exaggerated, reflected in the articles and commentaries of *Forbes, National Review,* and the *Wall Street Journal.* In short, Americans embrace moral and spiritual codes of behavior, but they also embrace moral freedom.

Can moral philosophy guide children (and adults) in their personal lives (or professional lives)? Educators are often uneasy about imposing certain values or virtues on students, but I believe that this is part of their professional responsibilities. Yet, they tend to shy away from this responsibility and make excuses why they would rather not get involved in moral education. As a group, they should set down the values and virtues they want to teach by allowing the parents and community the final measure and form of commonality.

Certain values can be agreed upon by both niche and diverse communities, even in the midst of new family structures and reconfigured racial, ethnic, and gender identities that now shape communities in which the schools serve.[1] The scope and depth of the curriculum will need to be changed at all grade levels, teachers will need to model appropriate and agreed-upon behaviors, and students will have to be held responsible for their behavior. The idea is to establish school policies and expectations for all teachers and students. The consequences of ignoring moral issues, under the guise of separation of church and state or that morality is subjective or eclectic (which it is), will mean the continual growth of school alternatives and choices that meet this need.

Right now, there is a moral vacuum in many public schools. Alfie Kohn would go one step further and argue that schooling has become extremely competitive, where students are no longer committed to helping each other, and parents have the attitude that only their child counts, and they don't want other students performing as well in school if it jeopardizes their child's chance to play five minutes more in the

---

1. Paul Shaker, "Literacies for Life," *Educational Leadership* (October 2001), pp. 26–29; Mano Singham, "The Science and Religious Wars," *Phi Delta Kappan* (February 2000), pp. 424–432.

basketball game or their chance to learn. White, middle-class parents have fought to preserve a tracking system that discriminates against and limits children of color out of honor and advanced classes.[1]

Jeannie Oakes goes one step further and maintains that middle- and upper-class parents may have nothing good to say about the likes of Pat Robertson and Rush Limbaugh, but when it comes to education issues they often sound like the Far Right. A lot of the hot issues among these people deal with direct and skill-based instruction versus abstract and discovery-based instruction, and preserving ability grouping and classes for the gifted and talented, sorting students, and providing letter grades, weighted grades, and class ranks for college admission purposes.[2] Other issues deal with suburban school desegregation, SAT preparation, school finance, school spending, and property taxes.

The purpose of schools is to educate, socialize, and help children and youth function in society. Cognitive learning and information-based skills are important, but they are not the be-all and end-all; they need to be tempered by moral constraints that recognize and distinguish between selfish behavior and proper behavior. Given the fact that most parents want what's best for their children, we need to constrain parents who send "quiet" messages to school administrators and pressure teachers, coaches, and principals so that their own kids are favored. The goal is to work for the vast majority of students, not a tiny minority whose parents are "connected" or like to complain.

**EPISODE  *B***

## Brain Research and Learning

The human brain can be compared to a shrink-wrapped Microsoft disk—a program with precise, coded instructions that evolution has written for the operation and maintenance of a person. The brain is likened to a computer, possessing about "100 billion nerve cells wired together with 100 billion interconnections."[3] There are about 1,000 different variety of *connections*, each with a special subset of instructions, which make us individually prone to exhibit love or hate, obedience or rebellion, intelligence or lack of intelligence.

Recent controversies involved in brain research include (1) the ages at which *synaptic densities* and *brain connections* peak (ranging from age 3 to puberty);

1. Alfie Kohn, "Only for My Kid," *Phi Delta Kappan* (April 1998), pp. 568–577.
2. Jeannie Oakes et al., *Becoming Good American Schools* (San Francisco: Jossey-Bass, 1999). Also see Evans Clinchy, *Creating New Schools* (New York: Teachers College Press, 2000).
3. Nicholas Wade, "The Four Letter Alphabet That Spells Life," *New York Times* (July 2, 2000), p. 4

(2) whether early visual and auditory experiences increase synaptic densities or numbers during or after puberty; (3) whether the use of language, and what type of language (formal, informal, oral, reading, TV, digital, etc.), training, and education increase the efficiency of connections; (4) whether there is a critical age period in which synapses that are developed influence how the brain will be wired and whether the synaptic densities are more susceptible to being eliminated after puberty; (5) what kinds of synapses are pruned when pruning begins, and at what rate, and to what extent does it effect behavior and memory; and (6) whether one can determine for sure whether people with greater synaptic densities or connections are more intelligent.[1]

In general, according to the research, an optimal brain requires that humans use as many synapses as possible before puberty or lose them afterward; that brain connections and intelligence have a genetic and environmental component; that connections used to a lesser extent during a critical period (some claim prior to age 3, some say prior to age 10 or 11) are more susceptible to being eliminated; and that the brain area undergoes considerable reorganization during puberty and these changes modify how people process information and behave after puberty.[2]

## Learning Styles

According to research, the way people think and learn is associated with different brain functions, such as preferences toward movement, intake (of foods or liquids), and reaction to sound and light. These brain functions result in areas of personal strengths and weaknesses, and, in some cases, different *learning styles*.[3] Yet, most teachers treat their students alike and teach as if they were all the same. In short, learning differences are not solely tied to ability factors; rather, all people have propensies that influence their thinking and guide their intellect. Just as baseball players have different batting styles, people have different ways of thinking and learning.

For example, some individuals learn best alone, and others prefer to learn in small groups and share information. Some students exhibit on-task persistence, whereas others fidget, tap, or doodle while taking notes in class or studying at home. Some learn best with "hands-on" activities and manipulative materials, and others are better able to digest abstract and verbal information. Some display preferences toward eating and drinking while reading or studying, and others need little intake. Some are "night owls"; others are "morning people," suggesting when individuals are most efficient in performing school work or studying. Many students process cognitive information

1. John T. Bruer, *The Myth of The First Three Years* (New York: Free Press, 1999); Peter R. Huttenlocher and A. S. Dabholkar, "Regional Differences in Synaptogenesis in Human Cerebral Cortex," *Journal of Comparative Neurology* (March 1997), pp. 167–178; and Rima Shore, *Rethinking the Brain: New Insights into Early Development* (New York: Families & Work Institute, 1997).

2. Ibid.

3. Douglas Carnine, "New Research on the Brain," *Phi Delta Kappan* (January 1990), pp. 71–75; Stephen Garger, "Is There a Link Between Learning and Neurophysiology?" *Educational Leadership* (October 1990), pp. 63–65.

with background music or when stretched out on the couch or even on the floor; others need a quiet place and to be seated upright behind a desk or table. Some seem to procrastinate, and need extra time to warm up, whereas others immediately jump into the assignment and perform meticulously. Hence, you need to observe your students in class and make adjustments in your instruction to suit the way each of them learns. There is no one ultimate way for all children to learn.

One of the more popular theories of the brain involves *left-right brain* or hemispheric functioning. Traditionally, teachers have taught students in a "left-brain" way—based on verbal symbolism, logic, and analytical thinking. Yet, a substantial percentage of students (40 to 75 percent, depending on the research study) are "right-brain" oriented; that is, they are more global than analytical, more deductive than inductive, less structured and more dependent on tactile or kinesthetic resources.[1]

According to the prevailing view, the right-brain thinker tends to rely on one or more of the following functions: (1) *visual,* in which the student "sees" information, doodles while listening to the teacher, draws lots of pictures and arrows when taking notes, and needs a quiet place for studying; (2) *auditory,* in which the student "hears" information, reads aloud and talks aloud when problem solving or writing, often studies with background music, and says things over and over to memorize information; and (3) *tactile* or *haptic,* in which the student learns by "moving and doing," doesn't like to listen to or read directions, prefers the floor or couch rather than a desk, needs frequent breaks when doing homework or studying, sometimes procrastinates, and takes notes in class but rarely studies them.[2]

Some caution is needed. Many students, it would appear, are equally proficient in left and right thinking, although they may have some difficulty in making switches. It is questionable whether auditory preferences always connote right-brain thinking. For example, "visual" activities, such as reading and spelling, are in part based on auditory discrimination. Auditory preferences might be more cognitive and related to verbally symbolic and logical thinking than the literature on brain theory suggests.

Related to different kinds of learning styles is the notion of different forms of intelligence, which leads to the theory of multiple intelligences (discussed later), not just intelligence based on tests of verbal and abstract patterns of thought. Similarly, there are ways of thinking and learning that are culturally bound, or, more precisely, associated with ethnic, racial, and immigrant factors. For example, cultural differences exist toward schoolwork; teacher authority; on-task effort versus social interaction; time orientation (coming early or late to class or meetings, and meeting deadlines); present versus future orientation; the value of hard work and studying; abstract versus visual, auditory, or tactile processing; physical space (perceiving the teacher as

1. John Abbott and Terence Ryan, "Constructing Knowledge, Reconstructing Schooling," *Educational Leadership* (November 1999), pp. 66–69; Laura Ellison and Betty Rothenberger, "The Multiple Ways of Teaching and Learning," *Educational Leadership* (September 1999), pp. 54–57.

2. Scott Baron, "Chaos, Self-Organization, and Psychology," *American Psychologist* (January 1994), pp. 5–14; Michael J. Bina, "Schools for the Visually Disabled," *Educational Leadership* (March 1999), pp. 78–82.

"pushy," when in fact the intent is to foster comfortable interpersonal space or personal relations); touching and kissing in public; role expectations and behavior toward people based on age, gender, job status, and family interactions; group and individual learning situations; and a host of other culturally laden values and behaviors that influence performance in school and how people act.

In short, learning styles differ from culture to culture, as well as among individual students, and possibly also on the basis of urban-suburban-rural patterns. Furthermore, many learning modalities are not recognized in classrooms, unless schools and teachers are sensitive to and respect diversity. Obviously, teachers need to adapt their instruction to coincide with the learning styles of their students, to capitalize on the students' strengths or preferences, and to accommodate all students. In a classroom of 25 or 30 students, the teacher has the daunting task of recognizing individual and group differences based on ability, needs, and interests, as well as cognitive processing and learning styles.

## Memory and Brain Expansion

"Who am I?" The question is either the start of a provocative thriller story, an existentialist inquiry, a plot in an artsy-craftsy movie, or a reason to purchase a book on memory exercises or a ticket to a memory fitness class to help our parents and grandparents remember where they left the car in the parking lot. But the appealing notion that our individuality is bound up in our memory runs up against the idea that memory is not reliable and it fades as we age.

As one psychologist puts it, what we commonly refer to as memory are "confabulations, artificial constructions of our own design built around . . . retained experience, which we attempt to make live again by influences of imagination."[1] Such a definition leads to all kinds of theories about memory loss, memory boosting, memory manipulation, and memory and imagination. It can lead to the theater of the absurd, a semantic cul-de-sac, and a postmodern conversation: "What?" to which the answer is: "This is what." And "What is this?" "This is what is." "Which is?" "What you want it to be." So a fork can temporarily be a knife; good teaching can be defined as a stroll in the park; and for an aspiring art student one red dot on a large white canvas or a series of Campbell soup cans can be construed as the ultimate in modern art.

Now, if you think this is a little silly, absurd, or mystical, there is always *Yogacara*, a mind-only school, in which you can find enlightenment and hear sermons that are reflected and rooted in Buddhism, the holiness of the Dali Lama, and ancient Chinese philosophy, that separates the self and the world and dates back a thousand years before Descartes's rationalism.[2] That kind of "trip" would certainly add to the conversations, stories, metaphors, and voices of the postmodernists; it might eventually allow participants (not only monks and the faithful) to become ferociously brainy and

1. David Wilson, quote in "When Memory Fails," *Economist* (November 25, 2000), p. 105.
2. Richard Bernstein, *Ultimate Journey: Retracking the Ancient Buddhist Monk* (New York: Knopf, 2001).

understand "ultimate reality." Am I talking about the meaning of life? No. I am playing with some of the cerebral ideas of revisionist thinkers who complicate rational thought and criticize traditional theories and research methods as western, white, male oriented, and technocratic, and who enjoy poking fun of scientific principles that encourage predictability and empirical answers to questions. I am providing them with a new idea of which way to go—basically to the East—and analyze some mountaintop view in Nepal or Tibet, or to contemplate the complexities of Buddhist truth or the Odyssey of life through the eyes of "The Great Tang," who lived a monk's life in the seventh century.

Reading about the brain or mind is obviously confusing. We are told that about one trillion neurons are ready to connect in a newborn's brain, and how "the wiring" takes place will depend on the baby's early experiences.[1] It is the experiences of childhood that determine what neurons are used and how they interconnect in the brain; the connections subsequently determine the potential and limits of cognitive capacity and other domains of learning such as social, moral, and psychomotor. The strategy for optimal brain development is to stimulate and use as many synapses and circuits as possible during childhood that correspond with traditional behaviorists and environmental theorists.

In a somewhat similar viewpoint, two psychologists declare that the brain consists of a "quadrillion connections supported by trillions of nerve fibers," its branching neurons and "protoplasmic kisses, [whereby a message] vaults across a sliver of space called a synaptic cleft and into the outstretched arm of another neuron."[2] In simple terms, we seek all kinds of memory aids, from tests and files to training methods and drugs, with the hope that we will come up with a smart pill for the brain. Right now, however, no imagery, no training method, no drug can save us from brain plaque and neurofibrillary tangles. According to researchers, plaques are the "litter" and "rubble" that clog our memory banks,[3] just like plaque forms around our teeth and arteries and leads to gum disease and heart problems. The popular remedy among Indian and Chinese scholars is to sip on warm water to clean out your system of all plaque. And, if you don't believe in warm water (with or without lemon), special chemical drugs, or genetic engineering, there is always the potential for a computer chip. In 10 to 20 years, we should have "smarter brains, happier brains, calmer brains, brains that are less forgetful" and less vulnerable to age, disease, and damage.[4]

There is no question that we will soon have drugs to enhance cognition, to compliment the many psychoactive and mood-changing drugs we already have on the

---

1. John I. Bruer, "Neural Connections: Some You Use, Some You Lose," *Phi Delta Kappan* (December 1999), pp. 264–277; B. Kanttrowitz, "Off to a Good Start," *Newsweek*, Special Edition (Spring 1997), p. 7; and Ronald Kulak, *Inside the Brain* (Kansas City, MO: McMeel Publishers, 1996).

2. Rudolph E. Tanzi and Ann B. Parson, *Decoding Darkness: The Search for Genetic Causes of Alzheimer's Disease* (New York: Perseus Publishers, 2000).

3. Ibid.

4. Erica Goode, "Rx for Brain Makeovers," *New York Times* (January 1, 2000), Sect. E, p. 27.

marketplace. We already have treatments for depression, schizophrenia, tangled nerves, and hyperactivity; in fact, we have raised a whole generation of children on Ritalin, which makes it easier for teachers and counselors to modify behavior and control students. We are on the verge of treating Alzheimer's disease and enhancing memory. Soon, we will be shaping and expanding intelligence, repairing and improving brain networks, and possibly using computers for a complete brain overhaul. The availability of all these new chemicals (and computer chips) will pose difficult ethical questions concerning their use by whom and for whom.

One might argue there is nothing wrong in increasing intelligence for kids who have trouble learning or eliminating from their a memory painful or emotional experience such as rape or the death of a parent. But equally important is, unless you believe in Nazi eugenics, human beings must come to terms with loss and emotional injury as part of growth and development. The best we can all agree on is the basic need for brains, what the scarecrow in *The Wizard of Oz* wanted. We can also agree on some form of memory improvement through conventional methods such as a two-hour course or reading 10 tips on brain exercises in a magazine or book, as well as some recognition that there are different forms of brain development, intelligence, and styles of learning.

## DNA, Genes, and the Brain Pool

When Watson and Crick discovered the mysteries of DNA some 50 years ago, the understanding of inheritance was advanced. As Crick stated, "DNA makes RNA, RNA makes protein and proteins make us." Until recently, we could only theorize about the process. Now, we have the knowledge to direct this process. Designer babies are set to follow in the wake of genetically modified crops, which promise better nutrition or environmental contamination, depending on one's politics and view of Green Peace. There is no doubt, however, that gene research has the capacity to change our lives, to extend it, and to improve our intelligence.

A dissenting view is expressed by Evelyn Fox Keller, who argues that genes no longer shape destiny but behave as second-tier players in the game of life. DNA is bequeathed from one generation to the next, and, except for mutations, explain our potential for human growth and development, including cognitive, social, moral, and psychological learning. But the exact coping process from parents to child stems from associated proteins that perform "proofreading" tasks. Without RNA and related proteins, the error rate that reflect in mutations would jump from one in 10 billion to one in 100.[1]

Although mutations are deleterious, occasionally they increase survival of species or populations within a particular animal grouping sequence and become the basis of adaptation by natural selection. Under stressful or hazardous conditions, DNA has evolved to create genetic variability in physical characteristics. The controversial aspect of the equation is whether it also leads to genetic variability in cognitive

1. Evelyn Fox Keller, *The Century of the Gene* (Cambridge, MA: Harvard University Press, 2001).

characteristics. If so, this leads us to the hereditarian or genetic school of thought, which has been squashed since the 1950s by the environmental school. The demise of hereditarian thinking coincides with the defeat of Nazism and the decline of colonialism around the world; it also coincides with the increased popularity of Piagetian and developmental theories of growth, followed by the compensatory education movement based on environmental theory and research.

## Culture, Geography, and "Smart" Thinking

On a global, much more theoretical level, growth and prosperity among cultures and civilizations can be explained by environment, or by the limits of geographical isolation. Given a make-believe world in which every individual has identical genetic potential, there would still be large differences in education, skills, and related occupations and income among people because of demographic differences, which, over centuries, shape human behavior and attitudes.

For Thomas Sowell, nothing so much conflicts with desire for equality as geography; it is the physical setting—reflected by large bodies of water, deserts, mountains, forests—in which civilizations, nations, races, and ethnic groups have evolved and in turn produced different cultures. Put simply, the people of the Himalayas have not had equal opportunity to acquire sea-faring skills, and the Eskimos did not have equal opportunity to learn how to farm or grow oranges. Too often, the influence of geography is assessed in terms of natural resources that directly influence national wealth. But geography also influences cultural differences by either expanding or limiting the universe of ideas and inventions available to different people.[1]

When geography isolates people—say by mountains, a desert, or a small island—the people have limited contact with the outside world; so, subsequently, there is technological and innovative advancement. While the rest of the world trades skills, ideas, and values from a larger cultural pool, isolated people are limited by their own resources and what knowledge they have developed by themselves. Very few advances come from isolated cultures, and those that do are usually modified and improved on by people who have learned to assimilate and adopt new ideas from other cultures.

The British, French, Portuguese, and Spaniards were tiny countries, compared to China and India, but the Europeans traveled the navigable waterways of their continent as well as the Atlantic. They came in contact with many countries and civilizations, including South America, Egypt, Turkey, India, China, and Japan—and thus gained from their knowledge. But the older civilizations did not draw from the Europeans or from each other and eventually those great civilizations (which were once more advanced, but isolated) were overtaken and conquered by the smaller countries that had expanded their knowledge base. Once Japan broke from its isolation, the country rose to one of today's economic powers. Similarly, the rise of the United States—in particular, its technology, innovations, and economic advances—is based on the history of immigrants, people coming from all parts of the world and ex-

---

1. Thomas Sowell, *Conquests and Cultures: An International History* (New York: Basic Books, 1998); Sowell, "Race, Culture and Equality," *Forbes* (October 5, 1998), pp. 144–149.

changing knowledge and ideas. It is this constant flow of different people from around the globe that helps create an American entrepreneur spirit and sense of innovation and creativity not enjoyed in more static, less dynamic countries.

New knowledge in the United States doubles about every 15 or 20 years. In many third-world countries, mules and horses are the main mode of transportation, and the local economy is picking berries, dragging banana trees to market, or cleaning out goat intestines that can be turned into leather. This is the real rural China, India, and Pakistan[1]—possibly representative of two-thirds of the world, a world that American students and teachers cannot fathom. This is not to say that these type countries don't have a corporate mentality, and a class of people who are both old-fashioned industrialists and a new brand of technocrats who are versed in computer software, media, and other high-tech and electronic ventures. What is less clear is the extent to which this new economic and human capital trickles down to the mass who live in poverty—both in the countryside, far from the "new economy" that deals with the exchange of knowledge and ideas, and in urban squalor, where old and new knowledge, ideas, and values collide. In third-world cities, East meets West and low-tech meets high-tech—causing a great cultural rift and the makings of revolution.

For 2,000 years, before the invention of railroads, trucks, and airplanes, water was the key for traveling and exploring. Up to the 1850s, it was faster and cheaper to travel by water from San Francisco to China than over land from San Francisco to Chicago. The Europeans, since the Viking era, understood that geographical isolation could be overcome by the sea or ocean. Given their capitalistic and religious zeal, and attitudes of superiority, they went out and traded with and colonialized other peoples and other cultures; subsequently, they made industrial and technological advances by adopting and modifying the ideas of other civilizations.

Anyone familiar with New York City, Chicago, or Los Angeles understands that these cities house people from a vast assortment of countries with different knowledge, ideas, and values. Far from "celebrating" their particular identities, most U.S. urban dwellers have contact with different people and become more "hip," "sophisticated," or "cosmopolitan" than their nonurban counterparts. Even kids who come from the backwaters of the world, say from the rice paddies of Vietnam or the mountains of Montenegro, quickly become enculturated into the American environment, especially if they settle in large cities and they step out of their parents' cultural and historical isolation. The computer and cell phone may increase our ability to communicate with people from around the world, but there is still limitation to exposure of new thoughts without actual contact with different people. In short, our thinking is shaped not only by our home environment and community but also by diverse people we come in contact with who reshape and expand our knowledge, ideas, and values. Those who come in contact with people from around the world assimilate more information than those who remain isolated in their urban neighborhoods, rural villages, and islands.

1. By Gucharan Das, *India Unbound* (New York: Knopf, 2001); Ma Jian, *Red Dust: A Path Through China* (New York: Pantheon, 2001); and Peter Maas, "Emroz Khan is Having a Bad Day," *New York Times Magazine,* October 21, 2001, pp. 48–51.

## Multiple Intelligences

Howard Gardner argues for a theory of *multiple intelligences* and contends that there are different mental operations associated with intelligence. But Gardner feels the search for empirically grounded structures or components of intelligence may be misleading, since it avoids many roles and skills valued by human cultures. He maintains that there are many different types of intelligence and that too often (at least in a technological society) we emphasize only verbal or linguistic factors. He outlines eight types of intelligence:

1. *Linguistic intelligence.* This ability is reflected in the effective use of language and literacy forms. For the oral language, this skill may be demonstrated by actors, politicians, newscasters, and public speakers. For the written language, writers of literary works, poets, journalists, playwrights, and editors would display this intelligence.

2. *Logical-mathematical intelligence.* This intelligence has to do with the ability to use numbers and arithmetic operations extremely well, such as that exhibited by mathematicians, statisticians, and accountants. These people also have the ability to reason, hypothesize, and theorize logically, such as that seen in scientists and engineers, and to engage in propositions and abstractions in thinking.

3. *Spatial intelligence.* This type of thinking is the capacity to deal with and reconstruct the experimental, nonverbal world to a high degree of successful performance. This would be a visual-spatial thinker negotiating or reconstructing the visible world, such as a painter, inventor, sculptor, architect, and designer. These people also have the capacity to pictorially or graphically represent visual/spatial ideas, and to orient themselves spatially, as would be the case with pilots, sailors, architects, builders, and chess players.

4. *Bodily-kinesthetic intelligence.* This ability is the craft of using one's persona—one's whole bodily self—to handle objects and excel at physical dexterity. This skill is exemplified in people such as dancers, athletes, mimes, surgeons, and artisans. These people use their bodies and physical dexterity to express ideas and feelings and can use their hands to create, transform, and manipulate objects and tools.

5. *Musical intelligence.* This ability is bestowed on those who have a strong sensitivity to such aspects as pitch, melody, rhythm, and tone of a musical piece. These people may be able to discriminate, create, and transform using musical forms or "language," such as a composer, music critic, and avid listener of music.

6. *Interpersonal intelligence.* This type of thinking is strongly manifested in those who work with people. Individuals with this capacity understand and interact well with others, such as would be in the case for teachers, ministers, counselors, social workers, and (hopefully) politicians. These people are sensitive to the feelings and needs of others, and respond well to verbal cues and gesture and facial expressions.

7. *Intrapersonal intelligence.* People with this ability have strong self-knowledge and perceptions of themselves so that they can skillfully plan and direct their own

lives. They know their strengths and weaknesses, their interests and motivations. People with strong intrapersonal intelligence might pursue such disciplines as theology, psychology, and philosophy, as well as the entertainment industry.

**8.** *Naturalistic intelligence.* The human ability to discriminate features among living things in the plant and animal kingdom and the ability to be sensitive to other conditions (such as stars, cloud formations, and types of vegetation) of the natural world are the capacities that make up this thinking. Such abilities were highly valued in the past, when humans were hunters, gatherers, and farmers. The same type of thinking is central for the natural scientist, biologist, botanist, as well as to the outdoor adventurist who climbs mountains, backpacks for weeks, hunts for bears in remote areas, sails or sky-dives in highly dangerous places with drinking water and flare guns (prepared for an emergency).

Guilford's Influence on Gardner    What Gardner has to say is not new, but rooted in the work of J. P. Guilford, who, in the 1950s and 1960s, formulated a theory of intelligence around a three-dimensional model called the *structure of intellect*. It consisted of six *products* (units, classes, relations, systems, transformations, and implications), five *operations* (knowledge, memory, divergent thinking, convergent thinking, and evaluation), and four *contents* (figured, symbolic, semantic, and behavioral).[1]

The three dimensions, produced a 6 × 5 × 4 model: six products, five operations, and four contents, yielding 120 cells of distinct mental abilities. By 1985, Guilford and his doctoral students had recognized and separated more than 100 abilities by factor analysis of standardized achievement and aptitude tests. Guilford concluded that the remaining cells indicated uncovered mental abilities. It is possible, however, that cognitive tests do not measure other mental operations or that such abilities do not exist.

The Guilford model is highly abstract and theoretical and involves administering and grading many extra tests. But rather than a single index of IQ (or of aptitude), we are required to recognize and report several scores. Thus, the theoretical issues surrounding intelligence and cognitive operations take on added complexity, much more than Gardner's theory of intelligence or Binet's and Weschler's idea of reporting one IQ score.

The point is, the idea of multiple intelligences stems from J. P. Guilford's work who, in turn, formulated his theory to challenge the idea of Charles Spearman's *factor of intelligence*—that is, intelligence is composed of a general factor *g*, underlying all mental functions, and a multitude of *s* factors, each related to a specific task.[2] To be smart meant to have lots of *g*, since it was an umbrella factor permeating all mental operations. Whereas Gardner feels the search for empirically grounded components of intelligence may be misleading, and delineates fewer components (eight in broad areas of life), Guilford maintains the criteria for intelligence can be quantified and consists of many (120) mental operations, or *cognitive processes*. The idea of 120

1.  J. P. Guilford, *The Nature of Human Intelligence* (New York: McGraw-Hill, 1967).
2.  Charles E. Spearman, *The Abilities of Man* (New York: Macmillan, 1927).

different mental operations confounds teachers, and thus remains a theoretical construct. Gardner is more popular with school people because his discussion avoids statistics and is more positive and democratic. He stretches the notion of what is important for human growth and development—more than cognition—fitting the progressive idea of the whole child, expanding the child's full human potential, opening academic and career doors, and encouraging low achievers who might otherwise be shunted aside by schools.

Beyond Gardner   Gardner's ideas provide a place in the school curriculum not only for the 3 Rs and academic core subjects but also for music, art, dance, drama, sports, and even social skills (winning friends, influencing people, negotiating, etc.). The latter bodies of knowledge and aptitudes have a place in our "other-directed" society and foster social and economic achievement and success in adulthood, including corporate America, the local and civic community, and the entertainment, artistic, and sports world. Academic merit is not the only avenue for social and economic mobility—which is a highly important factor in a democratic society that tries to foster excellence in many endeavors and provides multiple options and several chances for people to succeed. In a society that requires all the trains to run on time, academics is prized. Now, it's kind of scary, if in such a society, you can't find anyone at the train station who is physically impaired, learning disabled, or just plain slow in thinking or moving about. Excellence has been stretched beyond the pale of reason.

Subscribing to Gardner's ideas means not only being a cognitivist but also a *positive cognitivist,* if I may coin a new term. It means there are many opportunities and chances in life. Someone who can paint, dance, sing, act, or accurately hit a golfball 250 yards can rise to the ranks of a master. If encouraged and given a chance, and if many talents are recognized, then many of our potential school dropouts would not drop out. For those who do, this country allows second, third, and fourth chances to go to school and college. In the same vein, it allows individuals and companies to go bankrupt several times with minimal or no penalties—to try again and then again. There is no debtors' prison in the United States, and fingers and toes are not cut off by government officials, as in many other countries, for failing to pay a debt.

Those in charge of planning and implementing the curriculum are faced with the task of expanding their vision beyond intellectual and academic pursuits without creating "soft" subjects or a "watered-down curriculum." Teachers must nurture all types of talents and all types of excellence that contribute to the worth of the individual and society. They must be guided by reason and balance and consider the versatility of children and youth. They must also be aware of students' multiple strengths and abilities, and their multiple ways of thinking and learning. Indeed, there are many ways of reaching Rome and finding the end of the rainbow; fixating on one method is restrictive, myopic, and/or all-authoritarian.

What Gardner says has little to do with the traditional concept of intelligence; rather, what he says has more to do with aptitude and talent. In the final analysis, intelligence is reflected in the ability to function effectively in one's environment, to support oneself and loved ones, and to prosper and live a full life. In a hunting, fishing, or farming society, verbal skills play a minor role, and the importance of "muscle" power and "naturalistic intelligence" is noted. In a farming society, what counts is the ability to plow the soil and plant, not to read Plato or Kant. Given a technological and information society, however, most jobs and daily routines have a verbal and/or mathematical component needed to function effectively. Less than one out of 100,000 Americans can support themselves as baseball or basketball players, country western singers, artists, and dancers. People with these special abilities are few in number. Although they should be encouraged as children to maximize their potential in these special areas, like it or not, the vast majority of children and adults need to be schooled in cognitive bodies of knowledge that deal with verbal and numerical symbols. Why? Because present society requires those skills, and the vast number of employers reward those skills.

In a more positive and liberal vein, too often teachers do not recognize the skills and achievements associated with noncognitive domains—at the expense of low achievers who usually have difficulty in cognitive areas. Teachers dismiss too many students who are below average in reading or writing, overlooking the fact that many of them can develop other noncognitive areas of expertise. Indeed, there are many forms of learning and excellence. A viable society needs to reward both its scholars and bricklayers, its engineers and carpenters, and its verbal-spatial learners as well as its kinesthetic learners and socially skilled learners. Emphasis in schools on one or two preferred aptitudes or talents results in rejecting many potentially creative and gifted children—and limits the nation's future human capital.

**Beyond Intelligence: Cloning**  Few people today complain about in vitro fertilization, which caused quite a stir some 25 years ago. Few people would also complain about genetic engineering, DNA medicines, and organ transplants to fight human disease or extend life. Although Americans have great faith in science, they also have come to fear it, partially because of history and partially because of the movies and media. In particular, we have become suspect of the deranged or diabolic scientist running amuck, a Faustian search for knowledge (at the expense of spiritual or moral values), or a Frankenstein or Dr. Strangelove outcome of knowledge. Nazi experiments in death camps, Hiroshima, and now the nuclear bomb club and threat of war among its members, and fears of chemical, biological, and radioactive warfare add to the potential evil use of science. Indeed, scientists can be bought and sold by political leaders and political fanatics all day and night, just like police officers, politicians, and judges can be bought.

Should human tissues or body parts be used to save someone's life? Should smart babies be cloned? Should the sperm cells of Bill Gates, Ted Turner, Michael Jordan, or Papavochi be packaged and frozen, then used to generate human embryos—and on what scale? Once? Ten times? One hundred times? Or should we go the route of "the Andromeda strain"? Today, people and politicians are concerned with "embryo farms" and the commercialization of body parts, as well as the mad scientist out of control.[1] All these concerns have led to a U.S. ban on cloning and stem-cell research.

1. Sheryl Gay Stolberg, "It's Alive! It's Alive," *New York Times* (May 5, 2002), Sect. 4, p. 16.

Recombinant (genetic combinations, new combinations of genes in progeny that did not occur in the parents) DNA has not been banned. The field of biotechnology remains largely intact, and work on the human body and mind continues in ways that have the possibility of altering who we are and how we think. The concept of multiple intelligence now can be expanded to a much larger idea. With mood and memory drugs, gene splicing and gene engineering, we can expand our abilities to learn as well as the concept of gifted and talented to include a multiple range of abilities and aptitudes. There is no limit to a potential new top range of ability. In 10 to 15 years, students should be beginning education at levels more typical of students now several years older.

## Learning How to Learn

In this text, the concept of learning differs from the notion that the learner merely remains passive, reacts to stimuli, and waits for some reward. Here, the learner is regarded as active and able to monitor and control cognitive activities. He or she possesses new information through assimilation and integration with previous information. Without this integration, new information is lost to memory, and task performance dependent on the information is unsuccessful.[1] Learning new information results in modification of long-term memory. The responsibility for engaging in learning—including control, direction, and focus—belongs to the individual.

Cognitive structures are searched when students want to identify, categorize, and process new information. If the cognitive structures are disorganized, unclear, or not fully developed (for the person's age), then new information will not be clearly identified, categorized, and assimilated. On the other hand, new learning based on previous learning should be meaningful to students—in context with prior knowledge and real-life experiences, regardless of whether the students are low or high achieving.

High-achieving students have a more expanded prior knowledge base in terms of *in-depth knowledge* and *multiple forms of knowledge* than low-achieving students.[2] This mature knowledge base permits learners to integrate important and/or complex information into existing cognitive structures. Similarly, those students who are capable of learning on their own are better able to (1) *narrow* and place information into preexisting categories, (2) *sharpen* or distinguish prior information from new information to avoid confusion or overlap, (3) *tolerate* or deal with ambiguous and unclear information without getting frustrated, and (4) *assimilate* existing schemata to interpret problematic situations.[3]

1. John Flavell, *Cognitive Development*, 2nd ed. (Englewood Cliffs, NJ: Prentice-Hall, 1985); Robert Glaser, *Advances in Instructional Psychology*, vol. 4 (Hillsdale, NJ: Erlbaum, 1993).

2. Paul Cobb and Janet Bowers, "Cognitive and Situated Learning Perspectives in Theory and Practice," *Educational Researcher* (March 1999), pp. 4–15; Gaea Leinhardt, "What Research on Learning Tells Us About Teaching," *Educational Leadership* (April 1992), pp. 20–25.

3. John R. Anderson et al., "Perspectives on Learning, Thinking, and Activity," *Educational Researcher* (May 2000), pp. 11–13; Richard S. Prawat, "The Value of Ideas," *Educational Researcher* (August–September 1993), pp. 5–16.

A cognitive framework proposed by Weinstein and Mayer consists of eight comprehension strategies:

1.  *Basic rehearsal strategies.*  The ability to remember names or words and the order of things.
2.  *Complex rehearsal strategies.*  Making appropriate choices or selections (such as knowing what to copy when the teacher explains something or what to underline or outline while reading).
3.  *Basic elaboration strategies.*  Relating two or more items (such as nouns and verbs).
4.  *Complex elaboration strategies.*  Analyzing or synthesizing new information with old information.
5.  *Basic organizational strategies.*  Categorizing, grouping, or ordering new information.
6.  *Complex organizational strategies.*  Putting information in hierarchical arrangements (such as in outlining notes or homework).
7.  *Comprehension monitoring.*  Checking progress, recognizing when one is on the proper track or confused, or right or wrong.
8.  *Affective strategies.*  Being relaxed yet alert and attentive during a test situation and when studying.[1]

All of these learning skills combined represent knowledge about and control over cognitive processes—what some educators refer to as *metacognition.* The specific strategies deal with the identification, categorization, and integration of information.

Of all the specific strategies discussed, *comprehension monitoring* is often considered the most important. This skill permits a student to monitor, modify, and direct (and redirect) his or her cognitive activities. The student remains focused on the task, is aware of whether he or she is getting closer to or farther away from an answer, and knows when to choose alternative methods to arrive at the answer.[2] A student with good comprehension monitoring has developed self-correcting cognition processes, including how to determine what part of the problem needs further clarification, how to relate parts of a problem to one another, and how to search out information to solve the problem. In short, the student is able to identify what has to be done, focus attention, cope with errors, and make modifications in steps to work out a solution—all without losing control, getting frustrated, or giving up.

*Learning-to-learn skills* are basic thinking skills that are used in all content areas. Although some of these learning skills are generic and can be taught solely as

1.  Claire E. Weinstein and Richard E. Mayer, "The Teaching of Learning Strategies," in M. C. Wittrock, ed., *Handbook of Research on Teaching,* 3rd ed. (New York: Macmillan, 1986), pp. 315–327.

2.  John R. Anderson, "Problem Solving and Learning," *American Psychologist* (January 1993), pp. 35–44; Deanna Kuhn, "A Developmental Model of Critical Thinking," *Education Researcher* (March 1999), pp. 16–25. Also see Cathy Collins Block and Michael Pressley, *Comprehension Instruction* (New York: Guilford, 2002).

general strategies, without reference to content, it is impossible to avoid a certain amount of subject matter,[1] especially in the upper (secondary) grades. This assumption seems to make sense—for example, a good mathematical learner may not be as good in English or history. That does not mean there is no *transfer* of learning skills from one subject to another; rather, it is likely just *less* transfer. Bruner may have been right: Different disciplines have their own principles, concepts, and research methods that are distinct from other disciplines. Or, as Lauren Resnick claimed, what is learned in one area is not easily transferable to another area of learning because it is content based.[2]

Yet another school believes generic learning skills can be taught to most students and transferred across subjects. Most of such learning skills can be incorporated into regular classroom activities or taught in a special course that incorporates cognitive processes that cut across subjects. Separate programs designed to teach thinking include Adler's Padeia Program, Feuerestein's Instrumental Enrichment, Lipham's Philosophy for Children (discussed later in greater detail), and Pogrow's Higher-Order Thinking Skills (HOTS). These special thinking programs and others are designed to make all students independent learners in all subjects.[3] The training should begin early in the elementary grades, say around the third or fourth grade. It should continue thereafter with additional time devoted to these thinking skills, perhaps twice the allotted time by the sixth or seventh grade, when students must understand and organize increasing amounts of subject-related information. Learning skills cannot be postponed until high school, when the job of learning how to learn has become more difficult because of increasing academic deficiencies.

## Critical Thinking

One of the most important things a teacher can do in the classroom, regardless of subject or grade level, is to make students aware of their own metacognition processes— to examine what they are thinking about, to make distinctions and comparisons, to see errors in what they are thinking about and how they are thinking about it, and to make self-corrections. It is now believed that *critical thinking* is a form of intelligence that can be taught. The leading proponents of this school are Matthew Lipman, Robert Sternberg, and Robert Ennis. Lipman's program was originally designed for elementary school grades but is applicable to all grades. He sought to develop the ability to use (1) concepts, (2) generalizations, (3) cause-effect relationships, (4) logical

1. Heidi G. Andrade, "Using Rubrics to Promote Thinking and Learning," *Educational Leadership* (February 2000), pp. 13–19; Michael Crawford and Mary Witte, "Strategies for Mathematics: Teaching in Context," *Educational Leadership* (November 1999), pp. 34–49.

2. Lauren Resnick, *Education and Learning to Think* (Washington, DC: National Academy Press, 1987).

3. Allan C. Ornstein and Thomas J. Lasley, *Strategies for Effective Teaching,* 3rd ed. (Boston: McGraw-Hill, 2000).

inferences, (5) consistencies and contradictions, (6) analogies, (7) part-whole and whole-part connections, (8) problem formulations, (9) reversibility of logical statements, and (10) applications of principles to real-life situations.[1]

In Lipman's program for teaching critical thinking, children spend a considerable portion of their time thinking about ways in which effective thinking differs from ineffective thinking. After reading a series of stories, children engage in classroom discussions and exercises that encourage them to adopt the thinking process depicted in the stories.[2] Lipman's assumptions are that children are by nature interested in such philosophical issues as truth, fairness, and personal identity, and that children can and should learn to explore alternatives to their own viewpoints, to consider evidence, to make distinctions, and to draw conclusions.

Lipham's emphasis on reading and discussing philosophical/moral issues coincide with the objectives and procedures of the *Junior Great Books Program* for all grade levels (starting in the first grade), originally developed in the 1930s and continuously refined and revised. The emphasis is on good literature, whereby teachers are trained in teaching specific *reading* strategies, encouraging students to *think* about and *discuss ideas,* how to *listen* for different ideas and *build on* their own and others' ideas, how to reason and *use evidence,* and how to *write* persuasively and creatively. Although the program is based in Chicago, trainers are available for school districts across the country.

Lipman also distinguishes between *ordinary thinking* and *critical thinking.* Ordinary thinking is simple and lacks standards; critical thinking is more complex and is based on standards of objectivity, utility, and consistency. He wants teachers to help students change (1) from guessing to estimating, (2) from preferring to evaluating, (3) from grouping to classifying, (4) from believing to assuming, (5) from inferring to inferring logically, (6) from associating concepts to grasping principles, (7) from noting relationships to noting relationships among relationships, (8) from supposing to hypothesizing, (9) from offering opinions without reasons to offering opinions with reasons, and (10) from making judgments without criteria to making judgments with criteria.[3]

Robert Sternberg seeks to foster many of the same skills, but in a different way. He points to three categories or components of critical thinking: (1) *meta-components,* high-order mental processes used to plan, monitor, and evaluate what the individual is doing; (2) *performance components,* the actual steps the individual takes; and

1. Matthew Lipman, "The Culturation of Reasoning Through Philosophy," *Educational Leadership* (September 1984), pp. 54–56.

2. Matthew Lipman et al., *Philosophy for Children,* 3rd ed. (Philadelphia: Temple University Press, 1990); Lipman, *Philosophy Goes to School* (Philadelphia: Temple University Press, 1988).

3. Matthew Lipman, *Thinking in Education* (New York: Cambridge University Press, 1991).

(3) *knowledge-acquisition components,* processes used to relate old material to new material and to apply new material.[1]

Elsewhere, Sternberg distinguishes between creative, intelligent, and ordinary thinking. *Creative thinking* emphasizes taking risks, the courage of one's convictions and beliefs, and deep-seated personal resources need to believe in oneself. *Intelligent thinking* is the ability to define and refine problems, to think insightfully, and to discard irrelevant information and zero in on relevant information. *Ordinary thinking* relies on known knowledge and can use this knowledge for basic tasks and highly structured solutions and problems; the person is able to meet minimum standards and general requirements.[2]

Robert Ennis identifies 13 attributes of critical thinkers. They tend to (1) be open-minded, (2) take a position (or change position) when the evidence calls for it, (3) take into account the entire situation, (4) seek information, (5) seek precision in information, (6) deal in an orderly manner with parts of a complex whole, (7) look for options, (8) search for reasons, (9) seek a clear statement of the issue, (10) keep the original problem in mind, (11) use credible sources, (12) focus on the point, and (13) be sensitive to the feelings and knowledge level of others[3] (see Figure 3.1).

## Promises and Pitfalls of Critical Thinking

In general, teachers must ask students a great many questions; require students to analyze, apply, and evaluate information; take opposing sides to tease and test students; and require them to support their answers or conclusions. Supplementary materials, beyond the workbook and textbook, will be needed; it is recommended that teachers work together to develop such materials. By varying instructional activities, ensuring that groups are heterogeneous in abilities and skills, distributing relevant materials, giving instruction in constructing logical arguments, and encouraging students to rely on evidence, teachers can help students learn to think critically in a variety of academic situations.

According to researchers, "Giving children a sense of ownership in their classroom can lead to the kind of open and cooperative learning environment that most teachers dream about." This kind of classroom climate is important for developing "confident, active" learners who learn to rely "on their own inner resources."[4] Children

1. Robert J. Sternberg, "How Can We Teach Intelligence?" *Educational Leadership* (September 1984), pp. 38–48; Sternberg, "Practical Intelligence for Success in School," *Educational Leadership* (September 1990), pp. 35–39.

2. Robert Sternberg and Todd I. Lubart, "Creating Creative Minds," in A. C. Ornstein and L. S. Behar-Hornstein, eds., *Contemporary Issues in Curriculum,* 2nd ed. (Boston: Allyn and Bacon, 1999), pp. 153–162; Robert Sternberg, *Understanding and Teaching the Intuitive Mind* (Mahwah, NJ: Erlbaum, 2001).

3. Robert H. Ennis, "A Logical Basis for Measuring Critical Thinking Skills," *Educational Leadership* (October 1985), pp. 44–48; Ennis, "Critical Thinking and Subject Specificity," *Educational Researcher* (April 1989), pp. 4–10; and Ennis, "Critical Thinking Assessment," *Theory Into Practice* (Summer 1993), pp. 179–186.

4. Michelle G. Zachlod, "Room to Grow," *Educational Leadership* (September 1996), pp. 50–51.

---

## FIGURE 3. 1
### Teaching Learning/Critical Thinking Skills

---

I. **Defining and clarifying**

1. Identifying conclusions
2. Identifying stated reasons
3. Identifying unstated reasons
4. Seeing similarities and differences
5. Identifying and handling irrelevance
6. Summarizing

II. **Asking appropriate questions to clarify or challenge**

1. Why?
2. What is the main point?
3. What does this mean?
4. What is an example?
5. What is not an example?
6. How does this apply to the case?
7. What difference does it make?
8. What are the facts?
9. Is this what is being said?
10. What more is to be said?

III. **Judging the credibility of a source**

1. Expertise
2. Lack of conflict of interest
3. Agreement among sources
4. Reputation
5. Use of established procedures
6. Known risk to reputation
7. Ability to give reasons
8. Careful habits

IV. **Solving problems and drawing conclusions**

1. Deducing and judging validity
2. Inducing and judging conclusions
3. Predicting probably consequences

---

*Sources:* Adapted from Robert H. Ennis, "A Logical Basis for Measuring Critical Thinking Skills," *Educational Leadership* (October 1985), pp. 44–48; Ennis, "A Taxonomy of Critical Thinking Dispositions and Abilities," in J. Baron and R. J. Sternberg, eds., *Teaching Thinking Skills: Theory and Practice* (New York: Freeman, 1987), pp. 9–26; and Ennis, *Critical Thinking* (Upper Saddle River: NJ: Prentice-Hall, 1996).

must learn to listen to each other, to respect each others' conversations, and thoughtfully respond to what their classmates have to say; there must be room to think, to grow, and to build genuine concern and appreciation for others.

Similarly, David and Roger Johnson point out that students must learn to respect and value one another so they can learn from each other. Students must feel secure enough to challenge each other's ideas and reasoning, and they must be encouraged to engage in controversial discussions, debates, problem-solving activities, and decision-making activities.[1]

No one teacher can do the job alone. It is a process that takes years to develop. It behooves the school administration to establish the professional climate and the need for cooperation and communication among teachers (of all subjects and grade levels) to implement the goal of making students into critical thinkers. It takes a critical mass of teachers who agree, and have certain student expectations, that thinking counts more than facts, and that asking "Why," "How," and "What if" are more important than "What," "When," and "Who."

One might argue that all this fuss about thinking is nothing more than old-fashioned analysis and problem solving—what good teachers have been infusing into their classroom instruction for years. Moreover, it may be argued that teaching a person to think is like teaching someone to swing a golf club or cook a stew; it requires a holistic approach, not the piecemeal effort suggested by Lipman, Sternberg, and Ennis. Trying to break thinking skills into discrete units may be helpful for diagnostic proposals, and it may sound like a good theory, but it can also be argued that critical thinking is too complex to be broken down into small steps or discrete parts. Rather, as some researchers purport, it involves a wide range of strategic activities, such as cause-effect relationships; arguments in the forms of opinions, each supported with multiple forms of evidence; and knowing what one knows and how one knows it.[2] In short, the whole may be more important than the parts in describing or analyzing a student's mental functioning.

Perhaps the best way to teach thought is to ask students to explain their thinking, to require them to support their answers with evidence, and to ask them thought-provoking (Socratic) questions. Formulating thinking into discrete and generic skills, a special unit or course seems artificial. However, dividing thinking skills by subject matter is unwieldy and mechanistic. Hence, we are left with several options that have potential pitfalls. There is no sure argument or solution. We are forced to take educated guesses concerning the right approach.

Perhaps the major criticism of thinking skills programs has been raised by Sternberg himself. He cautions that the kinds of critical thinking skills stressed in school and the way they are taught "inadequately [prepares] students for the kinds of problems

---

1. David Johnson and Roger T. Johnson, *Learning Together and Alone,* 5th ed. (Boston: Allyn and Bacon, 1999).

2. Karoline Krynock and Louise Robb, "Problem Solved: How to Coach Cognition," *Educational Leadership* (November 1999), pp. 24–35; Deanna Kuhn and Susan Pearsall, "Relations between Metastrategic Knowledge and Performance," *Cognitive Development* (March 1998), pp. 227–247.

they will face in everyday life."[1] Further caution is needed. Thinking skills programs often stress "right" answers and "objectively scorable" test items; therefore, they are removed from real-world relevance. Most problems and decisions in real life have social, economic, and psychological implications—not just a cognitive spin. They involve interpersonal responsibility and choice.

How a person deals with illness, aging, or death or with less momentous events, such as starting a new job or meeting new people, has little to do with the way a person thinks in class or on critical thinking tests. But such life situations are important matters—for some, the essence of life. In stressing cognitive skills, educators tend to ignore the realities of life. Being an A student in school guarantees little after school and in real life. It certainly has little to do with being a good lover, possessing mental and physical health, being a moral, spiritual or good person, or earning a lot of money in our society—all in the larger scheme of life are more important than being "smart."

There are many other factors associated with the outcomes of life—and many of them have little to do with critical thinking or even intelligence. Thus, we need to keep in mind social, psychological, physical, and moral components of learning as well as "luck"—what some of us might call the unaccounted for variables in the outcomes of life. Given all the options and factors related to life, luck (good and bad) counts more then "smarts" or intelligence. Do we make our own luck? I guess type-A personalities think that they make their own luck, but no genius can swim against the tide: Events dealing with global affairs, the national economy, who gets elected to what political office, or where the next war, terrorist act, or traffic jam will take place. In simple terms, you cannot always determine or control who you will meet at the next party you attend. It could be your new lover or future spouse. Anyone with a few ounces of brains, mixed with old-style wisdom, understands that social and personal skills are more important than cognitive skills in the scheme of life, as well as how we get along with people and take advantage of events that have an impact on us.

## Thinking Outside the Box

Moving from conventional and ordinary thinking to the fringe, the way we learn how to learn, think, and innovate may change in the future, since the science and math we know may be incomplete, in need for reinterpretation and rearrangement. In fact, our science and math has led us down the wrong path, according to physicist Stephen Wolfram.[2] The mistake (phenomenologists, reconceptualists, radical critics, and ethnographic researchers will be happy to hear) is trying to describe the world with traditional scientific (Newton's world) and mathematical (Einstein's world) models.

Almost all western scientific and mathematical thought is based on abstract ideas related to time and space as a continuum that extends into infinity. So long as we keep to this continuum, we can describe things with precision. For example, we are able to

---

1. Robert J. Sternberg, "Teaching Critical Thinking," *Phi Delta Kappan* (December 1985), p. 277. Also see Robert J. Sternberg, *In Search of the Human Mind* (San Diego, CA: Harcourt 2000).

2. Stephen Wolfram, *A New Kind of Science* (Champaign, IL: Wolfram Media, 2002).

precisely describe the earth's trajectory around the sun; the time and place (within a few miles) where a space capsule will enter the earth's gravity and subsequently land; and the force with which a person falls from the Empire State Building or Eiffel Tower. But once we try to explain systems with greater complexity and numerous interacting variables, we run into a slippery slope and we start hedging our bets. This happens when scientists try to predict the force of a hurricane or the death toll of a potential atomic blast, when social scientists try to predict the end of a recession or when and if the Dow Jones will reach 15,000, or when educators try to explain all the classroom conditions and teacher-student interactions related to successful teaching.

In all these instances, the calculations are open to confusion, contradictions, and speculation. We are left with an array of variables that cannot be fully explained by the laws of Newton and Einstein, nor the logic of Descartes or Russell; we have an incomplete model for thinking and dealing with multidimensional and elaborate calculations, and where there is unpredictability.

Our theories, models, and equations do not fully explain how the universe works. Plato cannot save us, neither can Augustine or Aquinas, Bacon or Locke, nor can the doctrines of the Vedas (Hinduism) or Zen (Buddhism). The only thing that can save us, according to Wolfram, is the computer program that can deal with all known variables and their respective interactions. All we need are spreadsheets and lots of paper to generate unlimited, infinitesimal data. Indeed, the "computer geeks" who understand and manipulate little snippets of electronic information will hopefully revamp science and math and save humankind from its incomplete thinking.

Now, some of this sounds far-fetched and perhaps like I'm playing with your mind. It can be argued by rational and logical people that computer programs are nothing more than human inventions that understand little more than 1 and 0, and that the program is as good as the human mind. It is contended, however, that scientific and mathematical models got it wrong; our equations are artificial and based on flawed continuums. Time doesn't flow; it ticks. Space is not a surface, but a grid.[1] The world we know is best described not by scientific and mathematical equations, but by computer programs that can spit out tiny pieces of information that yield endless, infinitesimal, intricate data. Behold—the computer will capture the richness of our thinking, producing dribbles of information, taking an inch (space) or second (time), then halving it, again and again, into infinity.

## A Final Note: Listening to and Looking at Children's Drawings

I leave you with food for thought, something a bit more concrete, by looking through the eyes and artwork of fifth-graders in a minority school in New Haven, Connecticut. These are kids with imagination, creativity, and a sense of wonder. When asked to draw a day in their lives 20 years from now, one student drew his own body shop,

1. George Johnson, "You Know That Space-Time Thing?" *New York Times Book Review* (June 9, 2002), p. 10.

painted bright yellow, where for $90 you could get your car fixed. Another student painted two women, trading volleys on a tennis court, to win a trip to the moon. There was also Pokemon saving the human race from a host of volcanoes erupting at the same time; and a bare-chested man surrounded by a half-blue, half-green background, flying to his destiny with the verbal explanation, "That's my uncle."

There was a picture of a minivan, full of children with the verbal explanation, "My mother . . . buys a minivan and she takes us places. This [van] can fly, and only she can drive it. . . . It can go anywhere you want. You just push in the speed like you push in the speed on the treadmill, and it will go. . . . You don't have to drive, you can just tell it your destination and it will take you there."[1] There was another student with a picture of a framed diploma represented by some wavy lines on paper, a chair with wheels, a desk, and what appeared to be a computer and a file cabinet. Her explanation: "When I grow up to be a lawyer, I'd like to roll around on my chair and still be able to see the screen. . . . Being a lawyer you can make more friends. You'll help people and they'll remember, 'Yeah, that's the girl that helped me.' "[2]

How about this last one: a picture of a baby robot and mother robot (no father figure), a balloon, and a small purse or bag. Explanation: "The baby robot is made out of tin, and the mama is made out of copper. They'll probably be just like us; they don't take showers [but] they're be our friends. It's a New Year's Eve party. . . . They're listening to, probably, like sounds of machinery."[3]

What happened to these friendly, imaginative, positive-thinking kids? What went wrong in the home, school, and community so that many kids from the ghetto are left behind, grow angry, and lose their future? Think about it. Happy, bright, creative, fifth-grade students. Now, the flip side is that three-quarters of these kids in the class read below grade level. Is that the answer? Does it boil down to reading? Do we need to consult with some education guru? Given all the half-baked schemes for improvement, maybe we need to consult with Dr. Seuss, Timothy Leary, Master Po, or the Dali Lama. Surely, you don't need to be a genius or have the insights of the most successful children's author or be a Harvard professor, a Chinese war lord, or Buddhist monk to figure out that reading is the strongest link to school success.[4]

Are there other domains of learning that are important? For every Michael Jordan, Michael Jackson, or Jennifer Lopez who succeeds in sports or entertainment, a hundred thousand or more kids from the ghetto fail school because of limited reading skills—and subsequent learning and/or behavioral problems. Other things count, and they will be discussed in other chapters. However, I thought it was worthwhile

1. Jodi Wilgoren, "Through the Eyes of Children," *New York Times* (January 1, 2000), p. 17.
2. Ibid.
3. Ibid.
4. Timothy Leary was a Harvard University professor whose use of LSD was popularized in the media during the 1960s. Master Po was the mystical teacher and instructor of Master Cane, the martial arts expert who traveled the path in search of enlightenment in the TV show *Kung Fu*.

to recapture the world of young, innocent kids who have managed to remain hopeful. They provide us with subtle and simple reminders about our roles and responsibilities as parents and teachers.

## Summary

1. In classical conditioning, the S-R association depends on the conditioning of the response and stimulus. Pavlov and Watson represent this theory. In contrast to classical conditioning, no specific or identifiable stimulus consistently elicits operant behavior. Operant theory is best represented by the work of B. F. Skinner.

2. People can also learn through observing and modeling; this explanation of behaviorism is associated with Albert Bandura.

3. According to Piaget, four cognitive stages form a sequence of progressive mental operations; the stages are hierarchical and increasingly more complex. Piaget is also noted for his cognitive theory of assimilation, accommodation, and equilibration—namely, new experiences are modified and derive new meaning.

4. Moral knowledge can be acquired through academic content, but moral character takes years to develop and to reflect the whole person.

5. Whereas Piaget concludes there are three stages of moral development, Kohlberg contends there are six stages to moral reasoning. Both Piaget and Kohlberg view moral development as a socialization process that can be shaped, in part, by schools and society.

6. Students have different learning styles and different ways of thinking, including, but not limited to, visual, auditory, and tactile responses.

7. Our contacts with or lack of exposure to various cultures influence our thinking processes—how we perceive the world, and to what extent we make use of universal knowledge.

8. Whereas Charles Spearmen viewed intelligence as one general factor, Howard Gardner viewed intelligence in context with eight broad areas of life, and J. P. Guilford described it in terms of 120 mental operations and/or cognitive processes.

9. Students can be taught learning skills and critical thinking skills. The idea is for the teacher to move from facts and right answers to analysis and problem solving.

## Questions to Consider

1. In what ways do behaviorist theory and cognitive psychology differ in terms of how students learn?

2. Why might you think that Piaget's theories of cognitive growth influence elementary teachers more than secondary teachers? What is the difference between assimilation and accommodation of experience?

3. Should teachers be expected to teach moral education? If so, whose morals?

4. How does brain research influence teaching and learning?

5. What teaching methods can be used to improve students' thinking skills?

## Things to Do

1. Observe two or three teachers at work in the classroom and try to observe their instructional techniques. List those techniques that reflect a behavioral approach. Discuss your findings in class.
2. Observe the same teachers. Make a list of cognitive instructional techniques. Discuss your findings.
3. Some observers argue that Piaget and Kohlberg ignored women in developing their moral theories. Check the Internet to ensure the voice of women in moral education.
4. Describe your own learning style. What preferences do you have regarding movement, sound, light, and food when you study for a test?
5. School success is partially based on the students' ability to think critically. Identify four or five processes, or things teachers can do, to foster critical thinking among students.

## Recommended Readings

Cooper, James M., ed. *Classroom Teaching Skills,* 7th ed. (Boston: Houghton Mifflin, 2003). Teachers are viewed as planners, implementers, and evaluators of instruction; the emphasis is on cognitive psychology.

Darling-Hammond, Linda. *The Right to Learn* (San Francisco: Jossey-Bass, 2001). Ways for improving the teaching-learning process.

Dewey, John. *How We Think,* rev ed. (Boston: Houghton Mifflin, 1998). Originally published in 1918, the book is still relevant and readable today.

Kohn, Alfie. *What to Look for in a Classroom* (San Francisco: Jossey-Bass, 2000). How teachers can be more effective at helping students learn.

Philip, D. C. *Construction in Education,* 99th yearbook of the National Society for the Study of Education, Part I (Chicago: NSSE, 2000). Opinions and issues about how knowledge is constructed.

Piaget, Jean. *The Psychology of Intelligence,* rev. ed. (London: Broadway, 1950). An overview of Piaget's thinking about how people think and learn; based on environmental stimuli.

Skinner, B. F. *Reflections on Behaviorism and Society* (Englewood Cliffs, NJ: Prentice-Hall, 1978). One of many important books by Skinner, continuing the tenets of behaviorism.

# The School as a Socializing Agent

Chapter 4

*Focusing Questions*

1. How does society affect schools? How do schools affect society?

2. What are the major purposes of education? Which do you support? Why?

3. What are the core values and virtues that most Americans accept?

4. What are the major challenges teachers experience in teaching about morality?

5. Why are the concepts of social class, race, and gender so essential to consider in teaching and learning?

6. How do sex roles and sex differences influence social behavior and learning?

7. How does the peer group influence social behavior and learning?

8. How does the peer group influence teaching and learning?

9. What social priorities need to be addressed by teachers? What moral priorities need to be addressed by teachers?

## EPISODE A

Education is neutral (and depends on the practices, beliefs, and consequences derived). It can be used to cultivate totalitarianism, to promote democracy, to liberate the mind and encourage inquiry and innovation, or to restrict thinking and promote conformity and obedience. Imposition from above—based on religion, law, or traditional ideas from "elders" or rulers—opposes freedom of inquiry and the cultivation of individual thought. Learning that emphasizes a finished product, a timeless value, an external form of control, or a "true" way of thinking, with little regard either to the way the ideas were formulated or how the future will change the product or thought, is doomed to result in a static society—left behind by other more progressive or innovative societies.

If one believes in the rise and fall of civilizations, as expressed by Oswald Spengler and Arnold Toynbee, then such a society is bound to fall behind other societies, wither away, and even self-destruct. According to John Dewey, "The rise of progressive schools [in the United States] is a product of discontent with traditional education" with its emphasis on "conformity, obedience . . . and imposed knowledge. Books, especially textbooks, are the chief representatives of the lore and wisdom of the past."[1] Facts and acquisition of information characterize traditional learning and a static society, as opposed to learning by problem solving, inquiry, and experimentation, which are characteristic of progressive education and a democratic society.

## Education for Transmitting the Culture

The kind of education youth receive determines the quality of life in and the future of society. The transmission of culture is the primary task of the educational system of a society. The values, beliefs, and norms of a society are maintained and passed to next generations not merely by teaching about them but also by the embodiment of these elements of culture in the content taught by the teacher, the day-to-day school activities, and the overall operation of the educational system.

If society fails to transmit the culture, then memories held by its people die and their existence as individuals and a society fades into oblivion. People remember certain things with fondness or sadness, with grace or melodrama, through the passing years. Constancy and change are the tides that guide us, that set the moment against what might have been and what endures. Certain things are harbored in the family, ethnic or religious group, the larger society, whatever the vicissitudes of history— some noble and some horrible, some folk rituals and some laws, some stories and some fleeting images of people—until time itself washes them away, or into the safe-keeping of the next generation.

Different things are important to different people and different societies. Some of us are required to remember the Holocaust, others remember Hiroshima or the killing fields in Vietnam. Some of us can recall the Statue of Liberty welcoming us as we arrived in New York, others remember their first glimpse of the Golden Gate Bridge, and still others remember the neighbor who died yesterday—the same person who brought plum jam to our door when we moved into our house 10 years ago.

We are a nation of many nations, and many of our parents and grandparents are descendants of aristocratic empires, fascist states, or ethnic tribes. The nation's spirit of independence, its religious tolerance and vast resources, coupled with people's

---

1. John Dewey, *Experience and Education* (New York: Macmillan, 1938), pp. 18, 21.

desire to escape vindictive governments, political hardships, and squalid economic conditions, resulted in the continuous migration across the Atlantic in the eighteenth and nineteenth centuries followed by massive migrations after World War I. Besides the need to escape the old order, much of what built this country, according to Merle Curti, was "the romantic legend" of America—its rich abundance, golden opportunities, and freedom from "the bickerings of [corrupt] officials and clerics."[1] America has always been an asylum for the oppressed, and it was the mass of immigrants who indirectly promoted the need for free public schools. The schools were seen as the socializing agent for Americanizing immigrants and for dealing with the illiteracy of the foreign born.

Having grown less poor and more Americanized, many of our parents and grandparents went streaming out of the wretched old tenements in search of green pastures—first known as the wilderness beyond the mountains, later known as the West, and more recently as suburbia. The old ethnic neighborhoods changed, but many can still remember the old language, the old church, the family dinners, and the old school. It was the school that assimilated our parents and grandparents into a new race of people called Americans, with new values and virtues.

Indeed, it is the family's role to pass the old ethnic and religious culture to the next generation, and it is the school's role to pass the nation's culture—its folklore, art, and language—to the next generation. There are a host of methods to describe our history and culture, according to our world, our reality. Teachers are obligated to tell this story—so we don't forget our heritage, so we remain a people bound by common ritual, common custom, common law, and a common destiny. Life is not only birth, consumption, and decay, and civilizations don't just rise and fall. Teachers must spark the embers of the past, the romantic legends and the opportunities across the rivers and mountains, as well as across the urban tracks and slums. They must help students cultivate educated and liberated minds, and to appreciate the American culture, so that youth understand the past, the present, and the image of the future.

For John Dewey, education was about growing, with no end and no limit. "The criterion of the value of education is to the extent to which it creates a desire for continued growth and supplies means for making the desire effective in fact."[2] Education, then, is a process for the individual and society to grow, to develop to the fullest potential. Education also transmits the culture so that culture may change with the times, depending on how traditional or progressive it is. The essence of growth, according to Dewey, is tied to experiences; the richer and more meaningful the experiences, the more productive the growth and the better the quality of society.

In *Democracy and Education,* Dewey argues that education is "a continuous process of growth [and] a constant expansion of horizons." Lawrence Cremin aptly points out that Dewey perceived the main purpose of education in *social* terms (what I would call the Greek concept of education, serving the nation-state) and in terms of *personal* behavior, attitudes, and experiences. Education, experience, and growth were all cen-

---

1. Merle Curti, *The Growth of American Thought,* 2nd ed. (New York: Harper & Brothers, 1951), p. 259.
2. John Dewey, *Democracy and Education* (New York: Macmillan, 1916), p. 53.

tral to Dewey's purposes of education—and those purposes had to be continuously formulated and reformulated. Given this conception of growth, U.S. society—based on democracy—"can be defined simply as a society in which each individual is encouraged to continue his education throughout his lifetime."[1] Most important, in our society we give each student many chances and multiple chances to succeed, to try again and again, far different from most other industrialized or democratic societies that provide one chance at adolescence, either the fast or slow education track. The notion of second (and third or fourth) chances, a new beginning, is based on the founding principles of the nation—the rationale for the Declaration of Independence, the "Western Eden," the manifest destiny and the new frontier, and the flow of immigrants—the chance to start over, to find gold in the streets, to move from the pushcarts of Mott Street or Maxwell Street (immigrants) to the suburbs (their children), away from the old, homogenized neighborhoods.

The story of America is about opportunity, regardless of background, and is the main reason for the rise and prosperity of our country. The United States even provides the opportunity to avoid debt, go bankrupt, and start over again. Finally, twentieth-century evangelism (from Billy Graham to Pat Robertson) provides sinners the chance for redemption, and a new beginning. A great many B and C students in Europe and Asia are tracked into nonacademic slots, resulting in a major loss of human potential that perpetuates a pool of working-class citizens. It reflects the old aristocracy, the class theories and prejudice of the old world that has haunted so-called enlightened civilizations of Europe and Asia, and that has caused the lack of innovation, advancement, and eventual downfall of vast empires—ranging from Egypt, Persia, Rome, and the Ottoman Empire to China and Siam. Today, all these once great empires, which had hundreds and thousands of years headstart on the United States, are second- and third-rate powers.

Most Americans tend to regard education as synonymous with schooling. Actually, a culture may have no schools but still educate its young through family or special ritual and training. Schooling plays a major role in education in modern industrial and technological societies; it becomes increasingly important as cultures become more complex and the frontiers of knowledge expand. In traditional societies, almost everyone becomes proficient over the whole range of knowledge necessary for survival. In complex societies, people acquire different proficiencies and abilities; no individual can range over the entire body of complex knowledge or expect to be proficient in all areas of learning. In traditional societies, women are not encouraged to participate in formal schooling, and their roles are subservient to men. Theoretically, once society moves from "muscle power" (farming, hunting, fishing, or industrial) into a society based on "brain power" (that is, a society based on technology and information), the roles and relationships of men and women become more equal. Obviously, this does not take into account the reality of a double standard or a glass ceiling that may exist. Women on a fast track still have to keep a check on their weight, hair, clothes, and performance much more than men.

1. Lawrence Cremin, *Genius of American Education* (New York: Vintage Books, 1966), p. 19.

The techniques of education used by nonliterate peoples include overt training by elders, emulation of older children, attendance at ceremonies, observation of parents and elders doing daily tasks, and inculcation of proper values and conduct by codes of admonition and rewards. In modern societies, education begins at home, and school takes on greater importance as the child becomes older. The schools become the crucial facility for helping the young acquire an education, inculcating them with the ideas and institutions of the culture and bridging the gap between generations. In short, the school imparts the knowledge and tools necessary for survival, and ensures the transmission of values to future generations; it provides a sense of continuity and past experiences of the culture. School is a highly formal system for educating the young, an institution children are required to attend in order to be socialized and enculturated into the larger society.

## The Purposes of Education

The purposes of schools are basically to enhance the potential of the individual and to perpetuate society. In western society and in a democratic society like ours, there is greater tension between these two purposes because we believe in individual rights and self-realization. But we also know it is the schools' responsibility to promote the goals and needs of society—and that society must come first over the goals or needs of the individual. This tension or duality between the individual and society has challenged us for centuries, since Plato's *Republic*, whereby he proposed an ideal state characterized by loyal citizens who worked in unity and harmony to further the goals of society.

Thus, John Goodlad argues that "developing individuals to their fullest potential often has been argued as the antithesis of educating the individual to serve the state. . . . Whatever the schools may be able to accomplish in promoting [individual growth and enlightenment], they are simultaneously required to instill a sense of devotion to the nation-state."[1] All societies must promote their way of life to survive. The danger is, however, some nation-states may instill a sense of nationalism or ideology that dethrones individual rationality and individual rights. Hence, the difference between ends and means becomes obscure in such a society. Dewey understood this dilemma and stressed education for civic and moral responsibility. He also maintained that the state should not establish the aims of education without critical examination from its citizens, because he feared abuse if there was complete immunity.[2] It was the same fear our founding fathers had when they introduced a series of checks and balances to protect the people from the abuse of power from its own elected leaders. Hence, the citizens have a right to challenge and modify the aims of education and the right to control education at the local or community level—and this right has been delegated to them by the states.

1. John I. Goodlad, *What Are Schools For* (Bloomington, IN: Phi Delta Kappa Educational Foundation, 1989), p. 36.
2. Dewey, *Democracy and Education.*

One of the most famous statements on the purposes and nature of schooling is the "Cardinal Principles of Secondary Education," prepared by the NEA's Commission on the Reorganization of Secondary Education and published in 1918. Although the work of the commission was directed at secondary schooling, the statement is applicable to all levels of formal education and is still relevant today. The commission stated that "education in democracy, both within and without the school, should develop in each individual the knowledge, interests, ideals, habits, and powers whereby he will find his place and use that place to shape both himself and society toward ever nobler ends."[1] It influenced Lawernce Cremin's thinking when he declared that "the aim of education is not merely to make citizens, or workers, or fathers, or mothers, but ultimately to make human beings who will live to the fullest."[2]

The commission listed seven areas of daily living with which this broad purpose of the school programs were to be concerned: (1) health, (2) fundamental skills, (3) home membership, (4) vocation, (5) civic education, (6) leisure, and (7) ethical character. These seven cardinal principles of education reflect the rise of progressive education and the concept of the whole child—two major philosophical and psychological thoughts developing during this period. They also constitute a point of view worthy of consideration for all planning at all levels of education, K–12, for today.

Although we are frequently exposed to new reports from different government panels, task forces, and commissions, viewed historically the broad purposes of education reflect the social issues and problems of the times. It is true that over time the issues and problems shift; however, we still must come back to concerns for the individual and society—the community, state, and nation. There is no escape from these two broad purposes, and the best we can do is hope that we perceive and act on the issues and problems in a democratic, just, and wise manner.

## Mental versus Moral Purposes

Another duality or balancing act exists between cognition (or intellect) and morality (or moral reasoning). For Alfred Whitehead, teachers do not begin with purposes, goals, or aims. Teachers begin with ideas; they should be few and important, and they should be abstract and interrelated. The idea is to produce learners who "possess the culture and expert knowledge in some special direction." The overall aim of education, for Whitehead, is for the student to become knowledgeable and virtuous; that is, "the educated man" should also have "morality of mind."[3] This ideal is similar to Thomas Jefferson's education "bill for the diffusion of knowledge," introduced in the Virginia legislature in 1779, for the students of Virginia (and the nation): The state should provide public money and educational opportunities for common people, especially for

---

1. Commission on the Reorganization of Secondary Education, *Cardinal Principles of Secondary Education* (Washington, DC: U.S. Government Printing Office, 1918), p. 9.

2. Lawrence A. Cremin, *The Transformation of the School* (New York: Knopf, 1961), pp. 122–123.

3. Alfred N. Whitehead, *Aims of Education and Other Essays* (New York: Macmillan, 1929), pp. 1, 19.

bright students and economically less fortunate students—to promote classical education, good citizenship, and social progress.[1] The first purpose deals with the intellect, and the latter two overlap with moral decisions.

Ted Sizer takes the same position as Whitehead, in somewhat more modern form, when he argues that "less is more," "mastery of content" is more important than "collection of credits," and that the school's job "is less in purveying information than in helping people to use it, to exercise their minds."[2] Sharing the same views as Whitehead and Jefferson, he concludes that the overall purpose of school is the "education of the intellect" and "education in character"[3] Now, the education of the student in intellectual or cognitive terms is obvious; the moral factor is related to cultivating decent people who can act in a responsible, appropriate, and compassionate manner toward other people—in short, they do "the right thing." The need is to balance both the mental and moral aspects of thinking to help create a good person and good society, an individual and a nation that believe in, support, and defend democracy, freedom, and justice. This type of individual and society is a rarity, given the flow of history for the last 2,500 or more years.

Mass Killings: Moral Questions    Intellect without morality can lead to a great many social and economic problems in society, create dominant and subordinate relations among groups, and pit people against people. Without morality, there is no justice, no fairness, no compassion for the less fortunate. Without moral guidelines, there is minimal difference between human and animal behavior; in fact, the reason for man's inhumanity to man basically revolves around a lack of morality. At its worst, immorality can lead to a host of horrors that our arsenal of adjectives are not fully capable of describing—such as a observing gang of soldiers raping women or cutting off the testicles of male prisoners; a group of homophobic men nailing a homosexual to a cross, then hanging him high on a tree or setting him adrift on a river; or smelling the corpses of gas chamber victims.

Try to listen to the conversation of a man whose tongue has been cut out or see the live skeleton-like civilian prisoners of war or their corpses heaped on top of each other. Witness the bodies of those who were clobbered to death and left to rot in Argentina, Algeria, and Afghanistan. Some people who have a different view of reality would merely argue that words do not really count—numbers can fully explain these acts. Just keep on adding zeros. Multiply those horrors a thousandfold and another thousandfold, and we can start examining the evil of people and nations: the slaughter and carnage of mankind, the horrible and irrational racial, ethnic, and religious hatred—all which can be summed up as the triumph of evil over good. Our brains are equipped to deal with atrocities at the nation-state or tribal level by moving the blame from individuals to groups, from relatively unknown criminals or soldiers to better-known political and military leaders.

1. Thomas Jefferson, "A Bill for the More General Diffusion of Knowledge," in P. L. Ford, ed. *The Writings of Thomas Jefferson* (New York: Putnam, 1893).
2. Theodore R. Sizer, *Horace's Compromise* (Boston: Houghton Mifflin, 1985), pp. 63, 84.
3. Ibid., p. 84.

As students, teachers, or social scientists, our minds permit us to discuss or read about the genocide of one million or *more* Armenians by the Turks in 1915 (who still officially deny it ever happened), two million or *so* Chinese citizens killed by Japanese soldiers during the rape and plunder of Nanking in 1934; six million *plus* Jews exterminated by the Nazis between 1943 and 1945, and *about* two million Cambodian civilians who were victims of the killing fields in the mid-1970s. And what does *more, so, plus,* and *about* mean when we reach these numbers? And other than some footnote, what does the recent butchery in Bosnia and Kosovo and Rwanda mean? Here, we are talking about *only* one-quarter or one-half million victims. (The word *only* cannot be used in front of this tally, or any tally, because it would trivialize the dead; in fact, if we start lowering the count for any of these events, we might argue about diminishing the tragedy or significance—or transforming these deaths into some revisionist history.) In all of these cases, the victims were considered as subhuman by the soldiers, workers, scientists, and intellectual elite of the aggressor nation, even depicted in terms of insects and rodents that enabled willing executioners (soldiers and civilian bureaucrats) to slaughter without conscience or moral benchmarks and without regard to human life.[1]

How can people be so indifferent to these numbers? Few seem to care, and international amnesia usually sets in within six months; we just estimate the number of dead and talk about some court or war tribunal to mete out punishment, what the victors call justice. So, England imprisoned dozens of Turkish leaders involved in the Armenian genocide, only to exchange them for a handful of captured English soldiers; a few dozen Japanese and Nazi leaders were put on public trial after World War II.[2] Twenty years later, Pol Pot was turned over to an international tribunal and Slobodan

1. This enabled Japanese soldiers to beat, rape, and kill women and children, use them for bayonet practice, and then set them on fire. Similarly, this enabled German soldiers to gas Jewish victims, then tear their corpses apart for gold and civilian products like soap and elastic. It enabled Serbian soldiers to rape female victims and cut off the testicles of male prisoners of war.

What is the best way to describe these acts: Butchery? Barbarism? Evil? I don't believe we have appropriate words, models, or paradigms to fully describe these acts, or what life becomes under these conditions. Even worse, when all the raw emotions have subsided and the battle ends, the soldiers and bureaucrats who are responsible often have no sense of guilt or remorse. They excuse their behavior because they were fighting for the emperor/fuhrer (some cult figure) or an ideological and totalitarian concept that destroys their individual consciences.

Now almost everyone wants to believe his or her religion or nation is the best, or at least that is what people are educated to believe. That being so, how do we preserve human rights and human dignity, when the strong decide to bully the weak? I doubt if there is any social scientist or philosopher who can fully explain this madness, this instinct to hurt and kill others, as if they were a species lower than animals. Maybe movies such as *Planet of the Apes, Brave New World, Lord of the Flies,* and *Animal Farm* need to be repeatedly played for people to understand the message. Maybe they need repeated documentaries and pictures of the victims at Nanking, the Holocaust, or Killing Fields in Cambodia.

2. A couple hundred second-tier, less-visible Nazi war criminals were also tried in Frankfurt after the war.

Milosevic is facing a war criminal trial. (A few soldiers have also been convicted of war crimes in Bosnia, Kosovo, and Rwanda.) Is this really justice? And who is responsible for all the militarists who have prevailed over peacemakers from Gautemala and Uruguay to the Sudan and Somalia to Iraq and Indonesia?

What should be done with people who commit such acts? It seems relatively easy to convict one murderer for the slaying of another person. But how many people should be convicted when the loss of life is in the thousands? Hundreds of thousands? Millions? Is it sufficient to put two dozen political and military leaders on trial for the death of six million-plus Jews and another million or so gypsies, homosexuals, and mentally retarded people? If we keep punching and adding numbers, the dead in World War II total some 30 million soldiers and civilians. Who is responsible for these deaths?

So what! We punish or put to death a handful of governmental officials and generals who were committed to Nazi or Japanese fanaticism. Are the Cambodians or Croations worth less, so that punishing fewer people suffice? Are Africans worth even less, so that we have supported their dictators and gangsters under the guise of toppling Marxist governments, and now permit failed nation-states incapable of sustaining themselves to be run by corrupt warlords and bandits who call themselves political leaders?

How many of you even know Pol Pot, the dictator responsible for killing some two million Cambodians? Who remembers Jona Savimbi, the guerilla leader who traded diamonds for guns during the Cold War for 27 years? No one even knows or agrees how many millions were killed,[1] only that his gangsterism epitomizes the Continent's horrendous waste of resources and people. How many of you can recall one or more of the Nazi and Japanese leaders imprisoned or executed at Nuremburg or Tokyo? Why did the Soviet Union imprison and kill more of its own citizens (15 to 20 million dead) than Nazi soldiers (3.3 million dead) who invaded their homeland? Who apologized for Dachau or the Gulag? Who cares today? We transform mass death into a number and some kind of tragic event—and then soon forget. Perhaps at some cocktail party or in some college classroom we mention some morally obtuse point, or add some benign phrase to sum up the numbers or meaning. Hence, we rely on stories such as Ann Frank's diary to try to make sense of these numbers and events, and hope her voice or words have meaning for all the dead.

The international community wants to forget or limit justice to a handful of culprits so as not to encourage historical hatred nor the need for revenge—or prolong efforts to build peace. In the meantime, the world searches for an answer. Does it all start with an innocent ethnic or religious joke? What do teachers discuss in class or give to students to read to limit the madness and vile behavior that constantly rears its ugly head? What international organizations or justice system should be implemented to cause potential criminals and mass murderers to pause and reconsider their acts? Is there a way to control a person's instinct to kill, slaughter, plunder, and torture—what Freud would call the expressions of the *id*? According to Alan Dershowitz, "The

---

1. Howard W. French, "Exit Savimbi and the Cold War in Africa," *New York Times* (March 3, 2002), Sect. 4, p. 5.

world is full of evil people and it is important to stand up to evil."[1] Well, how do we stand up to nations that become infected by evil? What price should they pay? There are a host of intellectual and moral critics who are good at analyzing the yokes of injustice and irrationality to the maximum, but it doesn't seem to help.

Why is it that political leaders such as Lenin, Stalin, and Hitler and religious leaders like Bin Laden and the Ayatollah Khomeni are able to dupe the masses? What similarity is there in ideological conviction between political fanaticism and religious dogma? Faith, conviction, and zeal seem to dominate and overwhelm the vast majority of individuals. Why is it that the mass, including educated groups, fall victim to brainwashing and thought control? Does it all boil down to having food in your belly? Is it simple jealousy or hatred toward someone, some group, perceived as different?

Almost everywhere, the power of the state or religious order are deployed to mislead the masses, obscure and twist knowledge, and drown out the individual, while intellectuals fail in their duty to voice the truth or speak up. As for teachers, their duty is to ensure the perpetuation of the nation-state, to accept the norms of the community, to keep their noses clean, not to jeopardize political and social stability or question the "truth." The question arises: How far should teachers and schools question the political and social order, the purposes of the nation-state, or the behaviors of the clergy?

According to radical and neomarxist educators, the teachers and schools do an inadequate job in raising questions about the political and social order. Even worse, democratic nations fail to properly analyze global events leading to the totalitarianism, and fail to take quick measures to prevent militaristic or religious powers from rearranging or trying to rearrange the world order. According to one historian, the world is run by fools and morally inept leaders, thus permitting the rise of left wing and right wing regimes.[2] In this connection, neomarxists would argue that American schools are run by inept educators who continue to perpetuate the dominant-subordinate relations that exist in our society.

**Education and Democracy**   Thomas Jefferson, Horace Mann, and John Dewey all understood that democracy without education was impossible. To secure the blessing of liberty to ourselves and our posterity, as idealized by the Declaration of Independence, Jefferson advocated for an educated citizenry. Horace Mann's call for free schools was basic for establishing a national identity and for promoting a democratic society. John Dewey, in *Democracy and Education,* recognized the relationship and set forth the notion that democracy itself was a social process that could be enhanced through the school. All three giants envisioned school in America as an instrument of democracy.

No doubt, democracy without education is fruitless, but education without morality is perilous. It will inevitably lead society down a gloomy road where materialism and greed triumph over the ideal of a community based on caring and compassion and where political cynicism and corruption triumph over personal integrity

1. Alan Dershowitz, *Letters to a Young Lawyer* (New York: Basic Books, 2001).
2. Piers Brendon, *The Dark Valley* (New York: Alfred A. Knopf, 2002).

and social justice. Morality must be defined, agreed upon,[1] and taught by teachers and schools on a secular basis. To shrink away from this responsibility under the misguided notion that it may lead to conflict with the school and community or overlap with religious doctrines is outdated and means we will most likely continue to repeat the horrors and injustices of the past.

Children at every grade level can and should be taught the differences between right and wrong, personal responsibility, how their beliefs and behavior affect others, as well as abstract principles of ethics, law, religious freedom, human rights, and justice. In deciding to emphasize morality, to give it similar importance as the intellect, teachers need to consider the developmental theories of Piaget, Kohlberg, Erikson, and others. When organizing the content and experiences of subject matter, teachers must consider the cognitive and moral development of their students and the relationship that exists between intellectual and moral reasoning (see Chapter 3).

## Freud: The Id versus the Superego

Teaching about morality is rooted in the lessons of Freud's psychoanalytical view of the individual and society. In Freud's description of the self and the socialization process, he begins with the egocentric, aggressive, pleasure-seeking infant. He described not only sexual and aggressive urges, which he believed were biological givens, but all bodily functions as well as the *pleasure principle* as the concern of the *id*. Modern society, by way of parents, interferes with children's pleasure-seeking activities; their demands for food are met only at certain times, they are forced to control their bowels, and their masturbation is restricted. Teachers in school serve the same restrictive role for society as do parents in the home. As children struggle to accommodate to these and other social demands, there begins to develop what Freud called the *ego*. The ego is the rational part of the self that interprets information through the senses and finds socially acceptable ways of satisfying biological needs.[2] (Being a

---

1. The question arises: Whose morality? Although the question is a red herring, it must be addressed. The need is to consider the beliefs, customs, and attitudes of the local community, while considering the nation at the same time. In short, the answer involves a balancing act, and it needs to be addressed on a regular basis in a democratic society. In static society, one that is dominated by religious or totalitarian thought, philosophy, morality, and education are imposed from above and from outside the school/community—the school is merely an instrument of the religious or political order.

This is how schools operated in the New England colonies under puritan scriptures and how it operates today with the madrassahs (religious schools) under militant Islamists. The puritans and militant Islamists have at least one common thread: the wrath of God or Allah and the predestination of a few to salvation who are true believers, and many to damnation. There is a different definition of justice and morality between the puritans and militant Islamists, but the definition is still imposed from above, and the schools are still institutions designed to further religious orthodoxy. Of course, there is the obvious difference that puritanism eventually led to democracy, and militant Islamism eventually led to the Taliban.

2. Sigmund Freud, *The Standard Edition of the Complete Works of Sigmund Freud* (London: Hogarth Press, 1953).

bully in the schoolyard is no longer socially acceptable, but playing football and knocking the sense out of the opponent is still acceptable.)

As children grow up, their desires are still powerful, but so are their fears. Realizing that their parents (and other adults) have enormous power over them, they conform to what their parents (teachers, police officers, etc.) want them to do. They begin to internalize their parents' (and teachers') concepts of right and wrong, including their moral ideas. They learn to repress socially unacceptable ideas and, ideally, to redirect their energies into socially approved channels. The *superego,* or conscience, develops at this period; it forces the id underground. The desires and fears of childhood, which are stimulated by the reemergence of sexuality in adolescence, remain active in the unconscious, influencing the way the individual behaves throughout life.[1] Later in life, the superego is internalized by the norms and beliefs of society. The id continues to press for gratification. The ego serves to control these lustful (sexual and aggressive) drives, while at the same time modifying the unrealistic demands of the perfection-seeking superego. Driven one way by biological needs, the other by the norms of society, we are (at least most of us), according to Freud, forever discontented.[2]

In short, society must control the individual's id, his or her impulses and pleasures, by developing a superego. Society must impose restrictive norms and beliefs among members of society so that they become morally responsible. Religious institutions probably do the best job in instructing masses of people for the purpose of controlling the id and enhancing morality. But they can also encourage tyranny by demanding one "true" interpretation of reality and subsequently suppressing human thought and behavior.

The history of religion is rampant with controlling the minds and behavior of people—relying on the tools of torture, denunciation of neighbor by neighbor, and mass execution by fire and sword.[3] To be sure, the medieval campaigns to root out heresy and heretics, the grotesque march to wipe out Catharism,[4] the Crusades in the

1. The notion of unconscious behavior influencing conscious behavior is a powerful concept that most psychologists (and members of society) refused, initially, to accept. It took many years, after much evidence, for the idea to be accepted. To that extent, Freud may be considered, along with four others in the last 500 years—Galileo, Thomas Paine, Charles Darwin, and Martin Luther King—whose ideas threatened the social order, and thus encountered major resistance from their peers, the Establishment, and/or the larger society. It would take many years before society would accept their ideas as plausible or correct. Freud (and Darwin) are still considered controversial among many people, almost as much so when they originally proposed their original ideas.

2. Sigmund Freud, *Civilization and Its Discontents* (New York: W. W. Norton, 1961). (Originally published in German in 1930.)

3. Stephen O'Shea, *The Perfect Heresy* (New York: Walker & Company, 2000). Also see Richard Bernstein, "Early Lessons in Tyranny, Repeated in Modern Times," *New York Times* (October 23, 2000), p. E7.

4. Each victim holding the shoulder of the man ahead of him, with the eyes of all but one gouged out, and their noses sliced off. Only their leader was left with one eye—to lead them—implemented by Simon de Montfort, "a man with God on his side" who had official church approval.

Holy Land, the Inquisition, and the religious conversion of the human mind and spirit in parts of Latin America, Africa, and Asia provide the model (the goals and methods) for twentieth-century totalitarian control of the mass at the expense of individual consciences and individual dignity. Much of the unification of Europe, including its wars and empire building, is based on the sword and faith of the Gospels. It also includes ruthless efficiency to eliminate "nonbelievers" and "impure" blood, causing a great deal of second-class citizenship of the medieval polity and historical horror and controversy in modern times.

## Morality and the Role of Teachers

Obviously, morality means different things to different people, which is one reason why teachers shy away from their responsibility of teaching about morality. The fact is, there are certain moral principles and values such as hard work, courage, compassion, teamwork, and patriotism that can be agreed upon by the vast majority of Americans. Involvement of the community, and the presence of multicaring and fair-minded adults greatly help, but teachers and administrators must also learn to communicate effectively with parents, to make all parties reinvest and work together in the school and community. It means that adults (parents and teachers) take time to understand each other, to slow down and form bonds to build trust and respect, and then to listen and compromise for the good of children and youth.

The idea is for teachers and schools to educate (and socialize) students to be concerned with "doing the right thing," not just "doing things right." The job of teachers is not only to provide students with knowledge and skills but also to instill values and virtues—to build character by shaping students' attitudes and behaviors. Cognitive and moral messages must be fused in teaching. Both messages should not be separated; in fact, much of the content—knowledge and ideas—teachers discuss in class have moral implications that are often ignored because of the feeling of treading on thin ice. People unmistakenly believe that morality borders on or overlaps with religious messages—sometimes there is a mix and sometimes there is complete independence. Educated adults should be able to make the separation.

Morality in this country starts with selected passages from the Bible, such as Ecclesiastes, Exodus, Genesis, and the Ten Commandments; these ideas are found in the old testament and are accepted as the foundation of major religions of the world, including but not limited to Judaism, Christianity, and Islam.[1] Morality is highlighted by Anglo law—such as the Magna Carta, *The Federalist*, the Declaration of Independence, the U.S. Constitution, and, more recently, by the charters of human rights organizations. (*Note:* Anglo law provides for basic rights of common people and also provides for checks and balances in government. Political leaders can be voted out, even

---

1. I am recommending the Bible for some of its passages, not its interpretation, which is full of landmines and quicksand. For example, revisionist history of the Bible argues Exodus did not happen as described; the violent and swift conquest of Canaan never took place; and David and Solomon were nothing more than second-ranked, local chieftans. See Israel Finkelstein and Neil A. Silberman, *The Bible Unearthed* (New York: Free Press, 2001).

impeached, by rule of law—not by military takeover or revolution.) If the students are intellectually capable, it also includes the works of Dewey (*The Virtues*), Darwin (*The Moral Source of Man*), Hume (*Of Justice and Injustice*), Kafka (*The Metamorphosis and Justice*), Kant (*Conscience, The First Principals of Morals,* and *Moral Imperative*), Maimonides (*On Evil*), and Wiesel (*Night* and *Man's Search for Meaning*).

Morality is taught in classrooms not by teaching a series of facts, not by memorizing a host of sermons or speeches, not by insisting on some ideology or making "true believers" or "cult followers" out of the common folk. Morality is taught by discussing and analyzing folklore, songs, poetry, art, film, and literature. It is our artifacts, methods of communication, and expressions of feelings and emotion that determine who we are as people and as a society. Most intellectuals and people connected with the arts would argue that a nation's greatness has little to do with military or economic power, but rather with the "quality of civilization,"[1] or its artistic achievements, which is a related method of measuring the type and quality of society. Put in different words, the artist is an agent of morality—creatively describing society and challenging assumptions, sometimes shocking the bourgeoisie and establishment, and stimulating cultural, spiritual, and noble pursuits of a nation.

Moral Content    The teaching of morality starts at kindergarten with folktales such as "Jack and the Beanstalk" (an English folktale), "Guinea Fowl and Rabbit Get Justice" (African folktale), "Coyote Rides the Sun" (Native American folktale), and "The Mouse and the Wizard" (Hindu fable), and the stories, poems, and fables of the Grimm brothers, Robert Louis Stevenson, and Langston Hughes. To be sure, teaching Johnny to read or think by assigning "Dick and Jane" workbooks or "cat and mouse readers" is senseless; the idea is to encourage good reading at an early age, to give students a way to begin reading and thinking about various emotions and feelings of self-respect, community, and social good.

In the eighth grade, students should be reading the books listed in Figure 4.1 and by the twelfth grade, they should be reading the authors listed in Figure 4.2. In the eighth grade, reading ability more readily enters into the selection process, so there is need to be more precise with recommendations. As one moves up grade levels, reading improves, and so there should be more variety and options among and within authors. In some cases, there is the possibility of reading three or four essays or books from one author.

These books can be read in traditional history and English courses or in an integrated course such as Junior Great Books, World Studies, and American Studies. Harry Broudy refers to this type of content as a *broad fields approach* to curriculum; he organizes the high school curriculum into five categories, including "moral problems" that address social and moral issues.[2] Florence Stratemeyer and her coauthors

---

1. Rochelle Gurstein, "The Artists and the Aristocrats," *New York Times Book Review* (April 22, 2001), p. 60. Also see Rochelle Gurstein, *The Repeal of Reticence* (New York: Hill and Wang, 1996).

2. Harry S. Broudy, B. O. Smith, and Joe R. Bunnett, *Democracy and Excellence in American Secondary Education* (Chicago: Rand McNally, 1964).

━━━━━━━━━━━━━━ FIGURE *4.1* ━━━━━━━━━━━━━━
**Twenty-Five Recommended Junior Great Books—Read by Eighth Grade**

1. Maya Angelou, *High School Graduation*
2. Pearl Buck, *The Good Earth*
3. Truman Capote, *Miriam*
4. James Fennimore Cooper, *The Last of the Mohicans*
5. Charles Dickens, *Great Expectations*
6. Anne Frank, *The Diary of Anne Frank*
7. William Faulkner, *Brer Tiger and the Big Wind*
8. William Golding, *Lord of the Flies*
9. John Kennedy, *Profiles of Courage*
10. Martin Luther King, *Why We Can't Wait*
11. Rudyard Kipling, *Letting in the Jungle*
12. Harper Lee, *To Kill a Mockingbird*
13. Jack London, *Call of the Wild*
14. Herman Melville, *Billy Budd*
15. George Orwell, *Animal Farm*
16. Tomas Rivera, *Zoo Island*
17. William Saroyan, *White Horse*
18. John Steinbeck, *Of Mice and Men*
19. Robert Louis Stevenson, *Dr. Jekyll and Mr. Hyde*
20. Harriet Tubman, *The Underground Railroad*
21. Ivan Turgenev, *The Watch*
22. Mark Twain, *The Adventures of Huckleberry Finn*
23. John Updike, *The Alligators*
24. H. G. Wells, *The Time Machine*
25. Elie Wiesel, *Night*

developed a curriculum based on 10 "life situations," comprising the ability to deal with social, political, and economic forces.[1] Joseph Tykociner outlined 12 basic areas in knowledge, including "integrated areas" or what he called "philosophical and aspirational sciences."[2] Mortimer Adler divided the curriculum into organized knowledge, intellectual skills, and understanding of ideas and values. The latter deals with its discussion of "good books" (his term), and not textbooks, and the Socratic method of questioning.[3] Finally, Ted Sizer has organized high school curriculum into four broad areas, including "History and Philosophy" and "Literature and the Arts."[4] The different courses of study by these authors represent a way of organizing and com-

1. Florence B. Stratemeyer et al., *Developing a Curriculum for Modern Living* (New York: Teachers College Press, 1947).
2. Joeseph T. Tykociner, *Outlines of Zetetics* (Philadelphia: Dorrance, 1966).
3. Mortimer J. Adler, *The Paideia Program* (New York: Macmillan, 1984).
4. Sizer, *Horace's Compromise.*

FIGURE *4.2*

**Fifty Recommended Great Book Authors—Read by Twelfth Grade**

| | | |
|---|---|---|
| 1. Aristotle | 18. Goethe | 35. Melville |
| 2. Austen | 19. Gogol | 36. Mill |
| 3. Cervantes | 20. Hemingway | 37. Mohammed |
| 4. Chaucer | 21. Homer | 38. Nietsche |
| 5. Confucius | 22. Hugo | 39. Paine |
| 6. Conrad | 23. Hume | 40. Plath |
| 7. Dante | 24. Ibsen | 41. Plato |
| 8. Dickens | 25. Jefferson | 42. Rousseau |
| 9. Dickinson | 26. Kafka | 43. Shakespeare |
| 10. Dostovsky | 27. Kant | 44. Steinback |
| 11. DuBois | 28. King | 45. Swift |
| 12. Ellison | 29. Lincoln | 46. Thoreau |
| 13. Emerson | 30. Locke | 47. Tocqueville |
| 14. Freud | 31. Machavelli | 48. Tolstoy |
| 15. Faulkner | 32. Madison | 49. Voltaire |
| 16. Flaubert | 33. Malcolm X | 50. Wiesel |
| 17. Gandhi | 34. Marx | |

bining traditional history and English courses into an interdisciplinary area of study; great books and great authors can be added to this approach.

In general, the content of the courses deal with moral and social issues; ideas that deal with life and how to live life; thoughts that are elegant, witty, and weighty, and make us think and reflect; and dilemmas that help us understand ourselves, our society, our universe, and our realities. By engaging in purposeful discussion, agreeing and disagreeing with the ideas expressed, synthesizing and building on ideas through conversation and consensus, questioning and testing arguments, and supporting evidence to bolster opinions, students can gain immense insight in making personal decisions and choices. The content should also help students accept personal responsibility for their behavior, and appreciate religious and political freedom and economic opportunities that exist in this country. Ultimately, the idea is to respect and promote human rights and social justice among all people and nations.

As teachers, we need to involve all students in these great ideas and books. But we cannot overemphasize the written word, because there are other methods for transmitting our culture—the values and virtues that describe the kind of people we are now and wish to become in future generations. If we rely only on good literature, we will lose more than half—possibly two-thirds—our student population who we often label as disadvantaged, deprived, educationally challenging, slow, low achievers, learning disabled, semi-illiterate, and non-English speaking or limited English speaking. Unintentionally, schools have enhanced this divide between concrete and abstract thinkers, by tracking students and because so many students come to school unable to read and understand good literature.

I prefer not to get into a debate about "whole language," in which children are encouraged to read for enjoyment and without extensive drill, and the "phonics" approach, which relies on drill and practice. In the latter case, the schools view reading not as things children are "naturally wired" to do, but as acquired skills, like learning to drive a car or play tennis, that requires structured, sequenced, and reinforced learning. I would argue, at the risk of simplifying the controversy, that good teachers (teachers who know how to teach reading) matter more than the curriculum materials or reading approach developed by the schools. Some say that investing in effective teachers may be all that is necessary to teach reading to "nonreaders" so they can appreciate good literature. Good teachers can produce better readers, regardless of the pedagogical approach or reading program provided by the school.[1] Rather than blame students, perhaps the reason we have so many poor readers is we have so many poor teachers. It's a thought, not a fact—for a fact is little more than how we perceive the "truth."

Considering Figures 4.1 and 4.2, we can make the same kind of lists for great works of poetry (Robert Frost, Carl Sandburg, Emily Dickinson), songs (Irving Berlin, George Gershwin, and Bob Dylan), art (Rivera, Picasso, and Goya), drama (*Les Miserables, Doll House, Enemy of the People*), and film (*Gallipoli, Grapes of Wrath, The Joy Luck Club, A Man for All Seasons, Sunshine, Sophie's Choice,* and *Snow Falling on Cedars*).[2] The vast majority of "nonreaders" and "slow" learners have emotions, feelings, and thoughts, and can hear and see, and can learn through audio and visual materials. Film is probably the most powerful medium to get the message across to these learners—and there are "great films," just as there are "great books." Often, teachers feel that films or movies use up precious time in class, and they fail to recognize that even the poorest households have VCRs. Just as schools distribute textbooks to students, teachers should be distributing videos for home use, or using the school after 3:00 P.M. or on Saturdays for viewing selected movies that deal with larger social/moral ideas and issues concerning people and society.

Public television offers another option for nonreaders and readers alike. In particular, the Public Broadcasting Service (PBS) produces a host of interesting video stories, most of which teachers and schools are unaware. There are more than 1,000 topics to choose from, including 350 award-winning documentaries (ranging in 90-minute to 17-hour segments). In addition, there is an on-line directory of some 40,000 video segments, cross-referenced and linked to national and state standards.[3]

Among PBS topics to choose from are Greek and Roman civilizations; the rise of western civilization; the story of the English; Asian civilizations; major religions, including several on Christianity and Islam; stories of great American and European au-

1. See Richard L. Allington and Peter H. Johnston, *Reading to Learn: Lessons from Exemplary Fourth-Grade Classrooms* (New York: Guilford, 2002); Michael Pressley et al., *Learning to Read: Lessons from Exemplary First-Grade Classrooms* (New York: Guilford, 2001).

2. The argument can be made that one or two of these selections are not classics. The point is, they are "great works" in that they were made by talented artists and depict important messages.

3. *PBS Video: Catalog of Educational Resources* (Spring 2002).

thors of the nineteenth and twentieth centuries, including a large collection of American short stories; the Civil War; War in Europe (from World War I to Bosnia); war with Nazi Germany and several stories about genocide and gas chambers; the Cold War and the Vietnam War; American presidents from Washington to Reagan; twentieth-century political leaders, such as Churchill, Roosevelt, Ghandi, and Martin Luther King Jr.; stories about American immigrants, and several on black history and black culture; and themes dealing with freedom, justice, power, and terrorism.[1] Most of the stories and themes have powerful messages and are aimed at viewers ranging from preadolescent (middle school) to adult age.

All learners have a social lens and can reason in a social/moral vein. In our role as teachers, as reformers who wish to elevate morality in our classrooms and schools, we need to move toward practices that promote caring, character, civic virtue, diversity, and social justice—ideas and policies that promote the common good. Where do we begin? If the Bible is too risky, and if the Ten Commandments is too risky (and the decision should be school based), then start with Anglo law, for it is Anglo law that made this country what it is—where there is individual dignity, individual rights, and individual opportunity.[2] Where else are individuals protected from the tyranny of the rich, the tyranny of the majority, the tyranny of religion—in short, the tyranny of ideology? Only in America (and in a few other western countries) is an individual innocent until proven guilty. Only in this country is a suspect protected by the Miranda law. Only in America (and in a few other western countries) can a freedom-fighting artist criticize and stand up against the "reactionary Establishment" without being banned, exiled, or tossed into the gallows. And only in America can an individual stand up against the tobacco industry, oil industry, or insurance industry.

Moral Dilemmas and Choices    How do moral dilemmas relate to the life experiences of a first-grader? Perhaps by beginning with a moral/legal dilemma discussion: Jack and his dad go hunting for deer one weekend. Jack's dad aims for a deer and unintentionally kills Johnny's father, who is alone and also hunting for deer. (Johnny is Jack's classmate). Jack is the only witness. Should Jack lie to the authorities to protect his father? Should Jack's dad be imprisoned? For how long? Should Jack's family be required to help support Johnny's family? The difference between Anglo law and non-Anglo law is most fundamental to the outcomes.

We are now in the fifth or sixth grade. Abba, four retired rock stars from Sweden, recently turned down $1 billion by refusing to reassemble as a group and perform 100 rock concerts.[3] One billion dollars split four ways means that each Abba singer would probably rank within the top 500 American households, and perhaps 1,000 households worldwide. Abba has no price, which is highly unusual, because

1. Ibid.
2. Anglo law means the average person has basic rights, including protection against arbitrary action by officials; the right of the citizen to participate and make decisions in government is originally rooted in the "rights of Englishmen" and was carried over to the New World, called the "English Colonies."
3. MTV Program, January 23, 2001.

the overwhelming majority of people do have a price. It is worth noting, however, that the issue is not morality; rather, it deals with ethics, which is a by-product of or overlaps with morality. (The difference between ethics and morality is a philosophical quibble and depends on which treatise one prefers.)[1]

Now, on to the eighth or ninth grade. The nation's Supreme Court justices have a price. Five pro-state rights judges denied the state of Florida (and its 2 million voters) the right to count ballots, and thus indirectly *selected* George W. Bush as president despite the fact that the people of Florida and the nation, according to critics, had *elected* another person. It is worth noting that the issue has nothing to do with justice, but politics. Certain people—based on race, class gender, or political clout—have a better chance of winning an election, getting admitted into a prestigious college, or getting away with a crime (including rape, accidental death, or inside stock trading). The problem is that the court system is supposed to level the playing field and provide justice, but sometimes fails because of social or political pressure.

Children (or adults) who continuously lose the race in a playground, fail tests in school, or are on the losing end of a social or political issue have somewhat more clarity than is generally possible for people who continuously win the race, get good grades, or are accepted by the majority culture or power elite. Black students for the last 200 years and Jewish people for the last 6,000 years understand what I'm talking about: The victims of continued discrimination (and even worse, oppression) bring to the situation a different slant or view, which is often unsettling to the "winners" or majority populace—and often denied by the latter group.

As for film, the major question to consider is: At what age or grade level can students appreciate and conceptualize good and evil, man's inhumanity to man, by seeing *Sophie's Choice*? Too complicated? Then go with *Schindler's List*. If *Snow Falling on Cedars* is unavailable, then go with *The Joy Luck Club*. If *Gallipoli* is too depressing, then go with *Papillon, A Day in the Life of Ivan Denisovish*, or *The Deer Hunter*. And if you never heard of *The Power of One*, then try *To Kill a Mockingbird, The Rainmaker, A Civil Action*, or *Enemy of the State*. Despite someone's chronological and/or geographical distance, it is hard to remain neutral or cool about the messages of these movies.

The point is, a good education should take on the characteristics of good art. Not only should it teach people to respond to changes in society but also to crises (like the WTC) and help to better understand what is happening. A good education transmits the past and present, what Dewey called the culture, in a way that it can be used in the future. On the surface, this sounds more like perrenialism, but the transmission involves the academic core subjects taught in school as well as minor subjects (e.g., music, drama, and art). Bruner used the term *disciplines* to describe essential subject matter, and Sizer used the term *areas* or *departments*. Every school and every teacher must first understand this larger concept about education and art and then plan and find their own way.

1. For those who need to know the finer moral/ethical points in life or metaphysics, I refer you to Aristotle's *Nicomachean Ethics*, Machavelli's *The Prince*, Kant's *First Principles of Morals*, and Dewey's *The Virtues*. See Chapter 3.

Education, like good art, should present to learners ideas and values that make them think about life and death, peace and war, good and evil, equality and inequality, justice and injustice. Good education (like drama and movies discussed earlier) should influence the students' minds and hearts. Likewise, good art first transmits then transforms the viewers (or readers) and makes an imprint on their memories or makes their memories come alive. By jogging one's memory, by creating an emotion or graphic snapshot, one can integrate prior and new experiences. Words are not the only medium for emotions and thoughts. A photograph, picture, statue, painting, or musical score can have the same effect on feelings and memories—in fact, this is the medium for helping us remember the past and stirring revolutions.

What Picasso achieved in "Guernica," Brecht in "Mother Courage," and Dmitri Shostakovich in his Seventh Symphony called "Leningrad," were stories—hidden subtopics dealing with protest, war, and totalitarianism. Of course, there are other important works, narratives of life, that focus on larger moral and social issues. Great literature is what good education is about; it is responsive to basic themes in being alive, people find themselves submerged in it, and the messages encapsulate and articulate emotions and thoughts essential to the human spirit.

Teachers have a choice; it is a choice that has been offered them throughout the ages. They may uncritically accept the tendencies of the times in which they find themselves and implement school programs that mirror current forces. They may uncritically accept the ideas of pressure groups that seek to further their own interests and promote their own causes, sometimes at the expense of students and society. As Harry Broudy put it, "There buds a suspicion that the reformers are not without their own axes to grind; hidden axes, to be sure, but axes nevertheless."[1] Or they may try to ensure a more enlightened place for students to learn—not only more desirable educational outcomes but also a more desirable process, a better school, and a more humane society. What we teachers need to do is to look into the eyes of our students, to care for them, to decide what they should know, and to match the content with appropriate moral messages.

We need to work together as a team to try to ensure a better place for students to learn. We need to care for our students, to make contact with them as individuals, and to help them awaken their minds and explore new ideas. We also need to decide what students should know (content), what they are capable of learning (abilities), and how they best learn (process). We need to integrate cognitive and moral learning and this mix and match should depend on each teacher's philosophy as well as knowledge of subject matter and pedagogy. The importance of philosophy is worth noting, since it will enter into almost every important decision about curriculum and teaching—decisions about content, homework, testing, grading, tracking, and more. Ideally, the teacher's philosophy should coincide with the school's philosophy and the community's philosophy; otherwise, the teacher will become unhappy and possibly be perceived as part of the "out" group, or even as a troublemaker. (This agreement

---

1. Harry S. Broudy, *The Real World of Public Schools* (New York: Harcourt, Brace, 1972), p. 8.

assumes the school/community philosophy is moral or good as well as relevant to the needs of the learners.)

As teachers, we can continue to remain placid and indifferent, concerned more about administrative trivia or whether we are entitled to another free period during the school day. Or, as teachers, we may reflect on the tendencies of the times, and act to shape our students and the world around us. Indeed, there is a danger to individuals and society in an education that accepts uncritically and acts unthinkingly. Teachers can remain powerless people in a powerful society, or they can adapt a more professional role in their work environment, and enhance the minds and moral fiber of their students.

As the world becomes more complex, more connected, and more burdened with problems, it becomes increasingly urgent to propose changes that deal with classroom and school reality, and to educate a new generation of students who are wiser and more humane than those who teach them. Dewey and Whitehead would simply say: Each generation should go beyond its predecessors and improve society, and it is the role of teachers to see to it that it happens.

Life is what you make of it! Teachers should not worry about speaking up and acting on their thoughts—or loosing their jobs at a time when more than 100,000 teachers are needed each year for the next 10 years to replace the graying teaching force and the projected increasing student enrollments. We teachers need to network among ourselves and with the parents of our students and the members of the community to effect change and reform. According to Jeanne Oakes, we need to look at reform not as a set of techniques or recommendations, but as an idea.[1] The reform I am talking about is not due to the shortcomings of good intentions among teachers; rather, it involves their inability to marshal sufficient commitment to their intentions or ideas. As teachers, we can take shortcuts and make all kinds of compromises to make our lives easier. Why rock the boat? As parents, we can turn our kids loose in the neighborhood, sending them down the block to learn from their peers (or other adults). Or, we can reinvest in our schools and community, taking time to integrate education with scouting, sports, and other groups and institutions that foster adult bonds with children and integrate home life with school life.

## Changing American Society

David Riesman's *The Lonely Crowd* appeared 50 years ago; its central thesis coincided with the most important change shaping American culture: moving from a society governed by the imperative of production and savings to a society governed by technology and consumption (which in turn led to the rise of the Motorolas and IBMs of the world and shopping centers and regional malls around the country). The character of the middle class was shifting, and Riesman conceptualized and described its change and new habits—from inner-directed people who, as children, formed be-

1. Jeannie Oakes et al., *Becoming Good American Schools* (San Francisco: Jossey-Bass, 2000).

haviors and goals (influenced by adult authority) that would guide them in later life, to other-directed people who became sensitized to expectations and preferences of others (peers and mass media).[1]

The book was expected to sell a few thousand copies in college social science courses, but wound up selling over 1.5 million copies by 1995—making Riesman the best-selling sociologist in U.S. history.[2] For the next 25 years, inner-directed and other-directed ideas would surface as popular conversation on college campuses and at cocktail parties in the West Villages, Harvard Squares, and Hyde Parks of the country. The ideas helped explain "flower power," Woodstock, and a new generation of middle-aged men and women like Willy Loman, Mrs. Robinson, and Beth Jarrid.[3]

Riesman formulated three major classifications of society in terms of how people think and behave: traditional, inner, and other directed. The *traditional-directed* character prevailed in a folk, rural, agrarian society. Primitive tribes, feudal-era Europe, and present-day third-world countries, especially isolated villages in Asia, Africa, and Latin America are examples—although the Internet is likely to break down its isolation in terms of ideas and issues. Although these societies varied, they were and still are dominated by centuries-old tradition. Little energy was directed toward finding new solutions to age-old problems. Almost every task, occupation, and role were substantially the same as they had been for countless generations past, and each was so explicit and obvious that is was understood by all. Each person knew his or her station in life (women were generally in second place, or worse, in terms of education and power), and each was obedient to tradition. In most cases, the individual was not encouraged to use initiative beyond the limits and defined position of society; education was reduced to rituals, storytelling, and preservation of old customs, beliefs, and norms.

For the greater part, these countries (especially in places such as the Sub-Saharan Africa and former Soviet republics in Asia) have always had to fight for America's attention, and, depending on changes in geopolitics, have often fallen off the map. Which teachers among us know the issues involving Chad, Eritren, Uganda, Zimbabwe, Kazakhstan, or Kurdistan? (Probably the only black African political leader known by a majority of U.S. teachers is Nelson Mandela because of media exposure and the controversy surrounding apartheid.) Before the war on terrorism, it is hard to believe that most American high school students ever heard of al-Qaeda or could locate Afghanistan on a map, given the fact that such students lacked in-depth knowledge of Asian civilizations and world geography.[4]

1. David Riesman (with Nathan Glazer and Ruel Denny), *The Lonely Crowd* (Garden City, NY: Doubleday, 1953).

2. Todd Gitlin, "How Our Crowd Got Lonely," *New York Times Book Review* (January 9, 2000), p. 35.

3. The references are to the movies: *Death of a Salesman, The Graduate,* and *Ordinary People.*

4. E. D. Hirsh, "Seeking Breadth and Depth in the Curriculum," *Educational Leadership* (October 2001), pp. 22–25; Allan C. Ornstein, "Curriculum Trends Revisited," in A. C. Ornstein and L. Behar-Horenstein, eds., *Contemporary Issues in Curriculum,* 2nd ed. (Boston: Allyn and Bacon, 1999), pp. 265–276.

The Renaissance, the Reformation, the Age of Enlightenment, and the commercial and industrial revolutions ushered in discovery, innovation, change—and a new dynamism characterized by the landing of the pilgrims, America's Declaration of Independence (and the French Revolution), followed by American nineteenth-century westward expansion, Darwinist thinking, and early twentieth-century colonial expansion. Conformity to the past no longer dominated intellectual thinking or predetermined the behavior of men and women. Experimentation and progress (including American pragmatism and progressive educational thought) became important patterns of conduct and behavior. Within this shift came an *inner-directed society,* characterized by increased personal mobility, population shifts, growth and expansion, accumulation of wealth, exploration, and colonization. Tradition gave way to individual initiative; the strong survived and even conquered the weaker or more traditional societies; in fact, this is one explanation for Manifest Destiny and the near annihilation of Native Americans, as well as U.S. "Big Stick" policy in Latin America.

The prevailing values of inner-directed society also highlighted puritan morality, the work ethic, individualism, achievement and merit, savings and future orientation, with the nuclear family and other adults (teachers, police officers, clergy, etc.) knowing best and influencing the behavior of children and youth. On a sour note, however, minorities were "invisible," out of sight, segregated—on the other side of the urban tracks or buried in blighted, rural towns; women knew their place, subservient to men and aspiring to become typists or teachers (until they married); and gays and lesbians were in closets, also locked out of sight.

Finally, *other-directedness* is the emergent character of American society, evolving since the post–World War II period. It is the product of a social and cultural climate that has come to support and encourage teamwork, group integration, gregariousness, organizational behavior, and homogenized suburbs—and to disparage the individualism and independence of inner-directed virtues. The other-directed psyche aspires to fit and belong to the group—whether it is "Big Blue," the local PTA, or the golf club—to be accepted by peers. Conformity is extracted from peers as well as the mass media and popular culture (in the "Pepsi generation," the "Gap world," and Calvin Klein ads, everyone looks and acts the same). Conspicuous consumption and display of wealth are important to other-directed persons; nontraditional and highly provocative models (Dennis Rodman, Prince, Marilyn Manson, etc.) are popularized through the media—at the expense of traditional and so-called normal behavior and values.

In the other-directed society, parents and other adults have less influence over children than they did in the inner-directed society, and adult knowledge is diminished relative to children's knowledge. First television, and now the Internet, provide young people with access to information that in the past was mainly limited to adults; the information barrier between children and adults is increasingly shattered, or at least made porous, and in some cases the children know more about certain subjects than the adults.

Education, leisure services, and entertainment come together with increased consumption of words and images from the new mass media and flow of communications. Increasingly, relations with the larger society and with various subcultures are mediated by emerging ideas—resulting in rapid synthesizing of new fads and tends. The individual is atomized and depersonalized by large and/or loud groups, often confused and confounded by the bombardment of new images and ideas from the mass media and popular culture. Recent writers have described this shift in culture in terms of the "organization man," "future shock," "greening of America," and "postmodern world."

## Postmodern Society

The new world we live in (at least in the United States) is a place where our fundamental beliefs and rational arguments are challenged by modern beliefs and language not common to the scientific and technological community. Rather, one relies on cultural meanings and class differences, social and political context, metaphors, qualitative data, accusations (e.g., "you're a racist") and chaos theories (the unpredictability of people and events). Henry Giroux would merely argue that there are different realities that periodically intersect and on other occasions collide and cause conflict.[1] Indeed, there is no longer a common culture or agreed core of values that bind us together, considered "universal" or generic; different social/cultural groups are accentuated within society. In fact, each group demands a greater share of the pie and is willing to pull down the other group for its own benefit—quite different than in the past, when people favored a rational, scientific approach to organizing information, a common national identity, and equality of opportunity (an equal or fair chance) to succeed.

Fifty years ago, equality of opportunity meant an equal start for all children, but the assumption was that some would go farther than others. "Differences in backgrounds and abilities, as well as motivation and luck, would create differences in outcomes among individuals, but children born into any class would have the opportunity to achieve status as persons into other classes."[2] The postmodern view, today, favors entitlements (sometimes at the expense of work and productivity) and demands equal results for groups with unequal backgrounds and abilities, even if it means changing the concepts of merit or handicapping our brightest and most talented minds.

Today, we live in a society where diversity and pluralism dominate discourse and diminish conventional norms and values transmitted by larger society, including the concepts of traditional family, church, and national sentiments. In *postmodern* society, according to David Elkind, language is used to "challenge universal and regular laws that govern the physical and social worlds" with which we are familiar.[3] For the last 400 years, universal principles (such as Newtonian physics) and rational thought (such as Descartes' reasoning) have guided and transformed our scientific and social

1. Henry A. Giroux, *Theory and Resistance in Education* (Westport, CT: Bergin & Garvey, 1983).

2. Allan C. Ornstein and Francis P. Hunkins, *Curriculum: Foundation, Principles and Issues,* 3rd ed. (Boston: Allyn and Bacon, 1998), p. 54.

3. David Elkind, "School and Family in the Post Modern World," *Phi Delta Kappan* (September 1995), p. 10.

thinking. Now, all of these fundamental concepts are labeled as technological rationality and viewed as machine theory.

In technological and scientific societies, according to critics, schools become distributors of cultural capital; they play a major role in distributing various forms of knowledge, which in turn leads to discrimination by one group over others, as well as power and control over others.[1] Under the guise of objectivity and generalizable situations, it is argued by postmodernist thinkers that artistry, drama, poetry, and qualitative research have been disparaged. The world is evolving—and uncertainty, irregularity, and even chaos assume new importance for reinterpreting our physical and social worlds.

In the new world, there is no one language common to all. Language is used to convey political and social messages; it contains cultural meaning that is used to address specific issues dealing with class, gender, and race; moreover, the three terms become fused with "liberation" politics—all which become part of the folklore and heart of postmodern theory. The idea is to be relevant, not necessarily objective, and to reconceptualize, reinterpret, and rewrite contemporary social science and education theory—and link this new theory to liberation causes. The world, through language and cultural messages, is turned upside down, inside out. Most people believe that our universal principles and rational thought have resulted in (1) human progress, (2) exploration and innovation, and (3) democratic institutions. Postmodernists (especially neomarxists, critical pedagogists, and reconceptualists), however, argue that there are fundamental ideas of the West that have led not to human progress but to human exploitation and oppression, not to exploration and innovation, but to colonization and slavery, not to enlightened democracy but to class differences, male dominance, and racial polarization.

Postmodernism is a world in which irregularity becomes legitimatized and worthy of exploration as the regular, and differences (as opposed to conventional norms) and particularity (as opposed to commonly accepted theories or principles) are legitimized and transform our scientific and social worlds. It is a world where the social structures of society—such as social relations, cultural formations, and institutional arrangements—are reconceptualized and reinterpreted so that the exploited and oppressed can be emancipated; it is a world where traditional structures—family, school, the larger society—are dethroned for new family forms, school choices, and pluralistic groups.[2]

Postmodern ideas include several academic names, most noted are *neomarxism*, *postcolonialism*, and *desconstructionism*. With the latter orthodoxy, the basic idea is that knowledge is a social construct relative to time, place, and one's belief system.

---

1. Michael Apple, *Ideology and Curriculum* (Boston: Routledge & Kegan Paul, 1979); Paulo Freire, *Pedagogy of the Oppressed* (New York: Herder & Herder, 1970); Freire, *The Politics of Education* (Westport, CT: Bergin & Garvy, 1985); and Ivan Illich, *Deschooling Society* (New York: Harper & Row, 1971).
2. Henry Giroux, *Teachers as Intellectuals* (Westport CT: Bergin & Garvey, 1988); Peter Mclaren, *Revolutionary Multiculturalism* (Boulder, CO: Westview Press, 1997); and Mclaren, "A Pedagogy of Possibility," *Educational Researcher* (March 1999), pp. 49–54.

The belief system is colored by one angry word, if I may editorialize: *Raceclassgender*. Given our social lens and social biases, everything is relative and nothing is what it seems to be. Reality is what the individual or group wants it to be. There is no objective reality, no truth unless one believes in religious or political dogma.

The pen I'm using to formulate these words is not a pen, rather some phallic symbol. The American prison system, we are told, is comparable to the Soviet gulag. Shakespeare, Chancer, Cervantes—the great works—is nothing more than elitist literature, construed as part of ethnocentric, western, and mainstream culture which needs to be reconceptualized, reshaped, and replaced by minority and female authors. Schools are institutions administered by people in power to maintain the status quo; therefore, they discriminate against the under class, and are designed to train a continuous flow of workers who will maintain the system. Schools are also the arm of the law, devised to keep kids off the street, and a place for brainwashing them so they buy into and defend the system. Hence, just about everything is open to reinterpretation and revision.

**Postindustrial Society: Bits and Bytes**    Postmodern society includes what Daniel Bell called "post-industrial" society, and is produced by information and technology.[1] The singular feature of this new society is the importance of knowledge (including the transmission, storage, and retrieval of it) as the source of production, innovation, career advancement, and policy formulation. Knowledge becomes a form of power, and those individuals or nations with more knowledge have more power.

Emerging from the old industrial society, driven by the motor and how much horse power could be produced, postindustrialism was (and still is) a knowledge-based society, driven by the production of information and the preeminence of professionals and technicians. In a society based on "brain power" rather than "muscle power," meritocracy and mobility tend to be equalized among men and women. (This assumes equal educational opportunities and minimal job bias.) The stratification structure of this new society produces a highly trained research elite, supported by a large scientific, technical, and computer-proficient staff—all retrieving, manipulating, and producing knowledge. Given the computer and the Internet, brain power can be marketed on a global basis, and people in China or India can compete for knowledge-based jobs in the United States without ever having to come to American soil.

Although Daniel Bell gets much of the credit for developing the original concept of the postindustrial society, his ideas are rooted in articles that appeared in the 1948 *Bell System Technical Journal* and in the 1952 *Scientific American* magazine in which Claude Shannon (certainly not a household name) described his mathematical theory of communication.[2] Shannon proposed the term *bits* to represent "binary digits." A bit was a choice: "on" or "off," "yes" or "no," "stop" or "continue," "one" or "zero." Whereas some information was continuous and based on sound waves (such as phonograph records, radio, and television), other information was not continuous but discrete (such as smoke signals, telegraph, and teletype). On and off, yes and no, suggested

1. Daniel Bell, *The Coming of Post Industrial Society* (New York: Basic Books, 1973).
2. Bell gave no credit to Shannon.

that circuits could transmit bits of information based on logic. Eventually, bits led to bytes for storage capacity, and subsequently to kilobytes, megabytes, and gigabytes.[1]

Information, in a true sense, is neutral, just like education is neutral by itself. Although information systems and random numbers are meaningless by themselves, they are packed full of information when strung together and lead to new fields of information and power based on information. The medium is not really the message, as the cliché goes, rather it's bytes of information that count. (Originally, it was bits of information, but like the wheel in discussing the history of horse power, bits is now passé when it comes to the storage of information.)

## Remembering Rockwell: The "Old Days"[2]

I grew up in the 1940s and 1950s—a world where Norman Rockwell was popular and idealized what was supposed to be but never really was.[3] American inner-directed society and family life were portrayed in his paintings. He illustrated a Newtonian world where values were regularly transmitted by the family, peer group, church, and nation. Boys were boys and girls were girls; they could squabble without threat of litigation. Rockwell's portrayals of Stockbridge, Massachusetts (and other small towns), were safe, orderly, and antiseptic: Trees were trimmed, houses were cute and picture perfect, and there was no display of poverty or social unrest. Children played together, went to church with mom and dad, and ate dinner at the table as a family. They had regular haircuts and check-ups with the local dentist and doctor; later they went off to college (dressed in a suit) and fought our wars (without burning draft cards or defacing the American flag). Children were "normal," families were "normal," and social protest was not part of Rockwell's landscapes. Just about everyone seemed hard

1. James Gleick, "Bit Player," *New York Times Magazine* (December 30, 2001), p. 48.
2. The next several headings deal with protestors, gurus, heroes, and cult figures from the last 50 years, as well as art, film, TV, movies, music, and magazines—a slice of popular life to describe American society. Because of the artistic, musical, and media flavor, the discussion centers on history and pop culture. The 19- and 20-year-old students will be challenged, while older readers may reminisce about the "good old days," although they were not good for the majority of the disenfranchised and disenchanted populace. Nonetheless, this quickie glimpse into the past—based on bits and bytes and fading memories—has merit, since pop helped shape society, which in turn impacted on youth culture and schools.
3. If you can't recall or identify with Norman Rockwell because of your age, then think about mom or dad talking about "the old days"—at the hop or the neighborhood corner, staying out all night long and watching the submarines in the backseat of a car. Those were the days when the average teacher earned $3,000 (1950 salary) and the average worker $2,930 (*Digest of Education Statistics*, 1971, Table 56, p. 41.) A Coke cost $.10, movies cost $.25, and a new Impala convertible $1,500 (the monthly rent today for a studio apartment in many large cities). Listen to the Platters, the Kingston Trio, or the Everly Brothers sing. Whip out the old family album that shows mom or dad in younger and tighter clothing, a size 5 or 32 waist, seated next to the family RCA radio or Philco (45) phonograph player. Think about Buddy Holly and *Peggy Sue,* Jackie Robinson, and Jolt'n Joe—or a world without rollerblades, cell phones, FedEx packages, or Nike cross-trainers—and without plastic money!

working, church going, and patriotic. The only reference to race and ethnicity, or any kind of social or global concerns, came in his post–*Saturday Evening Post* era, his declining years, when he was illustrating for *Life* and *Look* magazines and married to his third wife, the socially conscious Molly Punderson.

Rockwell's world—sentimental, romantic, white, small town and suburban, Christian, a nuclear family, and highlighted by regularity and predictability—is a bygone era. The first hint of cracks in Rockwell's world—a straightforward life with values documented by small town U.S.A., religious fundamentalism, and the dominant mood of social and political conservatism—came via intellectual protest. It was apparent in the writings of Theodore Dreiser, Charles Beard, Sinclair Lewis, Walter Lippmann, Henry Mencken, George Bernard Shaw, and Oscar Wilde, as well as in the pages of the *Atlantic Monthly, Commonweal, The Freeman, The Nation, The New Republic,* and *Saturday Review*—all based in Boston and New York and comprising slender constituencies.

In 1953, Arthur Miller's play, *The Crucible,* hit Broadway. Set during the Salem witch trials to the anticommunist hunts of that time, the play had a timeless message few could miss. The witch-hunt idea helped explain America's twentieth century. Although written and analyzed as a reaction to the growing power of McCarthyism,[1] it could have also jolted memories of the lynchings of blacks, the Scopes Trial, the Know-Nothing Party, the Japanese interment camps, and the execution of Sacco and Venzetti and later the Rosenbergs. The witch-hunt idea was rooted in religious, ethnic, and religious intolerance, under the guise of making America safe from people who didn't seem to fit into Rockwell's ideal world: fair-skinned images where blondes had more fun and were more readily accepted in private clubs, the blue-suit bank and church crowd, and the watering holes for the "now crowd" (the Rolex and champagne set).

While Miller's play was on Broadway, songwriter Irving Berlin was being criticized by the conservative and religious right as the Jewish immigrant (although 40 years in the country) who had no right to compose the song *God Bless America,* now the number-one song played in schools and sporting events in post–9-11 society. *The*

---

1. For those of you who may not understand McCarthyism, it was aimed at choking and targeting liberal intellectuals. Many people lost their jobs because they were branded as being "pink," "red," or "Communist"—unAmerican. Miller knew he was a target, and in 1956 he was called before the House Committee on Un-American Activities. While Miller chose an American metaphor used in the Salem witch trials, people from Soviet Russia under Stalin and from China under Mao can identify with the play. And so can people from smaller, far-off places: half of Africa, half the Middle East, and half of Latin America—in short, more than two-thirds of the world population. It matters little if we are talking about Albania or Argentina; San Salvador, Somalia, or Sri Lanka; Iraq, Iran, or Indonesia; Mozambique, Malaysia, or Myanmar (formerly Burma), its all the same. The Committee on "Truth," "Crime," or "Justice," some government agency, will beat you down, scramble your brain cells, and reeducate you, or if not, then kill you.

The irony is most American students have no understanding of this system of "justice" and "political purity," and most teachers are either political naïve or educationally unequipped to discuss these issues.

*Crucible* also provided a clue to those who had no idea how McCarthyism was able to rear its ugly head and thrive. It was a search-and-destroy mission against liberals, especially artists, writers, actors, filmmakers (and even professors) whose imagination and creativity conflicted with Rockwell's world—a homogenized white and conservative world, a world of social innocence and religious truth, and a mass of people (later called "middle Americans" and "the silent majority") yearning for certain traditional values in the midst of change and confusion.

The vast majority of educational thinkers never raised the issue of the McCarthyism witch hunting and ethnic/religious intolerance. They were reluctant to oppose the dominant social and political mood of the country. Even progressive philosophers were remiss. In separate books, Counts and Bode came the closest in contending that progressive education had left its social ideals behind.[1] Counts warned that progressive schools had become play schools and failed to address social-welfare issues, the great crisis of the day. Bode also warned that progressivism had put too much emphasis on the child at the expense of social issues and democractic philosophy. The controversy in education among progressive educators centered on the activity movement and project method, to the extent that the curriculum should be student or subject centered, and how behaviorism could be incorporated into the larger Progressive movement. Surprisingly, in a little volume entitled *Individualism Old and New,* John Dewey warned against social protestors and labor organizers as having "Bolshevik" leanings, who he also labeled as "befuddled cranks." He urged that a collective character was essential to the solution of political and social conflicts.[2] In fact, Dewey was not concerned about diversity or pluralism; he argued that the schools should assimilate the immigrants into the larger U.S. culture.

Today, as the United States again takes measures to seek out and destroy the hidden evil among us, all those who would threaten the American way of life, check your local listings and headlines for another revival similar to the scenes in *The Crucible.* Sinclair Lewis was correct: It can happen here, although he purposely wrote the title of his book as *It Can't Happen Here.* Watch how the country starts profiling and reacting against ethnic Americans who look a little different, practice a different religion, speak with an accent, and have "funny sounding" and strange last names. Watch how the witch hunts resurface if we have another terrorist attack that reflects an extremist version of Islam.

Either the nation we live in becomes more politically controlled and less free or we simply learn to tolerate greater risks. Given option one, a top-down government policy may curtail the liberties of Muslims living in America. Unless we are willing to fly naked in the air and all subscribe to a strict honor code to maintain civil order when we enter tunnels, large buildings, and sporting events, all which is doubtful, be prepared for a twenty-first century witch hunt—or at least a new round of conservatism that curtails our freedom.

1. Boyd H. Bode, *Progressive Education at the Crossroads* (New York: Newson, 1938); George S. Counts, *Dare the Schools Build a New Social Order?* (New York: John Day, 1932).
2. John Dewey, *Individualism Old and New* (New York: Capricorn Books, 1929).

## Forgetting Rockwell: Enter the 1960s

As Rockwell's world came to an end, disillusionment and criticism mounted and the stage shifted from small towns to big cities. A host of pressure groups and minority groups began to appear on the stage, each pushing its own agenda, each vying to be heard, each seeking media attention. Americans began to confront society, to challenge the social and political order. Upon entering this "space-time" capsule, it is hard to bring together the ideas and insights of this decade. It was a whirlwind!

The 1960s produced the "beat generation" and the writings of Allen Ginsburg and Jack Kerouac,[1] and a strange mix of innocent and outrageous people who spread the counterculture through the arts, tore up the Bible, grew marijuana in their backyards, meditated, and urged America to make love, not war. Although Ginsburg and Kerouac were counterculture messiahs, a number of other minor intellectuals—wives, homosexuals, and unemployed artists, painters, and writers—played out their parts at college campuses, cocktail parties, and off-beat coffee shops.

Then came the radical students (such as the Students for a Democratic Society [SDS] and the Weathermen) who grew up in working-class and middle-class neighborhoods and small suburban towns. Now enrolled in the elite colleges—such as Columbia, University of Wisconsin, and Berkeley—they seized university buildings, urinated out windows, demanded a "relevant" curriculum and diverse faculty, and shut down the ROTC and military research. A spin-off movement produced the radical (or underground) revolutionists, such as Abbie Hoffman and Jerry Rubin, who brought together the largely separate and antagonistic cohorts of bohemia, the new Left, hippies, and rock stars to produce an antinuclear, antiwar, antiracist, anticapitalist sentiment—basically an antiestablishment view of their elders. Although the radical student movement was mainly political, and enlisted the assistance of liberal intellectuals of the era, the radical revolutionist movement was characterized by psychedelic love speaking and love making, demonstrations in big cities[2] and small towns, and musical festivals from Monterey, California, to Woodstock, New York.

The 1960s also produced the civil rights movement, including Martin Luther King Jr. and the Southern Christian Leadership Conference (SCLS), Stokely Carmichael and the Student Non-Violent Coordinating Committee (SNCC), Eldridge Cleaver and the Black Panther Party, Malcolm X and the Black Muslim Party, and, finally, black rage and black riots from coast to coast. Carmichael and Hamilton maintained that racism among Europeans and Americans had been formed and widely disseminated as a means for justifying the political subordination, economic control, and miseducation of blacks.[3] The white teachers, white social workers, white

1. James Campbell, *This Is the Beat Generation* (Berkeley: University of California Press, 2001).

2. Chicago's demonstration in 1968 drew the most media attention because it involved the Democratic Convention and pitted Abbie Hoffman and the "Chicago Seven" against Mayor Richard Daley, "the biggest boss" mayor of the nation, and his so-called facist police force in a duel of personal wits, politics, and the judicial system.

3. Stokely Carmichael and Charles V. Hamilton, *Black Power the Politics of Liberation* (New York: Vintage Books, 1967).

landlords, and white police officers were all agents of the same white racist society. Cobbs and Grier attributed the mental health problems of blacks to white racism in every corner of the country, and it was now considered healthy for blacks to act out their rage against whites.[1] The Kerner Commission, organized in 1967 to investigate the urban riots, warned of a racially divided nation.[2] A larger number of whites began to drift from Rockwell's sanitized and safe image of America and came to accept their responsibility in the lack of black progress (instead of blaming the system or black behavior and black family structure).[3] But as the cities erupted, the mayors complained and the Congress and the president began to lose enthusiasm for the War on Poverty. The connection between community programs and violence grew in the minds of many politicians, and it was questioned whether taxes should be used to employ agitators who trained other agitators.[4]

When the conflict in Vietnam became a full-fledged war, all the great hopes of the War on Poverty came to a slow halt; the war became center stage. The "best and the brightest" (David Halberstam's term of nearly 35 years ago[5]) of the Kennedy and Johnson administrations led the nation into the conflict but were unable to properly weigh the costs and benefits of different options and sunk us deeper into the rice paddies and jungles of Vietnam. This was the first war televised on a daily basis to the American public, and the bloody images of the battles and the blunders of our foreign policy led to massive antiwar demonstrations at home and got in the way of social reform.

President Johnson and his closest advisors, Secretary of State Robert McNamara and National Security Advisor McGeorge Bundy, knew the Vietnam war was unwinnable without full-scale bombing of Hanoi and then the possible entry of mainland China into the war. Nonetheless, our leaders were digging in deeper and sending in hundreds of thousands of ground troops into combat, knowing many would die in vain. Johnson's Great Society would linger and his mood swings and whining would drive aides such as Bill Moyers and Richard Goodwin to consult with psychiatrists.[6]

Today, it serves little purpose to analyze our misfortunes in the war—whether key battles might have been planned and fought differently, or whether a different diplomatic strategy could have saved South Vietnam. The war, today, is like a folk legend memorialized by Hollywood and Public Broadcast System documentaries and veterans who seek to legitimize their sacrifices. It makes little difference, now, to hypothesize whether Halberstam was correct in maintaining that it was American arrogance and overconfidence that got us into the war, or whether it was international stupid-

1. William H. Grier and Price M. Cobbs, *Black Rage* (New York: Basic Books, 1968).

2. *U.S. Riot Commission Report* (Washington DC: U.S. Government Printing Office, 1968).

3. Edward C. Banfield, *The Unheavenly City* (Boston: Little, Brown, 1970); Daniel P. Moynihan, *The Negro Family* (Washington DC: U.S. Government Printing Office, 1965).

4. Banfield, *The Unheavenly City*; Daniel P. Moynihan, *Maximum Feasible Misunderstanding* (New York: Free Press, 1969).

5. David Halberstam, *The Best and Brightest* (New York: Ballantine Books, 1993).

6. Michael Begchloss, *Reaching for Glory: Lyndon Johnson's Secret White House Tapes, 1964–1965* (New York: Simon and Schuster, 2001).

ity and George Kennan's "containment policy" against the Soviet Union or the "domino theory" involving third-world countries turning communist (starting with the Eisenhower administration and continuing with the Kennedy, Johnson, and Nixon administrations). It doesn't matter now—it matters only that the quagmire split America by its seams. The net loss was 58,000 American soldiers and about $550 billion to fight what Johnson knew in 1965, and McNamara admitted 30 years later in his own book, was a losing war.[1]

## New Art, New Movies, New Philosophers

As America lost its innocence, Rockwell's paintings fell out of favor and were replaced by the erotic and ecstatic spontaneity of other artists. The "low-brows" and off-beat coffee-house crowd gravitated to Peter Max and Andy Warhol. The "high-brows" and Park Avenue crowd welcomed the works of de Kooning and Pollock. The new art flung in the viewer's face, with paint splattered on the canvas, rows of soup cans and soda bottles, and dots in the middle of squares depicted as modern art with all kinds of high-modern ideas and seas of new consciousness. Most of it was junk, at least from Joe Public's perspective, but the critics and auction houses lapped it up as the new image and thought of American art. Indeed, it was a new era—no longer "ordinary" or "average," but rather spontaneous with flashy artists and celebrities created by "pop-op" and gay life.[2]

Not only did Warhol successfully transfer the aesthetics of gay subculture to the mainstream, and use sexual symbols on canvas as an inspiration for *pop art* but, along with de Kooning and Pollock and other modern artists, he managed to move *abstract expressionism* into second place.

Warhol was the most provocative and surreal among the new artists, the antithesis of Rockwell's "normal" world with which ordinary Americans could identify. The pop painter's images were purposely outrageous—fragmented body parts, male nudes, hernia repairs, torsos, nose jobs, car wrecks, suicides, electric chairs, racial assaults, paintings made from urine, and abstract famous figures from Marilyn to Mao.[3] What Warhol sought to do was to create a new "normal" world in which he and other outsiders could fit (one reason today why so many different people come to live in New York City); it meant tearing down accepted values and virtues of middle America—all the images and models teachers are supposed to represent to their students.

1. Robert McNamara and Brian Vandemark, *In Retrospect: The Tragedy and Lessons of Vietnam* (New York: David Mckay, 1996). As a side note, the North Vietnamese loss was estimated to be 1.5 to 2 million soldiers and civilians. Ho made no apologies and had no loss of political power, because his nation had a different value on life and was willing to absorb more combat losses than the United States, since they were fighting closer to home and interpreted the war as liberation from a colonial super-power.

2. One writer asks: How gay was Warhol? He answers, "As gay as you can get." See Wayne Koestenbaum, *Andy Warhol* (New York: Viking, 2001).

3. Holland Cotter, "Everything About Warhol But the Sex," *New York Times* (July 14, 2002), Sect. 2, pp. 1, 32.

During this period, other artists such as novelist Truman Capote and entertainer Liberace were clear about their sexual preference, challenged the psyche of the majority populace, and turned celebrity into homoerotic art and metaphors. Although the three of them might be considered the trilogy or sovereigns of "swish" for that era, their works transcend this label and their popularity lasted for decades. But it was Warhol who put gay identity in everyone's face, as a badge of honor. He did so, in the 1950s and 1960s, before gay liberation, Gay Pride, and gay parades, when to do so meant to be ostrasized by many colleagues. Warhol didn't care, or pretended not to, and thus became a political figure. In education, Paul Goodman was a comparable figure who made his gay identity clear during the same period—and flipped from college to college.

The 1960s tilted mainstream America to the political left and bolstered media influence, the ethic of the "now" generation, a host of happenings, sit-ins, street marches, protests, acid and LSD trips, yoga and meditation, big bands, loud music, and all sorts of preachers and prophets who sang or voiced highly charged lyrics or words to those who would listen. Summing up this part of society and young generation was the lyrical advice, "If you're going to San Francisco, be sure to wear some flowers in your hair." Society was also described in the lyrics, "All across the nation, such a strange vibration, there is a whole new generation, with a new explanation." Little Richard, Jimi Hendrix, and Elvis Presley were just as popular to American youth as Billy Graham, Pat Robertson, and Jim and Tammy Baker were to the older, more conservative crowd. When the Beatles arrived in New York in 1964, it was "groovy," but the Vietnam war and urban riots, coupled with the assassination of John and Robert Kennedy, and then Martin Luther King Jr. and Malcom X, created a serious mood that blanketed the country.

Intellectuals tried to make sense of what was happening, and many became overnight sensations and the talk of television shows and cocktail parties, then in academic circles, followed by the world of Archie Bunker and the "silent majority." Similarly, intellectuals tried to make sense of the changing American society in magazines such as the *Partisan Review, Commentary, Transaction,* and *Dissent,* which no more than a few hundred scholars and professors read. But some of the intellectuals eventually gained access to a national audience through television talk shows; they were allowed, for the first time, to startle and befuddle the public with claims and counterclaims, and a host of prescriptions that must have sounded like castor oil or viewed like a Woody Allen movie (sheer frustration) to Americans now itching for instant answers. In simple language, "What was," "What is," and "What might be" were being challenged by all sorts of "knowledgeable" folks.

The most interesting intellectuals of the period were probably William Buckley on the right, who was the editor of the *National Review* and a super-verbalizer, and who no one fully understood because of his self-indulgent digressions and hubristic vocabulary, and Pat Moynihan, then a Harvard professor, and Irving Kristol, the editor of *Public Interest,* both who became for a time the conservative right's favorite liberals as their views shifted to the right and they were dubbed "neoconservatives." There was also Gore Vidal, a throwback to the Roosevelt era, whose parodic prose and archaized quotations were just as confusing as Buckley's chatter. (No one really

knew for sure when these two critics were joking or serious.) Although not an intellectual, nor a light-weight, *Playboy*'s Hugh Hefner was quick to reinvent Freud's
"pleasure principle" as the driving force behind the 1960s. The irony is that Hefner's
lifestyle became ho-hum compared to a new wave and cast of characters parading in
our faces out of Manhattan and San Francisco's multisexual, multidrug-addicted
world: drag queens, male prostitutes, cross-dressers, transvestites, crack addicts, and
methodone addicts.

A new group of television talk shows, low-minded biographies, and quickie
books crammed with photos emerged on American bookshelves—each hair splitting
their particular social theories, spiritual and uplifting messages, and personal struggles around race, class, and gender. Each spokesperson tried to outdo and outplay the
other, spread his or her own message and metaphors, perform intellectual judo flips,
and handicap the other "intellectual heroes." How alien it all seems now—all the talk
shows, intellectual trajectory and overheated oratory that was taken seriously at the
academic level and among government policymakers.

There may no longer be anyone in America like Allen Ginsberg and Jack Kerouac
or Abbie Hoffman and Jerry Rubin, or Martin Luther King Jr. and Malcom X, or Betty
Friedan and Gloria Steinem, but America is not the same for them having been here.
We rarely encounter these people in textbook pages today. Their breath is stilled, their
voices silenced, but the converse dictum is alive and well: The harmony and rhythm of
the living are modified by the words and deeds of these dead. Most of the philosopher-
kings of the era are quiet now and have disappeared from the public eye. In their place
a "hipper" type of thinker has emerged—well dressed, the epitome of cool, the image
of a quick-witted 40- or 50-year-old news anchor or talk host (e.g., Fox's Brite Hume
and Bill O'Reilly, CNBC's Chris Matthews and Brian Williams, and CNN's Aaron
Brown and Connie Chung). Americans who still identify with the traditional networks
and older anchors—Rather (age 71 as of 2003), Jennings (64 years), and Brokaw (63
years)—have a listening audience whose median age is 58 years and regarded by the
younger, more hip, audience as one or two steps from the grave.

Whereas the older intellectuals were considered somewhat irrelevant and out of
place outside of the Northeast, this new breed of the mass media personalities have
the knack to deal with and summarize emerging ideas, bloated digressions (keeping
the other person on track), and wearisome thoughts in 30-second sound bytes. The
words we now hear are packaged so that the "average" viewer from the heartland
of the nation can relate to the thoughts and associations of the speaker. These people
speak to us at the ninth- or tenth-grade level, quite different from the theories, hypotheses, and prose of the old philosopher-kings.

And who needs to read any more, given the new breed of television personalities
and shows that entertain us and make us aware of world events in 30 or fewer minutes? Earlier high school generations found relevancy in books such as *Catcher in the
Rye, Zen,* and *Catch 22.* No contemporary readings seems to have galvanized today's
teens. Once we get beyond first-tier colleges, professors bemoan how little their students
read and the lack of their core or intellectual knowledge base. Ask college students to
discuss Louis Brandeis, Thomas Hart Benton, Sinclair Lewis, Walter Lippmann, Lewis
Mumford, Thomas Mann, or Eugene O'Neil. It's like speaking to a wall. I guess young

people, today, await artificial intelligence to alter their shortfall in general knowledge as surely as the earlier generation signed up for walking on the moon.

So, we come to the end of the Rockwell era and transcend beyond the abstract, post–Warhol world, and we ask, how does it all fit into our "simple," mundane world? By the late 1960s, the shift in thinking from optimism to pessimism was keenly represented by Stanley Kubrick's movie *2001: A Space Odyssey.* The 1968 movie represented a dark, dangerous, and destructive view of humanity—illustrated by extraordinary imagery and special effects. Kubrick's view of the future, often enigmatic and gloomy for the last 35 years, parallels the terrorist attack on the World Trade Center. The image of Kubrick's monolith—a mysterious, blurry, technological object pointing to the stars—has reappeared at "Ground Zero" in the form of several black-glass building slabs surrounding the twin-tower rubble.[1]

The vision of the future, depicted in Kubrick's last picture and released in 2001, *AI: Artificial Intelligence,* is a bleak and mysterious rendering. In the final scene, a robot child flies into the "Forbidden Zone"—over the rubble caused by World War III. There, partially sunken below the water line, is the World Trade Center. In both of Kubrick's movies, the viewer is dealing with the potential of technology—a tool for both creation and destruction, both peace and war, both good and evil—which can be influenced by other factors such as aliens or human politics and religion. Indeed, the advancement of humankind from the ape to man is based on humans' intelligence and technology—both which can be used for making weapons and committing mass murder or improving the human condition and extending life.

In the aftermath of both the movie and year 2001, it would seem that the black monolith is still part of our existence. I recall more than 30 years ago walking out of the movie *2001: A Space Odyssey* exhausted and somewhat confused and unsure about all the messages and points of the movie. As New York, the United States, and the free world recovers from 9-11, beyond 2001, there remains among us a certain amount of disbelief and bewilderment—the same kind of feeling generated by that movie. Aliens have not descended on earth, but people since the beginning of time continue to channel their tools and intelligence to commit murder and other vile acts. This melding of hate and technology (the cause of humankind's savage and ruthless behavior) is the main ingredient that separates humans from the ape in the course of evolution, what Darwin refused to accept or buried within his mind. In different words, the human species is the most savage and ruthless animal, and it is the emotions (potential for hate) and intelligence (potential use of technology) that makes them the most dangerous of all the animals.

In both films (*2001* and *AI*), there is an ambiguous ending; the parallel with reality is uncomfortably similar. The future of the next generation has some ambiguity as the world of Islam clashes with the western world. Unfortunately, the world has not changed much since 1968, except that the means of destruction has advanced more rapidly. Along the evolutionary continuum, from ape to human to robot, how-

---

1. Alexander Gorlin, "Tragedy and the Movie Monolith," *New York Times* (December 30, 2001), Sect. 4, p. 6.

ever, the means of destruction has advanced exponentially. Instead of counting the dead in tens or hundreds, we now count them in terms of thousands, hundreds of thousands, even millions. The body counts become a number, a "mathematical truth," to measure our inhumanity and ruthlessness.

Not only is there always the possibility of World War III but there is also the potential of a nuclear meltdown, the depletion of the world's resources, global climate changes, the melting of the ice cap and subsequent flooding, a worldwide virus, and a host of other scenarios—all which can reverse the evolutionary continuum from robot to human to ape. By reversing the march of time, we will return to the stone age and fight our wars with sticks and stones. Now, that aspect of quantum theory was never discussed by Einstein, although he was aware that time could theoretically move backwards. Of course, there is hope. At the end of *2001,* an elderly and "intelligent-looking" astronaut is transformed into an embryonic child gazing at the earth, which some of us who were less confused by the movie might interpret as the rebirth of humanity, and as a second chance to find the bright side of the new millennium.

## Confronting the Zeitgeist[1]

What happened to Pocahontas, Cinderella, the school marm, and Sylvia Ashton-Warner's *Teacher*?[2] What happened to the "infant room," the "play school," and all our warm and fuzzy ideas of teaching and schooling? Can you recall when teachers earned $100 a month and could not wear lipstick or dresses above their ankles? What happened to the charm of small-town America, when being with the "right people" meant running the show or being religious? Do you remember all the moss-laden landscape of yesterday—the white picket fence, the church choir, the Boy Scouts, the Four-H Club, the school hop, a family of four with a mom and dad? Do you recall your high school graduation? What happened to our dreams and hopes? Do you recall when you could eat blueberry pie without guilt or fear of tipping the scale? Oh, for the old days, when Mr. Rogers taught us short, simple sentences—about charming rural and suburban life—when the country was separate from the city and there were no tract houses, no chain stores, and no one ever got divorced twice. Can you recall those days?

The good old days have been replaced with the harsh realities of a postmodern world—diversity, pluralism, urbanism, nonsecularism, divorce, different family forms—where normalcy is considered atypical or out of step; even deviancy is considered normal or cutting edge—evidenced by new art, music, the entertainment industries. Ludacris, Terrell Owens, Rod Strickland, Eminem, Madonna, Cher, Howard Stern, and Monica Lewinsky are models to emulate in this new world—what some traditional folks might say is perverse, or at least stretching the boundaries of decency.

With the exception of Lewinsky, who is a chubby young woman, trying to slim down, find her way in life, and regain her self-esteem, the others go to lengths to be

---

1. Meaning the climate of opinion, the spirit of the times.
2. See Sylvia Ashton-Warner, *Teacher* (New York: Simon and Schuster, 1963).

cool;[1] their worst fear is to be uncool, or even worse, boring, for they would lose their audience and millions of dollars. Their behavior—unusual, exaggerated, peculiar—is all about money and remaining in the limelight. Some of us—who vote conservative, regularly read the *Reader's Digest,* and attend fundamentalist sermons—may not agree with what these people represent or the messages they send to our children. But in terms of dollars, these new models are seemingly successful and representative of postmodern values—highlighted by hip-hop music, raw sexuality, pills and drugs, and outrageous behavior—what some artists or social scientists might call the post-Warhol expressionist show or post-Woodstock crowd.

Fifty years ago, dark lipstick was considered risqué. Today, men get facials and use nail polish, and women wax their bodies or cover their bodies in glitter. Suburban teenagers who used to "hang out" at the malt shop, now pierce their tongues and noses. Middle-aged women decorate their eyes with plastic jewelry, and both women and men of all ages tattoo their bodies—which was once the trademark of motorcycle gangs and punk rockers who, because of their "weird looks," were once unable to perform on Milton Berle's or Ed Sullivan's television shows.

And along comes William Bennett, the former head of the Department of Education under the Reagan administration. He writes and speaks about old values and virtues that characterized the traditional nuclear family and church, as well as traditional and national sentiments: honesty, thrift, fidelity, hard work, saving, responsibility, clean living, patriotism, and heroism.[2] These are inner-directed values that correspond with the first half of the American twentieth century—still part of the core values of the heartland or what others may call middle America or the silent majority. These people live along the highways and byways of America, in rural counties, small towns, "Yankee" villages, farms, and urban ethnic enclaves that still follow family/church rituals and folkways.

Bennett's tone is moral, religious, capitalistic, Protestant, and pro-American, not only a throwback to Riesman's inner-directed society and Rockwell's world but also

1. One female reviewer reprimanded me for making such a disparaging remark about Lewinsky. Let me set the story straight. I have problems with the attention Lewinsky still receives, including her 2002 HBO story entitled "Monica in Black and White," and her continuous sympathetic coverage in the magazines (*Time, New Yorker,* etc.) and newspapers (*USA Today, New York Times,* etc.). Overlooking her adolescent-like behavior on television what some people might dub as "cute" or "witty," the constant media attention to this woman and her college speaking sessions among law students and women-study groups is an insult to every hard-working professional or 9-to-5 office woman. Her story and subsequent media attention is based solely on her sexual indiscretions, and I object to the sympathy and money she receives while other women work for a living.

Tammy Faye Baker, another sad case, struggled to upgrade her image. I had no trouble discerning how much of Tammy's "wounded-woman persona" was fake, and the same is true with Lewinsky's behavior, which was calculated to ensure sympathy and project a new image made to sell herself or some product. For a summary of the HBO coverage, see Carla James, "Telling Her Own Story," *New York Times* (March 3, 2002), Sect. 2, pp. 11, 37.

2. William Bennett, *The Children's Book of Virtues* (New York: Simon and Schuster, 1995); Bennett, *The Broken Hearth: Reversing the Moral Collapse of the American Family* (New York: Doubleday, 2001).

rooted in the themes of William McGuffey, whose popular *Readers* (which were also moral, pro-capitalistic, Protestant and pro-American) sold over 120 million copies between 1836 and 1920 and were used in a few school districts up to the 1960s.[1] Alas, Bennett's ideas are an updated version of McGuffey and reflect the conservative "reform" agenda affecting middle America, people who graduated from McGuffey to the *Reader's Digest,* who prefer the "normalcy" of Norman Rockwell over the "non-normalcy" of Andy Warhol's world, whose models include Pat Robertson, John Wayne, Colonel Sanders, and Sam Walton, and presidents Reagan, Bush, and Bush.

## EPISODE *13*

## Postnuclear Family

The story of American immigration is characterized by Ellis Island and millions of people from all over the world, uprooted and coming to the "promised land" with all their belongings in their hands, having no prospective jobs, but lots of optimism and faith in the American dream. The small farmer, shopkeeper, peddler, and painter, the illiterate and the literate, all came from the Old World to breath freely in the New World and to bequeath to their children the opportunity of a better tomorrow. The story of the immigrant children studying long hours in school and at home to become doctors, lawyers, and corporate chiefs is based on the folk culture and nuclear family of the American immigrant—children pleasing mom and dad, bringing honor to the family, rising from rags to riches. The pictures and displays at Ellis Island remind us of these images—a history that the vast majority of homogenized Americans today do not understand or relate to because they no longer fully appreciate or know their own roots or the history of America. It's a sad commentary—how quickly Americans forget and take for granted their liberties and way of life, while hundreds of millions of people across the oceans and south of our border want to emigrate to this country.

As the 2000 census was tallied, many Americans were shocked and disappointed that the nuclear family (mom and dad and the children living under one roof) now comprises less than 25 percent of the households in the United States.[2] Now, every married male can lay claim to being in an imperiled minority with the need for some favorable treatment—a laughable stereotypical person (Homer, Al Bundy, etc.).

Divorce rates continue to hover over 50 percent, but a vast majority of former spouses remarry for a second and even third time. These are trends that have produced, according to one social critic, "nearly as many stepfamilies as nuclear families."[3] Within these new blended families, we have a growth of stepsisters and

1. Ornstein and Hunkins, *Curriculum: Foundations, Principles and Issues.*
2. Joe Queenan, "Nuclear Dad: Last of My Kind," *New York Times* (June 17, 2001), Sect. 9, pp. 1–2.
3. Alex Kucznski, "Guess Who's Coming to Dinner Now," *New York Times* (December 23, 2001), Sect. 9, p. 1.

stepbrothers, and former spouses and family members who 20 years ago would have nothing to do with the other are now finding it practical to stay connected, especially during holidays. American divorce culture has traveled far beyond *The War of the Roses* or *Kramer vs. Kramer.* Although postdivorce life may not be as cozy as depicted on *The Brady Bunch*, former spouses seem to be in closer contact with one another, exhibiting a new tolerance because of the children. Indeed, it is not surprising in some households to find "Dad and wife no. 2 [sitting] down with mom and her new beau" and all the stepchildren from the blended marriages, at the holiday dinner table.[1]

In addition, the likes of Robert Young in *Father Knows Best* is being replaced by the unwed couple—a man and pregnant girlfriend living together with no plans for marriage. (She only wants a baby because of her biological clock.) Today, there are about 5.5 million unwed couples living together, a 72 percent increase over the previous decade.[2] The figures include gay and lesbian couples, although the increase is mainly due to couples of the opposite sex, and some of these couples have children. Profamily and church groups obviously view this trend as evidence of moral and social decline.

Indeed, Rockwell's popular art was a form of escapism in a sugary-coated world—no more real than *The Andy Griffith Show* (Mayberry or "Life as I would like it") or Cinderella's story (the young maiden marries Prince Charming). Perhaps because there were so many people seeking simple-minded answers and fairy-tale opportunities, Dr. Spock was popular with moms and dads alike. He told parents they could use common sense to discipline and help children grow and develop. He saw children as innocent and immature, and, just like Rockwell and Griffith, in need of parental guidance and support, which the nuclear family was expected to provide. Spock's "how to" book outlined for parents (and other adult authorities) methods for protecting and supervising children—and children fell in line and embraced parental and adult authority. Indeed, James Dean's movies were popular among teenagers in the 1950s because he rebelled against parental and adult authority; later, Elvis Presley jolted the social order (and all the "decent" people) as young girls embraced his lyrics and watched his hips, in stark contrast to American family values that stressed morality, conformity, and keeping up with the Joneses. Not only did Ed Sullivan have trouble with Presley's moves and gyrations, but so did Aunt Ida and Aunt Mary, mom and dad, and more than half of America.[3]

Recall that I grew up in the 1950s—in an idealized, magical, and stable world of unbridled optimism. The literature for children was *Winnie the Pooh, Peter Pan*, and *Tom Sawyer.* Popular TV programs were *Howdy Doody, Captain Video*, and *Magic Cottage*, and for the daring and heroic there was *The Cisco Kid, The Lone Ranger,*

1. Ibid.
2. Daniel Voll, "Unwed Dad: Marriage Is Just a Maybe," *New York Times* (June 17, 2001), Sect. 9, pp. 1–2.
3. Hollywood made efforts to reduce national concern over the likes of Presley, Brando, and Dean by pushing clean-cut figures such as Troy Donahue, Pat Boone, and Tab Hunter—blonde, blue-eyed, sincere-looking guys who would never take advantage of someone's daughter. As rock and roll gained popularity, all the "chaste" and "pure" crooners and actors lost popularity; their TV gig ended and their acting was reduced to cameo performances.

and *Flash Gordon.* On Broadway, adolescent rebellion was portrayed by the music and dancing of *West Side Story* and later *Grease.* According to David Elkind, childhood was seen as a playful period where children should enjoy themselves—where parents set limitations and knew what was best for children and where they provided an abundance of time, patience, and love.[1]

Given the nuclear family of the post–World War II period, up to the Eisenhower years, Mom stayed home and displayed her maternal and caring instincts by raising children and cooking and cleaning—exhibited by the "Betty Crocker" mentality and later on TV by June Cleaver in *Leave it to Beaver.* Dad brought home the "bacon" and was considered rational, knowledgeable, hardworking, and head of the family—best represented by Robert Young in *Father Knows Best* and by James Stewart in *It's a Wonderful Life.*

I do recall a crack in the armor, a female model that did not fit the strict moral code or custom of the day. Wonder Woman, the first popular female comic character, was sort of a tough, super-heroine woman, the counterpart to Superman, Batman, and Captain Marvel. She was created in 1941 by a male psychologist named William Marston who asserted that the Amazon woman represented a new type of woman who would eventually "rule the world."[2] The early editions inferred lesbian intimacies among her female friends from the Amazon Island. On Paradise Island, where she lived, there were no men. Wonder Woman asserted this is "where we play many binding games [and] is considered the safest method of trying a girl's arms." Wonder Woman was representative of the new feminism about to explode on the American scene, and she appeared on the cover of the first issue of *Ms. Magazine.* The Amazon giant looked and acted the part of the new woman, somewhat similar to Nancy Sinatra's boots and shorts and, before that, Betty Davis's piercing eyes and cigarettes.

As for blacks, they knew their place: Women were seen as Aunt Jemima and Butterfly McQueen (in *Gone with the Wind*) and men as *Amos 'n' Andy.*[3] Hispanic

1. David Elkind, *Ties That Stress: The New Family Imbalance* (Cambridge, MA: Harvard University Press, 1994).

2. Les Daniels, *Wonder Woman: The Life and Times of the American Princess* (New York: Chronicle, 2001). Wonder Woman's favorite expression was "suffering sappho," a passing resemblance that her author William Marston maintained that "women enjoy submission." Although Hugh Hefner might agree, and *Playboy* illustrated the point, Gloria Steinem (who has always been one of my favorites) and *Ms. Magazine* might have a different spin about female positions, female silence, and female behavior.

3. At that time, given Jim Crow laws, white America defined what and who black Americans were. Although blacks have gained considerable political power, racism is still alive and well, and much of America still stereotypes blacks, although the perceptions and labels have changed in the last 50 years.

Race as a category is both a social and political label, whereby those in power are able to assign characteristics or qualities that infer a stereotype or label and then have those characteristics or qualities bolstered by institutional structures and social relations that in turn affirm the stereotype. The process is designed to control and predict the behavior of the powerless group (and has included degradation and discrimination). See Glen C. Loury, *The Anatomy of Racial Inequality* (Cambridge, MA: Harvard University Press, 2002).

Americans and Asian Americans did not exist on television unless you tuned in to *I Love Lucy* and got a glimpse of the "hot-blooded," handsome face of Desi Arnaz, or unless you managed to see a rerun of Charlie Chan, portrayed by Warner Oland. By and large, minorities did not live in "our" neighborhoods, certainly not in the "Magic Cottage" or later in "Mr. Rogers' Neighborhood." With the exception of the Census Bureau once every 10 years or Glazer and Moynihan in *Beyond the Melting Pot,* no one really bothered to distinguish among nonwhite ethnics; it was not until 35 years ago that Andrew Greely and Michael Novak made the distinction and social scientists took notice of white ethnic groups.[1] For the greater part, however, the social problems of American society were (by the 1960s) to be defined in terms of poverty and race—and ignored the group consciousness of white ethnics; later, gender was added to the list of "oppressed" minorities.

In recent years, according to Gloria Steinem, there has been backlash against women's advances—a hostility that includes rock lyrics that degrade women and support bombing abortion clinics, from Internet porn to media meanness that jeers and humiliates women for their looks (Linda Tripp), weight (Camryn Manheim), physical condition (Janet Reno), hymophobic look (Hillary Clinton), or sexual digressions (Monica Lewinsky).[2] Powerful men may be criticized and even lampooned in the media, but not with the intent of proving their inferiority by highlighting their "rolly-polly" waistlines or vanishing hairlines, not by exposing their physical vulnerabilities or ridiculing their sexual indiscretions.

Actually, the age of innocence began to peel off in the mid-1950s, when actor James Dean died on a California roadway, and when Dodgers' owner Walter O'Malley moved the "Bums" out of Brooklyn for a few bucks. This was the same person, who 10 years ago risked his business and fortune and hired Jackie Robinson over the groans and howls of all the other baseball owners. Then B. B. King, Jackie Wilson, and Little Richard descended on the scene, and along with the rhythm and blues craze, they were warm-up acts for Martin Luther King Jr.[3] The lyrics and animated dancing did not lead to delinquency or decadence, but rather to democracy and dreams.

The "good" life, the Puritan society Rockwell painted, was coming to an end. Rockwell tried to paint more "serious" and "relevant" subjects by painting Ruby Bridges, a young black girl on her way to a newly integrated school in New Orleans, reflecting the post-*Brown* (1954) era. His painting signaled the end of his identification with the common white folks of Stockbridge he painted.[4] It coincided with the

1. Nathan Glazer and Daniel Moynihan, *Beyond the Melting Pot* (Cambridge, MA: MIT Press, 1963). Also see Andrew Greeley, *Why They Can't Be Like Us?* (New York: Institute of Human Relations, 1969); and Michael Novak, *The Rise of the Unmeltable Ethnics* (New York: Macmillan, 1972).

2. Gloria Steinem, "Lovely to Look Upon—Or Else," *New York Times,* (January 16, 2000), Op Ed p. 17. The parenthetical examples are my own.

3. Some people might say that rock 'n' roll started with Muddy Waters's blues and Sonny Boy Williamson's harmonicas followed by the sounds of Chuck Berry and Bo Diddley. In either case, the white audiences heard the beat and music which changed the world.

4. "Reassessing the Art of a 'Lightweight'," *New York Times* (November 7, 1999), pp. 1, 54.

nation's turn of events and pending social crisis. As the decade came to an end, James Conant, in *Slums and Suburbs,* warned that social dynamite was building in the cities,[1] a concept with which Rockwell's people could not identify. On the heals of Conant's book, the Eisenhower years were also coming to a close; the War on Poverty and civil rights movement was about to have an impact on the right-minded, moral-minded, ordinary folks of America.

## Dad: Popular but Misunderstood

Not until *Ozzie & Harriet* were wives and husbands treated as equals on TV, epitomized by the fact that this was the first couple on TV to sleep in the same bed. *The Honeymooners* took women's status a step further by Alice and Trixie continuously challenging and putting down their respective husbands—turning Jackie Gleason and Art Clooney into buffoons—almost a white *Amos 'n' Andy* act. Today, of course, many TV husbands are treated as idiots or cavemen, starting with the popular Archie Bunker in the 1970s *All in the Family* and more recently with Homer in *The Simpsons,* Al Bundy in *Married with Children,* and Jake Mallow in *Unhappily Ever After.* Periodically, men exhibit power on television, but they are still denigrated. Indeed, Mr. Burns, the business tycoon in *The Simpsons,* is a better known robber baron than Rockfeller I or Ford I—certainly better known than Ayn Rand's super-capitalists or the current list of CEOs in *Forbes.*

It is fashionable today to make fun of and ridicule men—ironically, the same kind of men who are part of Tom Brokaw's *Greatest Generation,* Stephen Ambrose's *D-Day,* and Stephen Spielberg's *Saving Private Ryan.* These were men from all parts of the country who rose to the occasion, put their lives on the line, and saved the world from the horrors of the Third Reich. Afterwards, the survivors went home, went on with their lives, and didn't talk about their deeds. The public rarely understood these men, and they were dubbed by intellectuals, in a culturally biased and prejudicial way, as part of the "bourgeois" and "working class," and later as part of the "silent majority" and the "shoot'n, hunt'n crowd." In their declining years, they were merely written off as "crusty old men," silly and outdated, and portrayed by Jack Lemon and Walter Matthau. The vast majority never read Aristotle, Plato, or Homer, nor could they distinguish good wine from mediocre wine, but they understood the implications of the racial Nazi doctrine without ever reading Wagner, Nietsche, or Heidegger. The vast majority did not and could not understand feminism, much less gender politics, but they were faithful to their wives and family.

The 1950s was the last decade when families were expected to remain intact—men and women were supposed to marry and live happily every after until death did they part. The result was a great many unhappy spouses—unloving marriages for the sake of the children, the church, or "the Joneses." Of course, women who didn't marry were "old maids," "spinsters," or "school marms." Lesbian, gay, bisexual, or

---

1. James B. Conant, *Slums and Suburbs* (New York: McGraw-Hill, 1959).

transgender people, or the broader notion of "queers," were not "out"—but still locked in closets.[1]

## New Family Types

Historically, U.S. society and schools have drawn support from the nuclear family (two parents living with the family), which grew to prominence in Western society during the last two centuries. The nuclear family has been described as highly child centered, devoting its resources to preparing children for success in school and a better life in adulthood than that of the parents.

Today, the notion of family is very different. Given the popularity of diversity, pluralism, and irregularity, the nuclear family is an anomaly. Overall, about half the youth under age 18 have been in a single-parent family for some part of their childhood.[2] The nuclear family has been replaced by many different family forms—usually without a father at home—all claiming to provide enriching child-rearing experiences and all refusing to admit to the potential detrimental effects of a single female-headed household, divorced family, remarried family (with half-brothers and half-sisters), gay and lesbian adaptive families, and so on.

Given today's alternative communicative and cultural contexts, the claim is that the traditional nuclear family is far from ideal, often loveless and dysfunctional, while the modern, postnuclear family provides love and support for children. The fact is, however, parent-child interaction has declined 40 percent in the last 20 years, 75 percent of women with children were working in 2000 compared to 18 percent in 1950, and the number of latchkey children, ages 6 to 14, has soared to 70 percent.[3]

In some intellectual and gender-visionary circles it is now "hypercorrect" for women not to rely on men for economic support or even for having children, since sperm banks exist. Society is pushing the frontiers of cloning. It is also marching toward the day when women, married or single, will be designing babies—eliminating

1. In the same way that blacks can use the word *nigger* to make various points and whites cannot without the potential of being labeled racist, possibly even losing their jobs, most heterosexuals are not allowed to use the word *queer*. In both subtle and blatant ways, what can be said in print or public is not only determined by context but also by the identity of the messenger. This obviously creates a double standard in the social sciences, literature, and the arts. To be sure, James Baldwin, H. Rap Brown, and Dick Gregory have used the word *nigger* in their books and titles, and Colleen Copper, Cindy Pawon, James Sears, and Eve Sedwick comfortably use the word *queer* in their comments and writings, as do James Baldwin, Truman Campote, and Oscar Wilde. *Neurotic, hysterical,* and *bitch* are other loaded and potentially liable words.
2. Stephanie Coontz, "The American Family and the Nostalgia Trap," *Phi Delta Kappan* (March 1995), pp. K1–K10; Lynn Smith, "Giving Context to Issues '90s Families Face," *Los Angeles Times* (November 12, 1997), p. 3.
3. David Blankenhorn, *Fatherless America* (New York: Basic Books, 1955); Peter Brimelow, "Marriage Rings and Nose Rings," *Forbes* (February 10, 1997), pp. 140–141; and Allan Ornstein and Daniel Levine, *Foundations of Education,* 8th ed. (Boston: Houghton Mifflin, 2003).

genes for undesirable traits and adding genes for desirable traits—and in the process altering the DNA of generations to come. This will not be the work of some mad scientist squirreled away in a dungeon lab or hidden below the ocean floor (as with Lothar, Joker, or Dr. No), nor by some eugenetic offspring of Dr. Frankenstein or Dr. Mengles, but by legitimate government-sponsored agencies and big-business biogenetic companies. And, as we live longer, will traditional marriages survive 70 or 80 years? Will we invent other relationships or family forms to supplement what we used to call marriage and the nuclear family? Given the politics of diversity and feminism, the new notions of normality and liberated behavior, sex transplants and Internet porn, the nuclear family seems on its way out.

Even when couples remain married, what some might call a "traditional" family, there seems to be a plentitude of lust, a yearning for extramarital affairs, that has infected the working and middle class. These are the same people who, during the Rockwell days, fit the mold of Ozzie and Harriet and Mary Tyler Moore and Dick Van Dyke. Although today these people still attend church services, they no longer believe or care that they might burn in hell. These people are better educated than those from Rockwell's period, but they seem to have a greater sense of incompleteness.

If I was gay or lesbian, I might argue that the nuclear family no longer demonstrates moral superiority compared to those who have opted for other family configurations. If I was a spiritual healer or epidemologiest, I might give some advice, point to television trash shows, or even blame the water we drink for this new morality. If I was an irate parent, I would look to the schools and the permissive attitude that provides a choice and dispenses pink and purple condoms to high school students. And if I was an owner of some out-of-the-way motel, or a fancy hotel, I would probably give out gold and platinum membership cards, two-for-one weekly specials, or sell computerized playmates. I might also hire some high school student to place ads on auto windshields in nearby shopping malls.

Sounds silly or warped? Well, in the post-Rockwell era, with only 25 percent of households in the United States living under a single roof as a nuclear family, marriage can be viewed as some sort of "emotional endurance test." In postmodern, postcolonial literature, where there is a redeployment of vocabulary, black is not black, white is not white, a male (or female) is not necessarily a male (or female), and normal sexual boundaries are no longer normal. In this new "intellectual" world, the boundaries of marriage become stretched with a new language of "sexual space," "geography of sex signals," "global patterns and traveling," and other weighty, radical, or perverse matters, depending on one's politics, level of generosity, and the rules of "scholarship" that are evolving at a given moment. And, the latest warrior of free speech and civil liberties is Harris Mirkin. He turns normalcy upside down and argues there is nothing wrong with adults involved in sex with children. The panic is much like the way people once viewed female sexuality, premarriage sex, and homosexuality.[1]

1. "Pedophilia for Progressives," *Wall Street Journal* (June 6, 2002), p. 14.

## The Peer Group

Whereas family relationships constitute a child's first experience of social life, peer-group interactions soon begin to make their powerful socializing effects felt. From play group to teenage clique, the peer group affords young people many important learning experiences—how to interact with others, how to be accepted by others, how to influence others, and how to achieve status in a circle of friends. Peers are equals in a way parents and their children (or teachers and their students) are not. A parent or teacher can pressure and sometimes force young children to conform to rules they neither understand nor like, but peers do not have formal authority to do this; thus, the true meaning of fairness, cooperation, and equality can be learned more easily in the peer setting.

A major tenet of cooperative learning is based on peers learning together, communicating and helping each other, working as a group to achieve specific (in this case academic) goals. Johnson and Johnson, the major authorities on the subject, envision cooperative learning as a means of increasing cooperation and socialization and reducing competition and individualization.[1] Actually, the idea is rooted in John Dewey's notion of education and democracy. Peer groups increase in importance as the child grows up and reaches maximum influence in adolescence, by which time they sometimes dictate much of a young person's behavior both in and out of school. Some researchers believe that peer groups are more important now than in earlier periods, partly because many children have little close contact with their parents and other adults, and few strong linkages with the larger society.[2]

Other researchers note the influence of the peer group as early as the first grade, and the need to introduce rules and behavioral expectations early in the primary-grade levels that create "a respectful, caring, learning community." The idea is for the children in a class to feel safe, valued, and respected by building a sense of peer respect, responsible behavior, and self-control within the classroom and school.[3] This is an issue involving not only socialization but also moral character—attitudes and behaviors that need to be introduced and modeled as early as possible by the teacher, and infused throughout the school. Teachers should not underestimate the power of the young mind and heart to understand social and moral choices.

To foster peer relationships that support rather than impede learning, teachers need to conduct activities that encourage students to learn cooperatively. In addition,

1. David W. Johnson and Roger T. Johnson, *Joining Together,* 7th ed. (Boston: Allyn and Bacon, 2000); Johnson and Johnson, *Learning Together and Alone,* 5th ed. (Boston: Allyn and Bacon, 1999).

2. Janis B. Kupersmidt et al., "Childhood Aggression and Peer Relations in the Context of Family and Neighborhood Factors," *Child Development* (April 1995), pp. 361–375; Malcolm Gladwell, "Do Parents Matter?" *New Yorker* (August 17, 1998), pp. 56–65.

3. Ruth Charney, Marlynn Clayton, and Chip Wood, *The Responsive Classroom* (Pittsfield, MA: Northeast Foundation for Children, 1997); Patricia Horsch, Jie-Qu Chen, and Donna Nelson, "Rules and Rituals: Tools for Creating a Respectful, Caring Learning Community," *Phi Delta Kappan* (November 1999), pp. 223–227.

teachers should promote children's interaction with peers, teach interpersonal and small-group skills, assign children responsibility for the welfare of their peers, and encourage older children to interact with and assist younger children. They need to encourage their students to care for each other, to expect helping others learn, and to do what is right, rather than rely on rewards or punishment—in short, to build a sense of community in the classroom and school. Such steps promote character development and may even help counteract peer pressure for antisocial behavior.

Teachers need to introduce age-appropriate and nonlitigious solutions to limit bullying and sexual harassment practices (which were once ignored or considered "cute" by some educators). Teachers must also respond to the growing religious and ethnic diversity in classrooms and schools. (By 2010, today's minority students will constitute 50 percent of all students in grades K to 12 and more than 60 percent in grades K to 8.)[1] Teachers must be prepared to meet the unique needs of a growing diverse student population. Even teachers of single-culture classrooms need to help their students understand, appreciate, and interact with other cultures, unless they expect these children to live in cocoons for their entire lives.

## Peer Culture and the School

Regardless of the type of school or grade level, the classroom is an "accidental" group as far as its participants are concerned. Students are brought together by accident of birth, residence, and academic (or reading) ability, rather than by choice. The students of different classrooms are participants in a miniature society because they happen to have been born about the same time, live in the same area, and are assigned by the school to a particular room. The teacher may not be in this particular classroom entirely by choice; however, she or he had the opportunity to choose her or his profession and school district. The students have no choice in their assigned classroom or whether they participate; they are compelled to attend school. Student "dorks" and "nerds" have to interface with "jocks" and good-looking personable boys and girls, immature kids have to mingle with mature kids, and various ethnics and nonethnics have to learn to respect and get along with each other. The classroom lacks the characteristics of a voluntary group—far different from the school yard or cafeteria, which more than likely may exhibit certain cliques or groups held together by free choice of association and mutual interests, goals, or even ethnicity.

Of course, it is a nightmare for most students to sit alone in the cafeteria, have no one to eat with, or be ignored and left out in school activities. As Philip Cusick points out, "The single most important thing in school is to have friends," to be part of a group. Not to have friends, or to be repeatedly shunned by the peer group, results in many students disliking school. (Students who were interviewed by Cusick

---

1. Norman R. Yetman, ed. *Majority and Minority: The Dynamics of Race and Ethnicity in American Life,* 6th ed. (Boston: Allyn and Bacon, 1999). Also see Robert C. Johnston and Debra Viadero, "Unmet Promise: Raising Minority Achievement," *Education Week* (March 15, 2000), pp. 1, 18–21; *Projections of Education Statistics to 2010* (Washington, DC: U.S. Government Printing Office, 2001), Figures 10–11, pp. 10–11.

referred to "hating school.")[1] One can see the task of the teacher in a better perspective by remembering the accidental and mandatory nature of the classroom—and the power of the peer group.

The classroom is the place where children and youth must learn to get along with peers and to learn the rudiments of socialization and democracy. A student learns his or her own needs are not the only needs that have to be met and his or her own views are one of many. Compromise, tolerance toward others, and positive peer relationships conducive to learning and future social living must be introduced and modeled by the teacher. The influence of peer consensus and teacher (adult) approval are subtle but are constantly in the background. Over time, this influence shapes the students' attitudes and behaviors toward each other—and how they respect and work with others. See Teaching Tips 4.1.

In a classic text on the sociology of teaching, originally published in 1932, Willard Waller discussed the authority given to the teacher by both law and custom. However, because of the shift from an inner-directed to an other-directed society—most notably a decline in all forms of adult authority—a teacher's word is less authoritative and respected today.

In describing the teacher's role, Waller maintained that "conflict is in the role, for the wishes of the teacher and the student are necessarily divergent, and will conflict because the teacher must protect himself from the possible destruction of his authority that might arise from his divergence of motives." Waller analyzed the teacher-student relationship as a "special form of dominance and subordination," an unstable relationship that was "supported by sanction and the arm of authority."[2] The teacher was forced into this role to limit the students' impulses and to preserve order in the classroom. A harsh analysis of what teaching is about, Waller's thoughts must be put into perspective; he wrote during an era of growing child psychology and progressive thought, which he opposed. A good teacher, today, affirms the child's identity, nurtures the child's needs, and gives students a say in shaping their environment, but Waller thought that if the children in the classroom weren't controlled by the teacher, they would consort against him or her. He maintained that the teacher "not adapt to the demands of the childish group . . . but must force the group to adapt to him."[3]

## Peer Group and Social-Class Factors

A number of researchers have studied adolescents in school and have stressed the idea of social status and stratification among students. They have generally found that three student groups tend to dominate extracurricular activities and the most peer prestige: the jocks and cheerleaders, the government-newspaper group, and the music-drama group. In general, good-looking and personable boys and girls tend to fall in one or more of these three groups.

1. Philip A. Cusick, *Inside High School* (New York: Holt, Rinehart, 1973), p. 66. Also see Cusick, *The Educational Ideal and the American High School* (New York: Longman, 1983).

2. William Waller, *The Sociology of Teaching*, rev. ed. (New York: Wiley, 1965), p. 383.

3. Ibid., p. 384.

## Principles for Improving Schools

A number of important principles result in school effectiveness and excellence. Based on recent efforts to improve schools and reform education, many principles are listed below that school leaders and teachers can adapt for improving their own schools and education of students.

1. The school has a clearly stated mission or set of goals.
2. School achievement is closely monitored.
3. Provisions are made for *all* students, including tutoring for low achievers and enrichment programs for the gifted.
4. Teachers and administrators agree on what is good teaching and learning; a general and agreed-upon philosophy and psychology of learning prevails.
5. Emphasis on cognition is balanced with concerns for students' personal, social, and moral growth; students are taught to be responsible for their behavior.
6. Teachers and administrators expect students to learn and convey these expectations to students and parents.
7. The school day and school year is increased approximately 10 percent (or about 35 to 40 minutes per day and 15 to 20 days per year). This amounts to 1½ to 1¾ additional years of schooling over a 12-year period.
8. Additional remedial reading and math classes, with reduced teacher-student ratios, are provided for all students in the lowest 50th percentile on state or national tests. These additional classes replace physical education, study hall, foreign language, and elective courses—or if extra money is provided, they are part of an after-school or weekend program.
9. Teachers are expected to make significant contributions to school improvement; they are paid extra for staying after school and planning curriculum.
10. Administrators provide ample support, information, time for teacher enrichment, and time for teachers to work together. Individual lunch breaks and preparation periods are discouraged; the focus is on socialization and collegial planning.
11. A sense of teamwork prevails; there is interdisciplinary and interdepartmental communication. The emphasis is on group activities, group cooperation, and group morale.
12. Incentives, recognition, and rewards are conveyed to teachers and administrators for their efforts on behalf of the team effort and school mission.
13. The interests and needs of the individual staff members are matched with the expectations and norms of the institution (school/school district).
14. The staff has the opportunity to be challenged and creative; there is a sense of professional enrichment and renewal.
15. Staff development is planned by teachers and administrators to provide opportunities for continuous professional growth.
16. The school environment is safe and healthy; there is a sense of order (and safety) in classrooms and hallways.
17. There is agreement that standards are needed, but they are not imposed by outside "authorities" or "experts"; rather, they are implemented (or at least modified) by teachers and administrators at the local level.
18. Teachers are treated with respect and as professionals. They are trusted to make important decisions that deal with standards and involve teacher evaluation and accountability.
19. Parents and community members are supportive of the school and are involved in school activities, including some form of curriculum planning.
20. The school is a learning center for the larger community; it reflects the norms and values of the community, and the community sees the school as an extension of the community.

In his classic study of *Elmtown* (a pseudonymous Illinois town), August Hollingshead studied the relationship of social-class differences, academic achievement, and peer prestige. He divided the group, some 752 high school students, into five social classes, ranging from I upper, II upper-middle, III middle, IV upper-lower, and V lower-lower. Hollingshead found that as many as two-thirds of the students classified in the two highest social classes were in the college preparatory curriculum, and only one-tenth of the two lower groups were in this track. More than half the students in the two highest classes had mean grade scores of 85 to 100, and the remaining had mean grade scores of 70 to 84. Less than 15 percent of the two lower classes had mean grades of 85 to 100, whereas about two-thirds had 70 to 84 averages, and one-fifth had 50 to 69 averages.[1]

When it came to school participation, students of the highest social classes dominated student government, social activities, and extracurricular activities. Except for those who participated in sports, almost all the lower-class students felt disenfranchised in school: They had no fun in school, disliked the place so much that "many could not stand to come," and many spoke about and actually dropped out of school (104 out of 305). The result was that lower-class students, feeling rejected by the middle- and upper-class students, formed their own subculture—reminiscent of the Broadway play *Grease* starring John Travolta and the movie *Rebel without a Cause* starring James Dean.

A similar relationship between social class and school adjustment was found in Robert Havighurst's classic study of another midwest community called *River City*. Patterns of school progress—in terms of grades, school participation, detention, special behavior classes, attendance, and who drops out, graduates, and goes to college—were related to social class, with major distinctions between Class I (low) and Class IV (high). The distinctions were clearly established at the elementary school level, and the gap widened with each passing grade level. By examining the grades of sixth-grade students, Havighurst concluded, "It is possible to discover the probable dropouts with considerable accuracy, and also to discover those who will go farthest in school . . . and go on to college."[2]

The need to mention these two classic studies is twofold. The period during the *Elmtown* and *River City* studies was much simpler, less materialistic time, and the gaps between social classes were not as evident as today. Yet, there were notable differences among students by social class in terms of adjustment and being accepted in school. In these two studies, an average of $4,000 to $5,000 separated the highest and lowest social classes. Today, the average income gap is $80,000 to $100,000, a factor of twenty, which highlights and increases social-class differences in terms of norms, attitudes, behavior, social adjustment, spending, and conspicuous consumption. It certainty creates differences about how students perceive each other: how they dress, whether they shop at K-Mart or J. Crew, how they act, where they live, whether siblings share one bathroom at home or each have their own, and which students expect to go to college and which students are unsure.

1. August B. Hollingshead, *Elmtown's Youth* (New York: Wiley, 1949).
2. Robert J. Havighurst et al., *Growing up in River City* (New York: John Wiley, 1962).

Recall that the students in both studies were white and lived in the same community. Nonetheless, lower-class students felt excluded and rejected by the dominant middle- and upper-class student power group. Members of the lower class hung out together, formed their own cliques, kept to themselves, and were rarely involved in school activities. Today, when the income and social-class factor is compounded by race, the differences become more noticeable, as evidenced by innocent behavior of black or Hispanic students sitting by themselves or on one side of the cafeteria and a separate white group sitting in another part of the cafeteria. Check your own college cafeteria to see how the seating arrangement stacks up by race.

## Peer Group and Racial Factors

Despite so-called good intentions and efforts to provide equal educational opportunity for all minorities, the clash of attitudes and behavior is exasperated by race. The fact is, whites rarely open their schools and communities to black students and black families. A great difference exists between tolerating blacks, abiding by the law, and welcoming them.

Given the shrinking white world we live in—from 13 percent in 2000, to 9 percent by 2010, and to 5 percent by mid-century—there is need to understand, respect, and get along with people of color. The fertility rate in Southeast Asia is 7.8 children per female; the average fertility rate of whites is 1.7 children per female, which illustrates the reason for the world decline of the white population.[1] This decline is most pronounced in Europe, which has a 2000 white population of 727 million and is projected ("medium rate") by 2050 to be 603 million. This unprecedented drop represents a loss of 17 percent, which has serious social and economic implications. The "low" (and most likely) projection puts Europe's population at 556 million, a loss of 24 percent, unless its willing to take in a large number of Middle Eastern and Asian Moslems and black African immigrants.[2]

White populations in western and technological countries continue to shrink and populations of color in poor countries continue to accelerate (the fastest growing in Africa). For example, the Congo will increase from 49.1 million in 1998 to 160.3 million in 2050 (226 percent change); Ethopia from 59.7 million to 169.5 million (184 percent change); Ghana from 19.1 million to 51.8 million (170 percent change); and Uganda from 20.6 million to 64.9 million (216 percent change).[3] All the old legacies of "separate" and "unequal" in the United States and "colonialization" and "white supremacy" abroad are viewed as self-destructive in nature. Although the health and

1. David E. Sanger, "In Leading Nations, A Population Bust?" *New York Times* (January 1, 2000), p. 8; Harold Hodgkinson, "The Demographics of Diversity," *Principal* (September 1998), pp. 23–34.

2. Ben J. Wattenberg, "Burying the Big Population Story," *International Herald Tribune* (May 18, 2001), p. 9.

3. Leslie Gaton, "Report on States," *New York Times* (February, 2, 2001), p. B-10; Harold Hodgkinson, "Educational Demographics," *Educational Leadership* (January 2001), pp. 6–11.

vitality of America depend on technology and efficiency, they also assume a good political and economic relationship with Africa, Asia, and Latin America—the nonwestern, people of color of the world—as well as people of all races and ethnic
groups getting along in our own country.

Although the United States is the only western country (along with Australia), expected to grow in population in the next several decades, by 2050 the majority (white)
populace in the United States will be in the minority and the minority population
(blacks, Hispanic Americans, and Asian Americans) will be in the majority.[1] Put in different terms, about 65 percent of the U.S. population growth in the next 50 years will
be "minority," particularly Hispanic and Asian, because of immigration trends and fertility rates. In fact, from 2000 on, the Hispanic population will increase twice as fast
as the black population because of Hispanic immigration trends (whereas blacks have
no comparable immigration pool). Thus, by 2010, there will be more Hispanic students than black students in U.S. schools.[2] Most of this population growth will take
place in 10 states (with the main shift in California, Texas, Florida, and the New
York–New Jersey metropolitan area). If someone still wants to live in a homogeneous
white enclave, however, he or she can ship out to the mountain states and great plains
of the West, and watch John Wayne movies where the white cowboys always win.

With the surge of technological advances, there is a blurring of time, place, and
activity—what some business people call "telecommuters" who work in remote
places. Theoretically, you can live and work on top of the Cascade Mountains or some
villa in Bali, with the use of phones, fax machines, and computers. So long as you have
electricity, one can live in the hills of West Virginia, the beaches of the Marshall Islands, or the riverbanks of the Nile—away from companies' home offices in New
York or California. In the year 2000, according to one estimate, 24 million Americans and 10 million Europeans were occasionally or regularly telecommunicating.[3]
So if someone wants to escape or live in some exotic place, perhaps in a closet or a
mountaintop away from "city life" or cultural diversity, it is possible.

Given this brief lesson in demography and the subsequent need to learn to work
together with diverse groups in this country and in the world, we need to understand
that for many low-income, black students, academic achievement is linked to acting
"white"; in still other cases, sports, especially among boys, is emphasized at the expense of academic studies. The dominant norm and behaviors of the peer group
put pressure on others to reject white behavior and act black—even if it is self-
destructive. This preference or attitude is referred to as *cultural inversion*—a tendency
for minorities who feel at odds with the larger society to regard certain behaviors,
events, rituals, and meanings as inappropriate for them because these are represen-

1. "Fastest Growing Countries," *New York Times* (January 1, 2000), p. 8.
2. Between 2000 and 2010, the Hispanic population should increase 9 million compared
to the black population increase of 3.8 million. See Hodjkinson, "The Demographics of Diversity."
3. Kevin Voigt, "For Extreme Telecommuters, Remote Work Means Really Remote,"
*Wall Street Journal* (January 31, 2001), p. B-1.

tative of the dominant culture of white Americans.[1] At the same time, minorities who feel they have been forced into subordination, and stripped of their culture, value other forms of behaviors, events, rituals, and meanings—often those opposite of the larger (or dominant) society, as more appropriate for themselves. Thus, what is appropriate or rational behavior for the in-group (black) members in a particular community may be defined in opposition to out-group (white) members' practices.

*Victimization or Defeatism*    John McWhorter has elaborated on the theme of cultural inversion in a controversial book called *Losing the Race*. Its thesis is that poor academic achievement among blacks has more to do with their own negative attitudes than the effects of prejudice or poor schools. Black students, even at elite colleges, McWhorter claims "are really disinclined to think that hard about subjects, other than their own victimization." Besides this "cult of victimization," two other defeatist patterns prevail among black students of all social classes: the "cult of separation," which makes blacks think that whatever whites do, they should do the opposite, and the "cult of anti-intellectualism," which holds that academic excellence is a white thing.

These three patterns of thinking and behaving are rooted in the history of segregation, slavery, and unequal schooling. But today, McWhorter maintains that such attitudes have taken on a life of their own, and their negative effects are worsened by racial preferences and quotas, which tell blacks they do not have to be as competent as whites to get a job or advance on a job. Moreover, since black students as a group consistently score lower than whites and Asian Americans on standardized tests, the majority of other students figure "they [blacks] are not just plain dumb."[2]

Although McWhorter has been criticized by other black social scientists as presenting an oversimplified theory about black bias against braininess,[3] one cannot ignore the fact that the vast majority of black students are not welcomed by their white counterparts in schools or communities. At best, they are accepted because of the law, and only in a minority of cases are they treated as individuals, for "content of their character," as Martin Luther King Jr. had hoped. Black students have been told repeatedly in many different ways by many different white adults who work with children and youth—including teachers, social workers, police officers, judges, and others—that they don't measure up and/or are social problems.

In fact, part of the victimization process may have something to do with the way the majority population stereotypes or labels black students—"dumb," "lazy," "delinquent," and reading and classroom management problems. At the adult level,

1. John N. Ogbu, "Understanding Cultural Diversity and Learning," in A. C. Ornstein and L. S. Behar, eds., *Contemporary Issues in Curriculum* (Boston: Allyn and Bacon, 1995), pp. 349–367; Debra Viadero, "Even in Well-Off Suburbs, Minority Achievement Lags," *Education Week* (March 15, 2000), pp. 22–23.

2. John H. McWhorter, *Losing the Race: Self Sabotage in Black America* (Oakland, CA: Marcus Books, 2000).

3. David J. Dent, "Spelling Trouble," *New York Times Book Review* (November 26, 2000), p. 28; Jack E. White, "Are Black Biased Against Braininess?" *Time* (August 7, 2000), p. 81.

black males, according to black social scientists, are seen as "athletes, preachers, and singers." That's the so-called positive stereotypes. They are also seen as "robbers, rappers, mentally deficient and sexually well endowed." The problem is, being smart is a "white thing." As for black criminal behavior, that is viewed as a response to white racism. For black men who fail in their family responsibilities, that is also viewed in terms of white racism.[1] Victimization, defeatism, and separation can all be viewed not as a psychopathology but as a healthy response to an unhealthy social situation. This would explain away McWhorter's perspective.

The fact that white families on average are seven times (75.3 vs. 11.0 percent) more likely to be categorized into the middle and upper class than black families and eight times (75.3 vs. 8.9 percent) more likely than Hispanic families,[2] and that upper-class daddies have more connections to get John and Teddy into Harvard and George into Yale, affirmative action merely levels the field. The problem is that it levels the field, or discriminates, at the expense of lower-class and middle-class whites, not the rich who can afford to be liberal and support affirmative action policies. The policies help reduce black rage, to the extent that some blacks feel whites need to learn they are saving themselves. But it certainly creates resentment among a majority of lower-class and lower-middle-class whites who feel the direct effects of the policies. Indeed, it is convenient for the rich to have a buffer among the "silent majority" or "middle Americans"—the same people who build our bridges, fight our fires, protect our streets, and fight our wars.

The problem, according to Shelby Steele, is that instead of tying affirmative action policies to social class, or what I would call a poverty index or economic need, we have decided to give resources and preferential treatment to victims of racism. Even President Johnson's Great Society used poverty in lieu of race as the benchmark for funding; but the concept of welfare rights, affirmative action, entitlements, and now reparations have been tied to race since the early 1970s, justified by past racial discrimination.[3]

Poverty and deprivation came to be seen as "evidence" of racism, and not as a family or community problem to overcome. To some extent, it can be argued that the welfare system is designed to perpetuate dependency, fatherlessness, and poverty—to be used as evidence of racial oppression and its need for continued entitlements. The entire civil rights industry deals with helping the victims of past discrimination at the expense of poor whites who make up nearly 70 percent of the poverty class. In fact, the entitlement industry can win money and special treatment in many institutions of society without ever having to show progress in dealing with poverty, since poverty is not the issue in the civil rights movement or with affirmative action.

1. Ellis Cose, *The Envy of the World: On Being a Black Man in America* (New York: Washington Square Press, 2002); Gerald Early, "The Way Out of Here," *New York Times Magazine* (March 3, 2002), pp. 12–14; and Laury, *The Anatomy of Racial Inequality.*

2. Tom Zeller, "Calculating One Kind of Middle Class," *New York Times* (October 29, 2000), Sect. 4, p. 5.

3. Shelby Steel, "Making Color Blindness a Reality," *Wall Street Journal* (March 29, 2002), p. 18.

In a diverse nation, the demands of the strong and vocal group cannot be ignored—no matter how radical or exaggerated the claims. The misery and exploitation that slavery brought on blacks is beyond debate, and so is the history of Reconstructionism of the nineteenth century[1] and "Jim Crow" laws and segregation of the twentieth century. As a white person, however, I find it hard to accept that black America still feels the impact of slavery. As for Jim Crow and segregation, many minority groups in America have suffered discrimination. Although racism still persists, it is hard to ignore individual and family responsibilities. It is also hard to accept that blacks still need a "blank check," such as affirmative action (which is 30 years old) and now reparations, to make up for 140 years of history. At what point is the "debt" paid and forgotten, or does it just continue ad infinitum?

Giving the color of my skin, I am open to criticism. But the issues I raise are the same that some black commentators have argued in public, including Thomas Sowell, the best noted, and which John McWhorter and Shelby Steele now raise. My biggest concern is that the quota, entitlement, and preferential treatment supporters could, if they haven't already, weaken the concept of excellence and merit to the point of hurting the social fiber of society. Maybe what we need to do is find another social cause, free of racial and gender needs. Ted Turner once reminisced about saving the world: saving the whales, saving the forests and environment, saving Anartica, stopping the population bomb, and ridding the world of nuclear weapons. When asked why he was so interested in saving whales, he answered, "Well, if we could stop killing the whales, maybe we could stop killing each other."[2] Turner is more positive than the author who contends we've been at each other's throat, vying for a larger share of the economic pie, since the "caveman days" when there was more than one tribe to fight over some mountain range, river, or food.

## Socialization, Gender, and Student Achievement

In a landmark study on adolescent culture, James Coleman examined 10 midwestern high schools and found a powerful peer influence among adolescents. As many as 54 percent of the boys and 52 percent of the girls found it hardest to accept parental disapproval; 43 percent of both sexes were most concerned with their friends' reactions, and teacher disapproval was of concern only to a small percentage. Coleman interpreted these data to mean that the balance between parents and peers reflects the transitional experience of adolescence—leaving the family, but not completely, for the peer group, and consequently being influenced both by parents and friends.[3]

Students surveyed by Coleman favored such activities as dating, talking on the telephone, being in the same class, eating together with friends in school, "hanging around together," or just being with the group outside of school—activities that are

1. Juan Williams, "Slavery Isn't the Issue," *Wall Street Journal* (April 9, 2002), p. 17.
2. David McTaggart, "The Radical Do-Gooder," *New York Times Magazine* (December 30, 2001).
3. James S. Coleman, *The Adolescent Society* (New York: Free Press, 1961).

still relevant today. Esteem was gained by a combination of friendliness and popularity, an attractive appearance and personality, and possession of skills and objects (cars, clothes, records) valued by the culture. The images of the athletic star for the boys and the cheerleader for the girls were most esteemed, and the brilliant student, especially the brilliant female, was unimportant and fared poorly as a dating choice. Coleman concluded that the peer group had a low commitment to the basic goals of the school and to some degree was a subversive element in adult society; in fact, students with the most status were less adult oriented (less concerned about parent or teacher approval) than the rest of the students.

Although most data on peer status infers that students from middle-class, relatively well-educated families tend to have the most status in schools, Coleman found that the correlation between a student's family status and his or her school status was modified by the socioeconomic composition of the schools. He wrote, "The leading crowd of a school, and thus the norms which the crowd sets . . . tends to accentuate [the] background characteristics already dominant, whether they are upper or lower class."[1] Other research tends to confirm the same conclusion; that is, the effects of academic achievement and social acceptance within each school are closely related when achievement is valued by the dominant group.[2] On the other hand, there seems to be a tipping point where the values of academic achievement can be threatened—such as if another group with sufficient numbers is unruly, unable to achieve, or possesses different values and behaviors that conflict with achievement in school.[3]

Fifteen years later, Coleman, as chair of a 10-member presidential panel on youth, pointed out that extended schooling in U.S. society accentuates the self-consciousness of youth and makes the transition to adulthood more difficult.[4] Schools have the paradoxical effect of developing a substantial group of young people who have a preference for the continuation of irresponsible and even deviant behavior— at least considered deviant by adult society.

Prolonged schooling isolates young people from adults and thus tends to shift socialization from the family to the peer group. Excluded from the major institutions of society, young people are "outsiders," and consequently they adopt the political and social views of outsiders. An outsider, according to Coleman, has no stake in the existing system. Whereas youth once wanted to hurry their childhood to arrive at adulthood, the opposite has begun to be true. Once they learn to live by their own subculture, many youth are reluctant to leave it and become assimilated into the adult culture from which they were never really a part. In effect, many students become alienated from the adult world because of the way the schools are organized.

1. Ibid., p. 109.

2. Geneva Gay, *Culturally Responsive Teaching* (New York: Teachers College Press, 2000); Thomas L. Good and Jennifer S. Braden, *The Great School Debate* (Mahwah, NJ: Erlbaum, 2000).

3. Banfield, *The Unheavenly City;* Nathan Glazer, "For White and Black, Community Control Is the Issue, *New York Times Magazine* (April 27, 1969), pp. 36–37ff; and Andrew Hacker, *Two Nations* (New York: Ballantine, 1995).

4. James Coleman et al., *Youth: Transition to Adulthood* (Chicago: University of Chicago Press, 1974).

## Conformity and Female Adolescence

In both studies, Coleman was sensitive to the way bright female students were discouraged to take subjects such as math and science, and were not always taken seriously by their teachers. Moreover, they were at a disadvantage in the "dating game" and were often forced to act dumb or yield to male "smartness." Being sweet, personal, and well dressed was much more important for being accepted by boys and being part of the power clique than being smart.

One might argue that the social conditions have changed for female students, and their academic achievement is welcomed by their peers and teachers. Although there are plenty of data to suggest that teachers and professors have always encouraged girls to academically excel, historically there has been an underlying bias against girls entering certain male-dominated professions such as architecture, medicine, and law. Although things are different today, and female students are taken more seriously in high school and college, there are data to suggest that high school girls are still under pressure to conform to certain ideas of what is properly "feminine" and to avoid other behaviors. There is still an ideal of womanhood, starting at junior high school, that renders girls (and later women) different from and usually subordinate to boys (and later men).[1]

It is no secret that as girls proceed through adolescence (junior high school), they generally lose the assertiveness, independence, and academic edge they had over boys during childhood.[2] It is still somewhat of a mystery, and there are conflicting reasons why it happens, but many teenage girls lose their voice and self-esteem. Blame can be placed on sexual discrimination or harassment, the advertising and movie industry, undervalued intelligence, and mother-daughter, father-daughter, and/or boy-girl relationships.

Nevertheless, there is still pressure on girls to be cute and thin, to be part of the party crowd, and to do what "everyone is doing"—smoke, drink, pet, and so on—in order to be accepted by boys and become part of the power clique. Many mothers are still grooming young women to become good wives, good mothers, and good caregivers—and this pressure starts at preadolescence, at the junior high school level, and intensifies at the high school level. Too many mothers are more concerned about their daughters' weight gain, breast buds, and sanitary supplies than getting good grades. According to one commentator, a 10- or 11-year-old who is "wearing a bra and a maxi pad" will need some loving support from mom and dad, and "frank talk about how to handle unwelcome sexual attention, but there needs to be less emphasis on what their bodies look like but what they can do."[3]

Childhood is short enough, and one can only wonder about the effects of kids bombarded from every direction by sexually explicit magazines and movies, "dumb blonde" commercials and ads, rock lyrics, MTV videos, and provacative fashions. If

---

1. Susan Laird, "Coeducational Teaching: Taking Girls Seriously," in A. C. Ornstein, ed., *Teaching: Theory into Practice* (Boston: Allyn and Bacon, 1995), pp. 354–372.

2. Lyn M. Brown and Carol Gilligan, *Meeting at the Crossroads* (New York: Random House, 2000).

3. Eugenia Allen, "What to Tell Your Daughter," *Time* (Octotober 30, 2000), p. 70.

young girls' bodies push them into adulthood before their hearts and minds are ready, what is forever lost? How many girls are lost to a permanent culture of poverty because of teenage pregnancy? How many others are victims of sexual abuse and violence, subsequently affecting their education and employment? What percentage of family abuse, date rape, and rape on the street is never reported? In the United States, we are probably talking about one-third of all girls, possibly one-half, up to the age of 21. If we discuss second- and third-world undeveloped nations, we are probably talking about 1.5 to 2 billion females who remain uneducated, have little control over their bodies, and become marginalized by society because of cultural and religious traditions. On an international level, rape has usually been considered a weapon of war, and only since 2000 has it been ruled by the United Nations as a war crime.[1]

It is nice to be protected by gender and geography, and not have to count "victims" or "perpetrators," but it is impossible to remain impartial to this mass waste of the mind, body, and spirit. Part of the problem is that many victims live on the "other side of the tracks," invisible and without a voice, or in far-off countries that we get a glimpse of for 30 seconds on the news. There is no depth to these glimpses and sound bytes—so the knowledge has no substance, the facts become meaningless, and the truth becomes smothered. High school students in America (and even many of their teachers) have no comprehension of reality outside their own world—where the majority of women are treated as chattel, forced into poverty and prostitution, and deprived of education. Since the ancient world—under tyranny, totalitarianism, and/or tradition—women have been forced into a secondary role: as chattel, as objects to physically or sexually abuse, as sexual slaves, and deprived of property, education, and/or the right to vote.

Here we are in our postmodern "cosmopolitanism," according to David Elkind, where women rights have overturned traditional male-female roles, and there is an acceptance and valuation of diversity[2] and equal educational and occupation opportunities for all men and women—black, brown, red, yellow, or white. But even assuming a normal childhood, with loving parents, there is still too much emphasis on girls' sexual changes and bodies, how girls look, and whether they will be accepted by boys and become part of the party crowd and power clique than about their own independence and identity. Only a small percentage of girls, usually academic types or girls who have strong interests outside of school, can feel secure enough not to be part of an "in group" but rather to form their own social group, which often excludes boys. Researchers point out that athletic girls also seem to have high self-esteem, and to some extent, that athleticism serves as a countermeasure to body preoccupations; in fact, athletic girls do well in academics (they feel empowered) and are less likely than nonathletic girls to engage in substance abuse, develop eating disorders, become pregnant, and drop out of school.[3]

1. This decision came about largely due to the pressure of human rights and feminist organizations, and by the creation of war crime tribunals for the Balkans and Rwanda.

2. David Elkind, "The Cosmopolitan School," *Educational Leadership* (January 2001), pp. 12–17. Quotes around *cosmopolitanism* are mine.

3. Jean Zimmerman and Gil Reavill, *Raising Our Athletic Daughters* (New York: Random House, 1999).

Most of these problems are induced by pressure from mothers and peers. An attitude of gender neutrality or gender blindness is likely to cause us to miss, or even reinforce, these subtle problems and biases. It is another thing, however, for women to view "normal men" as latent rapists who consider love and romance as a form of hatred and torture, who reject marriage and children as a form of servitude, or who advocate homosexuality as a form of diversity. This kind of discussion by radical feminists, to explore forms of male aggression and female oppression, possibly reflects female frustration and anger. Actually, it may even be self-destructive and lead to dysfunctional relations with men. Under the guise of questioning traditional male-female roles, and given the nature of gender rhetoric, there is the potential for building fences. The goal is for men to understand that women should have the same chances as men, and they should be able to choose low-paying or high-paying professions. But male bashing, antimarriage ideas, and unchecked freedom without morality does not necessarily lead to a rose garden or to feminist nirvana.

The fact is, however, that men are still not doing 50 percent of the housework, child care, or geriatric care; also, it is difficult for mothers to stay glued to the fast track in corporate America, given their family and social responsibilities. Peggy Ornstein, a "second wave" feminist (distinguished from the younger X Generation and the older feminists such as Billie Jean King, Betty Freidan, Germaine Greer, and Gloria Steinem)[1] goes so far as maintaining that women need to begin to see single life as a viable alternative with its own rewards, costs, and challenges. What she shows is that women have a wide range of ambition levels, and these levels wax and wane over the years, and for some women it conflicts with their career aspirations. The women with the most frustration are those whose ambitions continue at high levels and their desire for children continue to rise. For most women, having children is the apex of fulfillment, but for some it means the evaporation of a waistline and career.[2]

Society has come a long way since Coleman described some of the issues facing girls in high school; but today, girls are still dealing with the issues of self-esteem, identity, and sexuality—what lipstick and nail polish to use, how much make up to wear, how to cut their hair, how to say no, when to say yes, and a host of personal issues with boys and fathers.[3]

The bottom line is that more than one-third of professional women over age 40 are childless, according to a new study, many because they worked and waited too long to get married or have children, or thought they could not balance children with a fast-track career. Many of these childless "liberated" women now feel unfulfilled. Some old-fashioned men respond with, "I told you so—you wanted too much"; in fact, there are many women who call me a "retrofeminist," "antifeminist," or "paper-bag

1. Given 5,000 years of both subtle and strong prejudices against women, I have come to realize these women, through a complex amalgam of political, economical, moral, and religious considerations, have helped fashion one of the biggest and most powerful revolutions in the world, which is still emerging in front of our eyes, as part of human and global activity.

2. Peggy Ornstein, *Women on Sex, Work, Kids, Love, and Life in a Half-Changed World* (New York: Doubleday, 2000).

3. Karen Lehrman, *The Lipstick Proviso: Women, Sex, and Power in the Real World* (New York: Doubleday, 1997).

intellectual" for suggesting that women pay attention to their biological clocks and focus on finding husbands with whom to have children.[1]

The question arises (as a male, I think I may be on thin ice): How do smart, ambitious women balance their careers with marriage, children, and home life? Jane Austen and Emily Dickinson expressed this concern in their writings and letters, and every female athlete, female professional, and First Lady has had to wrestle with this problem. It's a real issue for today's women, far more so than women's studies or even title IX, which may be hard for some female professors to swallow or admit.

The fact is, schools are unable to prepare women for both a career and children, or to prepare them for nonmarriage or, even worse, no children. Starting in adolescence, the schools need to help create a feminine identity that is dependent on neither husband nor child, but rather fosters independence and promotes the fact that that identity means different things to different women.

Recently, women are beginning to reject their traditional choices and models, breaking away from low-paying professions based on "dedication," "care-taking feelings," or "love of children." This means many smart, independent women who otherwise would be entering classrooms are now joining the corporate world, as well as the legal and medical fields. Given the fact that two-thirds of U.S. teachers are women, what impact will the loss of many bright women have on the teaching profession? Entry standards have been questioned for the last 50 years, since the Conant and Korener reports; now, they should be questioned even more with these career shifts among women.

As the "new, new woman" and the "postmodern woman" emerges with six earrings and orange stripped hair, or possibly with black gladiator attire, or with a red dress, red shoes and red glasses—exhibiting new confidence and heightened self-esteem—boys and men are going to have to make adjustments. Many professions and corporate boards are going to be making room for both conventional and nonconventional women—as sure the tides turn and the seasons change. A key to western progress and power is the growth of female power, and the utilization of 50 percent of a nation's resources and brains.

## Male Roles and Sex Differences

Not only does society demand conformity to its basic norms and mores, it also assigns specific roles to each of its members, expecting them to conform to certain established behavioral patterns. A good example of this type of socialization is found in sex roles—that is, the ways boys and girls and men and women are "supposed" to act. Sex roles vary from culture to culture, but within a given culture they are rather well defined, and, what's more, they are enforced through an elaborate schedule of selective reinforcement.

An important and historical contribution to the notion of sex roles has been made by David Lynn, who differentiated between parental identification, by which the child

---

1. Sylvia Ann Hewlett, *Creating a Life: Professional Women and the Quest for Children* (New York: Miramax Books, 2002).

internalizes the personality characteristics of his parents, and sex-role identification of a given sex in a specific culture.[1] The initial parental identification of both male and female children is with the mother, but the boy must shift from his original mother identification to establish the masculine role identity. However, in an increasingly large number of homes, fathers are not present or, in the case of divorce, serve as models only on weekends. Even in traditional two-parent homes, the boy, if lucky, gets to interact with dad for only a few hours of the day. Besides, most fathers participate in some roles that until very recently were defined in American society as feminine (washing dishes, cleaning, child care, etc.)

Thus, sons must distinguish the masculine role from the stereotype spelled out for them by society through a system of reinforcements and rewards. As a result, as a boy's identification with the mother role diminishes, it is gradually replaced by a learned identification with a culturally defined masculine role. This is accomplished mainly through negative admonishments, such as "Don't be a sissy," which does not tell him what he *should* do instead, however. If he is lucky to have a father who has time, and knows what to do, the boy will probably adopt healthy behaviors. However, researchers remind us that a boy sometimes pays a heavy price when his father holds him to an impossible standard of manhood[2] or when his peers feel he is unathletic, too sensitive, or "not one of the boys"—what some schoolyard kids would call a "nerd" or a "dork."

The girl simply learns the female identification as it is presented to her, partly through imitation and partly through the mother's reinforcement and reward of selective behavior. The boy has the problem of making the proper sex-role identification in the partial absence of a male model, and this is even more difficult in a *female-headed household* where the father is completely absent. Overall, single-parent families now constitute close to one-third of all households with children under age 18. Much of the recent increase in single-family households reflects the growing divorce rate, which has quadrupled in the United Sates since 1960, and the growing illegitimacy rate among the black underclass. Only 33 percent of black children under age 6 were living in two-parent households in 1996, compared to 50 percent in 1968. This compares with 75 percent of white children under age 6 living in two-parent households in 1996, compared with 95 percent in 1960.[3]

The point is, the girl acquires a learning method that basically involves a personal relationship and identification with the mother. By contrast, the boy must define his goals, restructure some of his experiences, and synthesize underlying masculine principles. The result is greater learning problems for boys, especially black males, and a

1. David B. Lynn, "Sex Role and Parental Identification," *Child Development* (March 1963), pp. 555–64; Lynn, "Divergent Feedback and Sex-Role Identification in Boys and Men," *Merrill Palmer Quarterly* (January 1964), pp. 17–23.

2. Dan Kindlon and Michael Thompson, *Raising Cain: Protecting the Emotional Life of Boys* (New York: Random House, 2000).

3. *America's Children* (Washington, DC: Federal Interacency Forum, 1997). Beth A. Young and Thomas M. Smith, *The Social Context of Education* (Washington, DC: U.S. Government Printing Office, 1997).

greater dependency on their mothers. When children reach school age, they find that the schools are largely staffed by females, especially at the elementary level, which is a critical age in child development. The schools are dominated by female norms of politeness, cleanliness, and obedience. The curriculum and classroom activities are female oriented—safe, nice, and antiseptic. The school frowns on vulgar language and fighting; it suppresses the boys' maleness and often fails to permit action-oriented, tough sports, at least until high school. Thus, the disadvantage that the boy finds at home in developing his masculine identity is often compounded by the schooling process.[1]

In this connection, Patricia Sexton was among the first to present controversial data showing that schools are feminizing institutions that discriminate against the male and subvert his identity.[2] Her data show that approximately three out of four students regarded as problems are boys, and since teachers tend to fail problem students, approximately two out of three students who fail are boys. The male student who is a high achiever tends to be "fat and flabby" (her words and somewhat generalized), especially at the elementary and junior high school level. Those who gravitate to masculine activities, such as conflict sports and mechanics, tend to do poorly in academic areas—and they are often at odds with their teachers, who are predominantly female (and with male teachers, too, who, by virtue of their role, tend to enforce the feminized school norms).

## Boys and Girls Today

Sexton maintains that the schools' values and the resulting discrimination against boys, compounded by the mothers' inability to relate to sons in helping them establish a healthy male identification, are negative and cumulative. In part, this explains why boys largely outnumber girls in school dropout rates, deviant and delinquent acts, mental illness, and suicides.

Although Sexton's conclusions may be somewhat overgeneralized and extend beyond her data, and even considered dated, there is no question that girls receive higher grades throughout elementary school, with the gap being gradually reduced in high school. More boys are nonreaders, more boys fail, more boys are considered learning disabled, more boys are disciplinary cases, more boys are on ritalin, and more boys drop out of school. And more men than women are prisoners or have mental breakdowns, and men die at a younger age than women. No doubt sex roles and sex differences in school are at least in part related to role expectations that are incorporated into the self-concept very early in life. However, there is research that suggests that such roles may also be biochemically related and may stem from inherited predispositions of males and females as well as maturation differences.[3]

1. Allan C. Ornstein, "Who Are the Disadvantaged?" *Young Children* (May 1971), pp. 264–272.
2. Patricia C. Sexton, *The Feminized Male* (New York: Random House, 1969).
3. Natalie Angier, "Genes May Account for Social Skills in Girls," *New York Times* (June 12, 1997); Lynn Friedman, "The Space Factor in Mathematics: Gender Difference," *Review of Educational Research* (Spring 1995), pp. 22–50.

There is more evidence, of course, that social adjustment is related to physical growth and development; girls develop much more rapidly than boys during childhood and preadolescence. There are plenty of data illustrating that junior high school girls are often four or five inches taller than boys, and start to go through sexual changes while boys still have squeaky voices and little or no pubescent hair. When it comes to dealing with the opposite sex, one commentator writes, "boys may often react in clumsy, immature and basically clueless ways."[1]

Of course, some females will insist that boys never grow up and that they remain clueless—hopeless or helpless—even when they are men. This view is embedded in our culture; it appears in many popular TV shows, including *Everybody Loves Raymond* and *King of Queens;* many Broadway shows, among them *Caveman* and *I Love You, You're Perfect, Now Change,* and *The Odd Couple;* and in such movies as *City Slickers* and *Grumpy Old Men. Titanic* was a box-office smash, not only because it was a great love story but also because Jack did it right; he was not clueless. (Of course, some women would argue we know Jack for only a few days, and that the phrase *clueless boys* or *clueless men* is a redundancy.)

But, indeed, boys (and girls) do grow up. Sometimes they sink to the lowest forms of humanity, directing unbelievable cruelty toward others, and sometimes they ascend to the highest forms of human dignity and courage. However, for the last 5,000 years, most humans have lived in the shadows of political autocracy and tyranny, as barbarians, peasants, slaves, serfs, or ignorant workers—trapped by the greed and corruption of a few powerful people. The fact is, we all grow up, and it is important to be guided by a sense of morality. The absence of this content from the curriculum tends to lead to all kinds of discrimination, persecution, and hatred based on gender, race, or religion. Indeed, the concepts of equality, civil and human rights, laws, and social justice have little or no meaning to people who have few or no moral benchmarks. It must also be noted that barbarians, peasants, slaves, serfs, and workers are mainly followers, victimized by despots and tyrants. Indeed, it is the nation-state's leadership (usually male) that creates the ethos for morality or immorality.

Unquestionably, girls and women have been discriminated against in the past, especially in the workforce, and their identity and independence often have suffered in marital relations. In general, women of previous generations lost their individuality in their subservience to men, especially in traditional and inner-directed societies. Black women in America and women of third world countries have suffered the most. Although change comes slowly, the civil rights movement followed by the feminist rights movement in the United States has led to tremendous gains for women in our society as well as all industrialized nations. Nonetheless, the tide of the feminist movement set in motion a new ideology. Since the 1980s, schools have been continuously told how they have short-changed girls in terms of self-esteem and career pursuits. Worst among the faults were that textbooks described few females in professional roles (other than teachers and nurses) and positions of power, and that girls had been discouraged from taking math and science courses in high school and

1. John Greenwald, "What About the Boys?" *Time* (October 30, 2000), p. 74.

college. A plethora of gender-equity programs, highlighted by Title IX, as well as text-book and curriculum changes, became part of the school reform movement.

The fact is, today, boys continue to get less attention in the classroom than girls, get lower grades, and have lower self-esteem. Boys are 50 percent more likely to re-peat a grade than girls, represent two-thirds of the children placed in special educa-tion programs dealing with social and emotional problems, and are twice as likely to be given ritalin for attention deficit disorders or controlling behavior.[1] And talk about a crisis in self-esteem: Boys are twice more likely to drop out of school, and young men (ages 15 to 24) are five times more likely to die from homicides and six times more likely to commit suicide than young women.[2]

The gender problem starts early in school. By the third grade, boys' drawings are three times more likely to portray the teacher in a negative demeanor (17 percent of boys, 6 percent of girls). Boys are more likely to depict teacher behavior, when ad-dressing the class, in terms of discipline (59 to 41 percent) and to depict students in a traditional way—alone at desks in rows—than showing students in clusters or groups. And boys more often depict the teacher standing alone at the blackboard[3]—distant from the class.

According to the 1998 Metropolitan Life Insurance survey, by the time students reach junior high school (seventh grade), boys are at a disadvantage in schools com-pared with girls in the following ways: (1) lower expectations, (2) less confidence, (3) less support from teachers, (4) less positive feedback from teachers, (5) less help-ful comments from teachers when they answer incorrectly, and (6) less likely to say they expect to go to college.[4] Similarly, about two-thirds more boys than girls (31 vs. 19 percent) complain that teachers don't listen to them. As for teachers, they perceive girls as more confident, more focused in their academic studies, and more likely to go to college.[5] Interestingly, these results coincide with reality. More girls than boys enroll in AP courses in high school (14 vs. 11 percent) and go on to college—comprising 56 percent of the enrollment at the bachelor's and master's levels.[6] In short, school is kinder to girls, no matter what the common view, and it is boys who need special attention and shoring up.

1. Teachers and schools overdiagnose and overlabel students in terms of learning and be-havior. If Huck Finn and Tom Sawyer were alive today, they would be on Ritalin and in spe-cial education for hyperactivity. Edison, Einstein, Dylan, and Ringo would be designated as learning disabled, partially because of the school's inability to deal with nonconforming stu-dents, or kids who see the world differently from their teachers. Given a class of 25 or 30 stu-dents, most teachers have difficulty in dealing with quick-witted and/or creative students.
2. Diane Ravitch, "Girls Are Beneficiaries of the Gender Gap," *New York Times* (De-cember 17, 1998), p. 21.
3. Gerald W. Bracey, "Poverty and Achievement," *Phi Delta Kappan* (December 1999), pp. 330–331.
4. Geoffrey Canada, "Raising Better Boys," *Educational Leadership* (December–January 2000), pp. 14–17.
5. Gene Koretz, "School Is Now Kinder to Girls," *Business Week* (March 2, 1998), p. 32.
6. *The Condition of Education 1998* (Washington DC: U.S. Government Printing Office, 1998), Table 26, p. 90; *Digest of Education Statistics 2000* (Washington DC: U.S. Government Printing Office, 2001), Table 173, p. 202.

All of these gender differences are usually treated as nonissues since they are considered politically incorrect by the majority of social critics, contradict conventional wisdom that girls are thought to be at a disadvantage in schools, and directly oppose feminist politics that charge that schools harm girls. It is further aggravated by the media's gullibility and the rhetoric of groups defining themselves as oppressed minorities.

## From Dick and Jane to Harry Potter

As we all know, reading is tied to academic success, and the inability to read is tied to academic failure. Why is it that nationwide 47 percent of fourth-grade boys fall below the basic reading level (i.e., they can hardly read), compared with 36 percent of girls?[1] Is it their genes? Brain size? Social roles? The question is: What is left for them to read?

Young girls, long ignored in adventurous and exciting literature (only one or two steps above "Dick and Jane" who used to visit the zoo or their grandmother in the country), now enjoy a plethora of girl-featured books. Much of today's school books now show that half the football and soccer team characters and half the pirate characters are female, including the team captain and head pirate. In the new *Paper Bag Princesses*, a spirited girl saves herself from a dragon without assistance from a prince. In line with the new gender sensitivity, even *The Little Engine That Could*, a powerful and phallic symbol in classic children's literature, for years a *he*, is now a *she*.

The masculine ideal of action, self-confidence, teamwork, and "manly" or "smart" heroes who nab villains, outwit ghosts and giants, explore the Amazon or climb the Himalayan Mountains, or duel against wizards, monsters, or space aliens have all but disappeared from school shelves. Even more horrific, according to one critic, would be a story where the male hero fights Zulu tribes or hunts grizzly bears or wolves[2]—because it might be considered politically incorrect (i.e., racist or environmentally insensitive). Similarly, a male hero can no longer fall victim to poison darts or some wild animal in some far off land and with his last-gasp sigh, "Never mind me; stick to it lads" or "Be sure to protect Judy," because some civil rights group or animal rights group may protest.

The strong male model or hero is out of fashion, regardless of whether it is Tarzan (highly ethical, somewhat wild or uncivilized), John Wayne (spirited, proud American, hunt-and-shoot type), General Patton (savvy, headstrong, brash) or Arnold Schwartzeneger (strong, powerful, violent). All these male heroes do things their way and come from the rough and tumble crowd—but according to some "gender sensitivity" observers, they are one or two levels above the caveman. Nonetheless, from *Sparticus* to *Brave Heart*, from *Conan the Barbarian* to *Rambo*—these prototypes have been popular among males of all ages. These type of heroes, however, have been eliminated from grade school films, literature, and library shelves because of attitudes and behaviors related to socializing—what some call *feminizing* boys and some call an outrageous interpretation of the socialization process. The only thing left for men

1. Ibid.
2. Danielle Crittenden, "Boy Meets Books," *Wall Street Journal* (November 26, 1999).

to do, on the weekends is to watch the football game—grunt and cheer and escape in a world of modern cavemen and gladiators.

Daniell Crittenden puts it this way: "Today, the zeal for adventure idealized in [action-oriented tales] would be hastily treated with Ritilin. And of course, we must deplore all references to pen knives, slingshots, and BB guns, however useful such items may be when . . . walking the plank."[1] Even the classics have been targeted for the trash can—such as Twain's *Huckleberry Finn,* Rudyard Kipling's *Kim,* Robert Louis Stevenson's *Treasure Island* and *Kidnapped,* Tom Aldrich's *The Story of a Bad Boy,* and Franklin Dixon's (pseudonym) *Hardy Boys.* The adventures of Huck Finn are considered racist and riddled with negative stereotyping; Kipling is considered a white imperialist; Stevenson's novels "feature" guns and tobacco; Aldrich's main character resides in an in-tact family, somewhat irrelevant and offensive in today's postnuclear society; and Dixon's heroes express too much male heroism and machoism—which today can lead to "bullyism" and "gender insensitivity." No wonder that disappointed boys give up on books and retreat into the competitive and fantasy worlds of Nintendo, Sega, and Doom.

For good reason, Harry Potter's children's books are popular—all toping the *New York Times* best-selling list.[2] Harry's popular and mystical schoolboy world stems from Tom Hughes's *Tom Brown's School Days,* published in 1857 and the more recent magical world of J. R. R. Tolkien, who authored *The Hobbit* and the trilogy *Lord of the Rings* in the 1940s.[3] Harry is not subliterate, nor a jock, nor a particularly good student. He has his problems. His parents are dead and he lives with mean-spirited relatives. He is surrounded by bullies and he doesn't fit in well with his classmates. But he wears sneakers and jeans—not pirate clothes or breeches—and lives in the suburbs—not some faraway land. He is like many other average boys seeking adventure and struggling with their identity; most importantly, he lives in a world free from adult and teacher constraints. Eventually, Harry discovers that he is brave, kind, compassionate, and ethical. He fights wizards, warlocks, and witches—and faces villains and dark forces. He saves the world!

It's a testament to Scottish author J. K. Rowling that she writes about boys as boys and is not afraid of the anti-boy lobby. She liberates boys instead of lecturing, chastising, or restraining them.[4] Although some educators want to ban Harry, since he is involved with death, despair, and witches and wizards,[5] Harry's school is much more interesting than the school boys attend in U.S. society. At Hogwarts School, Harry gets involved in bizarre intramural sports that date back some 700 years and are designed to promote magical understanding in the art of witchcraft and wizardry,

1. Ibid.

2. These include *Harry Potter and the Sorcerer's Stone* (the first and most popular one), *Harry Potter and the Chamber of Secrets, Harry Potter and the Prisoner of Azkaban,* and *Harry Potter and the Goblet of Fire* (the longest and most recent one, published in 2001). Three additional books are scheduled to be published between 2002 and 2004.

3. Both Hughes and Tolkien were British authors, as is Rowling. Most of Tolkien's work is based on Viking and Scandanavian folklore.

4. Crittenden, "Boy Meets Books."

5. Paul Gray, "Wild About Harry," *Time* (September 20, 1999), p. 67.

and triumphs over dangerous dragons and wicked wizards, including Lord Volde-mort, who has gone posthuman.

Although critics feel Harry Potter books are "long on clichés" and "short on imaginative vision," the ultimate fear is that the Potter books will replace good lit-erature in the school, and that "hip" readers and "relevant" educators will celebrate another confirmation of the "dumbing down" of the curriculum. Although it is doubtful if Harry Potter can really cast a spell on his readers, J. K. Rowling seems to write the same kind of fiction (escapism) that attracts millions of adult readers to Stephen King's bizarre and frightening world. Nonetheless, can 35 million Potter readers,[1] soon to be 40 million readers, be wrong? Most people who respect num-bers would say no; elitist readers and cultural critics would say yes. And so we have the theme of America education—freedom to disagree and voice our opinions, with-out burning books or being hauled off to attend some "mind-bending" or "brain-rescuing" school that reinforces the "truth." Horace Mann and John Dewey never spoke about democracy and education in this way, but in order to attain our ideals as a nation through democracy, free thought in classrooms is paramount to the pur-pose of schooling. Anyway, three cheers for Harry, *The Hobbit,* and *The Lord of the Rings*—reading materials that kids enjoy.

## The Culture of the School

Although each school in the United States reflects the culture of the larger society (namely middle-class values, beliefs, and norms), it also has its own culture—its own ethos or way of thinking and behaving that it reinforces and rewards. Some schools emphasize highly traditional goals and "essential" subjects, and other schools may be more progressive and emphasize student participation and encourage music and art. In many rural and suburban schools, sports dominate student activities and in part define pride and spirit of the community; the Friday night basketball game or Saturday afternoon football game attracts a large portion of the local residents. In an-other school, however, the emphasis may be on community service and intramural sports; fine arts may have a definite place in the curriculum.

Education in school, compared with that in the family or peer group, is carried on in relatively formal ways. Groupings are formed not by voluntary choice but in terms of age, aptitudes, and sometimes gender. Students are evaluated and often labeled—and sometimes mislabeled. Indeed, one-third of a teacher's professional time in school (not counting time outside of school) is devoted to preparing and adminis-tering tests, grading papers, and evaluating students.[2] Interestingly, teachers rarely, if ever, enroll in a course on testing and evaluation.

1. Harold Bloom, "Can 35 Million Book Buyers Be Wrong? Yes," *Wall Street Journal* (July 11, 2001), p. 16.
2. Peter W. Airasian, *Classroom Assessment: Concepts and Applications,* 4th ed. (Boston, McGraw-Hill, 2001); Allan C. Ornstein and Thomas J. Lasley, *Strategies for Effective Teach-ing,* 3rd ed. (Boston: McGraw-Hill, 2000).

## Conformity in Class

Students are told when and where to sit, when to stand, how to walk through hallways, when they can have a bathroom pass, when they can use the pencil sharpener, when they can have lunch in the cafeteria, and when and how to line up and exit the school at the end of the day. The emphasis is on the teacher controlling the behaviors of students. It is the teacher who decides who will speak and when, who will go to the front of the line and back of the line, and who receives what grade. To be sure, grades can be used as an instrument for controlling behavior in class—at least for students who are grade oriented.

Getting through school for many students, then, means to subordinate their own interests and needs to those of their teachers. Willard Waller described it as a contest and a conflict between adult and youth cultures in which the teacher, to preserve his or her own authority, had to win.[1] Charles Silberman, 30 years later, described it as a useful learning experience for students—"a necessary aspect of learning to live in society." But he warned that teachers and schools sometimes translate this "virtue into a fault by . . . excluding the childs' interests altogether."[2] One way students cope is they learn to live in two worlds—one with peers and the other with adults. In this connection, Dewey observed, "Children acquire great dexterity in exhibiting in conventional and expected ways the *form* of attention to school work . . . while reserving the inner play of their own thoughts, images, and emotions for subjects that are more important to them, but quite irrelevant" to adults.[3]

Just like teachers learn to cope with and control their students, students learn similar strategies for dealing with their teachers. By adolescence, children are very adept in observing and manipulating adults, and they do an excellent job in classrooms, sometimes without their teacher's knowledge. Don't ever think that the 25 or 30 students you are teaching are not sizing you up and judging your weaknesses and strengths—assessing what they can get away with and how they can outwit you. It's a classroom game—involving not only who is smarter but also who is in control. In many inner-city schools, students are in control and teachers experience frustration and even symptoms of battle fatigue—one reason for the large turnover of beginning teachers in these type of schools (nearly 50 percent in the first five years).[4]

## Coping and Caring

Some students, however, survive in classrooms and schools by turning off or withdrawing into apathy. One way for students to avoid the pain of failure or the lower

1. Waller, *Sociology of Teaching.*
2. Silberman, *Crisis in the Classroom,* p. 151.
3. John Dewey, *The Child and the Curriculum* (Chicago: University of Chicago Press, 1902).
4. Joel A. Colbert and Dianna E. Wolff, "Surviving in the Urban Schools: A Colloborative Model for a Beginning Teacher Support System," *Journal of Teacher Education* (May–June 1992), pp. 192–199; Allan C. Ornstein and Daniel U. Levine, "Social Class, Race and School Achievement: Problems and Prospects," *Journal of Teacher Education* (September–October 1989), pp. 27–33.

expectations of teachers is to persuade themselves that they don't care. Thus, threatening some students with lower grades has no effect on them. Sadly, most students who claim they don't care initially did care. The point is, repeated failure coupled with receiving unfavorable remarks and grades in a public arena (say, in the classroom) takes its toll on all people. The effects are worse for young children because they have fewer defense mechanisms against adults and less ability to ward off learned low expectations for themselves.

Unquestionably, negative stimuli have a much greater impact on all people than positive stimuli. You can turn a person into a vegetable in a few days, but it takes many years to make a doctor, lawyer, or CEO. Teachers can change a child's behavior in a matter of weeks, through comments, gestures, and other body language, turning a young, motivated student into an unmotivated and self-doubting student who easily exhibits frustration and no longer likes going to school. The younger the child, the easier it is for a teacher's negativism to influence student behavior.

The idea is to encourage different intellectual abilities and other skills and aptitudes of all students in class, not to make one group feel "smart" and the other "dumb." The best approach, observe Oakes and Lipton, is that "teachers can assure students that, although no one in class will be 'good' on all [problems or tasks], each student will be good on at least one."[1] Other researchers have found that when teachers stop publicly judging students, students begin identifying each other and themselves as "smart" in some areas, weakening previous negative expectations. However, when evaluation of tasks distinguishes between successful and unsuccessful student performance, or when students are organized into ability groups, classmates begin to make the same distinctions.[2] The goal is for all students to assume that everyone in the class is competent in one or more areas, and that everyone has something to contribute.

In this connection, a few progressive schools have eliminated all elementary school grades in order to reduce labeling of students and academic expectations of themselves. Grades basically create "winners" and "losers," and usually the same winners and losers. Over time, students get the message—it's called *dropping out.* Robert Slavin puts it in a slightly different, more moderate way: "In the usual, competitive reward structure, the probability of one student receiving a reward (good grade) is negatively related to the probability of another student receiving a reward."[3]

For this reason, one educator urges a school progress or mastery report card, without grades, on which a list of descriptors or categories are listed and the teacher describes what the student can do by checking off terms such as *yes* or *no* or *outstanding, satisfactory,* or *unsatisfactory,* or, even better, writing a narrative describing the student's

---

1. Jeannie Oakes and Martin Lipton, *Teaching to Change the World* (Boston: McGraw-Hill, 1999), p. 204.

2. Elizabeth Cohen and Rachel Lotan, *Working for Equality in Heterogeneous Classrooms* (New York: Teachers College Press, 1977); Lisa Delpit, *Other People's Children* (New York: Teachers College Press, 1995).

3. Robert E. Slavin, "Classroom Reward Structure: An Analytical and Practical Review," *Review of Educational Research* (Fall 1977), pp. 650–663.

progress and problems.[1] Imagine, no grades, no labels every school year, no one always playing right field or batting last every time, no one finishing last or next to last in every school yard race, until he or she gets the message and says "I don't like this game. I don't want to play anymore"—and drops out. This nongrading approach could continue until students enter junior high school, usually seventh or eighth grade.[2] Then, grades, percentages, and rankings need to be used to prepare students for the reality of high school; likewise, high schools want to have knowledge of the students' abilities so they can track them and devise programs relative to their needs.

Oh, the wonders of tracking—who is "fit" and "unfit," who is "bright" and "slow." The schools have been labeling kids for the last 200 years, much more so since Binet devised his IQ original test in 1905. Kids who usually win the race, or get good grades, don't really know what it feels like to be judged "less than average," "inadequate," or "slow" by peers and teachers. Given the academic success of most teachers (i.e., they have graduated from college), I wonder if teachers fully understood how their judgments and evaluations affect lower-achieving students.

## Culture of the Classroom

In his study of elementary schools, Philip Jackson found a diversity of specific subjects but few different types of classroom activities. The terms *seatwork, group discussion, teacher demonstration,* and *question-and-answer period* described most of what happened in the classroom. Further, these activities were performed according to well-defined rules, such as "No loud talking during seatwork" and "Raise your hand if you have a question." The teacher served as a "combination traffic cop, judge, supply sergeant, and time-keeper." In this cultural system, the classroom often becomes a place where things happen, "not because students want them to, but because it is time for them to occur."[3] Life in classrooms, according to Jackson, is dull. It is a place "in which yawns are stifled and initials scratched on desktops, where milk money is collected and recess lines are formed."[4]

Similarly, in John Goodlad's study of schools, he and his colleagues describe the following widespread patterns: The classroom is generally organized as a group that the teacher treats as a whole. The teacher is the dominant figure in the classroom and makes virtually all the decisions regarding instructional activities. "Enthusiasm and joy and anger are kept under control." As a result, the general emotional tone is "flat" or "neutral." Most student work involves "listening to teachers, answering the teacher, or writing answers to questions and taking tests and quizzes." Students rarely learn

1. Allan C. Ornstein, *Secondary and Middle School Teaching Methods* (New York: HarperCollins, 1992).
2. In lieu of grades, I would recommend a report of the children's abilities, needs, and interests, coupled with strengths and recommendations; the report would be in narrative form and would not grade or rank the student.
3. Jackson, *Life in Classrooms,* pp. 8–9, 13.
4. Ibid., p. 4.

from one another. Instruction seldom goes beyond "mere possession of information." Little effort is made to arouse students' curiosity or to emphasize problem solving.[1]

Such systematic emphasis on passive learning by rote is in opposition to most contemporary ideas of what education should accomplish. You might ask: Why, then, do so many classrooms often function in this way? I ask you to think about it in terms of your own teacher preparation, student preference for passive learning, and the bargains and compromises between students and teachers—in short, to take the easy way out. Passive learning requires no extra teacher time for planning creative classroom activities. Often, there is a tacit conspiracy to avoid active learning and rigorous standards because this involves extra work by teachers and potential conflict with students.

Thus, classroom patterns suggest boring and repetitive interactions between the teacher and students—instructional activities divorced of human feelings and emotions. It suggests a place where students must restrict their feelings and emotions, learn what behavior pleases the teacher, and learn what strategies and methods to use to get through the day—often with the least amount of work. In this connection, John Holt talks about how students adopt strategies of fear and failure. For most students, it means pleasing the teacher; for others, it means outwitting the teacher; for still others, it means doing the work as quickly as possible, like taking medicine and getting it over with.[2]

Given all these negative attributes of how classrooms operate, it is little wonder that many teachers often lose their students' interest after 10 or 15 minutes of instruction: "Students doze off, stare out the window, or stare past the teacher, while others doodle, pass notes, or throw 'spitballs'—or just pass time in classrooms."[3] What remedy or behavior do you as a student exhibit in class when you are bored? As a teacher, do you expect your students to be different? Can you look squarely in the looking glass and ask: What changes are you going to make to improve your instruction?

Since much of this section has focused on negative aspects of school culture, I should emphasize that many positive statements can be made about schools in the United States. Most schools provide an orderly learning environment, and most students learn to read and compute at a level required to function in society. Relationships among teachers, students, and parents generally are positive. Almost all students become better persons and productive members of society as a result of schooling, despite all the criticism. The vast majority of students receive a high school diploma, and most proceed to some form of postsecondary education.

## The Planned and the Unplanned Curricula

What students learn in school extends beyond the panned curriculum, sometimes called the *formal* or *explicit* curriculum. The planned curriculum is represented by goals of the school; this is translated into the subjects students are supposed to learn,

---

1. John I. Goodlad, *A Place Called School* (New York: McGraw-Hill, 1984); Goodlad, *Educational Renewal* (San Francisco: Jossey-Bass, 1998).
2. John Holt, *How Children Fail* (New York: Putnam, 1964).
3. Ornstein, *Secondary and Middle School Teaching Methods*, p. 20.

and the prescribed objectives of the courses and classroom lessons. But curriculum scholars have observed that the school also transmits an *informal* or *hidden* curriculum, one that is not intended or stated in the planned curriculum but dominates the relationships and interactions of the students with each other and with their teachers in classrooms and schools.[1]

If we consider only the planned or official curriculum, evident in written documents, course descriptions, and teachers' lesson plans, we wind up ignoring the powerful influence of the hidden curriculum. Although not written or found in any list of school goals or course descriptions, students are influenced by the attitudes and behaviors of their own culture; it may not be taught by teachers or encouraged by the school, but students know, at least in a general way, that it exists, and they often construct more powerful and emotional learnings from the hidden curriculum than the formal curriculum. Indeed, the hidden curriculum is built around the peer group and competes with the teacher's planned curriculum. It influences thinking and behavior in classrooms, more than most teachers realize, sometimes even conflicting with the ethos and main values of the school and larger society.

Teachers and schools put too much emphasis on grades, and unwittingly create an atmosphere where the hidden curriculum elevates grades over learning, the right answer over understanding, facts over ideas, conforming behavior over independent behavior, and getting on the honor role rather than helping others. Given the competitive nature of our schools and society, critics argue that the hidden curriculum encourages some students that "beating the system" or "winning" is more important than anything else.[2] To be sure, students are not born to cheat on tests; rather, pressure to succeed in school fosters the problem. For some, the idea is to get into Harvard, Yale, or medical school, even if it boils down to giving classmates the wrong answers on a test or for homework. For others, it means winning the state championship, even if it means throwing at someone's head in a baseball game or tackling someone to put him out of the football game—possibly on a stretcher.

## Half-Forgotten Memories: One Last Sermon

Finally, the idea of literacy must be expanded to include not only basic or functional literacy, traditionally referred to as the *three Rs,* but also cultural literacy, scientific literacy, computer literacy, and moral integrity. Most importantly, we live in a society that demands informational and technological skills. Anything else, under the guise of "relevancy," "life experiences," "cultural identity," "ethnic heritage," or "political correctness," short-changes the student population.

    1. Elliot W. Eisner, *The Educational Imagination,* 3rd ed. (New York: Macmillan, 1995); Colin J. Marsh and George Willis, *Curriculum: Alternative Approaches,* 3rd ed. (Columbus, OH: Merrill, 2003); and Ornstein and Hunkins, *Curriculum: Foundations, Principles, and Issues.*
    2. William Bigelow, "Inside the Classroom," *Teachers College Record* (Spring 1990), pp. 437–448; Alfie Kohn, "Fighting the Tests: A Practical Guide to Rescuing Our Schools," *Phi Delta Kappan* (January 2001), pp. 348–357.

These other approaches belong in the home, community, or church, in the evenings or weekends, as part of ritual, folklore, or ethnic (religious) custom. Even bilingual programs in school must be limited—say, to three years as New York City schools are planning.[1] Black power, black pride, and black language do not belong in the formal curriculum—neither does Korean power and pride, Polish power or pride, or white power or pride—and neither does a bilingual language program where parents are encouraged to keep their children in the program because of politics or ideology.

The school's job is to prepare all students to function effectively in the larger society, not to emphasize tribal identities. The idea is to recognize that we are "many people," but to emphasize we are "one nation." As Oscar Handlin once wrote, "The transition from rural to urban surroundings is difficult in itself, and is complicated by serious cultural discrepancies between the old life and new."[2] But 20 years later, Nathan Glazer pointed out that America had become a multicultural nation; the schools, instead of trying to assimilate immigrants or minorities into a common culture, must learn to be more sensitive to the culture of immigrants and minorities. Given the diverse nature of society, "we're not sure what values [are] American values."[3] But conservative commentators (e.g., William Bennett, Lynne Cheney, E. D. Hirsh, Diane Ravitch, etc.) are concerned about the potential for disunity, disharmony—and as Arthur Schlesinger asserts in *The Disuniting of America* and as Robert Hughes in *The Fraying of America*.

These same conservative commentators are concerned that most American students don't know their own history and culture; moreover, many multiculuralists and radical educators from the political left frown on anything that might hint of western culture—criticized as white, Anglo, male, imperialist, and racist. The outcome is that American history courses are no longer part of the required curriculum in most colleges, and students can satisfy such requirements by taking courses such as Environmental Politics, Global Policy Studies, Urban Life, and others.[4]

Thus, in a Roper survey among the top 55 colleges in the country, only 40 percent of college seniors knew that the Battle of the Bulge was a World War II event, only 34 percent knew that George Washington commanded the American forces at Yorktown (37 percent thought it was Grant), and only 22 percent could identify that a "government of the people, by the people, for the people" came from Lincoln's Gettysburg Address.[5]

Remember, these data were compiled from college seniors from the nation's elite colleges! Now if these students can't get their American history facts and ideas

1. Lynette Holloway, "Levy Sets Out Plan to Adjust Bilingual Class," *New York Times* (December 20, 2000), pp. B1, B3.
2. Oscar Handlin, *The Newcomers* (Garden City, NY: Doubleday, 1959), p. 62.
3. Nathan Glazer, *We Are All Multiculturalists Now* (Cambridge, MA: Harvard University Press, 1997), p. 7.
4. "The Pilgrim's Magna Carta," *Wall Street Journal* (November 23, 2001), p. 15.
5. Ibid.

correct, how do we expect our college populace to defend the values of freedom and democracy? If the agenda is political, and the platform is "multicultural understanding" or "race relations," then the values of western civilization become suspect and we get into new explanations and word games. For example, those who use the word *terrorist* are held suspect or condemned on the grounds that "one man's terrorist is another man's freedom fighter"; those who disagree that *education is corporate controlled* are viewed as agents of the establishment or racist—insensitive to immigrants, minorities, women, and others.[1] These word games may work in a college environment, but they don't work well in the real world—and are often considered dysfunctional.

Improvement in economic and social status, for most immigrants and minorities, depends on education and functioning in the situation where jobs exist. For every one person who gets a job playing basketball or singing country western songs, 100,000 or more jobs will require the ability to communicate formally—read, speak, write, calculate, and compute—no jive talk, no hip-hop talk, no trash talk, no limited or broken English. Posters of ethnic heroes and knowledge of folk history and folk culture might work in a special course or in school, and it might also improve a person's identity, but it doesn't work in most jobs. We are moving in a multicultural direction and acceptance of many cultures, but the focus of school, and the skills required for most jobs, is to read, write, and communicate in English and work with computers.

Yellow, brown, and black ethnic groups will not be totally assimilated into the "melting pot" in my lifetime, as John Dewey once thought would happen in his lifetime with all ethnics; color prejudice and primitive, tribal instincts will not go away. His associate Jane Addams understood this, since she worked closely with immigrant populations in her settlement house in Chicago. There is a hodgepodge of nationalities characterized by race and ethnicity that has brought displacement, disorientation, and conflict to Europe for centuries; in fact, it has dragged down the old world. This poisonous combination of *nationalism* and *racism* must be swept away in the new world, with the help of education, which ideally includes moral content and great literature—where there is a flow of ideas that deal with life. Indeed, we are all Americans, entitled to certain blessings and rights resulting from civil and religious liberty, and the schools must reinforce this snapshot of life.

We are here for a short period of time. When we are young, playing childhood games in the schoolyard or listening to snatches of heavy rock or metal music, we don't dwell on or have references to death. But how we succumb to the passing years, with sadness or grace, hatred or charity, or disrespect or respect toward other groups, to a large extent depends on our education and life experiences—who we become.

The responsibility of schools in America is to help all ethnic, racial, and religious groups come to terms with the larger culture of America, to appreciate the national

1. Paul Goodman, in his 1964 text *Contemporary Mis-education,* was the first to refer to education as corporate controlled, a frequent criticism voiced by today's critical pedagogists, neomarxists, and radical theorists. No credit is given to Goodman by this new group of radicals.

identity, to escape from a ghetto mentality, our ethnic or religious tribes—the darkness, hatred, and horrors of the old order, the other side of the world where our parents, grandparents, or great-grandparents escaped. The history and memories of the old order—rooted in religious and ethnic hatred, economic disparities and greed, and political strife and genocide—are ever-present in our textbooks and classroom discussions, but they are never dwelled on. Rather, they are glossed over and sanitized in a few pages or short teacher-student dialogue. At best, in some advanced history or English course, taught by an unusual teacher, the doors are opened a little, letting only a little darkness and madness spill out.

The result is that our children and youth lack a full understanding of the dark side of humanity and don't come away from school appreciating the nation's character or believing in American values and virtues. The United States is far from perfect, and has plenty of room for improvement—and that is what schools are about—to help create a better tomorrow. Along these lines of thought, our students need an intimate entry, as early as possible, to great ideas, great books, and great films (and music, art, photography etc.) in order to become thinking persons, to understand the cultural, social, and moral conundrums and vicissitudes of life, and to work at and become better persons.

Alas, I end this chapter by telling you not to despair. We are the lucky ones! Over the course of 250 years ago, this nation has grown from a small cluster of colonies, a ragtag collection of people and a makeshift army, to a mighty and wealthy nation—the most influential one in the history of humankind and on the present world stage. How was this possible? Does it boil down to accident, luck or design?

Could the answer be simply what Otto Von Bismark, the Prussian foreign minister once muddled: "God has special providence for fools, drunks, and the United States of America." The United States has been blessed, indeed, perhaps not in the way meant by Bismark. De Tocqueville, perhaps the most influential and profound visitor and observer of America, put it in more realistic terms. Whereas a "permanent inequality of condition prevailed" in the old world, and where the social conditions tended "to promote the despotism" of the monarchs and ruling class on the masses, the "principle of democracy" prevailed in the United States.[1]

Some 170 years later, another foreign chap, this time an immigrant from the far-off land of India, Dinesh D'Souza (someone much more conservative but just as idealistic as De Tocqueville) commented: "America is a new kind of society that produces a new kind of human being. That human being—confident, self-reliant, tolerant, generous, future-oriented—is a vast improvement over the wretched, fatalistic and intolerant human being that traditional societies have always produced and that Islamic societies produce now."[2] One need not agree with everything that D'Souza says, given the fact that he hails from India where there is a history of conflict with the Muslim world, but one gets the idea about the American progress and power, and that much

---

1. Alexis de Tocqueville, *Democracy in America*, vol. 3 (New York: Knopf, 1945; originally published in 1835), p. 89.
2. Dinesh D'Souza, *What's So Great About America* (Washington, DC: Regnery, 2002).

of it has to do with the separation of church and state, which de Tocqueville also noted when he visited the American shore in the 1830s. Indeed, America has produced a rich, dynamic, tolerant, democratic society that, according to D'Souza, "is now the hope of countless immigrants, and a magnet for the world," and also, if I may add, the hope for world peace, world stability, and western civilization.

Given a war of words and ideas in many fields of study between "liberals" and "conservatives," "visionaries" and "technocrats," and "blue" and "red" voters, I would opt for the description of de Tocqueville and D'Souza, and hope that teachers also adapt this view of history. I certainly understand that the view of American history and society is based on a person's self-identity and self-interest, and thus determines what that person sees or doesn't see. However, I don't think I'm blind. When all is said and done, my paradigm recognizes "the huddled masses and tired poor," so vividly described by Emma Lazarus and etched in the Statue of Liberty, yearning to be free, coming to America, changing the landscape, and forming a new colossus.

## Summary

1. The purposes of education are influenced by changing social forces, but there tends to be a balancing act between developing the potential of the *individual* and improving *society*.

2. Another balancing act or duality is the need to stress *intellectual* and *moral* matters. Most schools, however, emphasize learning in the cognitive domain and deemphasize the moral domain.

3. In the last 50 years or more, American society has changed from an *inner-directed* society to an *other-directed* society, and now to a *postmodern* society.

4. The American family is changing from households headed by two adults to households headed by one adult. In an age of diversity and pluralism, the nuclear family is being replaced by many different family forms.

5. Elementary schools tend to discriminate against and feminize boys, as illustrated by a host of statistical and comparative data between boys and girls in terms of academic achievement and school behavior.

6. The country is taken by the Harry Potter phenomenon, who continuously faces Herculean tasks that test his magical prowess, daring, wits, and ability to cope with and overcome danger.

7. The peer group becomes increasingly important as children proceed through adolescence; it has an important influence on social behavior and academic achievement.

8. Social class, race, and gender influence social behavior and academic achievement. Both girls and boys experience various sex-role pressures in school.

9. The culture of the classroom and school tends to stress passive and conforming behaviors; students adopt to the environment by exhibiting various strategies, ranging from manipulative and pleasing to withdrawing and hostility.

10. Schools change slowly, much slower than other institutions in society. The methods and techniques of teachers have not materially changed in the last 50 years.

## *Questions to Consider*

1. How do education and schooling differ?
2. How do socializing experiences in school differ in inner-city, suburban, and rural schools?
3. What are the main purposes of education?
4. What might schools do to alleviate some of the pressures related to black students linking academic achievement to "white" behavior? What might schools do to alleviate some of the problems related to boys and girls growing up and relating to each other?
5. How did the hidden curriculum affect your behavior in school?

## *Things to Do*

1. Contact a local school district to obtain a document concerning its purpose or goals of education. Share this information with the class and discuss the implications of the school's purposes.
2. Print out a recent article from the Internet on family life or family composition. Discuss in class what you have learned from the data.
3. Interview school officials in your community to determine what they are doing to improve gender issues in school.
4. Observe a classroom at a nearby school or at your college. How would you assess whether learning taking place in the classroom was passive or active?
5. Which arguments in the chapter did you find most persuasive? Why? Which arguments do you criticize most? Why?

## *Recommended Readings*

Corno, Lyn, ed. *Education Across a Century,* 100th Yearbook, Part I. Chicago: National Society for the Study of Education, 2001. Social and historical themes of education in the context of the present and future.

Foshay, Aruthur W. *The Curriculum.* New York: Teachers College Press, 2000. The planning of curriculum for the purpose of maximizing human potential.

Goodlad, John. *A Place Called School.* New York: McGraw-Hill, 1984. A classic treatise on the nature of schooling, what happens in classrooms, and how teachers teach.

Kohn, Alfie. *What to Look for in a Classroom.* San Francisco: Jossey-Bass, 2000. The author raises serious questions about what's wrong with classrooms and schools, and what can be done to improve them.

Ogbu, John U. *Minority Education and Caste.* New York: Academic Press, 1978. An analysis of how social class and race influence academic achievement.

Orfield, Gary, and Elizabeth H. Debray, eds. *Hard work for Good Schools.* Washington DC: Brookings Institution, 2001. Reform issues related to improving Title I schools.

Schlechty, Phillip C. *Shaking Up the Schoolhouse.* San Francisco: Jossey-Bass, 2000. The nuts and bolts in improving classrooms and schools, and supporting educational reform.

# Schooling in America: Part I

## Chapter 5

## Focusing Questions

1. Who qualifies as an education icon? What risks does an author run when he or she criticizes an icon?

2. How did the ideas of leading philosophers and educators of the eighteenth and nineteenth century shape schools?

3. How did American democratic ideas contribute to the rise of the common school movement?

4. In what way did American nationalism during the first half of the nineteenth century influence schooling?

5. What ideas or practices from Jefferson and Webster coincide with your own philosophy of education?

6. How did the western frontier of America influence schooling?

7. What unique problems were evidenced in the nineteenth century as elementary and secondary schools expanded?

8. How did racial and gender factors limit social and educational opportunities in the past?

9. How would you interpret or square the concept of universal education with student enrollments in the nineteenth and twentieth centuries?

## EPISODE A

Whether we are talking about the principles of dieting or exercising or the principles of theoretical physics or cloning, we are talking about ideas that shape life. The cutting edge of physical science is not about the completely unknown. It is found where we have a continuous thread of past discoveries, where we understand just enough to go one step further by asking the right questions, taking educated hunches, improving an existing machine, or modifying the right formula. In *Einstein's Unfinished Symphony,* the author points out that the concept of $E = MC^2$ was a breakthrough formula to explain the relationship of energy to matter. However, it was preceded by a host of scientific principles and discoveries related to gravity, lightwaves, and cold fusion.[1] Breakthrough discoveries, including the more recent ones (such as the atomic bomb, moon landing, DNA and cloning), were built on an accumulation of ideas over several decades and involving several scientists. The fact that one person (e.g., Bell or Edison) or one group (e.g., Watson and Crick) may get most of the credit overlooks hundreds of other people whose ideas influenced these scientists.

Similarly, the cutting edge of social science theories is based on an accumulation of previous ideas that can be traced back to various time periods and people. What we read is filtered through a personal and cultural lens, and modified by the power of language, critical thought, and the previous and experiences and current intentions of the reader. When we examine our schools, today, we need to remember there is a host of antecedents—a history of people and ideas—which helps explain and trace human affairs. We will perform this examination in the next two chapters.

## Reexamining Three Icons: Rousseau, Cremin, and Dewey

The rise of universal schooling in America can be traced to many different periods, philosophies, and statesmen, including Socrates, Plato, and Quintilian, and, more recently, Rousseau, Jefferson, and Mann. From his early readings of *Great Men and Famous Women,* President Truman concluded that *great individuals* made history—and he felt that both Roosevelt and Churchill shaped world history. For the same reason, Truman feared General MacArthur and his influence in foreign policy, and dismissed him before he could lead the nation down the road to war with mainland China. President Carter was influenced by *War and Peace,* the notion that great events are determined by *common ordinary people*—their hopes, dreams, fears, and prejudices determine, in a quiet way, the destiny of the world.

Both points can be argued in the political arena, as well as the educational arena. For example, did Horace Mann really spearhead the common school movement or was it the common people who shaped the common school movement? It was Thomas Jefferson who framed the Declaration of Independence, but had he not been alive, would there have been someone else to write it? In the final analysis, Sidney Hook's idea that history is determined by a mix of events and people seems plausible, although there are turning points and key people that shape trends, ideas, and discoveries. Elie Wiesel, described as a "messenger of mankind," when he was awarded the Nobel Prize in 1986, believes events are determined by a nation's or a

---

1. Marcia Bartusiak, *Einstein's Unfinished Symphony* (Washington, DC: Joseph Henry Press, 2000).

person's education and experiences, rooted in its history, philosophy, and literature, and by what its teachers have to say to its youth. "The past reverberates in the future. Sophocles and Shakespeare have much to tell you about human cruelty and suffering"[1]—about life in general.

Authors have choices in where to start the flow of thought or the period (or the year) of a movement. In Lawrence Cremin's classic book, *The Transformation of the School*, progressivism in American education begins in 1876,[2] coinciding with the aftermath of the 1874 U.S. Supreme Court decision that permitted states to establish and support public high schools with tax money, and John Runkle's idea of introducing manual training on a mass scale for students who were less academic and wished to pursue a practical education. This was "the key," according to Cremin, "to a new balanced schooling that would . . . marry the mental and manual, thereby preparing people realistically for life in an industrial society."[3]

The idea of a *universal education* was based on the theories and influential leadership of Thomas Jefferson, Noah Webster, and Horace Mann. This concept of free education for the nation's children and youth represents the main glue of progressive thought. Jefferson's idea of universal education was based on political reasons, for promoting democracy, since he felt it could not survive unless the citizens were educated. Webster's reasons were based on cultural nationalism, the need to break from English culture and customs, and to build a national language and national identity. As early as the 1820s, Mann saw universal education as a means of socializing and enculturating the country's growing immigrant population. Thus, Cremin's history of progressivism, which starts in 1876, seems arbitrary. Obviously, to criticize Cremin is to push the education envelope and to invite criticism. And why not? Socrates, Descartes, and Voltaire made it very clear that we all sit on a riverbank of ideas, some popular and some unpopular. We have the natural instinct to fish for new thought, and some of us (professors, for example) get paid to fish and play with ideas that flow by. Let me, then, fish and play a little more—forming a new thought about John Dewey, who obviously influenced Cremin.

Dewey, in one of his lesser known books, *Schools of Tomorrow*, traced progressivism to Rousseau's ideas about the child's natural goodness and natural development.[4] But Rousseau was much more concerned about social and political inequality, society's corruption, and the need to politically and socially reform society than to pay attention to schooling. It was Pestalozzi and Froebel, two European educators, who took Rousseau's ideas and popularized them into pedagogical practices that became part of American progressive education. As Dewey wrote, "Pestalozzi and Froebel were the two educators most zealous in reducing inspiration got from

1. Elie Wiesel, "Dear Students," *Newsday* (November 7, 2001), p. A45.
2. Lawrence A. Cremin, *The Transformation of the School* (New York: Random House, 1961).
3. Ibid., p. 26.
4. John Dewey and Evelyn Dewey, *Schools of Tomorrow*, rev. ed. (New York: E. P. Dutton, 1962).

Rousseau into the details of schoolroom work." They took Rousseau's "idea of natural development and translated it into formulae which teachers could use from day to day."[1]

However, I would add that Pestalozzi and Froebel, as well as Dewey, took Rousseau's ideas about (1) teaching through the senses, (2) exploring the child's surroundings, (3) emphasizing the child's needs and interests (as opposed to the teacher's words), and (4) aligning teaching methods and the curriculum (although the latter term was not coined until the turn of the twentieth century) to the child's stages of development. Furthermore, much of Dewey's early theoretical practices (prior to *Democracy and Education*) at the laboratory school, which he headed at the University of Chicago, were based on Rousseau's ideas, yet only minimal credit was given by Dewey.[2] Although much of Dewey's ideas can be directly traced back to Rousseau, ultimately much of universal education can be traced to Plato. Even Rousseau asked his readers to turn to Plato for advice on educating the masses,[3] as well as to shape the child and uphold the purposes of the nation-state.

There was a great paradox in Rousseau's political doctrine, a totalitarian aspect of the general will: A state is established when individuals place themselves "under the supreme direction of the general will," and whoever refuses to obey the general will be "forced to be free."[4] These statements suggest that the general will (or the majority) can become tyrannical.[5] Not only is Rousseau's majority "forced to fall back on notions of coercion and constraint," according to one historian,[6] but also Nietsche crafted the Teutonic "superman theory" to oppose the general will, relying on Rousseau's political doctrine to provide a rationale for a "totalitarianism response to modern life."[7] So, if great minds have their flaws and follies, then it is not the worst thing to be a little critical of dead gurus and spiritual leaders of progressive thought.

The discussion, so far, throws cherished ideas into question, but the intent is to illustrate the original point about social science ideas—where they begin, how the dynamic flow of ideas are traceable, who influences whom, and how current moments of time and thought can be expressed with different shades and meaning from the past. Historians, social critics, and academics should fish for ideas that flow by, and thus they will retain the vestiges of a lost world, deal with flawed memories, and struggle with the visions and virtues of men and women who are now dead but whose ideas are the foundation of education.

1. Ibid., p. 45.
2. John Dewey, *The School and Society* (Chicago: University of Chicago Press, 1899).
3. Cremin, *The Transformation of the School.*
4. See the *Social Contract,* Book I, chapters 6 and 7.
5. A personal letter to me from Jerome Reich, a retired European historian, February 12, 2001; J. L. Talman, *The Origins of Totalitarian Democracy* (New York: Secker and Warburg, 1952).
6. Keith Ansell-Pearson, *Nietsche Centra Rousseau* (London: Cambridge University Press, 1991), p. 94.
7. J. Merquior, *Rousseau and Weber* (London: Routledge & Kegan Paul, 1980), p. 36.

# The Rise of Universal Education

It is essential for every nation to educate the younger generation to promote its own culture, religious and political institutions, and economic growth. Mann, Webster, and Jefferson all understood it, although they had different reasons, ranging from promoting Rousseau's form of democracy (government by the people) to Plato's republicanism (the need for a strong nation-state.)[1] In contemporary times, this is comparable to comparing the political, social, and education ideas of Kennedy, Johnson, and Clinton with Reagan, Bush, and Bush. The Puritans in New England and the Calvinists and Quakers in the middle Atlantic states also understood the need for educating the masses, although their reasons were religious and moral.

## Colonial New England Education

Education in colonial New England is the starting point for universal education in the United States. The schools established in New England were closely related to the Puritan church and sought to educate children in God's commandments and to resist the temptations of the world, especially the devil's work. In fact, the child was regarded as naturally depraved—almost the exact opposite of Rousseau's ideal that children were naturally good and that adult society, especially urban society, was the problem. In order to civilize the child to the ways of society, the Puritan teacher constantly disciplined the child and could yield a firm rod. Schooling was intended to cultivate respect for the laws of the theocratic state and respect of property. Since religious persons were educated, and only the wealthy owned property, education was based on maintaining a class-based society. Most of the people in New England formed their ideas from England, which had (and still has today) a class-based society partially rooted in the differences between private and public schooling, as well as the House of Lords and the House of Commons.

There was also a general economic rationale for school in New England, which was reinforced by the Puritan ideal of hard work. The citizen was economically productive—a hard-working farmer, manufacturer, or trader—rooted in the English idea of promoting the commonwealth and colonial empire. Hard-working children and adults would further the ends of the church and capitalist class—highlighted by the schoolchildren's reading of *Book of the Common Prayer, New England Primer,* and the *Horn Book.*

1. Some observers would argue that Plato's education enhanced a class-based society in which the academic elite received most of the education and others (soldiers, auxiliaries, and workers) received much less education. True, but this type of academic elitism, where a person's education is determined by intellectual capacity, is similar in some ways to Jefferson's idea of who should receive a free high school and college education, and is reminiscent of old-fashioned Essentialist philosophy apparent in the writings of Arthur Bestor's *Educational Wastelands* and James Conant's *The American High School Today,* which characterized the post-*Sputnik* era. For each type of student, according to Plato, there was an appropriate educational track—not much different from Bestor's and Conant's idea of separating the vocational student from the average, the college bound, and the talented and gifted.

As early as 1642, Massachusetts required parents to make certain that their children could read and understand the principles of religion and laws of the New England commonwealth. In 1647, the state legislature (the General Court) enacted the Old Deluder Satan Act, which required every town of 50 or more families to appoint a teacher of reading and writing. Towns of 100 or more families were to employ a teacher of Latin so that students could be prepared for entry to Harvard College.[1]

It is obvious that the Puritans did not want an illiterate class to grow in colonial America. They feared that such a class might comprise a group of underclass, dependent, poor people, which would be reminiscent of that in England and other parts of Europe, and which they wanted to avoid. They also wanted to ensure that their children would grow up being committed to traditional customs and religious doctrines—thus there was need for literacy.

But the Puritans had a limited view about freedom. They did not want religious freedom that opposed their doctrine nor freedom for the Native Indians who opposed their expansion plans. The high clergy tossed Roger Williams out of New England, just like the Anglicans had previously tossed him out of England. Why? He attacked religious persecution, denied that civil authorities could enforce spiritual laws, and insisted in land rights for the working class in England and later for Indians in America. Considered an annoying, highly confrontational person who disagreed with the Establishment (Anglicans and Puritans alike), Williams was still able to negotiate a charter for Rhode Island with the English Parliament.[2] His ace was not his social or writing skills, but rather it was the influence of his surrogate father, Sir Edward Coke, who codified much of English law and understood court intrigue when Charles I was the head of State.

The Town School    All (white) boys and girls were expected to attend the town school from age 6 to age 13 or 14. Attendance was not always regular, since weather conditions and the need for farm labor during certain growing periods superseded compulsory attendance.[3] In general, the students learned reading, writing, and spelling by reading the *New England Primer* and *Horn Book,* which were also fused with religious passages. They also learned how to add and subtract, memorized the Ten Commandments, the Lord's Prayer, and several other religious sermons. Write two researchers, "The somber caste of the Puritan religion and morals was evident as students memorized sermons and learned their ABC's through rote and drill."[4]

The town school was originally designed to enhance the social control and religious doctrine of the Puritan community. Although the town school promoted the

1. Nathaniel Shurtleff, ed. *Records of the Governor and Company of the Massachusetts Bay in New England,* vol. 2 (Boston: Order of the Legislature, 1853).

2. Mary Lee Settle, *I, Roger Williams* (New York: Norton, 2000).

3. George H. Martin, *The Evolution of the Massachusetts Public School System* (New York: Appleton, 1894); Allan C. Ornstein and Daniel U. Levine, *Foundations of Education,* 8th ed. (Boston: Houghton Mifflin, 2003); and Joel Spring, *American Education,* 10th ed. (Boston: McGraw-Hill, 2002).

4. Allan C. Ornstein and Francis P. Hunkins, *Curriculum Foundations, Principles, and Issues,* 3rd ed. (Boston: Allyn and Bacon, 1998), p. 65.

idea of universal education, a dual-track system (similar to England's) was created where upper-class boys (girls were excluded) attended the Latin grammar school to prepare for Harvard College and later Yale. A boy would enter the school at age 8 or 9 and remain for 8 years. The classics, Latin and Greek, rhetoric and logic, along with science and mathematics were stressed—which had the makings of a modern perennialist curriculum. It was this tough-type academic curriculum that set the tone for the American high school until the introduction of Abraham Flexner's modern curriculum in 1916. A religious atmosphere also prevailed with the "master praying regularly with his pupils" and quizzing them thoroughly on the sermons.[1] As Samuel Morrison reminds us, the Latin grammar school was one of the closest links of colonial America to European schools of the Renaissance.[2]

Latin Grammar School   Latin grammar schools prepared students for college and subsequently for professional careers—ministry, law, medicine, and so on—much like high school academic programs prepare students for college today. The tough academic curriculum of the school, with its stress on the classics and Latin, set the curriculum tone for American high school until the beginning of the twentieth century, and thereby restricted the number of students attending and graduating high school (see Table 5.1).

The current relationship between course offerings of high schools and college admission requirements, as well as the habit to require college aptitude tests such as the SAT or ACT, were set in motion more than 200 years ago. Writes Ellwood Cubberley, the best-known educational historian of the first third of the twentieth century and cultural elitist, "The student would be admitted into college 'upon Examination' whereby he could show competency 'to Read, Construe, Parce Tully, Vergil and the Greek Testament, and to write Latin in Prose and to understand the Rules of Prosodia and Common Arithmetic,' as well as to bring 'testimony of his blameless and unoffensive life.' "[3] In other words, good morals and good character—what today would be expressed in an applicant's letters of recommendation and community service—also counted. But perhaps what counted more was family connections, certainly not an unfamiliar concept today.

## The Middle Colonies

In the middle colonies, unlike New England, no common language or religion existed. Writes George Beauchamp, "Competition among political and religious groups retarded willingness to expend the public funds for educational purposes."[4] No one sin-

1. Newton Edwards and Herman G. Richey, *The School in American Social Order,* 2nd ed. (Boston: Houghton Mifflin, 1963), p. 102.

2. Sammuel E. Morrison, *The Intellectual Life of Colonial New England* (New York: University Press, 1956).

3. Ellwood P. Cubberley, *Public Education in the United States,* rev ed. (Boston: Houghton Mifflin, 1947), p. 30.

4. George A. Beauchamp, *The Curriculum of the Elementary School* (Boston: Allyn and Bacon, 1964), p. 34.

—————————————————— TABLE *5.1* ——————————————————
## Percentage of Students Enrolled in High School and College, 1900–2000

|  | 14- to 17-Year-Olds Enrolled in Secondary School | 17-Year-Olds Graduating High School | 18- to 21-Year-Olds Enrolled in College |
|---|---|---|---|
| 1900 | 11.5 | 6.5 | 3.9 |
| 1910 | 15.4 | 8.8 | 5.0 |
| 1920 | 32.3 | 16.8 | 7.9 |
| 1930 | 51.4 | 29.0 | 11.9 |
| 1940 | 73.3 | 50.8 | 14.5 |
| 1950 | 76.8 | 59.0 | 26.9 |
| 1960 | 86.1 | 65.1 | 31.3 |
| 1970 | 93.4 | 76.5 | 45.2 |
| 1980 | 93.7 | 75.4 | 46.3 |
| 1990 | 95.8 | 85.4 | 48.5 |
| 2000 | 97.9 | 87.5 | 53.7 |

*Source:* From *Digest of Educational Statistics, 1982, 1985–1986, 1989, 1998* (Washington, DC: U.S. Government Printing Office, 1982, 1986, 1989, 1998), Table 35, p. 44; Table 9, p. 11; Tables 6, 49, pp. 13, 62; Tables 6, 8, pp. 15, 17. *Projections of Education Statistics 2008* (Washington, DC: U.S. Government Printing Office, 1998).

gle system of schools could be established. What evolved instead were parochial and independent schools, related to different ethnic and religious groups, and the idea of community or local control of schools (as opposed to New England's concept of central or districtwide schools). The current notion of cultural pluralism and diversity thus took shape some 200 years ago in New York, New Jersey, and Pennsylvania.

Religious tolerance flourished in the middle Atlantic states, as opposed to the "self-evident truth" and uniform doctrine imposed by the Puritans in New England. Schools were operated by several different churches and they were open to all children, including girls, Native Indians, and blacks.[1] There were also private, independent schools for boys and girls those who could pay for it. In the private school, outstanding teachers (called masters) earned a comfortable living, about two or three times more than a carpenter or blacksmith. The free market system prevailed, and teachers with appropriate academic credentials were paid handsomely for their

1. H. Warren Button and Eugene F. Provenzo, *History of Education and Culture in America* (Englewood Cliffs, NJ: Prentice-Hall, 1983).

services, very different from today, whereby semi-skilled laborers make as much or more than most teachers. (In California, first-year prison guards earn more money than freshmen teachers with a master's degree. In New York City, average salaries for sanitation workers exceed teachers' salaries.)

The teachers, unlike those in New England, opposed the views of child depravity and respected the dignity of the child. Although most colonists gave little thought in educating black slaves, a number of religious sects in the middle Atlantic colonies, especially the Quakers and Moravians, found slavery morally oppressive and were forbidden to own slaves. Schools were established for blacks in the late 1600s in these communities, and other black children were taught with white children.[1]

Anthony Benezet, one of the leading Quaker educators, argued that blacks were "generously sensible, humane and sociable, and that their capacity is as good, and as capable of improvement as that of white people." Benezet, along with Quaker John Woolman, "were the first American abolitionists . . . and worked to save the souls of white and black children alike."[2]

Although American colonial opinion was divided about treatment of Native Indians and blacks, Benjamin Franklin's view eventually prevailed. Although he also came from Pennsylvania, a middle colony, he worried that the white world was outnumbered by Africans and Asians, and according to Joel Spring, "considered expansion into North America as opportunity to increase the white race."[3] One interpretation for Franklin's antislavery position is that he feared the black population increase in North America, since there was "opportunity, by excluding all Blacks and Tawnys, of increasing the white race."[4] Thus, the naturalization Act of 1790 excluded from citizenship all nonwhites, including blacks and Native Indians.

## The Southern Colonies

In the southern colonies, schooling followed a different pattern than the New England or middle states. Private tutors were employed to teach the children of the upper class. Sometimes plantation owners funded a small schoolhouse in which nearby families sent their children to receive an education. Those who could afford to pay were expected to do so for the good of the community. In general, plantation and property owners did not believe in providing schools at public expense for all children—except for poor families. This view of education might be considered the forerunner of charity funding; however, it also placed a stigma on public or free education.[5] In effect, the demands of an agrarian economy and the stigma attached to

1. Edgar W. Knight, *Education in the United States* (Boston: Ginn, 1929); Samuel E. Morison, *Growth of the American Republic* (New York: Oxford, 1969).

2. Button and Provenzo, *History of Education and Culture in America*, p. 38.

3. Joel Spring, *The American School: 1642–1996,* 4th ed. (Boston: McGraw-Hill, 1997), p. 35.

4. John Best, ed., *Benjamin Franklin on Education* (New York: Teachers College Press, 1962); Spring, *The American School.*

5. Lawrence A. Cremin, *Traditions of American Education* (New York: Basic Books, 1977); James M. Hughes, *Education in America,* 3rd ed. (New York: Harper and Row, 1970).

public schools kept many poor children from attending school. Black slave children had more legal and social disadvantages placed on them and much of their schooling rested on the good will of their owners.

The southern system of education, besides being elitist in its emphasis on private schooling, was designed to support and enhance slavery by keeping the black populace ignorant and maintaining a white working underclass. Few political leaders in the South seemed concerned about public schooling for the masses; in fact, the extreme or libertarian view was illustrated by Virginia Governor William Berkley, who, in 1671, argued in a public document to authorities that educating the poor would result in "disobedience and heresy" and bring conflict or "sects into the world," aimed at bringing down the government and property classes.[1]

## Jefferson: Education for Citizenship

Faith in the agrarian society and distrust toward the proletariat of the cities were basic in Thomas Jefferson's idea of democracy. A man of wide-ranging interests that embraced politics, agriculture, science, and education, Jefferson assumed the state had the responsibility to cultivate an educated and liberated citizenry to improve social conditions and ensure a democratic society. In "A Bill for the More General Diffusion of Knowledge," introduced in the Virginia legislature in 1779, Jefferson advocated a plan that provided educational opportunities for boys and girls and both common people and landed gentry "at the expense of all."[2] To Jefferson, formal education was largely a state or civic concern rather than a matter reserved to religious or upper-class groups. Schools should be financed through public taxes. He also wanted the state to control education, because he feared that religious institutions, such as in New England, were dogmatic and unwilling to encourage critical or scientific thinking. At all costs, he wanted to avoid religious indoctrination and promote free expression of opinion. The fact that Jefferson's views prevailed, that the church and state were separated, is one reason for American progress, social mobility, and secular law which protects the common folk.

Jefferson's plan subdivided the counties of Virginia into wards, each of which would have a free elementary school to teach reading, writing, arithmetic, and history. He rejected the reading of religious materials, including the Bible, since elementary schoolchildren by reason of their immaturity were unable to fully understand the spiritual or moral implications. He did put great faith in moral education when children could fully reason, describing it as education for "good conscience, good health, occupation, and freedom in all just pursuits."[3] These four characteristics of Jefferson's moral education would become part of the Seven Cardinal Principles of

1. Henry Steele Commager, *Documents of American History*, vol. 1 (New York: Crofts, 1934), p. 114.

2. Thomas Jefferson, "A Bill for the More General Diffusion of Knowledge," in P. L. Ford, ed. *The Writings of Thomas Jefferson* (New York: Putnam, 1893), p. 221.

3. Thomas Jefferson, "Notes on the State of Virginia," in G. Lee, ed. *Crusade Against Ignorance: Thomas Jefferson on Education* (New York: Teachers College Press, 1961), p. 95.

Secondary Education, presented in 1918 by the NEA, which could be summed in twentieth century "educationeze" as ethical character, good health and physical fitness, vocational education, and civic education.

For Jefferson, this teaching of morality was largely based on appraising history, to analyze human actions—other people and other nations—and to use this understanding as a benchmark for students to judge their own personal actions and the actions of others. For Jefferson, who epitomized the Age of Enlightenment, *education* (a blending of knowledge and reason) and *morality* would foster a free society; these two ingredients would provide its citizens with the understanding and virtue to fulfill the obligations and duties as free people.

Also provided for in Jefferson's proposal was the establishment of 20 grammar schools at the secondary level, for which gifted students who could not afford to pay tuition would be provided scholarships. There, the students would study Latin, Greek, English, geography and higher mathematics. Upon completing grammar school, half the scholarship students would be assigned positions as elementary (or ward) school teachers. The 10 scholarship students of highest achievement would attend William and Mary College. These youth would become the leaders and statesmen for promoting the interests of the Republic. Jefferson's plan promoted the idea of school as a selective agency to identify bright students for continuing education, as well as the future idea of equality of opportunity for economically less fortunate students.

Jefferson forcefully expressed his view in the "A Bill for the More General Diffusion of Knowledge": "Those persons who nurture [their] endowed with genius and virtue should be rendered [or educated] . . . to guard the sacred deposit of the rights and liberties of their fellow citizens . . . without regard to wealth, birth, or other accidental condition . . . whom nature hath fitly formed and disposed to become useful instruments for the public, it is better that such should be sought for and educated at this common expense of all."[1] In the final analysis, Jefferson had the greatest faith in educating the common citizen for promoting democracy, more than the need for the talented to attend college for it was "the people [who] are the ultimate guardians of their own liberty."[2]

Jefferson's three-tier system of education—first educating all citizens; then the artisans, craftsmen, and business people; and then political statesmen—is somewhat similar to Plato's plan in *The Republic*. The Greek philosopher envisioned a perfect state that also educated three classes—workers and warriors, academic elites, and philosopher-kings (to lead the state)—each contributing to the general welfare of society. Also, each person's contribution would be defined in intellectual abilities, and not social circumstance or accident of birth.

The difference between Plato and Jefferson is, however, that the former relied more on philosopher-kings in administering and shaping society than did Jefferson, who put his faith in political leaders and statesmen. Plato did not believe the people had the knowledge or virtue to govern themselves, and so put his trust in the state

1. Jefferson, "A Bill for the More General Diffusion of Knowledge," pp. 220–221.
2. Jefferson, "Notes on the State of Virginia," p. 96.

(seeds of fascism). Plato, like Hamilton and Voltaire, mistrusted the "herd" (Hamilton's expression) and believed that the spirit of a nation always resides in a small number who put a large number to work and tell them what to do. This legitimizes a lot of power in the hands of a few—and a propensity to nationalistic and religious zeal at the expense of democratic ideals. Jefferson put his trust in the people, maintaining they had the most to gain or lose in the final analysis. In his notes to the people of Virginia, he maintained that the man with the plow had more "common sense" than members of the natural aristocracy or intellectual elite who had been selected and educated by the school and college system. Similarly, he felt the people had an innate sense of morality and justice, and could distinguish right and wrong just as well, "often better than the latter [or political leader], because he had not been led astray by artificial rules,"[1] and, if I may add, political compromise and temptation of power and payoff.

Jefferson was more knowledgable and better read than Plato. Jefferson had 6,500 books in his private library;[2] Plato may have had 100, possibly 200. Perhaps Jefferson was the most intellectual and best-read American president; he was fluent in several languages and he had the advantage of reading the social and political theories of Locke and Rousseau, who were the driving force of the Age of Enlightenment. Both Locke and Rousseau had disdain toward the aristocracy and both believed that the political order should be based on a contract between the people and the government, which would rule by the consent of the majority. It was Locke in the *Two Treaties of Government*, in 1689, who first argued that all persons possessed inalienable rights of "life, liberty, and property," and it was Jefferson who used the first two words and changed property to "pursuit of happiness" to frame the Declaration of Independence.

Rousseau argued for a secular society against an established church, which became one of the cornerstones of the U.S. Constitution. It was Rousseau who objected to distinctions based on wealth and property and preferred "noble savages," or common folk, free and uncorrupted by social inequality. Jefferson would not condemn the accumulation of wealth, and linked it to the establishment of government and national prosperity, but he would argue, as Rousseau and Locke had, for the natural rights of citizens. Rousseau felt that schools interfered with learning and promoted traditional customs and norms that led to social restrictions and discrimination based on class, and he would abolish schools if he had his way. "For Rousseau, nature made formal education unnecessary; the best education was to let nature unfold, to permit the child to follow his own instinct and desires."[3] Many progressive educators shared similar views about the child's instincts and desires, starting with William Kilpatrick

1. Thomas Jefferson, "To Peter Carr, with Enclosure," in Lee, ed. *Crusade Against Ignorance*, p. 146. Also see Spring, *The American School: 1642–1996*, p. 58.

2. Harold Evans, "White House Club," *New York Times Book Review* (January 14, 2001), p. 31.

3. Robert J. Schaefer, "Retrospect and Prospect," in R. M. McClure, ed. *The Curriculum: Retrospect and Prospect*, Seventieth Yearbook of the National Society for the Study of Education, Part I (Chicago: University of Chicago Press, 1971), pp. 3–25.

and Harold Rugg in the 1920s and 1930s; however, it was the "neoprogressives" or "radicals" of the 1960s and 1970s, such as Paul Goodman, John Holt, and Ivan Illich, who wanted to abolish schools as they currently exist, similar to Rousseau's theme.[1] Although we can question the value or success of schools, especially for reaching and teaching lower-class students, what the critics offer in lieu of schools tends to be fuzzy—more rhetoric than reality.

Jefferson, on the other hand, like Horace Mann and John Dewey, had more faith in schools. Despite their limitations, schools were considered the major institution for promoting the purposes of a democratic society. Given the relationship of free schooling and democracy in America, all children were to be encouraged to continue their education for as long as possible, preferably throughout their lifetimes. Indeed, this was Jefferson's platform, as well as the thoughts of Mann and Dewey. Plato, on the other hand, had less faith in formal schools; rather, it was socialization and life experiences that (similar to Rousseau's beliefs) led to knowledge and molded character and virtue.

Neither Plato nor Jefferson's ideas were implemented by their contemporaries, partially because they were too forward thinking than those people of their period. Indeed, when someone expresses sentiments that are considered too extreme or radical by most members of a democratic society, the majority will modify or reject those views. For Jefferson's southern contemporaries, free education at public expense, and whereby birth was not a qualification for political leadership, was considered a step toward state socialism and the demise of the property class. And it was the property class, about 10 percent of the male population, that voted for independence.

Jefferson's proposal for Virginia was similar to Benjamin Rush's proposal for Pennsylvania, which, in 1791, called for free elementary schools in every township of 100 families or more, a free academy (Latin grammar school) at the county level, and free college at the state level for the future leaders of society.[1] The public would pay for the expenses, but, in the end, Rush argued that the education system would reduce taxes because a productive and well-managed work force and entrepreneur force would result. Today, we refer to this work force and entrepreneur force as *human capital*, and many argue that human capital is more important than economic capital in determining economic productivity and social progress of a nation.

Like Jefferson's, Rush's proposal was not enacted. Nonetheless, the ideas indicate the type of education theorizing characteristic of the young nation. The two proposals demonstrated the purpose of education to promote good citizenship, social progress, and utilitarianism. The classical curriculum and its religious tone were, in effect, beginning to decline. Rush and Jefferson were both concerned with equality of educational opportunity—that is, they proposed universal education for the masses of children and youth as methods for identifying students of superior ability who were to receive free secondary and college educations at public expense.

Before leaving the topic of Jefferson, it is important to note that a 2001 Gallop poll asked Americans to identify its "greatest U.S. president." Thomas Jefferson re-

1. Benjamin Rush, *A Plan for the Establishment of Public Schools* (Philadelphia: Thomas Dobson, 1791).

ceived about 1 percent of this vote—about one-tenth the percentage for Bill Clinton and one-fourth for Jimmy Carter. Either the historical memory of Americans is pretty close to zero, or the recent controversy regarding whether Thomas Jefferson fathered a child with his slave Sally Hemmings,[1] is the reason why one of the longest celebrated presidents is now in disfavor. Remember, this president is the principal author of the Articles of Confederation, the Declaration of Independence, the doctrine of the separation of church and state, the Northwest Ordinance, and the Constitution, as well as the driving force behind the construction of the White House and the purchase of the "wild lands" of the Louisiana Territory, which increased American boundaries by tenfold and led to American westward expansion for the next 100 years.

Many recent Jefferson biographies get credit for having insights into his flawed character, and it makes for interesting reading. But other than Truman, Ford, and Carter, I don't know any one president whose behavior comes close to living by the Golden Rule or the Ten Commandments. In the blurred postmodern world we find ourselves in, two questions arise: Have writers ascribed to Jefferson's character that are not really his but more political in nature? Given that almost all humans have partially flawed character qualities, should not the biographer focus on the larger issues and not bog down on half-truths, false positives, or superficial dribble? And which giant among us—including Victor Hugo's inspector Jevert, who asserted he always tried "to follow the letter of the law," or even Mohammed, Gandhi, and Martin Luther King, whose followers believed they preached the "truth" and marched for rules of "right conduct"—could pass a lie detector test completely confirming their character and morality?[2] So why pick on Jefferson for conduct we are not even sure about?

## Webster: Schoolmaster and Cultural Nationalism

The United States differed from most new countries struggling for identity in that it lacked a shared cultural identity and national literature. In its struggle against the cultures and ideas of the "old" world, the new nation went to great lengths to differentiate itself from England. Noah Webster passionately called on his fellow Americans to "unshackle [their] minds and act like independent beings. You have been children long enough, subject to the control and subservient to the interests of a haughty parent. . . .

1. Jefferson gets a "bum rap" under closer scrutiny, according to respected historians. Most of the alleged affair is based on a letter from Jefferson's granddaughter, which scholars believe was altered. The DNA linking Jefferson to Hemmings's son Eston merely shows that one of two dozen Jefferson males in Virginia was the father, including his much younger brother, Randolph, or one of Randolph's five sons. The statistical probability is much less to point to Thomas, who was 64 years old when Eston was conceived. For a quick overview, see Robert F. Turner, "The Truth about Jefferson," *Wall Street Journal* (July 6, 2001), p. 14.

2. Mohammed was considered a warmonger and pedophile by his critics. Gandhi and King were considered to be womanizers, the latter much more than Jefferson, but their files were buried by the press. (FBI director Hoover sent names and pictures to Mrs. King in an attempt to embarrass and stop the Rev. King—to no avail.)

You have an empire to raise . . . and a national character to establish and extend by your wisdom and judgment."[1]

In 1789, when the Constitution went into effect as the law of the land, Webster argued that the United States should have its own system of "language as well as government." The language of Great Britain, he reasoned, "should no longer be our standard; for the taste of her writers is already completed, and her language on the decline."[2] By the act of revolution, the American people had declared their political independence from England, and now they needed to declare their cultural independence as well.

The Revolution aroused bitter feelings toward the English, which persisted in the American press and was encouraged by the increased vogue of French etiquette, art, and literature, and in the view that speaking French was a sign of an educated and enlightened person. It was the ideas of the French philosophers, such as Diderot, Rousseau, and Voltaire, that helped Americans throw away their intellectual crutch toward England.

The new national self-consciousness led to an independent religious view, a break from the strings of Europe, and especially England, and the belief that an independent nation should print its own Bible and own version of the New Testament in 1777. As Merle Curti wrote, the "American Bible helped [provide] tangible evidence that God's printed word could issue from Philadelphia [where it was published] as well as from Oxford."[3] Similarly, the argument was made, first by Bishop Berkeley in 1731 and then by Joel Barlow, the composer of the patriotic poem *Columbiad,* at a Yale commencement in 1778, that the supremacy in the arts and sciences would eventually transfer from Europe to the United States. The new nation was even being compared to the classical cultures of Greece and Rome by American poets and artisans of the period.[4] As one famous orator at Harvard in 1797 asserted, the United States was destined to become "the Athens of our age, the admiration of the world."[5]

With this backdrop, Noah Webster, a Connecticut schoolmaster, declared in 1783 that "Europe is grown old in folly, corruption, and tyranny." For America to adapt the customs and laws of the "old world would be to stamp the wrinkle of decrepit age upon the bloom of youth, and to plant the seed of decay" upon the nation.[6]

1. Hans Kohn, *American Nationalism: An Interpretive Essay* (New York: Macmillan, 1957), p. 47.

2. Noah Webster, *Dissertations on the English Language* (Boston: Isaiah Thomas, 1789), p. 27.

3. Curti, *The Growth of American Thought,* p. 146.

4. Oscar A. Hansen, *Liberalism and American Education in the Eighteenth Century* (New York: Columbia University, 1926); Allan Nevins, *The American States During and After the Revolution* (New York: Macmillan, 1924).

5. Joseph Perkins, "An Oration Upon Genius, Pronounced at Harvard University," July 19, 1797 (Cambridge: Harvard University Press, 1797), p. 9.

6. Noah Webster, *A Grammatical Institute of the English Language,* Part I (Hartford CT: G. F. College, 1783), p. 14.

Realizing that a sense of national identity was conveyed through a distinctive national language and literature, Webster set out to reshape the English language used in the United States. He believed that a uniquely American language would (1) eliminate the remains of European usage, (2) create a uniform American speech that would be free of localism and provincialism, and (3) promote American self-conscious and cultural nationalism.[1] The creation of an American language would become the linguistic mortar of national union and national spirit; it would, however, have to be phonetically simple to render it more suitable to the common people.

Webster directly related the learning of language to organized education. As they learned the American language, children also would learn to think and act as Americans. The American language that Webster proposed would have to be taught deliberately and systematically to the young in the nation's schools. Because the curriculum of these Americanized schools would be shaped by the books that the students read, Webster spent much of his life writing spelling and reading books. His *Grammatical Institute of the English Language* was published in 1783. The first part of the *Institute* was later printed as *Noah Webster's American Spelling Book,* which was widely used throughout the United States in the first half of the nineteenth century.[2] Webster's *Spelling Book* went through many editions; it is estimated that 15 million copies had been sold by 1837, and another 15 million by 1875. Webster's great work was *The American Dictionary,* which was completed in 1825 after 25 years of laborious research.[3] Often termed the "schoolmaster of the Republic," Noah Webster was an educational statesman of the early national period whose work helped to create a sense of American language, identity, and nationality. His need to promote patriotism and an American language through the public schools, and to impose certain political and moral values became the model that Horace Mann was to adopt in the 1820s and 1830s.

## The Rise of the Common School Movement

The common school movement is often associated with Horace Mann. Although he popularized the idea in the 1830s and 1840s, the movement was rooted in the United States by the turn of the nineteenth century, as certain social and political forces gave impetus for the need of a free, universal system of education.

As early as 1795, Connecticut established a school fund, although the towns were not required to provide the schools. New York, Pennsylvania, and Virginia followed

1. Henry R. Warfel, *Noah Webster: Schoolmaster to America* (New York: Macmillan, 1936).
2. Henry Steele Commager, ed., *Noah Webster's American Spelling Book* (New York: Teachers College Press, 1962).
3. Robert K. Leavitt, *Noah's Ark, New England Yankee and the Endless Quest* (Springfield, MA: Merriam, 1947).

Connecticut's lead and had provisions for school funds before creating a statewide system of education.[1] By 1815, Massachusetts' parents paid tuition (called a *rate system*) for school if they were able. If they were not, the town paid the bill. This created a stigma, or in Merle Curti's words, a "pauper's label." Progressive reformers, led by James Carter, urged the elimination of tuition and the substitution of a free, tax-supported system of schools.[2] In Wisconsin, one-teacher, one-room schools existed and became the forerunners of a state system of free schools.[3] And there were "Hoosier" schools in Indiana, the first state in the Union (as early as 1816) to require in its state constitution "that public schools be open to all," including blacks.[4] (In the 1840s, the Supreme Court of Indiana repudiated the provision in favor of racial segregation.)

In short, according to Diane Ravitch, "Horace Mann and his generation of reformers may have been the articulators rather than the initiators of a trend that was already well grounded."[5] It was the context of the times, not the man, that provided the impetus of the common school movement—that is, if I may say, the rise of *Webster's nationalism* and the need to establish a school system free from European influence; the expansion of *Jefferson's republicanism* and *Jackson's democracy* and the need to educate the common folk and prevent an ignorant mass or "mob" from toppling the political or economic system; the *industrial revolution* and the need for an educated work force; *westward expansion* and the rise of equality and the disdain toward Eastern elitism and private schooling; increased *immigration* and diverse populations and the need to assimilate the new Americans into the "American" way; and the need to replace the *religious influence* that still prevailed for secular and public schools.

## Horace Mann: Common Schools, But Not a Common Man

The common school was established in 1826 in Massachusetts when the state passed a law requiring every town to choose a school board to be responsible for all the schools in the local area. Eleven years later, the Massachusetts legislature created the first state board of education, and Massachusetts organized the public or common schools under a single authority. Connecticut quickly followed the example of its neighbor. These early common schools were devoted to elementary education (not high school) with emphasis on the three Rs. The movement was spearheaded by Horace Mann and rooted in the ideas of American progressive thought, particularly that of Rush, Jefferson, and Webster. It was a movement that expanded state by state—not a national or federal concept.

As a member of the Massachusetts legislature and later as the first Massachusetts Commissioner of Education (1837), Horace Mann skillfully rallied public support for the common school by appealing to various segments of the population. To enlist the

1. R. Freeman Butts and Lawrence A. Cremin, *A History of Education in American Culture* (New York: Holt, Rinehart, 1953).

2. Merle Curti et al., *A History of American Civilization* (New York: Harper & Bros., 1953), p. 235.

3. Fredrick M. Binder, *The Age of the Common School* (New York: Wiley, 1974).

4. Clarence Thomas, "Never Give In," *Imprimis* (November 2000), pp. 1–2, 5.

5. Diane Ravitch, *The Schools We Deserve* (New York: Basic Books, 1985), p. 186.

business community, Mann sought to demonstrate that "education has a market value" with a yield similar to "common bullion." The "aim of industry [and] wealth of the country" would be augmented "in proportion of the diffusion of knowledge."[1] Workers would be more diligent and more productive. Mann also established a *stewardship theory,* aimed at the upper class, that the public good would be enhanced by public education. Schools for all children would create a stable society in which people would obey the laws and add to the nation's political and economic well-being. To the workers and farmers, Mann asserted that the common school would be a *great equalizer,* a means of social mobility for their children. To the Protestant community, he argued that the common school would assimilate ethnic and religious groups, promote a common culture, and help immigrant children learn English and the customs and laws of the land.[2] Mann was convinced that the common school was crucial for the American system of equality and opportunity, for a sense of community to be shared by all Americans, and for the promotion of a national identity.

Slowly, Horace Mann won. In 1852, Massachusetts adopted a law requiring every child to attend school for a certain period of years. Some critics argued that this compulsory attendance was an encroachment on family life, but Mann's view prevailed: If the American republic was to survive, it was essential that public education be taken seriously and be supported by public taxes. The biggest opposition came from parents of children attending private and religious schools, who felt they would be double taxed. In the end, Americans opted for compromise and choice—not a state or federal school ideology that discourages private schooling and not a church-dominated school system (which prevailed in Massachusettes until the 1820s). Other states took notice of Mann's success, and soon had their own Horace Manns and statewide system of education (which tended to center on the elementary schools).

Although Mann accepted the traditional curriculum, his ideas about pedagogy were different from the dominant philosophy that was rooted in classical learning and strict obedience to the teacher. Mann fused together the ideas of Rousseau's *Emile* and Pestalozzi's *How Gertrude Teaches Her Children,* emphasizing the naturalistic interests and needs of the child, and providing an education suitable to the child's age consisting of interactive and natural activities (later developed by Kilpatrick and Rugg and called the "activities movement") and social participation (which Dewey later called "group participation" and "socialization").

Mann also sought to reconcile academic instruction with social values and moral instruction, and to that extent he was also influenced by Rousseau's social contract (an educated populace) and ultimately by Plato's *Republic* (liberal arts and moral education). The need for some balance still plagues the American populace, and, given our heterogeneous population, there is no firm agreement on what values or morals and whose values or morals to teach. Mann believed that children could be shaped and assimilated into the American social system (the larger society) and that character (or morals) could be modified to build a "good" and "just" society. It was (and still is) a

1. V. T. Thayer and Martin Levit, *The Role of the Schools in American Society,* 2nd ed. (New York: Dodd, Mead, 1966), p. 6.
2. Johnathan Messerlie, *Horace Mann: A Biography* (New York: Knopf, 1972).

practical necessity if diverse members of a community and nation were going to get along and preserve their freedom. He was also influenced by his whig ideology—that government should promote public works (e.g., railroads, canals, and bridges), and schools should be organized to promote national and industrial productivity.

Like Dewey, later, Mann felt that children needed to be taught self-discipline and freedom of choice, but also the responsibility of choice, in order to prepare for future democratic citizenship and "voluntary compliance with the laws of reason and duty" and the laws of this land.[1] Without moral fiber, the only glue that keeps the political and social cement in place is an ideology or an "ism," which can become excessive and dangerous. Certainly, the lessons of the twentieth century call for Dewey's system of *Democracy and Education,* which is also rooted in the works of Mann, Jefferson, and Rousseau. See Teaching Tips 5.1.

Although the pattern for establishing common schools varied among the states, and the quality of education varied as well, the foundation of the American public school was being forged through this system. The schools were common in the sense that they housed youngsters of all socioeconomic and religious backgrounds, from ages 6 to 14 or 15, and were jointly owned, cared for, and used by the local community. Because a variety of subjects were taught to children of all ages, teachers had to plan as many as 10 to 20 different lessons a day.[2] Teachers also had to try to keep their schoolrooms warm in the winter—a responsibility shared by the older boys who cut and fetched wood—and cool in the summer. Schoolhouses were often in need of considerable repair, and teachers were paid miserably low salaries. By then, most elementary school teachers were women, and they were hired in part because they would work for less money than men, because there were few jobs open to educated women. Thus emerged the image of the "school marm," dedicated, gentle, unmarried, and underpaid. It was an image that was to prevail until the 1960s, when teachers became militant in an attempt to improve salaries and working conditions, and the media focused on picketing and striking teachers. And why not? Teachers are entitled to eat steak, if they wish, and they are entitled to the same comfort and respect given to their European and Asian counterparts. Should married teachers have to work one or two part-time jobs to supplement their income and make ends meet.

## Faith in the Frontier and Common Man

In New England, the state legislatures encouraged the establishment of school districts, elected school boards, and enacted state laws to govern the schools. But it was on the frontier where the common school flourished, where there was faith in the common person and a common destiny. The one-room schoolhouse "eventually led to one of America's most lasting, sentimentalized pictures—the 'Little Red Schoolhouse' . . . in almost every community." It had problems and critics, but it symbol-

---

1. Cremin, *The Transformation of the School,* p. 12.
2. Andrew Guilford, *America's Country Schools* (Washington, DC: National Trust for Historic Preservation, 1985).

# Teaching Tips 5.1

## The Need for Historical Perspective

All professional educators need a historical perspective to integrate the past with the present. Not only does an understanding of history help us not repeat the mistakes of the past, but it also better prepares us for the present, both in terms of the abstract and real world. There are many other reasons to have an understanding of history (and the history of education), such as:

1. The development of ideas in education is part of our intellectual and cultural heritage.
2. Our notion of an educated person is too narrow and technical; we need to expand the idea that an educated person is one who is steeped in an understanding of the humanities and social sciences, which stems from history.
3. A discussion of various theories and practices in education requires an understanding of historical (as well as philosophical, psychological, and social) foundations.

4. An understanding of history helps us appreciate and understand national and international events.
5. History can be studied for the purpose of understanding current pedagogical practices.
6. In developing a common or core curriculum, a historical perspective is essential.
7. With a historical perspective, teachers and curriculum specialists can better understand the relationship between content and process in subject areas.
8. Through the use of history, we have more opportunity to include a moral dimension to our teaching and learning.
9. The history of education permits practitioners to understand relationships between what students have learned (past) and what they are learning (present) and what they need to learn (future).
10. The study of education history is important for its own theoretical and research purposes.

ized the pioneers' spirit and desire to provide free education for their children. "It was a manifestation of the belief held by most of the frontier leaders that a school was necessary to raise the level of American civilization."[1]

This small school, meager in outlook and thwarted by inadequate funding and insufficient teachers, nevertheless fit with the conditions of the American frontier—of expansion and equality. Abraham Lincoln, the son of an illiterate, dirt-farmer and a mother who died when he was 9 years old, epitomized the best qualities of the frontier person—hard-working, honest, moral, and a believer in the common man. However, he had only one year of formal schooling (he was self-taught), and the vast majority of the patrician class in the big cities of the North and South considered him a backwards "bumpkin." But Lincoln's rise to the presidency is the essence that distinguishes America from its European cousins: the Horatio Alger heroes of our nation versus the sorting-out process of the "old" order based on hereditary privilege

---

1. Hughes, *Education in America,* p. 233.

and social hierarchy—and the subsequent waste of human talent and stagnation of that society.

According to Lincoln's most famous biographer, Lincoln attended a "blab school," the kind of school in which the common person's children—even those born in log cabins—could begin their "readin," "writin," and "cipherin,"[1] and could advance to limitless achievements. It was a school local citizens could use as a polling place, a center for Grange activities, a site for dances, and a location for community activities; it was a school controlled and supported by the local community. The traditions built around the common school—the idea of neighborhood schools, local control of schools, and government support of schools—took a firm hold on the hearts and minds of Americans. America's confidence in the common school helped fashion the public schools later in the nineteenth century; it also influenced our present system of universal education.

After the purchase of the Louisiana territory from France in 1803, the West opened for expansion and development as Congress encouraged settlement by offering free or cheap land for settlers. It was a difficult journey, usually by covered wagon, full of hardships and risks—and only those who wanted to start a new life were willing to head to the western frontier. Displaced factory workers, unskilled laborers, and farmers immigrating from Germany, Norway, and Sweden comprised the bulk of the new settlers. Observed by two educators, the West became "the country of the common man," the purest place for freedom and democracy.[2] Put in different terms, Horace Greeley advised, "Go West young man" and find your fortune.

Blacks also gained by moving west. Former slaves had the chance to break from their "Maafa Remembrance"—that is, the horrors of the trans-Atlantic slave trade, and to build a new life for their families (keenly depicted in *Gabriel's Story,* a recent novel of a black teenager coming of age on the American frontier).[3] The shared hardships of the landscape and the constant presence of Native Indians underscored the surprising commonality of blacks and whites trying to survive and build a future. However, compared to other immigrants who could change their names and wash away their old customs and attire to blend in and become "new Americans," blacks never had the luxury to forget their race. Nonetheless, the early West created a certain amount of equalness among its inhabitants in their daily lives and challenges by the fact they were cut off from the rest of civilization.

1. Carl Sandburg, *Abraham Lincoln: The Prairie Years* (New York: Harcourt, Brace, 1926), p. 19.

2. Button and Provenzo, *History and Culture*, p. 51.

3. David A. Durham, *Gabriel's Story* (New York: Doubleday, 2001). *Gabriel's Story* was Durham's first novel. In his second novel, *Walk through Darkness* (New York: Doubleday, 2002), the young black author writes about slave identity, slave uprisings, slave violence, and hatred toward white America. The author is a skillful, powerful writer whose characters extend beyond simple black and white roles. Reflect on the way he describes William, an escaped slave: "Even if he were granted all the freedoms of the nation he wouldn't fully understand how to use them. Though he would be allowed to speak he would have no voice. He would never be able to debate the finer points of a French garden . . . or be so confident as to imagine an entire lifetime shaped by his own inclinations." Durham is worth reading.

The American Civilization Grows    The rich were not motivated to go west; they were comfortable in their eastern surroundings and did not want to face the rugged terrain and the hardship of travel. Starting over was for the sod-buster farmer, rugged miner, adventurer, trapper, hunter, and cowboy—the person willing to roll up his or her sleeves and go to work. The western movement can be viewed as the edge of the western world, the place where the shambles of European liberalism might have one last chance to succeed. It was a kind of class war, where the peasant and "bourgeoisie" class of the old order could live without the stratification and privileges associated with the monarchy and nobility of the ruling class. In stratified societies of Europe, in the classrooms of Eton and Exeter, the amount of education received by a child largely depended on his or her class. In the run-down parts of society and among the masses, talent, merit, and hard work rarely made a difference. The individual was kept down by his or her class, and society paid dearly for instilling the doctrine of heredity and privilege.

The history of education in the United States, and especially in the West, was a long and hard campaign to break from the European system of education, and to reward merit, talent, and effort. One hundred years later, this great fight to democraticize American education was to be called *equal educational opportunity*. Jefferson understood that the full development of talent among all classes could be developed in the New World, and especially among the common class. "Geniuses will be raked from the rubbish," he wrote.[1] He added that the common people of America had the opportunity for thinking and discussing social and political problems closed to them in the Old World. Mann understood it, too, and argued that education was the chief avenue where "humble and ambitious youth" could expect to rise.[2] This is a major reason why immigrants all over the world dream about coming to America—for their children's future.

But the notion that differences in class were due to differences in hereditary remained in the background. In the 1880s, Herbert Spencer, an English philosopher, maintained that the poor were "unfit" and should be eliminated through competition and the survival of the fittest. At the turn of the century, English author H. G. Wells linked peasant immigration to the country as the downfall to America. "I believe that if things go on as they are going, the great mass of them will remain a very low lower class," and the U.S. population "will remain largely illiterate industrial peasants."[3] From the 1950s through the 1990s, psychologists such as Shockley, Jensen, and Herrnstein, placed heavy emphasis on heredity as the main factor for intelligence—and the reason why the poor remained poor from one generation to the next. Although the arguments were written in education terms, the implications were political and implied class warfare, and, most disturbing, it resulted in a stereotype of black mental inferiority, thereby putting blacks on the defensive.

1. Thomas Jefferson, *Notes on the State of Virginia, 1782* (Chapel Hill: University of North Carolina, 1955), p. 14.
2. Maris Vinovskis, "Horace Mann on the Economic Productivity of Education," *New England Quarterly* (April 1970), pp. 550–571.
3. H. G. Wells, *The Future of America* (New York: Harper & Bros., 1906), pp. 142–143.

The western movement can also be viewed as one of numerous migrations of Europeans to many sparsely, somewhat uncivilized lands. Behind this "European invasion" is the assumption that the land was free for military veterans, and to be sold cheap to farmers and speculators who would develop it. There was no need to buy the land from the American Indians; it was purchased from the French and belonged to the U.S. government, so the theory went. The idea was to claim the land and occupy it. One historian, Walter Webb, put it this way: "The frontier movement [was] the invasion of land assumed to be vacant as distinguished from an invasion of an occupied or civilized country, and advance against nature rather against men."[1]

The West was a huge parcel of land, more than one million square miles (stretching from the gulf of Mexico to Canada from Appalachia to the northwest Pacific coast), more than six times the size of the original 13 colonies. "Inherent in the American concept of [the] frontier [was] the idea of body of free land which [could] be had for the taking."[2] The movement was so rapid and extensive that Merle Curti maintained that it actually "drained the population from [Eastern] seaboard regions."[3]

**The Winning of the West**    Both Jefferson and Jackson had immense faith in the common man, and it was Jeffersonian democracy followed by Jacksonian democracy that flourished in the West. When Jefferson spoke of the American people, he meant the American farmer, who was to be the backbone of American democracy. Jackson meant the frontier people, including farmers, plain people, and those with "vulgar whims" of the lower class.[4] He rejected the status of class and the view of a democracy led by gentlemen and landed gentry, which Alexander Hamilton, Aaron Burr, James Monroe, and John Quincy Adams all favored. Based on hindsight, Jefferson and Jackson took the most favorable position—recognizing all classes and hoping plain people and lower-class people would become educated through the schools and gain proper faith, morality, and knowledge to self-govern—as the nation broke from its European traditions and forged westward in the territory he had purchased from the French.

American historians would even argue that if the English colonists had been limited or hemmed in along the coast, American social and political development would have followed the class consciousness and lack of social/economic mobility followed by European countries.[5] It was lawyers who made the laws, who, by background and education, were conservative, patrician, and generally accepted traditional European laws of nature (latter to be called *Darwinism*) and property rights. But these lawyers were forced to translate many of their patrician ideas into the reality of the New

1. Walter P. Webb, *The Great Frontier* (Boston: Houghton Mifflin, 1952), p. 2.
2. Ibid., p. 3.
3. Curti, *History of American Civilization*, p. 148.
4. Curti, *The Growth of American Thought*; Vernon Parrington, *The Colonial Mind: 1620–1800* (New York: Harcourt, Brace, 1927).
5. Charles A. Beard and Mary R. Beard, *The American Spirit* (New York, Macmillan, 1942); Fredrick Jackson Turner, *The Frontier in American History,* rev. ed. (New York: Henry Holt, 1950). Originally published in 1893.

World—an American West that had an abundance of land to settle, a mysterious wilderness, vast natural resources, and primitive conditions being populated not by the wealthy but the frontier people and agrarian people who believed in equality and rejected the aristocracy. It was here, in the new world, where the principles of the French Revolution and European liberalism could flourish.

It was the fluidity of life, the hard work, the independence, the new opportunities, the forces of nature, the steady growth of prosperity, and the belief in the rights of individual that led to an egalitarianism. This sense of equality could never be achieved in the eastern cities, much less in Europe, where class prejudice, elitism, and etiquette of the more cultured and upper class ruled. In the slums of U.S. cities, it was not unusual for entire immigrant and lower-class families to live in one small room (10 × 10 feet), in buildings without water or heat, with minimal light and ventilation. Disease, alcohol, and crime characterized the city slums—far different from the open landscapes, fresh air, and log cabin homes (averaging 1,200 to 1,500 square feet) on the frontier. While the west was romanticized for its rich resources and vast land, popularized by folklore, ballads of the west, and stories of Buffalo Bill and Wild Bill Hitchcock, the East was seen as controlled by greedy industrialists and bankers, where products were produced at the expense of labor—producing a new class of "have nots" called factory workers and later union workers.

Hypothesizing about the Past     Rousseau would have been at home on the frontier. The soil, the forests, the rivers and mountains, and the wilderness were his kind of landscape, his natural environment where the individual could develop and flourish. The frontier was the antithesis of urban life that Rousseau disparaged and felt would eventually corrupt man and limit the child's natural growth. Jefferson also had great faith in agrarian democracy and believed cities were overcrowded, filthy, and corrupted by the search for profits among merchants and patricians. As a southerner, where land was plentiful, he felt that in the free air of the country, small farmers could flourish and work with country gentlemen to create a stable society. Plato, however, believed that equality would promote despotism of the masses. He felt that common people needed to be restrained and be guided by philosopher-kings with the help of intellectuals, but that the state was to exist to serve man—a marked departure for that period in which man existed to serve the state. Like Jefferson, Plato believed that through education, citizens would gain appropriate knowledge and morality to function in Athenian democracy. The difference is, Jefferson had more faith in the common man, whereas Plato put more faith in an oligarchy and academic elite.

How would these three giant philosophers react to the passing of the frontier, and transitional generations benefiting from education? There was a major difference between Plato's republicanism, Rousseau's romanticism, and Jefferson's enlightenment. Plato was at home in the big city-state of Athens, with its inventory of manuscripts and artistic objects, and the buzz of people in the marketplaces. He would have flourished in the big cities of Boston, Philadelphia, and New York. Rousseau would have preferred the Old West, seeing it as a "beautiful prison," cut off from the rest of the world, and he certainly would have appreciated Thoreau's *Walden,* Ernest Thompson's *On Golden Pond,* and Thomas Benton's water-colored landscapes. Jefferson was comfortable in the big cities of America and Europe (in fact, he lived parts of his life in Paris and enjoyed its "gentler" social life); he was also at home in small, rural communities, the hard path: where people quarried the earth, cleared trees, built their own homes, plowed and grazed the soil, and hunted elk and moose.

Rousseau would have appreciated Thoreau's words: "I went to live deliberately, to front only the essential facts of life, and to see if I could not learn what it had to teach, and not, when I came to die, discover that I had not lived." He would have cheered the rustic, outdoor, communal life of the American Indians and Eskimos who hunted and lived off the land and water. He would have accepted and lived the life of a Quaker, Friend, or Mennonite, farming the land, cutting trees, framing and erecting their own cabins—and forsaking the evil ways of city life. Rousseau, today, would be at home in Woodstock, New York, as well as Woodstock, Illinois—seeing and enjoying nature, whereby, as Thoreau put it, you could "in a summer day [sit] in the sunny doorway from sunrise to noon, rapt in revery."

Thoreau, like Rousseau, had a way with words. But if we consider that most Americans no longer have time to pick blackberries or mushrooms, much of what both nature lovers have to say is, at best, cute, a little idealistic, and perhaps has an edge in the way they describe how others live, particularly urban dwellers. Then, I think of my ride on the Long Island Expressway, heading west, into Manhattan, and what I call "the road to hell."[1] Maybe the log cabin doesn't look so off-kilter, and the hunters, fishermen, and farmers may know something about life that I haven't learned to appreciate.

Jefferson, much more than Rousseau and Plato, would have accepted the passing of the frontier, where the sons and daughter first went to common schools and then to colleges and universities to become doctors, lawyers, and accountants. Life was not easy on the frontier; there was exposure to ungrateful and cruel winters, possible hunger, sickness, and death. Thus, Jefferson would have cheered the rise of today's new generation, performing medical miracles, fighting over words and phrases and representing clients, sitting behind desks and clicking computers and shuffling papers, and becoming somewhat "flabby" and affluent by age 30.

Jefferson would have seen all this as progress, although he would have understood what had been lost; he was too educated and too cosmopolitan not to understand the authenticity of the hard life—on the plains, by the rivers, in the wilderness, on the hills and mountains. Rousseau would have despaired, seeing men and women removed from nature and the physical life; he would have flatly rejected the notion of golf and tennis—games for a "soft" generation of people. Rousseau would have died of a broken heart had he lived long enough to endure American progress and American culture by the mid-twentieth century. However, he would have saluted the writings of Theodore Dreiser (*An American Tragedy*), F. Scott Fitzgerald (*Peace of*

---

1. The perfect question is: Why travel to hell? I guess it has something to do with my soul mate. Actually, my preference is to pedal down some obscure highway where I can hear frogs and crickets—and give my readers a dutiful description of weather changes, landscape, traffic conditions, and the people I meet along the way. Indeed, I cannot think of America as a single place—so much is so different and contradictory—and there is so much to see.

*Soul, This Side of Paradise, The Great Gatsby*), Sinclair Lewis (*Babbitt, Elmer Gantry, It Can't Happen Here, Main Street),* and John Dos Passos (*U.S.A., Manhattan Transfer, Three Soldiers*), who denounced America's commercialism and conformity, its materialism and "meritocracy," its urban blight and degenerate lifestyle. Rousseau would have rejected the new American, somewhat comfortable and distant from the land, speaking idle chit-chat, drinking "designer" coffee, and measuring their lives and status by the number of toilets in their houses. He would have chastised all the people who now had "gentler" lives and deaths than their ancestors, and who had grown soft, corrupt, and vulgar. Rousseau would have called for SWAT teams to swoop down on all the robber barons, CEOs, and dot-com wizards who move around money and produce nothing and make nothing—the "few who wind up with the savings of many," to repeat one of Eugene Debs's better ditties.

Since Plato was an advocate of a strong nation-state, his greatest concern today would be media images, mass propaganda, and American politics—or how the press treats liberal and conservative government officials. Because Plato was cultivated and lived in the city, I suspect that so long as his philosopher-kings (today's statesmen and leaders) had the opportunity to craft policy, he would accept the mobility of the offspring of the common folk (his working class) and feel at home with yuppies and guppies (graying yuppies) now driving around in BMWs, talking about the differences between Merlot and Cabernet, while nibbling on their chocolate-covered strawberries and chatting about the latest exhibit at Soho or the meaning of life at some cocktail party. Plato, I believe, would have toasted the "riches" of the upper class, and viewed their status as, in J. P. Morgan's words, "the reward of toil and virtue."

## Blunt Talk about Gender Equality

It was in the West, on the frontier, where the surplus of men enhanced the status of women, and where the latter performed essential work in the home, school, and community who built the nation.[1] The customs of the "old order" faded in the West. It was the hard work of farm families and frontier people, coupled with a sense of independence and freedom, where the concept of equality of sexes was realized; in the East, the ideal women did not work. The analogy has some similarities to feminism today: The idea of a *working woman* who "gives" and participates as an equal at home, as opposed to a *lady* who "takes," does not work, and is less independent. (The difference is subtle, but most feminists can appreciate it.) Still, very few women were considered as "somebodies," and a great many talented and smart women had to find fulfillment through their husbands' careers. The vicissitudes of being ignored and understanding one's place in the social order, combined with domestic violence, homophobia, and the iron grip of tradition and religion dominated women's lives—both on the frontier and in eastern cities.

For every Molly Brown or Susan B. Anthony who chose to break ranks from the male world and chose to remain single, for every Eleanor Roosevelt and Germaine Greer who emerged from the shadows of their husbands and forged their own

1. Curti, *The Growth of American Thought.*

identities, there are millions of American females, probably billions all over the world, who spent their whole adult lives being a woman in the home, in search of a man to love and be loved by, to have babies with, to live "happily ever after" by fetching, cooking, and cleaning, without wanting to be a woman at home. What an upsetting idea for many men to think about—women wanting their own identities, wanting to create their own professional lives, seeking achievement with or without a man—simply wanting choices in life, love, and work that men have always taken for granted.

The West may have provided a few more options for women, based on the spirit of equality and independence, but few had the opportunity to emerge as Athena, on the top the Acropolis, or as Henrik Ibsen's *viking woman,* or in modern times as Ruth Bader Ginsburg, Madame Aldrich, or Susan Walters. Not until the 1990s could women "go into the phone booth" (to steal a line from Nuala O'Faolain, the Irish novelist and feminist) and "come out as Lois Lane," fully transformed. As metaphors go, not until the 1990s could women graduate from college (the new phone booth for women) and expect to compete in the male world of business, industry, law, and medicine. Although there is still a glass ceiling in many sectors of the economy, the *expectation* of an educated woman becoming a teacher has been shattered in the last 10 years or so.

The evolution of the new female role on television serves as an example. Gone is the daffy *I Love Lucy,* the sexually suppressed and neurotic *Our Miss Brooks,* the cute blonde in *I Dream of Jeannie* and the bubbly, zany *Mary Tyler Moore Show.* In their place are smart, super-athletic, and fully empowered heroines (and none of them is a teacher!). Sydney Bristow, in *Alias,* has one life as a graduate student with a boyfriend and a strained relationship with her father—a pretty normal life. She also lives another life as a super-charged spy who jets off all over the world—running, fighting, and overpowering the bad guys. Bristow has the courage, confidence, and ability to emerge on top in a world of espionage and double agents, and she does so without the help of a fairy godmother, prince, or husband.

There is also *Buffy the Vampire Slayer* and her brainy friend Willow whose supernatural gift is likened to her lesbian awakening. The new sisterhood also includes the female warrior *Witchblade,* who successfully battles with medieval wizards and warriors and modern-day crooked male cops and detectives. She sometimes solves crimes and manages to have a romantic relationship with ancient or mystic lovers and a modern-day FBI agent. Then there is *The Practice.* Lara Flynn Boyle plays Helen Gamble, the hard-driving, tough, sophisticated district attorney, and Kelli Williams plays Lindsay Dole, the rational, brainy senior partner of the law practice. Both women are in full control of their personal lives and careers; moreover, Lindsay is able to mix her career with marriage and motherhood. Although, statistically, she is representative of a minority of women today, she oozes the American dream among most college-educated women who aspire to have a "normal" marriage, nuclear family, and professional career.

All of these women are antithetical to the teacher model; these women overpower (some with tricky martial arts skills) and outsmart their male counterparts, show emotion, have a sense of identity and independence, and exhibit a keen sense of loyalty and duty to ordinary people, and for doing the right thing. (It also suggests that fewer brainy, fully empowered women will choose teaching as a career.) Some of you might think I have made an unwarranted leap, but the generalization remains that female college graduates have many more career options than they did 20 or 25 years ago. Certainly, their social status is quite different from the traditional opinion that regarded women as intellectually inferior to men and that limited their educational opportunities and equality with males.

From the colonial period to the end of the twentieth century, outspoken feminists have taken women to task for accepting their second-class economic and social status, for resigning themselves to a "retrogressive" function within the family. Only recently have women magazines been criticized for containing little discussion of these issues, and for focusing on sex tips, cooking tips, and cosmetic and weight-reduction tips—all related to catching and pleasing a man. Their present focus continues to detrimentally influence the social and psychological identity and independence of women, and the way they relate to men.

Depending on one's opinion, only recently can American women blow away the dust of prejudice and tradition, embedded in history and custom for thousands of years, and emerge as a somebody, fully self-actualized persons. Breaking from a husband's shadow, free from "women's work" at home, is a some what brazen idea, and still shocks many men. One hundred years ago, even on the western frontier, this type of talk had no place—except buried deep in some maverick mind or blurted after many bottles of beer—only to lament for another time, another life, another dream that got lost along the way. Of course, many women in the history of this country are famous for something, but most of them have been forgotten, buried in some library stack or encyclopedia.

Mary *WHO?*   A good example of a woman buried by her male counterpart, and by the boys in the press box, was Mary Harris. A labor organizer who worked with and was overshadowed by Eugene Debs in the 1920s and 1930s, Harris was dubbed "Mother Jones" by union workers in the North and a "saint" by coal miners in the South. Harris also organized labor in Chicago and New York against the capitalist class, used vile vocabulary to describe the Fords and Rockefellers, and regularly stared down gun-toting, company-headed thugs at union rallies who were intent on disrupting her public speeches.[1] Construed as a "nut" by the "boys" who ran the country and as "notorious" by the "boys" who printed the news that was "fit to print." Harris was rarely taken seriously by polite and educated society. To be sure, the conventional views of womanhood for that era filtered through the stories of Harris—not much different from when the "boys" today describe some "troublesome" or "tough" woman. There are a host of stories similar to that of Harris and

1. Elliot J. Gorn, *Mother Jones: The Most Dangerous Woman in America* (New York: Hill and Wong, 2001).

Debs, not much different when we compare the work of Jane Addams and her settlement house in Chicago with John Dewey's lab schools.[1]

The likes of Mary Harris and Jane Addams have swelled the ranks of working women in the last two or three decades. Many are unknown—with names like Nancy, Susan, and Patricia—self-reliant, independent, living in the places as far away as Manhattan and Montana, Boston and Boise. Patricia Henley's novels are vivid descriptions of the "new" woman. She has written two award-winning books about women who live in the West and who have problems with men: Boyfriends and husbands take them for granted and cannot fulfill their emotional needs.[2] The men are rugged types who drink and hunt, and don't always come home. One of her characters, Kit, asks why she chooses a man who is handicapped. The response from her caseworker is: "They're all handicapped. This one just shows." When these women get fed up with their men, they don't go into depression. They pack up and leave; their lovers and husbands are fungible, similar to the way men have often treated women.

In Antonya Nelson's short stores of females, we find the modern women seeking the dream of fulfillment—career, husband, and children—who are usually crushed by their experiences. Their men are often superficial, some with tattoos and body odor, and others who are older and cannot always deliver. Most of her women make love with their men in a monotonous way, with stilted monologues, each having a mechanical "sense of what is to happen next."[3] Most of her women, have been "dealt a bad hand"; their choices are limited by economics, hard labor, and, if I may add, tradition and choices they make and inevitably regret. Most prefer to escape the life they were born into and wait for some "Prince Charming" who never appears or can never reach this idealized benchmark—and thus they live a life of failed dreams and losing habits.

The men they choose in the stories break their hearts and ruin their lives, and they are forced to reinvent themselves between lovers and husbands. Others are saddled down with children, exhausted, and know they will simply never have a chance to have their own life and identity. They are personally, socially, and intellectually isolated by their ambitions—and often suffer in silence. Their lives are tied to their children and husband—a bitter truth that many feminists today wrestle with in their attempt to find both love and meaningful work that so often escapes them.

1. With the exception of Catherine the Great and the queens of England and Scotland, men get most of the headlines. The state of New York, for instance, has high schools named after Eugene Debs and John Dewey, but none for Mary Harris and Jane Addams.

I have no survey data to support my beliefs, but I estimate that no more than 10 percent of American teachers under age 40 (and outside of New York) know about Eugene Debs. If more than 1 percent have heard of Mary Harris, I would be surprised. Just about every education student knows something about John Dewey, but I don't know if one out of five of the same people have heard of Jane Addams. Yet, Addams was more actively involved in the city of Chicago and through her social work had an impact on far more people than Dewey did at the lab school.

2. Patricia Henley, *Hummingbird House* (New York: MacMury, 1999); Healey, *Workshop of the Germon Heart* (New York: MacMurran, 2001).

3. Antonya Nelson, *Female Trouble: A Collection of Short Stories* (New York: Scribner, 2002).

If you're a Freudian psychologist or feminist, it is easy to put the blame on fathers. The party-line theory among *Vogue* heroines and feminists such as Germaine Greer and Camille Paglia is that whatever is wrong with women—whether they are neurotic, hysterical, masochistic, or quarrelsome—it all stems from their relationship with their fathers. Poor dad; to take a line from Paul Simon, there are "55 ways" for fathers to ruin their daughters' careers and relationships with men, and only one or two ways for them to succeed in raising daughters who can follow their own paths and have a full and happy life on their own terms. I guess that makes me a cad and a candidate for all kinds of guilt trips and psychological neurosis.

Back to the Frontier   Returning to the western landscape, social and political equality could find an outlet, compared to Europe, where Tocqueville believed there was "permanent inequality" perpetuated by arrogant people and abstract truths that were never enacted in principle or law.[1] To be sure, de Tocqueville envisioned the American west as the "crucible" of American democracy. In theory, inequality and class consciousness had no place in rural American life, where people had to wake up at 4:00 A.M. to till the soil, or where people had to fend against an Indian attack. People didn't win points on the prairie if they were cultured or could discern good wine from lousy wine, speak French, read Latin, or cite Shakespeare. Similarly, class differences had no place in a one-room schoolhouse where students might walk several miles, fetch firewood to heat the room, and where there was a no-nonsense approach to teaching and learning. Nonetheless, women were still second-class citizens, and were given the vote 50 years after the black man.

I hope all people today can understand this waste of talent. I am sure most of us are filled with memories of people who lived and died, and never fulfilled their potential for a host of reasons related to inequality or some "ism." Call it stupidity, hypocrisy, or male bias, but it was not until the early twentieth century that women were given the vote and treated equally on a political basis, and were given full citizenship. Schooling is supposed to alter social relationships, improve the minds and morality of people, and promote democracy—at least Jefferson hoped it would. And, had he fully succeeded—or had Mann, Dewey, Rugg, or Counts succeeded with their progressive ideas (somewhat "radical" for their day[2])—what a triumph of moral conscience!

And so the people of the West with their so-called unconventional and lower-class habits and behaviors welcomed the common school movement. The people simply assumed that common schools would help the children of common people achieve a stable government and were necessary for improving the level of American civilization. But if given a choice between hard work or education as a means for prosperity, most frontier people, in the 1800s would have more faith in hard work—reflecting Puritan morality. Nevertheless, the agrarian and frontier people had great faith in schooling, and it was the "little red schoolhouse"—the idea of a neighborhood

1. Alexis de Tocqueville, *Democracy in America,* rev. ed. (New York: Knopf, 1945). Originally written between 1834 and 1840.
2. Dewey, Rugg, and Counts all had FBI files, and you can make a sure bet that Senator McCarthy would have investigated them had they been alive in the 1950s.

school, the concept of local control and local support of the school—that took a firm footing on the western soil, in the hearts and minds of independent, frontier people.

## Secondary Schools

In the early nineteenth century, the academy began to replace Latin grammar schools; the latter was an elitist institution and served as a prep school for college for wealthy children and a few bright children of the poor. By the middle of the century, the academy was the dominant secondary institution. If offered a wide range of curricula, and it was designed to provide a practical program for terminal students as well as a college preparatory course of study. By 1855, more than 6,000 academies had an enrollment of 263,000 students,[1] more than two-thirds of the total secondary school enrollment of that period.

**The Academy**    Originally an invention of Benjamin Franklin, the academy was intended to offer a practical and diversified curriculum for those not going to college. To some, it was the "poor man's" opportunity for American students. "One of the main purposes" of the academy, according to Ellwood Cubberley, "was the establishment of . . . subjects having value aside from mere preparation for college, particularly subjects of modern nature, useful in preparing youth for the changed conditions of society. The study of real things rather than words about things . . . became prominent features of the new course of study."[2] In other words, the practical or functional was emphasized over the theoretical or abstract; vocational and commercial subjects were taught in lieu of college preparatory subjects. What started as a thorny, obscure idea eventually turned into a full-blown movement that challenged education elitism.

By 1837, as many as 72 different subjects were offered by the academies of the state of New York. But the academy had veered to the right and become part of the educational establishment. The different subjects were mainly tough and traditional, such as Latin, Greek, mathematics, natural science, philosophy, geography, English grammar, composition, rhetoric, and logic (among the top 15 in rank order),[3] so that the institution inadvertently served the chief function of preparing students for college. Writes Elmer Brown, "The college preparatory course was the back bone of the whole system of instruction" in the better academics. Although practical courses were offered, "it was the admission requirements of the colleges, more than anything else, that determined their standards of scholarship."[4] And, stated Paul Monroe, "the core of the academy education yet remained the old classical curriculum . . . just as the

---

1. Knight, *Education in the United States;* Theodore R. Sizer, *The Age of Academics* (New York: Teachers College Press, 1964).
2. Cubberley, *The History of Education,* p. 697.
3. Newton Edwards and Herman G. Richey, *The School in the American Social Order,* 2nd ed. (Boston: Houghton Mifflin, 1963).
4. Elmer E. Brown, *The Making of Our Middle School* (New York: Longman, 1926), p. 230.

core of the student body in the more flourishing academics remained the group preparing for college."[1]

The era of the academies extended to the 1870s, when they were replaced by public high schools. The academies, nevertheless, served as finishing schools for young girls—with courses in classical and modern language, science, art, music, and homemaking. Also, these schools offered the "normal" program for prospective common school (elementary school) teachers by combining courses in classics with principles of pedagogy. A few private military and elite academic academies still exist today.

The High School  The common school movement was originally limited to elementary schools. The first public high school was founded in 1821 in Boston, and several northern states had such high schools by 1850. But high schools did not become major institutions until after 1874, when the Michigan court ruled, in the *Kalamazoo* decision, that the people could establish and support high schools with tax funds if they consented. Moreover, it permitted all children, irrespective of race or sex, to attend these schools. This concept of equality was based on Michigan legislation, dating back to 1841, which first required public schools in every district of the state, including for "colored children."[2] There was some initial resistance—the fear that public taxes for the high schools would only benefit a small portion of the youth population—but after the court decision, the high school spread rapidly and compulsory attendance laws were established on a state-by-state basis in the late nineteenth and early twentieth centuries.

The idea of required high school attendance for all youth, based on the nation providing educational opportunity for all students, was a major educational reform. However, the idea was not easily adopted, since many critics viewed it "as an unwanted encroachment of the state on the family."[3]

The high school curriculum emphasized traditional academic courses, which was considered inappropriate for the vast majority of students who would never go on to college. "What possible reason," wrote Diane Ravitch, "would a future farmer or machinist have for learning history or science or literature? Educators believed that the failure to introduce vocational courses would cause students to drop out in droves."[4] The critics were wrong; enrollments grew from 200,000 students in 1890 to 520,000 in 1900, passing the one million mark in 1912. By 1900, the number of public high schools had soared to 6,000 while the number of academies had declined to 1200.[5] However, as late as 1900, only a small fraction of the total youth population was enrolled in public high schools. See Teaching Tips 5.2.

1. Paul Monroe, *Founding of the American Public School System* (New York: Macmillan, 1940), p. 404.
2. Thomas, "Never Give In."
3. Curti, *History of America Civilization*, p. 236.
4. Diane Ravitch, *The Schools We Deserve* (New York: Basic Books, 1985), p. 148.
5. Edward A. Krug, *The Shaping of the American High School: 1880–1920* (New York: Harper & Row, 1964); Daniel Tanner, *Secondary Education: Perspectives and Prospects* (New York: Macmillan, 1972).

# *Teaching Tips 5.2*

## Characteristics of an Ideal Curriculum

**An ideal curriculum**

1. Deals with stages of human growth and development and corresponding needs and interests of learners.
2. Consists of core knowledge and learning skills.
3. Enhances critical thinking, creativity, and independent thought.
4. Considers the intellectual, aesthetic, and moral dimensions of content.
5. Deals with the major ideas and values of American and Western society.
6. Examines historical and philosophical aspects of society and the issues of modern life.
7. Emphasizes great books and great authors from a national and internal perspectives.

8. Recognizes, accepts, and provides for individual and social/cultural differences among learners.
9. Develops and attitude of responsibility, honesty, hard work, and perseverance.
10. Appreciates humanistic, moral, and spiritual themes and constructive thoughts, attitudes, and behaviors.
11. Considers the problems and issues of the local, national, and international community.
12. Encourages students to take an active role in community and civic affairs, with emphasis on helping the elderly, pre-K, poor, and special-needs populations.

By 1900, the majority of children aged 6 to 13 were enrolled in public elementary school, but only 11.5 percent of those aged 14 to 17 were enrolled in public secondary schools, and only 6.5 percent of the 17-year-olds graduated. As previously shown in Table 5.1, not until 1930 did the public secondary school enrollment figure exceed 50 percent. By 1970, the percentage of elementary-aged children attending school was 98 percent, and the percentage of secondary-aged children was 93 percent (and 76 percent were graduating). The great enrollment revolution, or the concept of universal education for American elementary students, took place between 1850 and 1900; for high school students, it took place between 1920 and 1970.

It was not until 1954 that school desegregation was eliminated by the courts, a fight spearheaded by the NAACP and the legal work of Philip Kurland and Thurgood Marshall. And, as illustrated in Table 5.1, it was not until 1970, when three-fourths of 17-year-olds graduated from high school, might we conclude that equal education opportunity was available for the children of the common man. It was a revolutionary idea, but an evolutionary trend, as it took over two centuries before schools were open to all persons irrespective of national origin, color, or sex before the majority of common-folk children enrolled and graduated from high school. It was the principle of *universal education,* first echoed by Jefferson who believed that "freedom could rest secure on"; urged by Webster as a vehicle for uniting Americans into a common culture, free from the influence of Europe; what Mann's faith represented and believed would become the "balance wheel of social machinery" essential for "democracy and socialization" of American children, and for "assimilating children into American society"; and what Cremin (influenced by Mann) viewed as the "great equalizer of human conditions."

## EPISODE 13

## History 101: Topics Rarely, If Ever, Discussed

This chapter has discussed some people who history holds dear but who can be criticized in light of revisionary history. It is unfair to pick on Franklin's ideas about population growth, Jefferson's alleged affair with one or more black slaves, and Webster's harsh views of English and European life. They were ahead of their times—men who brought the ideas of the Age of Enlightenment to the colonies and post-Revolution period, and who helped build an American education system that provided free schooling for the nation's children.

Most important, they were instrumental in promoting the ideas of freedom and democracy, rooted in Anglo law. The notion of Anglo law is crucial because it provides a host of civil rights for the common people, checks and balances against ignorant or corrupt politicians, a legislative system for electing political leaders and providing peaceful change within the government, and a judicial system to indict and prosecute those who become tainted by political power and economic greed. One must understand that American colonists had a strong affinity to Europe, especially England. Isolated from each other, the colonies at first felt little common purpose or affinity. A citizen was loyal to his own colony and to the motherland. "He was a Virginian [or New Yorker] and English man; hardly an American."[1]

### Anglo-American Ties

The history of England is based on colonizing whole countries, entire populations, especially colored populations in Africa, Asia, the Middle East, Australia, and North America. The English colonial appetite is fueled by tales of cultural and racial superiority, highlighted by a host of kings and queens, lords and dukes, explained and rationalized by Darwin's and Spencer's ideas of biological evolution and survival of the fittest. These ideas were also fictionized and fantasized by Kipling's story of *Gunga Din* and his views of those strange people from India and Burma, as well as the "white man's burden"; Burrough's story of *Tarzan and the Apes,* and the ignorant and subservient black native African population; Sir Lawrence of Arabia's portrait of Arab folly and amusement of Arabic nationalism; right down to present times in the way the English treat the Irish, which is portrayed in the theme of civilizing the Irish and

1. Curti, *History of American Civilization*, p. 61.

considering them, since the 1600s, as "savages" along with the Indians of colonial America.

The English never required Jews to wear a yellow patch on their clothing, as did the Lateran Council of 1215 so "they would no longer be mistaken for first-class citizens of the medieval polity,"[1] or as the Germans required in order to make it easier for them to strip away first Jewish property, then their dignity, and then their lives. However, the English have been blood cousins of the Germans since the reign of William and Mary of Orange and the birth of Queen Ann and her marriage into the House of Hanover in the 1700s. To be blunt, the English have enslaved more people than their Teutonic cousins as they criss-crossed the world for the last 400 years. The English never built death camps or extermination camps, but they went out to "civilize" the "wild" Indians of North America, the "savages" of Africa, the "aborigines" of Australia, and the "yellow barbarians" of Asia. The British empire eventually declined as a result of two wars with Germany and was eventually ruined as a world power by the heavy costs of the wars. Perhaps England could have mobilized more effectively against Germany before it smashed its blows throughout eastern and western Europe. But then England would have lost time and resources in its own imperial pursuits—to colonize and impose its own brand of economics and politics on the Middle East, India (and what is now Pakistan), Burma, and parts of Africa and Asia (including Hong Kong, Singapore, and Australia). England concentrated its efforts on the navy in order to expand its geopolitics on the world at the expense of the army and air force.[2]

British armies and navies went around the world to build the glories of an empire and to civilize the "colored" people of the world in which Kipling considered the latter to be "wild . . . sullen . . . [and] half devil." Formulating the idea of *The White Man's Burden* in 1899, Kipling argued that it was the duty of superior countries "to civilize the inferior races."[3] This concept fed Queen Victoria's appetite for expansion, in which she reigned for more than 50 years, promulgating the so-called natural laws of imperialism, colonialism, and capitalism. Queen Victoria died in 1901 and never saw all the problems of the world left behind by this type of "altruistic" thinking. Kipling died in 1936 and had a sense of the decolonizing years and mess that were to follow after World War II.

But the empire expired and the Union Jack was hauled down again and again, across oceans and continents. Consider the partitioning of India and Pakistan. It was the fastest, most chaotic divorce in history between nations and religions. Sir Cyril Radcliff, an English lawyer, had 36 days to come up with a plan and to divide India and Pakistan, merely a political decision[4] and reference point to the ordinary Englishmen

---

1. Stephan O'Shea, *The Perfect Heresy* (New York: Walker & Company, 2001).
2. David P. Callco, "Exchange Rates," *New York Times Book Review* (March 25, 2001), p. 9. The fact that the English possessed a second-rate air force permitted the Germans to continuously bomb London and almost bring down the Union Jack during the early years of World War II.
3. See L. Perla, *What Is National Honor?* (New York: Macmillan, 1918); David Gilmour, *The Long Recessional: The Imperial Life of Rudyard Kipling* (New York: Farrar, Straus, and Giroux, 2002).
4. Urvashi Butalia, *The Other Side of Silence* (Durham, NC: Duke University Press, 2001).

and women to discuss in local pubs. But to the people of the subcontinent, it led to a bloody civil war, the death of more than one million people, and the largest uprooting of people (20 million) in history. Indeed, the forces of two cultures and religions collided, leading to an unending conflict where there is now the threat of nuclear war and where the U.S. Defense Department estimates there could be 15 to 25 million casualties, if such a war came to pass.[1]

Now, British historian David Cannadine, born 15 years after Kipling's death, has his own interpretation of the *Empire*. For him, it had nothing to do with racism or cultural arrogance, but more about class, status, and tradition. It was about honor, order, chivalry, knights and dukes, about horses and elephants, chiefs, sultans, and viceroys. It was an extension of antiquity, hierarchy, and the crown. Indeed, the Brahmin class structure and Indian hierarchy fit into British customs of class and hierarchy, along with the concept of ornamentalism, aristocracy, and British titles. Hence, Queen Victoria was dubbed Empress of India.[2] In the vast stretches of the old empire, in the postcolonialism of the twenty-first century, the ground now burns with nationalistic and religious fervor, in the Kashmir between India and Pakistan, in the Persian Gulf by Iran and Iraq, in Arabian deserts between Palestine and Israel, and in the jungles and mountains of Burma, Kenya, and South Africa—all once part of this empire.

The memory and effects of England's imperialism is ever present today. Certainly the Scots and Irish can detail hundreds of years of sadness and tears, but Americans gloss over it in classrooms and schools and view Britain as a unified and democratic country. I am sure that if their memories were not forgotten, William Wallace, an indigent Scottish knight of the fourteenth century, and Brian Boru, an Irish activist and rebel of the eleventh century, could tell us a thing or two about ordinary people who are passionate about freedom. The past is not always accurate, and memories are sometimes blurred, but the English are not the *sine qua non* of political freedom and social justice.

Perhaps we should not be so surprised at how Americans have treated blacks and Indians, given our political, historical, and cultural ties to England. Not withstanding race prejudice that exists around the world, how does one describe the roots of the injustices of slavery and the annihilation of the Native American civilization? If only the ghosts of Sojourner Truth and Fredrick Douglass or Geronimo and Crazy Horse could visit our classrooms. They no longer exist, but their memories should not be forgotten; however, most American students have little knowledge of them, and absolutely no idea of people like Wallace and Boru who lived and died for freedom. We need to understand our own history as part of the cultural and racial baggage Americans brought from Europe, especially from England, for it was belief in our cultural and racial superiority that was used to justify the bondage of blacks and the massacre of a proud Indian race that did not want to surrender their forests and rivers and mountains to the whites.

1. Nicholas D. Kristof, "August 1914 in Pakistan," *New York Times* (June 14, 2002), p. A37.

2. David Cannadine, *Ornamentalism: How the British Saw Their Empire* (New York: Oxford University Press, 2001).

Try to picture 16 hours of work, seven days a week, under the tutelage of the whip, because you are black. Try to think what it is like for you and your family to be tossed out of your home at gun point, and herded 1,000 miles away, placed on some barren wasteland too hot or too cold for the human condition, designed to make you economically and psychologically dependent until you become a nameless and nonfunctioning persona, because your face is red. How do we teach these episodes of American history to our children and youth? How many textbook pages are set aside—one paragraph, one page, one chapter—in describing this subjection of non-white and nonwestern cultures?

Always looking for better ways of educating our students, in recent times we have invented ethnic and plural studies, multiculturalism, and postcolonial studies to help describe our domination of other cultures. And sometimes we have provided ratio-nales ranging from "survival of the fittest," "manifest destiny," and "winning the West." Sometimes we hear the voices of subordinate groups: "racial quotas," "repa-rations," and "resistant theories." As part of postmodern and revisionary thinking, we hear the view that *expansion* always results in the mistreatment of "subject peo-ples," strikes at the principles of racial and ethnic tolerance, and is driven by greed. This is the problem with manifest destiny in the United States and the colonial ex-pansion of England. Thus, American and English history is seen as the history of im-perialism, racism, and aristocracy (in the colonial period, only white property owners could vote) by a variety of colored people around the world.[1]

Even our most popular heroes are seen in different light by revisionary critics. George Washington is considered a land grabber who managed to illegally accumu-late 20,000 acres of land originally earmarked for his enlisted men in adjacent areas that did not belong to Virginia. In *The Patriot*, Mel Gibson is the hero of the South Carolina fighting militia. In the real world, the rebels of South Carolina in 1775 killed unarmed, escaped slaves as their first encounter with the "enemy."[2] Similarly, Abra-ham Lincoln is the "devil" in disguise who initially believed that slavery was right and could be extended in the South, and his Emancipation Proclamation was merely an afterthought to encourage escaping slaves to enlist in the northern armies.[3]

All nations need to revisit their history and resolve issues that deal with war, geno-cide, and various forms of barbarism and other vile acts. We can always ignore our

1. The English might have a different and kinder interpretation. The "second empire" of India, Asia, Africa, and America (as opposed to the "first empire" which was based on war, blood, and death) was based on commerce and trade. It relied on capitalism, not conquest. It was intended to benefit both the colonizer and colonized, and to spread the concept of Eng-lish law. I guess this interpretation has something to do with whether you believe that the lib-eral minds of Adam Smith and Edmund Burke prevailed upon the "civilizing mission" of England or whether you feel it was the conservative thinking of Darwin, Kipling, and Queen Victoria that prevailed. As far as I'm concerned, the Empire was driven by power and profit.

2. Francis Jennings, *The Creation of America: Through Revolution to Empire* (New York: Cambridge University Press, 2001).

3. Lerone Bennett, *Forced into Glory: Abraham Lincoln's White Dream* (Chicago: John-son Publishers, 2000); Charles B. Dew, *The Imagined Civil War* (Chapel Hill: University of North Carolina Press, 2000).

dark side of history, like our European cousins. Only Germany has made an attempt to deal with its history. (I am not comparing the treatment of American Indians or blacks with the atrocities of World War II, although I do know some "trendy" professors in academia who might.) Indeed, politics comes in all shades and hues and is portrayed along a wide political continuum and racial color scheme.

Let it suffice to that if the dead could cry out, we would hear several million times over from people of all colors, classes, and religions—from the wild reaches and white mountain tops of India and Burma, to the yellow sandy desserts of the Middle East, to the green remote jungles of South Africa and Australia, to the blue rivers and redwood forests of North America—the agonies and groans of the dying, the lamentations of the wounded, and hearts filled with sorrow. We would hear their reflections of lost towns and villages that today no longer exist or nobody knows because of the myriad ways in which English invasions and English rule have caused a lifetime of migration, evacuation, and destruction around the world for hundreds of years. (Of course, the Spanish, Portuguese, French, Germans, and even Vikings are not so innocent. They were just as bold but less successful.)

You don't have to be Irish, Scottish, or Indian to understand English exploration around the world. All this sorrow has been has been caused by fidelity to the Crown, the field of glory, and whenever duty or the Empire called for sailors and soldiers to "civilize" and colonize other civilizations—about one-third of the globe. Indeed, the English were true elitists, believing in their own superiority, just like their cousins did under the guise of Nietsche's "superman" theory and later Nazism. On the other hand, to be fair to the English, most civilizations of all colors have historically conquered weaker civilizations and have exhibited more greed, racial hatred, and barbarianism.[1]

1. In terms of ruthless potential, the Hutu and Zulu tribes of Africa are not that different from the Persians, Romans, Turks, Germans, Chinese, Japanese, or Serbians. There is a cruel, disgusting gene buried in all of us. It periodically vibrates and surfaces—and twentieth-century Europe, given all its machines and masterminds, is the most ruthless time and place. In Europe, the heart of western civilization, we have witnessed in the last 100 years the most vile deeds and crimes people are capable of committing: the death of over 100 million people directly linked to war and totalitarianism. For a recent visual and vivid memory of man's inhumanity to man, specifically the violence and horrors of war, see the photojournalist book of Ron Haviv, *Blood and Honey: A Balkan War Journal* (New York: TV Books Inc., 2000). For a review of the past 100 years of plunder, final solutions, gulags, and ethnic cleansing, see Jonathan Glover, *Humanity: A Moral History of the Twentieth Century* (New Haven: Yale University Press, 2000).

Need a quick dose of human atrocity and gruesome abuses that characterize past or modern times? Just look in the mirror, determine your national or religious origin, synthesize your dinner table talk for the last 10 or 50 years, and that will determine who you hate. Man's inhumanity is part genetic, part environmental, often passed from generation to generation. Passions and disputes combine easily with personal ambition, economic grievance, and ethnic/racial/religious differences. This is the world we have inherited, characterized by old-fashioned hatred, evil, criminal stupidity, and greed. Most Americans have not attended indoctrination classes, but would say this nation is diverse, democratic, and secular, therefore, more tolerant and more often involved in defensive wars and humanitarian causes. Of course, there are people who despise us and would disagree, and so we have a new word, about 30 years old (since the 1972 Olympics), called *terrorism.*

Because of English-speaking folklore and legend as well as Anglo law and literature, and because in the last century we have fought together in two great wars, and
because we are staunch allies once more in the fight against international terrorism to
make the world safe for democracy, we bury this dark side of English (and Western)
culture. Besides, the literature of Shakespeare, Milton, Swift, and Chaucer is what
Americans tend to emphasize and embrace. (It might be called "high-brow" or "elitist" literature, typical for the "taste" of English educated and upper class, and American snobs, but it certainly beats the "bastard" norms the popular, romantic, or thriller
novel of the twentieth and twenty-first centuries which has great sales and says almost
nothing.) As literate Americans, we also stress the English Enlightenment, characterized by Bacon, Newton, Hume, Hobbs, and Locke. This part of our English heritage
is graceful and elegant, and the source of empirical rationalism (translated to mean traditional research methods adopted by academics), the Age of Reason, and the industrial revolution—ideas and values that Americans harbor in their hearts.

Of course, the English should also be given credit for having the longest-
established polity on earth. The key to its stability and duration down through the
ages, according to the celebrated historian Simon Schama, is that its government is
broadly based on including ordinary people into the process at the local and county
levels: From the tenth century on, and since the thirteenth century they have been sending the common folks to Parliament.[1] And, bringing the story to the present, you have
to marvel at the Beatles, the Rolling Stones, and Elton John, who have sung their way
into the hearts and minds of Americans, and the Cinderella story of Princess Diana.

Most important, England gave the world Winston Churchill, perhaps the most
effective political leader of the twentieth century, at least within the Western world.[2]
When he became prime minister at age 65, he had nothing to offer the English but
"blood, toil, tears, and sweat." Western civilization hung in balance and it was
Churchill, the overweight icon, the man who had flunked Latin, who said, "We shall
fight on the beaches . . . we shall fight in the fields and in the streets . . . we shall never
surrender." They were only words but they are words we shall never forget.[3]

1. Simon Schama, *A History of Britain* (New York: Miramax Books, 2001).
2. If you come from the other side of the world, you might rate Ho Chi Minh as the most
effective political leader of the twentieth century. Not only did he recognize and praise the
American system of government when he was a young revolutionist in 1927 (that America was
"a valuable [political] model for the Vietnamese to study") but he also managed to lead a tiny,
peasant country—nullifying the Japanese invasion in the 1940s, tossing out the French colonists
in the 1950s, keeping out the Soviets and Chinese who had imperialist designs toward Vietnam in the 1960s, and later defeating the Americans in the 1970s.
3. Churchill understood words. Bush, on the other hand, searches for the right sound
bytes and uses pompous phrases in search of an idea. Bush's ideas revolve around terrorism
and evil. Churchill's speeches were packed with meaning and were used to build spirit and
hope. He was a master of the English language, based on simple and short sentence structure.
He gave us a new vocabulary, including *Iron Curtain, peaceful coexistence, Cold War,* and *sum-
mit meeting*. Besides giving us words we will never forget, Churchill gave us the V-sign, bull-
dog growl, a six-inch cigar, and hundreds of memoirs for historians to mull over. See Roy
Jenkins, *Churchill: A Biography* (New York: Farrar, Straus & Giroux, 2001).

It is questionable whether the majority of the younger teaching force (under 40 years old) can identify the words with the man, or fully understand the context or times: what was at stake, why we are committed to the British, and why they are committed to their American cousins. Alone on a tiny island, Churchill stood up to the so-called master race, and bought the free world extra time—that is, until Americans realized the free world was at stake and were willing to travel across the oceans and sacrifice 300,000 U.S. men and women. Today, Tony Blair provides unwavering oratorical, diplomatic, and combat support for America, in its fight with the fanatical fringe of Islam. Indeed, there is history and culture that cements the Anglo-American world, and results in American teachers and textbooks skipping over, washing away, and/or rationalizing a lot of embittered memories that can be labeled by a variety of names or subjects: English "imperialism," "colonialism" and "domination" of a large segment of the world, and mainly involving third-world people.

Given the need to elevate moral character and social justice, at what grade level should teachers provide a clue of what the English and Americans meant by "civilizing" other people? Blacks call it "racism," and Muslims close to the Taliban, in search of an excuse for terrorism, call it an extension of the "Crusades." They also blame the English (and French) for secretly carving up the Middle East in 1916, which led to a great deal of political humiliation and tribal, ethnic, and religious conflict that endures today.[1]

## Global Ignorance

The Paperback Revolution and the Book of the Month Club—followed by the growing influence of the electronic era (first television, now satellite, cable, and Internet access)—bring a wild, politically laden, and emotionally toned world to viewers that educators cannot compete with and have never learned to fully utilize in the classrooms and schools. The fact is so few Americans, especially native-born Americans, have a global perspective. Most U.S. students, if given a set of geographical or historical questions with multiple-choice answers, would probably guess that Ceylon is a fancy appetizer or salad and that the Khyber Pass is a ski resort area in the Alps. We have relied more on popular magazines, talk shows and public television to entertain and educate us about the world around us.

The best we do is read *Newsweek* or *Time* to gain understanding of Islamic fundamentalism and the tens of thousands of madrassahs (religious schools) in the Moslem world. We don't speak their language and we don't read their literature. We are ignorant of the Moslem world, and for those of us who live on the fast track, we depend on CNN and network news—30-second sound bytes mixed with some three minutes of "in-depth" reporting. Considering that we are dealing with 1.2 billion people spread in more than 30 Islamic-dominated countries, our notion of understanding global diversity and multicultural education is a joke, surpassed only by our lack of preparedness by government and military leaders to short-circuit 9-11.

Are teachers equipped to critically analyze the global perspective? Much of the interpretation of history and current events reflects our own class and caste, and

---

1. Reference is to the Sykes-Picot agreement in 1916 and the subsequent division of the Ottoman Empire in the 1920s.

whether the teacher or learner is white or nonwhite, western or nonwestern. So much of our understanding of morality, of right and wrong, is based on the accident of geography and birth—and whether we are educated. Ironically, so much of our global "understanding" is based on a slogan or minced statement: "To make the world safe for democracy," "Better dead than red," or the "Axis of Evil." Sometimes it is based on a movie, such as *Private Ryan, Pearl Harbor,* or *Black Hawk Down*—what I would sum up as Hollywood's version of the world—or some TV docudrama about war or a biography of some political leader, military person, or some cult figure.

Our fight with Germany and Japan was simple. Our European allies were crumbling and democracy was at stake. Given a slightly different set of circumstances, the United States could have been a colony of the Third Reich or the Rising Sun. During the Cold War, the American rivalry with the Soviet Union was like a chess game, where moves were made to contain and checkmate the expansion of communism. Each party understood the behavior and verbiage of the other, and it was clear who was the enemy. Today, however, the United States is facing a group of loosely connected adversaries unlike World War II or the Cold War. They are not part of some evil empire or even some evil axis. The "enemy" consists of regimes and terrorist networks different from each other and driven by different ideologies—and different adversaries who are unpredictable and have a different rules of engagement than we do. In some cases, we are fighting a state; in other cases, we are fighting "the street" (underground terrorist groups). Although we can talk about religious or tribal differences, educated Moslems versus noneducated Moslems, moderates or extremists, or cultural misunderstandings, it all boils down to money and oil, less about freedom or orthodoxy, and still less about the understanding of historical events. Which view you adopt largely depends on your politics and mood, and how frank or friendly you are across geographical and cultural divides.

There is need to draw attention to the inability and unwillingness of moderate Muslims to criticize extremists, to publicly denounce them and hold them accountable in their respective countries. We have a silly, naïve image of ourselves—that we are a good people and nobody wants to hurt us. We fail to grasp that radical Islams' dislike toward Americans is all consuming, partially due to ignorance, religious fanaticism, conflict in culture and traditions, condescending superiority of Americans toward the nonwestern world, images of wealth and materialism portrayed by American television and American corporate policies, and the view that we hold secular law above God, representative democracy above Allah. What Americans must do is balance the claim that political and religious violence is foreign to the spirit of Islam with its anti-Americanism and historical theocratic crusades against the infidel. This kind of balancing act may not be easy to pursue in academic circles, but it is essential for political and international diplomacy.

According to one journalist who has been forced to live underground, thousands of radical Islam operatives live in the United States who are potential terrorists, and several Muslim fund-raising groups exist that make no distinction between raising money for schools or for terrorist operations on behalf of Hamas, Al Quida, and other groups.[1] We play down these activities because of historical guilt in treatment

---

1. Steven Emerson, *American Jihad* (New York: Free Press, 2002).

of Japanese citizens during World War II, present concern and debate over social profiling, fear of being labeled as bigoted, and the overarching education theories of "whiteness" as negative, and pluralism and multiculturalism as positive. Indeed, many on the political left have reacted with anti-Americanism rhetoric and concerns about patriotism, McCarthyism, and western imperialism.

Amid our economic expansion and military supremacy in the 1990s without parallel in American history, and with the threat of nuclear war dramatically reduced, we have gone asleep. The alarm went off in 2001. We are now challenged not by a super-power but by rogue groups that have no national identity, government apparatus, or tangible assets. Indeed, terrorist events in the United States can lead to economic and social deterioration, a collapse of national purpose and morale, and a lack of faith in the nation's destiny. We need to reset the alarm clock to 2011, and make sure we don't doze off or develop a self-deluding image of grandeur—and thus meet a similar fate that our Anglo cousins met between wars, when its empire and international power and prestige collapsed.

One must understand that history condensed in a page or chapter, or even in a book, requires authors to focus on one or another aspect of the past while excluding other aspects. Every chapter in this book, and in other books, and every work of history, social science, or education, even the most complex and comprehensive, omits much more than it includes. Writers and teachers alike always have to decide what is important and choose their words accordingly. Furthermore, as teachers, we are forced to compete with the mass media and electronic world, especially since so many youth (and adults) are "wired up."

In the next 5 or 10 years, every home will have the potential to have a "Me" channel—where each member of the family can program from a series of channels an individualized line-up of selections and shows assembled from all-but-infinite lists of programs pulsing through the digital web. The same digital force will most likely affect magazines and newspapers (even textbooks like this one), causing producers and publishers to narrow their focus and to provide multiple options for a wide variety of viewers and readers at the same time. The possibility of assigning specific school programs, homework, and academic enrichment will be immense, but it is questionable whether teachers will make use of this system of "Me" channels. (This view is based on how teachers in the past have underutilized television—the most effective mass medium and form of entertainment ever devised.)

If we have learned anything from the past, worldly philosophers (from Nietzsche to Heidegger) have flirted with and even collaborated with the forces of evil (i.e., final solutions, ethnic cleansing, etc.) while religious leaders have often remained neutral or obfuscated. American teachers have often remained silent or were very slow in addressing the philosophy of totalitarianism when a particular evil was in the incubating stages. This is true with Bolshevism, Stalinism, Nazism, Fascism, Maoism, Khmer Rougism, and Greater Serbanism, a list to which we must now add Islamic extremism. Totalitarian and fanatic ideas demand rebuttal from teachers—and they may need help from film and the History Channel. Teachers need to formulate and perform fresh moral roles, new thoughts related to 9-11, which deal with politics, diplomacy, globalism, and postcolonialism. Only a well-developed moral philosophy teaching will allow us to deal with what in society is worth protecting, to assure that America is not lulled into complacency, and at the same time to critically negate the images of television and the media that may oversimplify or stereotype contemporary politics and people, yet celebrate individual and group differences.

## Dealing with Whiteness

Colonists used the metaphors of a *subject people* in their petitions and *slavery* in their public debates to condemn the British. In their victory, Americans made freedom and liberty fundamental principles,[1] but the founding fathers were the offspring of the British and European traditions and permitted subject peoples and slaves to become part of this nation's history. Although the new nation was pluralistic and remarkably diverse with the arrival of European and African people, living among Native Americans, cultural and racial conflict was also part of its history. Our European ancestors had to adjust to a new social order in which cultural and racial domination had to be curtailed, far different than the old world order that was characterized by class distinctions and lack of social mobility.

The growth of the nation included a collection of the most diverse and motley group of human beings on a scale never imagined anywhere in the world before the 1600s. Confronted by people from all different parts of the world, from Scotland to Ghana, the early American colonialists had to rethink and reconceptualize their social and cultural world, their religious beliefs, customs, and language,[2] as well as their view of society and schools—and the relationship between education, mobility, and economic opportunity. Hierarchy, elitism, class distinctions and titles were unacceptable, far different from mother England and old Europe, because there was a mixing and melting of a diverse people—Europeans, Africans, and native Americans, and later Latin Americans and Asians. The new nation had to deal with its whiteness and at the same time create a nation that reflected a multicultural, multireligious society. It had to develop a system of education that was free of religious influence and that recognized diversity among the states and local communities. The concept of a ministry of education or a federal system of education was rejected, thus reducing the potential of a political or religious ideology influencing or seizing control of the schools.

The significance of the United States lies in the convergence of people from multiple nations and multiple religions coming together into one national story, one country indivisible, one nation becoming less white. Overall and over time, the nation has favored inclusiveness and not exclusiveness, pluralism and not homogeneity, assimilation and not domination. But critics can also show ways in which there was more misunderstanding than understanding, more mistreatment than fair treatment, more inequality than equality, and more injustice than justice. Thus, there is the clash between conservatives and liberals in interpreting American history and society.

---

1. James O. Horton and Lois E. Horton, *Hard Road to Freedom* (New Brunswick, NJ: Rutgers University, 2001).
2. Alan Taylor, *American Colonies* (New York: Viking Press, 2002).

There are many educators who take great pride in holding a mirror in front of us, to show only the cruel side of America. I cannot fathom and only have to fear to think of a world without the United States. Without this land, there would be no asylum for the wretched poor, little hope for the masses from distant places to escape from their oppression and misery, and the world would be possessed by one or more of the great evils—Nazism, Japanese imperialism, Stalinism, and/or Maoism. I would not exist, and most of you would be "subject people" or slaves. Sadly, however, many teachers and students alike take our human rights and our blessings for granted; many of us are ignorant of the history that molded America, and the spirit of reform that has guided the American political and social order.

Today, I write from the perspective of a third-generation American, proud and thankful that I am an American. Had Europe been a different place, I might have spoken a different language and had a different set of experiences and relationships. To this extent, I am a citizen of an ideal land because of the cruelty and hatred of man—which my ancestors were fortunate to escape with three or four bundles on their backs. As uneducated peasants, they never read Plato or Rousseau nor the writings of Jefferson, Webster, or Mann, but they understood that America was the asylum for the oppressed, regardless of their background—what other immigrants from other places also understood, and what foreign observers like de Tocqueville and Lord Byron said in words and what artists such as Irving Berlin, George Gershwin, and Rogers and Hammerstein have put to music scores and Broadway hits. Had my ancestors not understood the story of America, I would have no story to tell, no existence—one out of many millions reduced to incinerator dust. I don't think modern multiculturalists or speakers of immigrants—including Nathan Glazer, Oscar Handlin, C. Wright Mills, Michael Novak, or Ben Wattenberg—could say what I just said with any more appreciation, conviction, or passion toward America and our way of life.[1]

I also write as a global citizen who feels that human beings are 99 percent alike in terms of DNA and human characteristics, a map of 80,000 genes in every human cell. Yet, it is the 1 percent differences (usually based on race, sometimes on religion) that humans focus on. As a recent resident of New York City, with the greatest percentage of first- and second-generation immigrants than any other American city (more than 75 percent), I am aware of the world's diverse population. In a two- to three-block stretch in parts of Manhattan, Queens, Brooklyn, and the Bronx, some 40 to 50 different languages are spoken. You cannot find that type of diversity anywhere in the world; hence, New York is a microcosm of the world.

While the world population is expected to increase at 75 to 80 million a year, I am also well aware of a shrinking white world. Moreover, by 2025, as many as 75

---

1. Nathan Glazer, *We Are All Multiculturalists Now* (Cambridge, MA: Harvard University Press, 1997); Oscar Handlin, *The Newcomers* (Garden City, NY: Doubleday, 1959); C. Wright Mills, *The Puerto Rican Journey* (New York: Vintage, 1950); Michael Novak; *The Unmeltable Ethnics,* rev. ed. (New Brunswick, NJ: Transaction Publishers, 1996); Theodore Caplow, Louis Hicks, and Ben J. Wattenberg, *The First Measured Century: An Illustrated Guide to Trends in America, 1900–2000* (Washington, DC: AEI Press, 2000).

to 80 percent of the world's urban population (projected to be more than 6 billion people) will live in megacities of 25 million or more, in the cities of developing countries such as Beijing, Bombay, Cairo, Calcutta, Dhaka, Jakarta, Lagos, Mexico City, and Sao Paulo[1]—freewheeling places of outrageous contrasts—wealth (less than 0.5 percent) coexisting with abject poverty (about 90 percent) and the remaining working- and middle-class populations.

The cell phones, Internet, and cable TV that we are accustomed to are apparitions of the population of poverty, a world of color that is growing rapidly, and is the gulf where danger resides. Put simply, the disconnected world could overwhelm the high-tech, connected world. So long as these poor remain docile, they remain invisible to us—unaware and unconcerned about billions of people running through heaps of garbage and sleeping in streets, where the majority of children drop out of school by the sixth, seventh, or eighth grade and are called "street children," "beggars," and "no-hopers." Our education system is divorced from this global reality, yet this world (the third world) may weigh down the remaining world—what most of us call the Western world.

Despite the world increasingly speaking English and drinking Coca Cola, most of the inhabitants in developing areas of the world are rural immigrants and urban refugees within their own countries, many living in streets, drinking poisonous-contaminated water, sip by sip, people adrift and yearning for a better life and a little dignity. These people are the new proletariat—possessed by a growing dislike, jealousy, and even hatred toward Western values. These are the same kinds of people Europeans, and to a much lesser extent Americans, have exploited through colonization and capitalism. This is an obscure but serious trend: billions of people, about three-fourths of a growing world population, representing an inevitable force with a reason to rebel and bring down our way of life—not by invading armies but through social breakdown, health problems and viruses, rebellion from mountains and jungles, as well as overpopulated cities, nuclear terrorism, and/or cyber warfare.

Given our wealth and resources, and our belief in the rule of law, how do we prepare our children and their children for this age of uncertainty, of what endures around the world, and what might be. American students are unaware of the global village and feel they are on the top of the heap, but all around us there are ghettos and genocide, starvation and malnourishment, sickly and starving people living amidst rampant political waste, fraud, and corruption, a pending global apocalypse. Do American teenagers who visit Nike and Reebok outlet stores, or who shop at Eddie Bauer and the Gap, understand the thousands of foreign factories, many American, taking advantage of low wages and lax labor laws in the pursuit of profits? Do you think that the millions of teenagers who listen to the repugnant lyrics of Eminem and other hip-

1.   Roger Cohen, "Cities: Audis and Cell Phones, Poverty and Fear," *New York Times* (January 1, 2000), Sect. 1, p. 28; Ben J. Wattenberg, "Burying the Big Population Story," *International Herald Tribune* (May 18, 2001), p. 9. If we add 80 million per year until 2025, the total approximates 8 billion people. Eighty percent of 8 billion is 6.4 billion; 75 percent is 6 billion.

hop sounds,[1] coupled with photographs of multiracial sex acts or a sadomasochistic gay culture on VH1 or MTV, can make the leap and listen to the sounds and cries of the poor—a world away from them? In the past (and even today), Americans have been unable to make the leap to the other side of the urban tracks, one or two miles away, to what Michael Harrington some 40 years ago called the "invisible poor."[2]

Knowing that more than half of American twelfth-grade students cannot name the six New England states or where the United Nations is located, what percent of American high school students know that about 40 million third-world people are infected with HIV, 20 million children in third-world countries die of starvation each year, another 800 million people suffer daily from malnourishment and hunger, and that 1.2 billion people of the world (or about 25 percent of the third world) live on less than one dollar a day and 50 percent of these developing countries' population live on less than two dollars a day.[3] In 10 years, between 1987 and 1998, poverty (defined by the World Bank) increased 20 percent in Latin America, 40 percent in South Asia, and 50 percent in Africa. In Eastern Europe and central Asia, it increased more then 1,000 percent. In 20 third-world countries (10 in Africa), the life expectancy is expected to dip below 40 years.[4]

An angry urban proletariat is growing around the world as rural populations— namely, hundreds of millions of rural migrants—flood to grimy, overpopulated urban areas. There, they are assaulted by what is perceived as Western culture: luxury cars, nightclubs, sex and drugs, porno movies, gangs, and prostitution. Their daily existence is plagued by electric blackouts, unsanitary drinking water, overflowing sewage, and an assortment of five killer diseases—tuberculosis, typhoid, malaria, measles, and AIDS—annually killing some 54 million people worldwide.[5] It is not uncommon for

1. Despite his crude slurs about women, gays, and minorities, and despite his fantasies that promote murder, rape, and incest, including a defense of the Columbine killers, and his overall offensive lyrics, Eminem has won numerous Grammy Awards from the Academy of Recording Arts and Sciences. Some people believe that a nation's greatness is measured not only by its economic and military power but also by its artistic achievements, or what might be called the "quality" of its civilization. Put into report-card terms, I would rate American hard rock and metal music "A" for free expression and shocking the bourgeoisie, and "F" for its visual themes and values portrayed of American life. I suspect a good number of younger folks and jet-setting swingers would argue that I'm merely part of the older Establishment—along with Abbie Hoffman, Jerry Rubin, and the Woodstock generation—and my views are humdrum and no longer relevant.
2. Michael Harrington, *The Other America* (Baltimore: Penguin Books, 1963).
3. Based on 1998 World Bank data; "Poverty and Globalization," Center for Global Studies Conference, St. Johns University, April 16, 2001; Allan C. Ornstein, "Curriculum Trends Revisited," in A. C. Ornstein and L. Behar-Hornstein, eds., *Contemporary Issues in Curriculum,* 2nd ed. (Boston: Allyn and Bacon, 1999), pp. 265–276. Also see Howard W. French, "Whistling Past the Global Graveyard," *New York Times* (July 14, 2002), Sect. 4, p. 16.
4. Ibid.
5. Stephanie Flanders, "In the Shadow of Aids, A World of Other Problems," *New York Times* (June 24, 2001), Sect. 4, p. 3; Robert D. Kaplan, "A Nation's High Price for Success," *New York Times* (March 19, 2000), p. 15.

more than half of this new proletariat to live on rooftops, street alleys, and the out-skirts of the cities by garbage dumps. This is the world, the real world, that Americans do not understand or know, given the paradox of American prosperity.

As America preaches the gospel of freedom and democracy, and romanticizes market globalization, high-tech gadgets, and entrepreneur capitalism, there is a growing post–cold war proletariat class that infests, digests, and surrounds the cities of the most populated, underdeveloped countries: Bangladesh, Brazil, China, Egypt, India, Indonesia, Pakistan, and most of the African countries. Whatever their language, whatever their skin color, religion, or tribal descent, they resent the national government that often rigs elections, if there are any, and that is corrupt and unable to provide basic necessities of life. Because of economic and social conditions, plus political corruption and dictatorship, the value of life is not the same as in Western society. The result is that many of these people find salvation in revolution and guerilla warfare, and still others in religion that offers eternal hope for a better life, including extreme and fanatical groups that preach U.S. hatred. Most of the nations in the developing world are going to unravel, not all at once, but in piece-meal fashion. As we try to assist these countries and buy off their political leaders, it will be the challenge of modernity (with it comes Western culture) itself that will make so many of these people more bellicose toward the United States.

As for Africa, which houses the world's greatest concentration of poverty (and is beginning to splinter), the only way a citizen is going to rise above a higher existence is to get out. Despite all the rhetoric of American black radicals like W. E. B. DuBois, Marcus Garvey, Richard Wright, and Stokely Carmichael, the idea for blacks is not to return to Africa, but to make the trans-Atlantic voyage to America or Europe. Where all avenues of mobility have failed, because of continuous government corruption, waste, civil war, and diseases, Africans hope to go abroad for an education and decent job that Africa has denied them. The passport to social mobility in Africa is to leave and come back with an education and money. However, most blacks fortunate enough to obtain citizenship in England, France, or the United States do not want to return to Africa.[1] What the white world knows but refuses to say any more publicly, Africans will privately admit that theirs is a "Dark Continent." It is bound to remain dark for scores of more years.

Now there is nothing wrong to encourage African dance groups and art in black schools and communities in the United States, and there is a lot to be said for black children wearing a T-shirt of Kunta Kinte, the hero of *Roots,* or to know that the word *uhuru* means freedom. But it is counterproductive (uh-oh, here goes another white person giving advice to a black person) to expect Africa to solve psychological problems that blacks may possess because of American institutional racism. Black people in the United States want to redefine themselves without white labels ("dumb,", "lazy," "shiftless"), and they can do it without looking back to Africa as the road to prosperity or self-fulfillment, real or unreal, secular or spiritual. To talk about some sentimental notion about returning to Africa and being made whole rejects common sense and the flow of immigrants from Africa seeking a better life and

1. Caryl Phillips, *The Atlantic Sound* (New York: Alfred A. Knopf, 2000).

running from the squalor of a continent where the sun never rises. It flies in the face of African reality, a world described by one African commentator led by "dictators, murderers, and thieves,"[1] and, if I may add, a world ransacked by conflict, corruption, instability, starvation, and a medical/health nightmare.

## The "South": Latin America

The uneasy relationship between North and South America is depicted among many Latin American writers, referring to "the South" as the poor, illiterate, and oppressed—the have-nots, the barefoot, and the "bitten." Justice is like a snake, according to one Catholic archbishop and social critic, Oscar Romero from San Salvador, "It bites the barefooted."[2] On the surface, however, Latin America provides great hope, because all the countries, except for Cuba, are seemingly democratic and fewer people (36 percent of 225 million) live in poverty. The problem is that the gap between the landowners and the landless is as extreme or more extreme than in other parts of the world. Only 15 percent of South America's children make it to the ninth grade, despite increased spending in education. The increases in education spending tend to be less effective because Latin American governments concentrate spending on universities to mollify politically active middle-class students[3] who they feel are more dangerous than illiterate populations. This is a different type of payoff in which Americans provide aid to developing countries, knowing in advance most of it is siphoned off by corrupt political leaders and business opportunists.

Even with our neighbors to the "South," U.S. students (and many teachers) are ignorant about the coups, military takeovers, and fascist governments, one dictatorship after another through the years (the last 100 years), supported by American dollars, and with assassins, military police, and secret agents trained and armed by Washington. Indeed, the world's greatest peace-keeper is the largest maker and supplier of arms and airplanes—weapons of destruction for sale to the highest bidders and mass murderers who proclaim to be friends of the United States—from Guatemala and Chile to Saudi Arabia, Iran, and Indonesia. Must the need for political stability, an extension of Teddy Roosevelt's "Big Stick Policy," always win out over fundamental law, decency, and morality? Protest literature in Latin America is alive and well, but it has its limitations. It is difficult for American politicians and capitalists to assess judiciously in an era in which they are eager to extend the free market system as with Argentina, Chile, and Mexico.

One of the most widely read protest writers of Latin America is Eduardo Galeano, who has been denounced, banned, arrested, and subsequently exiled from his homeland in Uruguay. In his recent book, *Upside Down,* a series of questions

1. Rachel L. Swarns, "A Hint of the Coming Battle for Africa's Future," *New York Times* (July 14, 2002), Sect. 4, p. 3.

2. Isabella Fonseca, "A Land in Exile from Itself," *New York Times Book Review* (November 12, 2000), p. 32.

3. Anthony De Palma, "Poor Survive It All, Even in Boom Times," *New York Times* (June 24, 2001), Sect. 4, pp. 1, 14.

come to the fore:[1] How can we expect the survivors of the prisons and torture camps of all the dirty wars and dictatorships to believe that the best way forward lies in amnesia? Can democracy be built on forgetting all the torture, executions, and missing people of Latin America? In smaller counties like Guatemala, Peru, and Uruguay, the likelihood is that the victims and their families will meet their torturers on the streets. In many countries (including the three just mentioned), relatives are still searching for tens of thousands of bodies that disappeared during the last 25 years of state-sponsored reign of terror.[2] What then? American students and teachers have no idea what it means to live in Latin America or why so many Latin Americans from the intellectual class are anti-American.

Blacks in Latin America are in the worst economic condition. On a historical basis, the difference between slavery and racial hierarchy without slavery is slight. In many parts of the world, blacks were designated as subhuman, not as persons. Aluismo Azevedo, in *The Slum*, which was originally published in 1890, depicted life in Brazil. He referred to blacks as a *group* in comparing them to whites, rather as Portuguese or mulattos. Blacks were interchangeable and were described as *things*. Other than working in menial jobs, the only alternative for survival in *The Slum* was to sell yourself (as a prostitute) or betray your personal dignity and decency as a human being and become involved in theft, drugs or murder.[3]

Latinos for centuries have been obsessed with race, just as much or more as in the United States. In the eighteenth and early nineteenth centuries, Latin American mulattos who were wealthy could purchase "certificates of whiteness" from the Spanish or Portuguese monarchy. Money not only leads to power, but in South America it also led to a transformation skin color with new rights. Where the English language may have 4 or 5 different words to distinguish shades of color, ranging from "mulatto" to "mixed," in Spanish, there are 138 types and words.[4]

As a people, Latin Americans have been terrorized by dictatorships for the last century. In a world where big business and pirate plunder become indistinguishable, where God is blind and deaf, or where Kafkan "justice" rears its ugly head, political and military dictators become part of the landscape and bring a reign of terror to their people. The people cry and suffer forever—until they die. In the search to find the meaning of life, some of us may ask why. Why is that America has supported so many dictators and right-wing generals in Latin America, like Armas (Guatemala), Batista (Cuba), Peron (Argentina), Pinochet (Chile), Noriega (Panama), Stroesser (Uruguay), Trujillo (Dominican Republic), and others?

1. Eduardo Galeano, *Upside Down: A Primer for the Looking Glass World*, trans. by Mark Fried (New York: Metropolitan Books, 2000). Galeano has been writing protest literature since 1971, when he first wrote *Open Veins of Latin America*.

2. Juan Forero, "Government Tracing Deaths of Thousands in War with Rebels," *New York Times* (February 18, 2002), p. A3.

3. Aluisio Azevedo, *The Slum* (New York: Oxford University Press, 2000). Originally published in 1890.

4. Fonseca, "A Land in Exile from Itself."

Billed as anticommunists to the American public (including teachers who teach their students about Latin America), the dictators' military and police assassins are trained by the CIA and Marines, and become the "clients" and "borrowers" of the American government and American business. In their own countries, these despots became connoisseurs of terror and experts at random and anonymous killings; they understood that power flows from the barrel of a gun and dungeon interrogations. Justice is merely academic theory, a fantasy or dream to be taken to the grave. Protestors, dissenters, and individuals with minds (who think or question) live lives of desperation in which they fear being called in on any given day for interrogation, or having their doors broken down by the authorities, never knowing if they will be arrested for good—and disappear.[1]

In the world I describe, a free thought is liability, happiness is a fleeting moment, and power brings its own immunity. Every young woman in this ugly world, visited by some American tourists, has the potential to be subjected to the bed—to entertain political or police officials or to serve as a "playgirl" to both the locals and foreigners so she can earn enough money to feed herself. We can excuse this aspect of bedroom society by claiming that this is nothing more than the oldest occupation—and why all the fuss over flesh? The fuss is that when young women have no other options, the female body becomes part of the basis of rule and dictatorial power. Soldiers also plunder the countryside and rape women as if they were cattle or animals. Even worse, there is no sense of guilt or remorse when soldiers rape the "local stock" while fighting for their nation or tribe. If soldiers were troubled by such complexities, they would be lousy fighting machines.

John Rawls talks about justice, and that's all well and good, but I think Kafka is more accurate in perceiving it as the Big Lie, at least in most parts of the world. Piaget, Kohlberg, Sizer, and many others examine the notion of morality, and they do an excellent job for an American audience, but try to apply moral laws or moral thinking to a dictator's government or to an invading group of soldiers. It's a little like watching a Martian trying to use some theory or statistics to try to explain teenage dating. There may be a few crude patterns, but the complexity of the process is missing in the explanation.

Social scientists and academics may use a lot of words to describe the difference between justice and injustice, morality or immorality, but in a world terrorized by dictatorship (or war), most of these thoughts become nothing more than clichés. To live in Latin America, and in most parts of Africa and Asia, is to live in an ugly, upside-down world without morality as justice or fairness before the law. If there is one person who can tell you about military dictatorship in Latin America, about so-called committees on so-called law, truth, and justice, it is Eduardo Galeano, who came to his political awakening when he was 14 years old and saw Carlos Armas installed as president of Guatemala, armed by Washington and bolstered by the United Fruit Corporation.[2]

1. Galeano, *Upside Down;* and Mario V. Llosa, *The Feast of the Goat* (New York: Farrar, Straus & Giroux, 2002).

2. See Eduardo Galeano, *Guatemala: Occupied Country* (New York: Monthly Review Press, 1967); Galeano, *Upside Down.*

And so we return to the old, important question: Why? I can give you several philosophical explanations and sociological-sounding variations. To keep it short and simple, the one-word answer is *money*. In his poem *The Velocity of Money*, Allen Ginsburg made reference to this greed. Abba made a lighter statement in one of their songs, "Money, money, money. . . . It's a rich man's world." John Grisham's novel *The Summons* puts it in a blunter way: "I love money," says one of the lawyers in his story.

Unquestionably, the Rockefellers, Morgans, and Mellons did not rule by terror, but they were not against using goon squads to break up labor protestors. They did not inflict physical pain or literally kill people, but they did crush their competitors and acquired more riches than the dictators of Latin America and of other parts of the developing third world. These capitalists were not dictators, but they have been described as "robber barons," and their moral/ethical behavior make excellent primary sources for neomarxists to vent their rhetoric for liberation, not to mention extremist Islamic groups who wish to attack American capitalistic enterprises.

Women as Cattle    Given the history of rape and violence toward women, not only in Latin America but almost everywhere in the world, should abused women today have special asylum claims in the United States? We profess to be a nation in which those who have been persecuted in their own country can be guaranteed a new home. But the issue of asylum for women highlights the issue of violence and abuse that has been inflicted on women throughout the world since the dawn of civilization.

Every other woman from Vietnam to Serbia, from Guatemala to Iran can tell you about a lifetime of beatings from her father and husband; every second or third woman from the Middle East and Muslim world can tell you about female genital mutilation and devalued human status; every third or fourth woman from parts of the Asian Rim to eastern Europe can tell you about sexual slavery and forced prostitution with little hope for escape; and every fourth or fifth woman from North Africa can talk about the "herding" of women on a regular basis.

In totalitarian regimes, as in times of war, there are more barbarians than brainy people or people guided by moral principles; hence, women are the object of prey for the state militia and roaming armies. In times of peace, there is more abuse and sexual assault on women, as a matter of tradition, "a systematic form of persecution as those that make life unlivable for members of a hated religion or political movement."[1] In simple terms, there is a relationship between the "weak" and "strong" as there is between poor and rich throughout this world. In both cases, our sense of morality fails to grasp the issues involved, and we tend to focus on issues of race, ethnicity, religion, and membership of a political group when we deal with questions of immigration and asylum.

I don't believe Jefferson, Mann, or Dewey had gender politics in mind when they set forth the issues of democracy and education. I don't believe they considered the long history of war, religion, dictatorship, and tribal strife, as part of systematic persecution of women down through the ages, nor all the reign of terror imposed by dic-

---

1. Anna Quindlen, "Torture Based on Sex Alone," *Newsweek* (September 10, 2001), p. 76.

tators (Hitler and Stalin being the worst of the lot) nor corporate greed (the Swiss bankers and the U.S. Red Cross having the longest run at fooling the most people).[1]

Although Jefferson was concerned that women were made socially inferior by refusing them the educational opportunities that would establish their equality, it took World War I, with its need for the full support of women on the home front, to bringing about the women's rights to vote, more than 50 years after the right of black Americans to vote. Interestingly, Mann and Dewey wrote during the women's reform movement. With all their progressive thoughts, these education icons did not spend much time on the educational, economic, or political rights of women.

And now, almost all of us talk about gender politics. But for all the Marias and Rosas I know from Guatemala, Haiti, and Mexico who have been in the United States for the last five or six years, seeking a safe haven from countries in which being a female is reason for second-class status, even abuse and torture, I raise the question: Why have their appeals to become American citizens been delayed? My female counterparts at universities, and the female teachers I have taught, don't seem too concerned about Maria and Rosa who are seeking asylum. Their gender politics deal with textbook bias, math-science achievement scores, career opportunities, equal pay for equal work, child-care reform, abortion, divorce, and rape. Their silence about women seeking asylum from sexual abuse and torture provides tacit approval of female persecution in Latin America and other parts of the world.

## Global Economics: Profit or Promise?

Although unchecked population growth and lack of education in third-world countries are often considered factors in the increase of global poverty, critics argue that economic globalization or international capitalism increases inequality in poor countries. For them, open trade brings little prosperity to the poor nations and benefits only multinational corporations and their home countries. The reduction in protective

---

1. Billions of dollars have been stolen by Swiss bankers under the guise of "Can you produce a death certificate?" Other billions from thieves, drug smugglers, mass murderers, and tyrants have been transferred from victim countries to Swiss bank vaults. As for the Red Cross, billions of dollars have been stolen from donation money related to the victims of floods, fires, tornados, and, most recently, the WTC incident. In my view, the Red Cross is worse than any corrupt corporate entity, including Arthur Andersen, since the organization plays on the misfortunes of victims and the good will of others who contribute under the assumption that they are helping in a time of need. It's time to investigate the Red Cross and put a goodly number of their corporate fellows in the gallows. For example, of the $500 million raised by the Red Cross for World Trade Center victims and their families in a matter of six weeks, only $200 million was earmarked to the people affected by the tragedy, with the remaining to be "used to respond to future terrorist attacks." See Representative Charles Bass, *FDCH Press Release* (November 6, 2002). Now it is pretty vague and fuzzy to prepare for future attacks that may never come, but in the meantime, the Red Cross continues with commercials and pleas for donations without specifying their use. "Together we can save a life," says its CEO Bernadine Healy. See *Chronicle of Philanthropy* (November 1, 2001), p. 71.

trade barriers and subsidies put local and less efficient companies out of business or in an unwinnable competitive situation.

*Bloodsuckers, imperialists,* and *neocolonialists* are common words used by critics to describe the process. For every dollar lent to a third-world nation, the World Bank or International Monetary Fund makes three dollars for business profits. India, Pakistan, Brazil, and other developing countries must earmark approximately one-third or more of their countries' income for repaying these "humanitarian" loans, causing hyperinflation and market instability for these countries.[1] Whereas American homeless and poor sometimes sell their blood so they can eat, in several African and Asian countries, people sell their own body parts and organs to the rich—pushing the outer limits of humanity.

In corporate countries, the economies grew on an average of 4 percent annually from 1960 to 1995, promoting economic hegemony of a small number of Western countries and Japan over the rest of the world[2]—and also threatening traditional cultures and expanding the centralization of economic power among big-business interests. There are a few success stories—such as in Brazil, Korea, Malaysia, Mexico, and Singapore—bustling toward middle-class consumerism, but most third-world nations are saddled by high inflation, civil strife, health problems, lack of education opportunity, corrupt business practices, and political and military dictators who siphon off most of the country's wealth. The outcome is more than half the world's population, some 50 to 75 third-world countries (depending on the benchmarks used), from Costa Rica to Cambodia and from Macedonia to Mozambique, are saddled with grinding poverty and an economic system still too fragile to foster economic growth.[3] Many have to barter their resources for products and high-tech appliances from the West, which further drain their resources. Other nations have become the dumping sites of hazardous waste produced by western nations which further deteriorate their environment. Even countries that export oil, such as Iran, Nigeria, and Venezuela, have little to show for it. Nearly 50 percent of the populace in these countries are illiterate—drained either by tribal, racial, or religious factions or by leaders who have squandered or stolen much of the country's oil reserves.[4]

1. "Greed, Profit, and Globalization," *Korea Herald* (May 16, 2001), p. 3.
2. "Globalization, Employment and Labor Migration," Conference organized by the Center for Global Studies, St. John's University, May 2, 2002; Rick Rowden, "Corporate-Led Globalization and Its Critics," *Global Perspectives* (Fall 2001), pp. 11–14.
3. Social scientists, reporters, and critics have applied various labels to these countries: *third-world, developing, emerging,* and *newly industrialized,* which in turn leads to different benchmarks. Moreover, some of these countries, like Brazil, Malaysia, and Mexico are between first and third world. Advocates would claim this transformation is the essence of *globalization,* one of the positive stories and reasons to continue the globalization process. Critics would argue the poor people of these countries cannot defend themselves against corporate giants like Coca-Cola and McDonalds, and their culture is at stake. See Wu Hongying and Dao Schuling, "Sino-Third World Ties Need Improving," *China Daily* (November 21, 2001), p. 3; Robert J. Samuelson, "Globalization Up Close," *Washington Post* (May 9, 2001), p. 31A.
4. Burton Bollag, "Nigeria Universities Start to Recover from Years of Violence, Corruption, and Neglect," *Chronicle of Higher Education* (February 1, 2002), p. 40A; Motoko Sugiyama, "The Empowerment of Women and Children," *Global Perspectives* (Fall 2001), pp. 20–21.

Even Joseph Stiglitz, part of the inner circle of Clinton's economic advisors and chief economist at the World Bank, paints a flawed view of the principles of globalization in the same way Kennedy's and Johnson's "best and brightest" misjudged national security and Vietnam. Stiglitz describes a picture of rampant arrogance, simplistic economic theories, and disdain for foreign political realities that dooms globalization for the poorer countries. It has left hundreds of millions, possibly billions, of people worse off in 2000 than in 1990.[1]

Clinton's advisors, along with Bush's corporate barons today, thought they could transform poor countries overnight, that market fundamentals of supply and demand could eradicate generations of bureaucratic waste and corruption, and that capitalism would bring economic prosperity to an earlier generation that was communist ruled or ruled by corrupt fascist dictators. In short, the International Monetary Fund (IMF) provided financial aid, and in turn forced nations in Africa, Asia, eastern Europe, and Latin America to sell off government-decontrolled companies. They were decontrolled before the right time, resulting in economic recession and markets faltering throughout the world.

The only major third-world country not to accept Washington's aid or IMF money was China. It has embraced economic reform on its own method and time table. Russia, one of its biggest clients of Washington and IMF money, produced two-thirds more than China in 1990. By 2000, China produced two-thirds more than Russia.[2]

On the surface, many of these third-world countries are anti-American and anti-west, partially because of jealousy and the "blood-sucking neocolonialists" view attached to global capitalism. At the same time, the people of these countries crave and mimic nearly all things that are American, ranging from Gap jeans to Motorola cell phones. Analyzing multiculturalism on an international stage, education critics such as Paulo Friere and Peter McLaren provide an angry postmodern, postcolonialist analysis of capitalism in which the poor of the world wish to dismantle the political, economic, and social structures of the United States.[3] Part of the problem is that many third-world leaders assail white and western colonialism and oppression, but stand silently about their own autocratic violation of human rights, sanctioned torture and murder, and looted state resources and treasuries. Freire and McLaren overlook this double standard or bias and exhibit a great deal of anger, and sometimes it is hard to follow their language or thoughts, but then it is hard for Americans to understand the intense dislike some extremist groups and third-world populations have toward our way of life.

Friere, McLaren, and a number of other neomarxists and postmodernists are talking beyond education issues; therefore, many educators have trouble following their discourse. I must confess their sentences and phrases are sometimes difficult to follow. Nonetheless, no matter how irritating they become, they are on a different treadmill dealing with larger political and economic issues than just education. But

1. Joseph E. Stiglitz, *Globalization and Its Discontents* (New York: Norton, 2002).
2. Ibid.
3. Paulo Friere, *Pedagogy of Freedom* (Lanham, MD: Rowman & Littlefield, 2001); Peter McLaren, *Revolutionary Multiculturalism* (Boulder, CO: Westview Press, 1999).

their solutions are sometimes fuzzy, sometimes mystical, at least to the average person, and make little sense in the world of reality—schools and society (especially in corporate America where there are jobs). In academic life, bolstered by the influential publications that have moved to the political left, their ideas have appeal.

Moving beyond Philosophical Analysis to a worldwide stage, according to neomarxists and postcolonialists (a field concerned with the subjugation of third-world nations by the West), the United States is not a melting pot that respects other countries. Rather it is a colonist and capitalistic intruder driven by consumerism, hip-hop culture, racist attitudes, and a "big-stick" policy dating back to Teddy Roosevelt, who coined the expression. For the last 100 years, we have been manipulating other governments to satisfy our own corporate interests, and this process has been accelerated in the last 25 years with the rise of globalism. This view is obviously antimanagement, anticapitalist, and anti-American—a view not taught in American schools but voiced loudly in many schools outside the United States where "truth" is unraveled in a different way because of a different history, culture, and religion.

In the final flower of the search for enlightenment, the arguments of neomarxists, postcolonialists, and other radical intellects provide a basis for third-world terrorists. Killing innocent people is but a means to an end: to limit the expansion of the West and its capitalist and imperialist world—and subsequent destruction of the non-West.[1] For one author, the attack on the WTC is seen by extremist Muslims as hitting the symbols of American capitalism and globalism—its wealth and power—and an attempt to polarize the world's poor against the bastions of the rich. For millions of nonMoslem poor people, there was passive support for the WTC because they resent America's wealth (which is perceived as greed) and the nation's support of bad regimes (perceived as corrupt and as dictatorships). For some people saddled by grinding poverty and minimal opportunities, the terrorists were seen as heroes who had the gumption to fight back at the "big bully" of the world, and against the people who consume 25 percent of the world's resources while representing only 4.5 percent of the world's population.[2] Putting aside moral and national thinking, this angry global view of the world's poor should make us aware for the need of allies and the need to respect and assist the developing countries of the world in a way that provides their people with more rule of law and a redistribution of global wealth.

The counterpart argument is that the global market is inclusive and promotes racial, ethnic, and cultural diversity. Moreover, this diversity stimulates creativity, innovation, and economic success. The notion of multicultural, diverse companies is illustrated by international trade and World Bank literature; the Cisco, Ralph Lauren, and Nike commercials that display a mosaic group of sharp-looking, upscale, and healthy-looking people; the spirit and ads of the Olympics; and books by business gurus such as Peter Drucker and Tom Peters. Not only do people from Peru and Pak-

1. Hernando de Soto, *The Mystery of Capital* (New York: Basic Books, 2002); de Soto, "The Constituency of Terror," *New York Times* (October 15, 2001), p. 19a.

2. "Globalization, Technology and Poverty," Center for Global Studies Conference, St. John's University, April 26, 2001.

istan deserve a break at McDonalds, but also in this global village of money and power, even in the barren Mountains of Bodhgaya, somewhere near the "Road to Great Events," where the door to China closes and the door to India opens (or the opposite depending on the direction you travel), you can find a banner reading "Coca-Cola Welcomes the Dali Lama."[1] That is the ultimate "trip," showing the wide reaches of western capitalism.

Taken one step further, global economics, global markets, and global companies lead to a whole range of liberationists' claims (or myths, depending on your politics): curtailing or smashing national boundaries and racism. The dollar is green—not black, brown, or white. Capitalists want to wander the globe, sell to everyone, and hire all kinds of people who want to work. Given the world of Tao thinking, advocates claim the global and cosmopolitan corporations have become the rightful heir and major institution of the twenty-first century to fulfill the goals of the civil rights movement on a worldwide basis.[2] Jesse Jackson can't argue against this logic. Of course, such a description of global economics is from a management point of view and is rooted in Ayn Rand's view that capitalism is characterized by integrity and trust and that corporate America survives and grows by virtue and not vices. Now, I wouldn't hold much stock in this perspective, nor in the one proposed by Freire, McLaren, and other radical rascals who purport to represent the downtrodden of the earth. Somewhere between this either-or politics, hopefully, lies a resemblance of the "truth." But given the world of Excel spreadsheets used by corporate America for fraudulent and deceitful accounting tricks to wipe out the investments of hundreds of millions of small investors, the capitalistic model has been damaged and has lost significant credibility around the world.[3] America is in no position to preach to the rest of the world about political and economic corruption. If so, they are out of line.

## Global Perspective, Global Trends

Here in the United States, we feel the force of race, not the world's poor. Since the Civil War, this preoccupation with racial equality and race relations have gripped our social conscience and thus we have ignored the global underclass that is bound to become our biggest problem in the twenty-first century. As educators, we are almost totally ignorant of global poverty—and how it may influence our way of life, our democracy, trade, and prosperity. Our newspapers, from Boston to Beloit and from

---

1. Richard Bernstein, *Ultimate Journey: Retracing the Path of An Ancient Buddhist Monk* (New York: Alfred Knopf, 2002).

2. Thomas Frank, *One Market Under God* (New York: Doubleday, 2000); G. Pascal Zachary, *New Cosmopolitans and the Competitive Edge* (New York: Public Affairs, 2001).

3. As of June 30, 2002, U.S. stocks had fallen $8 trillion in two years, and Alan Greenspan—a disciple of Ayn Rand—was putting the blame on greedy investors who should have calculated better, and almost no blame on today's captains of big business. Indeed, Greenspan's "true colors" come through loud and clear. See "When Greed Was a Virtue," *New York Times* (July 21, 2002), Sect. 4, p. 12.

Seattle to Savannah, have been just as blind and ignorant—confining the news of global poverty, world hunger, and world illiteracy to the back pages or to an annual Sunday magazine story, possibly to a weekly review of world news, as in the case of the *New York Times*. Only since 9-11 have these stories been worthy of front-page news.

Without improvement in education, there can be little improvement in the social and economic conditions of the third world. The illiteracy rate reaches 1.2 billion, or about 20 percent of the world population,[1] mostly within African and Moslem countries where traditional society and religious custom keep women trapped and uneducated. Ironically, most American teachers are unaware that the United States and the free world are in a race against catastrophe in which international education is the only long-term hope available. Quick fixes and emergency food and health supplies have no long-term effect; education is the key to reducing worldwide poverty and ensuring modernity and democracy.

Do you think American students have any idea about the billions of beggars and "no-hopers" multiplying every 20 or so years, who may some day pull down their world? Do you think the next door neighbor's kid who is trying to make the freshmen basketball or baseball team, or even the high school graduate who just got accepted to Harvard, has any idea about world poverty and related trends? Our oceans once permitted us to take no notice of far-off people and places, but the problem is that today we are a global village and the oceans no longer protect us as they did 50 years ago, or even 5 years ago. The questions are: How can teachers compete with the soundtracks of recording artists who are in the forefront of the entertainment industry? How can teachers compete with the likes and reach of the corporate world? Overlooking the definitions of *artistry* and *profits*, do the entertainment and corporate worlds have a moral responsibility? And what about all the Americans, including students (and teachers), who live (or work) in Williamsburg or Watts or Westchester or Winnetka, who have no idea what is happening in the world around them? With 5 percent of the world population, do we have a right to continue to consume 25 percent of the world's resources?

Today, the United States bestrides the globe and extends its influence and leadership to the world stage. In fact, it now spends more on defense (at the expense of education and other human services) than the next 15 countries of the world. In fact, the United States has bases or base rights in some 40 countries;[2] we can move airplanes and battleships all over the world through our political and economic alliances. Nothing like this has ever existed—such disparity in power, and the ability for a nation to respond and mobilize to any far-reaching place in the world in a matter of hours in an emergency or days for a full campaign.

Even in times of recession, the United States is the leading economic engine; its health affects Europe, Latin America, the Asian Rim, and China—the economies of the entire world. We are the only superpower on the face of the globe, with the most

1. Ornstein, "Curriculum Trends Revisited."
2. Emily Eakin, "All Roads Lead to D.C.," *New York Times* (March 31, 2002), Sect. 4, p. 4.

powerful economy and army.[1] Our language and our customs (from our food to our movies) are the preferred model of the free-market system around the world. Not through military expenditures or force, but through economic, cultural, and political means, the United States extends its influence beyond its borders—a "Pax Americana" more influential than imperial Rome, Charlemagne's empire or the great empires of Persia, China, and the Ottomans. Today, we do not conquer people. We absorb people into the American way; we convert other people into Americans. And, the argument can be made that America has been converting or conquering other cultures and civilizations since Jefferson purchased the Louisiana Territory and Americans started moving westward. To be sure, historians may eventually envision twenty-first-century America as an empire, as well as a democracy, different from Rome and Britain—more powerful and far reaching. From an isolationist policy at the turn of the twentieth century, events have forced Americans to take an active political and military role in World War I, World War II, the Cold War, and now, post-September 11th.

America has become an empire—there is no country or group of countries that comes close to our cultural, economic, and military domination. Whereas most liberals and foreigners are critical of American foreign policy and have dubbed as as "colonialists" and "imperialists," a growing number of conservative scholars are embracing the notion of a full-blown empire.[2]

Patrick Buchanan's book, *America: A Republic, Not an Empire*, got it backwards. The 9-11 attack occurred because terrorists didn't think we would react. The solution to post-9-11 is to become more assertive and eliminate our foes. If nation-states are unable to control terrorist cells within borders, the need is to topple the government through covert methods. Trying to convert people into pro-Americans or believers of democracy takes too long. In an era of rogue states, terrorist groups, and nuclear weapons, the United States needs to change (restrict) its immigration policy

---

1. "Uses of American Power," *New York Times* (March 3, 2002), Sect. 4, p. 14. This global imbalance of powers is more skewed than all other empires at their height. Although the advantages of military power is obvious, it still needs its allies and friends in its Pax Americana view of the world. It must rely on international consensus, not American might alone. However, there is a dangerous counterpoint theory: the imperial and economic determinist vision of the triumph of democracy and capitalism. The need is for the United States to impose its will on the market economy (capitalism) and rogue states and belligerent nations (militarism) while it can, and not be befuddled or deluded by "liberal" theories in economics and politics. In up-to-date Machiavellian strategy, the argument is that America must use its unprecedented power to make the world a better place. It cannot sit idle, engage in appeasement, or watch history take its own course. Economic and military strength go hand in hand, and it must be mobilized to defend and spread the so-called gospel—democracy and capitalism. See Niall Ferguson, *The Cash Nexus: Money and Power in the Modern World, 1700–2000* (New York: Basic Books, 2002); Robert D. Kennedy, *Warrior Politics: Why Leadership Demands a Pagan Ethos* (New York: Random House 2001). Personally, I have trouble distinguishing if British historian Ferguson and American historian Kennedy and others like them (some of the U.S. military advising Bush) are simply espousing Machiavellian politics or the rhetoric and "logic" of Caesar, Napoleon, and/or Stalin.

2. Eakin, "All Roads Lead to D.C."

and assert its power with the help of moderate Muslim states. If we fail to act, we will face economic chaos on a worldwide basis, mass demoralization, and loss of our own personal freedom and liberties.

Imperial overreach is not a problem. Right now, all the world's major air forces and navies could not dent our military supremacy. Roman expansion was stopped, just like Persia, the Ottomans, Charlemagne, Napoleon, and the British, not because of over-reach, but because there were competing powers. There is no comparison today, no competing super- or semi-super-power.[1] Let me put in practical and gut-level terms. The only way to stop kamikaze attacks from continuing is to go after the aircraft carrier that is their base. Going after a needle in a haystack helps defend against but cannot fully stop terrorists; the only way of wiping out terrorism is to go after the haystack.[2] Terrorists who plot our demise live in a place, not off in space. If we deliver a military blow to the host state(s) of the terrorists, the message gets out to the rest of the world.

The world expects Israel to die a slow death, for its civilians to be murdered deliberately and without warning, and to refrain from using its full power. This has something to do with the politics of oil, and the traditional views that Jews are expected to live more securely in *time* than *space*. World contempt haunts them, where previously only stones and swords had reached them.[3] I don't believe the United States will be guided by world opinion if there is another major assault on its soil. A big test is taking place—involving religions, bombs, and computers, as well as lunatics who are willing to blow themselves up, and as to whether suicide strategy can succeed in balancing the power between the West and Islam radicalism, between high-tech and low-tech society, and in their fantasies to defeat the United States.

Complete victory over Nazism and communism were imperative for our existence as a free country; the same is required over Islamic terrorism—the same kind of extremism bred by the totalitarian mind. Make no mistake: Politics is driving religion—that is, Islam fundamentalism. It can be argued that a strategy based on industrial and military might, the winning strategy in the war against fascism and communism, cannot be counted on with the new threat—not with an elusive enemy with which we are faced. Is the richest and most powerful nation rendered helpless by an unconventional foe that has no national or well-defined physical assets, no geographical borders, and no government structure?[4]

Have we built a mighty military machine designed to fight a super-power while neglecting to deal with terrorist cells? Despite decades of preparation for nuclear war

---

1. Kaplan, *Warrior Politics: Why Leadership Demands a Pagan Ethos.*

2. Benjamin Netanyahu, "Three Key Principles in the War Against Terrorism," *Imprimis* (June 2002), pp. 1–4.

3. Joseph Roth, *The Wandering Jews* (New York: Norton, 2001). Let me add that in the late 1930s, Hitler asked all European nations to allow German Jews to immigrate to their country. There were no volunteers! When 920 Jewish refugees sailed to the United States for a safe haven in the early 1940s, Roosevelt denied their asylum—and sent them back to Germany. No country wanted the political refugees.

4. David M. Kennedy, "Fighting an Elusive Enemy," *New York Times* (September 16, 2001), Sect. 4, p. 11.

with a major adversary, 9-11 was an attack based on using our own technology against us. The choice of weapons—plastic knives and our own planes—underscores the newness of the threat. Most alarming is the prospect of continuous terrorist attacks and that, in our rage, we compromise our own freedom and liberties and vent our frustration toward Muslim Americans. But more disconcerting is that the 9-11 terrorists lived among us, drove a car with a Bin Laden sticker, and were trained by Americans to fulfill their mission; moreover, there are thousands of "sleepers" (future terrorists) who have been living among us for several years, attending our schools, drinking in our bars, shopping in our malls, driving on our highways. Not only are we unable to determine the next attack (when, where, what method), there is a new war—designed not to seize resources and territory but to cripple and demoralize American will.

If American teachers pussyfoot around 9-11 and fail to deal with this madness out of fear of being politically incorrect, or violating the principles of pluralism and multicultural policies, then they fall victim to the enemies of the United States and the civilized world. To argue that the United States is "to blame," "no innocent victim," and a "terrorist state," as Noam Chomsky argues, is bizarre. His perspective of the world (and there are other people in academia who subscribe to this off-the-wall perspective) is that all evil emanates from one source: the United States. Bin Laden, and other extremists groups involved in the World Trade Center and Pentagon carnage, is a result of U.S. policy.[1] Chomsky's logic is the type that blames a woman for being raped.

The only way to persuade people to stop blowing up buses full of children or office buildings full of people is to use international sanctions and boycotts, and to pressure for the change of political leadership. Indeed, the United States has the muscle to do it. If that doesn't work, because of the nature of the mindset of the culprits, you have to possibly blow them up before they blow you up—as we did in Berlin and Dresden, in Hiroshima and Nagasaki. This tactic sends a message to host nations that harbor these groups that they must control their extremists or suffer the consequences. I'm open to other options, so long as they are realistic. However, there are no normal diplomatic procedures, no standard rules of compromise or negotiation with people who are willing to kill themselves in order to kill you.

Scholars from the political left, and those who prefer to hedge their bets and sit on the middle of the fence, call this *Jingoism, Goldwaterism,* or *xenophobia.* They would argue that America's effort to promote democracy (and capitalism) is part of the imperialist western culture. And what do American teachers say? For the sake of freedom, we are obligated to take a stand, without sitting on the fence, because American interests and our way of life are at stake? Just as we are expected as citizens to vote, volunteer, participate, and serve, teachers are expected to fulfill certain responsibilities and duties when the country is threatened. Freedom is not free; it comes with a price. When innocent Americans are being blown up, and American communications, utilities, and infrastructure are at stake, there is no alternative perspective. We cannot remain in the state of denial or denounce U.S. policy as

1. Noam Chomsky, *9-11* (New York: Seven Stories, 2001).

repressive or downplay Islam extremism. Terrorism and suicide bombers cannot be stopped by self-restraint, admission of blame, fantasies of guilt, or compromise.

But just as we hold philosophers and poets in great regard, and shackle them to great ideals and ideas, we must be careful not to become prisoners to the thinking that holds us above international law or to stereotype Muslims as warmongers or terrorists. As we begin to ask ourselves why we were so unprepared and surprised by September 11, we should look at our intellectuals, including teachers, as part of the problem: 9-11 was not on their radar screen, so few of us were concerned with Middle Eastern or Muslim studies, and few of us knew about Bin Ladin, al-Qaeda, or the intifada. Bin who? Al who? Remember those days—before 9-11?

Having just crossed over to the new millennium, we expect several more American decades of prosperity and being the leader of the world. And that is dangerous. This kind of dialectical thinking is not unlike the Marxists, who saw the rise of communism as inevitable, or the Nazis, who were convinced the Third Reich would last 1,000 years. The greatest threat to our own future is us—our own stupidity, blinders, ego, and inept politics. The next greatest threat is to fail to summon up shades of the past, to forget the history of revolution and revolt. Despite our immense power, we cannot be the world's police force or fight terrorism without global allies, and to this extent we need to be global citizens and not pursue a policy of pure self-interest or random and constant exploitation of the world's resources. There should also be concern for military overreach, although some observers might argue that this represents dated or leftist-bashing concerns that go back to the Kennedy-Johnson administration, or even the Woodrow Wilson and "GI Joe" era. The final threat is the failure of teachers and schools to prepare the citizens of tomorrow for the world they will inherit. Can we bring prosperity to distant parts of the world or will we wither and decline like all other empires before us?

We do not live in a unipolar or culturally and racially uniform world—just the opposite. By 2050, the white world will comprise 4 to 5 percent of the world population. The more we think we can run the world, the more our friends will be put off and our enemies will become united. The more powerful and wealthier we become, the more we will be seen as dominating the world, and the more resentment will build from the rest of the world. The world's superpower should not expect to fight invading armies; rather, we are going to have to defend ourselves against third-world despots, thugs, drug dealers, international terrorists, and people sitting in front of computers seeking to disrupt our communication, utility, economic, and military systems.[1]

Nel Noddings would build an education system on the idea that different people have different strengths and that those strengths should be cultivated in an atmosphere of caring, not competing.[2] That might work for American students, who can read and write, who have three square meals, and who feel its "cool" to be tolerant,

---

1. See Steven Lee Myers, "On Empty Battlefields," *New York Times* (January 11, 2000), p. 2. Also see Robert I. Friedman, *Russian Mafiya: How the Russian Mob Has Invaded America* (Boston: Little, Brown, 2000).

2. Ned Noddings, *The Challenges to Care in Schools* (New York: Teachers College Press, 1992).

but how do American students deal with different cultures and distant others? Do we ignore them, like we tried some 30 to 40 years ago to ignore 20 percent of the world population (mainland China)? What *knowledge* should we be teaching? What *ideas* should we be discussing? What *values* should we be emphasizing?

How much time do teachers have for examining content that has no right answer, where time is needed to grapple with ideas, to express beliefs and feelings, and to listen to others with different or opposing attitudes? Given the high-tech world we live in, who has time to take a stroll in the park, to look at people come and go, to count the stars or marvel at the shape of the moon? Teaching and learning is about thinking, playing with ideas, listening to others, expressing feelings, and connecting with people. With outcome-based education, standards-based education, and right-answered teaching and learning, how many teachers can risk taking time out to maximize ideas and minimize facts? Sadly, the answers are obvious.

Some scholars would require that white students deal with their whiteness to reverse the course of their racism and notions of white supremacy.[1] Whereas most postcolonialists, postmodernists, critical pedagogists, resistance theorists, and neomarxists would lambaste whiteness and cloak all discussion in terms of white privilege and white power, others, who might be dubbed as "conservative" or part of the "dominant" class, would explore the concerns of white ethnics, the tendency to discriminate against whites under the guise of affirmative action,[2] and the psychological need among some intellectuals and reporters to gratify minorities by extending excessive respectability to their ideas and interpretations.

How do American teachers help their students understand about the great evils and atrocities that have happened and can still happen, that could have been prevented and can still be prevented. It requires not only an understanding of history but also philosophy, psychology, and moral responsibility. Academic standards for teachers are appallingly low, and I need only cite several well-known educators (such as William Bennett, Chester Finn, John Goodlad, E. D. Hirsh, Diane Ravitch, and even Secretary Rod Paige) to drive home the point that many, if not most, of our new teachers are unable to pass a basic test in math, reading, and writing at the national average. (Only one state, Virginia, sets a passing score at the national average. Passing scores for California, Florida, Louisiana, and Texas are set at the 20th percentile and/or at the tenth- to twelfth-grade level.)[3]

Some critics would simplify the problem by stating that bright students are scared off by the number of education courses required. Others would say that teacher

1. J. L. Kincheloe et al., *White Reign: Deploying Whiteness in America* (New York: St Martin's Press, 1998); Michelle D. Young and Jerry Rosiek, "Interrogations Whiteness," *Educational Researcher* (March 2000), pp. 39–44.

2. Adolph Reed, *Class Notes: Posing as Politics and Other Thoughts on the American Scene* (New York: New Press, 2001); Novak, *The Unmeltable Ethics;* and Norman Podhoretz, *Breaking Ranks: A Political Memoir* (New York: Harper & Row, 1979).

3. "A Better Class of Teachers: Secretary Paige Gives Teachers an F," *Wall Street Journal* (July 5, 2002), p. 12.

education puts the emphasis on *process* and not *content*; in fact, 27 states have no content requirement that teachers demonstrate for the subjects they become certified to teach. I would take the issue one step further: The need is to improve the pay and prestige of teachers, and thus attract better-educated personnel.

As educators, we are left with the need to invent new models and new dialogues, to explore our national and international options, to clarify what kind of schools and communities we want, to define what kind of people and nation we are, and to discuss what options and opportunities are there for improvement. Most of us are good judges of right and wrong, including the tank toppers in South Florida, the option traders in Chicago, the creationists in Kansas, and those who read the *National Enquirer* or *Village Voice*. Most Americans, regardless of their liberal or conservative labels, tend to do the right thing so long as they understand the issues. We are a diverse nation, almost as diverse as the world, and it is our liberal education and faith in humanity that should help us in the long run. But we probably will not come to the realization about the problems of the rest of the world, I am sorry to conclude, until we are thumped on the head or disaster looms on the horizon: 9-11 is a turning point in our history and our way of life. By George, it's time to wake up! Otherwise, one day, in a flash, it may be too late.

## $\mathcal{S}$ummary

1. John Dewey and Lawrence Cremin are essential educators for understanding the rise of progressive education. Both men were highly influenced by Rousseau.

2. Thomas Jefferson, Noah Webster, and Horace Mann, among others, emphasized the ideas of universal education, which later became transformed into the common school movement.

3. Many of the ideas of Plato and Jefferson were never implemented by their contemporaries, yet both had marked influence on American educational thought.

4. Noah Webster, the Connecticut school teacher, was instrumental in establishing an American spelling book, grammar book, and dictionary, which in turn helped the United States establish its own national language and educational system.

5. The concept of universal (free) education for all children started at the elementary school level in the New England colonies and eventually reached the high school level with the *Kalamazoo* decision in 1874.

6. Horace Mann, in the 1820s and 1830s, as a Massachusetts legislature and later as the first Massachusetts Commissioner of Education, spearheaded the common school in his state. The movement picked up momentum and moved to other eastern states, such as Connecticut, Pennsylvania, and New York; henceforth, it shifted to the heartland, where there was a much stronger emphasis on equality, built on the challenges of hard work and limitless opportunities.

7. It was in the frontier, the American West, where there was reliance on individual intelligence and achievement. The common person was free to choose and use his own judgments to arrive at solutions, rather than to appeal to some higher authority, such as a noble man in the old world or politician in the East.

8. Rousseau would have felt at home on the frontier—in the wilderness and among the natural resources. It was the place where the individual had limitless opportunities to develop, and every person had the inalienable right for self-development and improvement according to his or her capacities. It was this belief in freedom and equality that grew into the concept of egalitarianism and became incorporated into American educational practice.

9. There are dark sides all nations must confront, if the people are to retain a sense of decency, compassion, and morality. Our dark side includes the treatment of American Indians and American blacks. We cannot escape from the past; the idea is to confront it, learn from it, and avoid similar mistakes in the future. Politically, American women were treated as second-class citizens until they received the vote after the turn of the twentieth century. Economically, a glass ceiling still exists in many sectors of the economy, and therefore it can be argued that women are still economically second-class citizens.

## Questions to Consider

1. In what ways do I overstate or understate my views about Dewey and Cremin?
2. Which region had the greatest influence on American education: New England colonies, mid-Atlantic colonies, or southern colonies? Why?
3. What were some of the lasting effects on education that can be traced to Jefferson? Webster?
4. Why did the education ideas of Mann have such wide influence on American schools?
5. How did the frontier movement affect American education?

## Things to Do

1. Consult the Internet and note the ways in which different education authorities tend to interpret the New England (puritan) influence on American schools. Point out different interpretations.
2. Compare Jefferson's plan of education with the plans advocated by Plato. Which do you prefer? Why?
3. I purposely skipped over the Northwest Territory. Consult the Internet or one or two education history books and show how it influenced education in the United States.
4. Trace the main events of the common school movement in your state. Note the issues that arose and how they were resolved.
5. Review and reflect on the sections of the chapter dealing with race and gender. Then discuss in class my ideology and how it differs or coincides with your own views.

## Recommended Readings

Binder, Fredrick. *The Age of the Common School.* New York: Wiley, 1974. The rise of the common school movement and how it improved education in the United States.

Cremin, Lawrence A. *The Transformation of the School.* New York: Random House, 1961. A classic book on educational history and the rise of progressive schooling.

Curti, Merle. *The Growth of American Thought,* 2nd ed. New York: Harper & Bros., 1951. A comprehensive account of American intellectual thought involving social, political, and educational institutions; rarely discussed among educators, the book is a must for education historians.

Ornstein, Allan C., and Francis P. Hunkins. *Curriculum: Foundations, Principles, and Issues,* 3rd ed. Boston: Allyn and Bacon, 1998. A philosophical, historical, and social commentary of curriculum and instruction.

Ravitch, Diane. *The Schools We Deserve.* New York: Basic Books, 1985. A student of Lawrence Cremin, the author reflects on issues and ideas of educational reform; the tone is much more conservative than Cremin's progressive treatment of education.

Schultz, Fred. *Sources: Notable Selections in Education,* 2nd ed. Boston: McGraw-Hill, 1998. A collection of over 40 classic works that shaped American education.

Spring, Joel. *Political Agendas for Education.* Mahwah, NJ: Erlbaum, 2001. From colonial America to the Clinton Administration, the discussion centers on ideological issues of education—liberal and conservative, progressive and traditional.

# Schooling in America: Part II

## Chapter 6

## Focusing Questions

1. How would you describe the school curriculum at the turn of the twentieth century? Which student group benefited?

2. What forces led to the rise of progressive education? To the decline of progressive education?

3. How should we teach the structure of a subject?

4. How would you define (and teach) *humanistic learning* in schools?

5. What groups of students have been targeted for special treatment in the 1950s, 1960s, 1990s, and today? Why?

6. What are the major themes of recent policy reports on education? How do these themes differ from the *Sputnik* and Cold War period?

7. How would you describe the school curriculum at the turn of the twenty-first century? What student groups benefit?

## EPISODE A

We continue with our discussion of schooling in America with an underlying question, one that was first asked some 150 years ago by Herbert Spencer in his famous essay, "What Knowledge Is of Most Worth?" Spencer argued that science was the most practical subject for the survival of the individual and society, yet it occupied minimal space in the curriculum because impractical and/or ignorant traditions prevailed. Spencer also maintained that students should be taught *how* to think (and problem solve) and not *what* to think.[1] As we shall see below, Spencer's ideas were to influence John Dewey some 50 years later.

Many of Spencer's ideas about evolution and social progress (less intelligent, lazy, and weak people would slowly disappear, and heredity was the key to intelligence) created a furor—and they still do among observers today. However, his ideas fitted well with many thinkers of the second half of the nineteenth century, a period characterized by industrial growth, manifest destiny, and colonial expansion of European countries and the United States.

Spencer's original question about the worth of subject matter is more relevant today, because of the increased complexity of society. Actually, the question dates back the ancient Greece, when Plato and Aristotle questioned the value of knowledge in relation to citizenship and government affairs, and to ancient Rome, when Quintilian (influenced by Plato)[2] set forth the seven liberal arts—grammar, rhetoric, logic, arithmetic, geometry, astronomy, and music—as the ideal curriculum for educated citizens of public life: senators, lawyers, teachers, civil servants, and politicians. During the modern school period, these seven liberal arts have expanded to include many other subjects.

Finally, one must understand that Greek and Roman education (the latter influenced by the Greeks) cultivated contemplative knowledge, metaphysics, and rationality for purpose of nurturing the mind and body. The truly educated person had the power to think, to exercise reason, and to judge moral and ethical behavior. (This separates us from lower animals.) The good life was one of balance and moderation. This interpretation of knowledge and intellectual thought, promoted by Aristotle and Plato, was adopted by the medieval universities and by humanistic philosophers. It is the opposite type of knowledge concerned with utility, function, vocational education, and relevant education—which is trendy and becomes obsolete in a couple of years.

## The Transitional School Period: 1893–1918

From the colonial period until the turn of the twentieth century, the traditional curriculum, which emphasized the three Rs at the elementary level and classical studies at the secondary level, dominated the curriculum. The rationale for this emphasis was that the classics were difficult, and were thus the best source for developing mental abilities. The more difficult the subject and the more the students had to exercise their minds, the greater the subject's value. Such ideas of knowledge and subject matter, as well as mental rigor, were rooted in the philosophy of perennialism.

1. Herbert Spencer, *Education: Intellectual, Moral, and Physical* (New York: Appelton, 1860).
2. Plato also advocated several subject areas in his Republic, although there was greater emphasis on mastering reading, being involved in gymnastics, and displaying good rules of diet and hygiene.

Along with the classics, more and more subjects were added to the curriculum. As a result, there was a growing need to bring some unity or pattern for curriculum organization out of the chaotic and confused situation, especially at the secondary level, where subject matter was expanding the most. According to two educators, "Subjects taught varied from school to school. There was no uniformity as to time allotments, and grade placements of topics or subjects pursued" differed from school to school.[1]

A companion problem existed. Most children, even as late as the turn of the century, completed their formal education at the elementary school level, and those students who did go to secondary schools usually ended their formal education upon graduation. As late as 1890, only 14.5 percent of the students enrolled in high school were preparing for college, and less than 3 percent went on to college.[2] "The needs of more than 85 percent of the students were still being overlooked for only the top 15 percent; the discrepancy was more lopsided if the college track was considered."[3] Reformers began to question the traditional curriculum—the emphasis on mental discipline, the classics, and Latin.

## Reaffirming the Traditional Curriculum

With these unsettled issues as background, the National Education Association (NEA) organized three major committees between 1893 and 1895: the Committee of Fifteen on Elementary Education, the Committee of Ten on Secondary School Studies, and the Committee on College Entrance Requirements. These committees were to determine the specifics of the curricula for these schools; their reports "standardized" the curriculum for much of the twentieth century. In the words of Ellwood Cubberley, "The committees were dominated by subject-matter specialists, possessed of a profound faith in mental discipline." No concern for student "abilities, social needs, interest, or capabilities . . . found a place in their . . . deliberations."[4]

### The Committee of Fifteen
The Committee of Fifteen (on Elementary Education) was heavily influenced by Charles Eliot, president of Harvard University, who had initiated vigorous discussion on the need for school reform in the early grades, and by William Harris, then the U.S. Commissioner of Education, a staunch traditionalist (or perennialist) who believed in strict teacher authority and discipline. Both Eliot and Harris wanted the traditional curriculum to remain intact because they felt that the classics exposed students to great ideas, paramount for a democracy: The curriculum should be available to everyone, regardless of background, so long as they had the

1. V. T. Thayer and Martin Levit, *The Role of the School in American Society,* 2nd ed. (New York: Dodd, Mead, 1966), p. 382.

2. *Report of the Year 1889–90* (Washington, DC: U.S. Bureau of Education, 1893), pp. 1388–1389.

3. Allan C. Ornstein and Francis P. Hunkins, *Curriculum: Foundations, Principles and Issues,* 3rd ed. (Boston: Allyn and Bacon, 1998), p. 78.

4. Ellwood P. Cubberley, *Public Education in the United States,* rev. ed. (Boston: Houghton Mifflin, 1947), p. 543.

mental capability and drive. Eliot's plan, which was adapted by the committee, was to reduce the elementary grades from 10 to 8, which became the order of the day. The committee stressed the three Rs, as well as English grammar, literature, geography, and history. Hygiene, culture, vocal music, and drawing were given 60 minutes, or one lesson, per week. Manual training, sewing, and/or cooking, as well as algebra and Latin, were introduced in the seventh and eighth grades.

In general, the committee resisted the idea of newer subjects and the principles of pedagogy or teaching that had characterized the reform movement of progressive pioneers (such as Pestalozzi and Froebel in Europe, and Mann, Barnard, and Schurz in the United States) since the early 1800s.[1] The committee also rejected the idea of kindergarten and the idea that the children's needs or interests should be considered when planning the curriculum.[2] Any idea of interdisciplinary subjects or curriculum synthesis was rejected. Isolation of each branch of knowledge, or what John Dewey, in *Democracy and Education,* later referred to as "compartmentalization" of subject matter, was considered the norm; it still is today in most schools.

**The Committee of Ten**    The Committee of Ten (on Secondary School Studies) was the most influential of the three committees. Its recommendations best illustrate the tough-minded, mental discipline approach supported by Eliot, who was the chair. The committee identified nine academic subjects as central to the high school curriculum. As shown in Table 6.1, they were: (1) Latin; (2) Greek; (3) English; (4) other modern languages; (5) mathematics (algebra, geometry, trigonometry, and higher or advanced algebra); (6) physical sciences (physics, astronomy, and chemistry); (7) natural history or biological sciences (biology, botany, zoology, and physiology); (8) social sciences (history, civil government, and political economy); and (9) geography, geology, and meteorology.

The committee recommended four different programs or tracks: (1) classical, (2) Latin scientific, (3) modern languages, and (4) English. The first two required four years of Latin; the first program emphasized English (mostly classical) literature and math, and the second program, math and science. The modern language program required four years of French or German. (Spanish was considered too easy and not as important a culture or language as French or German.) The English program permitted four years of either Latin, German, or French. Both of these programs also included literature, composition, and history.

The Committee of Ten took a position and claimed that the latter two programs, which did not require Latin or emphasize literature, science, or mathematics, were "in practice distinctly inferior to the other two."[3] In taking this position, the committee

1. Carl Schurz established the first U.S. kindergarten in Watertown, Wisconsin; it was later adopted by William Harris when he was superintendent of schools in St. Louis, Missouri.
2. R. Freeman Butts and Lawrence A. Cremin, *A History of Education in American Culture* (New York: Holt, Rinehart and Winston, 1953); Robert S. Zais, *Curriculum: Principles and Foundations* (New York: Harper & Row, 1976).
3. *Report of the Committee of Ten on Secondary School Studies* (New York: American Book, 1894), p. 48.

========== TABLE *6. 1* ==========

## Secondary School Programs and Subjects Proposed by Committee of Ten, 1893

| First Year | | | Second Year | | |
|---|---|---|---|---|---|
| Latin | | 5 p.* | Latin | | 4 p. |
| English Literature | 2 p. ⎫ | | Greek | | 5 p. |
| English Composition | 2 p. ⎬ 4 p. | | English Literature | 2 p. ⎫ | |
| German [or French] | | 5 p. | English Composition | 2 p. ⎬ 4 p. | |
| Algebra | | 4 p. | German continued | | 4 p. |
| History of Italy, Spain, and France | | 3 p. | French, begun | | 5 p. |
| Applied Geography (European political-continental and oceanic flora and fauna) | | 4 p. | Algebra | 2 p. ⎫ | |
| | | | Geometry | 2 p. ⎬ 4 p. | |
| | | | Botany or Zoology | | 4 p. |
| | | | English History to 1688 | | 3 p. |
| | | 25 p. | | | 33 p. |

| Third Year | | | Fourth Year | | |
|---|---|---|---|---|---|
| Latin | | 4 p. | Latin | | 4 p. |
| Greek | | 4 p. | Greek | | 4 p. |
| English Literature | 2 p. ⎫ | | English Literature | 2 p. ⎫ | |
| English Composition | 1 p. ⎬ 4 p. | | English Composition | 1 p. ⎬ 4 p. | |
| Rhetoric | 1 p. ⎭ | | Grammar | 1 p. ⎭ | |
| German | | 4 p. | German | | 4 p. |
| French | | 4 p. | French | | 4 p. |
| Algebra | 2 p. ⎫ | | Trigonometry | ⎫ | |
| Geometry | 2 p. ⎬ 4 p. | | Higher Algebra | ⎬ 2 p. | |
| Physics | | 4 p. | Chemistry | | 4 p. |
| History, English and U.S. | | 3 p. | History (intensive) and Civil Government | | 3 p. |
| Astronomy, 1st ½ yr. | 3 p. ⎫ | | Geology or Physiography, 1st ½ yr. | 4 p. ⎫ | |
| Meteorology, 2nd ½ yr. | 3 p. ⎬ 3 p. | | Anatomy, Physiology, and Hygiene, 2nd ½ yr. | 4 p. ⎬ 4 p. | |
| | | 34 p. | | | 33 p. |

*Source:* From Committee of Ten, *Report of the Committee of Ten on Secondary School Studies* (Washington, DC: National Educational Association, 1893), p. 4.

*p. = periods.

indirectly tracked college-bound students into the first two or superior programs and noncollege-bound students into the latter two or inferior programs. To some extent, this bias reflected the committee's composition—8 of the 10 members represented college and private preparatory school interests.

The committee ignored art, music, physical education, and vocational education, maintaining that these subjects contributed little to mental discipline. In analyzing the effects of the committee's action, two curricularists wrote: "The choice of these subjects and the omission of the others from consideration was enough to set the course for secondary education" for many years and to indirectly set the tone at the elementary level, too. As "might be expected," the committee suggested that "the nine subjects be taught sooner" and that all subjects except Latin and Greek be taught at the elementary school level.[1]

Even though very few students at that time went to college, this college preparatory program established a curriculum hierarchy, from elementary school to college, that promoted academics and ignored the majority of students who were noncollege bound. In fact, the committee argued that the purpose of the high school was to prepare "a small proportion of all the children in the country [for college] who show themselves to profit by an education prolonged to the eighteenth year, and whose parents are able to support them while they remain so long in school."[2] Rather than viewing high school for all children, one critic maintains that the committee "viewed the high school as an elite institution," where about 5 percent of the cohort graduated.[3]

As the number of students enrolled in high school increased, from 14 percent in 1910 to about 50 percent in 1930, the proportion of students enrolled in academic subjects dropped form 78 percent to 64 percent.[4] Why? It has nothing to do with the influence of progressivism, as Diane Ravitch would have us believe, but rather when there is significant growth in numbers in any institution or profession, excellence and merit will often be balanced with equality and opportunity. Of course, today, the vast majority of students graduate and go on to one form or another of higher education. Even though we offer vocational, industrial, and/or technical programs, the academic program is still considered superior to and of more status than the other programs.

The Committee on College Entrance Requirements    When this committee met in 1895, it reaffirmed college dominance over the high school in terms of admission requirements and classical subjects for mental training at the high school and college levels. Consisting mainly of college and university presidents, including Eliot, the Committee recommended strengthening the college preparatory aspect of the high school curriculum, believing that it best served all students. (The committee, keenly illustrated its bias by

---

1. Daniel Tanner and Laurel Tanner, *Curriculum Development: Theory into Practice,* 2nd ed. (New York: Macmillan, 1980), p. 223. Also see Richard Pratte, *The Civic Imperative* (New York: Teachers College Press, 1988).

2. *Report of the Committee of Ten,* p. 51.

3. William Wraga, "Left Out: The Villainization of Progressive Education in the United States," *Educational Researcher* (October 2001), p. 34.

4. David L. Angus and Jeffery E. Mirel, *The Failed Promise of the American High School* (New York: Teachers College Press, 1999).

failing to recognize that the vast majority of students were not in the college preparatory track.) It also made recommendations regarding the number of credits required in different subjects for college admission. It served as a model for the Carnegie Unit as a means for evaluating credits for college admission, imposed on the high schools in 1909 and still in existence today in most high schools.

### Pressure for a Modern Curriculum

The common requirements of the three committees—even the terms *standards, academic subject matter,* and *excellence*—began to be criticized as a form of elitism. Sensitivity to the needs, abilities, and feelings of students took hold on American educational thought as progressivism became part of the school reform movement.[1] Although there was general agreement that a democratic society needed an informed citizenry, it need not imply a uniform curriculum or one that emphasized only traditional and tough subjects, or where only a small minority of bright students benefited at the expense of the majority. High standards, since the turn of the twentieth century, has been under attack, and is perceived today as even more threatening, since it shuts out a substantial portion of students based not only on class but also caste. Some critics have even argued that high standards challenge the concept of equal educational opportunity and reveal a certain degree of prejudice toward minorities as well as class dominance over working-class and lower-class students.[2]

Gradually, demands were made for various changes to be made in the schools to meet the needs of a changing society. The pace of immigration and industrial development led a growing number of educators to question the classical curriculum and the constant emphasis on mental discipline and incessant drill. This shift in curriculum was influenced by the scientific movement in psychology and education in the late nineteenth and early twentieth centuries, particularly the pragmatic theories of Charles Peirce and William James, the social theories of Darwin, Herbart, and Spencer, and the impact of Pestalozzi, Frobel, Montessori, and others on pedagogy. The movement rejected the mental discipline approach and classic curriculum (both of which stressed that certain traditional subjects were best for disciplining the mind), as well as faculty psychology (that is, enhancing the "faculties," or mind, of the child through stimulation of the senses.) Instead, the new scientism put emphasis on vocational, technical, and scientific subjects—fitting into the concurrent age of industrialism and big business.

Increased pressure against the traditional curriculum was evident at the turn of the century—with the educational ideas of John Dewey and Francis Parker, the Gestalt psychology and child psychology movements (which focused on the whole child), the learning theories of behaviorism and transfer learning (which involved connections between stimuli and responses), and the progressive movement in schools and society. The argument eventually appeared that the classics had no greater disciplinary or

---

1. Diane Ravitch, *The Schools We Deserve* (New York: Basic Books, 1985); Ravitch, *Left Back: A Century of Failed School Reform* (New York: Simon and Schuster, 2000).

2. Marion Brady, "The Standards Juggernaut," *Phi Delta Kappan* (May 2000), pp. 648–651; Peter McLaren and Ramin Farahmandpur, "Reconsidering Marx in Post-Marxist Times," *Educational Researcher* (April 2000), pp. 25–33; and Michael Young, "Interrogating Whiteness," *Educational Researcher* (March 2000), pp. 39–44.

mental value than other subjects, and that mental discipline (which emphasized rote, drill, and memorization) was not conducive to the inductive method of science or compatible with contemporary education theory.

Even Latin came under attack, by none other than old-time traditionalists (or perennialists). In 1917, for example, Charles Eliot, a former advocate of Latin, was saying Latin should no longer be compulsory for high school or college students.[1] Abraham Flexner, a former teacher of the classics who had become a celebrity with his exposé of the American medical schools, claimed that Latin had "no purpose" in the curriculum and that the classics were out of step with scientific developments.[2] Flexner, who had become a strong advocate of utilitarianism, argued that tradition was an inadequate criterion for justifying subject matter. In short, society was changing and people could alter the conditions around them; the stress on psychology and science and the concern for social-minded and educational reform made evident the need for a new curriculum, and thus came the rise of progressive education and scientific education

It was Edward Thorndike, the most influential learning psychologist of the era, and John Dewey, the most influential educator of the first third of the twentieth century, who argued that subjects could not be placed in a value hierarchy and that attempts to do so were misguided. Any study or body of knowledge was capable of expanding the child's knowledge and experience base—that is, being stimulated to develop his or her intellectual capabilities. Traditional subjects such as Latin, Greek, or the classics were no more valuable than music or art.[3] Try to tell that to a conservative educator, today, that math and science are no more valuable than music or art, and you are bound to get the same reaction as you might 100 years ago—disbelief!

One subject that seemed to be more important to Dewey was science, and here the influence of Spencer is noted. Science, for Dewey, was another name for knowledge, and it represented "the perfected outcome of learning—its consummation . . . what is known, certain . . . and what we think with rather than which we think about" is science or rationalized knowledge. Dewey considered scientific inquiry to be the best form of knowledge for society, especially one that was industrial (today it would be labeled technological), because it consisted of the "special . . . methods which the race has slowly worked out in order to conduct reflection under conditions whereby its procedures and results are tested."[4] He thus elevated the place in science in the curriculum. Similarly, in Dewey's book *How We Think,* his focus on "the method of inquiry," "rational thinking" and "problem solving," like Spencer, became synonymous with "intelligent behavior," and scientific thinking.[5] This type of cognition or processing is valued today by many educators, as it was close to a century ago with Dewey, although the term used now is *critical thinking.* (See Table 6.2.)

1. Charles W. Eliot, "The Case Against Compulsory Latin," *Atlantic* (March 1917), pp. 359–365.

2. Abraham Flexner, "Parents and School," *Atlantic* (July 1916), p. 30.

3. John Dewey, *Democracy and Education* (New York: Macmillan, 1916); Edward L. Thorndike, *Psychology of Learning,* 3 vols. (New York: Teachers College Press, 1913).

4. Dewey, *Democracy and Education,* p. 190

5. John Dewey, *How We Think* (Boston: D.C. Heath, 1910).

━━━━━━━━━━━━━━━ TABLE *6.2* ━━━━━━━━━━━━━━━

## Summary of Traditional and Contemporary Education: Philosophy and Curriculum

| Traditional Philosophy (Perennialism, Essentialism) | Contemporary Philosophy (Progressivism, Reconstructionism) |
| --- | --- |
| *Society and Education* | |
| 1. Formal education begins with the school; schools are considered the major institution of the child's education. | 1. Formal education begins with the family; the parents are considered the most important influence in the child's education. |
| 2. School transmits the common culture; individual's major responsibility is to society, performing societal roles; conformity and cooperation are important. | 2. School improves society; individual's fulfillment and development can benefit society; independence and creativity are important. |
| 3. Education is for the aims of society; it involves authority and moral restraint. | 3. Education involves varied opportunities to develop one's potential and engage in personal choices. |
| 4. Certain subjects and knowledge prepare students for democracy and freedom. | 4. Democratic experiences in school help prepare students for democracy and freedom. |
| 5. Education formulated mainly in cognitive terms; focus on academic subjects. | 5. Education concerned with social, moral, and cognitive terms; focus on the whole child. |
| 6. Values and beliefs tend to be objective and, if not absolute, then based on agreed standards or truths. | 6. Values and beliefs are subjective, based on the individual's view of the world. |
| *Knowledge and Learning* | |
| 7. Emphasis on knowledge and information. | 7. Emphasis on resolving problems and functioning in one's social environment. |
| 8. Emphasis on subjects (content). | 8. Emphasis on students (learners). |
| 9. Subject matter selected and organized by teacher. | 9. Subject matter planned by teacher and students. |
| 10. Subject matter organized in terms of simple to complex, centered on the past. | 10. Subject matter organized in terms of understanding relationships, centered on present or future. |
| 11. Unit/lesson plans organized according to topics or concepts. | 11. Unit/lesson plans organized according to problems or student interests. |
| 12. Subject matter is compartmentalized according to distinct fields, disciplines, or study areas. | 12. Subject matter is integrated; includes more than one related subject. |

continued

TABLE *6.2*
**(continued)**

| Traditional Philosophy (Perennialism, Essentialism) | Contemporary Philosophy (Progressivism, Reconstructionism) |
|---|---|
| *Instruction* | |
| 13. Textbooks and workbooks dominate; teaching and learning largely contained to classroom. | 13. Varied instructional materials; teaching and learning include community resources. |
| 14. Whole-group learning, fixed schedules, and uniform time periods. | 14. Whole, small, and individualized groups, flexible schedules, and adjustable time periods. |
| 15. Homogeneous grouping; tracking of students into special programs. | 15. Heterogeneous grouping; some tracking of students but widely differentiated programs. |
| 16. Passive involvement of students in assimilating what teacher or textbook says. | 16. Active involvement of students in seeking information that can be used or applied. |
| 17. Emphasis on uniformity of classroom experiences and instructional situations. | 17. Emphasis on variability of classroom experiences and instructional situations. |
| *Purpose and Programs* | |
| 18. Emphasis is on liberal arts and science. | 18. Mix of liberal arts, practical, and vocational subjects. |
| 19. Emphasis is on specialization or scholarship. | 19. Emphasis is general and for the layperson. |
| 20. Curriculum is prescribed; little room for electives. | 20. Curriculum based on student needs or interests; room for electives. |
| 21. Excellence and high standards; special consideration for high achievers. | 21. Equality and flexible standards; special consideration for low achievers. |

*Source:* Adapted form Allan C. Ornstein, "Philosophy as a Basis for Curriculum Decision," *High School Journal* (December–January 1991), pp. 106–107.

## Progressive Schools

Progressivism developed from pragmatic philosophy and as a protest against traditional thinking in education—namely, perennialist philosophy and the mental discipline approach to teaching and learning. The progressive movement in education was also part of the larger social and political movement of reform that characterized much of American society at the turn of the twentieth century. It grew out of the political thought of such progressives as Senator Robert LaFollette, Theodore Roosevelt, and Woodrow Wilson, as well as from the muckraker movement of the 1920s.

The educational roots of progressivism can be traced to reform writings of Horace Mann, and later to the work of John Dewey in the early twentieth century. In his most comprehensive work, *Democracy and Education,* Dewey claimed that democracy and education went hand in hand: Democratic society and democratic education are participatory and emergent, not preparatory and absolute. Dewey viewed the school as a miniature democratic society in which students could learn and practice the skills and tools necessary for democratic living.[1]

According to progressivist thought, the skills and tools of learning include problem-solving methods and scientific inquiry; in addition, classroom learning experiences should include cooperative behaviors and self-discipline, both of which are important for democratic living. Through these skills and experiences, the school can transmit the culture of society while it prepares the students for a changing world. Because reality is constantly changing, Dewey saw little need to focus on a fixed body of knowledge, as did the perennialists before him and the essentialists after him. Progressivism, instead, placed heavy emphasis on *how* to think, not *what* to think. Traditional education, with its "method of imposition form the side of the teacher and reception, [and] absorption from the side of the pupil" wrote Dewey, "may be compared to inscribing records upon a passive phonographic disc to result in giving back what has been inscribed when the proper button is pressed in recitation or examination."[2]

For Dewey and other progressivist thinkers, the curriculum was interdisciplinary in nature, and books and subject matter were part of the learning process rather than sources of ultimate knowledge. The role of the teacher was unique when operating under progressive thinking. The teacher served as a guide for students in their problem-solving and scientific projects. The teacher and students planned activities together (although Dewey later affirmed that the final authority rested with the teacher), but the teacher was to help students analyze, interpret, and evaluate data—to formulate their own conclusions.

## Warnings and Criticisms of Progressivism

The progressive movement became splintered into several different facets, including the child-centered, activity-centered, creative, and neo-Freudian groups. Dewey criticized these groups for misinterpreting and misusing his ideas. Just as he condemned the old philosophies that pursued knowledge for its own sake, he attacked those who thought knowledge had little or no value. Not only did he attack "traditional ideas as erecting silence as a virtue" but he also criticized those who sought to liberate the child from adult authority and social controls. He declared "progressive extremists"

1. Dewey, *Democracy in Education.*
2. John Dewey, "Need for a Philosophy of Education," *New Era in Home and School* (November 1934), p. 1212. Also see Dewey, *Experience and Education* (New York: Macmillan, 1938), pp. 18–22.

and "laissez-faire" philosophies to be destructive to the ideas of progressivism, and he warned that "any movement that thinks and acts in terms of an ism becomes so involved in reaction against other isms that it is unwittingly controlled by them."[1]

Dewey was not alone in his criticism of progressive educators. As criticisms mounted, Boyd Bode, another leading proponent of progressivism, warned his associates of the impending crisis in a book entitled *Progressive Education at the Cross-roads*.[2] He cautioned that "progressive education stands at the parting of the ways." The movement "nurtured the pathetic hope that it could find out how to educate by relying on such notions as interests, needs, growth and freedom." In its social and psychological approach to learning, in its "one-sided devotion to the child, it betrayed the child" and deprived him or her of appropriate subject matter. If progressivism continued its present course without changing its focus, "it would be circumvented and left behind."[3] Bode's words proved prophetic. More and more progressivists responded to the growing criticism and self-justifying theories and educational ideas that involved trivialities and errors.

Progressive education was both a movement within the broad framework of American education and a theory that urged the liberation of the child from the traditional emphasis on rote learning, lesson recitations, and textbook authority. In opposition to the conventional subject matter of the traditional curriculum, progressives experimented with alternative modes of curriculum organization—utilizing group activities, childhood experiences, problem-solving techniques, and the project method. Progressive education focused on the child as the learner rather than on the subject, emphasized activities and experiences rather than verbal and literary skills, and encouraged cooperative and group learning rather than competitive and individualized learning.

Now, all this good theory led to a great deal of discussions and counterdiscussions. On a practical level or mass scale, however, progressive education was more of an intellectual movement, popular among professors and their doctoral students, especially at Teachers College at Columbia University, and later at Ohio State University and the University of Illinois. The ideas of progressivism were expounded in committees and reports, and they generated thousands of books and articles on the subject, but little was actually done in the schools.[4] And although there were many shining examples of progressive schools—the schools in Dalton, Massachusetts; Winnetka, Illinois; Gary, Indiana; and several private schools such as the Fairhope School

1. John Dewey, *The Child and the Curriculum* (Chicago: University of Chicago Press, 1902), pp. 30–31.
2. Boyd H. Bode, *Progressive Education at the Crossroads* (New York: Newson, 1938).
3. Ibid., p. 44.
4. Perhaps the two best publications of all of them were *Schools of Tomorrow*, published in 1915 by John Dewey and his daughter Evelyn, which described many of the early programs of the movement, including Dewey's laboratory school at the University of Chicago, and the 1927 two-part series of the twenty-sixth yearbook of the National Society for the Study of Education, edited by Guy Whipple and entitled *Curriculum Making: Past and Present* and *The Foundations of Curriculum*, which brought together the leading proponents of the day to describe the ideas and practices of progressive education.

in Alabama, Francis Parker School in Chicago, and the Lincoln and Pratt schools in New York City—by and large, most schools remained highly regimented, drill oriented, teacher centered, and textbook centered. It remained that way because it was easier to teach that way.

## The Decline and Demise of Progressivism

Although the progressive movement in education encompassed many different theories and practices, it was united in its opposition to certain traditional school practices: (1) the authoritarian teacher, (2) excessive reliance on textbook methods, (3) memorization of factual data and techniques by drill, (4) static aims and materials that reject the notion of a changing world, (5) use of fear or corporal punishment as a form of discipline, and (6) attempts to isolate education from child experiences and social reality. However, Cremin points out that the movement's inability to outline a uniform theory of the purpose of schooling, or even to establish a set of principles, contributed to its downfall.[1]

Another factor related to its demise is that progressive education depended on highly competent teachers who could (1) implement the theories of Frobel and Pestalozzi; (2) diagnose the needs and interests of children; (3) consider the whole child, not just cognition; (4) incorporate many methods, materials, and activities into the daily lesson; (5) encourage students to explore, inquire, and problem solve—to learn on their own; and (6) connect with their students in a very special way—a humanistic and personal level. I could go on and provide more theory about what teachers were supposed to accomplish; sadly, there are more average and less-than-average teachers than highly proficient or above-average teachers. There is a statistical fact, evidenced by the bell curve. The inference is, there were insufficient members of highly competent and caring teachers to successfully implement progressivism in the schools.

Although progressive education failed to become the mainstream ideology in public schools, it did leave its mark. Junior high schools came into existence in many parts of the country; curricula were broadened to include courses of vocational, commercial, and general education; extracurricular activities were expanded; and greater emphasis was placed on student participation in their learning activities. The progressive education movement reached its high point during the years prior to World War II, when membership in the Progressive Education Association reached a peak of 10,000 members.[2]

## Essentialist Philosophy and Priorities

During the post–World War II era of the Cold War and Soviet *Sputnik* flight, the ideas and practices of progressive educators increasingly became a target of criticism, and the theories of John Dewey and his colleagues at Columbia University (where he had

1. Lawrence A. Cremin, *The Transformation of the School* (New York: Knopf, 1961).
2. Ibid.

moved from the University of Chicago) were blamed for most of the ills of American education. Progressive schools were pillared as "crime breeders," "time wasters," and "playhouses," and magazine articles with titles such as "Lollypops vs. Learning" and "Treason in the Textbooks" became the order of the day.[1] Essentialist critics claimed there was too much emphasis on psychological theories, the whole child, and general education at the expense of intellectual rigor. McCarthyism soon reared its ugly head and any person or group perceived as too progressive or liberal became suspect; school superintendents from Pasadena to Piscataway perceived as "pink" were ousted and replaced.[2]

## Emphasis on Academics

After World War II, during the era of the Cold War and the (Soviet) *Sputnik* flight in 1957, American education became a target for criticism. One must understand that the world in this period was perceived in terms of two giant blocks on the verge of war, with the potential for nuclear disaster. Citizens of both power blocks saw the rest of the world as friend or foe or neutral. With *Sputnik,* however, national pride was shattered, and there was the prospect of being the second-rate of the two powers. Our oceans no longer protected us, and there was the threat that our skies were penetrable. Then there was the Korean War in the 1950s, uneasiness with Mao's Red China, Khruschev banging his shoe at the United Nations and yelling in front of the television cameras that Russia would bury us, then Castro's Cuba and the Khruschev-Kennedy missile crises.

Society pressed the schools to respond to our national concerns; in fact, some people called it a crisis. The critics claimed there was too much emphasis on the "whole child" and "life adjustment courses" at the expense of critical thinking and academic rigor. In lieu of progressive pedagogy, play time at the elementary school level, and a general or broad education at the secondary level that stressed the whole child, the need was to return to the basics (or three Rs) at the elementary level and *essential* subject matter at the secondary level:[3] English, history, math, science, and foreign language, especially the latter three subjects. The need was to turn out sufficient scientists and mathematicians, and to push our bright students in order to beat the Soviets.

This would become the last hurrah in American society where the idea of *merit* was fully accepted and promoted as a national goal, and when *testing* and *tracking*

1. O. K. Armstrong, "Treason in the Textbooks," *American Legion Magazine* (September 1940), pp. 8–9ff; Ann L. Crockett, "Lollypops vs. Learning," *Saturday Evening Post* (March 16, 1940), pp. 105–106.
2. The most controversial book on the subject of progressive school superintendents forced out by citizen groups was written by David Hulburd, *This Happened in Pasadena,* written in 1951 about Superintendent William Goslin who was also the president of the American Association of School Administrators.
3. William Bagley and Issac Kandel, while at Columbia University in the 1930s, coined the term *essentialism* to voice their opposition to their progressive colleagues who were now dominating intellectual thought among educators.

of students would be considered the norm without question. No excuses would be accepted under the guise of equality or diversity, test bias or discrimination, and/or unequal treatment of students or programs. To argue, today, for anyone of these three ideas—merit, testing and tracking—is to risk being labeled a racist or elitist, and is criticized for reducing the options and opportunities of minorities. With the exception of Castro, all the major actors of the era are dead. Obviously, times have changed, but those tendencies of the times are worth reflecting on: To show the ebb and flow between and schools and society, and how the curriculum is shaped by the changing goals of a nation.

Powerful forces, such as Arthur Bestor, called for "a return to academic essentials and educational meritocracy." He declared that "concern with the personal problems of adolescents had grown so excessive as to push into the background what should be the schools central concern, the intellectual development of its students."[1] The title of his books *Educational Wastelands* (1953) and *The Restoration of Learning* (1956) conveyed the message of the day.[2] In *Education and Freedom*, Admiral Hyman Rickover questioned why Johnny could not read while Ivan could. For purposes of national interest, he demanded a "deemphasis of life-adjustment schools and progressive educationalists," and a return to the basics and "a beefing up of our science and mathematics courses."[3] At the same time, he compared American and European schools and concluded, "the [American] student must be made to work hard," at his or her studies, and "nothing can really make it fun."[4]

## Tough Subjects, Testing, and Tracking

Werner von Braun, the German-educated missile expert, offered testimony before a U.S. Senate Committee in 1958, urging the adoption of the European system of education that emphasized academic excellence. Testifying before the same committee on the same day, Lee DuBridge, then president of the California Institute of Technology, recommended that curriculum areas of science and mathematics be "singled out for federal support."[5] DuBridge urged schools to recognize, encourage, and provide special

1. Arthur Bestor, *The Restoration of Learning*, (New York; Knopf, 1956), p. 120.

2. Many other books of the same tone were written by other authors during this period—from mild criticism of progressive schooling such as Robert Hutchins, *The Conflict in Education* (1953) to harsh criticism, Albert Lynd, *Quakery in the Public Schools* (1953), Max Rafferty, *Suffer Little Children* (1957), and Mortimer Smith *And Madly Teach* (1949) and *The Diminished Mind* (1954). Bestor (professor of history at the University of Illinois) and Admiral Rickover (in charge of the first atomic submarine) had the most telling influence, that the chief purpose of education was intellectual; anything else led to "educational subversion." Life-adjustment courses and emphasis on self-esteem was tantamount to educational quakery and even losing the Cold War.

3. Hyman G. Rickover, *Education and Freedom* (New York: E. P. Dutton, 1959), p. 190.

4. Hyman G. Rickover, "European v. American Secondary Schools," *Phi Delta Kappan* (November 1958), p. 61.

5. Ornstein and Hunkins, *Curriculum: Foundations, Principles and Issues;* Daniel Tanner, *Secondary Education* (New York: Macmillan, 1971).

programs for students who are "unusually gifted and ambitious." The senators did not ask von Braun or DuBridge what schools or society should do with the intellectually less-able student. Fortunately for students of average skills, a relatively more moderate position, albeit one that still emphasized the gifted and intelligent student, was put forth at this time by several policymakers and educators alike.

A number of policy statements focused on academically bright students and high-order thinking during this period, although there was concern for every child, whatever his capabilities, as well as emphasis on the three Rs. For example, the White House Conference on Education in 1955 stressed the theme of academic quality and proposed that "education programs [must] fully exercise and develop the abilities of especially bright students."[1] Five years later, the President's Commission on National Goals gave top priority to science, mathematics, and foreign languages and called for "a testing program beginning in grade one if not before . . . and ability grouping from the earliest years of school. Every effort [was to be] made in and out of school to provide enrichment for the gifted student."[2] And in a report published on 1961 by the Education Policies Commission, the central aim "of all educational purposes—the common thread of education—[was defined as] the development of the ability to think."[3] Indeed, these commission reports, highlighting tough subjects and testing, would become the forerunner of the standards movement in education today.

One channel for serving able and motivated youth was the Advanced Placement of the College Entrance Examination Board. Testing was considered an important and valid yardstick for measuring performance and sorting capable from less capable students, then tracking them into programs according to their ability. The test industry was booming (and tracking was the uncontested norm), and by the mid-1950s, the College Board was offering advanced placement examinations to high school students for college credit in 12 subjects, mostly in math and science. Numerous advantages for these tests were cited, including the fact that these tests paid "attention to superior ability and stimulate[d] outstanding high school teachers to keep abreast of college requirements . . . and to keep after the abler students who can meet them."[4]

The two most influential educators of the period, John Gardner and James Conant, reflected the sentiments of the times. John Gardner, the president of the Carnegie Corporation (later to become the Secretary of Health, Education and Welfare, and then the founder of the public-interest lobby Common Cause), expressed the crucial need of the day in his 1956 Annual Report:

> It is not just technologists and scientists that we need, though they rank high in priority. We desperately need our gifted teachers, our professional men [and women],

1. *Proceedings, White House Conference on Education* (Washington, DC: U.S. Government Printing Office, 1955), pp. 5, 12.

2. *Goals for Americans, the President's Commission on National Goals* (Englewood Cliffs, NJ: Prentice-Hall, 1960), p. 85.

3. Educational Policies Commission, *The Central Purpose of American Education* (Washington, DC: National Education Association, 1961), p. 12.

4. *Advanced Placement Program* (New York: College Entrance Examination Board, 1956).

our scholars, our critics, our seers. The immensely increased demand for educated talent has placed a wholly new emphasis upon the role of colleges and universities in our life. Virtually the total future leadership of our society . . . is today being channeled through the colleges and universities. . . . [Concern for the advancement of society and] full use of human capacities will produce intensive efforts to salvage the able youngsters who are now lost to higher education.[1]

In Gardner's view, the welfare of society, the promotion of democracy, the emphasis on academic performance, and the funneling of bright students into colleges were all related; it was not until 20 years later in another publication, *Excellence: Can We Be Equal Too?*, did he soften his view and try to balance excellence with equality. For the Cold War period, however, he was compelled to stress the need for improvement of society, through nurturing gifted and talented students and expanding the role of institutions of higher learning by what he called, in his report, "the Great Talent Hunt."[2]

In 1953, as chairman of the Educational Policies Commission, Conant (then President of Harvard University) endorsed a progressive policy document that urged a student-centered, whole-child approach to learning. By 1959, Conant's vision was still to "provide a good general education for all the pupils," but there was also an emphasis now "on educating adequately those with a talent for handling advanced subjects."[3] In his famous study of the American high school, he wrote, "If the fifty-five schools I have visited, all of which have a good reputation, are at all representative of American public high schools, I think one general criticism would be in order: The academically talented student, as a rule, is not being sufficiently challenged, does not work hard enough, and his program of academic subjects is not of sufficient range."[4]

In the midst of great criticism toward schools, school people, and especially progressive theorists, Conant came to the defense of the educational establishment and saw little need for radically changing schools. Conant's influential book on the American high school was a blueprint for moderate reform: Tighten a few screws and a knock a few nails in place, but there is no need for major demolition or surgery. Conant merely called for upgrading the curriculum, especially mathematics, science, and foreign languages (not Latin or Greek but modern foreign languages); tightening standards and grades; pushing students to their maximum academic potential; grouping students according to their abilities; and putting more emphasis on educating gifted (top 3 percent of the student population) and talented students (top 20 percent), since they had the most potential to contribute to the national effort to halt the spread of world communism and safeguard American skies.

Many of Conant's ideas would be considered today as elitist and designed to discriminate against "average," "slow," and "low-achieving" students. Although

1. John W. Gardner, "The Great Talent Hunt," in *The Annual Report for the Fiscal Year Ended September 30, 1956* (New York: Carnegie Corporation, 1956), pp. 12, 20.
2. Ibid.
3. James B. Conant, *The American High School Today* (New York: McGraw-Hill, 1959), p. 15.
4. Ibid., p. 40.

Conant's vision was "to provide a good general education for all pupils." His emphasis on gifted and talented students, at best, might be considered a return to the mental discipline approach of the turn of the century; at worst, it would be seen as a subtle form of racism that would deemphasize the need for educating students who need to be "academically challenged" or who are "culturally different" (poor and minority students).

## Structure and Disciplined Knowledge

Reflecting the demand for academic excellence, essentialist educators of the 1950s and mid-1960s formulated the concept of teaching the structure of a discipline— originally designed to improve the science and math curricula so as to produce sufficient scientists, engineers, and technicians for the Cold War. *Structure* was defined as including the broad principles, concepts, and rules that define and limit a subject and control the methods of inquiry. By emphasizing structure, relationships would become clear, and teachers and learners would understand how elementary knowledge was related to advanced knowledge, how to reconstruct meaning within a subject area, and how to furnish the means for advancing new knowledge in the subject. Students were to be encouraged to see the structure of each subject area—what Joseph Schwab called the "substantive structure" and what Phillip Phenix called the "realms of meaning," or what I would call the logic and unifying ideas of a subject.

In stressing the cognitive aspects of learning and advanced knowledge, the advocates of structure tended to dismiss rote learning and memorization of information as well as the social and psychological needs of the learner. Wrote Phenix, "There is no place in the curriculum for ideas, which are regarded as suitable for teaching because of the supposed nature, needs, and interests of the learner, but which do not belong with the regular structure of the disciplines."[1]

By a discipline, the essentialist advocates meant a true body of knowledge, organized into a whole, and providing a basis for thinking in the content area and for generating new knowledge—new information, new ideas, and new principles and theories. Each discipline had its separate boundaries or content areas and its own way of generating research. This meant that the progressive ideas of interdisciplinary subjects or broad field subjects (such as social studies, language arts, general science, or civics) were considered irrelevant, watered down, and second rate. The idea was to train students to become little scholars in the various disciplines, to think like scientists or mathematicians, like historians or musicians, and later in college to train them to become real scholars in their respective disciplines.

Many of the early ideas of structure and disciplined knowledge were originally outlined in Jerome Bruner's classic book, *The Process of Education*. The very title suggests that education—more precisely, learning—should emphasize process or procedural knowledge, not specific content or tiny pieces of information. Bruner stated that

---

1. Philip A. Phenix, "The Disciplines as Curriculum Content," in A. Harry Passow, ed. *Curriculum Crossroads* (New York: Teachers College Press, 1962), p. 64. Also see Chapter 3 for an additional discussion of Bruner and the concept of structure.

the "curriculum of a subject should be determined by . . . underlying principles that give structure to that subject."[1] In short, the emphasis on structure and/or process closely resembled old-fashioned analysis and problem solving, combined with some academic rigor. Bruner pushed the boundaries of teaching and learning one step further in his emphasis on intuitive thinking, and it might be also argued he set the stage for present-day advocates of critical thinking. He maintained that the goal of learning was to *learn how to learn*—to utilize acquired knowledge to further new knowledge. As part of intuitive thinking, taking educated guesses was to be encouraged, as was hypothesizing and asking "what-if" questions. This thinking process was and still is similar to what scientists, mathematicians, and social science researchers do when they try to advance knowledge in their respective fields. Indeed, there is an inference of high-level thinking, and teaching and learning geared for the bright or talented student.

Once educators began to focus on knowledge-based, outcome-based, and standard-based education, once they became concerned with low-achieving students and with students who lack basic cognitive skills, it's easy to understand why the structure of disciplines, as a teaching strategy and curriculum design, lost its wide acceptance and reform aura. Today, few, if any, preservice teachers are exposed to this pedagogy and curriculum—that is, this *process of education*. The benchmarks for academic excellence have been lowered; the focus is on standards, which often turns into basic skills and a knowledge-based pedagogy and curriculum.

## Curriculum Reform

A most attractive notion of the disciplines approach expounded by Bruner was that "any subject can be taught in some effectively honest form to any child at any stage of development."[2] For example, the first-grade teacher can ask her students to rub their hands together and feel the heat produced," thus introducing a concept in physics (mechanical energy transforming to heat energy) that is commonly delayed until students have reached the eleventh or twelfth grade. In the same context, foreign language courses, which, prior to *Sputnik,* were usually introduced in the eighth or ninth grade, have now become part of the elementary school curriculum.

From their discussion at Woods Hole, Massachusetts, Bruner and his panel—comprised of scientists and scholars—formulated a host of national curriculum projects that centered on math and science. These included the Biological Science Curriculum Study (BSCS), the Chemical Education Material Study (CEMS), the Physical Science Study Committee (PSSC), and the School Mathematics Study Group (SMSG). The new wave of curriculum reform emphasized high-level subject matter and high-order thinking rather than students' needs, interests, and social problems.[3]

Most of the leaders of this movement made sweeping claims for the superiority of the new curriculum—what was later to be the basis for the "new science" and the

1. Jerome S. Bruner, *The Process of Education* (Cambridge, MA: Harvard University Press, 1959), p. 8.
2. Ibid., p 33.
3. Ornstein and Hunkins, *Curriculum: Foundations, Principles, and Issues.*

"new math." These ideas about new science and math filtered down to the elementary schools, and is still in vogue in many parts of the country. The general idea is to expose children at an early age to science and math concepts, rather than postpone them until junior high or high school. Similarly, the focus on gifted and talented students, part of the reform movement of the post-*Sputnik* period, led to an increase in advanced placement (AP) courses. Another increase in AP courses followed as an aftermath of the 1983 report, *A Nation at Risk,* which brought national attention to the need for educational excellence and higher academic standards for all students. (In 1982, 1.6 percent of high school graduates had taken AP calculus, 3 percent AP chemistry, and 1.2 percent AP physics. By 1998, the percents were 6.7, 4.7, and 3.0, respectively.[1])

The subject matter was reconstructed around disciplines with special methods of inquiry (that is, major principles and concepts). Science and mathematics—and, later, modern foreign languages—came to represent the highest disciplinary value, first evidenced by Bruner and the Woods Hole conference, and then by Conant's blueprint for the reform of the American high school. It was all intended to beef up the curriculum, especially at the secondary school level. The major legislation, called the National Defense Education Act (NDEA) in 1958, singled out science, mathematics, and modern foreign languages. (It was construed as a way of steering youth into these three academic fields and into college if they had the ability.) The focus on certain tough subjects (which suggested a hierarchy of importance) and bright students was often couched in terms of a free people surviving in a world in which communism was spreading and in which the American skies were at risk. The words sounded very similar to those associated with *A Nation at Risk,* 20 years later, which exhibited concerns that American manufacturing, economy, and standard of living were at risk because of economic competition from abroad. In both cases—*Sputnik* and *A Nation at Risk,* the threat was perceived on an international level—in the 1950s on a military basis, in the 1980s on an economic basis.

Most important, large sums of money for beefing up the curriculum were readily available for the first time from both the government and foundation sources. During the aftermath of *Sputnik,* William Van Til, the pipe-smoking Hoosier who was now professor and chair at New York University, wrote, "The end result was that both national interest and available funds [in education] coincided. The scholars had a genuine opportunity to reconstruct the content of their separate subjects."[2] This was particularly true at the secondary level.

1. *Digest of Education Statistics 2000* (Washington, DC: U.S. Government Printing Office, 2001), Table 140, p. 156.
2. William Van Til, "In a Climate of Change," in R. R. Leeper, ed., *Role of Supervisor and Curriculum Director in a Climate of Change, 1965 Yearbook* (Washington, DC: Association for Supervision and Curriculum Development, 1965), p. 16.
Van Til had published the best-selling foundations text, *Education as a Beginning,* while I was a doctoral student at NYU from 1967 to 1970. In 1976, I published *Foundations of Education,* which was later to go through eight editions (as of 2003) and become the number-one foundations text in terms of sales—about ¾ million sold in 27 years. Here, a tribute is made to Virgil Clift, Hilda Grobman, and Bill Van Til, who I studied with at NYU.

The Lessons of Reform   To many leaders of this period, it was clear that the way to proceed and reconstruct subject matter was to call together the scientific community and university scholars who most intimately knew the particular subjects, along with some curriculum specialists who might help with regard to planning and pedagogy. The problem is, the teachers were completely shut out of this reform movement; in fact, many of the new programs and materials were developed with the idea of being "teacher proof," which meant that the only thing teachers had to do was simply hand out the new materials and the students would learn. The so-called reformers and scholars overtly and covertly exhibited a condescending and biased attitude toward practitioners—toward the very people who were expected to implement the new curriculum. In short, the reformers wrote the teachers out of the education process, considered them as "objects" of reform, and often labeled them as "targets" instead of partners. The result was that teachers rejected many of the ideas of change and innovation during this period.

This biased attitude toward teachers was (and still is to a large extent) compounded by the teachers' daily routine, which provides little opportunity for interaction and communication with colleagues. According to John Goodlad, isolation results partly from the school's organization into self-contained classrooms and partly form teaching schedules that provide few collegial movements.[1] The countermeasure is for teachers to be willing to work after-school hours. However, where teacher unions prevail, especially in big cities, there is a tendency to reject required meetings after school, except for one or two sessions per month for staff development.

Seymour Sarason has also commented on the isolation of teachers in the school organization and on how the isolation negatively impacts on teacher attitudes and the notion of change. He contends that the reality of the school has made teachers feel that professionally they are on their own. It is their responsibility, and theirs alone, to solve their own problems.[2] Reformers and scholars (most of them who have never taught in the schools) don't really know what it is like to teach and have little information about what goes on in other classrooms and schools.

This posture causes many teachers to view change introduced into the program from outside the school as interference and, even worse, as counterproductive to teaching and learning. Viewing their struggles as solitary, teachers often develop a psychological loneliness and a hostility to administrators and outside change agents who seem insensitive to the teachers' plight. This feeling of isolation and hostility is more pervasive in the big cities where the problems of teaching and learning are more difficult—often boiling down to classroom management and basic reading problems—and where there is a certain amount of demoralization and disconnected behavior among people.

Only recently has the educational literature analyzed that much of what goes on in an organization is governed by a culture, including a way of behaving and surviving.

1. John I. Goodlad, *The Dynamics of Educational Change* (New York: McGraw Hill, 1975); Goodlad, *Educational Renewal* (San Francisco: Jossey-Bass, 1998).

2. Seymour Sarason, *The Culture of the School and the Problem of Change*, 2nd ed. (Boston: Allyn and Bacon, 1981); Sarason, *The Predictable Failure of Educational Reform* (San Francisco: Jossey-Bass, 1993).

The school culture is not opposed to change or innovation; indeed, schools have evolved considerably in policies, programs, and functions and have responded to the changing demands of society.[1] But schools also have survival mechanisms or what some old-time social scientists call *maintenance and stability* functions, and these survival mechanisms are self-reinforcing and more established than change mechanisms.[2] The culture of school establishes certain restrictions and regularities on teachers and administrators; to effect reform, reformers cannot interfere with or violate the established norms and behaviors of the organizational. This is basic organizational theory that reformers and change agents outside schools sometimes forget. See Teaching Tips 6.1.

Curriculum Fizzle   The quest for reform and proliferation of special projects in math and science were followed by other projects in the social sciences and humanities, planned and designed to embrace the discipline approach. But the search for structure in English, history, music, foreign language, and other subjects proved unattainable. Even in science and mathematics, the idea of a disciplinary structure eventually waned.

The reformers, of course, would never admit that part of the demise of the disciplinary approach was linked to the fact that teachers did not actively participate in any phase of curriculum development and eventually closed ranks against these reform packages. Educators have come to learn, sometimes the hard way, that for change to be effective, teachers must be committed to it and they must see that it has professional value to them. Teachers often judge change by how it will address the immediate needs they encounter in their daily work, and not by some theoretical value or reform slogan. To a large extent, successful change is more a function of people and organizations than of technology or even money.[3]

Another reason for the failure of the disciplinary approach was that it focused on bright and talented students, at the expense of slow, immigrant, and/or disadvantaged students who needed help in basic skills and content. In an effort to beat the Soviets, and subsequently beef up the curriculum, educators failed to grasp the fact that they were earmarking most of the curriculum reform ideas to the top 20 or 25 percent of the student population. Once they discovered poor and minority students, and subsequently a large number of students deficient in basic skills, the purposes and programs of schooling dramatically shifted.

The next challenge was the limited number of teachers sufficiently prepared in their subject or discipline who could grasp and properly use pedagogy related to teaching about the structure of their respective subjects. Such teaching methods called for in-depth knowledge of their own fields of study, and the ability to translate sophisticated principles and concepts into relationships for their students to grasp. This

1.  Carl D. Glickman, *Renewing America's Schools: A Guide for School Based Action* (San Francisco: Jossey-Bass, 1998); Robert G. Owens, *Organizational Behavior in Education*, 6th ed. (Boston: Allyn and Bacon, 1998).

2.  Daniel Katz and Robert L. Kahn, *The Social Psychology of Organizations* (New York: John Wiley, 1966); James G. March and Herbert A. Simon, *Organizations* (New York: John Wiley, 1958).

3.  Warren Bennis, *Changing Organizations* (New York: McGraw-Hill, 1966); James M. Kouzes and Barry Z. Posner, *Credibility: How Leaders Gain and Lose It* (San Francisco: Jossey-Bass, 1993).

# *Teaching Tips* 6.1

## Planning the Curriculum

1. *Organize committee.* The curriculum committee may be organized by subject, grade, school, or district.
2. *Assess needs.* Focus on needs of students, occasionally on teachers. Survey parents and teachers to establish needs. Consider changes taking place within society.
3. *Identify school problems.* Identify three or four problems that influence teaching and learning, and in turn, affect curriculum.
4. *Invite specialists.* Five specialists are worth considering: subject consultants, learning theorists, test specialists, technical (computer) experts, and community representatives. Specialists should help in identifying needs and schools problems, as well as in establishing goals, objectives, and/or standards.
5. *Review accepted goals, objectives, and standards.* Student needs and school problems influence the goals, objectives, and/or standards. Evaluate the statements of other school districts, state departments of education, and professional organizations for the purpose of improving your goals, objectives, or standards.
6. *Review curriculum philosophy.* The committee should consider the prevailing school philosophy and the extent to which the school wishes to emphasize subjects, students, and learning domains: cognitive, affective, psychomotor, moral, etc.
7. *Review content.* Content for all subjects and grades needs to be periodically validated (or questioned), pruned, and updated. Content can be discussed in terms of knowledge, concepts, ideas, and values the committee considers worthwhile to stress.
8. *Align curriculum.* Focus on content—how it can be better aligned to the school goals, objectives, and standards—as well as curriculum philosophy.
9. *Consider implementation process.* Teachers and supervisors must consider how to adapt and better implement curriculum. Consider ways of improving scheduling, team teaching, instructional materials, methods and media, supervision, and staff development.
10. *Consider curriculum evaluation.* This refers to whether the planning and implementation process has produced the desired program effects—that is, if the teachers or school have properly addressed the goals, objectives, and standards. Does the program work? How can it be improved?

assumed a certain amount of expertise both in subject knowledge and in pedagogical knowledge that most teachers did not possess (and still do not). They may possess one part, but not both parts, of this teaching equation.

Some 30 years later, a whole cottage industry related to teacher preparation, based around *subject* knowledge and *pedagogical* knowledge, was to take shape and be spearheaded by Lee Schulman and his former doctoral students who studied with him at Stanford University.[1] In short, Schulman pointed out the need to prepare teachers in

---

1. Lee S. Schulman, "Knowledge and Teaching: Foundations of the New Reform," *Harvard Educational Review* (February 1987), pp. 1–22; Schulman, "Ways of Seeing, Ways of Knowing: Ways of Teaching, Ways of Learning About Teaching," *Journal of Curriculum Studies* (September–October 1991), pp. 393–396.

content or "deep" knowledge (what Bruner and Phenix called "structure"), as well as teaching strategies or "process" (what Bruner and Phenix called "procedural knowledge"), which include the most useful forms of representing and communicating content and how students best learn the content of the subject. Today, the demand for teachers is critical, and in some states, such as New York and California, policymakers are willing to throw student teachers and uncertified teachers into the classroom to fill body counts. Thus, it is ludicrous to expect many teachers to be well prepared in their subject area and related pedagogy.

The fourth reason for the failure of the discipline movement in curriculum and teaching was a matter of timing. A new reform movement was shaping up on the American social and educational landscape: The fermenting seeds of the coming War on Poverty and civil rights movement, and the growing awareness of America's poor and minority students.

## Reconstructionism: The Warning Bell Is Sounded

The 1960s and early 1970s ushered in a period in which the social conscience of America burst forth, coinciding with concerns over poverty, racial discrimination, and equal educational opportunity. New aims and educational priorities surfaced to meet the climate of change. With the majority of students not going on to college and with a large percentage of students dropping out of school or graduating as functional illiterates, serious problems could be anticipated if our aims and priorities continued to be narrowly directed at our most able students. The shift to the problems of poor and disadvantaged students continued to accelerate until this school population became the number-one concern in education.

Exemplifying the change was Michael Harrington's small book, *The Other America;* it had a major impact on John Kennedy's social thinking and helped spark the War on Poverty.[1] Subsequently, billions of dollars in federal programs were spent on educating the disadvantaged, along with funding for social and community programs to help improve or reconstruct society. A much-needed popularization of governmental and scholarly reports, Harrington's book jolted many policymakers and moved educators to take a hard look at the relationship between poverty, education, and social policy.

Harrington estimated that between 40 and 50 million Americans lived in poverty (one-quarter of the population). In this category he put the needy, the aged, and the sick; the workers rendered useless by technology; the workers exempt from minimum wage protection; the uprooted migrant farm worker; the ghetto dweller who is the victim of racial discrimination; the uneducated youth; and other economic outcasts. Not since Dickens had anyone captured so vividly the problems and lifestyles of the poor—but this time the poor were Americans. Moreover, Harrington argued that poverty in America is no longer "cyclical"—that is, it is no longer temporary, as in the Depression—rather, it was becoming "structural"—meaning there were few chances to escape from it and it was becoming an inherited curse for part of the young

1. Michael Harrington, *The Other America* (Baltimore: Penguin Books, 1963).

generation. He spoke of "an enormous concentration of young people, who if they do not receive immediate help, may well be the source of a kind of heredity poverty new to America."[1]

Although the number of poor was challenged by numerous authorities and councils—including the government, which put the figure of poverty in America at between 30 and 35 million—Harrington's point was that a piecemeal, individual case approach could not solve the problem; massive funds and a full-scale program were needed. The poverty group was not limited to blacks; it also included poor whites—in fact, as much as 70 percent of the poor were white, he contended. Because they were white, they had low visibility; nobody paid much attention to them.

Harrington blamed the system for creating and maintaining poverty; America's affluent industrial society victimized the poor. He struck at the American conscience by declaring that for the first time society had the material ability to end poverty but lacked the will to do it. And so, President Kennedy's War on Poverty, and later President Johnson's Great Society, were meant to be the answers.

## The Roots of Inequality

Given a history of Christian ethics and duty ("to get rich by honorable methods," "to use money to relieve the poor and advance God's word"),[2] coupled with a touch of secular morality and a dose of reality, the wealthy have always understood that is serves their interests to provide philanthropy and charity to the less fortunate. These ideas are rooted in religious doctrines of puritan theology prior to the Revolution and in the patrician thinking of wealthy landowners during the Revolutionary period.

The concept is also evident in the doctrine of stewardship and civic responsibility of the rich and powerful businessperson for so-called good and noble reasons. The Rockefellers, Carnegies, and Vanderbilts preached both the natural law of economics, which gave them the right to crush their competition, and the guarantor of community well-being—giving back to the community and helping the poor. It is also rooted in the social and economic doctrines of Herbert Spencer and the biological doctrines of Charles Darwin, who reinforced this type of corporate wealth and stewardship in the late nineteenth century.

The inequality between rich and poor has always been justified in American society, first by the puritan doctrine of Henry Beecher that hard work and wealth come with sweat, and later by the nineteenth-century gospel: "God has intended the great to be great and the little to be little. The [working] man who is not fit to live on bread and water is not fit to live."[3] The difference in wealth between rich and poor is reflected and condoned by America's belief in liberty and the pursuit of happiness. It is reflected in the inalienable rights of the Declaration of Independence; in the laws of nature; in the natural rights of people (to acquire property); in Ben Franklin's quaint

1. Ibid., p. 183.
2. David S. Gregory, *Christian Ethics* (Philadelphia, 1875), p. 244.
3. Henry Ward Beecher, quoted in *New York Times* (July 30, 1837), cited in Paxton Hibben, *Henry Ward Beecher: An American Portrait* (New York: Doran Publishers, 1927), p. 326.

philosophy of self-improvement and expressions in *Poor Richard's Almanac;* in the nineteenth-century writings of Harvard professor Irving Babbit and Yale professor William Graham Sumner; in Ralph Waldo Emerson's concept of individualism; in Herman Melville's distrust of democracy; in Margaret Fuller's notion of "genius thriving without training"; in economic laws of competition and survival of the fittest espoused by John Stuart Mill (*Political Economy,* 1844), John Bates Clark (*The Philosophy of Wealth,* 1886), and Herbert Spencer (*Essays,* 1892); in the cult of the self-made man (biographies of several millionaires who made the climb from rags to riches); and in the stew of platitudes and ill-conceived bigotry of Henry Ford, mentioned on a regular basis in his own newspaper, *The Dearborn Independent;* and in the virtues of greed and a capitalist class advanced by Ayn Rand.

In education, these social-class distinctions have been evidenced by (1) Ben Franklin's rationale for vocational training; (2) the McGuffey readers, reflecting Protestant and business virtues of hard work and getting ahead through one's efforts; (3) Commissioner of Education William Harris's speeches and texts about the principles of self-help, competition, capitalism, and sanctity of private property, and his criticism of socialism which restricted individual merit; (4) the prevailing perennialist philosophy of hard work, mental discipline, and the cultivation of the intellect as the dominant thinking of education from the colonial period to the turn of the twentieth century (rooted in Aristotle's behalf that "learning is no amusement, but is accompanied with pain"); and (5) the hereditarian views of the two most eminent psychologists of the period—G. Stanley Hall and Edward L. Thorndike.

Social scientists such as Clark and Spencer, social and religious preachers such as Beecher and Sumner, and "robber barons" such as Rockefeller and Ford all had a disdain toward the poor and working-class population. The poor were the underclass because they lacked the brain power (mental discipline) or muscle power (diligence and sweat). The masses were flawed in terms of religious spirit, Protestant work ethic, moral upbringing, and/or mental capacity.

The kingdom of God, highlighted by 200 years of American religious doctrine, was not merely in heaven, but it also could be realized by hard work on earth; this puritan and Protestant ethic was transformed to the doctrines of American industrialism and capitalism. Any interference with natural laws, economic competition, supply and demand, and concessions to socialism or the rights of labor would reduce social and economic progress and increase inefficiency. In the words of Merle Curti, the progressive historian who summed up American social thinking during the 19th and early 20th centuries, deviation from this doctrine would lead to "depression, unemployment, falling prices, and other artificially induced ills."[1]

It would take the utopian and romantic thinkers of Edward Bellamy in *Looking Backward* (1887); the analysis of ruthlessness in big business by Henry Lloyd in *Wealth Against Commonwealth* (1894); the exposé of public and business corruption by Lord Bryce, in *American Commonwealth* (1888); the fervor of progressivism and muckracking articles in *Collier's, McClures,* and *LaFollette Weekly,* to name a few, and newspaper writers such as Joseph Pulitzer and William Randolph Hearst who wrote

---

1. Merle Curti, *The Growth of American Thought,* 2nd ed. (New York: Harper & Bros., 1951), p. 638.

for the masses; and the work of Louis Brandeis and Oliver Wendell Holmes to curb big business and provide safeguards to ensure that the economically weak would not be crushed. By the turn of the twentieth century, a progressive philosophy and social legislation highlighted by the Teddy Roosevelt and Wilson administrations increased the powers of the national government at the expense of big business. In fact, Roosevelt maintained that democracy would be doomed without government intervention to protect the "little fellow" from the excesses of the rich and powerful. At the same time, educational progressivism toppled the philosophy of perennialism, largely due to the writings of John Dewey, George Counts, William Kilpatrick, and Harold Rugg.

But today, as we listen to the ideas of Milton Friedman's free market system being espoused by contemporary economists, D'Sousa's idea of the natural goodness of capitalists and capitalism, the hereditarian ideas of Herrnstein and Murray in *The Bell Curve* (which connect social and economic position with genetic inheritance), and the Republican *laissez-faire* view of economics that limits government regulation in banking and business sectors, we sense that the applecart in economic inequality was never turned over. Even worse is the Bush tax plan, which has repealed the inheritance tax and thus enriches America's millionaires and billionaires while hurting 95 percent of the families who struggle daily to make ends meet. Warren Buffett, one of the world's wealthiest Americans, likens it to "choosing the 2020 Olympic team by picking the eldest sons [and daughters] of the gold-medal winners in the 2000 Olympics."[1]

Although we have come closer than any other nation in promoting the idea of meritocracy and social mobility, we are still at the mercy of big-business interests. We also have an increasing aristocracy of wealth, which means it is not heredity based on intelligence but on the possession of resources (including the right to attend mom's or dad's alma mater) being passed down from one generation to the next.[2] Actually, the wealthy and business community have always put the masses in their place. There is no point in citing facts or appealing to a sense of justice or morality; the system is rigged by the rich and powerful all over the world to keep the *herd* (Hamilton's word) at the bottom of the heap. It's been going on since the slaves rolled the stones uphill to build the pharaoh's pyramids. This unpleasant reality is developed in the poetry of T. S. Elliot, who combined his own insights with a Christian perspective. All the declared values of human life were illusory, for the poet, but God so loved the world that he was willing to give up his only Son for the world's redemption. Elliot's disgust with humans and the world is reflected as a theme in his famous poem, *The Wasteland*.[3]

It is true that the middle class and working class are better off in the United States than elsewhere, and the poor are better off in the United States than elsewhere, but the former do not get a significant share of the resources and the latter get almost none at all. Whatever expenditures get redistributed through progressive taxes, about 50

1. David C. Johnston, "Dozens of Rich Americans Join to Fight to Retain the Estate Tax," *New York Times* (February 14, 2001), p. 1.

2. If a college applicant can get 10 extra points (out of 100 total) because mom or dad went to the college, the argument can be made that minority status is worth 10 or more points in the admission process.

3. Denis Donoghue, *Words Alone: The Poet T. S. Eliot* (New Haven: Yale University, 2001).

percent goes to social legislation for daily life, not for things on which quality depends. The best example is President Bush's tax-reduction package. Its effect was not on the economy, as promised, but for the pleasure and benefit of the wealthy class. A single person earning $1,000,000 receives $46,758 in savings when the tax cuts are fully phased in. (Most of the tax cuts won't take place until 2005.) A single person earning $500,000 receives $23,621. A single person earning $60,000 (such as a teacher) receives $752. If married with two children, then the person realizes $1,900 in savings.[1] Two-thirds of the population will receive nothing at all, including all the families who live in poverty or just above the poverty line; moreover, the plan did nothing to cut social security or Medicare payroll taxes, which affect the poor the most. It is pretty clear that many voters, if presented with this proposal now, would be strongly opposed, and some who voted for Bush's economics might recast their votes.

In the meantime, President Bush continues to exploit 9-11 events by arguing for the rich and super-rich, bigger defense spending, more oil independence, and drilling for oil in the wilderness, and cuts in social services to compensate for growing deficit spending. No one seems to remember that just a few years ago, prior to the arrival of the Bush administration, this country had the biggest monetary surplus in its history. The federal government now has a major deficit, sending the Euro-currency up more than the dollar and the U.S. dollar spinning downward.

As for teachers, their real income may rise or fall based on salary negotiations and inflation, but they will never experience real prosperity. Like most workers, they have to work more hours (work a part-time job) or marry a spouse who earns more money to satisfy their needs. Indeed, there are very few teachers living in 4,000-square-foot homes or driving around in Mercedes automobiles. Ted Sizer touches on this problem when he describes his prototype teacher *Horace,* who works in a wealthy suburban school district, earns a good teacher salary, and who has a wife who earns more money than he does. Yet, he still has to work part time in a liquor store to make ends meet.[2] Unwittingly, Horace's predicament is an indictment of how this nation treats and what it thinks about teachers. Harrington's analysis was not as earthshaking as Kennedy and Johnson thought, but a confirmation of American social and economic history.

## The Focus on Disadvantaged Students

In 1961, Conant wrote *Slums and Suburbs.* Only two years before, Conant had advocated academic rigor and upgraded academic subjects, as well as greater attention to the top 20 percent of high school students. Now, he urged educators and policymakers to pay closer attention to less able and inner-city children. He pointed out that half the children in slum neighborhoods dropped out of school in grades 9, 10, and 11; that the per-pupil expenditure in inner-city schools was less than half the expenditure in the privileged, wealthy schools of suburbia; and that there were 70 professionals per 1,000 pupils in privileged schools and only 40 professionals per 1,000 in inner-city schools.[3]

1. "What the Tax Cuts Would Mean for Different Families," *New York Times* (February 9, 2002), p. A20.
2. Theodore R. Sizer, *Horace's Compromise* (Boston: Houghton Mifflin, 1984).
3. James B. Conant, *Slums and Suburbs* (New York: McGraw-Hill, 1961).

Dropout rates, lack of vocational skills, and soaring unemployment rates at that time among black youth were leading to serious frustration in the American ghettoes. Conant coined the term *social dynamite* and warned that conditions were reaching an explosive point in the ghettoes of the cities. He wrote, "I am concerned we are allowing social dynamite to accumulate in our large cities. . . . Leaving aside human tragedies, I submit that a continuation of this situation [youth out of school and out of work] is a menace to the social and political health of large cities."[1] Five years later, Conant's warnings were to echo loudly in many urban areas across the country—the term was called *urban riots*. (During this period, I also recall Stokey Carmichael, Eldridge Cleaver, and H. Rap Brown using the term *urban revolution* to make a political statement, and saying that every political revolution has certain elements of violence and warfare.)

It should be noted that Conant was referring to the wealthiest suburbs, not the average suburban schools. Per-pupil expenditures and teacher costs in much less affluent suburbs parallel expenses for city schools. Also, pupil expenditures in the last 20 years have shifted to favor disadvantaged populations in big-city schools, as a result of funding programs of the states and federal government and the general concern for educating poor and minority students. In several states, today, inner-city schools obtain as much or more money for special programs and teaching positions than outer-city or less needy schools, and are at or near parity with the mean suburban (but not the wealthy suburban) school in per-pupil expenditures and teacher-student ratios. Of course, this does not mean the output is similar among the different school types. (For example, New Jersey spends an average of $13,000 per inner-city student, as much as it does for its suburban students and twice the national average, but 57 percent of inner-city high school students failed state proficiency exams in 2001.)[2]

Disparities were more evident during Conant's era. Because of his prestige and reputation as a leading educator, Conant's book was extensively reviewed and widely read by policymakers as well as educators, who, in turn, helped clarify many issues related to educating the disadvantaged and set in motion the needed funds for inner-city schools. Conant was to make one fatal error in his analysis of inner-city students and schools: his recommendation to improve and expand vocational schooling for slum children who were unable to meet the demands of an academic program. Indirectly, he was advocating tracking of students by ability, which years later was harshly condemned by the many educators as a form of racism, and increasing vocational schooling, which was also condemned as perpetuating a second-rate program on minority and working-class student groups.

The same year Conant published the eye-opening *Slums and Suburbs,* a former union activist in Detroit, then a professor of education at New York University, published a major study called *Education and Income*. The book challenged the American dream and promised that low social status or economic income was not a serious barrier to the education of any child of normal intelligence.[3] The fact that Kenneth Clark, the black psychologist who was instrumental in the *Brown* v. *Board of*

1. Ibid., p. 2.
2. "The Education of Jim McGreevey," *Wall Street Journal* (October 31, 2001), p. 14.
3. Patricia C. Sexton, *Education and Income* (New York: Viking Press, 1961).

*Education* decision, wrote the foreword to the book highlighted attention. Using the Detroit school system as the focus of her study, Sexton pointed out that American schools had become less efficient and less able to serve as the instrument of social mobility; in fact, she argued that the schools solidified and intensified social-class distinctions—a somewhat new idea at that period of time.

Referring to the 1957 census tract, Sexton categorized the Detroit elementary schools by average family income of $3,000 to $11,055, and then combined these levels into four major groups ranked from lowest to highest as follows: (I) $3,000 to 4,999, (II) $5,000 to 6,999, (III) $7,000 to 8,999, and (IV) $9,000+. Table 6.3 indicates that achievement scores tend to go up as income levels rise, and dropout rates decline with increasing income levels. Students in all 242 schools in the two lowest income levels were achieving below grade level; furthermore, the differences between groups I and IV tended to widen with each passing grade level. Low reading levels also were associated with income. In the lowest group of schools, 96 percent of the students

## TABLE *6.3*

### Income Differences and Elementary Schools in Detroit

| Schools by Average Family Income Groups | Number of Schools in Each Group | Iowa Achievement Test Mean Scores | | | Percent of Students Reading Below Grade Level | IQ Mean Scores with Ranges from 2.0 to 6.0 |
|---|---|---|---|---|---|---|
| | | *Fourth Grade* | *Sixth Grade* | *Eighth Grade* | | |
| I. ($3,000+) | 135 | 3.48 | 5.32 | 6.77 | 96% | 2.79 |
| II. ($5,000+) | 107 | 3.73 | 5.61 | 7.38 | 82 | 3.31 |
| III. ($7,000+) | 85 | 4.42 | 6.47 | 8.22 | 5 | 4.55 |
| IV. ($9,000+) | 20 | 4.84 | 7.05 | 8.67 | 0 | 5.09 |

| Income Groups | Number of Gifted Students per 10,000 | Detention Students per 10,000 | Special Behavior Classes per 10,000 | Percent of Nonpromotions | Percent of Dropouts |
|---|---|---|---|---|---|
| I. ($3,000+) | 0 | 85.7 | 37.7 | 7.4% | 15.5% |
| II. ($5,000+) | 3.6 | 40.2 | 14.8 | 4.9 | 3.0 |
| III. ($7,000+) | 27.0 | 6.9 | 4.2 | 2.9 | 1.5 |
| IV. ($9,000+) | 78.0 | 2.7 | 0 | 1.2 | .7 |

*Source:* Adapted from Patricia C. Sexton, *Education and Income: Inequalities in Our Public Schools* (New York: Viking Press, 1961), pp. 24, 28, 39, 54, 60, 71–72, 97.

were reading below grade level, whereas in none of the schools in the highest group did students have a mean score below the national grade level. IQ mean scores for children in the first and fourth grades were grouped into five equal categories, from 2.0 to 6.0, and it was found that these scores directly related to income groups, too.

Sexton also compiled data on other school variables. She found that gifted students came exclusively from schools in upper-income groups; the number of gifted students per 10,000 was 78 for group IV and zero for group I. Detention students came mainly from low-income schools, 86 per 10,000 students compared to 2.7 per 10,000 for upper-class students. Special programs designed for students who were considered behavior problems were attended by 38 per 10,000 students in schools in the lowest income group and not one in the highest category. The nonpromotion rate was six times higher in group I than in group IV. Thus, from the standpoint of school *success*—say, achievement, reading, and IQ scores—and giftedness, the trend that favors upper-class children is established at an early age. And from the standpoint of school *failure*—say, detention, behavior problems, nonpromotions, and dropping out—the trend among low-income children is established early in their school careers, too. Indeed, the gap between both groups tends to widen at the secondary school level.[1]

Interest Fuels: The Field Expands    Interest in the disadvantaged, which started in the early 1960s, continued to gain momentum throughout the remaining parts of the century. Four other major players helped establish early interest in the field. Robert Havighurst, from the University of Chicago, who previously had interest in social-class differences, studied the Chicago high schools in 1964 and showed that reading ability was closely related to the socioeconomic level of the school; however, race was a factor in determining reading scores and low achievement even when class was controlled. Social-class ranking of schools was also a factor in determining the percent of high achievers and the percent saying they expected to go to college.[2]

1. On a personal level, Sexton was a career woman and full professor in a period when only super-women rose to full professorships at major universities. She had to claw her way to the top. Sexton's feminist philosophy, which was atypical for the period, clashed with my young notion of "pretty ladies" who were ideally more restrained and less vocal. She wanted to educate men and I wanted to charm women. Politically, we clashed on many occasions. I wound up getting a C in Sexton's course (even though I was better versed on the subject of social class and education than my classmates), the lowest grade I ever received in 60 hours of graduate study at NYU. With 35 years of hindsight, our differences could have easily been reconciled by allowing Sexton to make her pronouncements about strong and intelligent women who are put down by weak and shallow men in families relationships, schools and colleges, and churches—most vividly by the latter who historically have condemned women to nunneries, often when they were young and impressionable, and sometimes when they were mature, but usually under force or theology. With greater forbearance for Sexton's foibles and greater delight in her tales, and with some praise to the feminine mind, I would have fared better in her class. I should have known better, since I was an ardent fan of Henrik Ibsen at that period in my life.

2. Robert J. Havinghurst, *The Public Schools of Chicago* (Chicago: Board of Education of the City of Chicago, 1964).

In a 1962 book on the disadvantaged, Frank Riessman, from New York University, popularized the idea that the disadvantaged had their own culture (an idea rooted in Allison Davis's work in the late 1940s) and a number of positive characteristics that had been overlooked: exceptional physical orientation, hidden verbal ability, creative potential, group cohesiveness, extended family relations, informality, sense of humor, frankness, freedom from self-blame and parental overprotection, and ability to manipulate others and their environment.[1] He argued, like Davis had, that this culture was in conflict with the schools.[2] (Later, I would argue that the differences in culture, translated into certain conflicting attitudes and behaviors between students and teachers, was a cause for classroom management problems in inner-city schools; a conflict existed between the culture of lower-class students and middle-class teachers, and most teachers were unprepared to handle these differences in the classroom.)[3]

By using the words *deprived* and *disadvantaged* in his book to describe these positive characteristics and culture, Riessman unintentionally endorsed the contrasting standards of middle-class schools and society. Perhaps for this reason, in subsequent writings (mid-1960s) on the subject, Riessman used the term *poor* youth in the mistaken conviction that it was a more positive term. Educators, in fact, have been playing around with these terms for the last 30 or so years, in search of more positive descriptors—*culturally different, educationally challenging, overlooked children, at-risk children* and other euphemisms—so as not to be criticized by their peers for being culturally biased or worse.

Harry Passow, from Columbia University, shifted interest from the gifted student in the 1950s to the disadvantaged student in the 1960s (similar to Conant's decision). Through a number of urban education conferences held at Columbia University, Passow proceeded to compile and publish the proceedings in a number of books of readings: The two most prominent books were *Education in Depressed Areas* (1963) and *Education of the Disadvantaged* (1967). His books emphasized social, psychological, and cognitive factors related to educating the disadvantaged—vividly showing that these children lacked basic skills primarily caused by environmental factors in the home and community.

The work of Martin and Cynthia Deutsch at New York University and Columbia University was instrumental in showing how lack of auditory and verbal discrimination in preschool children and early elementary school children were critical factors in determining the lack of reading and language development among lower-class and disadvantaged groups.[4] Heavily influenced by the classic works of Piaget

---

1. Frank Riessman, *The Culturally Deprived Child* (New York: Harper & Row, 1962).
2. Allison Davis, *Social Class Influence Upon Learning* (Cambridge, MA: Harvard University Press, 1949).
3. Allan C. Ornstein and Philip D. Vairo, *How to Teach Disadvantaged Youth* (New York: McKay, 1967).
4. Martin Deutsch et al., eds., *The Disadvantaged Child* (New York: Basic Books, 1967); Deutsch et al., eds., *Social Class, Race, and Psychological Development* (New York: Holt, Rinehart and Winston, 1968). The Deutschs' early works were also published in the two Passow books previously cited, as was the work of J. McV. Hunt.

and also by a lesser-known environmentalist by the name of J. McV. Hunt at the University of Illinois-Champaign, the Deutschs (along with Benjamin Bloom) helped move discussion away from the hereditary school (which was predominant in the pre-1950s) to the environmental school to explain the reasons for school failure among poor and minority children.[1]

The Deutschs' research, along with Piaget and Bloom's work, were instrumental in highlighting the need for early child intervention programs and shaping the compensatory education movement in the early and mid-1960s. Thus, the Elementary and Secondary Education Act (ESEA), passed in 1965 (as part of President Johnson's Great Society), immediately provided $1 billion in Title I funds, frequently called *compensatory funding* to supplement and improve the education of poor and minority children.[2]

**Inequality Continues**   Some 25 years later, Johnathan Kozol spent two years touring some two dozen dreary and decaying schools in big cities from New York to Chicago, from Detroit to San Antonio. As a comparison, he visited suburban schools in wealthy suburbs outside of these cities (i.e., Rye, New York, and Winnetka, Illinois) and other suburban communities where classrooms overflow with the latest technology and almost every student seems destined for an Ivy League college.

Kozol had gained his reputation in his early best-selling book, *Death at an Early Age*. In the book, he condemned the attitudes and practices of Boston teachers and administrators toward inner-city black students, and he concluded that they were racists. Kozol's exposé corresponded with the period of the urban riots, college campus unrest, and protests against the war in Vietnam. Writers whose voices were antiestablishment—including voices against teachers and schools—were treated as

---

1. Benjamin S. Bloom, *Stability and Change in Human Characteristics* (New York: Wiley, 1964); J. McVicker Hunt, *Intelligence and Experience* (New York: Ronald Press, 1961); Hunt, *The Challenge of Incompetence and Poverty* (Urbana: University of Illinois Press, 1969).
2. By the mid-1960s, interest in the disadvantaged had snowballed, and by the late 1960s, coinciding with the urban riots across the country, government reports strongly suggested an impacted crisis in schools and society, and an impending social upheaval. The needs of disadvantaged students, in less than one decade, had become the number-one education priority—and it has continued to involve a large amount of interest not only among educators but also among businesspeople and politicians. By 1970, Title I money totaled $2 billion per year, or about $200 extra per disadvantage child. By 1980, Title I expenditures were more than $3 billion per year, and other federal compensatory expenditures, K–12, totaled another $2 billion or more, a total of about $500 extra per disadvantaged child. By 1990, compensatory spending was at $5.3 billion, plus another $6 billion was earmarked for vocational and postsecondary disadvantaged students. In 2000, under the Clinton administration, K–12 expenditures for poverty schools had soared to $8.5 billion. About 16 to 20 percent of all big-city school spending today comprises federal money. See Allan C. Ornstein and Daniel U. Levine, "Compensatory Education: Can It Be Successful?" *NASSP Bulletin* (May 1981), pp. 1–15. Also see *Digest of Educational Statistics 1990* (Washington, DC: U.S. Government Printing Office, 1990), Table 327, p. 343; Fred Lunenburg and Allan C. Ornstein, *Educational Administration*, 3rd ed. (Belmont, CA: Wadsworth, 2000), pp. 246–250.

heroes. Hence, Kozol (and other social critics, see page 351) gained popularity among young education students and liberal professors in academia.

At the heart of Kozol's new book, *Savage Inequalities,* was the thesis that public schools are public institutions, which means that the same equality of education offered in the slums of Harlem or Watts should be similar to the quality offered in the privileged suburban communities of America.[1] We may tolerate inequalities in the private sector, as a form of capitalism, but the facilities served by government should comprise similar standards throughout the country, certainly throughout a particular state. The disparities Kozol chronicled, sadly, reflected the same disparities that Conant and Sexton described in the early 1960s—when the problems and inequalities of slum and suburban schools were first discovered. Obviously, the inference was that there had been little or no change!

Even worse, the racial segregation that existed prior to *Brown* v. *Board of Education* in 1954 is the same today, even closer to conditions addressed in *Plesssy* v. *Ferguson,* in 1896, in which the court accepted segregated schools. The policies adopted under the Reagan era, and, if I may add, under the Bush and Bush eras, have turned back school integration more than 100 years.[2] Racial segregation persists in most big cities (which are predominantly minority) and their surrounding wealthy suburbs (which are predominantly white).

The strongest indictment of the government's insensitivity to black and Hispanic children (i.e., the students of big-city schools) was reflected by their own voices, which Kozol quoted. We learn that these children feel they are being short-changed by schools and society, and they know they are not wanted by and are being kept out of privileged communities. In places where minority students are bused, many are separated in "special" classes. Few get the opportunity to enroll in honor or advance placement classes.

The differences in the spending between inner-city and privileged suburban schools can be summed up by the differences of class size, books and computers, teacher salaries, and general classroom and school conditions—from cracked windows and leaky roofs in many inner-city schools to the campus-like set-up in many

1. Johnathan Kozol, *Savage Inequalities* (New York: Crown, 1991).
2. Now, if you or your folks belong to the country club on the hill and can break 80 after 18 long "rounds," frequent Ducasse when you visit New York, or don't care for New York but know the difference between *bavette cacio e pepe* and plain old green linguini, or simply voted red in the Bush-Gore election, then you are going to see red with this last sentence. If, on the other hand, you enjoy *West Wing,* believe that fine dining is the blue-ribbon special at the local diner, or have a poster of Karl, Eleanor, or JFK in your bedroom, then you will accept this last statement without further remarks. If you frequently get pulled over by the police when you are driving 30 miles an hour through Manhasset, New York, Lake Forest, Illinois, or Hillsborough, California, or if you have been labeled the personification of a criminal libido by some social worker or social scientist, or simply graduated from one of the many "separate and unequal" schools of Gotham City, Chicago, or Los Angeles, then absolutely no explanation is needed about school integration. As for the laws of the land, "The buck stops at the White House," to paraphrase an older and wiser president. I guess perceptions of life depend on what side of the fence you sit.

privileged suburban communities.[1] Indeed, families move to these school districts because of their superior facilities, and prices of homes in these communities reflect the success of these schools. Once people arrive, most have no concern for children other than their own and how their children can get into Harvard or Yale.

Moving beyond Kozol, you cannot expect an appeal to conscience, fair play, or social justice to work; the only thing that really pushes the American people and power structure to modify their attitudes and behaviors is the fear of violence or some threat to their existence. But even that tactic has limitations with highly privileged suburban dwellers. If they live far enough away from "battle zones," with enough working-class and middle-class barriers, they will not do anything, because they will not experience hostility or anger from the impoverished. Let the working stiffs and lower-echelon bureaucrats of America deal with the creeping expansion of poverty and race in their neighborhoods and workplace.

These privileged people may be polite and affable, and others may be prim and proper, but they know the right words and how to work the system. You will not change their behavior unless you can threaten their way of life—their country clubs, golf games and tennis matches, neighborhood parties and charity balls. (I lived with these people in an insulated, Yankee suburb for 15 years, and my kids went to an elitist public high school that looked more like a college campus than a high school, with about 25 percent of its personnel having their doctorate degrees, with state-of-the-art technological and sports facilities, and with the surrounding neighborhood containing large, traditional, graceful Tudor and Normady homes and lush green landscaping.) The people who come closest to describing this type of suburban school is Sara Lawrence Lightfoot in *The Good High School* (1983) and Philip Cusick in *The Educational Ideal and the American High School* (1983), both who describe top-rate and affluent high schools.

The suburbanites I am talking about use the law, work their political and social connections, hire consultants or special service agencies, and offer donations to advance their education goals, maintain their social system, and retain their superior schools so their children will have more than an equal opportunity. While inner-city children are focused on learning basic reading and literacy skills, while the average high school student is worried about getting into college and obtaining some scholarship money, these suburban kids have been groomed for years to get into an Ivy League college. Their parents, teachers, and administrators, in various degrees, have been directing these students toward a global, technical, and financial perspective in school and college. Their schools have their own brand of education, their own spelling lists and reading lists, their own way of teaching reading and writing, their own way of grouping and tracking students, and their own way of promoting socialization and community service. It is called *the Winnetka way, the Rye way, the Radnor way, the West Dover way,* and so on. Some of you who drink Grand Marnier or Chateau de Cognac know what I'm talking about; others who drink Pabst or Milwaukee Beer have no clue.

---

1. This disparity reflects a 30-year span, from Conant's *Slums and Suburbs* to Kozol's *Savage Inequalities*.

Poor children, immigrant children, handicapped children, and minority children have always been considered extra baggage in which the more fortunate have been willing to partially support and pay for their social, health, housing, and welfare programs in order to sedate them and prevent a revolution. If there would be a revolution in this country today, it would be based on increased taxation and redistribution of income, and it would require that business executives play by the rules or suffer severe consequences, including stripping away their fortunes. The rich are even willing to help fund the schools of disadvantaged children through taxes, so long as they are free to use their own money to maintain their style of life and their style of schooling—and be permitted to continue inequality.

Given a touch of morality and some sense of justice and/or common sense, it is in the best interests of the upper-middle class and wealthy class to provide money for those at the bottom of the social and economic scale in order to provide some hope and social mobility so that they don't rebel and topple the system.[1] The rich are willing to give up a few dollars in taxes so long as their children can read and can make it to top colleges and universities that open doors that most people don't know exist. To put it in different terms, the common school movement is alive and well, but certain schools are more privileged than common and some are more equal and others are less equal. Don't underestimate the power and influence of wealthy people, prestigious schools and colleges, and other "blue-blood" institutions. There are "golden" tickets that give certain people an edge over others. Intelligence is only one factor in life. As one Harvard alumnus has to say, "The place makes the person," or as American Express reminds us, "Membership has its privileges."

**EPISODE 13**

## Growing Priorities: New Disadvantaged Groups

The focus on the disadvantaged extended into the remaining decades of the twentieth century, and the number continued to grow. For example, in 1950, 10 percent of students were classified as poor or minority in the 25 largest school districts. In 1960, the number was 33 percent; in 1970, it was 50 percent. In 1980, the number increased to 70 percent; in 1990, it was 85 percent; and by 2000, it was estimated at 95 percent. This direction reflects immigration trends that since 1970 have been about 90 percent nonwhite, as well as middle-class and white flight from the cities to the suburbs, and financially stable retirees and older couples (whose children no longer attend school) moving from the Frostbelt to the Sunbelt.[2] All these trends in-

1. This type of thinking goes back to the patrician thinking of President Jefferson who understood that democracy needed an educated and upward-mobile populace.
2. Allan C. Ornstein, "Urban Demographics for the 1980s," *Education and Urban Society* (August 1984), pp. 477–496, Also see Gregor Acs and Megan Gallagher, *Income Inequality among America's Children* (Washington, DC: Urban Institute, 1999).

dicate tremendous financial shifts of wealth, tax revenues, consumption of goods and services, and jobs—which have a snowball effect in generating greater disparities between cities and suburbs and major regional shifts to the Sunbelt.

Most urban property taxes (as well as those of some poor suburbs) are alarmingly high, about 33 to 100 percent higher per capita than taxes in adjacent middle- and upper-class suburbs. High property taxes make it difficult to attract middle-income residents and new jobs to broaden the tax base. As the cities lose their middle-class population and businesses, their tax base is further undermined. They are forced to cut city services, including education, to balance their budgets; these cuts drive away more middle-class citizens and businesses and more tax revenues. The cycle reinforces itself, and this is one reason for the decline of many urban schools. Financing has become the major problem for many city schools, and recommendations for cutting costs and reducing wasteful programs have become important issues.

On the other side of the discussion, there is a growing amount of data suggesting there is no direct relationship between school spending and student performance. Higher per-pupil expenditures, new schools, smaller classes, higher teacher salaries, and increased curriculum/instructional expenditures have little to do with student performance.[1] Money might make a difference if it was spent properly and under the right circumstances, but if the goal is to increase student performance, then we have to look at some sensitive issues: dealing with individual student behavior, family responsibility, peer-group influence (gangs, drugs, and teen pregnancy), and influence of the TV and mass media.

Still, the sad fact is that the country is willing to invest more in prisons than in education. As many as 82 percent of the prison population dropped out of high school. In New York state, more black and Hispanic men are sent to prison than graduate from state colleges. California pays beginning prison guards higher salaries than beginning teachers. In 2002, more than 40 states were forced to consider budget cuts as a response to an unhealthy economy.[2] Some of there cuts affected programs and personnel in city schools, including tutoring and summer programs, which have an impact on student achievement, as well as hiring needed teachers to maintain small class sizes.

There is still another problem. The nation has become hypnotized by "white guilt" and "political correctness" and cannot have a two-way conversation about the persistent achievement gaps of black and white students, despite billions of dollars invested in compensatory education and other social remedies. Because of white guilt and political correctness, some people have the need to blame whites, the middle class and rich, and the Establishment for exploiting the poor, mainly blacks and Hispanics. White guilt can also hide all kinds of problems that are either embarrassing or

---

1. See Chapter 8 and the discussion dealing with Coleman, Jencks, Hanushek, Mayer, and Peterson. Also see Allan Odden, "The Costs of Sustaining Education Change Through Comprehensive School Reform," *Phi Delta Kappan* (February 2000), pp. 433–438.

2. Sandra Feldman, "Summer Learning," *New York Times* (March 24, 2002), Sect. 4, p. 7; Thomas Leahy, "Safe Communities, Successful schools," *New York Times* (December 23, 2001), Sect. 4, p. 8; and Robert Tomsho, "Tight Budgets Pose a Threat to Small Classes," *Wall Street Journal* (May 16, 2002), p. B1.

associated with individual, family, peer-group, and community responsibility—and permit nonwhites to introduce cries of victimization, oppression, and demands for quotas and reparations.

However, according to Shelby Steele, the great white advantage has been living within the larger society, adapting to its demands and changes, nurturing the individual values and habits of life that yield productivity.[1] This is the cultural capital hoarded by whites and middle-class families at the expense of blacks and browns, as well as the lower- and working-classes in the United States. The dominant group takes this cultural capital for granted and rarely thinks it exists among the majority of its victims; those with power organize their own schools to increase their cultural capital while they ignore the city schools of poor and minority students.

## Bilingual/Multicultural Education

America's *multicultural* and *bilingual* efforts were characterized by increased federal funding for Hispanic, Asian American, and Native American students; by the Bilingual Act in 1968, which expanded bilingual programs in American schools; and by the 1974 U.S. Supreme Court ruling in *Lau* v. *Nicholas,* which stated that schools must take steps to help students who "are certain to find their classroom experiences wholly in-comprehensible" because they do not understand English. The courts, as well as policymakers and educators, took an active role in providing educational opportunities for limited-English speaking (LES) and non-English speaking (NES) students. Despite controversies that surfaced concerning specific approaches and programs as well as recruitment of personnel, bilingual and multicultural education grew in importance during the 1970s. Congressional appropriations for bilingual education increased from $6.1 million in 1970 to $169 million in 1980. In 1990, appropriations were $203 million, and in 1999 it was $225 million, illustrating that these funds have now leveled off.[2]

The federal and state governments fund bilingual projects for more than 60 language groups speaking various Asian, Indo-European, and Native American languages, but the large majority (about 70 percent) of children in these projects are Hispanic. Although the United States continues to attract hundreds of thousands of immigrants from around the world each year, Hispanics represent the fastest-growing ethnic population in the country. In 1980, the legal Hispanic population was 15 million. Based on current immigration and fertility trends, as shown in Table 6.4, the Hispanic population should reach 30 million in the year 2000 (10.8 percent of the total population) and 47 million in 2020 (14.7 percent), surpassing the U.S. black population (14 percent) as the largest minority group. (Hispanics have a very strong sense of empowerment in many states, such as California, Texas, and New Mexico, and in some cities, such as New York, Miami, and San Diego, which turns the concept of minority status upside down and inside out.) On the heels of the Hispanic population is

1. Shelby Steele, "War of the Worlds," *Wall Street Journal* (September 17, 2001), p. 18.
2. *Digest of Education Statistics 1990,* Table 326, p. 337; *The Fiscal Year 2000 Budget* (Washington, DC: U.S. Government Printing Office, 2000), Appendix, p. 8.

---
## TABLE 6.4
### Total US and Minority Population, 1980 to 2020
---

|  | 1980 | | 2000 | | 2020 | |
|---|---|---|---|---|---|---|
|  | *Number* | *%* | *Number* | *%* | *Number* | *%* |
| White (non-Hispanic) | 181.0 | 79.9 | 200.3 | 71.7 | 205.6 | 64.9 |
| Black | 26.5 | 11.7 | 36.4 | 13.0 | 44.4 | 14.0 |
| Hispanic | 14.6 | 6.5 | 30.3 | 10.8 | 46.6 | 14.7 |
| Asian | 4.4 | 2.0 | 12.1 | 4.3 | 20.3 | 6.3 |
| **Total:** | 226.5 | 100.0 | 279.1 | 100.0 | 316.9 | 100.0 |

---

*Sources:* Adapted from *The Future Radical Composition of the United States* (Washington DC: Population Reference Bureau, 1982), Table 3, p. 14; Allan C. Ornstein, "Urban Demographics for the 1980s," *Education and Urban Society* (August 1984), Table 2, p. 486; and Fred C. Lunenburg and Allan C. Ornstein, *Educational Administration: Concepts and Practices,* 3rd ed. (Belmont, CA: Wadsworth, 2000), Table 9.3, p. 247.

the Asian group—the next fastest-growing minority group. The Asian population totaled 12 million in 2000 (4.3 percent) and will top 20 million in 2020 (6.3 percent), compared to 4 million (2 percent) in 1980.[1] Composition of the United States is undergoing considerable ethnic change—largely because of immigration trends—and the federal government is responding in the schools by requiring that the states and local educational agencies meet the needs of these children.

Controversies over bilingual education have become somewhat imbitterer as federal and state actions have led to the establishment of various bilingual programs. There are arguments between those who would "immerse" children in the English-language environment and those who believe initial instruction will be more effective in the native language. On one side are those who favor maintenance because they believe this would help build a constructive sense of identity; and on the other side are those who believe that cultural maintenance is harmful because it separates groups from one another or discourages students from mastering English well enough to function successfully in the larger society.[2]

1.  Harold Hodgkinson, "Educational Demographics: What Teachers Should Know," *Educational Leadership* (January 2001), pp. 6–11; Lynn Olson, "Children of Change," *Education Week* (September 27, 2000), pp. 31–36; Allan C. Ornstein, "Enrollment Trends in Big-City Schools," *Peabody Journal of Education,* 66 (1989): 64–71; and Ornstein, "Curriculum Trends Revisited," *Peabody Journal of Education,* 69 (1994), pp. 4–20.

2.  Nathan Glazer, "Where Is Multiculturalism Leading Us?" *Phi Delta Kappan,* 75 (1993), pp. 319–323; Rosalie Pedalino Porter, "The Benefits of English Immersion," *Educational Leadership* (January 2000), pp. 52–56.

Adherents and opponents of bilingual education also differ on the related issues of whether bilingual programs sometimes or frequently are designed to provide teaching jobs for native-language speakers and whether individuals who fill these jobs are competent in English. Observers who favor bilingual and bicultural maintenance tend to believe that the schools need many adults who can teach LES or NES students in their own language, whereas observers who favor transitional programs feel that very few native-language or bilingual speakers are required to staff a legitimate program.

## Disabilities and Special Education

During the 1970s, much activity and concern surfaced over special education, especially for students with physical disabilities and for students with learning disabilities. New pressure groups, new courses, advanced degrees, new certification requirements, and new teachers and faculty at colleges and universities stimulated recognition of special education, as have new policies and programs. The Education for All Handicapped Children Act (PL 94-142) of 1975 is the cornerstone of these policies and programs, and it has been expanded and amended several times, and, in 1990, was renamed the Individuals with Disabilities Education Act (IDEA).[1]

Students with disabilities (sometimes called *special education students, special need students,* and/or *exceptional students*) are defined by the original act as those who are mentally retarded, hard of hearing, deaf, orthopedically impaired, other health impaired, speech impaired, visually handicapped, emotionally disturbed, or learning disabled, and by reason thereof, require special education and related services. Full rights and protection of the law to 3- to 5-year-old children with disabilities was passed in 1986 and implemented in the 1990–91 school year.[2] Students with special needs must be provided with special education and related services at public expense under public supervision and direction. Schools must not only adopt policies that *serve* all such students but they must also conduct searches to *locate* such students.

Much of the recent debate on special education centers on how schools identify students who might be eligible for special education services and what related services are to be provided at the public's expense. In *Cedar Rapids* v. *Garret,* the U.S. Supreme Court ruled in 1999 that schools are required to provide medical equipment and nursing services during school hours. Because of this decision and related legislation (expansion of ADA and IDEA), the level of responsibility placed on principles and school personnel has increased and will most likely continue to increase.

As indicated in Table 6.5, the total number of special education students served by public funds has increased over 15 years, from 4.2 million to 6.0 million (or 13.1 percent of the public school enrollment), with 47 percent being served in regular classes (part time or full time), 21 percent in self-contained classes, and the remain-

1. Samuel A. Kirk et al., *Educating Exceptional Children* (Boston: Houghton Mifflin, 2000); Janet Lerner, *Learning Disabilities* (Boston: Houghton Mifflin, 2000).
2. Joseph Boyle, *Cases in Special Education* (New York: McGraw-Hill, 1997); Lundenburg and Ornstein; *Educational Administration.*

─────────────────────── TABLE *6.5* ───────────────────────

## Number of Students Receiving Public Educational Services by Type of Handicap, 1982 and 1999

| Handicap | 1982 | 1999 |
|---|---|---|
| Learning disabled | 1,622,000 | 2,789,000 |
| Speech impaired | 1,135,000 | 1,068,000 |
| Mentally retarded | 786,000 | 597,000 |
| Emotionally disturbed | 339,000 | 462,000 |
| Hard of hearing/Deaf | 75,000 | 70,000 |
| Orthopedically handicapped | 58,000 | 69,000 |
| Other health problems | 79,000 | 221,000 |
| Visually handicapped | 29,000 | 26,000 |
| Multihandicapped | 71,000 | 106,000 |
| Deaf-Blind | 2,000 | 2,000 |
| Autism | a | 67,000 |
| Developmental delay | a | 12,000 |
| Preschool handicapped (three to five years old) | a | 568,000 |
| **Total:** (all conditions) | 4,198,000 | 6,055,000 |
| **Percentage of public school enrollment** | 10.5 | 13.1 |

*Sources: Digest of Education Statistics 1987* (Washington, DC: U.S. Government Printing Office, 1987), Table 38, p. 49; *Digest of Education Statistics 2000* (Washington, DC: U.S. Government Printing Office, 2001), Table 53, p. 65.

*Note:* [a] = no data provided, not a recognized category in 1982.

ing in special schools or facilities.[1] The growth in the number of students requiring special education has been associated with the civil rights movement and its concern with making equal educational opportunity available to all students—not that more U.S. students have become handicapped. The numbers also include a somewhat large and fuzzy category, *learning disabled,* whereby many slow learners, underachievers, and precocious students are hastily slotted in this category—in part because of the overemphasis on testing and labeling students and the influence of special education advocates as a lobby and advocate group. Although *Brown* v. *Board of Education* in

1. *Digest of Education Statistics 1994* (Washington, DC: U.S. Government Printing Office, 1994), Table 53, p. 66; *Digest of Education Statistic 2000,* Table 54, p. 66.

1954 addressed the segregation of black students in separate schools, it also served as a precedent in establishing the rights of students with disabilities to be provided with equal educational opportunity under the umbrella notion of *mainstreaming.*

In terms of costs, special education expenditures rose steadily since the 1970s and into the 1990s. The average cost of educating a child with handicaps or disabilities is much higher than the national average for a normally functioning child—almost double the national average of $6,500 in 1997.[1] Although federal law requires local school districts to provide a free and appropriate education, the federal government, which originally contributed relatively few dollars to this effort, dramatically increased its funding in the 1990s, largely corresponding with the Clinton administration. Federal expenditures for special education increased from $70 million in 1970, to $1.5 billion in 1980, to $3.5 billion in 1990, to $7.6 billion in 1998, with estimates of $10 billion in 2000.[2] In real dollars, after inflation, this amounts to an increase of about 50 percent since 1980. Still, special education mandates place a heavy financial burden on the states and local educational agencies (which many school districts find burdensome). Of course, having let the genie out of the bottle, it would be considered mean-spirited to try to reduce spending for a student population in need of special consideration.

## Dwindling Concern for Bright Minds

Concern for the gifted and talented students reached a low point during the 1960s and 1970s, and continued throughout the closing years of the century. The commitment to educating the gifted and talented was slight compared to efforts directed at the disadvantaged and other special populations, such as bilingual, disabled, or learning-disabled students. As two authorities stated in 1976, only "a very small percentage of the gifted and talented population [was] being serviced by existing programs—[about] 4 percent of the 1.5 to 2.5 million children."[3] A similar statement was made 10 years later by another authority,[4] and the same statement (even worse) can be made today,[5] even among the likes of dot-com educators and globalists.

The breakdown of the federal budget and obligations for specially funded programs at the elementary and secondary levels, listed annually in the *Digest of Education Statistics,* does not even include gifted and talented students (even though it

---

1. *Digest of Education Statistics 1997,* Tables 43, 158, 169, pp. 58, 158, 172; *Eighteenth Annual Report to Congress on the Implementation of the Education of the Handicapped Act* (Washington, DC: U.S. Government Printing Office, 1998).

2. *Digest of Education Statistics 1993* (Washington, DC: U.S. Government Printing Office, 1993), Table 350, pp. 365–368; *Digest of Education Statistics 1998,* Table 363, p. 413.

3. A. Harry Passow and Abraham J. Tannenbaum, "Education of the Gifted and Talented," *NASSP Bulletin* (March 1976), pp. 4–5.

4. Donovan R. Walling, "Gifted Children: A Neglected Minority," *Curriculum Review* (September–October 1986), pp. 11–13.

5. Carolyn M. Callahan, "Beyond the Gifted Stereotype," *Educational Leadership* (November 2001), pp. 42–46; Personal conversation with James Campbell, President of the AERA, "SIG Research on Gifted and Talented," April 29, 2001.

lists just about every imaginable student group you can think of), because the expenditures are next to zero; it has no impact on the budget. Similarly, there is absolutely no federal legislation (Chapter 4 of the government *Digest*) concerning the gifted and talented among the 150 federal acts, amendments, and programs enacted between 1960 and 2000.

A low-funding priority and lack of trained personnel, coupled with few pressure groups for the gifted and talented, result in a scarcity of money and programs for these children—a complete about-face from the essentialist philosophy and post-*Sputnik* era, highlighted by the concerns of Bruner, Conant, and Gardner and by the criticism of Bestor and Rickover. Today, most people think that students who are gifted are smart enough to get by on their own, and that they don't need extra recognition or support. We often make the assumption that since these students perform at or above grade level, they are not entitled to receive extra help or to be motivated to learn at their full potential. It is a travesty to overlook and ignore these students—or to assume gifted and talented students are not entitled to instruction geared to their needs, interests, or abilities. Perhaps it reflects overt stupidity, perhaps covert jealousy, on our part as a people and a nation. At all levels of government, these students may be the real disadvantaged students—in terms of low education priority, program development, and funding. This group of students has no politician and no educator of influence, no political or social group, speaking for them. Although most teacher education programs require future teachers to take a special education course, there is no requirement to take any course for recognizing or teaching the gifted. Moreover, many teachers and schools are reluctant to provide additional support or facilities for the gifted because of "concern that other students or parents will accuse them of unfairness,"[1] elitism, or discrimination if a sufficient number of minority students are not enrolled in these courses.

From 15 to 20 percent of gifted and talented students have traditionally dropped out of high school[2]—some because of boredom, some because of personal baggage, and some because of pregnancy. Yet, these are the same children and youth who have the most potential to shape our future world, especially in areas of science, medicine, and technology. The future leadership for society should be from this bright group of students. The political, social, and business sectors need these people, and they should be nurtured at the school level.

What is saving us from our blind-sightedness and educational stupidity is brain drain from the rest of the world. A large number of our new crop of scientists, engineers, computer technicians, and physicians now hail from Asia. American students who enroll in science, technology, and medicine are largely derived from our immigrant population—first-generation youth who are driven to succeed, to fill the American

1. Susan Winebrenner, "Gifted Students Need an Education, Too," *Education Leadership* (September 2000), p. 54.

2. Based on dropout rates of the gifted and talented from 1962 to 1997. See Gary A. Davis and Sylvia B. Rimm, *Education of the Gifted and Talented* (Boston: Allyn and Bacon, 1998); Frederick B. Tuttle, *Gifted and Talented Students* (Washington, DC: National Education Association, 1978).

dream and their parents' aspirations and hopes. Across the country, in institutions of higher learning, Asian students' success in science, technology, and medicine is evidenced by statistical profiles of recipients of doctorate degrees. Asian students received 11.9 percent of all Ph.D. degrees in 1995. The breakdown by field of study in the social sciences, humanities, and education were 7.3 percent, 5.1 percent, and 3.0 percent, respectively. But in the so-called tough subjects, the percentages were as follows: engineering, 31.5 percent; life sciences, 18.5 percent; physical sciences, 25.3 percent; and mathematics, 22.0 percent. In medicine, Asians received 15.9 percent of the degrees; in dentistry, it was 15.1 percent.[1]

## Renewed Search for Relevancy and Humanism

Since the 1950s, there has been a large and sustained effort to reform schools, particularly curriculum and instructional methods, and to meet the needs of the disadvantaged. The decade of the 1960s was regarded by many educators as an era that would transform schools. Writing about the future of education, Robert Anderson, former school superintendent and noted Harvard professor, claimed that the 1960s would be considered "one of the major turning points in American education."[2]

Similarly, the New York State Commissioner of Education wrote in Arthur Morse's 1960 book, *Schools of Tomorrow—Today*, "Never before have so many approaches developed in such a relatively short period. . . . We are learning that many of the old ways of operating our schools are not necessarily the best ways."[3] Morse had borrowed his book title from John and Evelyn Dewey's *Schools of Tomorrow*, originally published in 1915. However, his description of schools, compared to Dewey's schools, were more conventional, full of "gimmickry and packaging than substantive change."[4]

The demand for relevancy and a new form of humanism came from students and educators alike. Concern for the disadvantaged was now compounded by urban riots and student riots in the mid-1960s and 1970s; the situation seemed to illustrate that the old method of focusing on subject matter was irrelevant, and even worse, that youth had become disconnected from adult society. The belief was that schools insisted on creating artificial boundaries between subjects and were more concerned with content within these boundaries than with what the student was interested in learning; the needs and interests of the student had taken a backseat to the focus on subject matter. It was further argued by the likes of Edgar Friedenberg that adolescents needed a good

1. *Digest of Education Statistics 1998*, Tables 274–275, 298–304, pp. 312, 324–327.
2. Robert H. Anderson, "Team Teaching in the Elementary and Secondary Schools," in A. de Grazia and D. A. John, eds. *Revolution in Teaching* (New York: Bantam, 1964), p. 127.
3. James E. Allen, "Foreword," in Arthur D. Morse, *Schools of Tomorrow—Today* (Garden City, NY: Doubleday, 1960), p. 6.
4. Charles E. Silberman, *Crisis in the Classroom* (New York: Random House, 1970), p. 160.

deal of freedom to fully develop, an idea originally rooted in Erik Erikson's developmental theories and what he called a "psychosocial moratorium" for personal growth, and a "search for something and somebody to be true to."[1] The critics were particularly concerned with how resources were being allocated—more for the military and technological ends rather for social and human ends. They attacked mathematicians and scientists at universities who worked for the government as part of the Vietnam war machine, and criticized mathematical and scientific subjects as irrelevant to the spirit of solving social issues. Moreover, many of the critics (including Friedenberg and Goodman, as well as John Holt and Herbert Kohl), seemed particularly attracted to romantic youth and lower-class life, while harshly criticizing middle-class teachers. In fact, one well-known education observer contended the criticism was based on an elitist and negative attitude toward *all* bureaucrats and civil servants.[2]

Representative educators who stressed the need for relevance contended that "most schools and school systems have become anachronistic. They are out of phase with everyday realities of their students' lives. They do not illuminate the concerns of youngsters. They are irrelevant."[3] And Mark Shedd, former school superintendent and professor at Harvard, argued, The trouble is "either the teacher does not recognize that the subject matter is irrelevant, if ever it was relevant, or he is unwilling to change, discard, or restructure his materials and procedure as relevance demands."[4]

Weinstein and Fantini, who were then at the Ford Foundation, wrote an important book that addressed humanistic concerns and needs of students and that the school served as a "vehicle for developing students' self concepts and mature images of themselves as members of the human family." For these educators, students' concerns drove the curriculum: "It [was] the . . . major factor in determining the basic organizing idea . . . and content areas of the curriculum."[5] The entire curriculum was to be organized around three personal and social themes: the learners' personal experiences, the learners' affective domain (feelings and interests), and the learners' social context in which they lived.

Similarly, Paul Goodman, in a more radical vein, described schools as factories of failure: "What prevents . . . children from learning how to read? It is almost demonstrable that for many children, it is precisely going to school that prevents [them from reading]—because of the school's alien style, banning of spontaneous interest, extrinsic rewards and punishments."[6] Describing school as a "universal trap" that failed to meet the needs of urban students, he concluded that these children are

1. Erik H. Erikson, *Identity: Youth and Crisis* (New York: Norton, 1962); Edgar Z. Friedenberg, *Coming of Age in America* (New York: Random House, 1965).

2. Silberman, *Crisis in the Classroom.*

3. Carlton E. Beck, *Education for Relevance* (Boston: Houghton Miffin, 1968), p. 238.

4. Mark Shedd, "The Kinds of Education Programs We Need," in J. G. Saylor, ed. *The School of the Future—Now,* 1972 Yearbook (Washington, DC: Association for Supervision and Curriculum Development, 1972), p. 57.

5. Gerald Weinstein and Marco D. Fantini, *Toward a Humanistic Education: A Curriculum of Affect* (New York: Praeger, 1970), p. 109.

6. Paul Goodman, *Compulsory Mis-Education* (New York: Horizon Press, 1964), p. 32.

"herded into a situation that does not fit their disposition, for which they are unprepared by their background, and which does not interest them; [they] simply develop a reactive stupidity very different from their behavior on the street or ball field."[1]

When one of the leading professional groups, the Association for Supervision and Curriculum Development, published its 1962 yearbook, *Perceiving, Behaving, and Becoming,* the discussion of humanism took on a very serious tone, one that was now adopted by the educational Establishment.[2] It represented a new focus for education, an approach to curricular design and instructional delivery that would allow individuals to become fully functioning persons. Arthur Combs, the chairperson of the yearbook, noted some key questions: "What kind of person would it be who has truly achieved the ultimate in self-realization? How do they come about? What factors went into making this kind of person?" He suggested that the curriculum be designed to stress human potential and to enable the student to be involved in the process of becoming. The emphasis was on empowering individuals—what today is called *postpositivistic thinking,* whereby a person is involved with his or her reality, participating in it, and is aware of the notion of becoming.

The 1977 yearbook of the Association for Supervision and Curriculum Development, entitled *Feeling, Valuing, and the Art of Growing,* also stressed the affective dimensions of becoming and humanistic educational designs. The yearbook made a case for social and personal development, indicating that we need to harness human potential and to allow it to fully develop. It suggested that educators must permit students to feel, value, and grow—to focus on the affective domain.[3]

The relevancy and modern humanistic tone was set in the introduction of the yearbook. It asked readers "to see the different levels at which affect may be present" with a series of some 25 follow-up statements, such as "consider the wholeness of the process; think about basic human processes—decision making, valuing, loving—as they relate to the affective; consider play as a source of insight; consider involvement as a means of drawing together various components of affect; build upon the fuller images of humankind," and so on.[4]

In response to the demands for curriculum relevance and humanistic education, many schools and colleges added courses in black studies, urban studies, sex education, drug education, and environmental education. Later, multicultural education, global studies, women studies, and gay studies were added to the list. Chaucer, Dante, Shakespeare, and the rest of the classics were dubbed as westernized, Euroethnic, and male-dominated literature, and many "slice of life" contemporary stories and plays were considered more relevant to young adults and to the ways of the current world. This was the first all-out assault on western literature (which was to gain greater mo-

1. Ibid., p. 28.
2. Arthur W. Combs, ed. *Perceiving, Behaving, and Becoming,* 1962 Yearbook (Washington, DC: Association for Supervision and Curriculum Development, 1962).
3. Louise M. Berman and Jessie A. Roderick, eds. *Feeling, Valuing, and the Art of Growing: Insights into the Affective,* 1977 Yearbook (Washington, DC: Association for Supervision and Curriculum Development, 1977).
4. Ibid., p. 5.

mentum in the 1990s to the present) by student rebels and the political left, who sought to condemn the accumulation of past achievements because they saw the common culture as reflective of the older generation and establishment—and that they saw as a trap and a need to put down.

The same critics of the classics, along with a host of "me too" educators, attacked standardized tests—including simple placement and diagnostic tests—as discriminatory, elitist, and instruments for tracking disadvantaged students (mainly poor and minority students) into second-class programs and perpetuating discrimination in society. Not only were the tests considered instruments of middle-class and white society, discriminating against and putting down lower-class and minority society, but so were many textbooks and teachers. Textbooks were viewed as irrelevant and as stereotyping all subordinate groups, especially ethnic minorities, women, labor and working-class groups, and gays, and even tilting the discussion in favor of Republican presidents and suburban living.[1] The attitudes and expectations of teachers were also questioned. Although textbooks today are much more inclusive of all groups—and in some cases may have tilted too far against boys, middle-class and white society, heterosexuals, and traditional values—teachers are still ridiculed for their behaviors, methods, and attitudes toward nonachieving groups. The popular term today is the *self-fulfilling prophecy*, whereby teacher expectations and behavior influence student outcomes.

Various new programs and courses in psychology with a "human orientation," sometimes called *third force psychology*, gained legitimacy and emphasized the sense of self, human values, the personal meaning of experiences, psychological health, and respect for human differences. This new third force was spearheaded by the works of Arthur Combs, Abraham Maslow, and Carl Rogers, who mixed a little old-fashioned progressivism with old-fashioned existentialism and gestalt psychology to arrive at these new human insights and images.[2] On a more extreme level, the new psychology also included transcendental thinking, meditation, yoga, Eastern philosophy and psychology, various mind-liberating experiences, and other "higher levels" of affective thinking, including hedonic behavior and freedom of expression. In describing this one new psychology, one educator wrote that "the sources and substance of man's knowledge [was] his subjective states of mind . . . feelings . . . and soul."[3]

1. Margaret T. Bernstein, "The New Politics of Textbook Adoption," *Education Digest* (December 1985), pp. 12–15; Bernstein, "The Academy's Contribution to the Improvement of America's Textbooks," *Phi Delta Kappan* (November 1988), pp. 193–198; Allan C. Ornstein, "Textbook Instruction: Processes and Strategies," *NASSP Bulletin* (December 1989), pp. 105–111; and Ornstein, "The Censored Curriculum: The Problems with Textbooks Today," *NASSP Bulletin* (November 1992), pp. 1–9.

2. Combs, *The Professional Education of Teachers;* Abraham H. Maslow, *Toward Psychology of Being,* 2nd ed. (New York: Van Nostrand Reinhold, 1968); Carl R. Rogers, *On Becoming a Person* (Boston: Houghton Mifflin, 1961); and Rogers, *Freedom to Learn* (Columbus, OH: Merrill, 1969).

3. George J. Mouly, *Psychology for Effective Teaching,* 3rd ed. (New York: Holt, Rinehart and Winston, 1973), p. 109.

Much of the underpinning for humanistic education and humanistic psychology first developed in the 1950s in opposition to the then dominant psychological school of behaviorism. This new psychological orientation emphasized that human action was much more than a response to a stimuli, that personal meaning was more important than rational methods, that the focus of attention should be on the subjective rather than objective nature of human existence, and that there was a relationship between learning and feeling. In the reawakening of humanistic interest, there was also large-scale reaction against scientific, logical, and technological thought and in describing social and psychological thought—a prelude to the current postmodernism that rejects Newtonian physics and Descartes' philosophy—condemned today as "western" and "male-dominated" thought.

These postmodern theorists "disrupt" the status quo of our thinking. Depending on what side of the social science or scientific fence we sit, we celebrate their views as revisionary and cutting edge or we write them off as silly and ideological. In the conflict over what is legitimate research, one group is preoccupied with going beyond traditional research and introducing qualitative and artistic methods, whereas another group wants to retain quantitative and scientific methods. One camp is willing to accept nonmeasureable variables, contextual (sometimes fuzzy) explanations, and abstract and unusual (even chaotic) thought; the other camp has a predisposition toward empirical data, probability and precision in explaining phenomena, and reasoned arguments. One group relies on opinion, stance, and ideology as expressive strategies and as a means for developing theories; the other group rejects this type of language, refers to it as politics, and prefers clinical and objective data as "true" data. One group sees the human side of its subjects and wishes to develop their voices and stories, whereas the other group is more technical and removed from its subjects for purpose of objectivity and validity. The intensity of the debate is keenly expressed in a recent tête-à-tête between Tom Knapp and Elliot Eisner, and between Tom Barone and Richard Mayer, in issues of the *Educational Researcher*.[1]

## Neoconservatism: Present-Day Warnings and Concerns

America's failure to heed Bruner's advice and Conant's warnings of the post-*Sputnik* era (moderate voices of reform) can be viewed by some as one reason why national attention has turned to a new wave of educational reform (sparked by the publication of *A Nation at Risk* in 1983), calling for educational excellence and higher education standards. In a nutshell, the concerns of the *Sputnik* era have resurfaced in the new millennium under the themes of "core curriculum," "academic curriculum," "standards-based education," "high-stakes testing," and "teacher accountability." The only difference is the international threat. Instead of being perceived in military

---

1. See the *Educational Researcher* (January–February 1999), pp. 18–20; (October 2001), pp. 24–32.

terms of guns and tanks, as in the *Sputnik*–Cold War period it is now perceived in economic terms, or human capital and the globalization of the world markets.

For present-day conservative critics such as Lynn Cheney, who heads the Council on Basic Education, as well as William Bennett, Chester Finn, and Diane Ravitch, who were all part of the Department of Education during the Republication Administration for 20 years (Nixon, Reagan, and Bush senior), it is the "touchy-feely" attitude of the previous generation that puts today's education system at risk. Our schools have failed, according to Ravitch, because academics have taken a backseat for the last century.[1] Progressive and humanistic theories, with their emphasis on a student-centered curriculum, are villainized by Ravitch in the same way William Bagley (one of the early essentialists) criticized progressivism in the 1930s and Arthur Bestor and Admiral Hyman Rickover criticized progressivism in the 1950s. Ravitch's argument—the need to toughen standards and stress an academic curriculum—reflects much of the current education reform efforts: the need for educational excellence and higher academic standards for all students.

During the cold war, there were two great giants and two great ideologies squaring off at each other. At the present, the United States "bestrides the globe like a colossus. It dominates business, commerce and communications; its economy is the world's most successful [even though it has lost its manufacturing prowess to second- and third-world nations such as China, Taiwan, India, and Mexico), its military second to none."[2] Yet, this colossus is uncertain and unsure about its political role across the oceans and its economical output at home. Having so much power, it does not know how to behave, to what extent it should involve itself as the world's police force, and to what extent it should act alone or in unison with junior partners. Having so much resources, the nation does not know how much money to spend on educating the future generation. Similarly, there is little agreement on which programs to emphasize and which programs need to be phased out so to avoid a "bottomless pit" in education policy. Given the massive brainpower among college students and need for hundreds of thousands of additional teachers, the nation also does not know how to attract the academic best, or even second best, to become teachers. Our school districts, some 15,000 in total, rely on outdated salary schedules to attract teachers—and it gets what it pays for.

A first-year teacher in 2000 with a master's degree earned, on average, $36,045. Individuals with master's degrees in telecommunications started at $79,000; in pharmaceuticals, $84,500; and in insurance, $90,000. After some 20 years or so (depending on the school district), the most a teacher can earn is, on average, $70,000. A top sales/marketing person in telecommunications can average $250,000; in pharmaceuticals, $450,000; and in insurance, $290,000.[3] Corporate life may have its drawbacks—office politics, gray and blue dress codes, and learning how to keep your mouth shut—but it is easier to understand the frustration of seasoned teachers with 10 or more years of experience. It is hard to eat dedication and love of teaching, to

1. Ravitch, *Left Back: A Century of Failed School Reform.*
2. "America's World," *Economist* (October 23, 1999), p. 15.
3. "MBA Payoffs," *New York Magazine* (unknown month, 2001), p. 53.

remain dedicated to a life of barely making do in a world of rising prices and consumerism, or to keep on saying "teaching has its own rewards"—a cliché I continuously hear among my education colleagues and students.

We need to provide a salary schedule for teachers that considers supply and demand (higher salaries for science and math teachers) and that is performance based and includes a career ladder for highly qualified and experienced teachers— amounting to at least $125,000 to $150,000, depending on the state and consumer price index. We need to provide an extra differential for teaching in difficult inner-city schools—to increase teacher supply in the cities; and, in turn, to eliminate ineffective teachers and not to assign new teachers and uncertified teachers (a common practice) to the worst schools.

A related idea would be to stiffen academic requirements of teacher education programs so we don't certify semi-illiterate teachers who are unable to pass simple basic skills tests. These data are troubling, since test score results show racial gaps in teacher tests in almost every state.[1] The next step is to stiffen licensing standards by developing a national test with academic teeth, to eliminate autonomous state standards, and to prevent school districts from hiring who they wish with no regard to preparation or competencies. Finally, we need to make teacher licenses portable, from state to state, to attract teachers in states that need them.

One thing is sure: Considering that we live in a highly technocratic, computerized, and scientific world, one in which knowledge has great impact on our standard of living, and in a world in which the push of a button can have an enormous impact on our lives, student enrollments in science and mathematics have serious implications for the future of our country. Although this statement could have been made 20 years ago (when *A Nation at Risk* was published) or 50 years ago (when *Sputnik* was launched), the words ring true today. We live in a "global village," and mainly through immigration and brain drain from other nations are we able to fill our scientific and technological needs. But, given that the *world* is now a global village— one that is highly interconnected and can be radically changed by a push of a button, a computer virus, an electronic or communications malfunction, or a nuclear meltdown—the stress on science, math, and technology is crucial. For the first 95 years of the last century, the technology of teaching did not change. Now, in the last 10 years or so, it is changing before our eyes, and it is hard to imagine how technology will shape teaching in the next 10 or 20 years.

## A Turning Point: Western and Islamic Worlds

We all know that the world has changed since 9-11. It is similar to Sarajevo and Pearl Harbor—setting a course of events and changing history. As we try to seek explanations in classrooms and schools, we should grow more appreciative of our own free-

1. Stephen Bauchero, "Law Could Worsen Teacher Shortage," *Chicago Tribune* (March 26, 2002), p. 14; Carl Campanile, "Racial Gap in Teacher Tests Brings Alarm," *New York Post* (March 31, 2002), p. 3. Also see Richard W. Riley, "Education Reform Through Standards and Partnerships," *Phi Delta Kappan* (May 2002), pp. 700–707.

dom, liberty, and tolerance toward diverse groups in our society. It is worth noting that our democratic way of life and values depend on our schools. Jefferson, Mann, and Dewey understood it, and I am convinced that most educators today understand it.

For Jefferson and many of his contemporaries, the religious persecutions of the sixteenth and seventeenth centuries are the equivalent of what slavery and racial discrimination has been for us. For Jefferson, freedom meant freedom of religion; for Martin Luther King Jr., freedom meant freedom from racial bigotry and discrimination. Our early leaders insisted on the separation of church and state, not to protect the church from the state but to protect the state from religious fanaticism. In short, we do not need God to tell us what is right or wrong. Each of us has a heart and a brain, and each of us can become educated about ideas and values that infer what is a good person and a good society. Each of us understands that moderate views must prevail over religious extremism; otherwise, we are doomed to fight crusades and holy wars. European history is ripe with this condition, and the Muslim world is now experiencing the need for the "silent majority" to act against the fanatic minority.

The United States, being a strong and wealthy society, incites envy because of its economic success, democratic ideals, secular rationalism, and freedom and ideals that threaten theocracy and autocracy.[1] The situation is compounded in the Muslim world because of their own lack of freedom and prosperity, and their religious intolerance expressed by growing radical Islamic groups. The fact is, recent Gallup polls of people surveyed in nine Muslim countries reveal that the majority of Muslims blame Americans for their own misfortunes and believe that the real perpetrators of 9-11 were either Jews, Christian fundamentalists, drug and mafia groups, the United States itself, or other "oppressed groups" and non-Muslim groups.[2]

Not only does this help explain the gulf between the two cultures or two parts of the world but it also illustrates the tendency for others to blame Americans for their own misfortunes. Concocting some conspiracy theory is one way for Muslim fundamentalist or radical groups to make sense out of their own plight and to explain what went wrong in their own society—why some are still living in caves or stone huts without toilets. It can be explained by 2,500 years of history: one-fourth of 1 percent exploiting more than 99 percent of the people within their own society—the way of the Muslim world and the world around us—compounded by their failure to fully utilize 50 percent (i.e., women) of their human resources for the last 500 years. To be sure, it has been 500 years (the medieval period) since Muslims fell from first or second place in science, art, and culture to near the bottom of the heap.

And so, when the Twin Towers collapsed, many Muslims cheered and said we deserved it. They were not all extremists, and some who cheered were living in the United States. Even worse, some of our European allies, and a few of our citizens, view our antiterrorist policies and our war against radical Islamic groups with alarm and trepidation. There are even a few academics and café intellects telling us that the new American patriotism is sort of a "red-neck" response to a misunderstood

1. Victor D. Hanson, "Classics and War," *Imprimis* (February 2002), pp. 1–5.
2. Erica Goode, "Finding Answers in Secret Plots," *New York Times* (March 10, 2002), Sect. 4, p. 3.

civilization that needs our understanding, not our bullets or rockets. When suicide bombers kill Israeli children in buses or in markets, some "Europeans say 'the Jews had it coming.' They've said it before, haven't they?"[1] Well, that's what a good many Muslims said about the attack on the United States that killed thousands of civilians: "They had it coming!" There is no point in asking for the reasons of this response, because there is no rational answer and no common view of what is right or wrong, not when religious fanaticism rears its ugly head.

Today, we are confronted with an enemy that is just as dangerous, just as determined as the original "axis of evil"—Nazism, fascism, and Japanese imperialism—and communism we had to defeat in the twentieth century. The United States had to save its European and Asian allies from these menaces, and we are forced to do the same now for the civilized world. On September 11, 2001, extremist Islamists attacked American and western ideals, beliefs, and values—whatever we hold dear. Once again, democracy is being tested, as it has been tested since the dawn of western civilization. As Plato asserted, "War is always existing by nature." War between nations is part of the human condition; it is much more tragic and fearsome if it becomes a war between civilizations, with Americans being pulled into the conflict as the major police force.

Thomas Friedman, who writes regularly for the *New York Times* on foreign policy, warms us that hatred in the Islam world is rampant, although it has not infected the majority of Muslims. A combination of population growth, terrorism, biological weapons, and weapons of mass destruction are descending on us. It might not be long before some terrorist tries to destroy Israel.[2] And there will be those who, again, will say, "They had it coming." The trouble is, there are lessons in history. It won't be long before another terrorist or group of terrorists come knocking at our door. Unless the moderates in the Muslim world get a grip on themselves, overcome their schizophrenia and display courage, and then shut down terrorist camps and religious schools that preach a holy war against the West, we are heading for protracted war, or potential World War III. Given the history of war, the history of religious fanaticism and aggression, and the clash of the two cultures over the last several centuries (which date back to the Crusades), we could be heading for a long nightmare.

The schools can modify the curriculum and introduce courses about the history, literature, and culture of Islamism, and teachers can help in the battle for the mind that explains the ideals of democracy and values of the West. Teachers and schools can ensure respect for diversity, but in the long run, Americans will have to face up to terrorism and deal with groups and nations that pose a threat to our existence. Our students need to understand that historical events are not linear. There were enough discernible trends leading up to 9-11. One historian points out hijacking planes has been around since the late 1960s and it has been used by Palestine and Muslim liberation groups, and other fringe groups, totaling some 500 hijackings. As for the idea

1. Raymond Sokolov, "A Surprise Attack at Breakfast: You Stupid Yanks!" *Wall Street Journal* (February 22, 2002), p. 16.
2. Thomas L. Friedman, "A Foul Wind," *New York Times* (March 10, 2002), Sect. 4, p. 19.

of flying planes into populous targets, the Japanese invented that idea in 1944 with 3,913 Kamikaze pilots. Between 1995 and 2000, there were more than 2,100 terrorist incidents, but only 15 occurred in North America and caused only seven casualties.[1] It was the success of the 9-11 terrorists that is new and has led to a wake-up call.

We should be wary of attaching too much importance to one event. We must stay with the big picture. Although we should try to predict possible scenarios, it is impossible to predict exactly what will happen. Ten years from now, I hope the dark clouds that are building dissipate and the world as Americans knew it is not much different—despite the trends that are now shaping the world.

## What Knowledge Is of Most Worth?

So we have come a full cycle and return to the original question: What knowledge is of most worth? When Spencer wrote his famous essay, he argued that science was the most practical subject for the survival of the individual and society, yet it occupied minimal space in the curriculum because classical, impractical, and ornamental traditions prevailed.[2]

Spencer also maintained that students should be taught *how* to think (or problem solve) and not *what* to think. But facts, more facts, and still more facts was the ideal method of teaching and learning, keenly expressed by Charles Dickens in his novel, *Hard Times*. Mr. Gradgrind, the school patron, demonstrates model teaching for the schoolteacher: "Now what I want is Facts. Facts alone are wanted in life. Plant nothing else, and root out everything else, this is the principle on which I bring up children. Stick to the facts, Sir!!"[3]

There is little difference between facts and some aspects of knowledge, but 100 years after the publication of *Hard Times* the issues were still being discussed. In a well-accepted classification of thinking and problem solving by Benjamin Bloom, knowledge was ranked as the lowest form of cognitive learning. However, he pointed out that the acquisition of knowledge is the most common educational objective, that teachers tend to emphasize it in the classroom, and test-makers tend to emphasize it on tests.[4] To help clarify Bloom, knowledge by itself has limited value and should be used as a basis or foundation for more advanced thinking, what he calls "problem solving." Of course, basic knowledge has some practical or functional value, but it serves only as the rudiment for more theoretical or abstract thinking.[5]

1. Niall Ferguson, "2011," *New York Times Magazine* (December 2, 2001), pp. 76–79; Ferguson, *The Age of Terror* (New York: Basic Books, 2002).
2. Spencer, *Education: Intellectual, Moral and Physical*.
3. Charles Dickens, *Hard Times* (New York: E. P. Dutton, 1894), p. 1.
4. Benjamin S. Bloom et al., *Taxonomy of Educational Objectives, Handbook I: Cognitive Domain* (New York: McKay, 1956).
5. The goal is to encourage advanced thinking—what the Greeks called "contemplation," what Dewey called "rational" and "reflective thinking," what Bruner and Schwab called "structure," what Adler and Sizer called "ideas," what Chall and Hirsh called "deep understanding," what learning theorists today call "critical thinking" and "high-order thinking," and what I simply call old-fashioned analysis and problem solving.

Knowledge is often construed as an index of intelligence and level of education attained by a person: Witness the popularity of *The $64,000 Question* and 40 years later *Who Wants to Be a Millionaire?* Facts drive such shows and listeners often comment on how "smart" someone is who answers several factual-oriented or knowledge-based questions. The point is, however, knowledge of facts is of little value if it cannot be utilized in new situations and for more complex learning; the learner (and teacher) need to make use of knowledge—as a base or tool for the pursuit of higher forms of cognition—often called *problem solving* by progressive educators (Dewey and Tyler), *inquiry-based* or *discovery learning* (Ausubel and Bruner), *formal operations* (Piaget and Vygotsky), and/or *critical thinking* (Marzano and Sternberg).

**Explosion of Knowledge**    Since the 1950s, many educators have continued to call attention to the explosion of knowledge. Every 15 years or so, our significant knowledge doubles. Although it cannot continue to double in the future, the explosion of knowledge—especially in health, science, and technology—makes it important to continuously reappraise and revise existing curricula. "It can be affirmed unequivocally," says Bentley Glass, "that the amount of scientific knowledge available at the end of one's life will be almost one hundred times what it was when he was born." Moreover, 95 percent of all the scientists who ever lived are alive today.[1]

Although Bentley packaged these remarks more than 20 years ago, his voice still rings true; in fact, it can be inferred that half of what a graduate engineer or computer specialist studies today will be obsolete in 10 years; half the pills dispensed today at the local pharmacist will be replaced or improved. I would venture to guess that half or more of what we need to know to function in scientific or technical jobs by the year 2020 is not even known today, by anyone.

The idea that knowledge is increasing exponentially or geometrically obscures the fact that the development of knowledge in many fields—especially science, technology, and medicine—is more typically related to "branching" (the creation of several subdivisions or specialties within fields), not just simple growth. Each advance in a particular field has the potential for creating another branch. In education, one can find some indicators of proliferation of several fields of study, or branches, sometimes identified by departments, programs, and/or core courses or minors, and within each field, or branch, are several specializations of knowledge and job titles. With this increase of knowledge, there are new professional journals, papers, and speeches, all adding to the proliferation of knowledge. The almost incredible explosion of knowledge threatens to overwhelm us unless we can find ways to deal with this new and growing wealth of information; new knowledge must be constantly introduced into each field of study or subject, while less important material is pruned away. In assessing the ongoing rush of knowledge, Alvin Toffler asserted some 30 years ago that knowledge taught should be related to the future: "Nothing should be included in the

---

1. Bentley Glass, *The Timely and Timeless* (New York: Basic Books, 1980). Also see Edward Teller, *A Twentieth-Century Journey in Science and Politics* (Cambridge, MA: Perseus Press, 2001). Cornering knowledge, not sharing it with others, made the difference or was the crucial factor in the outcomes of World War II and the Cold War.

required curriculum unless it can be strongly justified in terms of the future. If this means scrapping a substantial part of the formal curriculum, so be it."[1]

The question arises whether teachers are keeping up with the explosion of knowledge, at least the knowledge in pedagogy or content they teach. When I was younger and more feisty, I painted a harsh portrait of the teacher as it related to change and the explosion of knowledge:

> Had Rip Van Winkle been a teacher and slept for *fifty years* he could return to the classroom and perform relatively well; the chalk, eraser, blackboard, textbook, and pen and paper are still the main tools for most teachers, as they were a half a century ago—or longer. If Mr. Winkle's occupation had been related to one of three fields . . . science, technology, and medicine . . . and had he dozed off for five years, he would be unable to function effectively, for his knowledge and skills would be drastically dated.[2]

This statement was made *thirty years* ago, before the introduction of the computer. No question, the computer represents a significant change in the classroom and is essential for teachers to be competent. Yet, we all know that most classrooms don't have computers; the pen or pencil still makes the point, and a goodly percentage of older teachers (age 40 and over) are computer illiterate. To update matters, had Rip Van Winkle gone to sleep for 80 years (the original 50 + 30), he would still be able to bluff his way in the classroom. If he taught at the middle school or high school level, he would most likely need to do some last-minute preparation in his content area. But there are many teachers who teach out of license, and others who lack depth of knowledge in their content areas, and prepare by reading the homework assignment or textbook the night before teaching the lesson.

Research suggests that about one-third of all secondary teachers (grades 7–12) who teach math do not have a major or minor in math or related disciplines such as math education or science; about 25 percent of all English teachers and 20 percent of all science teachers have the same problem: Even if they are qualified to teach in a field (say, science), many are not qualified to teach a particular subject (chemistry or physics).[3] The situation is more alarming in big cities, where bodies count more than academic qualifications.

Essential Knowledge    If you will welcome or support E. D. Hirsh's idea of cultural literacy, then Mr. Winkle's content or subject preparation is basically intact, because more than 80 percent of the 5,000 items Hirsh recommends as important refer to events, people, or places in use for more than 100 years; about 25 percent of his essential knowledge deals with the classics. The inference is that Hirsch is against large-scale pruning and updating of the curriculum; as a modern-day essentialist, he

1. Alvin Toffler, *Future Shock* (New York: Random House, 1970), p. 132. Also see Alvin Toffler, *The Third Wave* (New York: Morrow, 1980).

2. Allan C. Ornstein, *Urban Education* (Columbus, OH: Merrill, 1972), p. 50.

3. Richard M. Ingersoll, "The Problem of Unqualified Teachers in American Secondary Schools," *Educational Researcher* (March 1999), pp. 26–37.

maintains there is a body of knowledge essential to learn for cultural literacy (what he calls "functional literacy") and "effective communication for our nation's populace. . . . Shared information is necessary for true literacy," and it has nothing to do with WASP culture (or the metaphors of domination) nor specific job-related tasks, but with the imperatives of a broad grasp and understanding of mainstream culture.[1] This argument, of course, omits pop culture and the contributions of media that influence our changing culture, as well as all ethnic and folk references.

Complementing his narrative is a compilation of essential items from history, geography, literature, and science, not to be memorized, as Mr. Gradgrind might have us do, but for students to know something about in context with their thoughts and speech. We don't have to know the fine details, but there should be some minimum level of understanding and competence, depending on the subject area and topic, for effective communication. Hirsh stresses the importance of scientific information at all levels of schooling; moreover, he has written a series of follow-up books on essential knowledge for every grade level. For him, and a growing number of present-day essentialists (Cheney, Bennett, Finn, Ravitch, etc.), knowing the facts increases students' capacity to comprehend what they read, see, hear, and discuss. The need for background knowledge is judged important for future communication and specialization. Finally, Hirsch argues that we have overlooked content and have stressed process—or thinking skills—with little regard for subject matter. The outcome has been a decline in national literacy.

The need is to transmit the shared knowledge and values of adult society to youth. Without the transmission of a shared cultural core to the young, conservative educators argue that U.S. society will become fragmented, and Americans' ability to accumulate and communicate information across the nation and to various segments of the populace will diminish, especially among immigrants and ethnic groups. We may all subscribe to multicultural education and recognize we are a nation of many nations, but this only increases the need for a knowledge base and an academic core to be taught to all students.

Returning to the Liberal Arts    A few years ago, Allan Bloom, in *The Closing of the American Mind*, voiced concern about education being relative to particular times and places, instead of being consistent with universal standards and subjects.[2] Like other perennialists, Bloom asserts that cultural relativism—with its emphasis on trivial pursuits, quick fixes, relevancy, and self-esteem—has eroded the quality of American education. Our media and educational institutions are marked by an easy-going, flippant, indifference to critical thought. Deprived of a serious liberal arts and science education, avoiding an engagement with great works and great ideas of the past, our youth lack educational depth.

---

1. E. D. Hirsh, *Cultural Literacy: What Every American Needs to Know,* rev. ed. (Boston: Houghton Mifflin, 1987), p. 10.
2. Allan Bloom, *The Closing of the American Mind* (New York: Simon and Schuster, 1987).

Indeed, if we want to ask ourselves how and where we went wrong, why we are in social and moral decline, Bloom offers a conservative analysis and sense of fundamental reform and what is crucial to the well-being of the nation. To remedy American education and to neutralize the problems caused by cultural relativism, Bloom, as did Robert Hutchins and Mortimer Adler over 25 years ago, seeks to reestablish the idea of an educated person along the line of the great books and great thinkers and to reestablish the virtues of a liberal education.

It is somewhat mind-boggling, even foolhardy, to downplay the importance of western culture (our own civilization) or the great books that purport our heritage and illustrate the great ideas, principles, and values that have evolved and shaped our culture over the last 2,500 to 5,700 years. (Where we trace our historical roots and culture largely depends on whether we start with the Hebrews or the Greeks or even with the Egyptians.) It is fashionable to criticize the great books as white, male, and Eurocentric, but western civilization is rooted in European history, philosophy, and literature—and, with the exception of the ancient Greeks, past civilizations rarely gave women equal education or equal status.

The great books approach, along with serious thinking and meritocracy, is disfavored partially because of white guilt and political correctness (discussed earlier). Many educators would like to stress what Robert Hutchins (former president of the University of Chicago) called the *liberal arts*, what Jeanne Chall (Harvard reading specialist) calls *world knowledge*, what E. D. Hirsh calls *essential knowledge* and *cultural literacy*, and what Bloom calls the *great books*. But educators are afraid of being labeled antiminority and insensitive to multiculturalism and diversity. Postmodernists, especially feminists and minorities, keep issues of gender and race alive as a means to curtail public discussion that differs from their vision. It is this vulnerability, even fear, of being labeled because of one's gender or race that makes it easy to substitute Plato, Locke, Kant, or Ibsen for lesser works by women and third-world authors.

Western civilization perceived by postmodernists has come at a price, according to Shelby Steele: the exploitation and victimization of people of color[1] and, if I may add, women. Therefore, a revisionary list of great books and liberal arts courses are needed to balance the literature of the dominant group. The cultural capital of women and minorities, their voice and stories, must be heard to "educate" those who need to be educated and to learn the "truth." It is this war in academia that holds hostage many educators from advancing the great ideas and great literature of western civilization, and leads, I am sad to say, to cultural relativism and the decline of liberal arts, reiterated by Bloom and Hutchins.

## Future Concerns: Teachers and Technology

In 1969, Postman and Weingartner published a provocative book, *Teaching as a Subversive Activity*, which had an impact on educators in the 1970s. On the first page of the book, they wrote, "Please be advised that page 61 . . . has been left blank deliberately" (p. 1). The purpose of the blank page, as explained on page 60, was to provide

1. Steele, "War of the Worlds."

the reader the opportunity to answer questions about "What's worth teaching?" and "What's worth knowing?" Actually, Ralph Tyler provided part of the answer 20 years prior to their book by pointing out that it's not what the teacher does or claims is important, rather "learning takes place through the active behavior of the student";[1] it is what the learner *does* that counts and what the learner *thinks* is important. This means that when the teacher organizes the content and classroom activities, he or she must also understand the interests and abilities of his or her students. Hence, this is nothing more than an extension of Dewey's view of how children best learn, and it takes us back to square one—the neoconservative attack on a student-centered curriculum and "soft education."

The key for determining what subject matter or content is most worthwhile is to ask what skills, knowledge, ideas, and values are important to effectively function in society. As society changes, so should the curriculum. The problem, however, is that the old curriculum rarely disappears; we merely add to old reading lists and/or reinvent old themes under new labels, such as *cooperative learning, core curriculum, team teaching, block scheduling, outcome-based education*—all of which date back 50 to 100 years. Even worse, very few schools or school districts take the *initiative* and revise curriculum on a regular basis. Tradition, textbooks, and tests (and college entrance requirements at the high school level) determine content; even worse, some criticism or outcry from the public causes school people to *react*. Part of the problem is that school administrators who should be taking the lead in curriculum making are rarely required to learn how to develop and design curriculum: Administrative certification requirements emphasize administrative theory and financial and legal issues. In some states, such as New York and New Jersey, an administrator doesn't even need a course in curriculum to become certified (so long as he or she enrolls in supervision courses).

For all practical purposes, teachers are often "deprofessionalized" and "deskilled" to teaching a prepackaged curriculum. It is an observation, first mentioned by Charles Silberman more than 30 years ago, that "teacher-proof" materials are often introduced into schools under the guise of reform because teachers are not trusted or considered capable. Mike Apple made a similar comment some 20 years ago, asserting that school administrators are bent on "proletarizing" teachers—controlling them, reducing their autonomy, putting pressure on them to conform, keeping a lid on their salaries, and so on.[2] Although Apple is writing from a neomarxist view, we must recognize that the professional identity of teachers continues to suffer; they are often demoralized by poor working conditions and relatively low pay. The fact is that teacher burnout and teacher turnover prevail in large numbers, despite claims of improved teachers training and teacher professionalism. (Working conditions, pay, and professionalism are worse in the cities than in the suburbs, because of big bureaucracy and limited finances. Similarly, teachers have much less input in curriculum matters in city schools; the curricu-

---

1. Ralph W. Tyler, *Basic Principles of Curriculum and Instruction* (Chicago: University of Chicago Press, 1949), p. 64.
   2. Silberman, *Crisis in the Classroom;* Michael W. Apple, *Teachers and Texts* (New York: Routledge & Kegan Paul, 1986).

lum is handed down to them from the central office, already packaged and stapled, just as it was reported some 30 years ago.)

Certainly, technology has changed the curriculum in terms of new skills and ideas to learn, but most students and teachers have superficial knowledge and some have limited exposure by lack of opportunity or choice. A number of states are now requiring proficiency in using technology in order to be certified to teach, and several school districts are offering on-line courses for middle school and high school students. The day may come when it will be easier to set sit in bed or on a couch at home than to go to class, especially if lectures become available on line. (Ohio has already moved in this direction with a new school, called the Electronic Classroom of Tomorrow [ECOT], sponsored by the Lucas County School District, and with a K–12 enrollment of over 2,000 students. The University of Phoenix is the largest provider of on-line college courses; it has some 87,000 students in 26 states.) The biggest problem is that the lack of socialization and creating a passive recipient of knowledge does little to improve problem-solving skills.[1] As of 2000, more than a dozen colleges and universities offered fully developed teacher preparation programs on line in an attempt to appeal to young adults who were changing careers or seeking advanced degrees; professors who teach these courses tend to report favorable feedback and evaluation of such courses.[2]

Do students learn more with computers? Of hundreds of studies involving computers and students in grades K–12, few have focused on learning outcomes. Several problems have been reported, however, ranging from dropped computers and broken monitors; misplaced accessories such as cards, disks, and batteries; technical problems like freezing, crashing, and misaligned printing (requiring the addition of an extra technician); physical strains among laptop users (back and neck); and the lack of proper teacher training.[3] Thus, one child's great new organizational learning tool can be another child's electronic headache. Being wired up and having access to unlimited information doesn't necessarily improve students' thinking, increase their reading of important books, or promote understanding of important ideas.

After wading through the hype about the potential of computers, research suggests that there is no academic improvement among most students who use computers.[4] A computer can make it easier for students to retrieve information, process words for a report, and communicate with people around the world, but it doesn't motivate them to learn or improve their learning. Increased time on the computer

1. Karen W. Arenson, "Going High Tech Degree by Degree" *New York Times* (January 11, 2000), p. 29; Leila Jason, "Is 8 am Too Early for You?" *Wall Street Journal* (August 22, 2001), p. 12; and Telephone conversation with Tom Lasley, Dean School of Education, University of Dayton, Ohio, November 27, 2001.

2. "Universities Offering Teaching Degrees, Credentials On Line," *Education Week* (February 14, 2001), pp. 1, 14.

3. Daniel J. Rocha, "The Emperor's New Laptop," *Education Week* (September 27, 2001), pp. 42, 46–47.

4. William M. Bulkeley, "Hard Lessons," *Wall Street Journal,* Technology Section (November 17, 1997), pp. 1, 4, 6; Rocha, "The Emperor's New Laptop."

often means spending time e-mailing, chatting, or browsing at the expense of school-work and reading books.

Actually, too many students are nestled in their respective time zones chatting with people on line in Boston, Chicago, and Los Angeles and exchanging intimacies (about hair color, breast sizes, tattoos) and ideologies (religious or ethnic-related sermons)—spending hours of "e-life" time that might have been spent otherwise engaged in homework and related academics. It is a world of instant messaging, a world that inadvertently pulls kids into a web of people they don't know, yet they converse sometimes for hours with these "virtual" strangers. Increasingly, parents are going to have to take responsibility and free their children from this escapism, from this world of squares and rectangles, and help them rejoin the world of reality—even if it means communicating occasionally with Luddites. Teachers and schools are going to have to find ways in (1) helping parents restrict the use of computers for children so they stay in touch with friends and family, (2) adopting age-appropriate guidelines for children's computer use, (3) educating children to make good choices about their computer use, and (4) equalizing access to computers for rich and poor students.

On a worldwide level, the Internet plays a role in the globalization of ideas, ranging from secretive and political messages to scholarly and medical publications from various countries. Instead of moving manuscripts and books on a ship or plane, a slow and inefficient way, the data can be sent digitally with e-mail from one country to another in a matter of seconds.[1] Ideas can be generated at maximum warp speed! There are translations (about 90 to 95 percent accurate) into English from European and Asian languages (there are fewer translations in the other direction). Far off, isolated places, such as Albania, Myanmar, rural China, and Indonesia can no longer remain untouched from the rest of the world. The spread of scholarly and democratic ideas, unfiltered information, is a reality.

The immediate downside or danger of the Internet is that hate messages can also be spread. People who gobble up these messages are often uneducated and seeking other people who hate all things and people they do. These people are seduced by digital information and take it for granted that if they learned it from the Internet, it must be true. In a world full of lies and anti-American propaganda, they now see the "truth." Friedman puts it in context with Muslim extremists spreading rumors (e.g., "The World Trade Center was a conspiracy by the XYZ group who support Bush"). Anyone or any group can stir passions among Internet users; or, as Friedman says, the Internet "infects people's minds with the most vile ideas. . . . [People] think it's [the Internet] the Bible."[2]

In basic terms, then, the Internet can move and exchange ideas in a flash, for good or bad, to educate or inflame people. It goes back to Dewey's analysis of education being neutral, and thus it can be used to foster democracy or dictatorship. It depends on purpose, context, and/or whether the user can independently think. If I may para-

---

1. Colin Day, "Globalizing the Exchange of Ideas," *Chronicle of Higher Education* (February 1, 2002), pp. 7–8.
2. Friedman, "Global Village Idiocy."

phrase Hamilton, he thought the masses or "herd" could not be trusted. Lenin, Stalin, Hitler, Mao, and Bin Laden and the Ayatollahs proved Hamilton to be right.

Given the world we live in, it's important for teachers to teach about democracy, understanding and respect for human rights, individual differences, and diverse customs and beliefs, and at the same time to examine and evaluate what brings us together as a nation and as citizens of the global village in which we are all interconnected in one way or another. Both the computer and the Internet are instruments for retrieving information and gaining knowledge. But the real promise for learning *how* to think, not *what* to think, and how and when to ask a question, and not to always say yes, lies with our teachers. For all the different views about what is a good education, and what knowledge is most worth, it goes back to our teachers and schools, showing students, and the world, that democracy and freedom are the cornerstones of civilization.

## Final Concerns: Modern Languages

Once more: What knowledge is worth learning? The number-one primary language in the world is Mandarin, followed by English, Hindi, and Spanish. Japanese ranks tenth and German and French rank lower. Nearly all foreign language programs in American schools offer Spanish, French, and German, and some offer Italian and Latin. As many as 58 percent of secondary students (grades 9–12) enrolled in a foreign language study Spanish, but fewer than .3 percent of U.S. high school students study Japanese, and about .1 percent attempt Mandarin.[1]

Failure to train students in Mandarin, the official language of China, is representative of our condescending and insulting attitude toward the nonwestern world and Asia, a dysfunctional foreign policy and close-minded attitude of ignoring the largest country in the world. What percent of American high school students study Hindi, the official language of the second-largest country? None! What percent of American high school students, except those in Islamic private schools, study Arabic and Farsi, the two major languages of the Muslim world? Next to none (less than .1 percent in Arabic and zero for Farsi). Also, about one-fourth of 1 percent of the public schools in the country have a community education program in Arabic or Farsi, usually meeting once or twice a week in the evening.[2]

During the Cold War, there was increased enrollments of Russian foreign language courses and other "security-related" courses such as math, science, and engineering,

1. Allan C. Ornstein, "Curriculum Trends Revisited," in A. C. Ornstein and L. Behar-Horenstein, eds., *Contemporary Issues in Curriculum,* 2nd ed. (Boston: Allyn and Bacon, 1999), pp. 265–267. See also *Digest of Education Statistics 2000,* Table 58, p. 69.

2. Dora Johnson of the Center for Applied Linguistics in Washington, DC, claims only two public high schools, one in Dearborn, Michigan, and the other in Houston, offer two or more years in Arabic. None offers Farsi. Personal conversation on July 23, 2002. Also see *Foreign Language Instruction in the United States* (Washington, DC: Center for Applied Linguistics, 1999), Table 9, p. 19.

at the college level. A sense of relaxation surfaced that coincided with the reduced threat of war with the Soviets. Thus, over the last decade, many schools of international relations shifted its emphasis from security to human rights, global economics, and environmental issues.[1]

As we move into the twenty-first century, it would be a shame that any modification in foreign language courses, from European or western languages to Mandarin, Hindi, Arabic, or Farsi, would be based on an international crisis—a reaction that the new enemy is either China, India, or the Muslim world. This type of thinking only creates new polarities: the United States versus China or the West versus Islam. Instead of modifying the curriculum because of new understanding of economic markets, of respect for other cultures and people, or the world is more interconnected, the curriculum may be changed because of perceived threats or fear. If so, that would be counterproductive—almost as counterproductive as framing the Chinese, Indian, or Islamic world in sweeping generalizations. One billion Chinese, one billion Indians, and one billion Muslims are very diverse. Although history does not change (it only gets revised or rewritten), political leaders and economic conditions do change, and subsequently, so does foreign policy and the need to communicate with and understand and respect other cultures.

In an age of multiculturalism, pluralism, and diversity, why is it that foreign language requirements for four-year college graduation has decreased from 34 percent in 1965 to less than 20 percent today?[2] Is it because the increasingly worldwide use of English dictates that we no longer have to learn other languages? Is it because the Cold War spurred the growth of foreign languages and now there is no Soviet threat? (If so, why didn't we offer Russian classes in high school when the Cold War was hot and heavy?) Is it based on difficulty of other languages or lack of willingness to break from Western tradition? Why, in a world in which western countries represent less than 10 percent of the population, do Spanish, French, Italian, German, and Latin (western and European languages) dominate 99 percent of all high school foreign language study? Given a shrinking western world, and a declining role in Spain, France, Italy, and Germany on the world stage, why do we cling to an outdated western view of superiority?

For all the multicultural buzzwords about respecting, understanding and appreciating other cultures, why is it that our class discussions and readings are limited to black culture (with a little sprinkling of Hispanic and Native American culture)? Is it because the depth of knowledge of another culture suggests more than the reading of one or two novels by James Baldwin, Malcolm X, or Toni Morrison, or watching a movie such as *Dances With Wolves*? Does it all boil down to political pressure and political correctness? Or is it just a matter of international innocence or stupidity? We

1. Eyal Press, "It's a Volatile, Complex World," *New York Times Education Life* (November 11, 2001), pp. 20–22, 35.

2. Telephone conversation with Laura Siaya, American Council on Education, July 24, 2002.

expect or hope that nonwestern civilizations will become more modern in order to spread democracy and capitalism. We expect them to wear Nike shoes and Yankee baseball hats and drink Coca-Cola, but we cannot learn their language.

Many Americans have no interest in learning difficult languages or languages other than those of western nations. We seem to need some foreign stimulant, some vague feeling that we should expand our horizons—something like a wartime concern, an economic imperative, or even some missionary calling. "Multiculturalism may not have prodded us to study cultures fundamentally different from our own," writes one observer, but the "war on terrorism" may be the catalyst.[1] For the last 100 years or more, the door has been closed to studying other cultures, despite the fact that about 700,000 immigrants from nonwestern countries have come to our shores each year since 1970. Given the global village we live in, the need to understand the world's inhabitants (so we don't kill each other or blow ourselves off the map), there is need for expanding global education and foreign language studies.

Language and Thought    Both Piaget and Vygotsky made it clear that language and thought are tied together, and that without language, rational thought is limited. Audio and visual stimuli might produce what Piaget termed the *sensorimotor* stage of cognition, which involves reflex operations and undifferentiated understanding in relation to environmental patterns. Such stimuli might also produce what Vygotsky termed *spontaneous concepts*—concepts that are not systematic, structured, or generalized into a larger mental framework. But language, in short, permits us to process and organize information, and to communicate efficiently with other people.

*The Tale of Genji* illustrates the need to know the language and culture of our global inhabitants. The novel takes place 1,000 years ago, during the Japanese imperial court where princes, monks, maids, and consorts lived a life of war, romance, and intrigue—exhibiting various virtues and rituals, and cultivating painting, music, and poetry in way that is difficult for westerners to fully comprehend. An elaborate social hierarchy existed in the court system, full of aesthetic nuances, polite behavior, and personal favors.[2]

During the eleventh century, Japanese writers and courtiers referred to this world as "above the clouds," a mystical place invisible to the peasants and working class but part of aristocratic and warrior society in which beauty was the main currency. Men and women, although involved in various complex relationships, rarely looked into one's face; style and aesthetics depended on nuance alone, not on verbal messages, and not body language. It was more subtle—the tint of a layered sleeve, the color or shape of an earring, the angle of a hair comb peeking beneath a chignon, the spray of a seasonal cologne, the way a drink was poured or handed to someone, a special blossom

1. Margaret Talbot, "Other Woes," *New York Times Magazine* (November 18, 2001), p. 24.

2. Murasaki Shikibu, *The Tale of Genji*, 2 vols., trans. by Royall Tyler (New York: Viking Press, 2001).

added to an intricately folded letter, the metaphor of a word in a poem or letter. *Mood* was more important than *action,* the latter considered simple and crude. The most important mood was the word *aware,* a heightened sense of the other person, a sensitivity toward beauty, a subtle refinement and understanding of nuance.

*The Genji* required the reader to understand and appreciate the mood. Without this knowledge, which in turn depended on understanding both the language and the culture, there was no true understanding of the novel. Many of the words lack a perfect translation, and to fully grasp the meaning of the book with all its subplots, one cannot rely on the English version or western thinking. The great Spanish novelist Miguel Vercantes wrote, "Reading a translation is like viewing a fine Italian tapestry from behind." Even if a translation is done well, many nuances are still lost. As Paul Harvey once said, "What about the rest of the story?"[1] The same dilemma exists when Americans try to comprehend the mind of an Asian or Middle Eastern person—regardless of whether the person is an international business person or a terrorist. The key to understanding other people from other cultures is to know their philosophy, their literature, and their language, not some political statement or metaphor about multiculturalism.

We can take painstaking detail in translating words, and rely on new and revised dictionaries, but we never fully grasp what the Asian or Middle Eastern mind thinks and why they think their thoughts. We can convey literal translations of their philosophy and literature, but the spirit, the mood, and the nuances are lost in the translations. Put bluntly, people who speak only English have nothing in common with people speaking in *The Tale of Genji,* chanting in a mosque, or silently contemplating in a Buddhist temple.[2] Moreover, we really don't fully grasp the view of the world as perceived by Mohammad, Buddha, or Confucius—what they have to say to the faithful and to billions of people. All religions preach peace, but few of the faithful practice what is preached. It often takes someone who is in the winter months of his life, losing his agility and five senses and approaching darkness, to seek peace—and usually it is personal, not a global vision.

Muslims view the world as if they have split personalities: one group is rigid, unconcerned about public or world opinion, and civil law and materialistic possessions

1. Both quotes cited in Jerry Jesness, "Not Just for Foreigners Anymore," *Education Week* (November 28, 2001), p. 33.

2. A similar situation exists in other forms of art—say, with the painter or choreographer who has a gift for creating with volume, color, and texture. The artist relies on certain images, often subtle—a mood or nuance that only the expert eye can fully understand. These images are reminiscent of Matisse's *Danse,* Bruegel's *Harvesters,* as well as with Alvin Ailey's *Revelations* and Paul Taylor's *Eslande.* Those who read *Revolution X* or *Superman* comics or feel that *Spin* and *Vibe* magazines are funky and radical or that *The Jerk* and *Pulp Fiction* are cool and artsy most likely lack the sophistication or ability to distinguish the aspects of the human condition that is timeless or to comprehend the idioms in *The Tale of Genji,* or the subtle images (mood and nuance) in the arts that go beyond the immediate moment, but still impart an aura of timelessness.

do not count, only spiritual law; the other group (the vast majority) is open-minded, sensitive about national and world opinion, and respects civil law and supports capitalism.[1] Buddhists view the world as a place of unfathomable darkness and suffering, similar to the western philosophy of Kafka and the poems of Milosz Czeslaw.[2]

Just like we do not fully comprehend the "average" person from China, India, Pakistan, or Iran, we lack the language, folklore, customs, and beliefs to fully grasp *The Tale of Genji;* likewise, we cannot fully grasp the minds of third-world populations and their religious and political ideologies. Some third-world people have been living in isolation for centuries, and some may still not have running water or sewers that work, but they have satellite TV—and therefore they understand the ideas of

1. Terrorism is not a part of mainstream Islam, and it is essential to avoid backlash against Muslim citizens in the United States. Poverty and illiteracy are determining factors in the Muslim split in personality. Whoever feeds the poor, and also educates them, controls their minds and behavior. In *Democracy and Education* (1916), Dewey pointed out that education is neutral and can be used to bolster many stances and ideologies. Even "true believers" can switch horses and change ideologies. During the closing days of World War II, Nazi scientists became Soviet scientists and others became American scientists overnight, including Von Braun and his V-1 rocket team that almost wiped out London. After the collapse of the Soviet Union, many communist supporters became advocates of capitalism because they had food on the table. Feed the poor and illiterate, and you can get most of them to stand on their heads all day, pick cotton, pile stones on top of stones all year, or blow themselves up with the belief they will find paradise and 72 virgins at their bedside. In some cases, you might need a whip or a boot to keep some troublemakers in the fold, but if you smile and stroke (reward and recognize) them, they will become "good soldiers"—and die for Caesar, Napoleon, the Fuhrer, Allah, or even the Cross. In this regard, we are no different from animals. Humans can be conditioned the same way Pavlov trained dogs, Skinner trained pigeons and rats, Roy Rogers trained Trigger, and the Lone Ranger trained Silver. The best stimuli for conditioning is food and water. Ask parents (and as teachers) who use cookies and candy to reward children and thus modify and shape behavior.

2. Milosz is somewhat unknown to the American audience, although for the last 70 years this 92-year-old Polish citizen might be considered by knowledgeable critics as the foremost European poet. His prose is steeped in the terror of the twentieth century, the horrors of war and the darkness of death camps. He is, in my view, the conscience of European civilization—writing about the hell it brought to the world with its wars, totalitarianism, and ethnic/religious hatred. See Czeslaw Milosz, *New and Collected Poems: 1931–2001* (New York: HarperCollins, 2001).

Both Kafka and Milosz would argue that language cannot fully grasp the reality and horrors of how people and nations behave. Descriptions of inhumanity rarely can be fully described in texts as artistically valid. Our language is inadequate; the best we can do is pretend that we can capture reality and the milieu of the day with descriptive prose, and this is what the philosopher, writer, and poet strive to capture. As teachers, we think that Greek tragedy, Shakespeare, or Steinbeck can provide us with glimpses of reality, the essence of life, and the tones of nuance. Personally, I doubt if they could fully describe Auschwitz, Hiroshima, or Kosovo.

the West and modernity. Because these people speak and read English, and some have even studied American history, philosophy, and literature at American universities, they understand us better than we understand them. Our knowledge of third-world nations is limited at the middle school and high school level to a chapter or a few pages in a history text, one or two novels by a third-world author, and some ethnic cuisine during a multicultural celebration in school or at a school-community festival hosting immigrant parents.

For the last century, the United States has been handicapped by traditional opinions of "the superiority of western culture," as well as its isolationist position related to its geographical separation from most of the world. A smug attitude prevails, even today, among a critical mass of American youth: If people are living in the same planet and same century as we are, they should know English. As we plunge into the future, the growing interdependence of nations made possible by technology, the energy crisis, supersonic airlines, and multinational corporations requires Americans to place greater emphasis on understanding other nations and cultures and learning non-western languages, particularly those involving the languages spoken by hundreds of millions and billions of people. To ignore the language of others is to remain partially ignorant about what happens elsewhere or to remain ignorant of events in countries with unfamiliar traditions and cultures; it represents a put-down of foreign people, it makes for many "ugly Americans," and it leads to all sorts of misunderstandings and anger toward the United States.

Right now, as I write this final draft, tucked away in an ivory tower, terror has wormed its way into the thoughts and language of Americans. Although such anxiety may be more evident in New York, and some people may still be concerned about ascending to the upper floors of skyscrapers, all Americans across the country are faced with longer lines at the airport as a reminder that the world as we knew it has changed. Indeed, smoking, drinking, and attending religious services are up—as well as all human-made "vices" to help people cope with a host of anxieties.

At the federal level, a reaction to the WTC has triggered the U.S. intelligence community to recruit speakers of Arabic and Farsi, the two major languages of the Middle East, and even the esoteric languages of central Asia, such as "Pashuto, Dari, Uzbek, and Turkmen."[1] Similar types of reaction took place after the Third Reich bombed London; including the need for German-speaking intelligence agents; the need for Japanese-speaking military and spy personnel after Pearl Harbor; and the need for Russian-speaking personnel after the launching of *Sputnik*.

Investing more money in recruiting spies who speak a foreign language has little to do with the view of a truly educated person having command of one or more foreign languages. It only reveals the inadequacy of our curriculum—when foreign-speaking spies cannot be recruited from our colleges because there are so few courses like Farsi or Arabic. Even worse, it highlights the junior high and high school curriculum that does not require a second language and settles for rudimentary knowledge (two or three years of study) even among college tracked students.

---

1. "The Spy Puzzle," *New York Times* (November 4, 2001), Sect. 4, p. 12.

## Summary

1. Prior to and at the turn of the twentieth century, a traditional curriculum—highlighted by Latin, the classics, and the mental discipline approach to teaching and learning—characterized American schools.

2. The traditional curriculum came under attack for its academic elitism, unusually high academic standards, and failure to meet the needs of the majority of students.

3. Both Edward Thorndike, the most influential psychologist of the period, and John Dewey, the most influential educator of the same period, argued that subjects should not be placed in a hierarchy of importance (the opposite view of traditional educators).

4. John Dewey spearheaded the progressive movement in the first half of the twentieth century; emphasis was on the needs and interests of the child.

5. Progressive education came under attack during the Cold War and *Sputnik* era. James Conant was the best-known moderate critic of this period, and Arthur Bestor and Admiral Hyman Rickover were most noted for the harsh criticism of progressive education and the philosophy of John Dewey.

6. During the 1960s and 1970s, emphasis was on talented and gifted students, as well as on college-bound students; testing and tracking of students was accepted and considered part of the norm. Demands for intellectual rigor led to a new way of organizing subject matter called *structure,* which bound a field of knowledge into *disciplines.*

7. Concern for disadvantaged students among academics appeared in the early 1960s, just prior to the War on Poverty and civil rights movement. The forerunners with the greatest impact on the field of urban education was socialist writer Michael Harrington, with his publication, *The Other America* (1963), and educators such as James Conant (*Slums and Suburbs,* 1961), Patricia Sexton (*Education and Income,* 1961), and Frank Riessman (*The Culturally Deprived Child,* 1962).

8. As interest in the disadvantaged expanded, additional groups such as immigrant children, bilingual students, and disabled students were added to our list of concerns. As a side outcome, interest in the gifted and talented student declined and has continued to take a backseat since the *Sputnik* and Cold War era.

9. Along with concern for the disadvantaged, school reform searched for relevancy and humanistic education. *Third force psychology* (or *humanistic psychology*) competed with traditional theories of behaviorism and cognition. Subject matter was deemphasized, and the needs of students were emphasized.

10. The question, "What knowledge is worth knowing?" was originally asked more than 150 years ago by Herbert Spencer and remains viable today; there is continuous need to reexamine the question, to consider changes in society, and to revise content.

11. Questions about the explosion of knowledge, the use of technology, and the mastery of different foreign languages lead to issues about education policymaking and the subsequent need to plan and revise curriculum. Before we can think about the *what* and *who* of the curriculum, we need to think about the *why.* Before we formulate our goals and objectives, we need to think about our values and the long-term implications of what we are trying to accomplish.

12. Americans lack a foreign language program that encourages or gives legitimacy to third-world countries (languages such

as Mandarin, Hindi, Arabic, and Farsi). Religious and ethnic differences are subtle and sometimes hard to distinguish, but there is nothing subtle about our failure to recognize the languages spoken by hundreds of millions of people. In simple, basic terms, our foreign language program is based on ethnocentrism, western bias, and worldwide isolation—and maybe even a little stupidity.

## $\mathcal{Q}$uestions to $\mathcal{C}$onsider

1. How did the Committee of Fifteen and the Committee of Ten influence curriculum for the twentieth century?
2. In what ways did the progressive movement influence American schools?
3. What went wrong with school reforms during the Cold War period?
4. Summarize the rationale for the concerns of educating the disadvantaged. What approach would you like to see adopted to meet the educational needs of the disadvantaged?
5. How has subject matter changed in the content area(s) you teach?

## $\mathcal{T}$hings to $\mathcal{D}$o

1. Interview teachers in a nearby school to determine whether they prefer a progressive or essential curriculum.
2. Invite a guest speaker to speak to the class about teaching the structure of a subject.
3. Interview a teacher at an inner-city school and examine the problems and possibilities of educating the disadvantaged. Report to the class.
4. Discuss in class your own school experiences as a high school student. Compare city and suburban school settings.
5. Read a magazine article or go on line and read an article about the explosion of knowledge. Organize a debate about how to improve content in your area of specialization or field of teaching.

## $\mathcal{R}$ecommended $\mathcal{R}$eadings

Butts, R. Freeman, and Lawrence A. Cremin. *A History of Education in American Culture.* New York: Holt, Rinehart and Winston, 1953. The role of school in American society, and the relationship of schooling and socialization.

Conant, James B. *The American High School Today.* New York: McGraw-Hill, 1959. An overview of American high schools during the Cold War period, and 21 recommendations for improving schools.

Dewey, John. *How We Think.* Boston: D. C. Heath, 1910. The moving from "knowing what" to "knowing how," from trivial pursuit to problem solving.

Harrington, Michael. *The Other America.* Baltimore: Penguin Books, 1963. The little book that sparked the War on Poverty.

Hirsh, E. D. *Cultural Literacy: What Every American Needs to Know.* New York: Random House, 1987. Includes 5,000 essential names, phrases, dates, and concepts for cultural literacy and effective communication.

Ornstein, Allan C., and Daniel U. Levine, *Foundations of Education,* 8th ed. Boston: Houghton Mifflin, 2003. A comprehensive overview of education trends and teaching and schooling in America.

Ravitch, Diane. *Left Back: A Century of Failed School Reforms.* New York: Simon and Schuster, 2000. A detailed attack on progressive education, and a call for national and higher academic standards of education.

# Social Stratification and Inequality

## Chapter 7

## Focusing Questions

1. What is the relationship between social class and mobility? Social class and educational achievement?

2. What are some reasons for and against using the SAT as a nationwide benchmark?

3. What are the major reasons for promoting excellence in our society? Equality in our society?

4. How can society reconcile excellence and equality?

5. Do the intellectual and social values of higher education outweigh the personal finances and sacrifices involved in obtaining a college degree?

6. What is your definition of *equality?* To what extent do you advocate equality of opportunity? Equality of results?

7. How would you define a *more effective school?* What are the key variables or factors in determining more effective schools?

8. Why is it wrong to rely mainly on property taxes as revenue sources for schools?

9. What fiscal problems characterize urban schools?

10. How do we improve race relations in this country?

---

EPISODE A

In America's complex society, a considerable degree of upward mobility from one social class to another implies there is equality, at least equality of opportunity. A substantial amount of stratification, however, gives evidence of inequality. The extent to which U.S. society, or for that matter any society, offers equality or inequality of opportunity will affect the kind of education available to students from various social and economic backgrounds. In turn, the education received by students will affect future mobility and stratification patterns within the society.

Equality and inequality can be discussed from social, philosophical, economic, and educational points of view. The issues in the idea of equality go back to the ancient Hebrews and Greeks, involving intense debate among intellectuals through the ages. In the United States, the pursuit of equality was first evidenced by the Puritans in the seventeenth century; subsequently, the Bill of Rights and the protection of minority rights originally involved religion—not social class and not race. Although religious persecution and controversies were more intense in the past, there are now signs that social and racial equality are now becoming a sacred idea, even "approaching dogmatic status" among many social scientists.[1]

In preindustrial society, inequalities were justified by achievement based on economic success. The birth of the American nation saw equalitarianism combined with excellence; equality of opportunity was professed as an ideal, but it was recognized that inequalities would emerge due to people's differing abilities. With growing doubts about this theory, a new egalitarian trend is emerging that deemphasizes *individual* merit and competence and calls for protection of specific *groups* defined as minorities. The traditional goal of equality of *opportunity* is being replaced in some circles by demands for equality of *results*.

## Historical and Philosophical Issues of Equality

With the exception of a few small, esoteric or utopian groups, all societies require some hierarchy of organizational structure with levels of superiority, subordination, authority, and power. In order to function and survive, they eventually adopt some form of inequality and restriction of individual behavior. Originally, these restrictions were not considered repressive but were presumed to be linked to the divine or natural order. When reason is applied to society, the hierarchy must be rationally legitimized and justified; it should conform, at least appear to conform, to the principles of justice.

In preindustrial society, such justification was based on ascription; differences of power, status, and wealth were believed to be derived from ancestry, birth, or caste. People were privileged or unprivileged by accident of birth and not for what they accomplished, and mobility from one class to another was severely limited. With the rise of industry and commerce, the role of ascription was replaced in modern western society by achievement, and ascriptive stratification was replaced by meritocratic stratification, wherein merit was awarded for achieving whatever society valued. The difference between an ascriptive and achievement-oriented society lies in the

---

1. Christopher Jencks et al., *Who Gets Ahead?* (New York: Basic Books, 1979); Daniel P. McMurrer and Isabel V. Sawhill, *Getting Ahead* (Washington, DC: Urban Institute, 1998).

yardstick for merit; in the case of ascription, it is belonging to a *group;* in the case of achievement, it is doing and performing on an *individual* basis.[1]

In modern western industrial and society, achievement as the legitimizing principle goes hand in hand with concepts of equality and mobility. For most Americans, legitimate equality is epitomized by equality of opportunity. It is recognized that all jobs in society are not equally pleasant or important; and, because different talents and abilities are required for different occupations, the reward system varies. With an unequal reward system, however, social stratification results; some people wind up with more money, goods, and power.

But the political left sees this stratification as producing a meritocracy that, in its own way, is as evil as any of the historic forms of aristocratic privilege. In his text on inequality, Christopher Jencks states that "the crucial problem today is that relatively few people view income inequality as a serious problem. We will not only have to politicize the question of income inequality but alter people's basic assumptions about the extent to which they are responsible for their neighbors and their neighbors for them."[2] Similarly, John Rawls equates justice with absolute equality and argues that if some citizens have more goods than others, it has been accomplished by the loss of freedom for those who have fewer goods.[3]

## A Change in Meritocracy

The phrase *postindustrial society,* coined by Daniel Bell, describes the scientific-technological societies evolving in developed countries in the second half of the twentieth century. The singular feature of such a society is the importance of scientific and technical knowledge as the source of production, innovation, and policy formulation. Emerging from the older economic systems in both advanced capitalistic and socialistic countries is a knowledge society based on the preeminence of professionals and managers. In the United States in the 1950s and 1960s, Bell notes, "this group outpaced . . . all others in the rate of growth, which was . . . seven times more than the overall rate for workers."[4] In the 1990s, computer and high-tech sectors outpaced the entire economy, reflected by a soaring NASDAQ market whose bubble burst in 2001. Nonetheless, the stratification structure of this new society produces a highly trained knowledge-based elite that is supported by a large scientific and technical staff.

The basis of achievement in the postindustrial society is education. Merit and differentials in status, power, and income are awarded to highly educated and trained

---

1. Alan C. Kerchkoff, *Diverging Pathways* (New York: Cambridge University Press, 1993); Yossi Shavit and Hans-Peter Blossfeld, eds., *Persistent Inequality* (Boulder, CO: Westview, 1993).

2. Christopher Jencks et al., *Inequality: A Reassessment of the Effect of Family and Schooling in America* (New York: Basic Books, 1972), p. 263.

3. John Rawls, *A Theory of Justice* (Cambridge, MA: Harvard University Press, 1971). Also see Deborah I. Rhode, *In the Interests of Justice* (New York: Oxford University, 2001).

4. Daniel Bell, *The Coming of Post-Industrial Society* (New York: Basic Books, 1973), p. 108.

experts with credentials; they are seen as the decision makers who will inherit the power structure in business, government, and even politics.[1] Achievement and mobility are also related to entrepreneurship and risk taking—what Ben Franklin would call hard work and Merrill Lynch or *Forbes* magazine might call "making money the old-fashioned way."

This trend toward a meritocracy of the intellectual elite has aggravated inequalities. Because of socioeconomic deprivation and limited education, poor and minority groups are unable to compete successfully in a society based on educational credentials and educational achievement. Without the appropriate certificates, they are not needed by the economy; not exploited, but underpaid for their services; not discriminated against, but not in demand. An achievement-oriented society based on academic credentials and standardized tests (which compare individuals in relation to a group score, say, on IQ, achievement, or academic aptitude) condemns many people who cannot compete on an intellectual or cognitive level to the low end of the stratification structure. It is the classic problem: The rich get richer and the poor get poorer—and gaps between the "haves" and the "have-nots" have dramatically increased in the last decade. Put in more precise terms, for the last 20 or 25 years, the top one-fifth of the population (or the income pyramid) has been improving their prospects while the remaining 80 percent has lagged behind.[2] Surprisingly, no one has rebelled. The majority have not imposed higher taxes on the wealthy; in fact, the opposite has occurred, partially because conservative forces more often than liberal forces have dominated the White House and Congress since the Nixon administration.

## Academic Merit and Testing

It is not surprising that those who find it difficult to compete within this credential-based system condemn the selection procedure based on it. Hence, the minority community, and the political left which generally supports their efforts, attack IQ tests and standardized tests of achievement and professional entrance examinations as culturally biased and as highly unreliable and invalid predictors of college and job performance. The rejection of measurements that register the consequences of deprivation has political and social implications; one strategy is to bury or deny the data.

In general, IQ tests have been eliminated from the schooling process because of their controversial nature (the way the tests were used to label children and assign them to "soft" or "dumbed-down" programs). Even though a record 1.3 million high school students took the SAT in 2000, an increasing number of colleges have stopped requiring them, including 6 of the top 25 liberal arts colleges. Moreover, the California, Florida, and Texas state university systems now base most acceptances on class rank,

---

1. C. Wright Mills, *The Power Elite* (New York: Oxford University Press, 1956); Thomas J. Peters and Robert H. Waterman, *In Search of Excellence* (New York: Warner Books, 1993).

2. John Kenneth Galbraith, "Economic Delusion, Political Disaster," *New York Times* (March 11, 2001), p. 15; Isabel V. Sawhill, "Still the Land of Opportunity," *Public Interest* (Spring 1999), pp. 3–12; and "What the Tax Cuts Mean for Different Families," *New York Times* (February 9, 2001), p. A20.

regardless of SAT scores, as a response to their states' end of affirmative action. It is like an end-run around a voter initiative to end affirmative action in university admissions.

By 2000, a record 280 colleges and universities ignored the SAT for admissions.[1] The result is that the College Board is under pressure to revise the SAT I (which measures verbal and mathematical reasoning, rather than specific academic content) because of the test gaps between white and Asian students compared to the minorities. There is still grumbling by some educators that the College Board lowered standards in the mid-1990s, when it made some statistical adjustments, and it is going to do it again to appease critics who argue that the test should be given less weight than other exams (such as the SAT II or the ACT, which measure academic content, not reasoning) or the focus should be on grade-point average and class rank.[2] Of course, many know but few will admit that a top-ranked student in an inner-city high school suggests far different academic ability than a similarly ranked student in a middle-class high school. For example, the percent of black students who took AP examinations in 1996 was 3.2 percent, compared to the white rate of 13.3 percent.[3] In short, between 1975 and 1995, the average SAT score of black students was 73 to 79 percent of the white students' score, and most of the reasons are still explained by household characteristics, not school characteristics.[4]

The SAT test does a good job of cutting through high school grade inflation and serves as a national benchmark to compare students among and within states (noting that different states and school districts have different academic standards). And we do need national benchmarks, since there is no federal system or ministry of education—no national uniform curriculum. But critics are concerned that colleges relying on the test discourage minority applicants and other students who may be qualified but don't test well; for the critics, the test is unfair, biased, and exclusionary.

Critics contend that the SAT measures aptitude, not achievement, and therefore favors middle-class students. In the midst of this criticism, the College Board is adding an essay component so that a perfect score will now be 2400 (instead of 1600). Although the colleges would like to see if prospective students can write a coherent paragraph, such a modest request is really "pie in the sky," given the fact that only about 25 percent of twelfth-graders nationwide write at grade level, according to national assessment testing data, but 63 percent of high school graduates go on to college (two or four years).[5]

1. "Rethinking the Big Test: No SAT Scores Required," *Time* (September 11, 2000), p. 52.

2. June Kronholz, "College Board Weighs Changes in SAT Exam," *Wall Street Journal* (March 22, 2002), p. 16. Starting in 2001, the University of California doubled the weight to SAT II scores; the switch was a boon to Hispanic students because one of the SAT II exams that qualify is Spanish.

3. *The Condition of Education 1998* (Washington, DC: U.S. Government Printing Office, 1998), Table 3, p. 7.

4. *Educational Achievement and Black-White Inequality* (Washington, DC: U.S. Government Printing Office, 2001).

5. *Digest of Education Statistics 2000* (Washington, DC: U.S. Government Printing Office, 2001), Table 185, p. 215; June Kronholz, "Math, Verbal and Writing," *Wall Street Journal* (March 22, 2002), p. 16.

Although critics will also argue that the test encourages guessing rather than thinking, and mainly assesses facts and knowledge (which is not really the case, since a good deal of the test content involves interpretation and analysis of reading selections, charts, and graphs), the real problem is that black and Hispanic SAT test scores continue to lag behind white and Asian American scores. Moreover, there are students who are either immature, rebellious, or bored with school, and who therefore receive poor grades. Some of these students come close to acing the SAT, and it is important to give them another chance to succeed and fulfill their potential.[1]

Someone might also argue that colleges make all kinds of concessions and excuses when recruiting top athletes; it is common knowledge that they have lower test scores and lower grades. If we can emphasize the recruitment of basketball or football players, why can't we also emphasize the recruitment of minorities for purpose of diversity—and throw out the SATs? The problem is twofold. First, if competition for basketball or football players gets in the way or exceeds competition for future scientists and poets, then something is wrong with our values:[2] That society will decline, as Rome did, once they began to prize chariot races and gladiators over intellectuals and artisans. Second, making minority status the key to opening the door to college, at the expense of nonminority status, is much more unfair, biased, and artificial than using a test to uphold some type of *objective* standard or *predictive* test of college performance. (No question, critics could argue over the words *objective* and *predictive*.)

If the importance of SAT scores is reduced, then other criteria are permitted to replace the test, such as minority status. According to the Center for Equal Opportunity in Washington, racial preferences play a greater role in college admissions than previously admitted to by higher education officials—and the preferences aren't minor. At the University of California, for example, which has now eliminated SAT requirements for admission, 300 points on the SAT separated successful white and black applicants; grade-point averages differed by more than a half point (i.e., the difference between 3 and 3.5 on a 4-point scale.) At the University of Michigan, it was 230 points, and at William and Mary, it was 210. SAT data obtained from 27 colleges

1. The most interesting method of getting around academic standards is the California state system, including top schools like UCLA and Berkeley. The system provides extra admission points for students who have experienced *adversity*—for example, immigration hardships; living in high-crime areas; having been a victim of a crime, especially a shooting; long-term or serious psychological or medical problems; and so on. If a student comes from a middle-class stable home, and mom or dad is a teacher, banker, or lawyer, that student should not expect to get admitted into UCLA or Berkeley unless he or she is a star athlete or has SAT scores above 1500. If a student has some personal or family hardships, or is of a minority status (not Asian American), SAT scores can be as low as 940 (380 below the average) and he or she will still be admitted. The greater the hardship, the better the chance for admission. Poverty as an admission index is not critical, since it would not help middle-class blacks and Hispanics and it could accidentally "pull in" low income whites and Asians. See Daniel Golden, "To Get into UCLA, It Helps to Face 'Life Challenges,' " *Wall Street Journal* (July 12, 2002), p. 17.

2. Thomas G. Donlan, "Putting Students to the Test," *Barron's* (March 12, 2001), p. 59.

show that the smallest gap between white and black students being admitted into same colleges was 70 points.[1]

Linda Chavez, president of the Center for Equal Opportunity, points out that the relative ratio favoring black over white students getting admitted with the same grades and test scores at North Carolina State was 177 to 1; at the University of Michigan, it was 174 to 1; and at the University of Virginia, it was 111 to 1.[2] To put this into some perspective, the relative odds that a smoker to nonsmoker will develop lung cancer is 14 to 1; the odds that a Hispanic student compared to a white student will drop out of school in grades 10 to 12 is 4 to 1, and for black students, the odds are 2 to 1.[3]

When we translate these point and percentage differences into the reality or life experiences of a white applicant, the outcome is a great deal of resentment, divisiveness, and stigmatizing. The message is that blacks (and any other minority that receives such overwhelming favorable treatment) cannot compete; they are not expected to succeed in schools or colleges, unless they are held to a lower standard.[4] The same kind of thinking and stereotyping about qualifications holds true on the job and with government contracting. Of course, most black and minority advocates would criticize any legislation or policy that reduces preferences based on skin color and ancestry. In the midst of the nation's attempt to ensure a politically correct diverse mix, and given the unpopularity of preferences among most Americans, we are left with a no-win situation—one that divides the country based on racial preferences.

## What Is Equality?

No country has taken the idea of equality more seriously than the United States. Politically, the idea is rooted in the Declaration of Independence and the Constitution. We have fought two wars over the definition of *equality:* the American Revolution and the Civil War. The origins of American public schools are also dominated by the concept of equal opportunity and the notion of a universal and free education. The rise of the "common school" was spearheaded by Horace Mann, who envisioned the schools as "the greatest equalizer of the condition of men—the balance-wheel of the social machinery."[5]

Equality of opportunity in this context would not lead to equality of outcomes; this concept did not attempt a classless society. As David Tyack wrote, "For the most part, working men did not seek to pull down the rich; rather they sought equality of

1. Robert Lerner and Althea Nagal, *Pervasive Preferences: Racial and Ethnic Discrimination in Undergraduate Admissions Across the Nation* (Washington, DC: Center for Equal Opportunity, 2001).

2. Linda Chavez, "Colleges and Quotas," *Wall Street Journal* (February 22, 2001), p. A22.

3. *Digest of Education Statistics 2000*, Table 106, p. 126.

4. Roger Clegg, "President Bush Can't Just Ignore Racial Preferences," *Chronicle of Higher Education* (March 23, 2002), pp. B13–B14.

5. Horace Mann, *The Republic and the School,* rev. ed (New York: Teachers College Press, 1957), p. 39.

opportunity for their children, a equal chance at the main chance."[1] Equality of opportunity in the nineteenth and early twentieth centuries meant an equal start for all children, but the assumption was that some would go farther than others. Differences in backgrounds and abilities, as well as motivation and personality, would create differences in outcomes among individuals, but the school would assure that children born into any class would have the opportunity to achieve status as persons born into other classes. Implicit in this view was that the "schools represented the means of achieving the goal . . . of equal chances of success" relative to all children in all strata.[2]

In retrospect, the schools did not fully achieve this goal, according to some observers, because school achievement and economic outcomes are highly related to social class and family background.[3] Had the schools not existed, however, social mobility would have been further reduced. The failure of the common school to provide social mobility raises the question of the role of the school in achieving equality—and the question of just what the school can and cannot do to affect cognitive and economic outcomes.

The modern view of educational equality, which emerged in the 1950s through the 1970s, goes much further than the old view. In light of this, James Coleman has outlined five views of inequality of educational opportunity, the first two representing the traditional notion and the latter three paralleling reconstructionist and revisionist philosophy: (1) inequality defined by the same curriculum for all children, with the intent that school facilities be equal; (2) inequality defined in terms of its racial composition of the schools; (3) inequality defined in terms of such intangible characteristic as teacher morale and teacher expectations of students; (4) inequality based on school consequences or outcomes for students with equal backgrounds and abilities; and (5) inequality based on school consequences for students with unequal backgrounds and abilities.[4] See Teaching Tips 7.1.

The first two definitions deal with race and social class; the next definition deals with concepts that are hard to define and hard to change; the fourth definition deals with school finances and expenditures. The fifth definition is an extreme and revisionist interpretation: Equality is reached only when the outcomes of schooling are similar for all students—those who are lower class and minority as well as majority and middle class.

When inequality is defined in terms of equal outcomes (both cognitive and economic), we start comparing racial, ethnic, and religious groups. In a heterogeneous

1. David B. Tyack, *Turning Points in American Educational History* (Waltham, MA: Blaisdell, 1967), p. 114.

2. Henry M. Levin, "Equal Educational Opportunity and the Distribution of Educational Expenditures," in A. Kopan and H. J. Walberg, eds., *Rethinking Educational Equality* (Berkeley, CA: McCutchan, 1974), p. 30.

3. Kathleen Bennett and Margarett D. LeCompte, *How Schools Work: A Sociological Analysis of Education* (New York: Longman, 1990); George Burtless, ed. *Does Money Matter: The Effect of School Resources on Student Achievement and Adult Success* (Washington, DC: Brookings Institute, 1996); and Jencks, *Who Gets Ahead*.

4. James S. Coleman, "The Concept of Equality of Educational Opportunity," *Harvard Educational Review* (Winter 1968), pp. 7–22.

# Teaching Tips 7.1

## What School Districts Can Do to Enhance School Improvement and Reduce Inequality

1. Identify the lowest (20 percent) performing schools in order to provide additional personnel and services.
2. Transfer highly qualified personnel (teachers and administrators) to target schools; pay an extra salary stipend to attract volunteers.
3. Increase the influence and authority of the school principal and hold the person responsible for school improvement.
4. Clarify goals or standards and use them as benchmarks for reform and change.
5. Target the lowest-performing students (50 percent) for afternoon tutoring, Saturday morning classes, and summer school.
6. Emphasize reading and literacy, even at the expense of music, art, physical education, and other extracurricular activities.
7. Develop partnerships between schools and universities and between schools and businesses.
8. Work with the parents and local community; encourage or require parental participation in school-community activities.
9. Provide staff-development activities at the school site, organized by experienced teachers and administrators.
10. Use videotapes and other observational techniques to analyze specific teaching behaviors and instructional activities in conjunction with self-evaluation and personal reflection.
11. Recruit new personnel to be mentored by experienced teachers.
12. Improve teaching conditions: Reduce burdensome extra class assignments, isolation of colleagues, and assignment of "difficult" classes to beginning teachers; increase collegiality and communication among teachers and proper supervision.
13. Examine curriculum on a regular basis (a 2- or 3-year cycle); modify, improve, and align it with the goals or standards of the school district.
14. Evaluate personnel on an annual basis to provide merit bonuses and other forms of recognition (pictures, plaques, news or magazine profiles, dinners, professional conferences and travel, summer employment, etc.) in addition to regular base salary; introduce some form of accountability. Remember positive strokes work better than negativism.

society like ours, this results in some hot issues, including how much to invest in human capital, how to determine the cost effectiveness of social and educational programs, who should be taxed and how much, to what extent are we to handicap our brightest and most talented minds (the swift racers) to enable those who are slow to finish to catch up, and whether affirmative action policies lead to reverse discrimination.[1]

1. Nathan Glazer, "The Affirmative Action Stalemate," *Public Interest* (Winter 1988), pp. 99–114; Allan C. Ornstein, "Are Quotas Here to Stay?" *National Review* (April 26, 1974), pp. 480–481, 495; and William G. Tierney, "The Parameters of Affirmative Action," *Review of Educational Research* (Summer 1997), pp. 165–196.

Indeed, we cannot treat these issues lightly, because they affect most of us in one way or another and lead to questions over which wars have been fought.

In his classic text on excellence and equality, John Gardner points out that in a democracy, the differences among groups cannot be dwelled on and we go out of the way to ignore them. He describes the dilemma: "Extreme equalitarianism . . . which ignores differences in native capacity and achievement, has not served democracy well. Carried far enough, it means . . . the end of that striving for excellence which has produced mankind's greatest achievements." Gardner also asserts that "no democracy can give itself over to emphasize extreme individual performance and retain its democratic principles—or extreme equalitarianism and retain its vitality." Our society should seek to develop "all potentialities at all levels. It takes more than an educated elite to run a complex, technological society."[1] Every modern society, as well as every ancient society, has learned this hard lesson, some only after tremendous bloodshed and loss of life.

The issues that Gardner raises will not go away, at least not in our democratic and heterogeneous society; they directly affect the social fabric of the country and have echoed loudly since the War on Poverty and the civil rights movement. They lead to hotly contested arguments in the media, often where frank discussion is curtailed; the worst culprits are college campus newspapers and forums—ironically a terrible place for academic freedom if the messenger moves too far to the right.[2]

Our Civil War pitted fathers against sons, brothers against brothers, blacks against whites, and northerners against southerners. Next to the Napoleonic Wars, it was the bloodiest war in the 1800s. It didn't start out that way, though. At the beginning, "fans" from both the North and the South went out to the Virginia countryside with picnic lunches to watch the spectacle of Bull Run, and ended up fleeing from the onrushing carnage, as did the Union troops. It took only a few weeks for the country to get the message, as stated by Secretary of War Edwin Stanton: "Champagne and Oysters on the Potomac" no longer is the day.[3]

David Eicher, a military historian, reminds us that more than 620,000 Americans died during the Civil War—more than 11 Vietnams. At Antietam, in one day, there were 26,190 casualties, the bloodiest and longest day in America.[4] Merle Curti puts it in this way: "Of the 2,500,000 soldiers involved, one in four were killed in action or died of wounds or disease." Its toll was enormous, equal to the number of American soldiers and sailors lost in *all the wars America fought*—including the American Revolution, the War of 1812, the Indian Wars, the Mexican and Spanish American

1. John Gardner, *Excellence: Can We Be Equal and Excellent Too?* (New York: Harper & Row, 1961), pp. 17–18, 83, 90.
2. Diana Jean Schemo, "Ad Intended to Stir Up Campuses More than Succeeds in Its Mission," *New York Times* (March 21, 2001), pp. A1, A17; David Horowitz, "Racial McCarthyism," *Wall Street Journal* (March 20, 2001), p. 16.
3. Jay Wink, "A Narrative of Hell," *New York Times Book Review* (September 16, 2001), p. 23.
4. David J. Eicher, *The Longest Night: A Military History of the Civil War* (New York: Simon & Schuster, 2001).

Wars, and two World Wars.[1] In terms of percentage of population at that time, 31 million in 1865, no other country in modern time lost as many soldiers vis-à-vis the total population until World War II—when modern machinery and human madness combined to create a larger catastrophe and waste of human life in Germany (5 million dead) and Russia (30 million dead).

America was ripped apart by the Civil War, first over the issue over federal and state rights, then over slavery. It still has emotional resonance, almost 150 years later, not only in terms of black-white relations, but also as it relates to many school and social issues, such as desegregation, federal and state funding, affirmative action, voting patterns and rights, the election of presidents and the selection of Supreme Court judges, and the formation of white-rights groups and black-rights groups—all doing battle over state rights, civil rights, and equality.

Almost 150 years later, the question still haunts us: What is equality? What is America all about? When I grew up, it was real simple—the prevailing philosophy was based on equality of opportunity. Individual merit and test scores counted, and no one received extra points or consideration for being "slow," "disabled," or "language deficient," or mentally or emotionally challenging. Educational policy statements focused on academically bright students during this period, and tests were used as a benchmark for sorting out capable from less capable students; scholarships were primarily based on merit—only a few were given for sports or financial reasons. Education was reflected in our national priorities with emphasis on science and math as well as high academic standards. That's how the country defeated Hitler and his master race, how we won the atomic bomb race against the German scientists' rocket race, and how we eventually won the Cold War and preserved our way of life.

But it is all over now. Milton Berle and Ed Sullivan are gone, Branch Rickey and Jackie Robinson are historical memories, and "father no longer knows best." Gone are the placid, tranquil Eisenhower years—when there were two separate societies, one black, one white—and when in the South there were separate toilets, separate counters, and separate schools. If *Time* is not mistaken, however, the confederate flag still flew high in 2000 over the state capitols in South Carolina, Georgia, and Mississippi.[2]

Today, given the context of the times, some of us would argue for equal results (not equal opportunity), group rights (not individual rights), and even reparations. Others, including most of my old friends from the schoolyard, and now their children, would still advocate equality of opportunity, where individual performance counts and produces differences in outcomes. The commitment to provide a fair chance for everyone to develop their talents remains central to the national creed for the vast majority of Americans; it has deep political roots, and, according to Isabel Sawhill, is what distinguishes us from the history and philosophy of Europe. Virtually no one favors equal distribution of income—for it would discourage hard work,

---

1. Merle Curti et al., *A History of American Civilization* (New York: Harper Bros., 1953), p. 323. I would add Korea and Vietnam to the list.
2. Matthew Cooper and Adam Zagorin, "Republicans and the Rebel Yell," *Time* (January 2001), p. 28.

savings, investment, and risk taking. Some form of inequality, based on abilities and talent, is the price we pay for a dynamic economy and the right of each individual to retain the benefits of his or her own labor."[1] The idea, for Sawhill, is not to address the symptoms or results of inequality, but to address the causes of inequality.

## Social Mobility and Social Structure

Social scientists study social mobility in order to ascertain the relative openness or fluidity of a social structure. They are interested in the difficulties different persons or groups experience in acquiring the goods and services that are valued in the culture and may be acquired through unequal contributions.

In *ascriptive* societies, the stratification system is closed to individual mobility because prestige (or status) is determined at birth. One's education, occupational status, income, and lifestyle cannot be changed. In an *open-class* society, although people start with different advantages, opportunities are available for them to change their initial positions. The life chances of a welfare recipient's child born in the slums differ considerably from those of a banker's child born in the suburbs, but in an achievement-oriented society the former can still achieve as much as or more than the latter.

The emphasis on vertical social mobility in the American social structure is one of the most striking features of our class system. Kurt Mayer maintains that the United States puts emphasis on social mobility, more than any other nation in modern times: "Americans have firmly proclaimed the idea of equality and freedom of achievement and have acclaimed the large numbers of individuals who have risen from humble origins to positions of prominence and affluence." Indeed, the belief in opportunity is so strongly entrenched in the culture that most Americans feel not only that each individual has the "right to succeed but that it is his duty to do so."[2] Thus, we look with disapproval upon those who make little or no attempt to better themselves—or who become "welfare junkies."

There is evidence of considerable social mobility in the United States. Studies of *intra*generational mobility—the occupational career patterns of individuals in terms of their mobility between jobs and occupations during their lifetimes—reveal that a very large proportion of American men have worked in different communities, different occupations, and different jobs. Nonetheless, there are certain limits to the variety of such experiences—most notably, occupational mobility is confined primarily to either side of a dividing line between manual and nonmanual occupations and between nontechnical/nonprofessional and technical/professional jobs; little permanent mobility takes place across this basic line.[3]

1. Sawhill, "Still the Land of Opportunity?," p. 4.
2. Kurt B. Mayer, *Class and Society* (New York: Random House, 1955), p. 69.
3. Otis D. Duncan, "The Trend of Occupational Mobility in the United States," *American Social Review* (August 1965), pp. 491–99; Seymour M. Lipset, "Social Mobility and Equal Opportunity," *Public Interest* (Fall 1972), pp. 90–108.

*Inter*generational mobility studies involve a comparison of social status of fathers and sons at some point in their careers (for instance, as assessed by their occupations at approximately the same age). From the 1950s to the present, the major studies show that about two-thirds of the American male population moves up and down a little in social mobility in every generation. If the son is not in the same occupational category as his father, the next most likely place is in either the occupational category immediately below or above, and in most cases it is above.[1] For example, 60 percent of the middle and upper class by the end of the 1980s came from working-class or farm families.[2] Factors contributing to these developments include the replacement of family-owned enterprises by public corporations, recruitment of management personnel from the ranks of college graduates, competitive promotion policies, and the demand for people with ability and mobility to cope with the complexities of the postindustrial society.

Although social and occupational mobility remain consistently high, economic mobility has slowed down in the last 25 years. Different reasons are given in various studies, but I would argue that money is being increasingly funneled to the top one-fifth of the population, actually the top 5 percent. With the exception of the 1990s, U.S. economy has suffered a slow-down compared with other industrialized nations, such as Australia, Germany, Korea, and Taiwan. Also, the tax burden has shifted to the working class and middle class, with tax breaks and benefits favoring the affluent—the top 5 percent, even top 1 percent.[3] The outcome is that it now takes two professional parents to buy the same goods and services that one wage earner was able to purchase in the 1950s and 1960s.

However, the studies that are educational and social in nature (including those by Peter Blau, Otis Duncan, and Martin Lipset in the 1950s and 1960s; David Featherman, Robert Hauser, and Marshal Smith in the 1970s and 1980s; and Michael Hout, Daniel McMurrier, Richard Rothstein, and Susan Mayer more recently), show that mobility from one generation to the next is the result of a combination of factors—education being only one factor. The other major factors are IQ, social class, and family structure.[4] Since we can't change existing IQ, social class, and fam-

---

1. Peter Blau and Otis D. Duncan, *The American Occupational Structure* (New York: Wiley, 1967); David L. Featherman and Robert M. Hauser, *Opportunity and Change* (New York: Academic Press, 1978).

2. Frank Levy and Robert Michal, *The Economic Future of American Families* (Washington, DC: Urban Institute, 1991); Mayer, *What Money Can't Buy;* and Daniel P. McMurrer et al., *Intergenerational Mobility in the United States* (Washington, DC: Urban Institute, 1997).

3. Galbraith, "Economic Delusion, Political Disaster"; Leonard Wiener, "Nice Surprises at Tax Time," *U.S. News and World Report* (January 22, 2001), p. 74.

4. As of 1990, 45 percent of all first births were to women who were either teenagers, unmarried, or lacking a high school degree. About one-third of all children were born out of wedlock, and it exceeds 50 percent in the 10 largest cities. The growth of never-married mothers can account for almost all the growth in child poverty since 1965. One need not be a genius to understand the economic consequences of such statistics. Although mobility is very fluid for most Americans, a sizable number are frozen at the bottom. See Daniel McMurrer and Isabel V. Sawhill, "The Declining Importance of Class," *Opportunities in America* (April 1997), pp. 1–3; Sawhill, "Still the Land of Opportunity?"

ily structure, public policy focuses on education, which in turn corresponds with our traditional faith in education. This does not necessarily mean that education is the key factor; rather, it is the most acceptable factor that society can tinker with in terms of reform and improvement in social and economic mobility. The other three factors are much more controversial and create many hotly contested debates that lead us down a path of emotions and ideology.

## The Value of Education

A vast amount of evidence shows that, on average, those who receive comparatively more years of schooling earn more income. Table 7.1 shows that in 1997, full-time working men who finished college earned twice as much as those men who did not finish high school ($48,616 vs. $24,726) and the same rates are true for women ($35,379 vs. $16,697). The spread increases as one goes up the education ladder; the median annual income for those with a master's and a professional degree continues to increase for both men and women. These differences have been constant over time, shown in the table with reference to years 1990 and 1997. The spread between men

---

### TABLE 7.1

### Median Annual Income of Full-Time Workers, 25 Years and Older, by Education Completed and Sex, 1990 and 1997

| | | | | | | | | |
|---|---|---|---|---|---|---|---|---|
| | | | | **Men** | | | | |
| | *Total* | *Less than 9th Grade* | *9th–12th Grade, No Diploma* | *High School Graduate* | *Associate Degree* | *Bachelor's* | *Master's* | *Professional* |
| 1990 | $30,733 | $17,394 | $20,902 | $26,653 | $33,400* | $39,238 | $49,500* | $73,300* |
| 1997 | $36,678 | $19,291 | $24,726 | $31,215 | $38,022 | $48,616 | $61,690 | $85,011 |
| | | | | **Women** | | | | |
| | *Total* | *Less than 9th Grade* | *9th–12th Grade, No Diploma* | *High School Graduate* | *Associate Degree* | *Bachelor's* | *Master's* | *Professional* |
| 1990 | $21,570 | $12,251 | $14,429 | $18,319 | $24,500* | $28,017 | $34,700* | $46,500* |
| 1997 | $26,974 | $14,161 | $16,697 | $22,067 | $28,812 | $35,379 | $44,949 | $61,051 |

*Estimated within $200+.

*Source: Digest of Education Statistics 1998* (Washington, DC: U.S. Government Printing Office, 1998), Table 380, p. 434.

and women at all educational levels is also shown—suggesting one of the main concerns of the feminist movement. The table also illustrates that all of these income differences, by education levels and sex, are constant over time.

Adults with higher levels of education are more likely to be employed than those with less education. The 1997 unemployment rate for adults (25 years old and over) who had not completed high school was 7.1 percent, compared with 4.3 percent for those who graduated high school and 2.0 percent for those with a bachelor's degree or higher. The difficulties in entering the job market for high school dropouts, under 25 years, is highlighted by the fact some 25 percent were unemployed in 1997, compared to high school graduates who were not in college, which amounted to 17 percent.[1]

Most educators share the public's faith in these income and education relationships. Education became the principal avenue of opportunity in the twentieth century. Although studies differ in the relative magnitude of the school-earnings effect,[2] virtually all studies of the subject show evidence of a significant school effect. This is even more evident for lower-class and minority groups, since the potential for earnings increase is greater than among working-class and middle-class groups.[3]

The emphasis on education in the United States is evident in the following trends: In 1998, 69 percent of all Americans graduated from high school, compared to 6.4 percent in 1900.[4] College enrollments more than doubled between 1960 and 1970, from 3.5 million to 8.5 million, and rose to 12.0 million in 1980 and 14.4 million in 1996.[5] In 1900, 4 percent of the population between ages 18 and 21 were attending college; it reached 50 percent in 1975 and 60 percent in 2000.[6] More than 95 percent of all American children from ages 7 to 17 were enrolled in school in 1996, and 92 percent of those from ages 5 to 17 were enrolled.[7]

These increasing enrollments, of course, do not necessarily indicate a proportionate commitment to the intrinsic value of higher education. The demonstrable economic rewards can make education attractive to those who would otherwise quickly terminate their formal educations when legally possible. With parental and peer pressure as well as equalitarian opinion added to the economic rewards, almost everyone is encouraged and expected to go on to higher education. It has become the thing to do, even if you don't know what to do. Certainly, it is important for the citizenry to be educated to their fullest potential, but there are some problems with mass higher

1. *Digest of Education Statistics 1998* (Washington, DC: U.S. Government Printing Office, 1998), Tables 382, 383, pp. 436, 437.

2. Henry M. Levin, "School Achievement and Post-School Success," *Review of Educational Research* (February 1971), pp. 1–20; Daniel U. Levine and Rayna Levine, *Society and Education*, 9th ed. (Boston: Allyn and Bacon, 1996); and Jencks, *Who Gets Ahead.*

3. *Digest of Education Statistics 1998*, Tables 382, 383, pp. 436, 437.

4. *Digest of Education Statistics 1998*, Table 101, p. 121.

5. *Digest of Education Statistics 1975* (Washington, DC: U.S. Government Printing Office, 1976), Table 79, p. 79; *Digest of Education Statistics 1998*, Tables 172, 186, pp. 196, 210.

6. *Projections of Education Statistics to 2008* (Washington, DC: U.S. Government Printing Office, 1998), Table 7, p. 30.

7. *Digest of Education Statistics 1998*, Table 39, p. 50.

education. Among them is an increasing oversupply of college-educated people vying for a shrinking number of jobs that require a degree. Second-rate college diplomas or degrees in large numbers also devalue all diplomas, especially since it has become increasingly difficult to test for academic outcomes and professional competence, without the cry of discrimination. The outcome is that some very talented college graduates wind up underemployed and frustrated by the vicissitudes of life.

## The Cost of Higher Education

I have elaborated on the investment returns of education, indicating that with increased education, one should expect to have better jobs and earn more money in one's lifetime. Although higher education has always highlighted those occupational and income differences, today an argument can be made that it offers no guarantee of doing so. Furthermore, the cost of higher education has dramatically increased in recent years, and it now means considerable sacrifice for the majority of parents and students.

These developments have fostered a new outlook toward higher education that was first expressed in part by Caroline Bird in *The Case Against College*.[1] She argued that college is a waste of time and money for the majority of students. At best, it is a social center or aging vat, and at worst, it is a young folks' home or institution that keeps young adults out of the mainstream of economic life for a few more years. The baby boom is over, but colleges and universities, having expanded in the 1960s and again in the 1990s to cope with the boom, now find a dramatic decline in their traditional market; they also are squeezed by the pressures of inflation and the recent stock market tumble. To keep their mammoth plants financially solvent, many institutions have begun to use hard-sell recruiting techniques and are lowering their standards to attract more students.

Bird's most persuasive argument 30 years ago against going to college is that it is no longer the best economic investment for a young man or woman. On the basis of 1972 census data, a man who had completed four years of college could expect to earn $199,000 more between the ages of 22 and 64 than a man who had only a high school education. If a 1972 high school graduate bound for an Ivy League college had put $34,181 (the amount his four years of college would cost him) into a savings bank at 7.5 percent interest (tax-deferred), compounded daily, by age 65 he would have accumulated a total of $1,129,200, or $528,200 more than the earnings of a male college graduate (the difference in earnings also compounded at 7.5 percent) and more than five times as much as the $199,000 extra the more educated man could expect to earn between ages 22 and 64.

Unfortunately, few high school graduates have the opportunity to bank all the money for their college education in advance, and those who do would probably attend college. Bird's estimates, based on Princeton's tuition, was skewed, since undergraduate tuition and residence at the average state university, according to the College Entrance Boards, was $1,790 per year and at a private university it was $4,568,

1. Caroline Bird, *The Case Against College* (New York: McKay, 1975).

including tuition, room expenses, and sundry expenses.[1] Only a few leading private institutions cost $8,500 a year when her thesis was developed.

Given the limitations of Bird's reliance on Princeton's tuition, let us examine it today in a slightly different perspective. About 50 percent of all undergraduates receive some type of financial aid; only 39 percent receive outright grants and fellowships, and 26 percent are provided with low-interest loans that have to be paid back.[2] For those who attend a private college, and receive no financial assistance, it can be safely assumed their parents can afford tuition, room, board, and related expenses or they would be attending a state university. In 2000–01, Princeton (as well as Harvard) cost $36,500 per year for education and sundry expenses. According to the College Board, tuition, books, room and board, and so on averaged $22,541 at private colleges and $8,470 at public four-year colleges.[3] Throw into the college mix an extra $2,000 for general living expenses (excluding clothing), and the cost is $24,500 at private colleges and $10,500 at public colleges. The government estimates the cost of college increases 3 percent a year.[4] Accepting this low-ball figure means that the nationwide cost for a four-year college education at a private institution was $102,453.

The big advantage of taking money set aside for college in cash, if it were possible to do so, would be that it could be invested in something with a higher rate of return than a diploma. The student who did not go to college in 2000–01 but banked his or her $102,453, who earned an average salary for a high school graduate, and who lived on his or her job earnings would at age 28 have earned $104,400 less on his job from age 22 to 28 than a college-educated person would. But that individual would have $102,453 (plus six years of interest)—enough to buy out the boss and to go into business for himself or herself. If he or she were smart enough to be accepted at an Ivy League or elite college in the first place, the individual might make more money in his or her lifetime without ever stepping on a college campus. Plumbers and electricians prove this point, as do local real estate developers, Burger King owners, and service station owners.

Jencks puts this into perspective with his argument that there is no real evidence that the higher income of a college graduate is due to a college education. College may simply attract people who are slated to earn more money anyway; those with higher IQs, better family backgrounds, and more enterprising temperaments. "Luck," or the unexplained variance related to income, may be more important than education.[5]

If a high school graduate became a butcher, baker, or candlestick maker, and banked the $102,453 at age 22 until age 64, to be used for retirement, at 7.5 percent return (tax deferred), the accumulation would total $2,296,600. If the money was banked at age 18, then the total funds available at retirement would be over

1. Allan C. Ornstein, *Education and Social Inquiry* (Itasca, IL: Peacock, 1978).
2. *The Condition of Education 1998*, Table 7, p. 25.
3. College Board.Com, "Trends in Education," "College Costs."
4. *The Condition of Education 1998*, Table 6, p. 24.
5. Jencks, *Who Gets Ahead?*

$3,067,000. On the other hand, a college graduate, from age 22 to 64 could expect to earn $645,000 to $1,000,000 more than a high school graduate—the range depends on specific assumptions and extrapolations about income differences.

The golden age of college ended at the outset of the 1970s, when the 25-year job market for college-educated people turned into a bust. Richard Freeman points out that when only a small proportion of young Americans attended college, the financial rewards for the college trained were sizable and stimulated many to extend their education.[1] In response, institutions of higher learning expanded (almost one new institution per week at the 1970–72 peak), and Americans flooded the halls of ivy. There was little incentive to examine the value of college education carefully when whatever was being taught was paying off in good jobs for graduates. Furthermore, going to college coincided with the democratization of schooling, the equalitarian philosophy of the day, and the notion of upward mobility—the kind of reasoning few people would oppose. However, it also meant that a large number of unqualified students were swept into college on this wave of new equalitarianism, thus further devaluing the college diploma both intellectually and economically.

When I graduated from college, John Kennedy was president. That may seem like the Dark Ages for some of you—before plastic money and moon landings—but only 11 percent of my age cohort held a bachelor's degree. The postwar economy was booming and there were three or four job offerings for every young professor searching for a job. In 2001, nearly 30 percent of the 21 to 25 age cohort have four or more years of college education, and a good number are underemployed as waiters, taxicab drivers, sales people, fast-food managers, and receptionists.[2] Economists say that between 1961 and 1970, the starting salary advantage of college graduates over wage and salary earnings was from 17 percent (in 1961) to a high of 24 percent (in 1968 to 1970).[3] By 1974, it had plummeted to 10 percent, and it continued to hover below that figure until the mid-1980s.[4] America was in the midst of recession. Today, we call it an *economic slow-down, a dot-com bust,* or a *mild recession,* but the starting salary advantage of college graduates is now again below 10 percent. Welcome once more to the world of college-educated waiters and taxicab drivers!

On a more professional level, it has become evident that the number of job offerings is not growing as rapidly as the increasing number of students graduating from college. The *annual* number of Americans with four or more years of college increased sixfold from 1940 to 1975, from 216,000 to 1.3 million, and to 1.8 million

1. Richard B. Freeman, *The Over-Educated American* (New York: Academic Press, 1976); *Projections of Education Statistics to 2008,* Table 15–1, pp. 38–39.

2. *Digest of Education Statistics 1998,* Table 186, p. 210; *Projections of Education Statistics to 2008,* Tables 16–18, pp. 39–41.

3. Richard B. Freeman and J. Herbert Holloman, "Declining Value of College Going," *Change* (September 1975), Table 1, p. 25.

4. Freeman, *The Over-Educated American;* George L. Perry and James Tobin, *Economic Events, Ideas and Policies: The 1960s and After* (Washington, DC: Brookings Institution, 2000).

by 2000.[1] This growth is expected to continue, reflecting high school bulging en-rollments, which is not expected to peak until 2111.[2] Coinciding with this growth of college graduates seeking work, most sectors of the economy that employ educated personnel have leveled off today, and even declined in some areas. A few sectors of the economy (computer science, pharmaceuticals, health services, and teaching) are still growing, but not enough to maintain high levels of employment for all college graduates. The new millennium has brought the nation an oversupply of highly trained and educationally qualified applicants for a shrinking (at least flat) employ-ment market.

During economy slow-downs, not only do college graduates find it more diffi-cult to get good jobs they were trained for (or think they were trained for) but also the relative advantages of the college degree and starting salaries of college graduates dip dramatically. On an economic basis (no social or intellectual considerations), the value of a college education declines, the investment has less economic reward, and the argument can be made that the money could have been invested in better places, such as a 7.5 percent tax-deferred insurance or mutual fund.

You might want to criticize me for making an anti-intellectual argument against a college education, and you might also add there are many other benefits of a college education. You have that right, and your opinion is as good as mine. But if you had the $100,000 available, to do what you want with it, and you had the guts, motiva-tion, and drive, how tempted would you be to take the money and run with it? About 15 percent of the CEOs from the top 800 U.S. corporations, especially the high-tech gurus such as Steve Bommer, Michael Dell, and Bill Gates, either never went to col-lege or are college dropouts.[3] Then, of course, there are the likes of Sam Walton, Ray Kroc, Steve Jobs, and Colonel Sanders, who never stepped on a college campus until after making tens of millions of dollars, and then to make a speech or a donation.

## The Great Divide

More than traditional forms of education are related to social and economic mobil-ity. We are living in a high-tech/information society in which the future "haves" and "have-nots," the "masters" and "peasants," the "lords" and "flies" will be based on knowledge of computers and technology—and how to generate and use knowledge. Human capital may no longer be defined as *intellectual capital* or *educational achieve-ment,* terms social scientists used in the last generation; rather, there is a new term on the horizon that is based on the *digital divide.*

In the near future, inequality or gaps between classes (the rich and poor) will be based on those with access to computers and the Web versus those without it. The

1. *Digest of Education Statistics 1974* (Washington, DC: U.S. Government Printing Of-fice, 1975), Table 115, p. 101; *Digest of Education Statistics 2000* (Washington, DC: U.S. Gov-ernment Printing Office, 2001), Table 257, p. 300.

2. *Projections of Education Statistics to 2011* (Washington, DC: U.S. Government Print-ing Office, 2001), Tables 27–29, pp. 69–71.

3. See *Fortune* (May 15, 2000).

real divide, according to Dinesh D'Souza, will be between those who "use these tools to acquire knowledge and those who don't."[1] To diminish the divide, to reduce future inequality, we need to teach students the value of knowledge: how to obtain it, how to organize it, how to modify it, and how to use it.

We are all well aware that whites and Asian Americans have higher incomes than blacks and Hispanics. We are also well aware that whites and Asian American students consistently score higher on standardized tests and have higher educational levels than traditional minority students. But we also should note that whites and Asians are more likely to be computer proficient and more likely to use the World Wide Web for pleasure, education, and work. They represent the majority of Internet surfers and the ones who respect and use technical and scientific knowledge in much larger numbers.[2]

In the past, the *nerds* and *geeks* were the kids who lacked peer status, got bullied or beat up in the schoolyard, and joined the chess team or math team. In my day, they were the ones who also played tennis, since they lacked the ability to play "real" sports. Well, times have changed—welcome to the World Wide Web. Today, there are plenty of computer nerds and geeks, and they have moved way up the totem pole of status, success, and respect. Those "invisible" or "pathetic" kids who got selected last and bat last on your favorite sandlot baseball team are now the "movers and shakers" of computerland and futureland. The kids who used to get bullied in the school yard or school hallway now have the last laugh.

In the post-Columbine High era, TV has returned *en masse* to high school settings, and thus *Freaks and Geeks,* on NBC, have had their own show. Besides media hype and super-hero fantasy, part of *Spiderman*'s success at the box office in 2002 ($114 million during the first weekend of its release) was that the hero, a high school kid, is transformed from a bookworm, social outcast, and dork (constantly diminished by his peers) to the toughest, coolest kid in school—the ultimate adolescent dream. *Spiderman* gives every adolescent nerd the idea of becoming a hero; in reverse, inside every super-hero (including Batman, Captain Marvel, Superman, etc.) in the original story is a nerd. While *Spiderman* is about teenage power, it is also about adjustment, acceptance, and attention, which is part of adolescents' developmental process—both for nerdy and cool kids.

When your screen or printer freezes, and you need some help, who are you going to call? Certainly not a ghostbuster, or the coolest kid, but a computer nerd. The person who performs the three or four occult keystrokes that unfreezes your computer in a few seconds is today's elitist, both in college and on the job. In reality, you don't always have to use a computer to function in college or on the job, so long as your verbal or math usage is superior. Language and math symbols are everything and everywhere; it is what lets us communicate with one another and helps us conceptualize and

1. Dinesh D'Souza, "The Return of Inequality," *Weekly Standard* (January 1, 2001), p. 33.
2. The U.S. government does not report home computer use for Asian American students, although it shows other ethnic groups. It does report SAT scores for several groups, including Asian students. Asian American students have an average math score of 565 and white students have 530 compared to blacks (426) and Hispanics (464). Here I'm assuming that computer usage and math scores mildly correlate. See *Digest of Education Statistics 2000*, Table 133, p. 149.

organize data. Language and math are what separates us from the slaves, barbarians, and peasants of the old world, and it is these twin subjects that split us apart today in schools as "achievers" and "nonachievers," college bound and noncollege bound, highly mobile and low mobile.

The gap that exists between those who efficiently communicate via language and math reflects class differences, but the gap is more dramatic with computers. The rich are on line much more than the poor. Social critics might argue that "access" is related to caste and class, and this reflects racial prejudice and socioeconomic discrimination within American society. Nonsense! That is political rhetoric. The simple truth is, at least according to D'Souza, Internet access is available to all people, and is "about as serious a problem as telephone access"[1] or, if I may add, television access. A poor family may not have three or four telephones or televisions in their home, but they have one or two. To put it in slightly different terms, the Internet is potentially an equalizer, but the ability to use a computer and access information is not equal.

Last year's computer model cost no more than a color TV set, and Internet use ranges from free to $20 a month, less than the cost of a monthly telephone bill. Anyone who wants to use a computer, acquire knowledge, and integrate information in his or her personal life or at work can. Whether the underclass in American society succeeds in becoming computer literate is one part of the equation; the second part is to appreciate knowledge, know how to obtain it, and know what to do with it.

Whereas both parts of the equation deal with class issues, the first part includes a cultural component. Here, it is worthwhile to note that significantly more Asian lower- and working-class children are on line than their American counterparts. The Internet seems to have made a whole nation of Japanese, South Korean, Taiwanese and Singaporean children and adults cybercrazy—logging on to the Internet—the highest per-capita ratios of Web users in the world.[2] So faddish are all things cyber that "cool" Asian and Asian American youth have adopted the Bill Gates scruffy nerdy look, while most other kids in the United States are seduced by the hip-hop urban look.[3]

At any hour of the day, Asian children are playing games, sending e-mail, doing homework, chatting, or even aimlessly browsing various sites and chatrooms. In a society still deeply influenced by conservative values, rooted in Confucianism and Buddhism, the anonymity and freedom of cyberspace has provided an escape from old-style attitudes that the young find oppressive. The bottom line is that about 20 percent of the Far Eastern students ages 10 to 18 may be Internet addicts, and about 33 percent would rather surf than socialize.[4] Though Web mania may seem a little extreme in some of the Far East rim countries, there is a certain amount of energy, creativity, and growth connected to computers; trends indicate that the future cyberspace and information society will gravitate away from the United States to other industrialized countries in Asia.

1. Ibid.
2. Donald MacIntyre, "South Korea Wires Up," *Time* (January 22, 2001), pp. 10–13, B12.
3. Ibid.
4. Ibid.

Not only will such a trend create more Web-crazed and wired-up Asian popula-tions on a per-capita basis than the American populace (hard to believe for some of us who live in big cities and watch people constantly walk and talk on their cell phones or click on their laptops in train terminals and airports), but it is also bound to affect future economic growth and put pressure on American schools to keep up with Asian schools on international tests. It is a no-win situation, since U.S. students are more concerned with socializing than chatting on line and prefer playing soccer, basketball, or football after school than studying math or science or connecting their computers into cyberspace. And *that* is more about culture than class!

## School Finance Reform and Equality

Evidence supporting the correlation between funding levels and student achievement remain weak and elusive because social class and home advantage are linked to the level of local school funding. In the real world, once we control for the effects of class and family, the separate effect of spending is weak, and it doesn't matter if the child enrolls in a high-funded or low-funded school district. The Heritage Foundation, a conservative think tank, and Erik Hanushek are the most-well-known proponents of this viewpoint among a host of others in the last 20 years.[1]

Money alone is not the answer for improving educational outcomes. A more com-prehensive or global approach might be that a variety of factors, in addition to money, affect student performance—for example, (1) *student input* (such as intelligence, prior achievement, and motivation); (2) *family background* (household headed by one or two adults, parent's [parents'] education level[s], number of siblings, number of bedrooms per sibling, number of books in the household); (3) *what schools do* (school size, class-room size, reading programs, tutoring programs, summer-school programs); (4) *what teachers do* (expectations and attitudes, teacher behaviors, instructional methods, teacher morale); and (5) *administrative input*—preparation, experience, and leadership.

"The simple fact is, money might make a difference if it was spent properly and under the right circumstances."[2] Regardless of the lack of relationship between school expenditures and student performance, *all* American children and youth are entitled to minimum and equal funding levels—an agreed benchmark that should vary only within the nation according to consumer price indices. Anything else means children are being cheated because of their parents' economic circumstances, and it should be considered by legislators and the courts as a form of discrimination and a violation of equal opportunity.

It is a well-known fact that state residence has a lot to do with the amount of money spent on education and the presumed quality of education received. In 1998,

1. Eric A. Hanushek, "The Impact Differential Expenditures on School Performance," *Educational Researcher* (September 1989), pp. 45–48; Hanushek, "A More Complete Picture of School Resource Policies," *Review of Educational Research* (Winter 1996), pp. 397–409.

2. Fred Lunenburg and Allan C. Ornstein, *Educational Administration*, 3rd ed. (Belmont, CA: Wadsworth, 2000), p. 355.

for example, New Jersey spent $9,643 per student, Connecticut spent $8,904, New York spent $8,825, and Alaska spent $8,271, whereas two states—Mississippi and Utah—spent half the amount, $4,288 and $3,969, respectively, per student.[1]

It is incorrect to assume that, based on dollars only, the education priorities of some states are higher than are the priorities of other states. We must ask what the states can afford, and this has a lot to do with the personal income of the state's inhabitants. See Teaching Tips 7.1 earlier in this chapter. Also, we must ask what the states spend on other services and functions (such as social welfare, housing, transportation, police and fire protection, medical outlays, etc.). In the first case, we are able to get a good idea of the states' financial ability to fund education; in the second case, we can determine the states' priorities. Finally, the cost of living must be considered.[2]

Large funding disparities also appear within most states. A few states (Hawaii, West Virginia, and Wisconsin) exhibit minimal differences, but large differences appear in many other states. In Alaska, Connecticut, Illinois, New York, and Pennsylvania, the differences are nearly $10,000 in student spending between the wealthiest and poorest school district. A school district located in a wealthy area or an area with a broad tax base can generate more local revenue than can poor school districts.[3] As a result, in many states, total expenditures per student may be two to four times greater in the five wealthiest school districts than the five poorest school districts. Within particular school districts, however, there is a tendency for the neediest school districts to spend more money per student. For example, among New York's 32 community districts, the 6 districts with the highest needs spent 5 percent more than the citywide median of $9,373, and the 6 districts with the lowest needs spent 6 percent less than the citywide median. The difference between the 6 highest- and 6 lowest-needs districts averaged $1,053 in the 2000–01 school year.[4]

This phenomenon exists despite the attempt by the federal government to favor poorer school districts through compensatory funding and despite the various states' attempts to redistribute school revenues through state funding methods and court-ordered reforms. The simple fact is, U.S. school funding is largely based on a local community's ability to fund education through property taxes, compared to most industrialized countries, where funding is relatively equal among students throughout the nation, province, or state.[5]

1. *Digest of Educational Statistics 2000*, Table 169, p. 191.

2. For example, Utah, the state with the lowest education expenditures per student ($3,969) devoted 33.9 percent of all its revenues to education, compared to New Jersey (30.3 percent), New York (23 percent), Alaska (21.5 percent), and Connecticut (26.1 percent), all of which spent over $8,000 (more than double) per student. In addition, the Consumer Price Index in Utah is more than half of Alaska and nearly half of the other three states. See Lunenburg and Ornstein, *Educational Administration,* Table 11–2, p. 358.

3. Lunenburg and Ornstein, *Educational Administration,* Table 11–2, p. 358.

4. Edward Wyatt, "Neediest Districts Spend the Most Per Pupil," *New York Times* (April 3, 2001), p. B4.

5. Kevin J. Payne and Bruce J. Biddle, "Poor School Funding, Child Poverty, and Mathematics Achievement," *Educational Researcher* (August–September 1999), pp. 4–13.

Municipal and Educational Overburden    Cities are plagued by what is commonly called *municipal overburden,* or severe financing demands for public functions due to population density and the high proportion of poverty and low-income groups. The result is that the large cities cannot devote as great a percentage of their total tax revenues to the schools as suburban and rural districts can. For example, in the early 1990s, Cleveland (Ohio), Detroit (Michigan), Gary (Indiana), Newark (New Jersey), and New York City spent less than 30 to 35 percent of all local tax revenues for school purposes, whereas the rest of their respective states were able to spend 45 to 60 percent of local taxes for schools.[1]

There is also the issue of *educational overburden.* A large percentage of the student population in city schools is in technical and vocational programs, which cost more per student than the regular academic high school program. Similarly, there is a greater proportion of students with special needs—namely, students who are poor, bilingual, and disabled—in city schools than in suburban or rural schools. These students require remedial programs and services, which cost 50 to 100 percent more per student than basic programs. Moreover, the need for additional services tends to increase geometrically with the concentration of immigrant children and poverty.[2] Therefore, city schools have to spend more educational resources per student than a similar-sized suburban or rural school, school district, or group of school districts comprising middle-class students.

Finally, city schools tend to have a greater proportion of senior teachers at the top of the pay scale than do their suburban counterparts. Many suburban districts have as a matter of policy replaced many experienced teachers to save money. They also experience a high turnover of pregnant teachers who do not return to the teaching profession. Cities have higher vandalism costs, lunch costs, desegregation costs, insurance costs, and maintenance costs (their buildings are older than suburban schools) per school than do other districts within the state. Both city and rural school districts spend more than suburban districts on transportation.

Legal Issues and the Courts    In *Brown v. Board of Education,* in 1954, the Court set aside the "separate but equal" doctrine and forbade the states to impose racial segregation in the public schools. Surely, "separate and unequal," with adjacent school districts spending two or three times more per student, is worse. Unless the Constitution, as it relates to schooling, applies only to black children, the *Brown* decision should also apply to lower-class and working-class children.

1. Joseph Cordes, Robert D. Ebel, and Jane Gravelle, *Encyclopedia of Taxation and Tax Policy* (Washington, DC: Urban Institute, 1999); George C. Glaster and Ronald B. Mincy, "Poverty in Urban Neighborhoods," *Urban Institute* (September 1993), pp. 11–13; and Allan C. Ornstein, "Regional Population Shifts: Implications for Educators," *Clearing House* (September 1996), pp. 284–290.

2. Michael L. Arnold, "Three Kinds of Equity," *School Administrator* (March 1998), pp. 34–36; Michael Fix and Wendy Zimmerman, *Educating Immigrant Children: Chapter 1 in the Changing City* (Washington DC: Urban Institute Press, 1993); and David H. Monk and Brian O. Bent, *Raising Money for Education* (Thousand Oaks, CA: Corwin Press, 1997).

It was only a matter of time that reformers would argue that social-class factors should also be related to fundamental rights and equal protection clauses of the Constitution. Although the 1971 *Serrano* v. *Priest* decision in California concluded that education was a fundamental right and that wide discrepancies in spending in neighboring school districts violated the constitution, the U.S. Supreme Court ruled (in a 5–4 decision) two years later in *San Antonio Independent School District* v. *Rodriguez* that education was not a fundamental right and that property wealth was not a suspect or illegal classification. The problem illustrated by the *Rodriguez* decision, and the subsequent school funding disparities among and within states is that fewer people speak for poor and working-class groups than they do for blacks and other minority groups.

Which congress person, senator, judge, or church member speaks for the lower class? I doubt if 1 out of 100 of you could name one person with political clout at the national level (possibly Ted Kennedy) who speaks for working-class or average Americans. The last "New Deal" politicians were Congresswoman Barbara Mikulski and Congressman Tip O'Neill, and both have long retired. A few old "war horses" such as Jimmy Breslin, Studs Terkel, Michael Novak, and Andrew Greeley are still alive and well; they voice (in print) the convictions and aspirations of the ordinary guy and still believe in government as the curer of social ills. For the most part, we are left with nonpolitical figures, caricatures such as Archie Bunker, Al Bundy, and Homer Simpson, and perhaps entertainers such as Johnny Cash, Bruce Springsteen, and Howard Stern to voice the concerns of the common folk, the "working-class stiffs" of America.

Although the states have been grappling with school finance and equalization formulas since the 1970s, outcomes are diverse and partly related to local differences in priority for education, funding methods or formulas to equalize spending, and states' interpretations of *Rodriguez*. With the exception of a few states—such as New Jersey, New York, and Vermont—the state courts and state legislatures have been reluctant to enact "Robin Hood" laws (that is, redistributing money); rather, they have attempted to add money for poor school districts from education lotteries, tobacco and alcohol taxes, and general sales taxes.[1]

Sadly, the range of actual increased student spending from 1970 to 1997 is similar in states where courts have tried to equalize spending and in states that have declined to do so or no litigation has been filed. Over this 27-year period, states with successful litigation experienced student spending growth of 54 percent, compared to 60 percent in states where courts refused to invalidate existing funding systems.[2] In other words, other variables—perhaps the threat of litigation or the historical reform attitudes of the state—factor into the equation.

The argument has been made that the education problems of lower-class and working-class children cannot be solved with more money. Like many institutions

1. Lunenburg and Ornstein, *Educational Administration*.
2. Rothstein, "Equalizing Education Resources on Behalf of Disadvantaged Children," in R. D. Kahlenberg, ed. *A Notion at Risk: Preserving Public Education as an Engine for Social Mobility* (Washington, DC: Century Foundation, 2000), pp. 31–92.

(hospitals, prisons, welfare, housing, etc.), the schools can and should do a lot better with the money now being spent. No doubt, also, that the parochial schools spend much less money than public schools, and they seem to do a much better job of raising student achievement.[1] Most disturbing is the fact that poor students in high-spending states in the Northeast and the Midwest already receive considerably more school funds than the most privileged students in low-spending states, such as the South—and there is no significant improvement among the poor. Furthermore, there is no significant differential in the academic outcomes of poor students in high- and low-spending school districts.[2]

In a recent court decision in the state of New York, Justice Leland DeGrasse drew a distinction that is often ignored in the professional literature: "Spending is meaningful when the money is properly deployed." Although there may be at best a causal link between funding and educational achievement, "the studies fail to take into account the cumulative effect of differences in spending over many years."[3]

Rather than looking at overall spending, the need is to look at specific factors, such as class size, teacher training, academic time, length of the school day, the focus on basic skills, reading, tutoring, and after-school programs, and so on. It is safe to assume that some factors have more impact than others and some of these factors over long periods of time may have dramatic impact. The need is to follow students and to separate specific school factors over a long period of time, which is costly, is time consuming, and requires more patience and less rhetoric.

All of these problems touch on inequality and the need for school finance reform. Since we are not going to redistribute money to achieve equality, as Christopher Jencks argued some 30 years ago in his book, *Inequality* (1972), we need a federal initiative that narrows differences in student spending between states, and state initiatives that narrow differences within states. Federal revenues for education need to be adjusted for child poverty, for the states' ability to fund education, and for consumer price differences between states. State revenues for education must be adjusted strictly by local wealth or income, with portions of state taxes and lotteries earmarked for equalizing spending within their jurisdictions. It is a simple decision, based on the principles of democracy and social justice and the special meaning America has always had for the world's oppressed and underprivileged; it is a decision long overdue.

1. Depending on the city and parish, Catholic high schools spend about $5,000 to $6,000 per student. As many as 95 to 99 percent of its high school students graduate, and about 50 to 60 percent apply to college. Minority students comprise nearly two-thirds of the enrollment and more than half qualify for free-lunch programs. See John E. Chubb and Terry M. Moe, *Politics, Markets, and America's Schools* (Washington, DC: The Brookings Institute, 1990); James S. Coleman, *Equality and Achievement in Education* (Boulder, CO: Westwood, 1990); and Coleman, "Public School Choice," *Educational Evaluation and Policy Analysis* (Spring 1996), pp. 19–29.

2. Rothstein, "Equalizing Education Resources."

3. Edward Wyatt, "Answering Those Who Say More Money Can't Help," *New York Times* (January 2001), p. B-6.

## Relationship of Education to Income

Education and income are related in a number of ways. Philosophically, two will be discussed here: the traditional and the revisionist.

**The Traditional View**  Traditionalists hold that most social and educational inequalities are not created by some central authority but arise out of the individual's innate or acquired skills, capabilities, and other resources. In a society based on unrestricted equality, where the government does not interfere, the individual with greater skills and capabilities will be at an advantage. There will be room for those who excel to climb to the top, but there will also be the possibility that others will not do well in school or will lose their jobs and drop a level or two in social stratification.[1]

In this view, education is conceived as a process involving the acquisition of skills and the inculcation of better work habits in order to increase the individual's productivity. Since income is related to productivity, the more education an individual has, the higher will be his or her income. Education also serves as a screening device to sort individuals into different jobs; the more highly educated individuals will obtain the better jobs. If we try to intervene and handicap one group or provide special privileges or entitlements for another group, we only cause false benchmarks, social ills, and maladjustment; society suffers in terms of lack of productivity.

A certain amount of inequalities will exist in society because not everyone has equal innate abilities or formal education. The explanation is as follows:

1.  There are marked differences in individual abilities; those who are more capable will achieve higher levels of education and thus better jobs. Stratification, based on individual merit and performance, will develop. Even in a society where there is inherited wealth, there will still be room at the top for those who are capable.
2.  In hiring, it is often difficult for employers to identify potential good employees, but they have observed the qualities that make present workers more productive on the job. Although the correlation between schooling and productivity is not perfect, competitive firms can offer individuals who have done well in school and have completed more years of schooling the better jobs.
3.  The more educated get the better jobs because they have been made more productive by the schools. In a modern, technological society, additional years of schooling constitute a signal of this greater productivity.
4.  As long as there is an excess number of applicants for a job, the employer has to use some criterion to decide whom to hire or promote. In some societies, it may be the applicant's race or ethnic group; in U.S. society, it is largely the amount of education. The more educated are not seen as necessarily the most productive; rather, education is a convenient criterion that most people would regard as fair and logical. See Teaching Tips 7.1 earlier in this chapter.

1. People such as Daniel Bell, Nathan Glazer, Irving Kristol, Daniel Moynihan, and Robert Nisbet—liberals from the Kennedy and Johnson era and who were still alive in 2002— would represent this view. Three of them graduated from the City College of New York, my old alma mater.

**The Revisionist View**   Various scholars representing the political left have argued that the traditional view is incomplete and inadequate. Although education often provides better jobs and higher incomes, it offers no guarantee of either. On some jobs, productivity has very little to do with education; other factors—such as personality, drive, common sense, and experience—are far more relevant than diplomas or degrees. Most important, with the passage of time there is a tendency for many people to be in jobs that utilize less education than they have (service industries, manual labor, the civil service); furthermore, on some jobs, educational advancement can catapult people out of employment, since they can be replaced by others who are just as capable but have less education and therefore command lower wages.[1]

A number of revisionists argue that schools have not promoted education nor social or economic mobility but have discriminated against and limited the life chances of the poor, racial and ethnic minorities, and women. They contend that members of these groups have always had a hard time in the schools. In the early 1900s, it was the European immigrants who were most likely to receive failing marks, to repeat grades, and to drop out of school; today, it is black and Hispanic students who are more likely to do so than white, middle-class students. Not only have the schools failed to recognize the legitimacy of cultures and classes different from the predominant middle class, but through reliance on intelligence tests, achievement tests, and vocational counseling they have also limited the educational opportunity of immigrant and minority groups. Revisionists ignore the evidence provided by the numerous ethnics who have risen to the top, and minimize the fact that other social indicators, such as family structure and environmental deprivation, also impact on school achievement.

A stronger revisionist view, which approaches Marxism, is that the educational system reflects the social and economic system. These advocates see American society as racist, sexist, and capitalistic, based on stratification and inequality, and maintain that the schools cannot be reformed until society is reformed. To them, the relationships among students, teachers, and administrators replicate the hierarchical division of labor and the discriminatory practices of society. Students are ranked, tracked, and sorted by social class, race, and sex, thus mirroring society. If people are trained to be subordinate and kept sufficiently fragmented in spirit, they will remain disorganized and unable to shape their material existence.[2]

Any kind of meritocracy is rejected on the grounds that it would undermine egalitarianism, and a good society and equality are virtually synonymous. Revisionists envision an egalitarian social system, to be achieved by replacing the capitalist system with enlightened socialism, income redistribution, affirmative action, quotas, and reparations. Not only does such a solution send the majority of Americans into their political trenches but such an approach to education condemns anything suggesting high standards or high-stakes tests as a mask for elitism and racism.

1. In this group, I would classify Ivan Berg, David Cohen, Colin Greer, Henry Levin, Joel Spring, and Paul Violas.
2. Some educators in this camp are Michael Apple, Paulo Frier, Henry Giroux, and Peter McLaren.

**EPISODE** *B*

## International Comparisons: Science and Math

Let us return to the question raised in the previous chapter: What knowledge is of most worth? Since the publication of *A Nation at Risk,* there has been a slight average increase in science and mathematics coursework among graduating high school students, ranging from two-tenths to four-tenths in one year (for example, 2.5 to 2.9 years).[1] But the data are not impressive when comparisons are made with high school seniors in other advanced, technological countries. Japanese, South Korean, and Hong Kong high school students, for example, average 1¼ science courses per year and 1½ math courses per year, including calculus and statistics.[2]

One result is that Japanese, South Korean, and Hong Kong students consistently outperform American students on international tests in science and mathematics, and the gaps increase in the higher grades,[3] in part because of the cumulative effects of more courses and more hours in science and math. In the last 30 years, there have been three international mathematics and science studies (TIMSS) comparing industrialized countries in grades 4, 8, and 12. The conclusion for all three studies is clear: The longer American students stay in school, the farther they fall behind their counterparts in most industrialized nations. In the last TIMSS report, U.S. fourth-grade students in math ranked 8th out of 18 among industrialized countries that participated; in science, the U.S. fourth-graders tied for third place. In eighth grade, U.S. students ranked slightly below average in math (23rd out of 38 industrialized countries) and slightly above average in science (below 14 countries). By the twelfth grade, American students scored last in math among 20 industrialized countries, and in science they scored below 16 countries. The international average math/science scores were 500; the U.S. average in math was 461, and in science it was 480.[4]

1. Government sources conflict and depend on the precise date and volume of *The Condition of Education.*

2. Kay M. Troost, "What Accounts for Japan's Success in Science Education," *Education Leadership* (December–January 1984), pp. 26–29; Herbert J. Walberg, "Improving School Science in Advanced and Developing Countries," *Review of Education Research* (Spring 1991), pp. 25–70. Also see *The Educational System in Japan* (Washington, DC: U.S. Government Printing Office, 1998); Marcia C. Linn et al., "Beyond Fourth-Grade Science: Why Do U.S. and Japanese Students Diverge?" *Educational Researcher* (April 2000), pp. 4–14.

3. *The Condition of Education 1998* (Washington, DC: U.S. Government Printing Office, 1998), Table 20, pp. 76–77.

4. E. Bronner, "U.S. 12th Grades Rank Poorly in Math and Science, Study Says," *New York Times* (February 21, 1998), p. A-1; Gerald W. Bracey, "The TIMSS Final 'Year Study' and Report," *Educational Research* (May 2000), pp. 4–10; *Digest of Education Statistics 1998* (Washington, DC: U.S. Government Printing Office, 1998), Tables 404–406, pp. 462–464; and Arthur Eisenkraft, "Rating Science and Math," *Education Week* (February 14, 2001), pp. 46, 48.

The picture worsens when education spending is compared on an international level. Among industrialized countries reporting education spending, the United States spends 4.8 percent of its Gross Domestic Product on education, ranking 10th among 20 industrialized countries. However, U.S. expenditures per student is much higher—second only to Switzerland.[1] In other words, other countries do not have the same resources as we do, but they make a greater effort by spending more of their GDP on education.

Looking at what the United States spends and what it produces, we learn sadly that our nation's output, as measured in the form of international test scores, is low compared to that of other industrialized countries. Even worse, countries such as Japan and South Korea rank low in education spending, about one-third less per student than the United States, yet they have the highest math and science scores. The inference here is that U.S. school expenditures do not correlate with academic output; other variables, what some might call excuses, are more important.

Among the common reasons or excuses given for the consistently low scores of American students are:

1. American twelfth-grade students average almost one year younger (18.0 compared to 18.7) than their international counterparts.[2]
2. Measuring the cumulative achievement on a short test may not sufficiently cover what students have learned. About 25 percent of the test items in math and science reflect topics not studied by American test takers.[3]
3. About 20 to 33 percent of American middle school and high school science and math teachers are teaching out of license; furthermore, nearly half of those certified to teach science and math teach subjects they are not qualified to teach.[4] For example, a science teacher may not be qualified to teach physics (only biology and chemistry) and a math teacher may not be qualified to teach calculus (only algebra and geometry).
4. American science and math textbooks are numerous—some above average, some average, some below average in quality—whereas textbooks in other countries are approved by the ministry of education so that there is consistency of coverage. Our textbooks emphasize *breadth* of topics, to please a wide audience (15,000 different school districts) at the expense of *depth* of topics. The outcome is that American textbooks (and teachers who rely on these textbooks) foster superficial learning of a large body of information. Students in other countries with a ministry, however, have more time to teach students to think about procedures,

1. *Digest of Education Statistics 1998,* Table 413, p. 469.
2. Bracey, "The TIMSS 'Final Year' Study Report."
3. Ibid., Jianjun Wang, "TIMSS Primary and Middle School Data: Some Technical Concerns," *Educational Researcher* (August–September 2001), pp. 17–21.
4. Richard M. Ingersoll, "The Problem of Underqualified Teachers in American Secondary Schools," *Educational Researcher* (March 1999), pp. 26–37; Stephen J. Friedman, "How Much of a Problem: A Reply to Ingersoll, 'The Problem of Underqualified Teachers,' " *Educational Researcher* (June–July 2000), pp. 18–24.

and to help students frame hypotheses, make predictions, and acquire skills to conduct experiments and contrast ideas and findings.[1]

5. American students have less homework (23 percent of eleventh-graders report no assigned homework, 14 percent do not do their homework, and 26 percent do less than one hour per day of homework) and engage in more social activities, out-of-school activities, and part-time jobs than their international counterparts.[2]

6. American students average 3.5 hours per day of TV viewing, not to mention computer surfing, and we know there is an inverse relationship between TV viewing and student achievement, especially after the second or third grade. (The positive effects of watching *Sesame Street* and other language skill programs become increasingly irrelevant after age 7 or 8.[3])

7. European and Asian students have a longer school day and school year, with European countries averaging 200 days and Asian countries averaging 220 days, compared to the United States, which has about a 180-day school calendar.[4]

8. Student poverty among American students it the highest, about 21 to 25 percent. It is nearly 50 percent higher than any other industrialized country; next comes Australia with 14 percent and Canada with 13.5 percent.[5] Moreover, poverty clearly correlates in an inverse relationship with student achievement. In addition, the United States has among the highest or highest student drug addiction, student violence, gang activity, and teenage pregnancy among industrialized nations.

9. Finally, the breakdown of the American family is well documented. More than 50 percent of American students live with a single head of household; it approaches 75 percent in big cities, where student achievement is the lowest compared to other parts of the country.[6]

10. It should not be assumed that the students taking the test in all countries are drawn from an estimated normal bell curve or ability distribution. Some countries—such as China, Japan, and Russia—may have certain political agendas, or sensitivity about "saving face," and be more selective in selecting students. Moreover, if you eliminate black and Hispanic students from the test pool, American white students compare favorably with European nations, and Asian American students compare favorably with students in Asian nations that score the highest in math and science.[7]

1. Eisenkraft, "Rating Science and Math"; Sandra H. Fradd and Okhee Lee, "Teachers Roles in Promoting Science Inquiry," *Educational Researcher* (August–September 1999), pp. 14–20; and Linn, "Beyond Fourth Grade Science."

2. *The Condition of Education 1998*, Table 37, p. 118.

3. Allan C. Ornstein and Thomas J. Lasley, *Strategies for Effective Teaching*, 3rd ed. (Boston: McGraw-Hill, 2000).

4. Ibid.

5. Payne and Biddle, "Poor School Funding, Child Poverty, and Mathematics."

6. Allan C. Ornstein and Daniel U. Levine, *Foundations of Education*, 8th ed. (Boston: Houghton Mifflin, 2003).

7. Wang, "TIMSS Primary and Middle School Data."

Although all of these reasons are valid factors for explaining the low scores in math and science achievement among American students on international tests, part of the problem must boil down to the limited amount of coursework in these two subject areas. If you want to learn how to drive a car, play tennis or chess, or read, you need to devote time—the more *instructional time,* the more proficient you should become. If Americans are so concerned about math and science, and we should because of the information technology age we live in, then we need to modify our curriculum and instructional time. This consideration must be weighed against a general belief among many educators that schools need to emphasize the whole child and the liberal arts, and that teachers should be paid on the basis of education and experience (with no differential for specific subjects such as math or science).

Similarly, if you want to learn more, or if you are serious about competing, the classroom size and the instructional ratios of the group count, over time. Obviously, one-to-one learning (a coach and student) is more effective than a five-to-one teacher/student ratio, and this small group is more beneficial than a class of 25 or 30 students. It boils down to money and social policy. *Inequality* (or social-class differences) is another factor we cannot ignore, because the world is not perfect. Points 8 and 9 in the preceding list reflect inequality, and as "excuses" go, affect student test outcomes. Inequality (or social differences) also affects learners' attitudes and behaviors, which relate to items 5 and 6.

Regardless of all the reasons and excuses, we are living in the midst of a work-force time bomb—growing illiteracy among U.S. workers that will subsequently influence our economic output. Not only are our junior and senior high school students outperformed by their international counterparts but the same holds true for American adults under age 40. For example, at the 56–65 age bracket, American adults rank 5th in literacy among 17 other industrialized nations; in the 36–45 age bracket, Americans rank 8th; in the 16–25 bracket, they rank 14th. Overall U.S. adult literacy ranks 10th out of 17.[1]

Most of the work-force literacy problems are reflected in our minority and immigrant populations. Hispanics scored 75 points lower than whites, and blacks scored 63 points lower. Native-born whites and Asian Americans were tied for second place in the international ranking in literacy. Immigrants account for 40 percent of the U.S. labor force, but they rank 74 points behind native-born Americans.[2] In short, American productivity is partially based on the GI Bill and pre-1950 immigrants who (90 percent) were largely from Europe and more skilled than today's immigrants who hail from nonEuropean and third-world countries. Soon, these older workers will be retiring and replaced by a less literate work force.

1. Aaron Bernstein, "The Time Bomb in the Work Force: Illiteracy," *Business Week* (February 25, 2002), p. 122. The 17 industrialized countries were from western Europe, Canada, and Australia. Test data are reported in a study conducted between 1994 and 1998 by the Educational Testing Service.
2. Ibid.

## International Inequality: The Urban Malaise

If you take a stroll in the ghettoes of the big cities—such as in Harlem, Southside Chicago, or Watts—there is the stench of urban decay; a sense of concentrated drugs, prostitution, and gang violence; and a feeling of helplessness and human failure. The dot-com bubble and economic boom of the 1990s never made it to the low end of the ladder. These ghettoes are the sort of place about which John Steinbeck and Tom Wolfe should have written—The Great American Novel—with the American themes of poverty, race, drugs, and sex. Politically, as citizens, we are all free and equal; in terms of economics, however, there are great inequalities in wealth and power; these inequalities are tolerated and reinforced by a philosophy (and political and economic system) characterized by utilitarianism, competition, excellence, and merit. These new principles, if taken to an extreme, lead to vast inequalities that should not be tolerated by a moral society, what John Gardner would call a "democratic society" or what John Rawls would call a "just" and "fair" society.[1]

Politically, Americans no longer think that anyone is naturally superior to anyone else (although it might be hard to convince a card-carrying Ku Klux Klan member or neoNazi youth member). Nonetheless, there is no monarch nor nobility who passes an inherited advantage provided by natural law, religious dictum, or military despotism. Our class system permits a certain degree of mobility, which in turn provides hope and belief in the "American Dream" and secures the existing system from being overthrown by the proletariat, as Marx would expect from the masses. Not all people may have equal ability or motivation, but every Tom, Dick, and Harry has the opportunity to own "a piece of the rock," to inherit Joel Barlow's *Vision of Columbus* (1787)—America's magnificent landscape—and to become "an artist, inventor, literary [person] as well as statesmen and military hero."

The poverty and inequalities that exist in American cities is nothing compared to the deprivation and misery that exists in the third-world cities such as Bombay, Cairo, Dhaka, Jakarta, Karachi, Lagos, and Sao Paulo—the vortex of urban problems of the twenty-first century. In the midst of these filthy, overcrowded, and wretched conditions, millions of families and homeless children are flooding these polluted cites. In search of jobs, or because of religious, ethnic, or tribal strife, these people have emigrated from rural, backwater villages, once populated by subsistence farmers, and are now living on rooftops, in street alleys, and by garbage dumps. They are surrounded by malnourishment, shortage of safe water,[2] overflowing sewage, and disease (especially AIDS). Some of these people may wear turbans or veils, but the majority wear cheap western-style polyester outfits rather than traditional clothes. Despite what they wear, the way these people live is unparallel and unknown to the American mind and eye.

1. Gardner, *Excellence: Can We Be Equal Too?*; John Rawls, *A Theory of Justice*, 2nd ed. (Cambridge, MA: Harvard University Press, 1999).
2. About 26 percent of Bangladeshis are drinking arsenic-contaminated water, 76 times the safe limit set by the World Health Organization. *New York Times* (July 14, 2002), pp. 1, 6. Clean water is also an issue in most parts of Africa, where people still use pond water and untested tube wells.

It is these places, what I call rotting cities or urban garbage heaps, where a new proletariat is being created—one in which the present government is unable to provide basic necessities. Although some of these governments have been celebrated in the West and in the United States as pro-American or "democratic," this new and growing proletariat sees their governments as corrupt, elected by ballot-rigging or overrun by military coups, and supported by U.S. dollars (which get diverted to the pockets of the politicians and military at the expense of the inhabitants). The paradox is that as government authority is weakened or overthrown (as in the case of Batista, Peron, Trujillo, Savimbi, the Shah), the people of the third world are being organized by regional, guerilla, or religious parties at the expense of national, progressive, or secular ones.[1] The governments in power must contend with, and in some cases actually reflect, extreme religious and left-wing political ideologies. In the meantime, the third-world proletariat grows larger—fostered by increasing poverty, illiteracy, and birthrates; and, it is being fueled by anti-American and anti-western sentiments, which are easy to induce because of the growing gap between the world's rich and poor, between the West and the third world.

For the greater part, the third-world cities are severely dysfunctional places, consisting of crumbling infrastructure, urban decay, drugs, and disease—and getting worse. It is happening slowly enough to avoid sudden catastrophe, but it is happening in front of our eyes. Anyone who wishes to deal with a dose of reality can read about it in the *New York Times*, the UNESCO reports, and sometimes in *Time* and *Newsweek*, or see it live on CNN and Fox news. You are not going to read about it in school textbooks, at least not for more than two or three pages, and very few teachers seem to have interest or time to discuss these problems in class for more than one or two days—simply because the curriculum doesn't allow time for it.

## The Third-World Is Growing

Dealing with global poverty is essential if capitalism is to continue to prosper; otherwise, the growing world poor will tip the scale and its weight will eventually bring down capitalism. At the present, capitalism is basking in its victory over communism, unaware that as global poverty increases, the third-world (65 to 75 percent of the world's population) countries gain in power and the potential to challenge the existing system.

The people of third-world countries are not burning the American flag or effigies of President Bush, nor are they rioting in the streets on a regular basis. Their anger toward the West and rich nations is loosely articulated, because these people, for the greater part, are working and struggling on a daily basis to exist and do not have time to take part in demonstrations. The people we do see demonstrating are riveting to the American audience, partially because of their anger toward the United States, partially because of their zeal, and partially because they seem to exist in another world so different from ours. For the most part, the world's poor believe, or are led to believe, that

1. Robert D. Kaplan, "A Nation's High Price for Success," *New York Times* (March 19, 2000), p. 15.

the United States is the cause of their squalor and misery, that their government cannot lead because of U.S. foreign aid and military. In their need to lash out at someone, to vent their subsistence existence, they are recruits for various anti-American movements, including totalitarian and religious extremists.

A few radical or neomarxist educators, such as Pablo Friere and Ivan Illich, both from Latin America, have hinted about capitalistic exploitation and a growing crisis between dominant and subordinate groups, white and colored people of the world, and the need for human liberation. Eventually, the capital-rich nations of the West will be challenged by "no-hopers"—people who have nothing to lose since life means very little in a society characterized by squalor and misery (which they believe America is to blame because of the way capitalism exploits). This "no-hopers" concept partially explains why it is easy to recruit guerilla soldiers intent on battling American-sponsored dictatorships who are anti-communist and pro-American; it also explains why terrorists are easily recruited from poor rural villages and urban hell holes.

The old elite, the wealthy in third-world countries, live a life walled off from the masses who are poor and who have migrated from rural shanty towns to urban squalor, where they now live on rooftops, street alleys, near garbage sites without running water or sewage. By 2015, more than 50 cities in developing countries will have populations of 5 to 10 million in which the poor have no land, no businesses, no machines, no tangible assets to create wealth—only the labor or sweat on their backs to offer presently at $1.00 or $2.00 a day for 12 to 14 hours of work.

According to neomarxist interpretation, Marx was right in claiming that capitalism strips workers of their assets, except their labor. They are unable to accumulate capital legally because they don't own property or other tangible assets, such as businesses that create capital and permit people to accumulate wealth. So the market is restricted, mobility is inhibited, and wealth is limited to those who control the property and other tangible assets. The only way for the poor to accumulate money is to deal in drugs, arms,[1] or some black-market product or become a corrupt government bureaucrat and provide some service for a fee.

It staggers the imagination of the American mind, but from Chile to Chad to Cambodia, from Peru to Pakistan to the Philippines, and from Uruguay to Uganda to Uzbekistan, the situation is similar. Democracy and free trade, the globalization of the world means, in blunt terms, the West dominating third-world countries. The reason is, there is no legal avenue for this poor population in third-world countries to acquire assets (or education) and break from their misery and squalor in a sufficiently large scale that can reverse worldwide growing poverty. Government officials in these countries are rarely held accountable; the powerful few—landowners, top military echelons, and drug lords—continue to rape the country and keep the poor in "chains," a metaphor described by Marx and Lenin and subscribed by today's neomarxist educators.

You need only to visit a third-world country as a tourist and see the entrepreneurial culture. Taxicab drivers are hustling you; vendors are trying to sell you their

1. Hernando de Soto, *The Mystery of Capital: Why Capitalism Triumphs in the West and Fails Everywhere Else* (New York: Basic Books, 2001).

goods in streets and flea markets, even behind garage doors; women are selling their bodies; and old people and children are begging. Everyone is trying to make a dollar, to keep alive. The vast majority are not trying to rob or fleece the tourist. The people are not lawless, nor are they demonstrating; they are working.

Educators claim that the key to alleviating poverty is through education; sociologists claim that the key is to limit population growth, and business people claim that the key is industry, technology, and free trade. Neomarxists (including de Soto) have a different spin, and it has some historical validity to it. They would like to redistribute the property, factories, businesses, and machines to the poor so they can accumulate capital—in short, so they can buy into the capitalistic system, instead of relying only on their labor, which amounts to continuous exploitation. The validity to the argument is that in the western world, this is how Australia and Canada were settled. People searched out and were able to acquire land for free by squatting and settling it. The American government permitted its immigrants to acquire large tracks of farm land for free or for a few dollars, and the English nobility sold 99-year leases for low rent on many rural estates to the "common folk."

As the third world continues to grow in population, the West, and especially the United States, will become the target for global hostilities. There are too many people wasting away, severely deprived, running from dying villages to cities that don't function and cannot serve their needs. The future is now, and it will get worse. Guerilla warfare, civil strife, and terrorism will become increasingly more commonplace, driven by people who have nothing to offer but the sweat on their backs and little to lose except for a life that has little meaning or merit in a world governed by corruption, famine, drought, and war. There is nothing for the world poor to grab on, to hope, except some totalitarian or religious idea that provides some kind of promise of a better world or better hereafter.

What do we tell American students so they wake up to world reality? How do we explain all the anti-American sentiments seen on cable television? How do our future citizens learn to deal with world anger, nations, and billions of people spearheaded by poverty, famine, and back-breaking labor? Even in boomtowns, the poor vent their anger at the West, and it becomes increasingly obvious in the media. Textbooks in the United States are currently censored and sanitized—and rarely reflect the political and economic realities of the world. Given different interpretations of the world, and that historical facts are little more than biases of the political left or right, how and what should American teachers do to prepare their students for globalization? The ice cap is melting, the air we breathe is polluted, prostitution and AIDS are a fact of life, the worldwide landscape has been continuously plundered, and third-world big businesses and politicians are often corrupt. Ask yourself how U.S. textbooks and teachers gloss over issues, or the way they interpret "facts," and then ask what makes for a sound education. How do we prepare the next generation of Americans for the world they will inherit? Indeed, the third world is growing in population and surrounding us! We are now unable to live in a vacuum or on an island; 9-11 shattered our protective layer.

Some of us are buying new cars and larger houses, and others are visiting shopping malls and purchasing the latest phones, faxes, and computers. But the applecart is bound to turn over by the growing imbalance of world economic scales. We have rogue nations that possess nuclear bombs, and others have access to biological chemical weapons. If you cannot recall the movie *On the Beach* or the television program *The Day After*, because of your age, think about Three-Mile Island and Chernobyl to remind yourself of a serious meltdown and the effects on air, food, and water supply. Global weather patterns know no national boundaries, and concentrated radiation or viruses can affect human populations at home or thousands of miles away.

In 1958, American intelligence predicted a doomsday scenario in which the Soviets attacked the United States with atomic bombs. Warnings of the attack came two hours before the Soviet planes appeared over U.S. soil. Major cities were targeted, and the results were devastating, reminiscent of the movie *On the Beach*. Approximately 20 percent of Americans died; major transportation, water, and sewer systems were immobilized; and the monetary and credit system collapsed, as bartering and looting became evident.[1]

Given today's era of computers and satellite communication systems, nuclear plants, and a high-tech infrastructure, it is almost impossible to speculate the damage and ripple effect of a major terrorist attack on fragile utility and high-tech sites, and without warning. Most Americans are unable to imagine the World Trade Center loss in dollars, jobs, and its effect on the national economy—somewhere between $250 and $500 billion. In the meantime, the U.S. government is preparing for a potential smallpox attack, and innoculating 500,000 health and medical people—the front-line soldiers of this possible war with terrorism. The government is also laying the groundwork to mass vaccinate the public, a policy abandoned 30 years ago.[2]

As for the "population bomb," Paul and Anne Ehrlich did an excellent job describing and projecting global disaster; the world ecosystem is in jeopardy and is having difficulty supporting the growing world population.[3] And who is the biggest user of world resources and warming the earth with carbons? It's the United States, where the doctrine of natural rights, inscribed into the imperishable words of the Declaration of Independence, permit and encourage "life, liberty, and the pursuit of happiness."[4] So damn the world, as one colonist lawyer, James Otis, said a long time ago, "we are entitled to all the rights of Nature." (Two hundred thirty-seven years later, a world wildlife leaflet on my desk tells me that the United States releases approximately 40,000 pounds of carbon dioxide per person annually; time to turn off the air

1. A top-secret Department of Defense plan, *The Doomsday Scenario,* was accidentally declassified in 1998 and published by historian L. Douglas Keeney.

2. William J. Broad, "U.S. to Vaccinate 500,000 Workers Against Small Pox," *New York Times* (July 7, 2002), pp. 1, 16.

3. Paul Ehrlich and Anne Ehrlich, *Extinction: The Causes and Consequences of the Disappearance of Specifics* (New York: Random House, 1981).

4. Partly because the United States dominates the world and partly because of its standard of living, there is a prevailing attitude among foreign policy and political leaders that it is entitled to consume 25 percent of the world's energy, while it comprises only 4 percent of the world's population. Such an obnoxious and hubris view leads to a lot of resentment among the rest of the world, especially among poor nations.

conditioner (which releases carbon emissions) and open the windows and breathe the "fresh" air!)

The point is, a parade of grim environmental realities makes for a long list, with the loss of large portions of vegetation, top soil, natural resources, and animal life (*Homo sapiens* included) as a real possibility in the twenty-first century. If these threats are acknowledged as real, no educational system hoping to prepare students for the world of tomorrow can ignore the environment (and population explosion) as an important subject. The good news is that the third world understands that the environment is globally connected; the bad news is that the United States is considered the worst culprit, and refuses to ratify the Kyoto climate change treaty. A paralyzing view by the world is that Americans want to do very little to change their lifestyle and habits—and to keep the environment safe from ruin. So, it may be argued that some rogue nation, terrorist cell, or individual nut may bring the world to the brink of catastrophe, but the United States may bring the world to a slow death. So long as you recycle your plastic containers, you get a good feeling and believe you are doing your job for the environment and humankind. We can also hope that Captain Kirk will beam us up to a new world—with all our molecules and information in place to start over.

Since Captain Kirk is an American invention, we can stretch our imaginations and claim the universe will be saved by American ingenuity and know-how. Of course, this opinion is laughable, even farcical, but some of us might claim there is an element of truth: The computer will save us. We already live in a world of pacemakers, cloning, computer chips, satellite tracking, and the Internet—so why not some genetic mutation or engineering that saves the world from environmental catastrophe? Now this view should not be totally dismissed, since some of us understand quantum physics and quantum computers, and therefore believe that the universe is manifested in Newtonian mechanics and that energy (kinetic and potential) can be conserved, modified, increased, and transported.[1] The "big bang" theory, Einstein's theory of relativity, Von Braun's work that got Americans to the moon, and the atomic bomb are all based on Newtonian principles—as well as the computers we use at home, in school, and at work. If you believe in postmodernism, or are predisposed to qualitative research such as art, voices, metaphors, biographies, and alternative realities, then you cannot get on board and beam up, because that would be the triumph of science, traditional research, and empirical knowledge.

## History, Culture, and Inequality

From the beginning of the nation, our founding fathers were concerned with great wealth and inequities. Thomas Jefferson feared that we might become a nation of gamblers who "spent their lives performing tricks with paper."[2] Benjamin Rush was

1. Tom Siegfried, *The Bit and the Pendulum: From Quantum Computing to the M Theory—The New Physics of Information* (New York: Wiley, 2001).
2. David Brooks, "Why the U.S. Will Always Be Rich," *New York Times Magazine* (June 9, 2002), p. 88.

concerned that big money would result in the nation's downfall; he put his faith into the Bible, science, and education to promote the enlightened mind and to advance morality and equality of people.

But these ideas were overshadowed by conservative doctrines. Ben Franklin's "Poor Richard" philosophy emphasized so-called capitalistic virtues of hard work, thrift, and savings: "A penny saved is a penny earned." It was the same type of education philosophy depicted in the McGuffey readers 100 years later. Alexander Hamilton emphasized the development of manufacturing and the accumulation of capital, as well as the virtues of a financial class that would foster trade and commerce. The Puritan doctrine—in contrast to the ideas of the American and French revolution, which ensured that people by nature were equal and potentially good—stressed innate differences in the abilities of individuals and assumed that people by nature were inherently depraved and motivated by self-interest rather than altruism.

For conservative thinkers such as John Adams, George Cabot, Henry Knox, Alexander Hamilton, and other federalists, the doctrines of equality written in the Declaration of Independence were considered high-sounding, unrealistic words that contradicted common knowledge. Obviously some people were not and never had been equal to others. So, John Adams "attacked equalitarianism of both American and French leaders as unrealistic and based on a false and untenable conception of human nature." Democracy, for Adams, was "unworkable and considered a step toward anarchy." Hamilton defended the need for a "strong central government to better serve the interests of the bankers and industrialists" against the mob. James Madison stressed "the innate diversities in the faculties of men" which explained the rise of people with superior abilities and the accumulation of property by the well born and educated.[1]

The transcendentalist movement, which began in the 1830s, was part of a larger romantic movement, which indicted the growing materialism of its nation, and the undemocratic aspects of industrialism at the expense of a laboring class. Concern for human exploitation and inequality characterized the writings of Ralph Waldo Emerson. Simplicity and the virtues of plain people were depicted by Henry Wadsworth Longfellow and Henry David Thoreau. Robert Frost and Mark Twain attacked the values of the Guilded Age, and humanitarians and social reformers such as Wendell Phillips, Peter Cooper, and Edward Kellogg at the turn of the twentieth century advocated social revolution in which wealth, instead of being accumulated in the hands of a few, would be distributed, and thus poverty would be abolished. Teddy Roosevelt keenly reflected the concern of malfeasance of business, that the only way to control the corporate giants was to regulate them. For him, the highest form of justice was to cushion the poor from business abuses, then heavily tax and distribute wealth so that all Americans could have a decent life. Inheritance of wealth and tax injustices led to greed, corruption, and lawlessness.[2] Profits gained by exploitation (sounds

1. Merle Curti, *The Growth of American Thought*, 2nd ed. (New York: Harper & Brothers, 1951), pp. 188–190.
2. Kathleen Dalton, "For T.R., Government Was the Solution," *New York Times* (July 14, 2002), Sect. 4, p. 3.

a little like Marxism)—and I would add fraud, deceit, and phony accounting procedures—was and still is "dirty money." In dealing with big business, President Bush today might learn a lesson or two from Roosevelt's ideas.

A teacher today at the top of the pay scale in large cities such as New York, Los Angeles, and Chicago earns about $75,000. If that's your income, then you might have trouble making ends meet if you have two or more kids to put through college, but you make more than 98 percent of the world's population. You might ask yourself, How do all the poor manage? There is no simple answer. But the United States is a country where teenagers have credit cards and spend $150 on sneakers, where well-heeled men spend $25 on a Cuban cigar and women spend $1,000 on a Gucci handbag, and still others spend $10,000 on a Piaget watch. This is the country where the people annually spend more money on landscaping and gardening ($40 billion) than the total federal tax revenues of India or China. This is the nation where the super-rich can spend more money on one meal (say, $500 per couple) in an upscale restaurant than what hundreds of millions of third-world laborers earn for the year. Such people in third-world countries have no time for polemics or protests. Yet, they can be easily led by a person or movement that promises a better future—or that brings down American materialism.

We are told that education will level the playing field among the "haves" and "have-nots." Wrong! Education cannot reduce the gap between the super-rich and the super-poor, the powerful few and the impotent mass. Only political, social, and economic reform can do so by redistributing capital and assets. At this point, reform has moved to another level, what I call overhauling the system and what some educators might call reconstruction, reconceptualization, and radicalism—a "pedagogy for the oppressed." (These are the words of today's neomarxists who wish to transform the teacher from a "clerk" and "public servant" to a "critical pedagogist" and "social reformer"—as in the old days with Brameld, Counts, and Kilpatrick.)

How much inequality is permissible in a country that boasts that it is guided by democratic and moral principles? Should the highest 5 percent own 50 percent of all the national wealth, and the bottom 25 percent own 5 percent, which is basically how the social/economic pyramid is shaped in this country? On an individual basis, should someone such as Sylvester Stallone or Tom Cruise earn $15 to $20 million a movie or should someone who hits a golf ball 300 yards down the fairway or hits a baseball 400 feet in the stands on a regular basis earn $25 to $30 million a year (with advertising and endorsements), while 40 to 50 million Americans live in squalor? Ayn Rand, Richard Herrnstein, and Dinesh D'Souza would welcome such a world, based on the doctrines of capitalism and individual achievement, and without apologies. That's a hard pill to swallow, at least with regard to my vision of the world, and the way I conceive morality, fairness, and what's good for society.

Should a CEO or boss earn 50 times more than his or her workers? And what about workers in China, India, or Indonesia? Should Eddie Bauer's CEO, Nike's CEO, or Polo's CEO, who employ third-world workers, earn 5,000 times more? In 1998, the top 700 executives in 365 companies (or the top 2 in each company) earned an average of $2.2 million in salary; however, some people (e.g., Stanford Weil, the CEO of the Traveler's Group) earned $230 million in salary, bonuses, and stock options;

others (e.g., CEO Robert Goizneta of Coca Cola) earned $110 million for the year. During this same year, the average teacher (nurse and social worker) earned less than $40,000 annually, and a school superintendent's average salary was $101,510, or 2.5 times more than the average teacher salary. The 226 superintendents in the largest school districts in the nation (25,000 or more students) averaged $126,631, with about an additional $25,000 to $50,000 in extra benefits and bonuses.[1] Of course, a lot of people moan and groan that school superintendents are overpaid. It if you consider the budget they administer and the personnel and students they oversee, some of these superintendents should be earning 10 to 20 times more than they are, especially in school districts comprising 25,000 or more teachers and 100,000 or more students.

Then there is Kevin Phillips's new book, *Wealth and Democracy*. He describes the dramatic increases in salaries and bonuses among the top 10 CEOs in the United States. The captains of industry were paid an average of $3.5 million in 1981 and $154 million in 2000, including stock options, bonuses, and other benefits—an increase of 4,300 percent in 20 years, compared to wages, which slightly more than doubled.[2] What do make of these astonishing trends? One might argue that "it's true, but there is nothing I can do," which is false. The masses of working people have the vote, and they can elect politicians who can prevent such a concentration of wealth by revising tax codes, eliminating off-shore tax loopholes, and prosecuting CEOs who bend the law and accountants who lie and cheat for their clients.[3] Indeed, the acquisition of wealth, since the age of Rockefeller, Morgan, and Vanderbilt, has always been the chief index of American civilization. In fact, it goes back to Christian duty to accept the worldly lot of the poor, that according to Rev. Joseph Morgan, in 1732, the poor should be content with their station in life and the rich should be sustained in theirs; "The accumulation of wealth is a public good."[4] It has been common to emphasize how capitalistic titans made immense fortunes through shrewdness, strength, and exploitation of others. In religious terms, "God in his wisdom and mercy turns our Wickedness to publick Benefits."[5] Bribes, scandals, fraud, and land stealing have always been part of big business since the post–Civil War period, according to many historians and social critics.[6] Why should it be different now given an army of well-paid, Ivy League–educated lawyers and accountants to protect CEOs from the arm of the law, from the public, and from their employees?

1. Lunenburg and Ornstein, *Educational Administration*.
2. Kevin Phillips, *Wealth and Democracy* (New York: Broadway Books, 2002).
3. For the 350 top CEOs, stock options were 3 million in 2001 compared to the stockholders' return of 3.6 percent. In addition, there were pensions and retirement plans, deferred compensations, and insurance policies that allowed executives to pass on their estate to their heirs free of income tax. See JoAnn S. Lublin, "Under the Radar," *Wall Street Journal* (April 11, 2002), p. B7.
4. Joseph Morgan, *The Nature of Riches* (Philadelphia: Dunn, 1732), pp. 14–15.
5. Ibid., p. 21.
6. Merle Curti, *The Growth of American Thought*, 2nd ed. (New York: Harper & Brothers, 1951); Allan Nevins, *The Emergence of Modern America: 1865–1878* (New York: Macmillan, 1927).

For any economist to argue that these new robber barons are worth what they get paid, because of their achievement or that they keep the engines of capitalism running, is outrageous. Just consider the greed, scams, market riggings, and fraudulent practices used by today's CEOs to hoodwink the public into thinking their companies are productive, long enough for these executives to cash in their stock options while their employees and the public are robbed of their pensions.[1] To say that such lopsided compensation doesn't matter because there is huge mobility among the working class ignores the growing concentration of wealth among the descendents of the super-rich, much more than the robber barons of the Golden Age ever dreamed or passed on to their children and great-grandchildren. The reason is simple: the super rich hire lawyers and accountants to evade hereditary taxes, achieved mainly through trusts.

So what does all this mean to Mr. Chips or the school marm who has something nice to say in class about American capitalism, social mobility, and the progressive tax system? Democracy is faltering, and they don't recognize it. We either reaffirm our traditional beliefs in democracy, with economic checks and balances to prevent the rise of a nobility class, or watch its slow demise in front of our eyes. *Demise* may be too apocalyptic. If so, then call it something else—*plutocracy, nobility,* or by some other name. Teachers (and their spouses) represent the largest concentration of voters among any other profession or union. They should become more actively involved in electing people who will try to reduce the concentration of wealth and preserve the spirit of democracy. A couple of "pep talks" by the president of the United States is not the answer. The answer lies with stiff laws and in our families, our schools and colleges, and the ethics we instill on our students. If we continue to remain silent on this issue, then Mr. Phillips and a few other think-tank experts at Brookings Institution or Rand Corporation soon may very likely be reporting the next book about America: *Upside Down Democracy, Plutocracy and Policy,* or *The Law of the Jungle.*

The basic problem is balancing the notions of equity (or fairness) with equality and inequality. This is not an easy task, and it takes us back to the philosophy of Socrates and Plato, right up to the present dialogue between postmodernists and neoconservatists. On a national level, reasonable people can hold different views on religion, politics, and morality and come to some consensus about equality and inequality. A broad consensus or a shared national view is permissible without the use of political power or political oppression to enforce consensus, because there is a connection among the people—cemented by history and custom.

As Americans, we generally believe that we have our own way of life; we tend to justify an extreme inequality of wealth on the basis of capitalistic and competitive principles because of the belief that our country (1) provides multiple chances to succeed, (2) recognizes and rewards multiple talents, (3) provides social mobility so that people can rise from rags to riches, and (4) considers that individual meritocracy benefits society. In fact, it is this fourfold belief that drives the engine in U.S. society and

1. Paul Krugman, "Plutocracy and Politics," *New York Times* (June 14, 2002), p. A37; Charles E. Morris, "Greed is Good, but Only Later," *New York Times* (June 9, 2002), Sect. 4, p. 4.

makes the difference why this young nation has achieved so much in so short a time compared to other civilizations that are 1,000 to 7,000+ years old (Egypt, Persia [Iran], Greece, India, China, etc.).

Although Americans don't accept the divine rights of kings and queens, or the superiority of the aristocracy, we accept vast differences in acquired wealth so long as it is based competition and achievement. We believe we are all politically equal, but we accept economic inequality and often blame the individual or home, and not the school or society, for the differences in economic outcomes or gap between prosperity and poverty. As educators, we take the position that gifted and talented students will become better educated and rise to the top. Given this scenario, where excellence is rewarded and achievement is based on intelligence or ability, many whites prefer to ignore racial factors and many males wish to ignore gender factors. All of us accept some degree of luck (Jenck's position), simply because it has a neutral ring to it—no race, gender, or class bias. Of course, all of us should be smart enough to know the difference between luck and discrimination.

Ironically, there are some Americans who might say there are no differences between the mass of workers and the pharaoh's slaves pushing the stones up the pyramids. Little has changed, especially if you consider that 5,000-plus years have passed. The argument is that blue-collar workers and low-end bureaucrats earn just enough to pay the rent and keep alive so that they can keep the system going for the wealthy—which has paralleled the history of all civilizations. You don't have to have a Ph.D. or be a card-carrying neomarxist to buy into this stance. Granted, western society provides disability benefits for those injured on the job. Nonetheless, many of the Archie Bunkers and Al Bundys of the world might reflect this view of the proletariat, along with many K-Mart and Cosco salespeople, hamburger cooks, waiters, cab drivers, and secretaries. These working people may lack the intellect to debate the philosophical issues, and to distinguish between Rousseau's democracy and Burke's aristocracy, or the best way to spread wealth, and they may lack the time to organize, march, and demonstrate, but they sense the system is unfair and partially rigged. Every now and then it comes up in conversation, with coffee or a beer, or in the songs of Willie Nelson and Bruce Springsteen—symbols of blue-collar pride and sympathy for the underdog. Our belief that this is the land of opportunity, reflected in the principles of Jeffersonian and Jacksonian democracy, reduces the possibility of a revolution and the violent overthrow of the government (a Marxist solution). It also prevents the majority of citizens to vote for a radical redistribution of income through the tax system—a solution that most critical theorists and neomarxists in education would favor (Apple, Friere, Giroux, Illich, and McLaren). I'm certainly in favor of taming the excesses of the rich, regulating the free-enterprise system, reducing fraudulent and deceitful corporate practices that hurt millions of working people, and eliminating the virtue of greed—what both Ayn Rand and Alan Greenspan advocate for a healthy economy. If we pay our teachers an average of $43,000 a year, then *no one* needs to make more than $1 million a year. No one is worth more than 24 times the value of a teacher, in term of service to society. (Possible exceptions are the president of the United States, a Supreme Court judge, Thomas Edison, Albert Einstein, and Jonas Salk.)

Across national boundaries, a shared view of equality and inequality, and what can be done to reduce extreme wealth and poverty, is more difficult to obtain. Many nations are characterized by a caste system based on color, gender, or hereditary status, rooted in centuries of tradition and ritual. There are differences in history, international law and customs, as well as 2,000 or more years of ethnic and religious strife and meaningless violence among different nation-states. This kind of historical chart makes it vastly more difficult for most nations to agree on anything beyond the date, time, and weather. The point is, extreme inequality between and within nations can be explained by differences in culture. There are some countries where the food, dress, and other customs have not changed for the last 1,000 years—where the influence of other civilizations and the intermixing of ideas have had limited impact. The differences can be very profound, which helps explain why more than half of the world is engulfed by extreme poverty and human misery.

Let me try to explain by providing you with examples from the perspective of different places and people. In the world I describe here, modernization and morality are dead—there is no justice. The places I talk about are not mythical places; they are real—and representative of two giant civilizations, two old cultures, the Chinese and Muslim worlds. After reading these stories, see if you can decipher the meaning of life and unravel the complexities of enlightenment, and determine why Buddhist monks and Chinese masters of martial arts in this part of the world are still seeking to know reality and truth.

Plunging into the Past    Almost every Chinese student has learned about the monk Hsian Tsang who 1,300 years ago sought enlightenment and traveled throughout Asia and the outreaches of the world (the West). It was a 10,000-mile journey, lasting 17 years, whereby Tsang brought home ideas that would profoundly affect Chinese philosophy and thought for centuries. Ma Jian, at 53 years old, deserted by his wife and cut off from his daughter, set out from Beijing to find enlightenment and self-realization by traveling the same path of the ancient monk. In his three-year odyssey, Ma Jian traveled on the rural fringes, meeting people steeped in poverty and personal debasement. But they were eager to speak to and hear the visitor from Beijing, the urban sophisticate, the former poet and painter.

In Guizhou Province, near the borders of Yunnan and Sichuan—places that no American has heard of except for a few with Chinese blood—Ma Jian wanders into a local Communist Party meeting where a father of four children is brought before the committee of "wise" men (communist bureaucrats) because he owes the state thousands of Yuan in family-planning fines. The decision is to confiscate the door, window panes, and roof tile of his house, as well as his farming tools, for payment of past fines. In addition, the men tie him to a table, cut open his abdomen, and snip his sperm ducts.[1] One is not allowed to go bankrupt and start over in the Chinese court system. This is payment in lieu of debtor's prison. This is what extreme isolation, poverty, and

1. Ma Jian, *Red Dust: A Path Through China* (New York: Pantheon Books, 2001).

lack of modernization breeds. This is Chinese justice—the same type of justice that prevailed 1,300 year ago.

In the village of Wa, near the Burmese (now Myanmar) border, Ma Jian stumbles over an old woman crouched by a pothole where a person is trapped. She is dropping potatoes to her son who fell down four days ago while picking berries to sell at the marketplace. No one helps.[1] On the other side of the divide, *character, compassion,* and *courage* are words that no longer have definition or meaning. People who live in rural wastelands and in isolation for centuries come to accept this type of existence and social order; tradition, geographical barriers, and a static culture have a way of cementing behavior and creating a stranglehold on progress. The divide between "haves" and "have-nots" have no meaning in a world where there is no satellite TV, no Ralph Lauren billboards or magazine pictures, no Gucchi gloves or belts. In Wa, there is little or no meaning to life that fits western philosophy, and there are few words in the English language that describe the tones, shades, and moods of this existence.

**The Present—Gone Bizarre**   Now we visit the world of *Blade Runner,* the grotesque sights and sounds of Afghanistan. This is the land that Alexander the Great and Genghis Kahn could not conquer, the same country from which the British and Soviets were driven out. Bibiarose tells her story, how she fled the Taliban with her family by bus just before the Americans arrived. Bibiarose and family left Kabul to avoid the bombing. Her husband was left behind because he had kidney problems and couldn't walk. She took her son and wife, their child, and two younger sons and daughters. At the border, the group ran into the Taliban soldiers, who started beating one of the younger sons because he had asked if he could get through. Bibiarose recalls, "I started crying and brought them my grandchild, lifted him up to them and said, take this small child and kill him, but don't hurt my son . . . who can work for the family." The soldiers beat her, too, for opening her mouth, and she fell to the ground with her grandson and went into shock. She doesn't remember crossing the border. At the time of the interview, she was extremely sick and could not afford medical care. Her daughter-in-law, Farhariz, speaks: "If she were to die, how would we go on? What would we do? How will we find the money to bury her? We had a nice home. We didn't live like this in Kabul. This is not our life."[2]

For other women, this is the land of Jihad (holy war in the name of God), where they send their sons to pray and read the Koran, and to become human bombs (mujahedeen) and commit martyrdom. Says Rehima, who belongs to a fundamentalist group, "For all my six sons, I wanted them to be mujahedeen. If they get killed it is nothing. This world is very short. . . . What will I do in this world? I could be in heaven, have a weekly meeting with God. . . . I am asking my husband if I can go to Kashmir and train to fight. I will suicide bomb [against] Americans and kill them."[3]

1. Ibid.

2. Alyssa Banta, "What They Were Thinking," *New York Times Magazine* (September 21, 2001), p. 36.

3. Alyssa Banta, "Jihad's Women," *New York Times Magazine* (September 21, 2001), p. 39.

For the first Afghan woman, Bibiarose, we are confronted with the memory of Sophie (in *Sophie's Choice*), who, at Auschwitz, had to choose whether her son or daughter would live while the other would die. It was a matter of Sophie placing them in different lines as she entered the concentration camp. She saved her son, only for him to later die.

Now, for Rehima, who is 35 years old, attractive and a teacher at a religious school in Peshawar (another place most Americans have never heard of), we get a sense of fanaticism. It is the same type of fanaticism that fueled Nazism and destroyed Sophie's family. However, this new fanaticism is taught at a religious school, or madrassah. (There are 10,000 madrassahs in Pakistan alone.) This is the heart of Muslim extremism aimed against the United States. Anger is loosely articulated on the streets, often because people are busy working and struggling to survive, and have little time to demonstrate—unless they get paid for it. This is a world where people feel that all humans should be equal, but they know they are not. Democracy and religious tolerance are not burning issues, since the entire land is overshadowed with squalor, despair, and government corruption.

This is a part of the world where humans suffer more than horses; this is a place where you don't want to vacation, where children as young as age 4 or 5 start working in pits and later in factories all day instead of attending school. Throughout Asia and the Middle East there are hundreds of cities where the youth are burdened by poverty, illiteracy, and anger—targets for the madrassahs. Here, inequality and equality are discussed in terms of "us" versus America. Given the philosophy of multiculturalism, pluralism, and diversity in American schools, how do American teachers balance things out without creating generalizations and stereotypes about the larger Muslim, nonextreme world that prefers democracy, religious tolerance, and prosperity for its people.

Into the Future   Now let us move from the past into the future. Here is a worst-case scenario, based on fiction and fantasy: a new world of anarchy, political strife, civil war, and violence. It is a world beyond Huxley's *Brave New World* and Orwell's *1984*. The future is based somewhat on Nevil Shute's 1958 classic *On the Beach* and Walter Mosley's 2002 *Futureland,* the latter of which combines high-tech society, racial and ethnic hatred, and post–9-11 fears. In the latter publication, the United States comes under attack; city dwellers live underground and sleep in tunnels and street alleys. Government breaks down, looting and crime are common occurrences. Terrorist groups plot to destroy blacks and Jews, and there are millions in the third world trying to destroy the western world.[1]

Someone in every family has a fatal disease, and there are long lines in stores to purchase whatever food and water is available. Bartering and smuggling are common. The roads are in horrible shape; nearly half of the cities lack running water and sewerage. Resentment and rage are everywhere, especially among the youth. Society is split into "haves" and "have-nots." The rich, few in number, have hired private "goon gangs" to protect their property and valuables. The poor sell pieces of themselves to

1. Walter Mosley, *Futureland* (New York: Warner Books, 2002).

survive. Convicted criminals are imprisoned indefinitely, sometimes for the small infractions. Mandatory sentences exist for a litany of infractions, and swift and public executions are evident in order to lay down the law. Military guards and police are highly visible and posted at government buildings, airports, railroad stations, utility plants, and major street crossings, Assassins are for hire. Guerilla soldiers as well as vigilante and dissent groups roam the cities and countryside, recruiting and plundering. Drivers are randomly searched and those without proper ID are jailed until their identity can be proven. The local economy largely revolves around smuggling—guns, ammunition, electronics, heroin, and hashish.

Drugs are rampant—leading to various fantasies, deviant and escapist behavior, and atrophies of the brain. Some of the youth are too drugged to do more than slump against a building or lie down, glassy-eyed. Older people and children are begging on the streets. Disinformation, security systems, and tracking systems are part of the government apparatus to "protect" the law-abiding citizens and to capture government criminals. Anyone who needs a physician must wait several months, unless this situation is life threatening. Except for the wealthy, anyone over 60 years must wait one to two years to be scheduled for surgery or a hospital, even if the person is a candidate for a heart attack. The average worker works 12 to 14 hours a day, and young children are working and not attending school.

Now welcome to the wide world of reality called the present. Beyond the western borders (United States and Europe) about 90 percent of what I describe (after the Mosley citation) exists in more than 50 percent of the world—driven by war, famine, and/or disease. And most of these people believe that somehow America is the cause of their plight. They usually don't blame their government, for their government has taught them to blame us and the western community. They blame their government, however, if it is pro-American; in their eyes, we are the "axis of evil" and anyone who stands up against the United States is an authentic hero—similar to the way people viewed Ho, Che, Mao, and now Bin Ladin. To a large extent, I am discussing the Muslim world, most of the continent of Africa, half of Latin America, and many other parts of the third world. It is a frightening world that the vast majority of Americans do not understand and it is descending on us, slowly but surely.

## Seeking a New Identity, Prescribing Violence

Part of the problem with the Muslim world, at least according to Amin Maalouf, is that *identity* (which leads to attitude and behavior) is often based on a false sense of self; identity is formed by the allegiances to which we subscribe and becomes the basis for who we are. If we feel that our allegiances are being criticized or attacked, our identity becomes modified in relation to our perceived enemy—the group we fear, resent, or even hate. Once a group (nation or religion) feels humiliated or oppressed, as does the Arab and Muslim world, the victimized group comes to interpret its identity around humiliation or oppression.[1]

---

1. Amin Maalouf, *In the Name of Identity: Violence and the Need to Belong* (New York: Arcade Publishing, 2001).

One of the driving forces of identity is history, and the Arab and Muslim world tend to view western culture and Christianity as a "big bully." The Arabic-Western cultural paradox and the Muslim-Christian religions paradox starts with the Crusades, followed by the Spanish Inquisition, Napoleon's Egyptian campaign, English and French protectariats and colonies in Asia and the Middle East in pre– and post–World War I, the English and French Suez Canal conflict in post–World War II, and American foreign relations with Israel and Iran (support of the Shah); Iraq (Desert Storm), and support of India since its partition from Pakistan.[1] Maalouf maintains that historically, Islam has been a tolerant religion, even in its political and cultural supremacy, whereas Christianity has been intolerant. The situation has been reversed and now the Muslims attack the West, and Islam has a stronghold of fanaticism because they feel downtrodden, humiliated, and victimized by the infidel. This identity crisis produces a particular interpretation that encourages redress, retribution, and revenge.

You cannot convince anyone personally involved in the World Trade Center tragedy about the authenticity of this interpretation of geopolitics. But for those who are sensitive to the long view of history, this view of the world must be recognized and understood (I'm not saying we have to accept it) as we plunge into the twenty-first century. Remember, these are people living in the same world as we are, breathing the same air, and who can potentially cause havoc in a world where national boundaries are no longer fully secured by border police or unapproachable because of physical barriers.

A similar treatise was offered by Franz Fanon, an Arab and Algerian psychiatrist living in Paris, after he was expelled from Algeria in 1956. The colonized experiences of blacks throughout the world led him to prescribe violence as good for the mental health of the victims. In his classic book, *The Wretched of the Earth,* it was argued that violence freed the native, the victim of white and western culture, from his inferiority complex and from despair and inaction; it also gave him self-respect and a chance to overcome his oppressor.[2]

The book became a bible for revolutionary slogans during the black nationalist movement in the United States in the 1960s and 1970s. It influenced Eldridge Cleaver, the leader of the Black Panthers, who wanted to kill the white "pigs," or police officers (the jailors of the black race) and who one said "Every brother can quote Fanon." Fanon influenced other extremist black leaders, such as Robert Williams of the Revolutionary Action Movement (RAM), Muglana Ron Karenga of US, and Jesse Gray of the Negro Action Group (NAG)—all who built their philosophy around Marx, Mao, and Fanon. Every black revolutionist of that era read and quoted Fanon, including H. Rap Brown, Angela Davis, Fred Hampton, Bobby Hutton, Bobby Seale, as well as more moderate black advocates such as Carmichael, Hamilton, and Malcolm.[3] It was a period of radical politics, black consciousness in the United States,

---

1. Note that the examples of history are by me, not by Maalouf.
2. Franz Fanon, *The Wretched of the Earth* (New York: Grove, 1963).
3. Allan C. Ornstein, *Race and Politics in School-Community Organizations* (Pacific Palisades, CA: Goodyear, 1974). Also see Eldridge Cleaver, *Soul on Ice* (New York: McGraw-Hill, 1968).

and the overthrow of colonization in Europe, leading Sartre (who was the number-one existentialist philosopher of the era) to write in the preface of Fanon's book: "To shoot down a European is to kill two birds with one stone, to destroy the oppressor and the man he oppresses at the same time."

Fanon's book on racism did not sell well in the Arab or African world at that time, because his intellectual peers were aware that African leaders were just as corrupt, violent, and oppressive toward their people. His belief that the peasants alone are revolutionary for they have "nothing to lose and everything to gain," a Marxist viewpoint, made sense for American black revolutionists. It also makes sense today for the Muslim proletariat living in abject poverty and becoming increasingly anti-West and anti-American because of the growing divide between the "haves" and "have-nots" and religious fundamentalism that preaches war and martyrdom.

Maalouf is an Arab and Lebanese reporter, novelist, and "home-grown" psychologist living in Paris who makes the same point that Fanon does about victimization and colonialization, and the subsequent need for Arabs and Muslims (for Fanon, the victims were blacks) to strike out against their enemy. He argues that the West does not want the rest of the world to be like it; rather "it just wants them [Arabs] to obey it." Similarly, Muslims feel that Christianity is based on the sword and the lack of free expression; moreover, Muslim extremists offer an alternative image, a response to their crippled identity, by rejecting western culture and Christian religion. As an Arab and Muslim, Maalouf asserts that no one should have to become defensive or a mental expatriate every time he opens up a book, watches television, or enters into a discussion with someone who is non-Arab or non-Muslim. People ought to be allowed to enter the modern world without being humbled or being stripped of their own identity.[1] Islamic extremism is a response to the infidel, one that rejects global colonialism and capitalism and challenges corrupt and despotic rulers, many of whom have been bought off by the West, particularly with American dollars.

Much of this new fanaticism among Muslims is the acting out against the enemy (the infidel West)—the kind of behavior that once characterized black nationalism against white America, highlighted by the black fist and the call of blacks around the world to unite against their white "oppressors."[2] Muslim extremism, according to Maalouf, is a horrible option but it provides relief and helps Muslims deal with a sense of inferiority and humiliation. As with Fanon's analysis of black nationalism, Muslim extremism helps Arabs and Muslims reduce their psychological suffering and embitterment, to act out their anger and frustration, to gain a philosophy of consciousness, and to strike out against the history of capitalism, colonialism, and Christianity. In parts of Afghanistan, Egypt, Indonesia, Iran, Pakistan, Palestine, Saudi

1. Maalouf, *In the Name of Identity*.
2. During the 1964 Olympics in Mexico City, John Carlos and Tommy Smith stunned the world when they entered the winners' circle and responded to the *Star Spangled Banner* with black fists. They were driven by idealism and considered to be heroes by the majority of the black community. Obviously, people with a different set of life experiences and subsequent view of the United States and world would have a very different reaction to the symbol generated by the black fist, and the behavior of Carlos and Smith.

Arabia, and northern Africa, especially in the religious schools run by militant Islam sects, this is an accurate and chilling view against the infidel. On the other hand, more moderate Muslims recognize that America is the most noble experiment in the world and is extremely important to the rest of the world as a safe heaven against mass extremism, mass ideology, and mass totalitarianism.

Anyone with an ounce of brain understands that the attack on the World Trade Center and the Pentagon was an act of war against the United States and the free world—the worst attack on the United States since Pearl Harbor—and one that actually did more damage. This was a day in our lives that almost everyone can say changed everything. Our world will never be the same. Although terrorists violate all fundamental values of civilized and free society, we need to understand that a nation-state, movement, or organization waging war today without technology is forced to fight on a different level with different rules of engagement. The British soldiers invaded the colonies in their red uniforms and shiny boots and marched on the open battlefield, ready to fire on the enemy in a sequenced and prescribed manner, and according to the rules of civilized society and gentleman soldiers. The American troops, a rag-tag army dressed in tattered and farm-patched clothing, hid behind trees and rocks, and resorted to unusual rules of engagement, including surprise and hit and run, all which were construed by the British as ungentlemanly.

I would argue that the world is a paradox, full of misunderstandings, subjectivity, and interesting comparisons. Let me explain. While Americans worry about whether the steak they ordered in some restaurant will come out medium rare, or whether they will have time to shop at the next Gucci clothing sale, there are billions of people worried about their next meal and whether the clothes on their backs will suffice for the winter cold. There are literally billions of people in the third world who can be radicalized by a political or religious zealot who feeds and clothes them and is intent on using this new force to challenge the Americans' way of life or to try to bring us down.

Allow me another comparison. In 1900, a nickel did not make you rich, but it gave you a sense of empowerment. If you were living in New York or Chicago, for five cents, you could buy a beer, a cup of coffee, a hot dog, three donuts, or an ice cream cone. John Rockefeller, the world's first billionaire, tried to improve his image by handing out dimes to children on the streets of Cleveland during his Sunday walks.[1] One hundred years later, in the impoverished third world of Latin America, Africa, Asia, and the Middle East, $1,000 can turn an impoverished teenager or young adult into a human bomb. The larger sum may have something to do with inflation or the reduced value of life among "true believers." But consider that there are some 3 billion people marginally existing on either $1 or $2 a day, and the number is growing because of the "population bomb." How much of a divide between "haves" and "have-nots" can the world tolerate without instability? What role does the United States play? Can it afford to remain isolationist, distant, or indifferent? How much of our resources should we share with third-world populations? What can

1. Roger Simon and Angie Cannon, "An Amazing Journey," *Newsweek* (August 26, 2001), p. 13.

educators do to prepare youth, the next generation, for the world of 2050 and beyond in which it is estimated that the world population will reach about 10 billion?[1]

## Inequality and Third-World Women

Throughout the world and throughout history, women have been marginalized by society—mainly a result of cultural and religious traditions that dehumanize them into third-class citizens (or objects)—depriving them of education, health, and equal rights in the workplace, church, marriage, and even on the world's main streets. Where there is extreme poverty and lack of education and democracy, women are often indiscriminately beaten and abused. Only in the western world, which accounts for about one-fifth of the world population, do they almost get a fair shake—at least protected by rational laws.

In a world where women are held hostage in many third-world countries, there is little chance to speak about peace or prosperity. There is a need to break the silence—of both shame and blame—and to give women equal rights. Only when women move forward toward equality will the third world, particularly the Muslim (and African) world, increase economic development, modernization, and democratic order. One social scientist points to a statistical model of Egypt indicating that if mothers with no education had at least completed elementary school, poverty would have been reduced by one-third. The United Nations has produced similar findings in other third-world countries where women's education is severely restricted because of tradition or religion.[2]

When women's influence increases, a number of trends are evidenced: The moderate center is strengthened, poverty is reduced and the middle class slightly increases, the potential for war is reduced, birth rates fall, and the education of children are enhanced—subsequently, there is political and economic stability and modernization. In reverse, where religious extremism surfaces, as in Afghanistan, Algeria, Bangladesh, Iran, Lebanon, Pakistan, and Palestine, moderate governments fall and economic instability increases.

Where a backlash against women surfaces, often uneducated, unemployed, or working-class men seize the public forum and abuse women; in some countries (in northern Africa), men "herd" women, and in other places (in the former Soviet republics, Eastern Europe, and parts of Latin America and Asia), men force women into prostitution.[3] The law and lord can be used for all purposes, both good and evil, so legal or religious scripture cannot be counted to protect women, even in western society. Under the guise of natural and divine law, people of many nations have viewed the abuse of and violence toward women as a recreational activity, encouraged the rape of women as an instrument of war, conducted medical and biological experi-

---

1. See page 430.
2. Barbara Crossette, "Living in a World Without Women," *New York Times* (November 4, 2001), Sect. 4, pp. 1, 5.
3. Although the exact numbers are sketchy, it is estimated that 2 to 3 million women a year are tricked or forced into the sex market against their will. Another 15 to 25 percent are abused by fathers or husbands; it is hard to agree on a percent because cases are underreported.

ments to advance their "scientific" theories, circumcised them to ensure their chastity and docility, and burned them at the stake as witches.

Given this tragic history of rape, abuse, and murder, the other side of the coin—sometimes portrayed in musical form or feminist literature—can be interpreted as a huge scream against thousands of years of women wallowing and drowning in sorrow. How do we make the leap to the other side of the world—from bondage to freedom, from being ignored or wrongly perceived by most thinkers, artists, and poets to being given new worth and expression to neglected female virtues? What needs to be done to transform girls from silent conformists to spunky individuals; from women who are dependent and attached to fathers or husbands to women who are independent and encouraged by fathers and husbands; from women who have been dealt a lousy hand consisting of much, dirty dishes and diapers to women with choices and careers and "wonder-women" characters; from women whose lives have been truncated by fate or failed dreams to women with fulfilled aspirations and who have followed their own path?

Forget the great glamorous women—Margaret Fuller, Eleanor Roosevelt, and Madam Albrecht; Mary McCarthy, Germaine Greer, and Susan Sontag; Ann Landers, Susan Walters, and Oprah Winfrey, or, my favorite, Gloria Steinem—the symbols of female aspirations, rule breakers, icons, and legends. The idea is to break the chains of *all* women—of all races, religions, and nationalities—including especially third-world women. To some extent, it means turning the world upside-down. It's a long road—from an idea to reality, from traditional social callousness and ruthlessness directed at women to ethics and laws that protect the sisterhood.

Even Madonna's harshest critics have to admit that she has a way with words and a social message. What can you say to Madonna when you meet her: "Hi, I have a new vibrator," or "Relax, I like gay men and bitch dikes." The principle is simple, full female independence, breaking from past traditions and conforming rules, from the male-centered universe, and it has nothing to do with Madonna as a person or any other artsy or jazzy voice. (Madonna is making this feminist point, besides making a shock statement to sell records.) Only in a progressive, fair, and just society, where men do not feel threatened, and where there is a strong belief in human rights, can women gain full freedom, full protection from discrimination and abuse, and full opportunity to achieve their human potential. I think Locke and Rousseau understood it by advocating that education be in accord with nature and their belief in natural law, which no human or divine authority could subvert. Ibsen wrote about it in *The Doll House* and *The Master Builder*—at a time when few people understood it; Babe Diedrickson lived it on the playing field with her athletic prowess; and Eleanor Roosevelt tried to implement it on a worldwide stage as part of the preamble to the United Nation's charter.

Certainly, there are other factors for Islamic militant recruitment and antifemale policies: poverty, illiteracy, corrupt governments and police officials, and the threat and dislocation of modernism. If democracy and education are to gain a stronghold in the Muslim world, and in other third-world countries, the role of women will become crucial. Although not all women are moderates or progressive (some choose traditional attire for religious reasons), as a group they represent the symbols of change and modernization. However, as long as there is a struggle against the infidel, or against western democracy and modernization, women will choose or be forced to forestall their own basic rights and freedom; traditional, religious, and nationalistic rhetoric will prevail.

It may be a man's world in the third world, but it is up to women to break the monopoly of men in the political, economic, and religious sectors. Most Muslims are moderate, lean toward western democracy and modernization, and accept the notion of educating women. Given the global village we live in, with the computer, fax, and cell phone, western women need to assert, communicate, and organize third-world women. There is a role for the United Nations and humanitarian organizations to play, and there is a role for American and other western teachers and professors to play, particularly at the teacher union and professional association level, and on the Internet highway. Some men are certainly willing and capable of helping, but what is really needed is an international Gloria Steinem to start a worldwide and peaceful female revolution. It is potentially a more powerful revolution—on a political, economic, and moral scale—than dreamed by Marx, Lenin, Che, or Mao, since it may reduce poverty, illiteracy, and the potential for war; increase democracy, modernization, and stability; and save the world from its own population time bomb.

War, Rape, and Prostitution in Europe    Historically, Western Europe is not 100 percent innocent in its abusive treatment of women. The Romans and Nazis were noted for their barbaric behavior toward conquered nations. Civilizations of poets, artists, writers, and philosophers were seduced by the ruthless and demonic powers of Caesar and the Fuhrer. There was a total moral collapse of two advanced societies in the heart of Europe. Ignorant laborers and beer-hall bullies in uniform plundered the countryside and raped "racial inferiors," while faithful comrades and military officers seduced almost any women at will for the privilege of extra food or toilet paper—what so-called decent men might call the "perks of tyranny." Nazi Germany was more barbaric, engulfed with more fanaticism, hatred, and terror; the worst atrocities of Europe's history were committed by the Nazis. Gifted men and women were hunted down in the smallest hamlets, then murdered, jailed, or deported, and so-called inferior women often became sexual or experimental objects for German S.S. killers and concentration camp thugs.[1]

A half century later, lawlessness characterized the chain of command of the Serbian army as it "cleansed" its ethnic neighbors. Once more, rape was used as a weapon of war, and for the first time, a war crimes tribunal has ruled that rape is a crime against humanity. Although these crimes can now be prosecuted, the question is how many will be prosecuted. Although rape has been identified as a war crime since the American Civil War, and briefly mentioned in the 1949 Geneva Convention,[2] military officers have often looked the other way or actually encouraged the

---

1. Michael Burleigh, *The Third Reich: A New History* (New York: Hill and Wang, 2001); Ian Kershaw, *Hitler, 1936–45: Nemesis* (New York: W.W. Norton, 2001).

2. Barbara Crossette, "A New Legal Weapon to Deter Rape," *New York Times*. As of 2001, the war crime tribunal in Hague convicted *three* Bosnian Serbs for rape and sexual enslavement. I repeat, *three* soldiers!

rape of women in occupied countries for the purpose of invoking authority and fear. Women organizations have brought pressure to the international community in recent years, and there has been a handful of convictions involving rape. Given the scope of rape, however, the number of convictions insult our intelligence.

There is no innocence even in the land of Bacon, Dickens, and Shakespeare, or in the homes of Descartes, Montesquieu, and Rousseau. When the "great" civilizations of England and France were like third-world countries, back in the 1600s and 1700s, the "low life" dominated the crowded streets of London and Paris. Here was a world where a person's possessions were in a box or on his or her back. The penal code was aimed at keeping the underclass in check, and many women were hauled to prison or shipped off on boats to the ends of the unknown earth (Australia, northern Africa, etc.) for stealing a loaf of bread to feed their children or a pair of shoes or socks to cloth them (not much different than the world described in *Les Miserables* by Victor Hugo.) Women were forced into prostitution in order to survive in prison, on the boats, and in the back alleys of the streets.[1]

In militia, rebel, and refugee camps around the world, from Bosnia and Kosovo to Rwanda, Colombia, and the Philippines, very little attention is paid to the rights of women in these camps, where they are almost always susceptible to abuse. The problem is that there are too few women making foreign policy, and when there is the opportunity, few push for international reform, for laws with teeth, and for more attention to gender balance on war tribunals and in federal or national prosecutors' offices.

I don't believe teachers anywhere in the world are prepared to deal with the issues of rape and prostitution in terms of the depravity and horrors of society. Not once in my formal education was the subject discussed, and I doubt it has ever been discussed in 99.9 percent of American high schools. The topic is often considered taboo in the classroom because of squeamishness and discomfort in discussing sexual abuses. People need to be educated on this issue—not after the fact, nor in some war tribunal. Women's organizations must pressure the schools to modify the curriculum. High school students, the future soldiers of nations, are mature enough (according to Kohlberg and Piaget) to examine these issues. The subject can be discussed in terms of history, literature, music, philosophy, morality, or civil rights.

Unquestionably, not all questions about good and evil have one "true" answer. Confucian ideals of loyalty to friends and family, Protestants' individualism and capitalism, Buddhists' ideal of contemplation, peace, and poverty, the Catholic Church's use of both the sword and fire as well as charity and compassion, and Islamics' notion of a holy war against the infidel suggest different concepts of good and evil. Cultural pluralists maintain that each way of life may not be wrong. Nonetheless, men and women of moral persuasion must band together and protect people from the evils of mad and depraved leaders and fanatic and brutal societies. The civilized world has no other choice, given all the evils facing humanity—rape, torture, genocide, mass murder, terrorism, and billions of people locked into poverty.

1. Sian Rees, *The Floating Brothel* (New York: Theia-Hyperion, 2002).

There are many questions and issues that teachers around the globe should be discussing in school and fail to do so because of ignorance, uneasiness, or lack of freedom. There are also benchmarks on how we should live on which reasonable people should agree, based on democratic and moral consensus. (We can never expect to get religious consensus.) The predominant view of pluralism, tolerance, and compassion, expressed by the great authors of all civilizations—what some of us from a western heritage might call *humanism, liberalism,* or *enlightenment*—is a means to a universal concept. Pluralism, tolerance, and compassion all suggest more than one way to view the world. However, the perspective still should have a moral consensus, a notion of what is right. Of course, when nations are bent on destroying each other, or driving one group into the sea, there is no sanity; universal concepts fall to the wayside. Our students (and the children and youth of the world) need to learn to make appropriate distinctions, given the free market of ideas and values.

The Diminishing Population Bomb    Recent population estimates show a decline in birthrates in many nations where poverty and illiteracy are still widespread. This trend appears to be linked to recent educational opportunities of women, growing awareness of women to gain control of their bodies, and the increased impact of world health organizations, along with women's rights. Most of the third world (and developing countries) are no longer crippled as much by traditional culture and religious doctrines that encourage large families; women from these parts of the globe are beginning to engage in contraceptive and other birth control methods, including the pill, as they gain information from international organizations and satellite television.

In Brazil, Egypt, India, and Nigeria, some of the world's most populated developing nations, there has been recent decline in birthrates, and revised projections indicate that the world's population may tip from 12 billion to below 10 billion within the next 50 to 100 years. In India alone, 2010 projections show that there will be 600 million fewer people than predicted prior to 2000; the fertility rate is now below 2.1, which is considered the conventional replacement rate. In Brazil, the fertility rate has dropped from 6.15 in 1950 to 2.27 in 2000[1]; predictions are that the rate will drop to 2.1 within the next 10 to 15 years. In China, government policy encourages one child per family. Where strong traditional and religious beliefs still prevail, especially in many poor Muslim countries, there is very little hope for population decline or any form of female equality.

Women in one village making a decision to have one or two fewer children is a small factor by itself. Compounded by millions of women, it has significant global implications. Just as women in most parts of the world are pushing for more education and greater rights (the two trends are interrelated), they seem to becoming more assertive about family planning. There is one single catalyst among all factors. Education is the key—leading to the transformation of a worldwide female population from being illiterate to gaining literacy—and subsequently affecting the thinking and actions of women.

1. Barbara Crossette, "Population Estimates Fall as Poor Women Assert Control," *New York Times* (March 10, 2002), p. 3. Also see Chapter 4.

*The Plot Thickens: From Population to Plastic Bombs*     I am sad to say there is another side to the role of women and the population bomb, one that is a little more frightening and deals with Jihad's women and martyrdom. In some of the larger cities of the Islam world, women attend high school and college, go to the movies (and even dream of Brad Pitt, Clint Eastwood, and Tom Hanks), eat at McDonalds, and even wear pants. But in many parts of Bangladesh, Indonesia, Iran, Pakistan, Palestine, Saudi Arabia, and Yemen, they attend religious schools steeped in Islamic fundamentalism and anti-American, anti-western sloganism.[1] Some of these students become candidates for terrorist schools. The number of estimated terrorists range between 100,000 to 250,000, all convinced that America is to blame for their misery and all trained and ready to commit suicide.[2]

Listen to Shafia, a 16-year-old Afghan refugee: "I have seen the images in the newspapers. . . . Perhaps God punished America for the wrongs she is doing in other countries. . . . Non-Muslims are all our enemy according to the Koran, so Americans are all our enemy. We hate America. . . . If I am provided the opportunity to get weapons, I will use them."[3] From her conversation, Shafia would be glad to use plastic bombs in an American airplane or in a crowded mall and die for Allah.

Perched in a safe office away from the trials of everyday life, writing these words, I conclude that Americans have a major stake in the struggle being fought over the minds and hearts of Islamic women and between the moderates and extremists of the Islamic world. With all the foreign aid and support we have given to Arab and Muslim countries, we find that we are misunderstood, perceived as a "big bully," and envied because of our prosperity and way of life. It is not so easy to understand, according to Thomas Friedman, who, in the Muslim world, is moderate and extremist. "Failure to make this distinction jeopardizes our future relations with the Arab and Moslem world."[4]

If the Muslim nations become increasingly theocratic states, we will head for war. The verdict of the Muslim masses is in favor of progressive Islamic states; it is up to the educated women of the Muslim world (women with children who want their children to live), along with the silent majority, to gain empowerment: to teach science, math, history, and literature—not just religion, not just the Koran, and not just military Mosque rhetoric. One would think that the moderate leaders would control the few extremists, but then the moderates fear that extremist fanaticism and hatred

1. Bangladesh, Indonesia, and Pakistan are the three most populated Islam countries.
2. In 2002, the value of a successful Palestine terrorist increased to $25,000, the payment promised to the family of a dead martyr by Hussain. For those academics who believe that Arab terrorists who blow up buildings or kill civilians in Israel are fighting for their homeland, or argue that terrorism in general is a political act or is justified under extreme circumstances, then I have one question: What happens when terrorists start blowing up our buildings and airplanes, poison our water supplies or farm crops, or target our tunnels, bridges, and nuclear plants? I am waiting to hear which Americans downplay these acts as "grievances" or as "misguided retaliation" to our "pax Americana" foreign policy. It's nice to increase the budgets for Middle East studies, and it is fashionable to talk about multicultural education, diversity, and even western imperialism, but we must also face the evils of terrorism.
3. Ibid., p. 40.
4. Thomas Friedman, "A Foul Wind," *New York Times*, Sect. 4, p. 19.

toward America would be turned around against them and they would lose control of the government.

Somehow I get the feeling that many of our so-called friends in power from the Muslim world double-talk and lull Americans into believing one thing while they wink and look the other way at Muslim extremism in order to maintain their own political status. While some academics remain in denial, the very same who dulled Americans to the dangers of Islam fanaticism and are now reaping windfalls in their books and speeches, the moderate leaders of the Muslim world may also be in a state of denial and lulling Americans into ignoring the future of Islam radicalism. In the name of Allah, or any other god or descendent of a god, a good many people can justify a good deal of extreme and cruel behavior. Just like education, religion can be used for many different purposes. The problem is, it is much easier to question the purposes of education or our education leaders, than it is to question the purposes of religion or our religious leaders both at home and abroad.

## Summary

1. *Social stratification* refers to the ranking of people in horizontal layers. This expression reflects the unequal distribution among the members of any society of certain scarce, divisible, valuable things, commonly including wealth, power, status, and education.

2. The *extent* of inequality of the distribution of wealth, power, status, and education is a matter of fact and therefore can be objectively categorized and analyzed. For our discussion, we have focused mainly on education.

3. The *reasons* for the same distribution (its equality or lack of equality) is a matter of judgment and subjectivity—and open to many interpretations.

4. The cost of higher education is questioned as it relates to employment opportunities, starting salaries of college graduates, and lifetime earnings. Admission policies of colleges, as they relate to the SAT and affirmative action, are also discussed in relationship to social stratification and equality.

5. Poorer school districts tend to receive more money from the federal and state governments than do wealthier school districts. The additional amount of revenue received, however, rarely makes up for the total difference in student expenditures.

6. Two strikingly different explanations have emerged to explain the existing social stratification or inequality in American society, as well as why certain groups either achieve or do not achieve in school. The first viewpoint, traditional and conservative, argues that people are rewarded on the basis of ability; it endorses equal opportunity and merit for *individuals*.

7. The revisionist and politically correct viewpoint—also overlapping with liberal-minority, radical, neomarxist, and postmodern philosophy—is critical of the economic and social system. It views inequality as exploitive and discriminatory—a result of the struggle for limited amounts of goods and services. It rejects the notion of achievement based on *individual* ability as a form of social exploitation; it seeks proportional and progressive equality of *groups* and endorses entitlements and preferential treatment of *groups* defined as minorities.

8. There are a host of reasons why American students have scored lower than their international counterparts on achievement tests. Of all the reasons discussed in the chapter, poverty in the United States is probably the most pervasive factor.

9. Cities of the third world are rock-bottom poor and dysfunctional places, where workers take on low-wage jobs and resentments come to the fore. Part of this frustration and resentment is fostered and fueled by religious ideology. This growing proletariat extends beyond the Muslim world and includes the large countries of the world such as in Brazil, China, India, Mexico, and Nigeria.

10. Whatever language third-world people speak, whatever their skin color or religion, they are living in extreme poverty—where extremism can be bred and aimed at western civilization.

## Questions to Consider

1. What are some problems related to defining or measuring the concepts of equality and inequality?

2. Discuss the implication of this statement: The closer society comes to the idea of equal opportunity, the more it will increase income gaps among people.

3. How can society achieve both excellence and equality? What limits must be placed on people in such a society?

4. What are some problems in trying to evaluate the value of an education?

5. Explain the concept of equalization from a school finance viewpoint.

## Things to Do

1. Have each student in class list the occupations of his or her parents and grandparents. Are the students in class upwardly mobile? What effect does a mother's social class have on the mobility of her children?

2. Interview a college counselor in your college to discuss potential dropouts. What are their ideological disagreements with the rest of society?

3. Organize a debate on the relationship between excellence and equality.

4. Invite a guest speaker to explain the future of computers in industry and education.

5. Invite a professor of Chinese, Indian, or Arabic history or culture to talk to the class about the "new" China, India, or Egypt.

## Recommended Readings

Barton, Paul A. *Toward Inequality: Disturbing Trends in Higher Education*. Princeton, NJ: Educational Testing Service, 1997. The influence of social class, educational achievement, and college attainment—disturbing trends as they relate to class, higher education, and equality.

Jian, Ma. *Red Dust: A Path Through China,* trans. by Flora Drew. New York: Pantheon Books, 2001. A three-year trip through China in search of enlightenment, understanding, and self-realization.

Jencks, Christopher, et al. *Who Gets Ahead?* New York: Basic Books, 1979. A description and analysis of the relationship of class, race, education, and mobility.

Kelly, Erin, ed. *Justice as Fairness: A Restatement by John Rawls.* Cambridge, MA: Harvard University Press, 2001. A restatement of Rawl's classic work, *A Theory of Justice,* originally published in 1971 and revised in 1999.

Maalouf, Amin. *In the Name of Identity: Violence and the Need to Belong.* New York: Arcade Publishers, 2001. The author, an Arab living in Paris, points out that much of the Arab identity is formed in relation to the people who they consider to be the enemy or infidel.

Ornstein, Allan C. *Pushing the Envelope: Critical Issues in Education* (Columbus, OH: Merrill, 2003). A half-serious, half-satire discussion of 27 major issues in education.

Phillips, Kevin. *Wealth and Democracy: A Political History of the American Rich* (New York: Broadway Books, 2002). How the wealthy have gained control of government policy and make politics a hostage of money.

# Class, Race, and Education

Chapter 8

# Class, Race, and Education

Chapter 8

## Focusing Questions

1. How does family environment influence academic achievement?

2. What is the relationship between schooling and mobility?

3. To what extent do you think luck plays a factor in determining economic outcomes?

4. How does the Coleman and Jencks reports agree (disagree) with your view of the influence of schooling?

5. What is your definition of *the culture of poverty?* How does poverty influence academic outcomes?

6. How would you define *a more effective school?* What are the key variables or factors in determining more effective schools?

7. Is affirmative action a reasonable social policy? Why or why not? Is there any way of improving this policy to avoid ideological clashes?

8. How do we improve race relations in this country?

## EPISODE A

The central social and political question in education since the 1960s has been how to provide equality for all persons considered to be of poor and minority status. Discrimination and prejudice, once considered only in terms of a black-white dilemma, has been expanded to include other minorities, women, people who have disabilities, the aged, and gay people. Concern for protections against racism and sexism is now common, and individuals, private and public institutions, and the federal and state governments are all involved.

Social class can be discussed as a separate classification. People and groups comprising a specific social class have many things in common with regard to shared values, attitudes, behaviors, and lifestyles. Social-class differences cannot be used to predict the behavior of individuals; the concept makes sense only for large groups. The grouping of people by class provides informed descriptions and analysis in how people interact in schools and society.

Differences in social class should not be attributed to any one single factor. Rather, the concept is based on a composite of factors, such as home and family background, cultural tradition, education, income, community factors, occupational status, or immigration factors. Any single-variable theory, such as a neomarxist view that regards social-class differences as being primarily based on economic factors or the view that assumes that all black-white differences in the United States are associated with racism or discrimination, is overly simple and frequently reflects an "ism" or ideology.

## Do Schools Make a Difference? Large-Scale Studies

The mid-1960s and early 1970s produced a series of large-scale studies, the biggest in education history, which basically showed that teachers and schools have minimal effect on student achievement. Over the years, the data have been ignored or buried by the liberal/minority community, because it lets teachers and schools off the hook, and implies there is little that educators (or society) can do to overcome the effects of poverty on education. In startling contrast to conventional wisdom, the studies by James Coleman and Christopher Jencks concluded that schools have little influence on children's intellectual achievements. The results of these studies are difficult to present concisely, since the analysis includes a host of variables and a large number of subgroups.

### The Coleman Report

The Coleman survey deals with 625,000 children and 4,000 schools, and the report is about 1,300 pages long, including 548 pages of statistics.[1] It is the largest educational research enterprise conducted in the United States, and almost everyone of whatever political persuasion can find something in it to quote. Coleman found that the effects of home environment far outweighed any effects the school program or the teacher had on achievement. The report analyzed the results of testing at the beginning of grades 1, 3, 6, 9, and 12. Achievement of the average Mexican American, Puerto Rican, American Indian, and black was much lower that the average Asian

---

1. James S. Coleman et al., *Equality of Educational Opportunity* (Washington, DC: U.S. Government Printing Office, 1966).

American and white student at all grade levels. Moreover, the differences widened at higher grades. The characteristics of teachers and schools had the least impact on black students among all other minority groups; teachers and school characteristics could not account for all the reasons why blacks, who started only six months behind in reading at the first grade, ended up 3½ years behind whites in reading at the twelfth grade.

The general approach used by Coleman sorts 45 school characteristics or variables into correlates and noncorrelates of student achievement (see Table 8.1 and Figure 8.1). For this purpose, a *correlate* was loosely defined as any school characteristic that correlates 0.2 or better with any one of three achievement measures—reading, mathematics, and general information. Of the 45 variables, 19 showed some relationship with at least one of three achievement tests, and 26 failed to do so.

The 19 correlates that tend to be associated with student achievement cluster around *student* and *teacher* characteristics, and especially around students; these are *hard-to-change* variables. Those that are unassociated with student achievement are by and large *school* characteristics and *easy-to-change* variables. In effect, the Coleman Report says that schools in general have little impact on learning, and the variables associated with learning, such as the students' or the teachers' mean verbal test scores, are difficult to change. Changes effected by spending extra money—such as teachers' experience, teacher turnover, student-teacher ratios, books and materials, tracking, and length of school day—are easier to bring about but have little relation to achievement. Thus, the correlation between expenditures per student and learning was essentially zero at each grade level examined, as Figure 8.1 (items 15–26) shows.

Coleman's findings raise difficult policy questions for the nation's educators. If increases in student expenditures, higher teachers salaries, reduced classroom sizes, and other conventional remedies for low achievement have virtually no effect, what grounds are there to seek increased funds for education? Compensatory education advocates were being told that extra spending basically makes no difference in outcomes because it does not correlate with student achievement. Reform advocates generally are being told that they need to come up with a better idea than increased spending.

Even worse, the data led to the conclusion that schools and teachers can do very little to effect changes in student achievement; rather, home characteristics and peer group influences are, in that order, the two major variables associated with achievement. In a subsequent interview, Coleman put it this way: "All factors considered, the most important variable—in or out of school—in a child's performance remains his family background. The second most important factor is the social-class background of the families of the children in the school. Those two elements are much more important than any physical attributes of the school."[1]

An important qualification of this conclusion is that schools seem to have greater impact on some minority-group children, as indicated in Table 8.1. Nevertheless, Coleman's finding of a small relationship between school facilities and student achievement,

1. James S. Coleman, "Class Integration—A Fundamental Break with the Past," *Saturday Review* (May 27, 1972), p. 59.

TABLE *8. 1*

**Coleman Report: Correlates of Student Achievement, Grades 6 and 9**

| School Characteristics | Groups of Pupils | | | | | | | | Total |
|---|---|---|---|---|---|---|---|---|---|
| | Mexican Americans | Puerto Ricans | Indian Americans | Asian Americans | Blacks North | Blacks South | Whites North | Whites South | |
| Student Body Characteristics | | | | | | | | | |
| Proportion of pupils with encyclopedia in the home | X | X | X | X | | X | | | 5 |
| Proportion of school's graduates in college | | X | | | | | | | 1 |
| Proportion in college prep curriculum | X | X | X | X | | X | | X | 6 |
| Average attendance as percentage of enrollment | X | X | | | | | | | 2 |
| Proportion of pupils who are white | X | X | X | | | | | | 3 |
| Average number of white pupils in preceding year | X | X | X | | | | | | 3 |
| Mean nonverbal test score | X | X | X | X | X | X | X | X | 8 |
| Mean verbal test score | X | X | X | X | X | X | X | X | 8 |
| Proportion of pupils who think teacher expects their best work | X | X | | | | | | | 2 |
| Proportion of pupils whose mothers went to college | | | X | | | | | X | 2 |

a conclusion that contradicts the opinions and ideology of reform advocates, has inspired a searching analysis of the topic and arguments for and against the report since its publication.

The major criticism leveled against the Coleman Report is that the criterion of academic achievement is almost exclusively a measure of verbal abilities, which are more

TABLE *8. 1*

**(*continued*)**

| School Characteristics | Groups of Pupils | | | | | | | | Total |
|---|---|---|---|---|---|---|---|---|---|
| | Mexican Americans | Puerto Ricans | Indian Americans | Asian Americans | Blacks North | Blacks South | Whites North | Whites South | |
| Characteristics of Instructional Personnel | | | | | | | | | |
| Teacher's estimate of quality of own college | X | X | | X | | | | | 3 |
| Teacher's verbal score | X | X | X | X | | X | | | 5 |
| Teacher's race | X | X | X | X | | | | | 4 |
| Teacher's preference for teaching middle class | X | | X | | | | | | 2 |
| Teacher's attitude toward integration | X | X | X | | | | | | 3 |
| Teacher's salary | | X | | X | | X | | | 3 |
| Finances and Program | | | | | | | | | |
| Per-pupil expenditure | | | | X | | | | | 1 |
| Comprehensiveness of curriculum | | | | X | X | | | | 2 |
| Mathematics offering | X | | X | | | | | | 2 |
| Totals | 14 | 14 | 12 | 10 | 3 | 6 | 2 | 4 | |

*Source:* Adapted from *Supplemental Appendix to the Survey on Equality of Education Opportunity* (Washington, DC: U.S. Government Printing Office, 1966), pp. 143 ff.

likely to be the product of the child's home than his or her school experience.[1] Another criticism is that it is difficult to find circumstances where one can measure and account for all the factors that result in student achievement.[2] However, most other studies rely on the same test measurements (reading and math tests) and use similar subgroups (based on class or ethnicity); when the results appear more positive, these so-called bias factors are not mentioned. If Coleman can be criticized for this bias, it follows that almost all other studies on school achievement are also misleading.

1. Henry S. Dryer, "School Factors and Equal Educational Opportunity," *Harvard Educational Review* (Winter 1968), pp. 33–56.
2. Sarah E. Turner, "A Comment on 'Poor School' Funding, Child Poverty, and Mathematics Achievement," *Educational Researcher* (June–July 2000), pp. 15–20.

FIGURE *8. 1*

**Coleman Report: Noncorrelates of Student Achievement, Grades 6 and 9**

**Student Body Characteristics**

1. Number of twelfth-grade pupils
2. Pupil mobility (transfers in and out)
3. Average hours pupils spend on homework
4. Proportion of pupils who read over 16 books the preceding summer
5. Teacher's perception of quality of student body
6. Proportion of students whose mothers expect their best work

**Characteristics of Instructional Personnel**

7. Teacher's socioeconomic status
8. Teacher's experience
9. Teacher's localism
10. Teacher's highest degree received
11. Teacher's absences
12. Amount of teacher turnover
13. Availability of guidance counselors
14. Pupil-teacher ratio

**Program, Facilities, Other**

15. Extracurricular offerings
16. Tracking
17. Movement between tracks
18. Accelerated curriculum
19. Policy on promotion of slow learners
20. Foreign language offering
21. Number of days in session
22. Length of school day
23. Number of science labs
24. Volumes per pupil in school library
25. School location (urban-rural)
26. Teacher's perception of quality of school

*Source:* Adapted from *Supplemental Appendix to the Survey on Equality of Education Opportunity* (Washington, DC: U.S. Government Printing Office, 1966), p. 143 ff.

Still another criticism pertains to Coleman's method of analysis, in particular his heavy dependence on regression analysis, which unavoidably leads to an underestimate of the effects of school investment.[1] When independent variables in a multiple repression analysis are related, controlling for the first will reduce the correlation of the second. For example, controlling for social class of the student indirectly controls also for part of the variation of school resources. The additional predictive power as-

1. Samuel Bowles, "Towards Equality of Educational Opportunity," *Harvard Educational Review* (Winter 1968), pp. 89–99.

sociated with the addition of school resources to the analysis thus represents a downward estimate of the real relationship between school resources and achievement.

These statistical problems were recognized by Coleman; it was for this reason that he permitted a low correlation of 0.2 to represent the level of acceptance, whereas most other studies would require a much higher correlation.[1] Moreover, Coleman accepted relationships on any one of three tests for any one of two grade levels as significant; each of the 45 variables had six opportunities to show a correlation with achievement. Had he required a higher correlation, or had he used only one test with only one grade level, there would have been almost zero correlates—a major factor to consider.

Most important, the reanalysis of the Coleman data by other investigators,[2] as well as other large-scale statistical studies of the determinants of student achievement,[3] show similar results. A large fraction of the variation in student achievement is accounted for in out-of-school variables, such as the students' community and home characteristics. Another large fraction is attributable to the so-called peer group effect—that is, the characteristics of the students' classmates. The blunt fact is that most student output is directly related to student input: High ability yields high achievement; low ability yields low achievement. Of the variation that is explained by school factors (usually no more than 17 to 20 percent), only part of this percent can be attributed to teachers (no more than 10 percent).[4] We will return to these percents later in our discussion.

## The Jencks Study

Whereas Coleman showed that there was not much schools could do to improve the achievement levels of students, Christopher Jencks went one step further and indicated that differences in school achievement as well as economic attainment are related more to socioeconomic origin than to schooling. In his four-year study of the reanalysis of the U.S. Census, the Coleman Report, Project Talent (a study of more than 100 high schools), and several smaller studies, Jencks concluded:

1. The schools do almost nothing to close the gap between the rich and poor, the disadvantaged or advantaged learner.
2. The quality of education has little effect on what happens to the students (with regard to future income) after they graduate.

1. A perfect correlation is 1.0. Most studies try to obtain 0.5 or higher correlations. The smaller the number of variables being considered, usually the higher the correlation because there is less noise and/or overlapping variables; the greater number of variables being controlled, usually the smaller the correlation.
2. George W. Mayeske et al., *A Study of Our Nation's Schools* (Washington, DC: U.S. Government Printing Office, 1966); Fredrick Mosteller and Daniel P. Moynihan, eds., *On Equality of Educational Opportunity* (New York: Random House, 1972).
3. Harvey Averch et al., *How Effective Is Schooling? A Critical Review and Synthesis of Research Findings* (Santa Monica, CA: Rand Corporation, 1972); Raymond Boudon, *Education Opportunity and Social Inequality* (New York: John Wiley & Sons, 1973); and Herbert J. Kiesling, *The Relationship of School Inputs to Public School Performance in New York State* (Washington, DC: Rand Corporation, 1966).
4. Ibid.

3. School achievement depends largely on a single input—that is, the family characteristics of the students—and all other variables are either secondary or irrelevant.

4. About 45 percent of IQ is determined by heredity, 35 percent by environment, and 20 percent by a covariance or interaction factor.

5. There is no evidence that school reform (such as compensatory spending or integration) can substantially reduce the cognitive inequality that exists among students.[1]

These are hard-to-swallow conclusions, and a number of social scientists and reformers would rather discard them. But committed to total egalitarianism, Jencks concluded that it would require actual redistribution of income to achieve complete economic equality regardless of ability. Considering his period, it was a major shift in thinking—from equal opportunity to equal results. Given the world we live in, "capitalist utopia" and "compassionate conservatism," it is hard to talk about increased or progressive taxation, or any other "Robin Hood" theory that takes from the rich and gives to the poor.

The main policy implications of these findings are that schools cannot contribute significantly to equality. Jencks maintains that educators at all levels of instruction are not improving the lives of students, but this is not really their fault; rather, the problem lies with the children's social class and other home characteristics. Economic equality in U.S. society will have to be achieved by changing not the schools but the economic institutions. The reforms of the 1960s and 1970s failed because they tried to effect changes that were not feasible.

Jencks's positions on heredity and environment, his support of standardized tests for predicting school success and measuring academic skills, his belief that schooling is without significant value, and his espousal of income redistribution, regardless of differences between those who are smart and ambitious or dumb and lazy, aroused criticism from the political left and right alike. The *Harvard Educational Review* devoted a feature issue to the study. In trying to answer his critics, Jencks strongly responded that those who are politically oriented or are advocating a specific position will "deplore anything that undercuts [their] arguments." He said that sufficient criticism had been leveled at the book so that educators, laypeople, and policymakers "feel free to accept or reject its conclusions according to their prejudices." The critics' arguments were unconvincing: "Most of the ideas they raise [were originally] covered in the text . . . or appendices." This does not necessarily mean that the study's conclusions were correct, but "the assumptions are plausible" and those who reject the data "are under obligation to offer an alternative view of how the world works, along with some empirical evidence that their view is more accurate then ours."[2]

In a related study, Jencks and Marsha Brown found few relationships between high school characteristics and measures of school effectiveness. Using portions of the Project Talent study (an extensive survey conducted during the early 1960s for purposes

---

1. Christopher Jencks et al., *Inequality: A Reassessment of the Effect of Family and Schooling in America* (New York: Basic Books, 1972).
2. Christopher Jencks, "Inequality in Retrospect," *Harvard Educational Review* (February 1973), pp. 104–105, 113.

of estimating the range and levels of ability among American high school students), they concluded that changes in high school characteristics are unlikely to change academic outcomes. Characteristics such as student expenditures, teacher salaries, teacher experience, and socioeconomic composition have little impact on cognitive growth between the ninth and twelfth grades and on college plans and occupational success.[1]

The Jencks and Brown study pretested and posttested some 4,900 students on six different reading and math tests in the ninth and twelfth grades in 98 high schools across the country. The researchers estimated the contribution of various high school characteristics to the variation of these test scores, and estimated how high school quality affected high school graduation, college plans, and career plans five years after high school. The findings indicated that high schools that are effective in boosting student performance on one standardized test are only marginally effective in boosting scores on other tests. The implication is that schools (and teachers) can teach toward a specific test, but they are generally unable to raise test scores across the board. Moreover, the increased test scores have nothing to do with students finishing their education, implying that inflating one test score by cramming or teaching to the test will not have long-term effects on the students' education. In the present era of testing and performance standards, Jencks's concepts and conclusions are classic: We can fool some of the people some of the time, by gearing our instructional time and review practices toward a specific test, but this will not modify student learning over long periods of time.

The fact that socioeconomic composition does not seem to affect student achievement scores is at odds with Coleman's conclusions, but the rest of the findings tend to coincide with the Coleman Report and the earlier Jencks study. The implications of this study by Jencks and Brown are that more money, smaller classrooms, more graduate work for teachers, higher salaries for teachers, socioeconomic desegregation, and possibly other traditional remedies do not have much effect on educational attainment. In effect, it mainly boils down to student input (not process) accounts for student output. Obviously, some people would argue that the idea is mean-spirited and contradicts the themes and dreams of what America is all about.

## The Duncan Model

Coleman and Jencks challenge both traditional and revisionist theorists who put more stock on the influence of education. Whereas the traditionalists argue that education is the main avenue of opportunity, the revisionists criticize it as a vehicle by which inequality is perpetuated by a "dominant" group that discriminates against and imposes tracking and testing barriers against the "subordinate" group. Both theorist groups probably overstate their cases as to the influence of education.

The correlations among occupation, income, and education are based on averages. The spread around the mean is considerable, which reduces the real predictability for each occupational and income group. In a classic study on occupational mobility of over 20,000 male Americans, Peter Blau and Otis Duncan show that the direct correlation between schooling and occupational status is a modest 0.32, but

---

1. Christopher Jencks and Marsha D. Brown, "Effects of High Schools on their Students," *Harvard Educational Review* (August 1975), pp. 273–324.

that when all variables are considered, education accounts for only 10 percent of the variation in occupational status.[1] Obviously, no one in education wants to hear this kind of news, especially dedicated teachers who expect to make a difference; likewise, most textbook publishers put pressure on authors to screen out this kind of research because it is too negative and may even effect textbook sales. It is considered prudent to kill off this kind of messenger, although Coleman and Jencks can be gingerly tolerated because of their stature and influence.[2]

Blau and Duncan further explain the relationship. A high school graduate, on average, has a lower occupational status than a man who has attended college. However, a considerable number of high school graduates have better jobs than do those who leave college before graduating as well as those who finish, and one-third do as well as those who do graduate work. At the other end of the scale, half the men who did not complete high school are doing as well as those who completed high school, although as an entire group the high school graduate earns more than the high school dropout.

In a related research project, Duncan found that education is only one of several variables influencing a person's occupational status and income later in life.[3] What accounts for the assumed relationship between education and occupation and income are a number of underlying variables related to education, such as family origin, family education, inherited IQ, and socioeconomic class. For example, parents with high incomes are able to provide more education for their children, just as they spend more on food and housing, and therefore the children of the affluent obtain more education and go on to higher-paying jobs. Parents with high educational levels themselves are more likely to expect and to motivate their children to continue further in schooling. There is also a relationship between social class and intelligence of parents and, in turn, the inherited IQ and education of children; thus, those with higher measured IQ scores are more likely to attain higher levels of education.

A synthesis of the relationships between intelligence, socioeconomic position, education, occupation, and income is indicated in Figure 8.2, a simplified version of the Duncan model.[4] To understand it, we must note that each variable can have an influence on another variable in two ways: direct and indirect. If we say, for example, that IQ has a direct influence on income, this means that after controlling for other variables, IQ would still have an effect on income. In other words, if everyone were alike on all variables except IQ, IQ would still influence income; its influence on in-

1. Peter M. Blau and Otis D. Duncan, *The American Occupational Structure* (New York: John Wiley & Sons, 1967).

2. Of all the introductory education texts, Ornstein and Levine's *Foundations of Education* devoted the most attention to Coleman and Jencks because of their sociological and urban background. However, there is no mention, along with all the other competitive texts, of Blau and Duncan and later Duncan and colleagues. For a lengthy review and analysis of Coleman, Jencks, Blau, and Duncan, see Allan C. Ornstein, *Education and Social Inquiry* (Itasca, IL: Peacock, 1978).

3. Otis D. Duncan, David S. Featherman, and Beverly Duncan, *Socioeconomic Background and Achievement* (New York: Seminar Press, 1972).

4. Actually, Duncan shows that several other variables—such as motivational level, the type of wife a man marries, and quality of schooling—are minor factors in increasing the ability to predict occupational status or income.

---

## FIGURE *8.2*
### Determinants of Social/Economic Stratification System

---

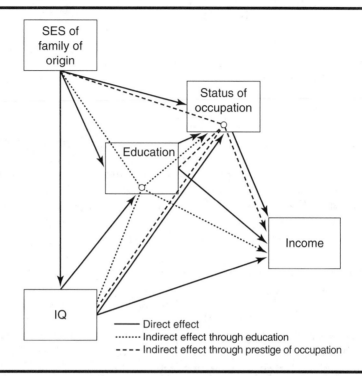

*Source:* Adapted from Otis D. Duncan, David Featherman, and Beverly Duncan, *Socioeconomic Background and Achievement* (New York: Seminar Press, 1972).

come would be direct or independent of the other variables, and it would be shown by a solid line in the figure. An indirect influence (shown by a dotted or broken line) occurs when one variable has its effect on a variable through another one. The best example of this is the influence of the variable of family origin on income; its influence is exerted indirectly through it influence on education and on prestige of occupation. It should be noted that one variable can have both a direct and an indirect effect on another variable; for example, IQ has a direct effect on income and an indirect effect on income through its influence on education.

The data on which the model presented in Figure 8.2 are based leads to the following conclusions:

1. Family origin or socioeconomic class is correlated with IQ, but the correlation is low, indicating that IQ is a result of other non-measured environmental or heredity variables.
2. A person's IQ has a direct influence on how much education he or she gets. Independent of education, IQ also has some direct influence on the status of occupation and income.

3. The socioeconomic status of a family has its main influence on education; it has some direct influence on occupational status and it has virtually no direct influence on income.
4. Education is highly correlated with occupational status (or type of job) and therefore has an indirect influence on income.
5. The main determinant of how much money a person earns is the status of his or her occupation. Education and IQ have less important direct effects on income; family origin has a greater impact.

## Unaccounted Factors: Luck

A large body of sophisticated research on social mobility within the past 20 years generally supports the preceding conclusions.[1] Of this research, the most controversial and well known is by Christopher Jencks, who studied the effect on income for the following variables: (1) father's occupational status, (2) father's years of schooling, (3) father's IQ, (4) respondent's IQ at age 11, (5) respondent's Armed Forces aptitude test, (6) respondent's years of schooling, (7) respondent's occupational status, and (8) respondent's income.[2] Jencks found that the number of years of school does not significantly predict income. For white males with the same family background and initial ability, an additional year of elementary or secondary education increases future income about 4 percent; an additional year of college, about 7 percent; and an additional year of graduate school, 4 percent. Controlling for IQ, the top fifth of the population earns seven times as much as the bottom fifth, whereas it should only account for 1.4 times as much; this suggests that other factors are related to inequality of income.

All the eight variables (including education and IQ) combined explain only 25 percent of the existing differences in income. This means that if everyone had the same family origin, if everyone had the same IQ and education, and if everyone had the same occupational status, most of the existing differences would remain. Jencks calls this *luck*. If, by "luck," one means all those variables not included in the Duncan model and not accounted for by Jencks, then Jencks is correct.

To call all these variables *luck*, however, is not a very good choice of words, because it implies that people have little control over their economic fates. Moreover, most of us in the business of education find it hard to accept that luck, or factors unrelated to schooling, has much influence (actually more influence than schooling) in the outcomes of life. To believe such a thought would mean that our professional jobs and efforts are somewhat meaningless. Jencks argues that two brothers who are brought up in the same family and who have approximately the same IQ and years of schooling may earn considerably different incomes. One becomes a surgeon who earns $500,000 a year; the other becomes a college professor who earns $100,000 a

1. See Allan C. Ornstein and Daniel U. Levine, *Foundations of Education,* 8th ed. (Boston: Houghton Mifflin, 2003); Susan E. Mayer, *What Money Can't Buy: Family Income and Childrens Life Chance* (Cambridge, MA: Harvard University Press, 1997); and Daniel P. McMurrer and Isabel Sawhill, *Getting Ahead: Economic and Social Mobility in America* (Washington, DC: Urban Institute, 1998).

2. Jencks et al., *Inequality: Reassessment of the Effect of Family and Schooling.*

year (my example, my figures). There is considerable difference in their incomes, but this difference may not be a result of luck; it could be the result of decisions over which both brothers had full control.

Rather than conclude that individual success is largely based on luck, it might make more sense to say that economic success is only partly related to family origin, ability, or education, and there are many other intangible factors—such as motivation, disposition, drive, and overall personality and people skills—influencing income differences among individuals. Of course, education cannot neutralize the wealth or political connections of the Kennedy, Bush, or Rockefeller families, nor can it neutralize the fact that someone steps into Daddy's franchise business that consists of 15 McDonalds restaurants or 5 Walmart-anchored retail centers. The list of factors is not endless, but it goes way beyond schooling. It is important for educators to understand and accept that there are limitations of what schools can do to bring about equality, despite the philosophy of Jefferson, Mann, and Dewey, and despite the faith all of us have in schools as the instrument of equality.

Although many may disagree with Jencks's reference to the unexplained variance of income as luck, he may be right in concluding that equalizing opportunity or equalizing education will not reduce inequality. Jencks, who is a revisionist, argues for the redistribution of income—taxing the upper-middle and upper classes and distributing revenues to the poor. Now, if that sounds un-American, or like some "Commie plot," then we have two other options to further the goals of equality: (1) quicken the pace of affirmative action and related requirements of quotas and (2) turn back the repeal of estate tax, which is even more difficult since the accumulation of wealth is sanctioned by religious scripture, robber barons, and those in political power.[1] Of course, we can always take the position that if the poor get poorer, so what, they can eat cake. If they keep their noses clean, live good lives (meaning don't cause trouble or challenge the system), and believe in Christ, Mohammad or Budda, they will be rewarded in the hereafter. I guess that is one way of sedating the poor. It has worked in the past, at least for the last 2,000 years.

## The International Educational Achievement (IEA) Studies

The first International Educational Achievement study evolved from an international conference in the 1950s at which researchers from a dozen countries agreed to assess children's achievement on a cross-national basis; it is the largest cross-cultural study on academic achievement. The first major survey, in the area of mathematics, involved 133,000 elementary and secondary students, 13,500 teachers, and 5,450 schools in 12 technological countries, including the United States. After this study, the researchers embarked on a six-subject survey of science, literature, reading comprehension, English and French as foreign languages, and civic education. Together with mathematics, these subjects covered practically all the principal subjects in the secondary curriculum. This survey involved 258,000 secondary students and 50,000 teachers from 9,700 schools in 19 countries (4 of them less developed).

---

1. For further explanation, see Chapter 6, pp. 331–334, Chapter 7, pp. 382–391, 413–419.

The data analysis in the math survey was complicated but tended to show that the teacher and school characteristics are relatively unimportant in determining math achievement. Student characteristics highly correlated with achievement, and the child's social class accounted for the greatest share of variation in learning. The study also showed that, at every age level and in most countries, boys outperformed girls in math.[1]

The six-subject survey was reported in nine volumes beginning in 1973. The reading survey is of most interest, at least to Americans. The conventional view of the relation of socioeconomic level to reading scores apparently holds true internationally. The general belief in the universal superiority of girls' reading hold ups only in the early grades; at the secondary school level, reading scores of teen-age boys and girls are similar. The relatively low scores of American students as compared to European students supports the general view that many students in the United States are disadvantaged and have basic reading problems.[2]

The data from all six areas tend to confirm the importance of a student's culture, and particularly the home, to achievement. The total effect of home background is considerably greater than the direct effect of school variables. At age 4 the overall average is .42 for home factors but only .26 for school (including the teacher); at age 10, it is .35 for home factors and .22 for school.[3] The data are also sufficiently detailed to conclude, as the science report does, "that learning is a continuous and cumulative process over generations."[4]

Put in different terms, human beings learn during all their working hours, most of which are spent at home and not in school; moreover, each generation provides and influences the intellectual growth for the next generation to rise to higher educational achievements. Not only is the child's family or home environment important, but so is the child's culture, which is rooted in generations of environmental (and genetic) change, and previous geographic isolation or intermixing (see Chapter 3). Significantly, the impact of schooling in context with culture is shown to be more important in science and foreign language than in other areas.[5] Since the Coleman and Jencks data are based on reading and mathematics scores in the United States, the suggestion that certain subjects might be more amenable to school influences (.26) is taken as an encouraging sign for those who feel that schools make a difference and educators should be held accountable.

1. Torsten Husen, *International Study of Achievement in Mathematics: A Comparison of Twelve Countries*, 2 vols. (New York: John Wiley & Sons, 1967).

2. Robert L. Thorndike, *Reading Comprehension Education in Fifteen Countries* (New York: John Wiley & Sons, 1973).

3. James S. Coleman, "Methods and Results in the IEA Studies of Effects of School on Learning," *Review of Educational Research* (Summer 1975), pp. 335–386.

4. L. C. Comber and J. P. Keeves, *Science Education in Nineteen Countries* (New York: John Wiley & Sons, 1973), p. 298.

5. William E. Coffman and Lai-min P. Lee, "Cross-National Assessment of Educational Achievement: A Review," *Educational Researcher* (June 1974), pp. 13–16.

Of course, there are many limitations to such a large-scale study. There is the question of common content across countries. (All 13-year-olds are supposed to have had the same amount of schooling cross-nationally but Americans have had less schooling in terms of days and hours per day.) Translation of content may be accurate, but it is difficult to assure that the vocabulary and resulting speed passages are similar. There is the sheer magnitude of the data; and because of the size of the population, there are numerous variables possibly not accounted for that may have affected the scores. With all of these problems, the studies still constitute probably the best models in existence for cross-national research on social institutions and social behavior. This fact should not be lost in the critique or criticism of these studies by secondary analysis.[1]

The revolutionary conclusions of the Coleman, Jencks, Duncan, and IEA studies threaten cherished beliefs about schools, particularly the notion of the benefits of universal education and the concept of equal educational opportunity. The research of the mid-1960s and early 1970s show that school reform has little effect on reducing social or economic inequality and differences in educational outcomes. Moreover, the notion of culture, touched on lightly by the IEA studies, is an interesting and thorny topic and rarely mentioned in the literature. Culture, here, is being distinguished from environment in that it has an historical and geographical component. Culture is also divorced of social class—formed over generations and exhibited by general attitudes, motivations, and behaviors of people. It helps explain, for example, why Asian American students study so hard (to please mom and dad and to carry on the family honor). It suggests that a family's instant climb from low income to middle income may not be enough to affect a child's achievement scores. For example, there are significant achievement and test-score gaps between middle-class black and white students that cannot be fully explained away by race or class. On a typical standardized test, the gap between blacks and whites is 75 percent, and the "gap shrinks only a little when black and white families have the same amount of schooling, the same income, and the same wealth."[2] We will discuss this topic later.

## Learning and Earning: 1980s and 1990s

Throughout the 1980s and 1990s, debate focused on whether schooling improved cognitive test scores and whether these outcomes had an impact on economic earnings. Basically, schooling explained only a modest amount of the variations related to academic achievement, highlighted by Coleman, and the latter explained a modest amount of the variation related to wages, highlighted by Jencks. It was true that employers valued what students learned in school and were willing to pay for it, but they also valued other skills.

Most of the variation in economic outcomes could be attributed to noncognitive factors, such as physical characteristics, personality, motivation, reliability, honesty,

1. Allan C. Ornstein, *Educational and Social Inquiry* (Itasca, IL: Peacock, 1978).
2. Christopher Jencks and Meredith Philips, eds. *The Black-White Test Score Gap* (Washington, DC: Brookings Institute, 1998), p. 2.

and creativity. Since social scientists had spent very little effort analyzing these characteristics, the cognitive factors remain masked (by noncognitive factors) and, for the time being, appear to be less than what educators would like to hear.

The negligible impact of schooling was bolstered in the 1980s and 1990s by Erik Hanushek's review of the research, which confirmed, like the Coleman and Jencks reports, as well as the Duncan model of social stratification, that schools had no measurable effect on students' test scores or future earnings, and that there was no strong relationship between school spending and student performance.[1] Whatever research showed that school characteristics or school spending had positive effects, the relationship was small or later shown to be contaminated by (1) methodological assumptions; (2) weighting procedures of school characteristics; or (3) unlike comparisons across schools, school districts, or states.[2] Despite these flaws in the research, student expenditures, smaller classrooms, and teacher experience (not salaries or education) had the most consistent effects; nonetheless, other studies showed contradictory or inconsistent results among these factors.[3]

The 1990s also revived the argument of hereditary with Herrnstein and Murray's 1994 publication of *The Bell Curve*. The authors argued that cognitive tests that predict life chances and economic earnings were measuring a collection of stable abilities, which psychologists, since Charles Spearman's research in 1904, often called *g*, for general intelligence.[4] The most important characteristic of *g* was the general ability to learn new skills and knowledge quickly and easily—exactly the type of "human capital" that employees seek and reward. It just so happens that "smart" people with a high *g* factor tend to go to school longer and get higher grades. It is not the latter (amount of schooling or high test scores) that are primarily associated with future earnings; rather, it is the *g* factor that leads to more schooling and better test scores. Even worse, the authors argued that the trait was biological or genetic, not environmentally based.

1. Emil A. Hanushek, "The Economics of Schooling," *Journal of Economic Literature* (Vol. 2, 1986), pp. 1141–1176; Hanushek, "The Impact of Differential Expenditures on school Performance," *Educational Researcher* (May 1989), pp. 45–51; and Hanushek, *Making Schools Work* (Washington, DC: Brookings Institute, 1994).

2. Ronald F. Ferguson, "Teachers' Perceptions and Expectations and the Black-White Score Gap," in C. Jencks and M. Phillips, eds., *The Black White Score Gap* (Washington, DC: Brookings Institute, 1998); Helen F. Ladd, ed. *Holding Schools Accountable* (Washington, DC: Brookings Institute, 1996); and Larry Hedges, Richard D. Laine, and Rob Greenwald, "Does Money Matter: Meta-Analysis of School Inputs on Student Outcomes," *Educational Researcher* (April 1994), pp. 5–14.

3. Gary Burtless, ed., *Does Money Matter? The Effect of School Resources on Student Achievement and Adult Success* (Washington, DC: Brookings Institute, 1996); Eric A. Hanushek, "Assessing the Empirical Evidence on Class Size Reductions from Tennessee and Non-experimental Research," *Education Evolution and Policy Analysis* (Summer 1999), pp. 123–144; and Ladd, *Holding Schools Accountable*.

4. Richard J. Herrnstein and Charles Murray, *The Bell Curve: Intelligence and Class Structures in American Life* (New York: Free Press, 1994). Also see Charles E. Spearman, "General Intelligence Objectivity Determined and Measure," *American Journal of Psychology* (April 1904), pp. 201–293.

The best analysis about education and earnings since *The Bell Curve* is by Mayer and Peterson (Mayer is actually a spin-off of the old Jencks team and Peterson is a Harvard professor) and by David Grissmer and his colleagues at Rand—and in the publications of Brookings Institute, Rand, and the Urban Institute. In general, these reports do not repudiate Coleman, Jencks, Duncan, and others, the notion of luck, or the unaccounted variance related to economic outcomes, nor do they bring comfort to the political left. We are told that schools help promote intergenerational mobility, although they do not provide sufficient or strong opportunity by themselves to break the general pattern of class structure. Given the information age we live in, where knowledge is crucial, formal education should increase social mobility in the future; however, we cannot dismiss growing economic inequality, especially in an era where students are completing more school years. Students at the bottom of the social order tend to be "frozen" into the status of their parents, but for those who are able to escape (the percentage is small), the schools are the chief route for success.

Mayer and Peterson fuel the debate by arguing that both aptitude and achievement results in adult success. But *aptitude,* they argue, is more important because people who learn more quickly are more useful to their employers than people who learn slowly or with difficulty. Their model also assumes that "the entire school curriculum is a prolonged aptitude test, and that the specific skills and knowledge taught in school have no economic value," because people who easily learn Latin are the same people who can easily learn algebra and computer skills, or master finance and banking skills.[1]

Most educators and policymakers prefer the *achievement* model, arguing that academic outcomes and schooling count, and that what you know counts more than how hard you need to study to learn it. The theory is, for this group, that outcomes count more than the process. Similarly, math or verbal scores count because employers seek someone who is versed in math or verbal skills, not because the scores are indicators for the workers' ability to learn something else. But Mayer and Peterson ask us to imagine two groups of adults with similar math (or verbal) scores: one with less math training but high aptitude and the other with better math training but low aptitude.

The achievement model assumes that both groups have equal opportunity to earn the same wages. The aptitude model assumes that the high aptitude/less math trained group can learn more math in the long run and can also function better in other content areas and thus earn substantially more than the low aptitude/better math trained group.[2] Most people have no problem with this analysis until they come to the realization that aptitude connotes heredity. Then, the conversation slows down or is stiffled.

Mayer and Peterson further maintain that schools can exert considerable influence on a child's experiences, and that these experiences have an effect on education achievement. Before we go around modifying the school environment—that is, altering the classroom and instructional experiences for students—we need to know how much achievement would vary if we treated all children alike, then how assigning children with different aptitudes to different environments would alter the

1. Susan E. Mayer and Paul E. Peterson, *Earning and Learning: How Schools Matter* (Washington, DC: Brookings Institute, 1999).
2. Ibid.

variance of achievement.[1] In this way, we could determine which alterations have the most influence, and how our resources can be earmarked to get the best results for improving achievement.

David Grissmer takes us to the final step in the debate about family and school characteristics, and the effect on achievement. He argues that there is such a thing as family capital and social capital. *Family capital* refers to characteristics within the family passed from parent to child, the quality and quantity of resources within the family, and the allocation of these resources toward the child's education and socialization. *Social capital* refers to long-term capacities existing within the community and school district that affect achievement, such as the peer group, parental trust in the community, the safety and support structures of the community, and the ability to support and pay for schools and social institutions (community centers, theaters, athletic clubs, etc.) within the community.[2]

Family capital is more important than social capital, according to Grissmer, and I would firmly agree, since the family doesn't change but the school and community can change (simply by moving), and the child's earliest experiences (which are essential) are rooted in the family. However, Grissmer points out that family and social capital are not independent, or randomly distributed, but are grouped together because of economics. "More social capital arises in communities and states having higher income and more educated families. Thus achievement scores across schools, communities and states differ partly because their families differ in their internal capacity to produce achievement and partially because families with similar characteristics are grouped in communities or states creating different levels of social capital."[3] To put it in different words, high-income families tend to cluster together in high-income communities that spend more money on schooling and have smaller classes and better paid, more experienced teachers.

Do school characteristics by themselves shape academic outcomes? Very, very little. It's family and social capital differences that lead to academic differences. For instance, a review of the NAEP results, which now test fourth- and eighth-graders in 44 states and are considered the best indicators we have for assessing national achievement, clearly show that achievement levels are directly related to family and social characteristics across states and only a tiny portion is related to what schools do. Moreover, it is difficult to discern which school policies are successful, because so much of the measures concerning school spending, classroom size, teacher education levels, and so on are related to family and social capital. There is some indication that changes in school spending and in classroom size count, but these results are "inconsistent and unstable . . . to guide policy" and sometimes even based on "noncredible estimates."[4]

And what do the recent scores in Texas tell us? It is worth noting because President Bush ran on his education record and boasted about statewide test scores in

1. Ibid.
2. David Grissmer et al., *Improving Student Achievement* (Santa Monica, CA: Rand, 2000).
3. Ibid., p. 18.
4. Ibid., pp. 29, 31.

Texas while he was governor. On the surface, they inform us that teachers and schools can improve student performance and reduce differences in average scores among minority groups in only four years, thus bolstering the achievement model.

Often referred to as the Texas Miracle, closer examination reveals intense test preparation in low-performing schools, large-scale cheating, and large numbers of students held back so that posttests show more improvement. Most important, each school selected the students and classrooms that would be tested, thus screening out low-performing students on the posttests.[1] Those factors are not unique. Other teachers, schools, and school districts involved in high-stakes testing, and showing large-scale or sudden gains, usually reveal similar findings that distort inferences from test-score gains.[2] It has become increasingly difficult to put stock in the results of any standardized test where stakes are high, when claims are being made for purpose of promoting a policy or program, or when black-Hispanic-white scores are being compared.

Overlooking the Texas Miracle, gains in reading and math across the country can be questioned because gains are not always real. Not only can we question the validity of the exam and exam procedures but we can also question whether gains are likely to continue each year, since it becomes increasingly harder to maintain gains. In fact, schools in Massachusetts that showed gains of at least 10 points in 1999–2000 showed a significant negative relationship (decline) the following school year (2000–01).[3] A school that does better the first time is more likely to do worse the second time and vice-versa. In reverse, the Chicago achievement scores dipped in 2000–01, then gained 3 to 4 percentage points in elementary reading and math, and high school reading, the following year (2001–02).[4]

## Implications and Policies

So we come full cycle. If education differences between groups have little to do with the way schools operate, or how much money is spent on schools or teacher salaries, what are we to do? How elaborate are we to make the efforts to wipe out these differences, and how successful can we hope to be, no matter how elaborate our efforts?

1. Debra Viadero, "Candidates Spar Over Test Gains in Texas," *Education Week* (November 1, 2000), pp. 1, 30; Stephen P. Klein et al., "What Do Test Scores in Texas Tell Us?" *Issue Paper* (Santa Monica, CA: Rand, 2000).
2. David J. Hoff, "As Stakes Rise, Definition of Cheating Blurs," *Education Week* (June 21, 2000), pp. 1, 14–15; R. C. Johnston, "Texas Presses Districts in Alleged Test-Tampering Cases," *Education Week* (March 17, 1999), pp. 22, 28; Jessica Portner, "Pressure to Pass Tests Permeates VA. Classrooms," *Education Week* (December 6, 2002), pp. 1, 20; and Erik W. Robelen, "Parents Seek Civil Rights Probe of High Stake Tests in LA," *Education Week* (October 11, 2000), p. 14.
3. Walt Haney, "Ensuring Failure," *Education Week* (July 10, 2002), pp. 56, 58.
4. Lori Olszewski, "Public Schools Best Post Scores in Years," *Chicago Tribune* (May 31, 2002), p. 16. Despite gains, nearly two-thirds of high school students and more than half of elementary students tested in Chicago perform below national levels.

Are our measures to equalize to include the restriction of opportunities for those groups who achieve at high rates? In order to provide increasing opportunities for those who find school difficult, are we to give them special status and special treatment? These are tough questions, and the answers to them are not easy to come by; in fact, they polarize policymakers and diverse groups within society. The fact is, there are people who have spent their professional lives studying race, ethnic, and class factors pertaining to education and economic differences. Although they have advanced degrees and have the ability to speak polite language, we find a growing number of social scientists who do not permit the tolerance or empiricism of science to enter into the discussion by which we try to prescribe the reasons for the differences and gaps between groups. Moreover, most of these academics are only interested in talking to each other, not to the larger public.

The data suggest that 17 to 20 percent of the variance related to student achievement pertain to what teachers and schools do; the remaining outcome of achievement has much more to do with social class, family background, and the peer group. The correlation of social class, family variables, and peer groups with student achievement is so high that some social scientists warn that it is difficult to separate with certainty how much impact the school or teacher alone has on students. Grudgingly, since the 1950s, there have been continuous attempts to separate these three variables from the others, and to show that schools in general have more impact on education outcomes.[1]

## Reaction 1: Deny It, Bury It

Basically, there are four reactions to the dilemma posed since Coleman, Jencks, Duncan, Hanushek, Grissmer, Mayer, and Peterson. The most common reaction has been to ignore or bury the data and to claim that the assessment tools and methodologies were biased. Continuing this line of reasoning, the strategy is to claim that this type of research is another way the white and conservative research community reinforces the power structure and refuses to deal with the inequalities of schooling and society. Moreover, the researcher cannot fully comprehend human behavior or action by simply taking the position as an "objective" person or "outside observer" who "sees" the manifestation of these acts or assesses the results of these acts.[2] The conclusions of Coleman, Jencks, Duncan, Hanushek, Grissmer, Mayer, Peterson, and others transfer the responsibility of education achievement on the family and student—that is, the client or victim, depending on your politics—and therefore the conclusions are considered not a sufficient reason or condition for an intelligent decision.

1.  Samuel M. Goodman, *The Assessment of School Quality* (Albany: New York State Education Department, 1959); Mayeske, *A Study of Our Nations Schools;* William G. Mollenkopf and Donald Melville, *A Study of Secondary School Characteristics as Related to Test Scores* (Princeton, NJ: Educational Testing Source, 1956); and Mosteller and Moynihan, *On Equality of Educational Opportunity.*

2.  Pamela A. Moss, "Enlarging the Dialogue in Educational Measurement," *Educational Researcher* (January–February 1996), pp. 20–28; Gerald E. Sroute, "Improving the 'Awful Reputation' of Educational Research," *Educational Research* (October 1997), pp. 26–28.

Putting aside this rhetoric, reformers who make this argument have failed to appreciate that the influence of teachers (about 10 percent) and teachers and schools combined (about 17 to 20 percent) is more than enough to make the difference between success and failure in life. In political hair-splitting terms, the difference between Bush and Gore in Florida was about 300 votes, which in turn decided the 2000 presidential election. With six million ballots cast in the state, the margin translated to a difference of about 1 out of every 20,000 votes, or one-twentieth of 0.001 percent. This difference, as minuscule as it was, is almost never perceived or appreciated in daily life.

Given the amount of uncertainty in an election, what researchers call "noise," what politicians call "voting irregularities," or what the person in the voting booth might call the "vicissitudes of life," this difference in the real world is barely perceptible and in the research world is moot; nevertheless, .001 percent decided the election and subsequently will impact on the history and politics of America and the world for generations. In your world, .001 percent will eventually influence your future personal security, your social security, your Medicare benefits, and the amount of taxes you pay.

It must be noted, again, that 17 to 20 percent in margins or outcomes is statistically significant. These percentages, for example, are enormous for a basketball game, given that 1 or 2 points (or 1 or 2 percent differences) in a 100-point game often determines the outcome. In a 100-yard dash or swimming race, the difference in winning or losing is often measured in milliseconds.[1] Given battlefield conditions or an auto crash, the differences of inches or split seconds can mean the difference between life and death.

In education terms, 10 percent right or wrong on a standardized reading test usually boils down to 4 or 5 questions since most tests are comprised of 40 or 50 test questions. The net result of (missing or guessing right) 4 or 5 multiple-item questions often translates into one whole grade level (e.g., whether someone is reading at the fourth- or fifth-grade level). On an IQ test, given the normal distribution of a bell curve, 10 percent can be the difference between being classified as having "below average" or "above average" intelligence. In a graduating class of 400 or 500 students, where 4.0 is a perfect score (all As) a GPA of 3.9 versus 3.8 equates to one-tenth of a point, or 1 out of 40 points. One-tenth of 1 point—that is, 2½ percent on a 40-point continuum—can be the difference of five numerical points at the top of the ranking (say 97 versus 92) because of skewed scores at the ends of the bell curve. (The scores are tightly bunched or compressed at the end of the bell curve and small differences in scores, every tenth of a point, are magnified and result in large differences in rank.) The 2½ percent difference means, in the real world of college admissions, being admitted into an Ivy League or non–Ivy League college, which in turn will have compounding effects for the rest of the students' occupational status and income.

1. In the 2000 Olympic games in Sydney, Australia, two American swimmers (Erwin and Hall) shared a gold medal in the 50-meter free style race, each with a time of 21.98 seconds. The actual difference between them was less than 0.01 second, which was about 10 times larger than the difference between the Bush and Gore vote in Florida.

In short, there are many factors in life that result in education outcomes, and 10 or 20 percent of the variance is enormous. To bury or ignore up to 20 percent of the variance because someone's politics would prefer to see a greater percentage related to what schools can do is self-defeating; at best, it is sheer naivete or stupidity; at worse, it reflects political shrill and puerile isms. It fails to consider the joint responsibility of students, parents, the community, as well as the role of teachers and schools. All of us have a stake in the outcomes of education for the prosperity and health of the nation. It is not racist or mean spirited to stop seeing poor or minority students as perpetual victims; rather, they (and their parents and communities) need to assume greater responsibility for their own education.

It is important to understand that education (or educational achievement) is not the only variable or even the chief variable related to economic outcomes. Duncan felt that schools alone amounted to 10 percent of the outcome, a little low and some critics would argue quite disturbing or misleading. Jencks hypothesized that 50 percent or more was unexplained or related to what others might call "luck." Indeed, a host of personal, social, and political factors fall into place to determine the outcomes of life. Michael Jordan is no genius; neither is Michael Jackson, Billy Joel, or Mick Jagger—and on and on. The fact is that ours is a heterogeneous society, where people who perceive themselves as members of a minority group compare outcomes (such as education or wealth) and become highly sensitive when they are dissimilar. In Japan or Sweden, this kind of sensitivity would be ignored.

Herrnstein and, more recently, D'Souza would have us believe that smart people will always rise to the top, especially if there is equal opportunity within society. The relationship between social class (and making money) and genetic inheritance cannot be legislated out of existence in a democratic society. In fact, as society succeeds in equalizing opportunity, the genetic factor becomes relatively more important.[1] These ideas stem from Darwin's doctrine of "survival of the fittest" and Spencer's "laws of nature" that the intelligent, strong, and hard-working species will survive and the less intelligent, weak, or lazy will slowly disappear. To equalize outcomes, society is forced to handicap smart people by implementing progressive taxes or quotas. The analysis deals only with social class and should not be assumed to covertly or cryptically express the racial inferiority of any group. But try to discuss the idea of academic achievement, heredity, or even quotas in a public arena, and the roof will cave in.

There is a political party line or liberal orthodoxy that must often be observed on most college campuses and in most government jobs,[2] not much different than the dialectic thinking of McCarthyism, only the limits of expression are turned upside down. It is conservatives who are treated as reactionary or racist—a threat to the welfare of society. The correct idea is to have a more optimistic view of the fate of the underclass, and we must learn to think and act accordingly, even if we have to bend

---

1. Dinesh D'Souza, *The Virtues of Prosperity: Finding Value in an Age of Techno-Affluence* (New York: Free Press, 2000); Richard J. Herrnstein, *IQ in the Meritocracy* (Boston: Little, Brown, 1973).

2. *New York Times* (March 21, 2001), pp. A1, A17.

the truth. Politics and passion are now proper tools and rules for engagement; facts can be bent to serve political interests and the strategy is to shut down or stifle competing political views. In education, the same type of thinking permits reformers to put the blame on teachers, schools, and society—and to ignore the responsibility of parents, youth, and especially poor and minority students who are often construed as the victims of teachers, schools, and society.

## Reaction 2: Poverty Problems Are Overwhelming

Another reaction is to admit that students born in poverty have so many problems that pile up and accumulate that they cannot fully make use of educational opportunities or experience the same upward mobility as most middle-class students do. Part of the problem has to do with the social pathologies and psychology of the "culture of poverty" that affects the mind and spirit—the attitudes, motivations, and behaviors of the children and parents of the poor.

Poverty is also related to policy, and thus some of us mourn the likes of Michael Harrington, who helped America discover the poor, and Cesar Chavez, who organized the poor. Both men spurred the spirit and idealism of Kennedy's "New Frontier" and Johnson's "Great Society." The 1960s were highlighted by the sweep of liberalism, and the belief that government could make a difference in the lives of the poor. The reason why some people had so little in the midst of plenty was thought to be a lack of government intervention. Thus was born the War on Poverty and a host of government programs designed around social welfare.

The critics of this social legislation asserted that welfare produced its own kind of dependency, as well as an unwillingness to work, increased illegitimate births, absentee fathers, drug abuse, and crime. The only ones who benefited were the bureaucrats who administered the programs and dispersed the funds. Poverty was not an issue of money but one of culture, which had to be changed by tough sanctions and policies designed to shape behavior.[1] But for those who remember the War on Poverty, and the creation of millions of jobs in the public sector, there are now a large number of third-rate jobs that simply do not pay a decent wage to make your way out of poverty. The jobs are often filled by immigrants who don't speak English, which, in turn, only increases the number of poor people and illegal immigrants in the United States. What America needs is sweeping welfare legislation designed to help the poor.

President Clinton provided false hope, according to one critic who worked for him, because he was only interested in his political welfare and calculated the risk for helping the poor as too high. He tended to make things worse for the poor in the midst of a booming economy and high-tech revolution.[2] Sadly, Clinton's legislation imposed limits on aid, pushed people into dead-end jobs, and reduced a long-standing guarantee of

---

1. See Daniel P. Moynihan, *Coping: On the Practice of Government*, rev. ed. (New York: Random House, 1971).
2. Peter Edleman, *Searching for America's Heart* (Boston: Houghton Mifflin, 2001).

assistance. Only a liberal in deep denial, or someone mesmerized by his charisma, could defend Clinton's policies.

The need is not to increase cash transfers to poor and working-class families with children, for this only draws low-income families out of jobs into welfare. A viable approach is to reward working families with children by creating earned income tax credits, implementing a national health insurance plan for low-income adults and children,[1] and guaranteeing child care for all children (age 3 and older) whose parents are working. It is unfair, however—nearly absurd—to think that the public schools can counteract the long-term effects of inadequate nutrition, housing, clothing, diet, health care, as well as general cognitive and social deficits, characterizing poor children. An enormous burden is placed on our teachers and schools when we expect them to "make up" for the inequality in U.S. society. Yet, Americans expect the public school system to "level the playing field" for all students, and to offer opportunity for upward mobility.

The fact is that schools with high concentrations of poor students are usually overloaded with enormous problems, ranging from (1) inexperienced and uncertified teachers, poor morale, and working conditions; (2) children who cannot read or control themselves in class; (3) children deprived by lack of sleep, food, and basic health care; and (4) children victimized by drugs, gangs, crime, and teenage pregnancy. All that is needed is a critical mass of poor students, about 30 to 35 percent, and the values and behaviors of this group will take over and prevail in the school.[2] It sounds harsh, but there is a level or point in the real world when a ship sinks, a building needs to be demolished, and a person dies. Similarly, there is a threshold point when the climate or ethos of a school deteriorates by the attitudes and behavior of students. There is a point when schools cannot have much positive impact, and that other social or psychological factors are more critical in determining academic outcomes. Indeed the "rags to riches" story has real significance for many immigrant groups, but it remains largely a fable for those immersed in the "culture of poverty."

The United States provides real potential for upward mobility that is unusual by international standards,[3] but the advantages to the middle class and upper class are more numerous and noticeable, and this will always be the case unless we wish to socialize society. Depending on whose figures you want to believe, 21 to 25 percent of

---

1. Surprisingly, this nation accepts some 39 million uninsured, including another 40 million aging adults, who have to cope with increasing drug costs. Given a democratic society, or a good society, how much health care do Americans have a right to? Medicare beneficiaries spend an average of $1,051 on out-of-pocket costs for drugs. See Robin Toner, "Why the Elderly Want," *New York Times* (June 23, 2002), Sect. 4, pp. 1, 14.

2. This tipping point is rooted in the classic studies of social class by Allison Davis, Robert Havighurst, and Lloyd Warner in the 1940s and 1950s; in the classic studies of equality by Samuel Bowles, Herbert Gans, and Frederick Mosteller in the 1960s and 1970s; and in the ethnographic studies of Philip Cusick, Elizabeth Eddy, and Sara Lawrence Lightfoot in the 1980s and 1990s.

3. Richard C. Leone, "Foreword." In R. D. Kahlenberg, ed., *A Notion at Risk: Preserving Public Education as an Engine for Social Moblity* (New York: Century Foundation, 2000), pp. v–viii.

American students live in poverty[1]—most of them in a "culture of poverty," from one generation to the next. We have put great faith in public schools to enhance social mobility and equality. Suggestions or evidence that this part of the American dream is at risk or in decline is at best disquieting to Americans and often produces controversial debates among intellectuals and policymakers. But those who live on the downside of advantage are more often destined to remain at the bottom of the heap. At the same time, never before in the history of the United States have so many immigrant children of multiple nationalities and colors done so well in entering the nation's most exclusive and elite colleges and performed so well—which to a large extent reflects culture and not class. Thus, culture can have both positive and negative influences on destiny.

Poverty Expressed through the Novel    How does someone explain the grinding effects of poverty to people who are accustomed to eating three square meals a day and having been sponsored by their parents throughout their youth and young adult life? How do students who have always had their diapers changed and noses kept clean since they were little kids, come to understand someone who has been sealed off by the tyranny of poverty—that poverty saps the individual's strength, the person's mind and body? There is no way the anecdotes of sociologists or indicators of social class reveal how poverty turns people into dots, peas, and amoeba—people wasted by the wrenching process of no hope, no choice, no future. So, how does a beginning teacher, with a working-class or middle-class background, full of idealism and seeking a larger purpose to the daily act of teaching, get to understand boys and girls who have been left behind by society, who society has always regarded as less than worthy, nothing more than a number, to a bureaucrat, business person, or researcher.

Allow me to provide you a short glimpse into the life of Mr. Potter, an illiterate taxicab driver living in Antigua. He could also be living in Harlem, southside Chicago, or Watts. Mr. Potter is an uneventful, nonscript person. He has been beaten down by loss and suffering that comes with poverty and lack of education. He created the author of the book titled *Mr. Potter,* but he played no part in raising her and in fact scarcely knew her. Ms. Kincaid was his illegitimate daughter, living among other half-sisters and half-brothers. Mr. Potter is speechless; he has nothing to say. His favorite expression is "eh"; at times, when he shows strong feelings, he remarks "ooohhh!" He is more sensitive to the variations of the sun (repetitive sameness of the Caribbean) than to the needs and interests of his children or other people. He notices nothing else, for this person who "said nothing to himself . . . and thought nothing to himself. . . . Nothing crossed his mind and the world was blank and the world remained blank."[2]

1. Harold Hodgkinson, "Educational Demographics: What Teachers Should Know," *Educational Leadership* (January 2001), pp. 6–11; Lynn Olson and Greg F. Orlofsky, "2000 and Beyond: The Changing Face of American Schools," *Education Week* (September 27, 2000), pp. 30–38.

Government figures are as low as 18 percent because of recent employment increases in single-parent families. See "Family Economic Well-Being," *New Federalism* (January 2001), p. 2.

2. Jamaica Kincaid, *Mr. Potter* (New York: Farrar, Straus, & Giroux, 2002).

There is no possibility for Mr. Potter to become self-actualized. He routinely eats, sleeps, grunts, and fornicates once a week. (He fathers numerous illegitimate children.) His pleasures are a clean shirt, an open window, and a breeze rippling on his face. It is impossible for him to harbor a novel thought, or to be interesting in a political or literary way. He has been reduced to nothingness, a disconnected person, a prisoner of poverty. Mr. Potter has never been in love, doesn't dream, doesn't express feelings, and doesn't ponder or question political or social issues—a middle-class luxury. He hardly cares about anything, so it is hard to care for him, to worry about him, or to try to improve his life. His story is a tale of sameness, uselessness, and futility. He has been beaten down, like a pancake.

For Mr. Potter, there is no need to escape, no journey to a promised land, as in Harriet Beecher Stowe's *Uncle Tom's Cabin* (1852); no sense of bitterness, as with Frederick Douglass' *My Bondage and My Freedom* (1855); no sense of hope as with Booker T. Washington's *Up From Slavery* (1901), no independent spirit, as with W. E. B. DuBois's *The Soul Of Black Folks* (1903); no fire or sense of rage, as with James Baldwin's *The Fire Next Time* (1963); no potential for violence or rebellion, as with Franz Fannon's *The Wretched of the Earth* (1963); no need for a revolution or power struggle, as with Carmichael and Hamilton's *Black Power* (1967); no need to honestly address the vexing issues of race and justice, as with Randall Kennedy's *Race, Crime and the Law* (2000).

The word of the novel is often incomplete and open to different perspectives and interpretations. Given this construct, and the consideration of time and place, Mr. Potter is a pathetic figure; he might as well as sleep through life. He is a man erased by the misfortunes of poverty, neglected and obscured by the power structure. He exists as an appendix to society. He is a "no-hoper." He has no personality, no status in the family, the community, or the church. Potter doesn't think of the future; he has no faith in his abilities or strength; he has no heroic designs. There are millions of poor people like him living in the slums of America. Some clean floors or toilets, some wash dishes or change bed sheets in hotel rooms, some cut grass or pump gas, some sell drugs, and some sell their bodies. Some travel downtown, others uptown, to forget all their troubles, all their cares. For the greater part, these people have been rendered hopeless by society, and their goal is to survive daily and stay clear from the arm of the law—the boot and whip, the gun, or the prosecutor's fury.

From the perspective of a prospective teacher enrolled in "Education 101," it is questionable if such a person can fully grasp the full force of poverty. It is doubtful that someone fully engaged in a debate over a subject-centered or student-centered curriculum, or the merits of whole language versus phonetics, has the knowledge, experience, or sensitivity to understand the cumulative effects of poverty. Similarly, it is doubtful if grossly underfunded schools, managed by bureaucratic and sometimes cruel policies, and staffed by many unprepared teachers, can make a dent. The question arises: Can we turn around the process to enable poor students on a large scale to develop their unique skills and talents before they grow up and become the Mr. Potters of America?

**The Rich Are Different**    People can get used to sleeping on the floor, eating rice and beans, or boiling worms and cockroaches for dinner. Others in New York City expect to dine at Le Beradine or Daniel's and order Dom Perignon or Cristal champagne with foie gras or beluga caviar for appetizers and white truffles or chateaubriand as an entrée. The bill: $400 to $500 per couple and $40 to $50 for parking. F. Scott Fitzgerald, in *The Great Gatsby*, made it very clear that the rich are not like you or I, and they certainly have different dining habits than teachers, or those stuck in urban ghettos or small towns whose idea of dining out consists of a Big Mac or a blueberry pancake special for $2.99, or those college students who dine with plastic forks and paper cups. Let's face it: $500 is the monthly food bill for a college student with money remaining for Saturday night drinking, and a round of golf once a month with a two-for-one coupon.

The rich are often the subject of stories and novels of a bygone era—about the charming life of the Victorian Age or the Old South, with attitudes and behaviors patriotically wedded in the past. The rich would not care if the rest of Europe or the United States sunk into the ocean, so long as their world were to continue. Their attachment to the status quo feels out of sync with the changing world, since the future they fear has arrived—the shifting political ground, the decline of their power, and the reshuffling of power and the culture at large.

There is still another group of rich whose stories unfold in contemporary settings—New York, Paris, Milano, and Frankfurt—present-day "Brahmans," some well bred and others who are "wheelers and dealers," mostly business tycoons who command CEO posts and sit in big board rooms and decide the fate of humanity by manipulating markets and prices. The world these people encounter generally has a different standard of morality and ethics, much different than the vision Plato, Kant, or John Rawls would describe.[1] In a different age, say 100 years ago, these capitalists were described by their critics as "cannibalistic plutocrats," "pirates," and "robber barons." Today, in an age of speech codes, rigidly enforced tolerance, and affirmative action, these CEOs espouse a business philosophy that sounds like a fundamentalist on the stump or a political candidate espousing the virtues of hard work, honestly, and rags to riches.

Then there are the super-rich who live in suburban horse country, or the Hamptons, the Cape, Newport Beach, the south of France or Spain, or in some castle along the English countryside. Money grows so fast with these people—faster than we can grow tomatoes and cucumbers—because of investments. As one critic observes, while most of us wear baseball caps and sweatshirts of our favorite baseball teams or colleges, the American youth who are part of this lifestyle wear caps and shirts of investment banks and mutual funds.[2] It is as if the emblems and logos of plebian culture have not caught on or been manufactured quickly enough the aristocrats' taste for clothing. "Mass" culture lags behind "money" culture, where people display their money on their heads and chests.

It was F. Scott Fitzgerald who some 75 years ago was able to capture the sinuous, leisurely, and extravagant life of the upper-upper class in stories such as *This Side*

1. John Rawls, *A Theory of Justice*, 2nd ed. (Cambridge, MA: Harvard University Press, 1999).
2. Caleb Crain, "Scott Fitzgerald Was Different," *New York Times Book Review* (December 24, 2000), pp. 9–10.

*of Paradise* (1920), *Flappers and Philosophers* (1920), and *The Beautiful and Damned* (1922). He was the first popular writer to put it in words—the rich are different than us—more "soft," "cynical," "spoiled," and "vulgar." As the flapper in the "Offshore Pirate" says of the possibility of being bribed with a platinum watch: "That sounds so nice and vulgar—and fun, doesn't it?" Gatsby had no illusions about the super-rich or money culture. But after *The Great Gatsby,* it can be argued that Fitzgerald's goal was to make money, as much as he could, and he didn't care whether the things he said were true or false, so long as they described the grandeur, and the lifestyle that drove him to Zelda and the promise of wealth. To be sure, money corrupts!

Both the men and women of the old rich and new rich come to accept the vices of their spouses, their fondness for drink, and their irresistibility to other lovers. But passivity or acquiescence is not a sign of remorse or defeat. Rather, it is a decision taken, a thought-out position, where the vicissitudes of life are negotiated and where personal relations are renegotiated—a certain compromise achieved to preserve a lifestyle. Only recently in western society, where women have achieved certain rights and protections under the law, are they now willing to file for divorce and cry on the witness stand, because of the indiscretions of their husbands or because they have become bored with the status quo. (Jack Welch's affair with the review editor of *Harvard Business Review* is a recent example of an "unappreciated" wife filing for divorce and demanding $1 billion; it makes for a fascinating and juicy case study in itself, exactly for what the Harvard Business School is most noted.)[1] Men in this financial bracket still prefer to go down with the ship, rather than give up parts of their fortunes. They tend to make more compromises with their spouses, or look the other way.

The old rich are snobs. In the old world, according to Joe Epstein, who admits it takes a snob to know one, snobbery had less appeal since just about everyone knew their place in the pecking order. Working people knew they were below the upper class. In the United States, snobbery is about asserting one's social and cultural superiority. Snobbery deals with taste and refinement, but much of it has waned since the upheavals of the 1960s,[2] particularly when the likes of George Bush—a WASP—portrays himself as a genuine cowboy with dirty boots. Even old-line, WASP institutions—prep schools, Ivy League colleges, private golf clubs, and Episcopalian churches—have recently allowed limited entry of ethnics. But snobbery continues to invent distinctions between old money and new money, among certain clubs and fraternities at colleges, at private golf outings and within private associations, and "old-boy" networks who are connected and think they know about style and substance.

I don't believe teachers understand this "rich person's world," since it is so different from their world of lesson plans, chalk boards, and crowded classrooms. Writers of educational subjects have frequently spoken about pedagogical methods and the need to master subject matter without any reference to the rich or any reminder of a class struggle that existed when the Rockefellers and Fords were crushing labor strikes, when Mother Jones (Mary Harris) and Eugene Debs were organizing work-

1. See James Bandler, "Harvard Editor Faces Revolt Over Welch story," *Wall Street Journal* (March 4, 2002), p. B1.
2. Jospeh Epstein, *Snobbery: The American Version* (Boston: Houghton Mifflin, 2002).

ers, or when the likes of Wal-Mart or Walgreen Drug Stores came to town, drove out the competition, and destroyed the lives of small business owners. Of course, someone like Bill Gates comes along and talks about some large donation for school reform and all is forgiven by the public.

The rich are different in other ways. They know when to jump ship and sell their stock, since they control or have inside information. The 2001–02 Enron, Global Crossing, Tyco, and WorldCom fiascos are the best examples, with top executives selling their stock right before the company's collapse and walking away with millions of dollars while their employees and stockholders watched their pensions and savings disappear.[1] Top executives from other big companies have been similarly insulated from losses with all kinds of "safety nets" that recession imposes on their workers. They also know when to jump in and buy depressed stocks in their companies, because they have inside knowledge that workers and average investors do not have. Moreover, they are highly compensated and highly diversified, much more diversified than the average employee who is encouraged by his or her employer to invest in the company's stock. Workers at Lucent, MCI, Motorola, McDonalds, K-Mart, and other companies have held their breath as their stocks and pensions have tumbled between 20 and 95 percent in just two short years (2001–02).

Then, of course, the rich are different when it comes to divorce. There is the story of Lisa Bonder Kerkorian, the 36-year-old tennis pro who demanded $320,000 a month in child support (for one 3-year-old child) from her former husband, the 84-year-old billionaire Kirk Kerkorian, who controls MGM and the Bellagio hotel in Las Vegas among other possessions. Among Ms. Kerkorian's "wish list" was $144,000 for travel per month, $14,000 for parties, $6,000 for dining out and $4,300 eating in, $2,500 for movies and other outings, and $1,400 for laundry. The whole family situation is absurd, with the rich spending $50,000 to $100,000 for parties for toddlers, complete with circus dancers, elephant rides, and cashmere socks for other toddler guests while departing.[2]

Obviously, something is very unfair about the social order—watching the rich exploit the working class or watching the rich fight over millions of dollars while the large majority of people have to worry about making ends meet. For those who earn less than $60,000 a year, who make up more than half the work force, it is pretty obnoxious and frustrating, to say the least. What the country needs to do, and have often failed to do, is to balance the concept of equality and equal opportunity, with some limits on capitalism, wealth, and acquired status. The moral and political question is: What are the right limits? We cannot afford to ignore this dilemma, because the answer to this question, and whatever balancing act we achieve, eventually decides the type of society we are and the happiness and quality of life we derive as a people.

It must be noted that the more wealth and acquired status that are permitted, the more resources and services are taken from the general population; the more economic

1. Louis Uchitelle, "The Rich Are Different: They Know When to Leave," *New York Times* (January 20, 2002), Sect. 4, pp. 1, 5.
2. Alex Kuczynski, "Can a Kid Squeeze by on $320,000 a Month?" *New York Times* (January 20, 2002), Sect. 9, pp. 1, 6.

gaps that are allowed, the fewer resources and services remain for the remaining society. *Laissez-faire* capitalism without subordination or a pure welfare state represents the far extremes we need to avoid. One situation puts too much wealth and power in the hands of too few, and the other situation reduces the health, vitality, and progress of society. Finding the golden mean or balancing the rights and needs of the rich and poor, is a philosophical question dating back to Greek civilization.

Differences in power should never be the crux for determining a balanced or fair situation, since the stronger and richer will always get their way. All kinds of theories and excuses have been manufactured to ensure the opposite, such as Tory conservatism (Adam Smith's *Inquiry into the Nature and Cause of Wealth of Nations* [1776]); social Darwinism (Elbert Hubbard's *The Message to Garcia* [1899] and Simon Patten's *Theory of Prosperity* [1902]); and unregulated capitalism and unrestrained free-enterprise business (Milton Freidman's *Capitalism and Freedom* [1962], Ayn Rand's *The Fountainhead* [1943], and D'Souza Dinish's *The Virtues of Prosperity* [2000]). All of these ideas are based on the cult of the elite—a natural aristocracy based on ability (not inherited wealth) to do the job, work hard, and rise to the top[1] (in doing so they are supposed to provide the best possible goods at the lowest possible price), and a mass of incompetents who are incapable of thinking on their own, earn according to their abilities and skills, and remain discontented.

Capitalism is where self-interest and competition meet—and become a self-regulating mechanism—so that government regulations are unnecessary. Capitalism is considered necessary for political freedom and democracy; otherwise, central controls and government coercion surface—the techniques of modern totalitarian states. In a free economy, according to a younger Alan Greenspan, government may step in "only after . . . fraud, . . . crime . . . or damage to the consumer,"[2] which basically puts the average person at the mercy of big business and assumes people in power are naturally ethical.

Much of this kind of thinking is "hocus pocus," designed to maintain a two-tier system (rich and poor) that leads to individual self-interest, economic oppression, and social injustice. Capitalism unchecked means that a small percent of people rise to the top in the form of a pyramid, while the masses remain at the bottom. Those in

1. Ironically, most wealthy people come to believe that the reason why they are economically successful, or rise to the top, is because of brains and hard work. They fail to consider macroeconomics, luck, political clout, and a host of questionable practices in which they or their parents participated—amoral practices, cash practices, criminal practices, pay-off practices, tax-evasion practices, and monopolistic practices—so common in big business. This is how the early Rockefellers, Vanderbilts, and Fords made their money and how the early Kennedys and Bushs made their money. Teachers are naive to teach that the capitalistic system merely rewards merit or "smarts," and that under the guise of American patrotism or heroism most business or Wall Street titans made their money the "old-fashioned way." The Puritan and Protestant gospel may have preached this doctrine, the McGuffy readers may have espoused this "wisdom," and William Bennett, the former head of the Department of Education may believe in it and call it virtuous, but that is not what business all about.

2. "When Greed Was a Virtue and Regulation the Enemy," *New York Times* (July 21, 2002), Sect. 4, p. 14.

America who remain at the bottom for three or more generations often become what social scientists call the "culture of poverty." The problem is that there is little opportunity today for the uneducated herd, a growing number within the American work force (some 40 million semi-illiterate workers). Increasingly, the uneducated will be left behind, with fewer and fewer opportunities.

Some sense of justice and morality must prevail in order to arrive at an economic compromise and fair solution. If not, the mob will eventually kill off the head(s) of state and overthrow the nobility, including the robber barons. It doesn't matter, according to history, if he or she is a pharaoh, caesar, emperor or empress, king or queen, shah, or general. Heads will roll. The beauty of our system is that people are permitted to go as far as their abilities and ambitions will take them, without obstacles associated with class, religion, or race—at least that is how the system is supposed to work. In this process, teachers and schools are instrumental in the "sorting" process. The process, of course, is flawed, because the rich have greater advantages and discrimination still exists; moreover, we do not have many good career options for those who lack ability or have below-average ability.

Obviously, if one has to, a person can get used to his or her economic plight and behave accordingly in order to survive. In the same vein, prisoners can get used to prison life, and soldiers can get used to life in the jungle or dessert—and in a short period of time. Similarly, prisoners at Devil's Island, like those caged by the Viet Cong 50 years later, got used to capturing and eating cockroaches and rats for purposes of protein. After two or three generations of living at the bottom of the heap, people will adopt a set attitudes and behaviors to conform to their world that other people outside the group cannot fully understand. Most of you reading this book have not experienced the culture of poverty, and only those who know such as world can close their eyes, recall those images and feelings, and fully grasp how long-term human misery can affect attitudes and behavior.

Imagine the world without toilets, only outhouses. Well, 100 years ago, there were no toilets—only sand piles of human waste. Today, we have households with one toilet and others with five or six—which partially determines the price of the house and separates us by class. To put it in neomarxist terms, there is the contrast between the luxury, extravagance, and conspicuous consumption of the few, the life of the working class who are often in debt, and the misery of the poor and shivering wretches of the unemployed, homeless, sickly, and drug addicted on the streets of many cities and away from the highways in rural America. Most of the poor have been "invisible," hidden from white and middle-class eyes.

Imagine the world with no television, no computers, no plastic money, no heart transplants, no fast food, and no "yuppie coffee." I remember such a world. People from my youth exhibited different expectations, different habits, and different behaviors because their world was different from the world of cell phones, microchips, and ATM cards. The point is this: People can get used to anything, except the shadow of death (starvation, drowning, hanging, etc.). Children who are poor act poor—and school has a different meaning and effect on them than it has on middle-class children. Our problem is, as middle-class teachers, we have a different perspective and set of expectations about schools than many poor inner-city and rural students. Despite the books we read and the rhetoric we espouse, most of us in education have different benchmarks than the poor. We don't fully understand what it is like to be poor and have to deal with the middle-class world of teachers and schools—what some critics (Paul Goodman and John Holt in the 1960s and Mike Apple and Henry Giroux today) would call the *caretakers* of the system.

Depending on the study cited, reading gaps between average scores of low-income and middle-income first-graders, measured in terms of ranking, starts six to nine months or one-half to three-fourths year behind, and it grows to two years behind by eighth grade. By twelfth grade, the difference is about three to three and a half years behind.[1] It hardly needs to be said that students who are unable to read are unable to succeed in school, and usually drop out of school. (Nationally, the dropout rate for high school students is 10 percent, but for students in the lowest income quintile, it is 25 percent.) In large cities, where there is high concentrations of poverty, the dropout rate is 25 to 40 percent, although it has tapered off since the mid-1990s.[2]

The implications of such studies call into question some of the myths and hopes about what schools can and cannot achieve. It raises questions about our original intentions (eliminate separate facilities and education outcomes will increase) regarding *Brown* v. *Board of Education,* in 1954, and all the other subsequent laws outlawing discrimination in almost every area of life. It raises feasibility questions about the War on Poverty and the civil rights movement of the 1960s, and particularly the Elementary and Secondary Education Act of 1965, which authorized grants for children of poor families and which led to billions of dollars in compensatory funding. Similarly, it raises feasibility questions about the No Child Left Behind Act of 2001, the most sweeping reform since the ESEA of 1965. Can increased education spending overcome the effects of poverty? Maybe Jencks was right. We need to redistribute money to eliminate poverty—and everything else we try to do is secondary, irrelevant, or wasteful—at least in large numbers it is.

## Reaction 3: Options and Choices Outside the System

The conservative model believes in capitalism and therefore recognizes there will always be an underclass. However, there is no question that these same people are aware of the potential for revolution, an angry proletariat rising up and dismantling tax loopholes, increasing environmental regulations, improving labor laws, and expanding housing, medical, and welfare programs at their expense. Having lost faith in public schools to solve the problems of inequality, conservative reformers have the foresight to look for other options, such as school choice, vouchers, and charter

1. Carl L. Bankston and Stephen J. Caldas, "Race, Poverty, Family Structure and the Inequality of Schools," *Sociological Spectrum* (January 1998), pp. 55–74; Richard D. Kahlenberg, "Making K–12 Public Education an Engine for Social Mobility," in Kahlenberg, ed., *A Notion of Risk,* pp. 1–8; and Richard Rothstein, *The Way We Were?: Debunking the Myth of America's Declining Schools* (New York: Century Foundation, 1998).

2. *The Condition of Education 2001* (Washington, DC: U.S. Department of Education, 2001), Table 23, p. 43; Kahlenberg, ed., *A Notion of Risk;* and Mayer *What Money Can't Buy.*

schools, which should lead to tax credits, increased competition, and enhancement of traditional values, which they also welcome. The conservative philosophy, spearheaded by William Bennett, Chester Finn, Diane Ravitch and Phillip Schlechty, seeks new avenues and remedies for reform—a restructuring and privatization of schools, where teachers teach and where there is high-stakes testing and accountability. It is a free market system that parallels competition and capitalism, rooted in the ideas of Milton Friedman and—once more, no joke—Christopher Jencks.[1]

For different reasons, the liberal/minority group sees hope in school choice and vouchers as a means for poor parents and students to escape from unsatisfactory inner-city schools, to provide more options in selecting schools (the rich certainly have more options), to stimulate improvement in public schools, and possibly to increase school integration. Their platform also includes high-stakes testing and accountability, but limited only to teachers and administrators (not students). The basic point is simple: Given the record of failure in public education for inner-city students, we should at least give other proposals and options a chance. In either case, regardless of political ideology, Joel Spring sees the demand for school choice, vouchers, and charter schools as the end of the common school movement in which all children receive "a common education that includes a common culture" and a common set of political and moral values.[2]

I would add that under the guise of reform and school improvement, we are vaulting into the saddle and riding mindlessly in many directions, with little attention to a systematic philosophy or set of values. American democracy is rooted in the common school movement keenly delineated by Mann, Dewey, and Cremin, and I fear that too many parents and even educators today are being seduced by the reporters of the *Wall Street Journal, Time,* and *U.S. News and World Report* who glibly acquaint us with education ideas without appraising all the facts.

In many schools, there are five or six major school reform initiatives on the table or in place, each with 25 or more subjects and subcategories. One observer summarizes the situation where "our principals are going crazy, and the system is on overload." Administrators, policymakers, and teachers all contribute to "this dilemma by proposing unrelated projects and making unrealistic demands on schools." The reason for all those new reform slogans, programs, and initiatives is because of "conflicting demands from diverse constituencies, constant changes in personnel and policies, and significant limits on time, resources, and available funding."[3] State

1. Milton Friedman, "The Role of Government in Education," in R. A. Solo, ed., *Economics and the Public Interest* (New Brunswick, NJ: Rutgers University Press, 1955); Christopher Jencks, "Education: Cultivating Greater Diversity," *New Republic* (November 7, 1964), pp. 33–40.

2. Joel Spring, *The American School: 1642–1996,* 4th ed. (Boston: McGraw-Hill, 1997), p. 401.

3. Thomas Hatch, "It Takes Capacity to Build Capacity," *Education Week* (February 14, 2001), p. 44. According to a 1999 survey of San Fransisco schools, 15 percent of principals claim they were involved with six or more different school improvement initiatives. In a different survey involving the states of California and Texas, as many as 23 percent of the administrators claimed they were involved in six or more different school improvement programs.

efforts to define and refine curriculum standards, and to impose accountability on educators, adds to this overload.

It is not common knowledge that the liberal/minority community is critical of the public schools, since the schools have not met the expectations and hopes of poor students. Many of their ideas are rooted in the ideology of Rousseau, who was highly critical of formal schooling—and viewed it as the basis for the "miseducation" of children and youth. To Rousseau, and to the "neoprogressives" and "radicals" of the 1960s (Edgar Friedenberg, Paul Goodman, Nat Hentoff, John Holt, Geroge Leonard, and A. S. Neill), nature made formal education unnecessary; the best education was to let nature unfold, to permit the child to follow his or her own instincts.[1]

The basis for education is not schools, for they are seen as restrictive and repressive institutions, even "imprisoning" and "enslaving" the child. Worse yet, the law requires that children attend school—and the argument is that school eventually destroys the dignity and self-worth of the child, especially poor children. It is the reason why Friedenberg would defend the student who puts a knife to the teacher and why Goodman would eliminate compulsory schooling. Hentoff would argue that poor children are dying in schools because schools are awful places—full of vermin and cockroaches, leaky roofs, faulty plumbing, and overcrowded classrooms. Both Holt and Leonard maintain that schools are designed to destroy the human spirit through control methods and boring classroom conditions. Holt would burn down schools, and Leonard would provide no school (rather, he would educate children in playgrounds, sidewalks, and small community sites). Neill provides the option for a private school, for children to have the freedom to act according to their own student-established rules rather than conforming to adult-imposed school rules.

Both Rousseau and the critics of the 1960s were critical of formal education and preferred other options. Neill was the only critic to go beyond intellectualizing the problem; he spent his whole professional life (40 years) running Summerhill (opening in 1924), a highly progressive English school where children could come and go as they pleased and do anything they wished (including not doing homework, attending classes, or taking exams), so long as they did not hurt someone else. Summerhill had no mission or set of goals; it was mostly a reaction against the system of the day. But it was not until the 1960s and 1970s that "free learning" and "alternative learning" began to spring up—part of the notion of relevancy, humanism, and school choice.

The home school movement today is rooted in this type of thinking—providing choices and options for parents who are unhappy with what public schools have to offer. Nationwide, there are about 1.9 million children taught at home, mainly from middle-class and/or religious backgrounds, and the ranks are growing at about 10 to 15 percent a year.[2] The movement, which is considered radical and antiestablishment,

1. See Allan C. Ornstein, "Critics and Criticism of Education," *Educational Forum* (November 1977), pp. 21–30; Robert Schaefer, "Retrospect and Prospect," in R. M. McClure, ed., *The Curriculum,* Seventeenth Yearbook of the National Society for the Study of Education, Part I (Chicago: University of Chicago Press, 1971), pp. 3–21; and Charles E. Silberman, *Crisis in the Classroom* (New York: Random House, 1970).

2. Flynn McRoberts, "The Economics of Karate," *Newsweek* (November 20, 2000), p. 62; Rebecca Winters, "From Home to Harvard," *Time* (September 11, 2000), p. 5.

is rooted in the ideas of Rousseau, who rejected formal schools, as well as the critics of the 1960s, who resented the establishment and described schools as coercive institutions—an arm of the law, military, or capitalistic system.

Today, those who debate issues about poverty and racism (Michael Apple, Paulo Freire, Henry Giroux, Ivan Illich, Peter McLaren, etc.) often resent being called *radicals* and *neomarxists*. But, if the use of those words leads to critical debates about how poor or minority children are victimized by school and society, then they are willing to play off these shock words. They want to stimulate discussion and reject any discourse that deals with inequality or keeps the mass of poor, working-class, and minority students imprisoned as an under class. Their goal is to create school options and choices in order to improve the conditions of poor and minority children—and to break the mold of established schooling, which they link to the middle-class and majority culture, as well as to the continuation of the capitalist or dominant class over the proletariat or subordinate class.

The fact is, most of these intellectuals fail to grasp that they no longer have clout with the educational establishment, policymakers, or government officials. Other than a few intellectuals, professors, and their students, no on really cares what they have to say, especially since most students perform well in school and most people feel capitalism and democracy go hand in hand. Not since Camelot and the Kennedy presidency have "the best and brightest" influenced policymakers or power brokers.[1] High-tech stockbrokers and analysts on CNN or Fox News have much more influence on voters than do intellectuals. For every person who watches *Meet the Press* or *Cross Fire,* there are probably 10 times more checking their retirement portfolio on CNBC's morning *Squawk Box* and evening *Edge.*

Today, according to one observer, there are more *meritocrats,* members of the baby boom and Generation X, whose coming of age and success were based on the SATs, studying, being self-made, and being high achieving.[2] These people, many who are now "preppies" and "yuppies," see affirmative action as a means of keeping good people out, and not as a tool to give good people the benefit of the doubt, or to bring them in. They believe that the poor do not want to work hard; rather, they want a free ride. They also see the reformer or intellectual as the crux of the problem—subverting democracy and the ideas of equality, as well as the notion of hard work and achievement.

## Reaction 4: More Effective Schools

In order to neutralize the skeptical and apologist attitudes of the education establishment, reformers have developed a literature on *more effective schools,* which purports that inner-city schools can successfully educate poor and minority students.

1. Neil Rudenstine, ex-Harvard president for 10 years (1991–2001), disagrees and contends that professors at his institution have much prestige and that their experience and advice are sought by government agreements and industry on a regular basis, and more than ever before. See J. Linn Allen, "Question and Answer: Education Needs Imagination to Meet Needs of the Future," *Chicago Tribune* (March 25, 2001).

2. Jack Hitt, "The Great Divide," *New York Times Magazine* (December 31, 2000), pp. 12–13.

Advocates in this camp pay attention to schools as institutions, the environment in which they operate, and usually defined success in terms of student achievement and usually focused on preschool and elementary schools. This emphasize corresponds with environmental research data indicating that intervention is most critical in the early stages of human development, because it is the most rapid period of cognitive growth (50 percent by age 4, another 25 percent by age 9, according to Bloom).[1]

Given the public concern for young children, and the fact Americans have sufficient wealth as a nation to meet the education and special needs of all young children, it is surprising that we lack a national and sustainable program that supports a public investment in infant and toddler education. The research is relatively consistent on the value of early childhood education and for children who are "at risk" and coincides with the developmental theories of Piaget and Bloom. In several European countries, there has been a trend toward nationalization of education services for all children from as early as 18 months in Sweden, 2 years in Belgium, and 3 years in Italy.[2] To date, most federal and state initiatives in the United States focuses on Head Start education for children 4½ and 5 years old. The problem is, only 36 percent of eligible children receive Head Start services,[3] bordering on a national embarrassment.

Right now the industrialized counties of Europe, Australia, and New Zealand spend, on average, one-half of 1 percent of their gross national product on education for early childhood.[4] Given the education benefits, exemplified by David Weikert's preschool study through age 27, the early childhood education studies in Europe, and the benefits to working mothers and ultimate savings to society,[5] it would seem to be to our advantage to extend prekindergarten education in the United States downward to age 3, to upgrade training in personnel and provide for certification, to ensure an agreed philosophy and pedagogy, to monitor the participation of parents and staff, and to pay sufficient wages to attract qualified personnel and reduce turnover.

As of the year 2000, about 2.6 million U.S. infants and toddlers were in some form of child care full time, or 35 hours a week. This care was based on private arrangements in child-care centers, (39 percent), and on care by relatives (27 percent), neighbors (27 percent), and nannies or babysitters (7 percent).[6] The Dependent Care Assistance Programs allows families to deduct up to $5,000 per year for child-care expenses for children age 14 and under. Who benefits? Certainly not the poor who rely on relatives and neighbors to provide care.

1. Benjamin S. Bloom, *Stability and Change in Human Characters* (New York: Wiley, 1964).

2. Michelle J. Neuman and John Bennett, "Starting Strong: Policy Implications for Early Childhood Education and Care in the U.S.," *Phi Delta Kappan* (November 2001), pp. 246–254.

3. Pauline B. Gough, "The Best Place to Start," *Phi Delta Kappan* (November 2001), p. 182.

4. *A Caring World: The New Social Policy Agenda* (Paris: OECD, 1999); *Starting Strong: Early Childhood Education and Care* (Paris: OCED, 2001).

5. Ibid. Also see David Weikart, *Significant Benefits: The High/Scope Perry Preschool Study Through Age 27* (Ypsilanti, MI: High/Scope Press, 1993).

6. "Nearly 5 million Infants and Toddlers in Child Care," *New Federalism* (June 2001), p. 2.

Given that the early years are so formative, it would be wise for the nation to commit to the care and education of its young and to make it compulsory, especially for "at risk" and poor children, to prepare or catch them up to grade level when they enter school. A few states, such as Massachusetts, Vermont, and West Virginia, are providing comprehensive programs for infants and toddlers, and the federal government in 2000 provided $3.5 billion in block grants to states to provide some child-care services to assist working women with children (73 percent of women between ages 25 and 34 are in the work force).[1] The outcomes are piecemeal and inadequate; we need more like $12 billion, twice the appropriations for Head Start, to ensure that all our nation's poor or at-risk children are receiving appropriate services and education.

The advent of school nutrition programs; extended day, weekend, and required preschool programs; required summer school for primary students (grades 1–3) to neutralize cognitive deficits as opposed to allowing them to increase; reading and tutoring programs; parenting education; and making class size and schools smaller—all are considered crucial.[2] The instruction that is recommended is prescriptive and diagnostic; emphasis is on basic skill acquisition, review and guided practice, monitoring of student programs, providing prompt feedback and reinforcement to students, and mastery-learning opportunities.[3] All of these instructional methods suggest a behaviorist, direct, convergent, systematic, and low cognitive level of instruction, as opposed to a problem-solving, abstract, divergent, inquiry-based, and high level of instruction. (Of course, come critics would argue that this type of instruction is second rate and reflects our low expectations of low-achieving students.)

The research on effective schools starts with the classic work of Ronald Edmonds, who, in the early 1980s, identified the characteristics of effective elementary schools in New York City in which there was (1) strong leadership, (2) an orderly climate,

1. Sharon L. Kagan and Lynda G. Hallmark, "Early Care and Education Policies in Sweden: Implications for the United States," *Phi Delta Kappan* (November 2001), pp. 237–245, 254; Sally Lubeck, "Early Childhood Education and Care in Cross National Perspective," *Phi Kappan* (November 2001), pp. 213–215; *Starting Strong: Early Childhood Education and Care.*

2. Lorin Anderson and Leonard O. Pellicer, "Synthesis of Research Compensatory and Remedial Education," *Educational Leadership* (September 1990), pp. 10–16; Allan C. Ornstein and Daniel U. Levine, "School Effectiveness and Reform: Guidelines for Action," *Clearing House* (November–December 1990), pp. 115–118; and William C. Symonds, "How to Fix America's Schools," *Business Week* (March 19, 2001), pp. 68–80. Also see Ronald Kotulak, "Teaching Them Early," *Chicago Tribune* (June 3, 2001), pp. 1, 9. Georgia was the first state to require pre-K programs for all 4-year-olds in the state. I would start with toddler programs at age 3.

3. Daniel U. Levine and Allan C. Ornstein, "Research on Classroom and School Effectiveness and its Implications for Improving Big-City Schools," *Urban Review* (July 1989), pp. 81–95; Allan C. Ornstein and Daniel U. Levine, "Urban School Effectiveness and Improvement," *Illinois School and Research Development* (Spring 1991), pp. 111–117; and Charles Teddlie and David Reynolds, eds., *Research on School Effectiveness* (Levittown, PA: Falmer Press, 1998).

(3) frequent monitoring of student progress, (4) high expectations and requirements for all students, and (5) focus on teaching important skills to all students.[1]

Other researchers of the same period extended the list of characteristics, the best example describing the Connecticut School Effectiveness Project by Joan Shoemaker: (1) a safe and orderly environment, (2) a clear school mission, (3) instructional leadership of the principal, (4) high expectation among the staff, (5) high time-on-task and student engagement in planned activities, (6) monitoring of student progress, and (7) positive school-home relations (and parental support.)[2] More effective schools were also identified in Chicago and Los Angeles where there was emphasis on (1) mastery learning, (2) reading programs, (3) curriculum skills and alignment with testing, and (4) homework and parent involvement with learning.[3]

In a review of six cities' reform initiatives, Paul Hill points out that the only consistent reform strategy across cities is the emphasis on student performance standards and staff development programs (which enhance new ideas and new methods of instruction).[4] He concludes that for schools to become more effective, they need to (1) define and use a consistent plan based on a particular philosophy or pedagogy so that teachers are clear on aims, goals, and strategies; (2) encourage parental and family engagement in their children's schooling; and (3) increase teacher responsibility for improving their own teaching practices and engagement in innovation. On a more theoretical level, Hill recommends that staff members from effective schools be permitted "to charge for help and advice given to other schools" in the district,[5] thus enhancing performance incentives and professionalism.

Twenty years later, after Edmonds's "kick-off," Casey Carter described 21 high-performing poverty schools across the country in his book, *No Excuses.* The overall message of his research was to reject the ideology of victimization or discrimination that dominates most discussion about poverty, race, and low achievement. Carter contends that the schools (18 out of 21 are elementary schools) profiled in his book do not reject standardized tests as discriminating against poor or minority children, but use them for diagnostic and benchmark purposes. They show that children can master the core subjects, especially reading and math, but some children learn at different paces and need extra time or tutoring.[6] The key to the success of these schools

1. Ronald R. Edmonds, "Programs of School Improvement," *Educational Leadership* (December 1982), pp. 4–11.

2. Joan Shoemaker, "Effective Schools: Putting the Research to the Ultimate Test," *Pre-Post Press* (1982), p. 241; William Gauthier, Raymond Pecheone, and Joan Shoemaker, "Schools Can Become More Effective, *Journal of Negro Education* (Summer 1985), pp. 388–408.

3. Daniel U. Levine and Joyce Stark, "Instructional and Organizational Arrangements that Improve Achievement in Inner-City Schools," *Educational Leadership* (May 1982), pp. 618–620.

4. Paul Hill, "Good Schools for Big-City Children," Research Paper published by the Brookings Institute, Washington, DC, November 2000.

5. Ibid., p. 14.

6. Samuel C. Carter, *No Excuses: Lessons from 21 High-Performing High Poverty Schools* (Washington, DC: Heritage Foundation, 2000).

is the principal, who establishes the school climate—where an orderly environment and good teaching are expected. "Finding the right principals, who in turn [are given latitude to] find the right teachers, may be the most important variable for eliciting high performing, high poverty schools."[1]

With the exception of compensatory programs such as reading or tutoring, the more effective school approach suggests very little additional cost and depends more on leadership of the principal, as well as the attitudes, motivation, and responsibility of the teachers, parents, and students. Money does not seem to be the answer; in fact, failure becomes a rationale to demand more money. The approach is not piecemeal or perceived as part of the compensatory movement (which cost billions of dollars and by and large failed). The focus is on a macrolevel—the entire school, not a specific program or specific teacher. The need is to analyze, modify, and improve the roles, values, and beliefs of *all* those concerned with the teaching and learning process. The idea is to create a school culture, an ethos, that the principal and majority of teachers believe in and are based on expectations of success. (See Teaching Tips 8.1.)

Thomas Sowell, a black economist, has been writing about successful inner-city schools for 20 years, starting with his first book, *Black Education: Myths and Tragedies*.[2] He rejects the notion of a "dumbed down" curriculum, "soft" courses, and "special courses" related to identity and ideology. He rejects the notion of culturally biased tests; rather, he contends they are realistic indicators of academic success and that children are learning. He rejects the notion of double standards and lowered standards under the guise of racial sensitivity and racial baiting among black students.

Writing before Johnny Cochran introduced the "race card," Sowell expects all teachers—both black and white—to be caring and competent and instill high academic standards, even if it means black students coming to the office to complain or make excuses. His overriding message is "there are no secrets," unless hard work is a secret. *Work* seems to be the only four-letter word that cannot be used in public today. Aside from hard work (and if I may add, good classroom discipline), "there is no emphasizing [one particular] educational theory" to what works but there are no lack of examples—past and present.[3] The fact is, although Sowell may deny it, the examples of success in poor and minority schools are few and far between. What we

1. Allan Meyerson, "Foreword," in Carter, *No Excuses,* p. 4. Although the report is uplifting and provides needed hope, the book and Heritage Foundation have been criticized by one reporter and editor for its political agenda and false impressions, false reporting of test scores, exclusion of students expected to score low in posttests, and misrepresentation of poverty schools (some which were middle class). The inference is if the school is all-black it must be poor, even if the homes, landscaping, and cars are well kept and somewhat expensive. "This 'blind spot' is typical of the way the data [were] rendered." The document is promoted around the country, showing positive test scores and positive profiles, despite the "wholesale cooking of the books." See George Schmidt, "No Excuses for No Excuses," *Phi Delta Kappan* (November 2001), pp. 194–195.

2. Thomas Sowell, *Black Education: Myths and Tragedies* (New York: McKay, 1972).

3. Thomas Sowell, "Minority Schools and The Politics of Education," *Imprintis* (January 1999), p. 4.

# Teaching Tips 8.1

## Indicators for Judging Effective Schools

Research indicates several common indicators of effective schools. The tips below are based on studies involving elementary and secondary schools. The indicators help establish precise parameters or yardsticks in establishing your own school profile.

### Elementary Schools

1. Scores on norm-referenced or standardized tests (reading/math scores)
2. Scores on criterion-referenced or school district (school) tests
3. Portfolios, writing samples, and other "subjective" measures
4. Valid measures of affective and social outcomes, such as self-concept, cooperative behavior, character development, and so on
5. Teacher and administrator opinions of student goal attainment
6. Opinions of students, parents, and community residents
7. Participation of students in extracurricular activities and participation of parents in school-community activities.*
8. Student awards and distinctions
9. Student attendance
10. Amount of reading material borrowed from media center or library
11. Quality of student performance in programs such as art, music, and drama
12. Community support and involvement in school programs

### Secondary Schools

1. Scores on norm-referenced or standardized tests (SAT/ACT scores)
2. Performance on minimum competency (or exit) tests
3. Student success in school; percent of students taking AP courses
4. Number and percent of students who go on to college or find employment
5. Teacher and administrator opinions of student goal attainment
6. Rates of student suspensions and other exclusions
7. Participation of students in extracurricular activities and intramural sports*
8. Student awards and distinctions
9. Student attendance
10. Student awards in academic, technical, or vocational competition
11. Quality of student performance in programs such as art, music, and drama
12. Awards for outstanding school programs

*Note:* *I subscribe to the view that competitive sports has nothing to do with school effectiveness. Actually, the focus should be on life-long sports and intramural games whereby the greatest number of students are required to participate. The so-called jocks, or top 5 to 10 percent of school ball players, should not dominate sports at the expense of the remaining student body. The school should not be a breeding ground for future "gladiators" or modern-day track stars, basketball players, and football players. I would put much more emphasis on swimming, biking, jogging, camping, fishing, tennis, golf, bowling, and similar sports.

need to do is to translate what we know works (common characteristics) to a larger scale and properly reward people (principals and teachers) for a job well done.

Instead of inner-city teachers being paid more money to attract quality, they are paid less money than suburban teachers—about 15 to 20 percent less in New York City than surrounding Nassau County suburbs, about 20 to 25 percent less in Chicago than adjacent Cook County suburbs. Furthermore, according to Arthur Wise, "we currently pay the same salary to qualified and unqualified teachers, a disincentive for individual teachers to prepare" and give their best efforts.[1] Why work hard when easier routes are available for the same compensation? Is everyone in education expected to be that idealistic and dedicated? If you want to ignore the economics of the situation, or if you think the answer to the last question is yes, you might as well live in "la la land."

The chain of events regarding salaries and qualifications has a greater negative impact with inner-city children than with suburban children, since the latter have better academic skills and support structures at home and therefore can learn on their own, even with unqualified or noncaring teachers. The fact is that effective teaching is more important in inner-city schools than elsewhere, and it is crucial if we are to build more effective school programs.[2] It also takes morale, a sense of collegiality and cooperation, for teachers to give their best efforts. The school must be a place where the leadership is perceived as fair, where good teachers are recognized and developed into better teachers, where inexperienced teachers and average teachers are mentored by experienced and above-average teachers, and where all teachers are treated as professionals and given extra support from their supervisors and administrators.

More effective schools is about more effective teaching. It means that we bring back our retired teachers as part-time mentors. It suggests that we pay "good" teachers more than "average" teachers, and that we think about allowing teachers and principals either to receive bonuses for merit or to negotiate salary and assignments, thus allowing the labor market to take its natural course, for the sake of professionalism and school success. It means that we break the "isolationist culture" that exists in most schools, and that people involved in teaching learn to listen and work with each other.

School people can influence children's development almost in the same way as competent parents. To be effective, schools need to create conditions and encourage teachers to relate cognitive and social development. Successful education starts at the early grade levels, builds on past and continuous experiences, and combines various

1. Arthur E. Wise, "Creating a High-Quality Teaching Force," *Educational Leadership* (January 2001), p. 20.

2. The fact is, however, 17 percent of New York City teachers are uncertified; that is, they have not yet passed a simple general knowledge test and teaching-skills test or they lack the necessary credits for a teacher license. These percentages compare to less than 5 percent who are uncertified in the remaining parts of the state. Even worse, 29 percent of minority teachers (blacks and Hispanics) are uncertified in New York City. See Carl Companile, "Racial Gap in Teacher Tests Brings Alarm," *New York Post* (March 31, 2002), p. 3. Comparable percentages exist for nearly every large city, such as Boston, Chicago, Dallas, Los Angeles, and Miami, and their respective states. See Allan Ornstein and Daniel U. Levine, *Foundations of Education*, 8th ed. (Boston: Houghton Mifflin, 2003).

domains of learning, not only cognitive. As James Comer puts it, we need a "pool of teachers and administrators who, in addition to having thorough knowledge of their discipline," they understand "how children develop generally and academically and how to support that development." (This is critical in high schools, where teachers are subject focused rather than student focused, and often ignore student developmental needs.)[1] Teachers must be able to engage parents of students and people in the community in ways that benefit student growth and development, and particularly their children's education. Providing vouchers, planning the curriculum, or imposing performance standards are infrastructure changes. (What Comer has been advocating is a *change in attitude.*) Teachers must become more professional and more collegial; likewise, they need to be adequately paid and recognized for their expertise and services.

Failure of programs and trendy policies—ranging from black English courses to credit for life experiences—must be rejected. Success is based on a positive attitude and hard work, and that is a matter of digging into one's mind and spirit, not someone else's pockets and not becoming a "welfare junkie" where there is an expectation of entitlement. Finally, it takes a partnership, what some observers call a "village" or a "school-community" of administrators, teachers, parents, and students to break the cycle of failure in low-income schools and low-income neighborhoods. It means that we all stop talking about blame, move forward with a positive and healthy attitude, and reflect on how we can improve our performance.

Probably the most important factor is the need for a strong principal with conviction, zeal, and a clear mission, who can stretch budgets and get more out of people than might be expected. Second, there is need for hard-working and dedicated teachers who expect students to learn. Next, parents must accept their responsibilities in providing support structures and a home environment that is conducive to proper socialization, personal growth, and learning. Finally, for students to achieve academic success, they must be held responsible for their actions, and accept that it takes self-control, self-reliance, no excuses, no laying blame on others, and no expectations of a free ride. It needs to be reemphasized that time on task, completing homework, review and practice, and studying are basic ingredients for academic success. This simply translates into Sowell's concept of *hard work,* or what Admiral Rickover, 50 years ago, and Thomas Edison, some 75 years ago, called *perspiration.*

Closing the book when the answers are not evident and watching television or shooting "hoops" all day with the "boys" is not the solution. The ghetto can provide only a limited supply of basketball super-stars, and a few others who use their bodies in lieu of their minds for earning a living. And, if you don't appreciate this honest talk, then keep in mind that it is the same one advanced by Jessie Jackson, John and Eunice Johnson, and Cornell West—three very different black voices. And if you don't know the Jacksons, the Johnsons, or West, then you lack the depth of knowledge to engage in this issue about the mind and body.[2]

1. James P. Comer, "Schools That Develop Children," *American Prospect* (April 23, 2001), pp. 30–35.
2. See Chapter 4, "Victimization or Defeatism," p. 217.

EPISODE *B*

## Race, Schools, and Society

Along with social class, the student characteristic that has been the subject of the most educational controversy and analysis is race, and the extent to which race (and sometimes ethnicity) is a function of differential school achievement and opportunities for schools. A number of reasons have been presented in the literature, since the 1950s, for why black students' achievement scores continue to lag considerably behind that of whites.

The conservative explanation includes a discussion of (1) *IQ* and the fact that as much as 80 percent of the variations in IQ can be explained by heredity; (2) *family instability* and related statistics dealing with female-headed households and its correlation with poverty, illegitimacy, fertility rates and teenage pregnancy, and welfare dependency; (3) *community problems and pathologies* involving juvenile delinquency, crime, and drugs, and the absence of a male model at home; (4) *black ideology*, which seeks a separate identity in opposition to "whiteness," criticizes black students who strive for good grades, and is obsessed with being "cool" in music, art, sports, attire, and general comfort—a form of subtle resistance and defiance against the dominant culture; and (5) an attack on *affirmative action*, which is seen as a form of quotas and reverse discrimination and leads to increased racial tensions.

Every one of these conservative explanations is viewed by blacks as an illustration of white resentment and racism. Despite the Constitution, the Civil War, and the Civil Rights Act, we are told by minority groups that racial discrimination is alive and well—institutionalized by the dominant society in its customs, norms, beliefs, and roles. Although there have been improvements in the last few decades, there are many racial issues that still need to be addressed—an argument that whites flatly reject and view as a "red herring," a strategy to make continuous demands on the larger society. Although the black community has hardly anything that approaches a monolithic view, most blacks view the difference in black-white education and economic outcomes as part of a political struggle that goes back to slavery. Hispanic American groups are more diverse, united only by an affinity toward language and the fact their performance in school is on the lower end of the bell curve. For the greater part, they do not feel oppressed with common historical grievances against white society. Although Hispanic Americans are concentrated in large cities and states, their common ethnic characters seem to be melting—like that of other immigrants—in pursuit of a place in American society.

On the other hand, a number of social scientists refer to *a deepening schism* among black families, a term originally used by the black economist Andrew Brimmer in a speech at Tuskegee University in 1970[1] and reintroduced by black educators such as

---

1. Andrew Brimmer, *The Deepening Schism*. Paper presented at Tuskegee University, Nashville, TN, April 1970.

Bark Landry and William Wilson in the mid-1980s.[1] While a growing, stable, successful black middle class is closing the gap on its white counterparts in term of education levels and income, there is also a growing, unstable, unsuccessful black underclass.

According to several studies of racial indicators, from the Moynihan Report in 1965[2] to the turn of the twenty-first century, there are either no or very slow catching-up projections for percentages of illegitimate births, female-headed families, children living with two parents, crime, and drugs—all which indicate a disintegrating family structure for lower-class blacks.[3] Although Moynihan focused on the breakdown of the black family and linked it to the abdication of the duties of black fathers, he went on to outline a "case for national action," which in many respects corresponds with policies that were later to be called "affirmative action." Nonetheless, as a white social scientist raising sensitive issues about the black family, he was unsparingly criticized for blaming the victim and being racist.

## The Conservative Perspective

The argument, first popularized by Moynihan, in the 1960s and 1970s[4] and further elaborated by both white social scientists (Nathan Glazer, Andrew Hacker, and Irving Kristol)[5] and black social scientists (Stanley Crouch, Stephen Carter, and Thomas Sowell) is that denial of black problems has become a successful strategy for liberals and blacks since the civil rights movement.[6] A literature of denial has steadily developed on the general theme that there is nothing wrong with black family arrangements. Whatever pathologies are admitted are seen as natural and as healthy adaptations to the history of subjugation and oppression.

Even more sensitive is that black student achievement scores continue to lag considerably behind the scores of their white counterparts in the same middle-class communities. "This is a tendency," writes one black social scientist, "documented across

1. Bart Landry, *The New Black Middle Class* (Berkeley: University of California Press, 1987); William J. Wilson, *The Truly Disadvantaged: The Inner City, the Underclass, and Public Policy* (Chicago: University of Chicago Press, 1987).

2. Daniel P. Moynihan, *The Negro Family: The Care for National Action* (Washington, DC: U.S. Government Printing Office, 1965).

3. Michael Flax, *Blacks and Whites: An Experiment in Racial Indicators* (Washington, DC: Urban Institute, 1971); Andrew Hacker, "American Apartheid," *New York Review of Books* (December 3, 1987), pp. 32–33; Hacker, *Two Nations* (New York: Ballantine, 1995); and Sarah Straveteig and Alyssa Wigton, *Key Findings by Race and Ethnicity* (Washington, DC: Urban Institute, 2001).

4. Daniel P. Moynihan, *Coping: On the Practice of Government* (New York: Random House, 1975); Moynihan, "Sources of Resistance to the Coleman Report," *Harvard Educational Review* (Winter 1968), pp. 23–36.

5. The 1960s and 1970s witnessed many liberal social scientists (e.g., Glazer, Hacker, and Kristol) labeled as *neoconservative*. In this connection, Norman Podhoretz, the editor of *Commentary Magazine* for some 20 years, wrote a memoir called *Breaking Ranks* in 1979, explaining his own intellectual and political conversion to conservatism.

6. See Thomas Sowell, "Minority Schools and the Politics of Education," *Imprintis* (January 1999), p. 4.

## TABLE 8.2
### SAT Scores by Race, 1987 and 1997

| Students | SAT Verbal | | SAT Mathematical | |
|---|---|---|---|---|
| | 1987 | 1997 | 1987 | 1997 |
| Average | 507 | 505 | 501 | 511 |
| White | 524 | 526 | 514 | 526 |
| Asian American | 479 | 496 | 541 | 560 |
| Black | 428 | 434 | 411 | 423 |
| Hispanic | 464 | 465 | 462 | 468 |
| American Indian | 471 | 483 | 463 | 477 |

*Note:* Scores range from 200 to 800 on each test; 501 to 511 is average.

*Source: Digest of Education Statistics 1998* (Washington, DC: U.S. Government Printing Office, 1998), Table 131, p. 146.

the country."[1] In the SAT, for example, the national average score is slightly over 500 for both the verbal and math test. For white students, compared to black students, the verbal score was 96 points higher in 1987 and 92 points higher 1997. In math, they were 103 points higher in 1987 and 1997. Hispanic Americans and American Indians also scored higher than black students in both SAT tests (see Table 8.2). All these differences in scores cannot be fully explained away by poverty, since black students in families with household incomes of $50,000 or more in 1995 averaged 489 points, and the national household income as well as white income was considerably less than $50,000.

The same pattern exists with the NAEP test scores (see Table 8.3), which, along with the SAT, are considered the best source of information on long-term achievement trends. Minorities have made substantial progress in narrowing test outcomes since the 1970s, but the gap between whites and blacks is discouraging, especially in math and science: Differences in proficiency are more than double in reading, 4½ times greater in math, and 6 times greater in science. The white-Hispanic gap is slightly narrower. Table 8.4 shows the racial/ethnic gap increases with the education levels of parents. In other words, "within-class" test-score gaps are evident in all class levels or measured by parents' education. However, the gap is wider among students with a parent who graduated from college than for students with parents who graduated high school or have less than a high school diploma.[2] Many black parents and teachers have decried the

1. John H. McWorter, "Why Black Students Lag Behind," *Wall Street Journal* (October 12, 2000), p. 14.

2. *Reaching the Top: A Report of the National Task Force on Minority High Achievement* (New York: College Board, 1999). I would venture to guess that black parents spend as much time or more time that white parents in educating their children to cope with racial and social problems created by life in America, whereas white parents can spend more time on education and social matters that are school related.

─────────────── TABLE *8.3* ───────────────

## Percentages of Twelfth-Grade Students within "Proficient" Achievement Ranges on the NAEP Tests, 1998

|                  | Reading | Math | Science |
|------------------|---------|------|---------|
| White            | 40      | 18   | 24      |
| Black            | 17      | 4    | 4       |
| Hispanic         | 24      | 6    | 6       |
| Asian            | 23      | 26   | 19      |
| Native American  | 24      | 3    | 10      |

*Source:* Adapted from *The Condition of Education 2001* (Washington, DC: U.S. Government Printing Office, 2001), Indicators 11–13, pp. 22-25. *Reaching the Top: A Report of the National Task Force on Minority High Achievement* (New York: The College Board, 1999), pp. 7, 9.

publication of these data, claiming the information leads to racial tensions within the schools and communities and unfairly continues the perception that blacks are dumb.

According to black social scientists from Franklin Frazier and Allison Davis in the 1940s, to present-day black social scientists such as Stephen Carter, John McWhorter, and Claude Steele, the problem is traceable less to present-day racism than to the legacy of past racism—an attitude that affects perceptions and behavior today. For example, Claude Steele contends that the way a person sees himself or her-

─────────────── TABLE *8.4* ───────────────

## Average Twelfth-Grade Reading Scores by Parental Education Levels, 1994

|                           | Less than High School | High School Graduate | College Graduate |
|---------------------------|-----------------------|----------------------|------------------|
| White                     | 274                   | 283                  | 302              |
| Black                     | 258                   | 258                  | 272              |
| Hispanic                  | 260                   | 265                  | 283              |
| White-Black Difference    | 16                    | 25                   | 30               |
| White-Hispanic Difference | 14                    | 17                   | 19               |

*Source:* Adapted from *The Condition of Education 2001* (Washington, DC: U.S. Government Printing Office, 2001), Indicators 11–13, pp. 22-25. *Reaching the Top: A Report of the National Task Force on Minority High Achievement* (New York: The College Board, 1999), pp. 7, 9.

self and how that person thinks other see him or her explains a self-defeating attitude generating when being tested. So-called hard parts of the test amplify frustration, build stress, and multiply doubts or just giving up.[1] Even worse, many blacks are haunted by the stereotype of black mental inferiority and anti-intellectualism, which can undermine achievement.[2] This inferiority complex is pounded into them by the dominant culture, the stereotypes promulgated in American novels and mass media, and in the publications of books about IQ, heredity, and scholastic achievement (the most influential of many being Herrnstein and Murray's *The Bell Curve*.)[3]

The fact that self-influenced, self-perpetuating feelings of black dumbness and black anti-intellectualism may be a factor in explaining why students of African and Caribbean backgrounds, who are subject to the same racism as black Americans, perform much closer to white achievement levels, even in poor schools.[4] Here we are, arguing the difference between class and culture; that is, over time (several generations), historical life experiences affect attitudes and behavior which becomes a part of culture, but it often is mistakenly lumped as part of class, since the latter can be easily identified and controlled in social science research by using income figures, welfare figures, and school lunch data.

Thomas Sowell puts it in a different way: The difference between black achievement and lack of achievement has more to do with solid academic preparation, hard work, a sense of confidence, and not turning one's mind inward or looking to blame others.[5] Hence, one's own attitude, expectations, and motivation count. This does not mean that history and social and political nuances are irrelevant. Rather, self-concept, self-identification, and self-determination have more to do with culture than class, more to do with motivation and personal achievement than social and political factors. The idea, then, is to shift responsibility to the individual, and not always refer to the social problems of society, or the cry of victimization and racism. The quicker minorities stop internalizing this attitude, the better off they will be and the less resentment of white students who feel they are not part of minorities' problems and who have to sweat and study because they have no entitlements. The idea is to follow the Nike commercial—"Just do it"—stop talking about the shadows of the dominant culture and stop making excuses.

Most blacks do not want to hear or deal with these subtleties, and merely conclude that the goal of racists "is not merely exclusion on the bases of race . . . , but to keep black people at the bottom arbitrarily and dictatorially," as they have done

1. For a brief overview of Claude Steele's research, see Clarence Page, "How a Poor Self-Image Can Stifle SAT Scores," *Chicago Tribune* (March 18, 2001).

2. John H. McWorter, *Losing the Race* (New York: Simon & Schuster, 2000); Sowell, *Black Education: Myths and Tragedies*.

3. Herrnstein and Murray, *The Bell Curve*.

4. McWorther, *Loosing the Race*; Thomas A. Sowell, *Race and Culture: Migrations and Culture* (New York: Basic Books, 1995).

5. Thomas A. Sowell, *Conquests and Cultures: An International History* (New York: Basic Books, 1998); Sowell, *Inside American Education: Knowledge and Decisions* (New York: HarperCollins, 1996); and Sowell, *Race and Culture*.

for centuries.[1] It is also argued that whites contribute to the problem because of their negative views about black achievement and the perception that minorities are unwelcome in predominately white schools and colleges. White teachers also contribute to the problem because of their lower expectations and tracking of black students. It is difficult quantify the overall negative impact of prejudice, but it is argued that the effect is real and it has both negative psychological and educational outcomes.[2]

For these and other reasons, blacks do not want to hear that they are ill served by racial quotas, either because they encourage special treatment or because as a group they cannot academically compete with whites. To maintain pressure on the political system, and the flow of government assistance, there is the black strategy as the perpetual victim: that all descendents of slavery are entitled to reparations—the last demand topping $4 trillion as compensation for past injustices their ancestors suffered.[3] (1) Were Africans involved in the slave trade traffic? (2) Were thousands of black Americans slave owners and free men? (3) Were many or most whites opposed to slavery? (4) Did most white ancestors immigrate to America after slavery was abolished? The answer is *yes, yes, yes,* and *yes.* But somehow these facts get lost behind successfully argued cases based on guilt by association or that appeal to some moral high ground.

## Black Subjects, White Social Scientists

The preceding analysis is threatening to black interests, and is one reason why blacks since W. E. B. Dubois's *The Negro Problem* (1903) to the present have rejected most social science theories and insist that the larger society persists in its own biased and self-serving accounts of the "black problem" (e.g., blacks depicted as "dumb," "shiftless," "pathological," and "violent") Kenneth Clark, a black psychologist who conducted the research for the plaintiffs in *Brown* v. *Board of Education,* claimed 35 years ago that there was "an invisible wall," erected by white society, those in power, "to confine those who have *no* power and to perpetuate their powerlessness"[4]—what others might refer to as *institutionalized racism.* White social scientists tend to focus on "objective dimensions" of urban ghettoes, emphasizing family breakdown and community pathologies while ignoring "subjective dimensions of resentment hostility, despair and apathy"[5] Similarly, they overlook the strengths of the black family and community.

The problems facing black families are not internal, as most white social scientists proclaim; rather, according to black social scientists, they are external and as-

1. Stokey Carmichael and Charles V. Hamilton, *Black Power: The Politics of Liberation,* 2nd ed. (New York: Random House, 1992), p. 47.

2. Geneva Gay, *Culturally Responsive Teaching* (New York: Teachers College Press, 2000); William G. Howell and Paul E. Peterson, *The Educational Gap* (Washington, DC: Brookings Institute, 2002); and Jeannie Oakes et al., *Becoming Good American Schools* (San Francisco: Josey-Bass, 1999).

3. "The Children of Slavery," *Economist* (December 23, 2000), p. 31.

4. Kenneth B. Clark, *Dark Ghetto: Dilemmas of Social Power* (New York: Harper and Row, 1965), p. 11.

5. Ibid.

sociated with the aftermath of slavery[1] and the continuous materialism and racism that emanate from the dominant society.[2] The reason black families have fared so much worse than white families in social science is that the subjects are black and the social scientists are white, and the latter have been victimized by their own white and western biases. Differences between blacks and whites are considered as deviations from the acceptable white norm; and, until recently, all nonwhite cultures have been regarded as subject to assimilation.[3]

The black family has many positive characteristics, among them (1) strong kinship bonds and family cooperation; (2) an attitude of self-help and the ability to cope with the "system"; (3) flexible family roles and confident females who can function as the heads of the families; (4) a strong work orientation; and (5) a strong religious orientation, especially in its role as a community organization and part of the civil rights movement.[4] (I would also venture to guess that black music, especially gospel and the blues, has helped blacks as an underclass group cope with their oppressive conditions and keep them together as a cohesive, functioning people.) Why black students fare so poorly in school has little to do with family arrangements, feelings of academics inferiority, lack of IQ, or academic ability—what is wrong is a "sick," racist school and society. Whites do not want to hear this kind of music, so the record needs to be played louder and more often, with the hope that if the message is heard enough times, some of the words will sink in and it will be a better world for blacks.

## The Racial Divide

The racial divide between blacks and whites is rooted in nearly 350 years of history,[5] and best described by de Tocqueville before the Civil War (which he predicted in 1834 would become a "revolution") in 1834 and by Gunnar Mydal (which he called the

1. James A. Anderson, *The Education of Blacks in the South: 1860–1935* (Chapel Hill: University of North Carolina Press, 1938); Virgil A. Clift, ed., *Negro Education in America* (New York: Harper and Row, 1962); and E. Franklin Frazier, *The Negro Family in the United States* (Chicago: University of Chicago Press, 1939).

2. Henry T. Frierson, "The Situation of Black Educational Researchers: Continuation of a Crisis," *Educational Researcher* (March 1990), pp. 12–17; Lee Rainwater and William L. Yancey, *The Moynihan Report and the Politics of Controversy* (Cambridge, MA: MIT Press, 1967); and Cornell West, *Race Matters* (New York: Random House, 1994).

3. Carmichael and Hamilton, *Black Power;* Joyce A. Ladner, ed., *The Death of White Sociology* (New York: Random House, 1973); and Michael Young, "Interrogating Whiteness," *Educational Researcher* (March 2000), pp. 39–44.

4. Andrew Billingsley, *Black Families in White America* (Englewood Cliffs, NJ: Prentice-Hall, 1968); James Blackwell, *The Black Community: Diversity and Unity* (New York: Dodd, Mead, 1975); and Robert B. Hill, *The Black Family: Essays and Studies* (Belmont, CA: Wadsworth, 1971).

5. The first slave ship arrived on American shores in 1619. Some black churches refer to the "Maafa Remembrance," meaning the unspeakable horrors of the trans-Atlantic slave trade, and others have new stained glass that depict Christ as a ship and African figures in biblical art. It is a way of helping young blacks deal with their slave past in a religious way.

"American dilemma") 110 years later. It is easy for whites, as the dominant group with most of the economic assets and educational capital, to say, "The past is behind us; let's move on as Americans." Now, a few blacks might say, "That sounds like a healthy, positive attitude." But for most blacks, a comment such as this is equivalent to skipping down the yellow brick road, hand in hand as one happy family, or singing *The circle of life* while listening to the Lion King pontificate some fairytale or fable.

No matter what whites do, the "race card" (claims of white racism) is used periodically by blacks, depending on the circumstances and the individuals involved. Whites are accused of not fully understanding black suffering and black ideology. Experience with the dominant power structure has hardened blacks' suspicions and resistance, even though racism today is much more subtle than the use of police dogs and the burning of crosses and churches.

The Ku Klux Klan is lodged in the cellar, today, under different Aryan-sounding names and slogans, but the aging black leadership (and some of our older colleagues in schools) remember the turbulent years of the civil rights movement. One doesn't have to be a genius to understand the tangled threads of culpability, how the law was used by big business and politically influential power brokers to keep blacks (as well as other immigrants) down, how there was a thin line between law enforcers and the Klan, between the rules of law and bigotry.[1] Eugene (better known as "Bull") Connor, and his Klan-based sympathizers dressed in blue may have played into the hands of the Reverend Martin Luther King Jr. and his marchers, but he was not the original organizer of the marches in Alabama. Although it was King who received most of the media attention and credit, the early lunch-counter sit-ins, boycotts, and marches were mainly organized by Ella Baker, an ex-NAACP organizer, and JoAnn Robinson, a professor at Alabama State University. They were cast aside by the male-dominated Southern Universities leadership Conference, and the sexist beliefs (keep the women behind the scenes to assist the male leader) that were typical of the period.[2]

King and other integrationists had to deal with more than the likes of working-class and low-end public officials who were overt racists. There was the power structure, epitomized by President Nixon's search for two Supreme Court judges in 1971. Nixon told John Mitchell that he wanted someone from the South, to capture its growing conservative vote in the next election. Beyond that, he had two criteria: "First, I don't want the man to be a racist. . . . But, you know I don't want a fellow who is going to go hog wild with integration, de facto segregation."[3] Overlooking the gender factor operating during this period, it was the go-slow attitude at the highest level of government that characterized (and still does) the nation's sentiment among the vast majority of whites—and why it took 25 or more years to integrate southern schools.

---

1. The most detailed and recent description of Birmingham revisited and the civil rights movement is by Diane McWhorter, *Birmingham, Alabama: The Climatic Battle of the Civil Rights Movement* (New York: Simon & Schuster, 2001).

2. Lynn Olson, *Freedom's Daughters: The Unsung Heroines of the Civil Rights Movement from 1830 to 1970* (New York: Scribner, 2000).

3. John W. Dean, *The Rehnquist Choice* (New York: Free Press, 2001).

## The Agony of History

Being on the wrong side of the so-called third revolution, southern whites, for the last 40 years, have been forced to confront themselves, to look into the mirror, and to analyze and reanalyze their past and present. This never happened in the North, especially among whites who were divorced from or indifferent toward the civil rights movement. The slave ships, the lynching and bombings, police brutality, and Jim Crow laws are not part of the personal and social history of the vast majority of whites, especially outside of the South. Hence, the archives and memoirs, poems, paintings, and songs—in short, the feelings, thoughts, and images—of black artists, writers, and poets are very different from the white world. Black images and words require a different unity of purpose and effect. It means narrating the daily life in the black community, past and present, balancing personal expression with social conscience and commitment, and balancing human tragedy and sadness with human aspirations and hope. It is a different theme, a different voice, a different metaphor, a different ideology than the art and narrative of the larger society.

Black social history, literature, and art are most likely going to feature slave life; the Underground Railroad; the 54th Massachusetts Regiment and the Tuskagee Flying Tigers; the Harlem Renaissance, the boycotts and marches of the 1950s and 1960s with stories of Martin and Malcolm, and possibly Rosa Parks, Phillip Randolph, Bayard Rustin, the spiritual songs of Herbert Brewster, Rosetta Thorpe, and James Cleveland, and the Delta Blues music of T. B. Walker, Sonny Boy Williamson, and Jimmy Reed; legendary boxers Jack Johnson and Muhammad Ali[1]; and the personal and abstract expressions of Richard Wright, Langston Hughes, and Jacob Lawrence. I am talking about major events and personalities of black society, but for many whites, I might as well be talking gobbledygook—and that is part of the problem. Of course, it is a tragedy when blacks don't fully understand their own writers and artists, especially in an era of identity politics and the notions of brotherhood, sisterhood, and solidarity.

Historically, most black artists, novelists, and poets lived in the shadow of their own melancholy, trying to free themselves from the constraints of white society and their own turbulent lives, confronting their oppressors sometimes obliquely and sometimes with

---

1. Both Johnson and Ali were the best boxers of their respective eras. They were arrogant, charismatic, and innately intelligent. Both men enjoyed fancy clothes, fast cars, and fast women, especially white women. Both waged a battle with America in the ring and in the courts, with the help of the media; in the public arena, it became a war of words. Their lifestyles, combined with their combative attitudes, threatened the white establishment. As a result, Johnson and Ali served jail sentences for questionable reasons—Johnson for crossing state lines with an unmarried women and having sex, and Ali for refusal to be indicated into the U.S. Army.

As boxers, both men had no equal during their lengthy reigns, as they effortlessly dispatched opponent after opponent. But both men fought beyond their prime and were defeated by lesser boxers. During their prime, however, they completely controlled all aspects of a fight, underlined with symbolic meaning for blacks as it related to society as a whole. Johnson and Ali must be remembered in context with black identity, black ideology, and black power.

rage, and retelling episodes and events from their lives and community in undertones. For some, it was a fine line between realism and absurdity, not because of a personal flaw but rather because of the inescapable harsh conditions imposed on blacks. For centuries, blacks had to wear masks and disguises, dance to someone else's tune, and often become tricksters, jive artists, informers, and hustlers in order to survive.

Given the context of the times, radio characters Amos and Andy were only trying to survive, and later James Baldwin, Elridge Cleaver, and Malcolm X were basically reacting and acting out their resentment and hostility toward white America, which forced the Uncle Tom image on blacks. One must understand that the political ideas of blacks are rooted in (1) W. E. B. DuBois, who challenged not only the traditions of racial segregation and the Uncle Tom stereotype but also the accommodationist ideology of Booker T. Washington, and (2) Richard Wright, who dramatized black life "as he knew it and lived it," gave his focus to feelings rather than to facts, and made it clear how words can be used for protest. Indeed, most black literature is protest.[1]

In the same context, O. J. Simpson was a hero because he beat the white system that for centuries had beaten down blacks. And although there is some diversity in the response of blacks, for the most part Rodney King is not a two-bit criminal but a hero, refusing to succumb to the Uncle Tom myth; the beast is the white police force and it is the battered body of King who represented the image of a black Christ and produced the Los Angeles riots. Both Simpson and King were symbolic of the existing racial divide between blacks and whites, rooted in slavery and based today on moral melodrama and the need to redress history.

In the post–civil rights era, the character of black victims and white villains is often oversimplified and sometimes considered too provocative for most whites to digest and accept. "White"-produced images such those in *Uncle Tom's Cabin, The Jazz Singer, Gone with the Wind, Red Badge of Courage,* and *Roots* permitted the white community to reflect and face moral issues. The more forceful words of Baldwin, Brooks, Ellison, and Hughes were acceptable to white liberals who could appreciate and interpret rougher and more realistic polemics. Black writers offered these people a means for understanding, forgiveness, and redemption—a way to cleanse their souls and transform their consciences and guilt at a time when such ideas were in vogue. It was a period when white liberals seemed to enjoy being verbally assaulted by black intellectuals, both at college campuses and at cocktail parties—perhaps a way of identifying with the downtrodden and victims of society. One observer contends that black intellectuals such as Baldwin made white liberals feel both sad and enlightened by these new insights—and they grew to like it.[2] I would venture to guess that many of them, including white females, were a little masochistic and had to show that they were the "Great White Hope" and could identify with black suffering by suffering themselves.

1. W. E. B. DuBois, *Dusk of Dawn* (New York: Schocken Books, 1940); Richard Wright, *Black Power* (New York: Harper and Row, 1954); and Wright, *Native Son* (New York: Harper and Row, 1940).

2. Carol Polsgrove, *Divided Minds: Intellectuals and the Civil Rights Movement* (New York: W. W. Norton, 2001).

Moving beyond Baldwin, Brooks, Ellison, and Hughes, there is now August Wilson, who has written eight plays (six which have made Broadway or off-Broadway), the most noted being *Jitney,* about the life of black gypsy cabdrivers. Wilson is positive, not negative; hopeful, not threatening to his white audience. He writes about black uniqueness, social history, and richness of human life. He writes as a black man first, a playwright second, with a mission to elevate black culture to equal its white counterpart. Wilson tells us that he uses music, speech, gestures, eating habits, social discourse, religious beliefs, sexual attitudes, and concepts of pain and loss, truth and justice, to promote and propagate black history and culture.[1]

Wilson purposely avoids writing about black pathologies, choosing rather to highlight the celebrated aspects, rituals, customs, and codes of conduct of black life. The characters in his plays believe in the American dream, and they constantly fight for the high ground, to improve their status. By doing so, they affirm the value and worth of themselves in the face of those who would prefer to keep them down and deny them access to a productive life and to rig the system with a set of customs and laws that produce hardships and injustices.

Both the novel and the theater are powerful conveyors of human values and human spirit, and they have often depicted racial and social inequities. The sources of language and drama provide us with a mirror to examine our moral and social values, and to gain new insights into aspects of society that keep us apart and/or produce stereotypes, hatred, and injustices. Whereas Henrik Ibsen was my favorite social critic and playwright when I was a college student, Wilson is my favorite social messenger today—making me think and rethink black-white relations. Sadly, for every college student (black or white) who is familiar with Wilson, I suspect 1,000 others read *Playboy* or *Vogue.* I fear, too, that the vast majority of teachers are racking their brains and twisting their tongues in some uncomprehending way, trying to figure out who August Wilson is. I straddle the border, fifty-fifty, on whether they have ever read Ibsen. The profession of teaching simply suffers from an army of poorly educated teachers, lacking a liberal arts education, who would rather have Oprah Winfrey or Katie Roiphe tell them what to read. Let me set the record straight: Wilson is worth reading; obviously, so is Ibsen.

Today, there is the tone and message of "intermediate explainers"—such as Eric Dyson, Jesse Jackson, John Ogbu, and Cornel West—where the "race card" is constantly played out and whites are repeatedly vilified. These mix of words separates blacks and whites and leads to as much white enlightenment as resentment, to as much social remediation as the stirring up of our tangled racial history. These explainers, according to supporters, would argue, however, that strong words are needed to illustrate the "pathology" of race and poverty—and for the enlightenment of the indifferent.[2] Still, rhetoric and reality between blacks and whites is much less today than it was during the early civil rights era. In short, progress has been made.

1. August Wilson, "Sailing the Stream of Black Culture," *New York Times* (April 23, 2000), Sect. 2, pp. 1, 36.

2. Adolph Reed, *Class Notes: Posing as Politics and Other Thoughts on the American Scene* (New York: New Press, 2001).

## Smiling Faces, Divided Minds

For centuries, the Jews in Europe had to endure under more oppressive conditions than blacks both in the ancient and modern world. The Jews and blacks were treated as subhuman by those who held the sword or whip, and even by members of polite society. Both groups have criss-crossed the world and have lived in ghettoes and have been victims of genocide. Members of both groups have been willing to surrender their identities, give up their families, deny their heritages, and to assimilate or "pass" and thus avoid the yoke of tyranny.

The movie *Sunshine* best describes the Jewish story over four generations in Hungry; despite all their achievements in business, law, military, and athletics, and despite their willingness to play by the rules of the dominant group and even to convert, they are never fully accepted. The black experience in America is best described by Ralph Ellison's *Invisible Man* (1947): the black man's inability to be accepted by whites and his continuous involvement in racial problems while at the same time trying to live a normal life where these problems are not allowed to invade every aspect of his life. It is also keenly described by Charles Himes's *The Third Generation* (1954), about a defeated father, an Uncle Tom derived from his inherited slave mentality, reduced to menial jobs; and his mother, on the brink of madness, confiding to strangers in white restaurants, "I destroyed my life by marrying a Negro."

All of these passages are merely snapshots, quick glossies, viewed from a safe distance, and read in the comfort of the reader's home. It is hard for most people to fully grasp the poisonous combination of anti-Semitism—centuries of religious persecution with the Vatican's silence or approval[1] and with government laws and programs that justify and promote it, and that end in the chambers of horror at Auschwitz. Likewise, it is nearly impossible for whites to fully understand the grinding effect of racism, also condoned by centuries of law, how it effects the mind and body, and how it builds resentment, frustration, and anger.

As educators, we are forced to rely on our own life experiences and the pitfalls of our generalizations and stereotypes in order to deal with the complexities and nuances of religion or race—people trying to live normal lives but always feeling under attack or potential attack. Once in a while, and only for a while, an "outsider" is allowed privileged and intimate entry into the lives of Jewish or black people. Since it is nearly impossible to be color blind and to erase the color line, race is a much more powerful factor in American society. The outcome is that it enables blacks to require whites to prove themselves by passing a litmus test for enlightenment, sensitivity, and sometimes ideological responsibility.

One must understand the contradictory nature of American society. With hundreds of hate groups existing under various Aryan and far-right conservative names, currently clicking their slogans and recruiting on the Internet, Jews and blacks are reminded of their inherited identities. By the time one adds up the score card, there are as many similarities as differences between the KKK and the S.S. Both had the law on their side and both organizations recruited good family men and church-goers. The

---

1. In the year 2000, Pope John Paul II apologized for 2,000 years of religious persecution.

vast majority of these men were not fanatics, deviants, adventurers, drug addicts, maniacs, sadists, or womanizers; they were recruited from working-class and middle-class society, and fit into normal society.[1] The S.S. was more ruthless, only because there was no morality left in Germany. The KKK did not have federal law on its side.

The South had U.S. Steel to keep southern blacks from organizing and joining unions, and the Nazis had the cooperation of IBM to provide print-out cards and machines to track down Jews in Europe and to ensure that the trains ran on time between fronts, from one city to another, and from cities to concentration camps.[2] Of course, no one cared to know how much cancer may have been caused by U.S. Steel's pollution, and no one has ever tried to calculate how many allied and civilian lives were lost because of IBM's profit-seeking technology that micro-managed German military and police operations. No one really cares, except maybe blacks or Jews, so the mainstream thinking is to write it off as rhetoric, hype, and exaggeration.

Another line of thought is to say that many other corporations have polluted the environment and discouraged unionization, and many other corporations and banks financially benefited from World War II and the Nazi war machine; moreover, there is no direct evidence that IBM consciously participated in crimes against humanity. Perhaps they looked the other way, but so did Chase Manhattan Bank, General Motors, and President Roosevelt, who failed to order the bombing of the railroad lines leading to the death camps and failed to provide asylum to a boat with several hundred Jewish immigrants and sent them back to Nazi Germany to die.

Although I am fighting anonymity, amnesia, and poor historical memories, there is no escaping from these stories. American Armenians have horrific stories to tell that date back 100 years. The Russians and Chinese have their ugly stories that date back to World War II and prior years, and the Croatians and Albanians have the most recent heart-breaking stories. Except perhaps for one or two pages about Nazi Germany, and one or two paragraphs about the recent destruction of Yugoslavia in some current history book, American teachers and textbooks rarely discuss these historical convulsions. We tend to forget or skim over these kind of events, especially if we were not victims or if we benefit from the luxury of late birth and geographical distance. Nonetheless, Europe and Asia are full of vile deeds and crimes committed by people—we have just ended the most ruthless and cruel century of history (because it had the most efficient armies, machines, and fanatics to kill the most people in the least amount of time).

Most Americans don't fully understand these stories, and to that extent we are all fortunate. We were never touched by such horrific events until 9-11. The bad news is that the World Trade Center is "small stuff" compared to what other countries have suffered and compared to future potential attacks; however, these recent events represent a turning point in our history and feeling of security.[1] Because foreign invaders

1. Lotte Kohler, ed., *Within Four Walls: The Correspondence between Hannah Arendt and Heinrich Blucher, 1936–1968* (New York: Harcourt, 2000); McWhorter, *Birmingham, Alabama.*

2. Edwin Black, *IBM and the Holocaust* (New York: Crown Publishers, 2001); McWhorter, *Birmingham, Alabama.*

have not arrived on our shores in our lifetimes (the last time was 1812), we have had the ability to examine these horrific stories as a "phenomenon of totalitarianism" or as so-called moral dilemmas (not as personal or life experiences involving plunder, rape, mass murder, ethnic cleansing or extermination). Although civilians have often been in the front lines, as causalities of war, Americans have had the oceans to protect us so that we can examine the facts of war in a "cool" and "objective" manner. These days, however, the war is happening at home, a major reversal that may not yet affect students in Montana or Nebraska who still feel insulated by geography and

1. Recent events, nightmarish as they seem, should perhaps be offered as a chance to understand the dangers of the world. There is enough anthrax produced in the world to kill every person on the planet ten times. One gallon of dried anthrax can wipe out our entire country. See William J. Broad, "Preparing America for the Reality of Germ Warfare," *New York Times* (October 21, 2001), Sect. 4, p. 4. Such a sobering thought can overshadow daily life and humdrum counseling programs.

Think of an act of war. A torpedo is fired, and a ship is sunk—1,000 sailors die. That sounds like a normal battle. Now think of an act of terrorism. A bomb-laden box containing anthrax arrives at a mail center or is placed in a suitcase on an airplane. The box explodes. There is nothing more to say. The world we know has just ended!

Sounds too extreme? How about a scenario straight out of the American intelligence community, originally considered top secret in 1958, at the height of the Cold War with the Soviet Union, and published in 1998 as *The Doomsday Scenario* by Douglas Keeny: The U.S.S.R. is capable of delivering weapons of mass destruction "anywhere in the United States," with TNT of millions of tons, as well as with "biological or chemical agents, and incendiary and high explosive" capabilities. Besides using aircraft or submarines, "clandestine [weapons] may be detonated without warning." It is possible to smuggle nuclear devices into the United States, place them in specific locations, and then control their firing.

Surface bursts would result in "widespread radioactive fallout," forcing Americans to take shelter for considerable periods of time and resulting in the death of "almost one out of five." Such an attack will cause a complete breakdown of the existing economic and political system. More workers will be involved in "disposing of the dead," taking care of survivors, and "cleaning up bombed areas" than producing goods or other services. All major infrastructure systems—including bridges, roads, tunnels, and municipal buildings—will either be impaired in peripheral areas or nonfunctioning in hard-hit areas. See "Blast from the Past: A Cold War Vision of a Nuclear Nightmare," *New York Times* (March 31, 2002), Sect. 4, p. 14.

The long and short of this scenario is that suicidal bombing in Israel is not only the Israelis' problem. If they fail in dealing with terrorism in their borders, there is no guarantee that it will not soon become a weapon that threatens our borders. A test is taking shape in the Middle East: Can terrorist attacks (whereby terrorists strap on nuclear devices and threaten an entire city or nation) on civilian populations topple a nation or cause it to cave in and accept absurd demands? Don't think it can't happen here. See Chapter 7, p. 412.

Teachers have no stomach to deal with these issues because of political correctness and fear of mislabeling or stereotyping a segment of the Arab or Muslim population as *terrorists*. Although the roots of terrorism can be defined and described in terms of political, cultural, nationalistic, religious, or military terms, there is a danger in ignoring or downplaying that it has serious implications for this country. At the very least, it is time to revise our world history textbooks and classroom discussions, and prepare America and the western world for a potential increase in terrorism and suicide bombing.

who feel different from someone living in New York or Washington, D.C., or along the East or West coasts. To some extent, though, the people from Montana and Nebraska have become New Yorkers by construing the Twin Towers as an assault on the United States.

In this country, European or Asian ethnic differences rarely influence classroom or school settings. However, black-white differences in historical and cultural perspectives spill over into inner-city classrooms and schools: White teachers are sometimes told they will never be fully qualified to teach black children, for they can never fully appreciate "blackness" and "black consciousness." This has little to do with professional or academic qualifications; it deals with the mind, the heart, the soul—the difference in feelings, attitudes, history, and culture. It is a different type of "race card" that enables liberal and minority groups to attend overrespectability for the need for black teachers in black schools.

In a way, this argument is like claiming you have to be French to teach French, Chinese to teach Far Eastern history, or Indian to teach about the Hindu religion. It suggests that a man cannot teach women's studies, and that a white English teacher is on very thin ice teaching about James Baldwin, Gwendolyn Brooks, or Toni Morrison. It also means that American teachers cannot or should not teach *Poetry* by Lao-Tzu, *Paradise of the Blind* by Duang thu Huong, or *Two Shores* by Carlos Fuentes. In simple terms, it means the vast majority of us are unable to fully understand or appreciate movies such as *The Joy Luck Club* or *Crouching Tiger* (an adaptation of the 1930s Chinese *Wuxia* novel by Wang Du Lu) or the music of Tan Dun and Chen Yi, who are prominent international composers. Based on logic, these are silly arguments, but logic is not the crucial ingredient; it is emotions, feelings, personal memories, and historical travesty that sometimes propel our thoughts and rhetoric.

The notion of blackness, black consciences, and black culture is a splinter theme from the original strategy of understandably blaming whites for the persistence of black problems, and continually raising the issue of victimization. The outcome of this dilemma is that no matter what statistics are used to show steady *improvement* (e.g., narrowing economic differences) or persistent *gaps* (e.g., standardized test scores), a critical mass of blacks will not be satisfied with the reasons and will point to the white society as the culprit. On the other hand, most whites feel they are being blamed or penalized for nothing they did, and they see themselves and their ancestors as immigrants who had to overcome their own ethnic, religious and economic difficulties.

## A Me-Too, Knee-Jerk Demand

Whereas the aim of the civil rights movement had always been to eliminate color consciousness from the law, to make it color blind, as the liberal movement became radicalized and as the integrationist movement transformed to black power in the 1960s and 1970s, the racial divide increased. By the mid-1970s, there was pressure to consider race in the law and in making decisions about who gets what job or into what college. This emphasis on race politicized other groups who perceived themselves as a political minority (that is, being historically discriminated against)—first Native Americans, Asian Americans, Hispanic Americans, and women, then other ethnic groups, later the disabled, and now homosexuals—all seeking special classifications and special treatment. Traditional notions of equality, meritocracy, and fairness have evaporated, as groups vie for educational and occupational advantages and a larger share of the economic pie.[1]

The irony of this ideology is middle-class parents telling the schools that their children are learning disabled and therefore qualify to take all standardized tests (including college admission tests) untimed—anything for a edge in our competitive society.[2] In Winnetka, Illinois, 10 percent of high school students are classified as learning disabled (the average expenditure was $14,400 per student for 2000–01); in Greenwich, Connecticut (a comparable suburb in terms of education spending), it was 19.8 percent. In Great Neck, New York, where student spending averaged $18,700, as many as 12 percent were classified as learning disabled. And the Dalton School in midtown Manhattan (which costs $22,500 per year) had 15 percent of its secondary students classified as having learning problems.[3] At the national level, about 5 to 6 percent of the total school population are labeled "learning disabled," representing about half the special education population. About 80 percent of the disabled have deficits in basic skills of dyslexia or hyperactivities.[4] The remaining are suspect, or at least they may be defined as disabled in one school district, but not in another.

The fact that the "learning disabled" category is overused is a minor criticism compared to the expenses in special education programs, which cost two or more times the amount of the traditional programs, depending on the need and school district. Even worse is the rising tide of litigation as parents battle with schools to get their children additional support and special treatment. In my time, where I was in

1. This kind of war, which has been going on since the civil rights movement, encapsulates a good deal of academic time and controversy. To put things into perspective, there is a new frontline: The stakes are higher and should make us pause and stop bickering over racial policies. The new trenches are in mailrooms, subways, bridges, nuclear utility sites, and airport terminals. We have all become one family, one nation, indivisible.

2. In 2001, the Educational Testing Service (ETS) announced it would no longer note the extra time provided for students with disabilities on the GRE and PRAXIS test scores for prospective candidates sent to colleges and universities. This is bound to affect the SAT, the merit scholarship test, and the advanced placement exam, which are administered by ETS but owned by the College Board.

3. Telephone conversations with Hank Bangser, Superintendent of New Trier High School, Winnetka, IL, April 18, 2001; Francine Sugar, Director of Program Development, Dalton School, NY, April 19, 2001; Kim Eves, Public School Information Officer, Darien, CT, April 19, 2001; Jessica Vega, Public School Information Officer, Great Neck Public Schools, NY, April 19, 2001.

In an article published in the *New York Times*, November 14, 2000, Arthur Levine, president of Teachers College, Columbia University, claimed that 36 percent of Dalton kindergartners were classified with learning problems. Francine Sugar claimed the figure was inaccurate, bordering on silliness, and that the placement data had been misinterpreted and also based on outdated information published about 10 years ago in the *Times*.

4. Rick Allen, "Learning Disabilities: At the Assessment Crossroads," *Curriculum Update* (Fall 2000), pp. 1–8.

high school and college, it was a stigma to be categorized as learning disabled. Times change, and given our competitive society, this new trend goes hand in hand with other middle-class parents holding back their children at the first grade to allow them to better develop cognitively and socially so they will have an edge over their peers. In the South and Southwest, the reason for holding back boys is to better develop physically so they can outplay their classmates and become football or baseball stars. Indeed, Americans are obsessed with winning.

Actually, the sweep of high-stakes tests across the country has run into opposition from parents who worry that their children do not test well and may not get into their first college choice, as well as from advocates of special education and disabled students, limited-English speaking, and black and Hispanic children who traditionally do not test well.[1] Approximately 35 to 40 percent of the nation's students are looking for various test accommodations—ranging from spell-check software, reading aloud reading comprehension tests, having unlimited testing time, and excluding themselves from taking tests.

The outcome is to artificially inflate test scores, give students an incentive to claim questionable handicaps, and penalize regular students who play by the normal rules. This goes hand in hand with many teachers and administrators caught violating test rules, helping students, and cheating (rescoring or omitting tests)—all of which may be the tip of the iceberg, given the testing and accountability movement taking shape in the nation's schools.[2] You don't have to be a Texan school teacher to understand that test scores, as the sole measure of student achievement, don't always tell the full story.[3] Any school district that makes dramatic gains overnight on statewide or NAEP tests is now suspect and rightfully so, unless you believe in magic pills, mystical illusions, or *pyogicra* (an Asian religion with emphasis on the mind and the ability to alter reality).

Further, an indication that racial quotas and group preferences have become a spoil system is the growing number of Italian Americans who have surnames that can pass for Hispanic, thereby successfully pursuing minority set-asides; Hawaiians who classify themselves as Asian-Pacific (who are sometimes entitled to favorable treatment) or Native Americans (to avoid being lumped into an Asian pool that sometimes does not receive special treatment); and reform educators who reprimand Hispanic parents who do not want their children to participate in bilingual maintenance programs.

John Leo, a veteran columnist for the *U.S. World News and Report*, confronts political correctness and diversity gone astray with a journalistic style rather than a social science eye. In *Incorrect Thoughts*, he provides his readers with a sad account of a Filipino high school student in Los Angeles who is reprimanded by school officials because he checked off "American" on an education form as his ethnicity. The

1. Daniel Golden, "Disabled Students Gain More Aid on Test," *Wall Street Journal* (February 1, 2001), p. 14.

2. Chris Pipho, "The Sting of High-Sakes Testing and Accountability," *Phi Delta Kappan* (May 2000), pp. 645–646.

3. See Kathy Christie, "Oh, No! Not Texas Again," *Phi Delta Kappan* (November 2001), pp. 5–6; Klein et al., "What Do Test Scores in Texas Tell Us?" Also see p. 453.

student is chastised again when, asked to bring his favorite family food, he showed up with a hamburger rather than some "native" cuisine.[1] The boy misunderstood the notions of political correctness and the politics of diversity; he had to be "educated." He could not be an "American," which, for many of us still stuck in the pre-1960s and believing in the concepts of the "melting pot," seems absurd. He had to stick to the ethnic category and party line, to project a sense of victimization so as to be entitled to special treatment.

In a another column, John Leo reports that political correctness has reached crazy proportions. Women in Europe and Australia have a new cause: They want men to sit down while urinating. It has little to do with the "splash" factor, but rather to keep them from standing up and asserting their masculinity—and, by extension, putting women in a degrading position. Standing up, we are now told, lends itself to a "nasty macho gesture," also suggesting male oneupmanship and male violence. There is a feminist movement to remove urinals from schools and colleges in parts of western Europe.[2]

Along these lines, another twist is the recent publication by Bandanna Books, which put out a revised edition of Walt Whitman's poetry with *he* and *him* changed to the unisex terms *hu* and *hum*. In the same vein, the editors of this book have changed *mankind* to *humankind* and *he* to *he or she*—all in the name of sexual neutrality. In the same way, *fat* boys are now *heavy* or *overweight* adolescents, and the *old man* is now the elderly *person*.[3]

Back at home, the University of California–Los Angeles in 2001 had a separate Lavender graduation, Raza graduation for Hispanics, as well as Asian American, African American, Iranian, and American Native graduations. Since the latter group was here earlier than other groups, their graduation was one day earlier than the other ones. Detecting possible criticism that the university was promoting the "balkinization" of the student groups, the administration referred to these events as "celebrations."[4]

Moving beyond the Leo perspective, most educators and social critics are quick to wave the banner of diversity. They fail to recognize that all minorities are redefining themselves in multiple ways. In the 2000 census, for example, 20 percent of blacks under age 30 classified themselves in more than one racial group, and because someone answering the survey could have listed anywhere from one to six races, there are now a total of 63 different racial classifications.[5] Certainly, Hispanic and Asian minorities are each united by language, but they include people on vastly different tracks, some already successful and some mired in the economic underclass. The sheer concentration of Hispanics in major states such as California, Arizona, Texas,

1. John Leo, *Incorrect Thoughts: Notes on Our Wayward Culture* (New Brunswick, NJ: Transaction, 2001).

2. John Leo, "You Can't Make This Up," *U.S. News and World Report* (August 21, 2000), p. 14.

3. See John Leo, "Heck Hath No Fury," *U.S. News and World Report* (June 17, 2002), p. 53.

4. John Leo, "Zones for All," *U.S. News & World Report* (April 23, 2001), p. 20.

5. Robert Fresco, "Census 2000: The Numbers Are In," *Newsday* (March 16, 2001), pp. E2–E3.

Florida, New York, and New Jersey changes the notion of minority status and powerlessness—just the opposite, since their numbers and political clout are geometric because of the size of the states where they reside and their respective impact on the House of Representatives and on presidential elections is proportionally much larger than their numbers.

Hispanics and Asians are divided by national origin, historical memory, shades of color and religion, and even "tribal" wars and genocide—just about every variable or factor that has characterized other immigrant and ethnic groups in their formation of an American identity. The Filipino boy discussed earlier understood the shades of gray in which American society and human reality are composed better than his teachers who were (and still are) guided by political correctness. He understood what America is about better than minority organizations that find a unified voice as an aggrieved minority on the national stage. The Filipino boy saw himself, first, as an American and did not want to know all "the minority stuff" of black, Hispanic, or Asian advocacy groups. The problem is, minority groups take the view that the legacy of the civil rights movement is to readdress issues of discrimination, and if you are a person of color, you need to be protected by the government, regardless of whether you arrived yesterday or 100 years ago.

In the same vein, Tiger Woods claims he is part *Ca*ucasian, *Bl*ack, American *In*dian, and *As*ian, what he calls *Cablinasian*. *Ebony* magazine and NAACP would prefer that Tiger declare himself black, and once convened a panel to contemplate what Tiger is. Tiger refused to participate; like the Filipino student, he understood the world is gray and mixed and did not want to be used by an advocacy group.

Although past memories are not always accurate, there was a time—nearly 40 years ago—when I drank Pizanno wine ($2.50/gallon) on the shores of Amagansett while Virgil Clift (my mentor at N.Y.U.) drank good bordeaux wine at French restaurants. Virgil was the first black professor of education at a major northern university, and we both gravitated to each other because of our minority status; it was the same time when I was a Johnny Cash fan, although few people knew about him, and when Virgil introduced me to black jazz at the Village Gate.[1] It was the time when there were "reform movements" in the country in which the distance between rhetoric and conviction, points and counterpoints, was much less so than now. Four strong themes have surfaced since Virgil and I first met and since the War on Poverty and civil rights movement descended on the American landscape in the mid-1960s:

1. It is very difficult to have a frank discussion in public and criticize any group that defines itself as a "minority." Certain issues and data get attention, which coincide with the ideology of political correctness, and contradictory explanations or findings are ignored or even hidden.
2. Among groups defining themselves as an "oppressed minority," there is a belief that anyone outside the group cannot fully appreciate or diagnose the minority experience. The researcher's treatment of the subject is considered suspect and

---

1. Allan C. Ornstein, "On Virgil Clift," *Peabody Journal of Education, 1* (1996), pp. 39–43.

even fraudulent. Any negative analysis is turned around to be the problem of re-searcher (or author), the result of a subjective and disdainful academic telescope.

3. Those members of the minority group who purport to unravel the problems of its respective group tend to do so for the enlightenment of the indifferent or well off, as well as to organize members within their group. Members who criticize their own group are considered to "sell out" and compromise their integrity.

4. Most arguments result in the "downtrodden" or "underclass" being analyzed as the victim of the dominant group. In some cases, there is admission that the mem-bers of the minority group need to develop habits of self-reliance and hard work, to overcome their obstacles the old-fashioned way, and to engage in self-help and develop organizations that help them function better individually and collectively as a group. For the greater part, however, there is still an expectation or demand for special consideration and that the dominant group should take more initia-tive for alleviating the victims' plight.

## Redefining Minority Classifications

It is a cliché to say American society has changed; it is like saying that change is in-evitable. We still live in a "melting pot"; J. Hector St. John (Crevecoeur's) letters, writ-ten in 1782, remain relevant: There is "the mixture of blood which you will find in no other country." The old immigrants more or less resided in their own neighbor-hoods in part because they felt comfortable doing so and they wanted to retain their old customs and values. The fact is, the Dutch, Swedes, French, and Germans lived in their own neighborhoods during the colonial and postcolonial period, just like the Irish, Italians, Greeks, and Jews did in the early twentieth century, just like the Croa-tians, Koreans, Mexicans, Poles, and Russians do today.

This kind of proximity in the nation's large cities has nothing to do with discrim-ination; rather, it reflects cultural, linguistic, and psychological needs and interests— a feeling of belongingness and community. It is self-imposed, and very different from the exclusionary policies of Bronxville or Tuxedo, New York; Darien or Greenwich, Connecticut, Hamilton or Dover, Massachusetts, Lake Forest or Kenilworth, Illinois, Bel Air or Hillsborough, California, or Hunt's Point or Medina, Washington. In all these communities, plus on the plains of Montana, Nebraska, and Wyoming, you can count on your two hands the number of Jews or Asians, or Hispanics, or blacks, or first-generation European immigrants.

My New Home: An Electric Jolt　New York City is the antithesis of "Yankeeville." The flow of immigrants to New York is mind-boggling: 43 percent of the residents were born outside of the United States, surpassing the precious record from the 1910 cen-sus.[1] The city is constantly reinventing itself because of this dynamic flow of people, energy, and ideas. It exemplifies how the super-rich and the super-poor, different eth-nic and religious groups, and people speaking multiple lists of language can live side by side in harmony.

1. "New York City," Metro Channel, November 13, 2001.

As a visitor, you quickly come to realize that New York City is a noisy, grimy and dirty, and overpopulated place, and there is too much traffic. Most of the street cart venders and souls in the subways and restaurants do not come from Europe and do not have blonde hair and blue eyes. You witness the flow of thousands of people on the street walking together, criss-crossing paths—a test of tolerance among so many newcomers and diverse people yearning to be free, to escape the old prejudices of the older countries.

New York City is the place where newborn Hispanic girls are called Ashley and newborn Asian girls are called Michelle (the number-one choice in New York for each group in 1999).[1] New York City is the place where Crevecoeur's letters, the Statute of Liberty, Ellis Island, and Glazer and Moynihan's *Beyond the Melting Pot* fuse in a meaningful way: where people from the four corners of the world come together, where they grow and prosper, and where they head out to the rest of America. New York City explains America to Americans and to the rest of the world. Visitors from all over the globe go to "the City" to take their pictures and visit museums—not to Bronxville, Greenwich, or Kenilworth, and not to the plains of America.

New York City is the world: where people learn to live together with their differences, with their own identities, and with respect for the identities of others. The city is an agglomeration of people; 125 languages (according to the major) are spoken. New York students do not need a course in multicultural education. You come to this city, as a visitor, to have your lessons in pluralism and diversity; the people living here accept people of all stripes, sizes, colors, sexual preferences—no matter how different they are. New York is the place where differences are celebrated. You can be who you are no matter how different you are. You can hip-hop on 42nd Street, dancing to the beat of the latest funky Caribbean music, in front of hundreds of tourists; or you can attend the opera at the Met or Lincoln Center and listen to the sounds of Bocelli or Pavarotti. You can hawk $10 look-a-like Rolex watches or sell "I Love New York" shirts, 3 for $10, a block from Tiffanys or Gucci's, where someone else might spend $100,000 on some luxury item. No one cares! Everyone in New York City can do their thing and reach their potential, where in more provincial parts of the country, you might be labeled, discriminated against, or held back because of your differences or because you're not part of the "old guard."

Sometimes resented by Americans because it is the most famous city in the world, New York has the most of almost everything. It is a cultural, entertainment, and intellectual force, and the economic and financial center of the nation. It is the world's art center, publishing center, entertainment center, theater and drama center, media center, sports center, and fashion center. It has more museums, schools, colleges and universities, theaters, restaurants, jewelers, and furriers than any other city in the world. It has the tallest number of buildings (the glass and steel center of the world), the largest transit and underground train system, and the largest fire department and police force (larger than most standing armies of the world), and it attracts more tourists and has more beautiful women than any other city. Next to the Boston-Cambridge area, it has

1. "The Melting Pot Works Magic on Baby Names," *New York Times* (January 12, 2001), Sect. B, p. 1.

the most international students, and next to downtown Cairo and Istanbul, it has the worst traffic jams.

New York is the warmest, most diverse, and most powerful city in the world. It is modern Athens and Rome rolled up in one metropolis. American icons and American heroes have all come to the city to be honored or to speak to its people. This is where America's monuments and American monumental people come together to fulfill their slogans and dreams. "Give me your tired and wretched poor," "I have a dream," and others. This is where you find survivors of Auschwitz and former Nazi soldiers, Irish rebels and British royalists, Croation freedom fighters and Serbian farmers living together on the same block, shopping in the same grocery store—living in new world and new nostalgia. I don't believe social science scholarship can fully catch the moment, describe the city, or even film it. You have to experience it, see it, smell it, and become part of the street hustle and bustle to fully grasp it.

Now listen to E. B. White's timeless description in *Here Is New York*. "It's noise, its glitter, its harshness, its tolerance." The city is a contradiction, congested, implausible. "Every facility is inadequate. The hospitals and schools and playgrounds are overcrowd, the highways . . . and bridges are bottlenecks." The city is "uncomfortable, so crowded, so tense." It's hard to get in to a restaurant, find an affordable apartment. "Buses are standing room and taxis are not to be found." But the city forms "a rich ethnic stew." It makes up for its inadequacies by "supplying its citizens with . . . the sense of belonging to something unique, cosmopolitan, mighty and unparalleled."[1]

Every imaginable city problem smolders in New York: infrastructure problems, pollution problems, traffic problems, race problems, crime problems, welfare problems, and education problems. But the noticeable difference or intensity of the problem(s) is not the problem, since they exist to some lesser extent in smaller big cities from coast to coast, but the truce, patience, and lack of bigotry. It is the city life, built on people, streets, and neighborhoods that makes the city different. It is the opportunities "to make it big" in finance and commerce, fashions and food, theater and art, publishing and writing, that draws young blood, like a magnet, from Maine to Mississippi, from Nebraska to New Mexico to the "Big Apple." Fresh talent and fresh ideas from other parts of the country are constantly injected into the City, making it the most vibrant city in the world.

New York is the heart and soul of America, and, since 9-11, it has become the symbol of America rising above a fiery graveyard. It best represents what the American dream is all about. The city is loved by visitors form all parts of the world; it reaches out to them and represents the best place where everyone can live, work, and prosper together. That is what this country is about—why it is so wealthy and why people from all over the world want to emigrate and even assimilate. People don't come to New York or to the United States to hold on to their old identities, or to be near people of their own group; they come for opportunity and a better life than in the place they left behind. Coming to New York means breaking away from the old ways. The children of the new arrivals have no desire to follow their parents' occupations or to speak the old language; they may cling to their people and live in "Lit-

1. E. B. White, *Here Is New York* (New York: Little Bookroom, 1999), pp. 14–15.

tle Italy" or "China Town" because of trust, business opportunities, and political clout, but in the end, American lifestyle shapes their lives and produces a new breed of Italian Americans and Chinese Americans—what I call *assimilated Americans*. Despite what cultural pluralists might say about the assimilation process or advocate in its place, America has been assimilating its immigrants for 350 years—and will go on so long as the flow of new arrivals continue.

**Ethnic and Folk Culture**    Although immigrant colors and countries have dramatically changed since 1965, the year when immigrant restrictions were relaxed, the impulse to assimilate into the larger society is still strong, as it has been for the last several hundred years. For those who made the long trip, whether it took eight weeks or eight hours (or less), the idea was to become an American. The difference today is that there is more pressure by the schools to retain one's racial/ethnic identity, and at the same time there is more tolerance toward minorities. Actually, there is an attempt by educators to highlight diversity and multicultural education, and to develop various claims, methods, and approaches to expand ethnicity and cultural pluralism.[1] We remain a hodge-podge nation, but for all immigrant groups, *education is essential*. Regardless of whether they come from Europe, Asia, Africa, or Latin America, no other nation is more dedicated to education. "Education has always been the pot of gold at the end of the rainbow."[2] Some 35 percent of U.S. students were members of minority groups in 2000, and it will climb to more than 50 percent by 2040,[3] thus reflecting the fact we are one of the only western and industrialized nations still growing in population because of immigration.

But the need for a balancing act, to convey various shades of color and to avoid the pitfalls of racial/ethnic stereotypes and discrimination, is crucial. Both right-wing white groups who espouse religious and racial hatred, and minority groups who persist in raising the banner of racism or ethnocentrism, and who view themselves as unhyphenated Americans, despite the different kind of blood flowing through their veins, are bound to cripple themselves socially and psychologically. Classifying race and ethnicity is more subjective than objective, more self-imposed by individuals than imposed by society—in short, based more on personal feelings and attitudes than precise mathematical or scientific categories.

Most of the immigrants today who yearn to breathe free and to prosper do not come from Europe; rather, they hail from "nonwestern" lands. In fact, about 90 percent of today's immigrants come from Asia, Africa, and Latin America. The noise is no longer from horseshoes, from ethnic European clubs and taverns, or from vendors who

1. See James A. Banks and Cherry A. Banks, *Handbook of Research on Multicultural Education* (San Francisco: Jossey-Bass, 2001); Carlos F. Diaz, *Multicultural Education in the 21st Century* (Boston: Allyn and Bacon, 2001); and Geneva Gay, *Culturally Responsive Teaching* (New York: Teachers College Press, 2000).

2. Sara Carbett, "The Long, Long, Long Road to Fargo," *New York Times Magazine* (April 1, 2001), p. 55.

3. Lynn Olson and Greg Orlosky, "Children of Change," *Education Week* (September 27, 2000), pp. 31–35.

speak Italian, Greek, or Yiddish. The folklore and language is very different, mainly from Hispanic and Asian cultures, with new music, new foods, new flavors, new customs. Much of the population growth and economic growth in the larger cities have to do with immigrant groups, not second- or third-generation Americans.

The nation's newest immigrants—Mexican, Korean, Indian, and Chinese—come from lost worlds and have different customs and beliefs than those old ethnics—Irish, Italian, Greek, Puerto Rican—who came to our shores generations ago. The new wave of immigrants are permitted to retreat into the images of their lost worlds, to cling to their traditions and culture, but they must learn to decide what works (and what doesn't) and what is relevant (and irrelevant) to their current needs. They must make adjustments to function today on streets such as Clark and Devon in Chicago and Delancey and Essex in New York City, and eventually on "Main Street" in suburban America. All these roads intersect, and they forge a new type of American, who leaves behind the lords and ladies, the landed aristocracy, the pretentious life they could never aspire or achieve in the old world, as well as the border warfare, political strife, and hunger that was once their world.

The mutations that develop represent the immigrants' accommodations to their new cities, their new homeland, to "Pax Americana." They may continue with their Indian or Chinese food and celebrate in September for the Hindu New Year and in mid-January or February for the Chinese New Year, but their children will attend American schools and watch American television (now considered the first education system, suggesting that children spend more time watching television than attending school) and eventually exchange curry dishes or oxtail dishes for Big Macs and a bucket of the Colonel's fried chicken and celebrate the "strange" American holidays of Christmas and New Years, and even Fourth of July and Thanksgiving.

Given all the criticism leveled by cultural pluralists and neomarxists in general, America has been constructed to absorb any group or any thing that comes along. The "founding fathers" who built this nation, despite all the liberal bashing that they were white, Eurocentric, male, and some even slave holders, gave their descendents something very special, peculiar, and seemingly implausible if history was to gauge the success of the experiment. They built a sort of perpetual, ever-increasing, rich, multiethnic, multireligious stew. They provided a massive dose of super-strength vitamins, to move people from a sense of confusion and despair to a sense of fulfillment and freedom, from a sense of uniqueness to a sense of belonging, from a harsh and untamed physical environment to a cosmopolitan and mighty legacy—a new breed of Americans. This is why this nation has been able to grow and prosper more than any other civilization. It is a remarkable story, but there is another side to it—one about which Americans need to be reminded.

We are all humans first; Americans second; men and women third; actors, lawyers, teachers, or bricklayers fourth. Then, we can talk about race, religion, ethnicity, and shades of color. Sidney Poiter, one of my favorite actors, was always referred to as a *black* actor, and Jackie Robinson was always a *black* baseball player. Those days are over, at least they better be over. Sidney Poiter should have been described in human, American, gender, and professional terms without the *black* adjective. The same goes for Jackie Robinson, who was my hero when growing up, and who I saw as a Dodger second baseman who batted third or fourth in the line-up.

Both remain in the shadows and favorite reaches of my memory. I was content to see them as humans and to judge them for their abilities. I don't know why, but few of my contemporaries who I played baseball or went to school with could make these distinctions. I can recall the cafeteria talk and locker-room talk. Perhaps it was the water they drank, the pollution or the blue-collar community, or some social disease that infected them and most of America before Rosa Parks got on a bus and started "all the fuss." Maybe my old classmates didn't understand the hateful fanaticism that has consumed the world. Maybe it was simply the tendency of the times.

As a nation, we all need to learn these lessons about people, or else we will drown as a civilization. Our decline will have little to do with the loss of Christian values, faith, and ideals (Toynbee's prediction for decline) or with the rise of gloom, defeatism, and anti-intellectualism (Spengler's prediction for decline); rather, it will have more to do with the inability of the western world to fuse with the Asian, African, and Latin American world; the inability of whites to understand, respect, and appreciate people of color. The esoteric abstraction of "Yankees" living in small secluded villages and towns—still hanging on to the old ways—is a covert, dangerous sentiment, the last flurry of American isolation and hypocrisy. These old families and communities need to open their doors to the world; their children cannot hold back the nonwestern and ethnic storm, the mixed blood swirling at their gates and fences.

There are many forks in the road to assimilation, and the themes of melting pot, mosaic, stew, and tossed salad to describe American society are as varied as its people. The word or concept is not crucial as some of us would like to think. Much of it depends on the upward mobility of minority groups, which in turn reflects whether the group becomes homogenized as new Americans or holds on to its separate identity. If, however, the group perceives itself as "oppressed," with common historic grievances toward the larger society, then the American concepts of equality, opportunity, and mobility needs to be reanalyzed and possibly reformulated. If the theme of oppression dominates, there is no satisfying that particular racial, religious, or ethnic group. On the other hand, more and more Americans are beginning to say that race, religion, and ethnicity should not be descriptions for categorizing people in any form or shape. We are reminded of Martin Luther King's dream: that children "should be judged not by the color of their skin but by the content of their character." It would be nice if some day we could achieve this goal.

## Closing Images and Interpretations

I did a lot of rambling and roaming when I was a younger man. Now, in the fall of my life, I have time to reflect and remember. In the aftermath of September 11, when I think about what separates us from the rest of the world, I think of *democracy, freedom, life and liberty, law, tolerance, dignity and rights of the individual, hope,* and *opportunity.* I am sure each of you has your own list, your own values, your own idea of America.

Where were you that day in September when the world stopped? Certainly every reader can delineate the place, the people, the memory. I still see the smoking ruins and collapse of the towers, the people who chose to jump out windows knowing full well what it meant, the firefighters who knew in their minds and hearts the outcome as they rushed to their deaths.

I think of Lincoln's words at Gettysburg "cemetery," which were repeated by several speakers across the country on the anniversary of September 11. I think of phrases such as *Four score and seven years ago, The unfinished work, The final resting place, that all men [and women] are created equal,* and that government should be *of the people, by . . . and for the people.* I think about how I used to repeat by rote these words when I was in school, and recall how a nation rose from the ashes and anguish of death and destruction. And so it is "fitting and proper" to remember the dead and to go on as part of "the living," to finish "the great task remaining before us," and to "provide a new birth of freedom."

It was the haunting lyrics of Lincoln's message, some 269 words, reflecting both great suffering and spiritual triumph, the mysticism and skill in his use of words and images, that made me appreciate the great struggle that profoundly affected the nation. Lincoln's address enriched the nation's literature, depicting heroic action, poignant humanity, the scars of the war, the nation's obligation to its dead, and its rebirth and principles of unity, liberty, and democracy.

As I reflect on President Lincoln—the man who was born in a log cabin, a simple farmer from the prairie, with one year of formal schooling—I think of America reborn from all the dead he came to honor at Gettysburg and at other battlefields and bloodbaths of the Civil War. I think it is "fitting and proper" that we remember and add all the dead at the World Trade Center, at the Pentagon, and in Shanksville, Pennsylvania—all the sermons, speeches, empty coffins, and last goodbyes as part of the "new birth," new spirit, and new hope of the nation.

Then, I think of the Lady in the Harbor, how breathtaking and proud she looks. I've never seen her look more magnificent than today, and I've never fully appreciated, until now, how my grandparents might have felt—and the millions of other immigrants, many who were outcasts and downtrodden—when she loomed in front of them.

So, Bartholdi's gigantic effigy has become the *welcoming lady,* her torch held high, touching the rising and setting sun—a symbol of American principles and freedom and hope to the entire world. Last week, when I flew home to New York, I gazed out the window as the jumbo jet made the last turn to descend onto the runway. I never had such a feeling—a feeling of love and adoration toward the Lady in the Harbor, beckoning at the entrance to America. For a split second, I thought of Athena, some 2,500 years ago, mounted on the top of the Acropolis.

I shall never forget the way she looked, Lady Liberty in the harbor who welcomed my grandparents nearly 100 years ago and provided a safe haven—hope and opportunity, birth and rebirth. She remains to me the spirit of America, welcoming old people and young people, from all walks of life, from all four corners of the world, 116 years after her unveiling. She is my favorite Lady and she still brings tears to my eyes and elicits complex emotions. She has become anchored to the passions and beliefs of all Americans, and of all the people clamoring to come to America—an image, a thought, a metaphor, an idea, a symbol—navigating adroitly between the past, the present, and the future.

## Summary

1. During the 1960s and 1970s, a number of large-scale and influential reports—including those by Coleman, Jencks, and Duncan—documented the minimal impact of schools on student achievement and future income. This literature is bolstered by the recent work of Grissmer, Hanushek, and Mayer and Peterson.

2. The more effective school literature is an attempt to counteract the original research of the Coleman/Jencks point of view. Several school characteristics appear to correlate with student achievement, the most important appearing to be the school principal's leadership and the teachers' attitudes and expectations of student achievement.

3. Discussions concerning race and academic achievement are often controversial and involve political ideology, slogans, and various explanations for the gap in achievement and test scores between black and white students. The explanations range from discussion about IQ, to black anti-intellectualism, to the racist nature of society.

4. We have always been a nation of many nations, and educators need to instruct their students in these matters without taking extreme positions, exaggerating, or presenting myths as truths. This is not an easy task; it involves some pruning of European history and literature without replacing it with "soft" or ideological content.

5. Most of today's immigrants came from the third-world countries of Asia, Africa, and Latin America. About 35 percent of U.S. students are members of minority groups. By 2040, minority students will comprise the majority of students in this nation's schools.

## Questions to Consider

1. What are some problems related to defining and measuring school variables related to improving educational outcomes? What argument appears to be the best for countering the Coleman and Jencks studies? Why?

2. What social policy can be implemented to unfreeze those caught in the cycle of poverty?

3. How can schools better promote the idea of equality?

4. What should be done to improve education in inner-city communities?

5. How do we teach the theme of diversity and cultural pluralism without balkanizing students into racial and ethnic groups?

## Things to Do

1. Interview a counselor in your college to discuss potential "dropouts." What are their ideological disagreements with the rest of society?

2. Use the Internet to find arguments for and against the Coleman and Jencks thesis on schooling and student achievement.

3. Examine one or more international studies to determine how American students rank among students of other industrialized countries.

4. Refer to the Internet and locate a recent study on more effective schooling. In what way do you agree/disagree with the findings?

5. Discuss in class: How would you summarize racial relations in the United States? What is the most pressing race issue?

## Recommended Readings

Carter, Samuel C. *No Excuses: Lessons for 21 High-Performing High Poverty Schools.* Washington, DC: Heritage Foundation, 2000. Twenty-one effective schools across the country are profiled.

Coleman, James B., et al. *Equality of Educational Opportunity* (Washington, DC: U.S. Government Printing Office, 1966). A classic government-sponsored report analyzing the achievement differences of selected minority groups in grades 1, 3, 6, 9, and 12; the conclusion is that schools have little influence on student achievement.

D'Souza, Dinsh. *The Virtues of Prosperity.* New York: Free Press, 2000. An offshoot of Darwinism, the author maintains smart people rise to the top and are paid according to the goods and services they produce.

Jencks, Christopher, et al. *Inequality: A Reassessment of the Effect of Family and Schooling in America.* New York: Basic Books, 1972. The basic position is that schools have little effect in reducing inequality; luck is more important than education in determining economic outcomes.

Kahlenberg, Richard D., ed. *A Notion at Risk: Preserving Public Education an Engine for Social Mobility.* New York: Century Foundation, 2000. Several recommendations for reforming inner-city schools and improving achievement among minority students.

McWorther, John. *Losing the Race.* New York: Simon & Schuster, 2001. Being a "culturally authentic" black American dooms you to the "cult of anti-intellectualism."

Sowell, Thomas A. *Black Education: Myths and Tragedies.* New York: McKay, 1972. Black students are ill served by racial quotas; good teaching and hard work for students are the answers.

# Index

Academic achievement (*see also* Achievement; Intellectual achievement and schools' influence):
among blacks, 217–219
and peer group, 220
of U.S. students, 92, 93–94
Academic merit and testing, 379–382
Academics and computers, 365–367
Academies, era of, 272–273
Accommodation, definition of, 126
Accountability (*see also* Evaluating teachers; Teacher accountability):
definition of, 80
Achievement:
model, 451
and peer group, 220
schools' influence on (*see* Intellectual achievement and schools' influence)
Acquisition of learning, definition of, 128
Activity-centered practices, 33
Adversity as criterion for college admission, 381
Affective strategies, definition of, 155
Affirmative action, 477
Africa, state of, 288–289
Age of innocence, society's, 192–193, 201–202, 204–205

Aggressive and violent behavior, 44–45, 113
Americanizing immigrants, 168
Anglo-American ties, 275–284
Anti-Americanism, 295
Anti-Semitism, 488
Aptitude vs. achievement, 451
Arab and Muslim view of western culture, 422–425
Art vs. science of teaching, 10–15
Ascriptive societies, 387
Assessment systems, 28
Assimilation, definition of, 126
At-risk children, 470–471
Autobiographies of teachers, 20–21

Barbarianism, 117–118
Behavior modification, 113
Behaviorism, 109–124
classical conditioning, 109, 119–120
in classroom situations, 114
connectionism, 110–111
hierarchical learning, 114–116
obedience experimentation, 116–119
observational learning and modeling, 113–114
operant conditioning, 112–113
and teaching, 120–124
Bilingual/multicultural education, 344–346

Biographies of teachers, 20–21
Biotechnology and human conditioning, 120–121
Birthrates, decline in, 430
Black ideology related to education, 477
Books, recommended reading, 180, 181
Brain research and learning, 142–162
cloning, 153–154
critical thinking, 156–161
DNA, 147–148
and the environment, 148–149
genetics, 147–148
learning how to learn, 154–156
learning styles, 143–145
memory, 145–147
multiple intelligences (Gardner), 150–154

Categorical checklist for observation, 67
Cellar and ceiling effects of testing, 73–74
Certification programs, 29–30
Character development, 131–135
Cheating, 138–140
Child-centered schools, 33
Children's drawings, 162–163
Citizenship, 49–50
Civic participation, 49–50
Civil rights movement, 195–196